SO-AFF-200

Program Composition	Example
Variable section	**var**
(predefined types)	*Count, I, Number : integer;*
integer	*Hours, Rate, Wages : real;*
real	*DeptCode, FirstInit, SecondInit : char;*
character	*OverTime : boolean;*
boolean	*OutFile : text;*
text file	*Dept : DepartmentName;*
(user-defined types)	*EmpCode : Digit;*
	Product, Item : List;
	ProductName : String;
	EmpRec : InfoRecord;
	Letters : CapLetterSet;
	InFile : EmployeeFile;
	FirstPtr, TempPtr : ListPointer;
Subprogram section	
Procedure definition	**procedure** *ReadCodes* (**var** *Department,*
	Employee : char);
	(∗ Read department & employee codes ∗)
	begin (∗ *ReadCodes* ∗)
	write ('Enter dept. & employee codes: ');
	readln (*Department, Employee*)
	end (∗ *ReadCodes* ∗);
	function *RoundCents(Amount : real) : real;*
Function definition	(∗ Round *Amount* to nearest cent ∗)
	begin (∗ *RoundCents* ∗)
	RoundCents := *round*(100 ∗ *Amount*) / 100
	end (∗ *RoundCents* ∗);
Statement part	**begin** (∗ main program ∗)
	statement-1
	.
	.
	.
	statement-n
	end (∗ main program ∗).

Data Structures and Program Design in Pascal

Second Edition

LARRY NYHOFF
SANFORD LEESTMA
Department of Mathematics and Computer Science
Calvin College

Data Structures and Program Design in Pascal

Second Edition

Macmillan Publishing Company
NEW YORK

Maxwell Macmillan Canada
TORONTO

Maxwell Macmillan International
NEW YORK   OXFORD   SINGAPORE   SYDNEY

Editor: David Johnstone
Production Supervisor: Ron Harris
Production Manager: Nick Sklitsis
Text Designer: Natasha Sylvester
Cover Designer: Natasha Sylvester
Cover illustration: Chris Stoffel Overvoorde

This book was set in Times Roman by Waldman Graphics, Inc., printed and bound by Arcata
Graphics-Hawkins. The cover was printed by Lehigh Press.

Copyright © 1992 by Macmillan Publishing Company, a division of Macmillan, Inc.

Printed in the United States of America

All rights reserved. No part of this book may be reproduced or
transmitted in any form or by any means, electronic or mechanical,
including photocopying, recording, or any information storage and
retrieval system, without permission in writing from the publisher.

Earlier edition copyright © 1988 by Macmillan Publishing Company

Macmillan Publishing Company
866 Third Avenue, New York, New York 10022

Macmillan Publishing Company is part
of the Maxwell Communication Group of Companies.

Maxwell Macmillan Canada, Inc.
1200 Eglinton Avenue East
Suite 200
Don Mills, Ontario M3C 3N1

Library of Congress Cataloging in Publication Data

Nyhoff, Larry R.
    Data structures and program design in Pascal / Larry Nyhoff,
  Sanford Leestma.—2nd ed.
      p.   cm.
    Rev. ed. of: Advanced programming in Pascal with data structures,
  c 1988.
    Includes index.
    ISBN 0-02-369465-3
    1. Pascal (Computer program language)   2. Data structures
  (Computer science)   I. Leestma,
  Sanford.   II. Nyhoff, Larry R.
    Advanced programming in Pascal with data structures.   III. Title.
    QA76.73.P2N94   1992   005.13′3—dc20   91-22551
                                                                              CIP

Printing: 2 3 4 5 6 7 8   Year: 2 3 4 5 6 7 8 9 0

PREFACE

Our first edition of this text, *Advanced Programming in Pascal with Data Structures,* was designed to meet the objectives of the course CS2 as described in the Curriculum '84 recommendations of the ACM (Association of Computing Machinery). It emphasized the application of software engineering principles to the design of structured algorithms and Pascal programs begun in our CS1 text: *Pascal: Programming and Problem Solving,* now in its third edition. A large number of examples consisting of algorithms, complete programs, and sample runs illustrated the application of these basic principles. This text continues to emphasize basic software engineering principles, but does so in an expanded and improved manner.

Recently, a new set of curriculum recommendations was published in *Computing Curricula 1991: Report of the ACM/IEEE-CS Joint Curriculum Task Force.* A major theme of this report is that the introductory computer science courses should include an introduction to the various areas of computer science. Feeling that this was an important objective in the early computer science courses, we included several examples and exercises from different areas of computer science in the first edition of this text. In this edition we have expanded and improved these examples, guided by the recommendations of Curriculum '91 and by suggestions made by reviewers and users of the first edition. These examples have been carefully selected to provide an overview of the discipline of computer science and to provide a foundation for further study in computer science. The topics include the following:

- Reverse Polish notation and generation of machine code
- Finite automata and lexical analysis
- Computational complexity of algorithms, illustrated by the analysis of standard searching and sorting algorithms
- A description of the software development process, including formal specifications and program validation and verification
- An introduction to correctness proofs of algorithms
- Simple systems concepts such as input/output buffers, parameter-passing mechanisms, address translation, and memory management
- Indirect recursion and parsing
- Symmetric linked lists and large-integer arithmetic
- String processing and data encryption schemes (DES and public key)
- Random number generation and simulation

- Abstract data types
- Object-oriented programming

A solid base is thus established on which later courses in theoretical and/or applied computer science can build.

A second recommendation of Curriculum '91 is that the introductory courses in computer science should include a laboratory component to supplement the class lectures. To meet this need, Professors Linda Elliott and Jane Turk from LaSalle University have prepared a lab manual to accompany this text. It contains sixteen lab modules and includes a disk containing all the programs, drivers, and data files referenced in the manual.

The major theme of the second computer science course described in the Curriculum '91 report is the study of data abstraction and data structures and implementations of these structures. It is in regard to these objectives that the current edition differs most from the first edition, so much so that we felt the former title no longer served as an adequate description of the text and thus the name change to *Data Structures and Program Design in Pascal.* Recent years have seen an increased emphasis in computer science on abstract data types (ADTs) and object-oriented programming. In the current edition, therefore, we have expanded and emphasized the use of abstract data types, using the structured data types studied in CS1 as building blocks. We emphasize the distinction between ADTs and their implementations by first studying each structure abstractly, describing the interface/definition part of a ''package'' (or ''unit'' in Turbo Pascal) for each ADT, and illustrating applications of the structure. After this, the implementation part of the package/unit is developed.

The major new features of this edition include the following:

- Increased emphasis on the formal specification of abstract data types and their use; for example, strings and stacks are presented as ADTs and ''packages'' in standard Pascal (units in Turbo Pascal) are given for processing these ADTs.
- More emphasis on software development in Chapter 1—in particular, more material on system design, coding and integration, validation, verification, and testing.
- New application of sets to finite automata and lexical analyzers.
- New treatment of strings as an ADT; a package of string operations is given for users of standard Pascal and a discussion of the predefined string data type is included for users of Turbo Pascal.
- A stack-processing package/unit is included.
- Queues are presented as an ADT.
- Discussion of algorithm efficiency appears later in the text.
- Reduced emphasis on array-based implementations of linked lists.
- Presentation of linked lists as ADTs and description of a package for processing linked lists.
- Revised presentation of linked stacks and queues, binary search trees, and hash tables as ADTs.
- Earlier treatment of binary trees.
- Expanded treatment of trees, including a discussion of tree balancing (AVL trees) and threaded binary trees.
- A new chapter to introduce object-oriented programming (OOP).

As in the earlier edition, we assume that the reader has completed a first course in programming that included at least the following basic features of Pascal: functions, procedures, text files, and arrays. The other structured data types—records, sets, and binary files—are described in separate sections of Chapter 2, which may be omitted or treated lightly if desired. For the most part, standard Pascal is used throughout the text—a brief summary of its features is given in Appendixes B, C, D, and F and on the front and back covers— but a few separate sections are devoted to features of other dialects of Pascal, and Appendix G provides a summary of the main variations and extensions in Turbo Pascal.

Supplementary Materials

A number of supplementary materials are available from the publisher. These include the following:

- A lab manual containing sixteen lab modules intended to supplement and apply the class lectures. It also includes a disk containing all the programs, drivers (testers) and data files referenced in the manual.
- An instructor's manual that contains solutions to the exercises in the text together with suggestions for using the lab modules.
- Data disks containing all the sample programs and data files used in the text. (Standard Pascal and Turbo Pascal versions are available.)
- Data disks containing all the exercises of the text.

Acknowledgments

We express our sincere appreciation to all who helped in any way in the preparation of this text. We especially thank our erudite editor David Johnstone, whose professional competence has kept us on course, whose words of encouragement have keep us going, and whose friendship over the years has made textbook writing for Macmillan an enjoyable experience. We must also thank our punctilious production supervisor Ronald Harris, whose attention to details and deadlines has compensated for our lack thereof and whose encouraging words and kind admonitions (when needed) have prodded us to action; working without him is almost unthinkable. And we cannot fail to note the many hours spent by Sheryl Lanser in preparing the manuscript and computer disks, making corrections, proofreading, and doing a multitude of other tasks, always with patience and a cheerful spirit; we thank her so much for all that she has done. The comments and suggestions made by the following reviewers were also valuable and their work is also much appreciated: Chuck Burchard, The Pennsylvania State University at Erie; Steve Hufnagel, The University of Texas at Arlington; Donald Marois, United States Military Academy, West Point; Laszlo Szuecs, Fort Lewis College; Harry Shea, University of Maine; George C. Harrison, Norfolk State University; David Valentine, Trinity College. And, of course, we must once again pay homage to our wives Shar and Marge, whose love and understanding have kept us going through another year of textbook writing, and to our kids, Jeff, Dawn, Jim, Julie, Joan, Michelle, Paul, Sandy, and Michael, for not complaining about the times that their needs and wants were slighted by our busyness. Above all, we give thanks to God for giving us the opportunity, ability, and stamina to prepare another new edition of this text.

L. N.
S. L.

CONTENTS

1

Software Development

Problem solving with a computer requires the use of both hardware and software. The **hardware** of a computing system consists of the actual physical components, such as the central processing unit (CPU), memory, and input/output devices that make up the system. **Software** refers to programs used to control the operation of the hardware in order to solve problems. Software development is a complex process that is both an art and a science. It is an art in that it requires a good deal of imagination, creativity, and ingenuity. But it is also a science in that it uses certain standard techniques and methodologies. The term **software engineering** has come to be applied to the study and use of these techniques.

Although the problems themselves and the techniques used in their solution vary, several phases or steps are common in software development:

1. Problem analysis and specification.
2. System design.
3. Coding and integration.
4. Verification and validation.
5. System maintenance.

In this chapter we briefly review and illustrate by means of a case study each phase of this **software life cycle,** describing some of the questions and complications that face software developers and some of the software engineering techniques that they use in dealing with them.

1.1   Problem Analysis and Specification

CPSC 152–Assignment 4

Due: Wednesday, March 11

One method of calculating depreciation is the sum-of-the-years digits method. It is illustrated by the following example. Suppose that $15,000 is to be depreciated over a five-year period. We first calculate the "sum-of-the-years digits," $1 + 2 + 3 + 4 + 5 = 15$. Then 5/15 of $15,000 ($5,000) is depreciated the first year, 4/15 of $15,000 ($4,000) is depreciated the second year, 3/15 the third year, and so on.

Write a program that reads the amount to be depreciated and the number of years over which it is to be depreciated. Then for each year from 1 through the specified number of years, print the year number and the amount to be depreciated for that year under appropriate headings. Run the program with the following data: $15,000 for 3 years: $7,000 for 10 years; $500 for 20 years; $100 for 1 year.

DISPATCH UNIVERSITY

To: Bob Byte, Director of Computer Center

From: Chuck Cash, V.P. of Scholarships and
        Financial Aid

Date: Wednesday, March 11

Because of new government regulations, we must keep more accurate records of all students currently receiving financial aid and submit regular reports to FFAO (Federal Financial Aid Office). Could we get the computer to do this for us?

The preceding assignment sheet is typical of the programming problems given in an introductory programming course. The exercises and problems in such courses are usually quite simple and are clearly stated. But as the preceding memo illustrates, this is usually not the case in real-world problems. The initial descriptions of such problems are often vague and imprecise. The person posing the problem often does not understand it well. Neither does he or she understand how to solve it nor what the computer's capabilities and limitations are. The first step in solving such a problem is to analyze the problem and formulate a precise specification of it. This analysis typically requires determining, first of all, what *output* is required, that is, what information must be produced to solve the problem. It may be necessary to answer many questions to determine this. For example, what must be included in the reports to be submitted to FFAO? Must these reports have a special format? Must similar reports be generated for any other government agencies or university departments? Must reports be prepared for mailing to individual students? Must computer files of student records be updated?

Once the output of the problem has been specified, one must then analyze the problem to determine its *input,* that is, what information is available for solving the problem. Often the problem's statement includes irrelevant items of information, and one must determine which items will be useful in solving the problem. Usually additional questions must be answered. For example, what information is available for each student? How will this information be accessed? What data will the user enter during program execution?

Besides the input and output specifications, additional information will be required before the specification of the problem is complete and the development of algorithms and programs can begin. What hardware and software are available? What are the performance requirements? For example, what response time is necessary? How critical is the application in which the software is being used? If fault-free performance is required, must a proof of correctness accompany the software? How often will the software be used? Will the users be sophisticated, or will they be novices so that the software must be extra user friendly and robust?

As the specification of the problem is being formulated, decisions must be made regarding the feasibility of a computer solution. Is it possible to design software to carry out the processing required to obtain the desired output from the given input? If so, is it economically feasible? Could the problem be solved better manually? How soon must the software be available? What is its expected lifetime?

If it is determined that a computer-aided solution is possible and is cost effective, then the statement of the specifications developed in this phase of the software life cycle becomes the formal statement of the problem's requirements. This document serves as the major reference document that guides the development of the software, and it is the *standard* or *benchmark* used in validating the final system to determine that it does in fact solve the problem. Consequently, this statement of specifications must be complete, consistent, and correct. For this reason, a number of **formal methods**—such as Z, VDM (Vienna Development Method), and Larch—have been developed for formulating specifications. These methods are usually studied in more advanced software engineering courses, and in this text the problem specifications will be stated somewhat less formally.

1.2 System Design

Once the specification of a problem has been given, a **design plan** for developing a program or a system of programs that meets the specification must be formulated. Whereas programs written in introductory programming courses rarely exceed a few hundred lines in length, software developed in real-world applications often consists of several thousand lines of code. In developing such systems, it is usually not possible to visualize or anticipate at the outset all the details of a complete solution to the entire problem. Instead, a **divide-and-conquer** or **modularization** strategy is used in which the original problem is partitioned into simpler subproblems, each of which can be considered independently. Some or all of these subproblems may still be fairly complicated, and this divide-and-conquer approach can be repeated for them, continuing until subproblems are obtained that are sufficiently simple that complete program units can be developed for them. Thus, an important part of the design plan is identifying these subproblems and determining how the modules that solve them can then be combined into a **system** that solves the original problem. This **top-down design** approach to software development is reviewed and illustrated in the case study in Section 1.6.

Two important aspects of system design are the selection of appropriate data structures to organize the data to be processed by the system and the design of the modules that comprise the system. Because the computer has no inherent problem-solving capabilities, this phase of the problem-solving process requires ingenuity and creativity. In this section we take a quick look at this phase, reviewing some of the basic concepts introduced in a first programming course.

The structures used to organize the data in a given problem are often *predefined data structures* or, as they are called in Pascal, *structured data types.* The most common of these, and one with which you should already be familiar, is the *array*. Nearly every high-level programming language provides arrays as predefined structures. Arrays are used to organize data items that are all of the same type, for example, a collection of test scores (integers) or a collection of names (strings). They may be *one-dimensional,* in which case each item in the array is accessed by specifying its location in the array, usually by enclosing it in brackets or parentheses and attaching it as an index to the array name. Arrays may also be *multidimensional,* in which case access to an element requires using more than one index to specify its location. For example, in Pascal, if *Score* is a one-dimensional array of integers and *Sales* is a two-dimensional array of real numbers declared by

```
const
    MaxScores = 100;
    MaxRows = 10;
    MaxColumns = 10;

type
    ListOfScores = array[1..MaxScores] of integer;
    Table = array[1..MaxRows, 1..MaxColumns] of real;

var
    Score : ListOfScores;
    Sales : Table;
```

then the fifth score can be accessed with the array reference *Score*[5], and the entry in the first row and third column of *Sales* can be accessed with *Sales*[1, 3].

Another predefined data structure that you may have already studied is a *record,* which differs from an array in that the items in a record need not be of the same type. Records are thus useful in organizing nonhomogeneous collections of data items. For example, a student record might consist of an identification number that is some positive integer; a name that is itself a (*nested*) record consisting of a last name (string of length 16), a first name (string of length 12), and a middle initial (character); an address that might also be a record consisting of strings of various lengths; a grade point average that is a real number; and other items of information of various types.

Some languages provide still more predefined data structures. For example, you have probably used *files* and may also have studied the *set* data type in Pascal. Even though the language in which you do most of your programming is rich in predefined data structures (and Pascal is such a language), sometimes it will be necessary to organize the data into a structure that is not provided in the language. For example, *strings, stacks* and *queues* are user-defined structures that may have been introduced in an earlier course. A large part of this text is devoted to studying in detail these and other data structures.

In addition to organizing a problem's data into structures, modules must be designed to process this data and to produce the required output. An important part of the design of a module is the development of algorithms that carry out this processing. The selection of data structures and the design of algorithms that are correct, well structured, and efficient are at the heart of software design. These two aspects of software development are equally important and, in fact, are inextricably linked; neither can be carried out independently of the other. Indeed, Niklaus Wirth, the originator of the Pascal language, entitled one of his texts

Algorithms + Data Structures = Programs

The word **algorithm** is derived from the name of the Arab mathematician, Abu Ja'far Mohammed ibn Musa al Khowarizmi (c. A.D. 825), who wrote a book describing procedures for calculating with Hindu numerals. In modern parlance, the word has come to mean a "step-by-step procedure for solving a problem or accomplishing some end." In computer science, however, the term *algorithm* refers to a procedure that can be executed by a computer, and this requirement imposes additional limitations on the instructions that comprise these procedures:

1. They must be *definite* and *unambiguous* so that it is clear what each instruction is meant to accomplish.
2. They must be *simple* enough that they can be carried out by a computer.
3. They must satisfy a *finiteness* property, that is, the algorithm must terminate after a finite number of operations.

In view of the first two requirements, unambiguity and simplicity, algorithms are usually described in a form that resembles a computer program so that it is easy to implement each step of the algorithm as a computer instruction or as a sequence of instructions. Consequently, algorithms are commonly written in **pseudocode,** a pseudoprogramming language that is a mixture of natural language and symbols, terms, and other features commonly used in one or more high-level programming languages. Because it has no standard syntax, pseudocode varies from one programmer to another, but it typically includes the following features:

1. The usual computer symbols $+$, $-$, $*$, and $/$ are used for the basic arithmetic operations.
2. Symbolic names (identifiers) are used to represent the quantities being processed by the algorithm.
3. Some provision is made for indicating comments, for example, using the Pascal convention of enclosing them between a pair of special symbols such as ($*$ and $*$).
4. Key words that are common in high-level languages are allowed, for example, *read* or *enter* for input operations and *display, print,* or *write* for output operations.
5. Indentation is used to set off blocks of instructions.

The finiteness property requires that an algorithm will eventually halt; that is, it will terminate after a finite number of steps. In particular, this means that the algorithms may not contain any infinite loops. For example, if an algorithm includes a set of statements that are to be executed repeatedly while some boolean expression is true, then these statements must eventually cause that boolean expression to become false so that repetition is terminated. Also, when an algorithm terminates, we obviously expect that it will have produced the required results. Thus, in addition to demonstrating that a given algorithm will terminate, it is also necessary to verify its correctness.

As a practical matter, simply knowing that an algorithm will terminate may not be sufficient. For example, an algorithm for playing a winning game of chess that at each stage of the game examines every possible move to determine whether or not it is a winning move will terminate but will require so much time that it has no practical value. Useful algorithms, therefore, must terminate in some *reasonable* amount of time. In Chapter 6 we will consider some techniques that are useful in estimating the computing time of an algorithm.

The analysis and verification of algorithms and of the programs that implement them are much easier if they are well structured. ***Structured algorithms*** and ***programs*** are designed using three basic control structures:

1. *Sequence:*   Steps are performed in a strictly sequential manner, each step being executed exactly once.
2. *Selection:*   One of several alternative actions is selected and executed.
3. *Repetition:*   One or more steps is performed repeatedly.

These three control mechanisms are individually quite simple, but in fact they are sufficiently powerful that any algorithm can be constructed using them.

Algorithms that are carefully designed using only these control structures are much more readable and understandable and hence can be analyzed and verified much more easily than can unstructured ones. To illustrate, consider the following unstructured algorithm:

ALGORITHM (UNSTRUCTURED VERSION)

(∗ Algorithm to read and count several triples of distinct numbers and print the largest number in each triple. ∗)

1. Initialize *Count* to 0.
2. Read a triple x, y, z.
3. If x = end-of-data-flag then go to step 14.
4. Increment *Count* by 1.
5. If $x > y$ then go to step 9.
6. If $y > z$ then go to step 12.
7. Display z.
8. Go to step 2.
9. If $x < z$ then go to step 7.
10. Display x.
11. Go to step 2.
12. Display y.
13. Go to step 2.
14. Display *Count*.

The "spaghetti logic" of this algorithm is vividly displayed in the first diagram in Figure 1.1.

In contrast, consider the following structured algorithm. The clarity

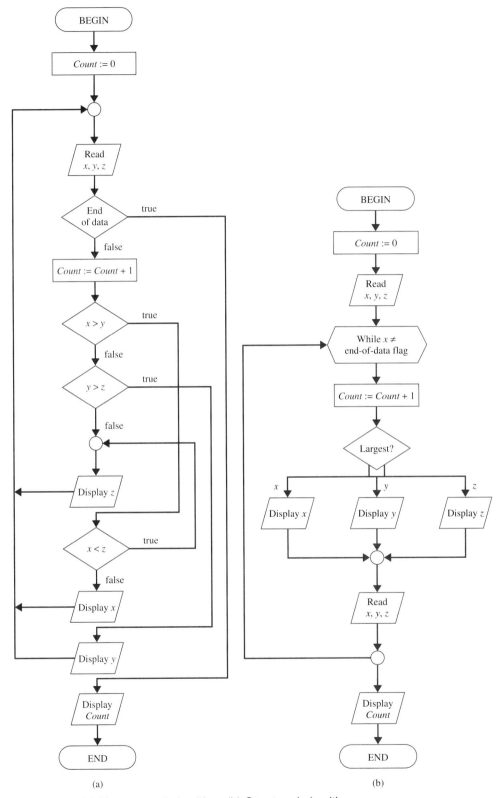

Figure 1.1 (a) Unstructured algorithm. (b) Structured algorithm.

and simple elegance of its logical flow are shown in the second diagram in Figure 1.1.

> **ALGORITHM (STRUCTURED VERSION)**
>
> (* Algorithm to read and count several triples of distinct numbers and print the largest number in each triple. *)
>
> 1. Initialize *Count* to 0.
> 2. Read the first triple of numbers x, y, z.
> 3. While $x \neq$ end-of-data-flag do the following:
>   a. Increment *Count* by 1.
>   b. If $x > y$ and $x > z$ then
>   Display x.
>   Else if $y > x$ and $y > z$ then
>   Display y.
>   Else
>   Display z.
>   c. Read next triple x, y, z.
> 4. Display *Count*.

1.3 Coding and Integration

Coding is a synonym for programming and is the process of implementing data structures and algorithms in some programming language. If the algorithms and data structures have been well designed, this translation process is nearly automatic. **Integration** is the process of combining the resulting program units into a complete software system. As we noted in the preceding section, the development of large software systems is done in a top-down manner in which a problem is partitioned into a number of subproblems and individual modules are developed to solve the subproblems. Integration of these units to form a complete system is usually carried out incrementally by adding them to the system one at a time. If an error occurs when a new module is added to the system, the developer can be reasonably confident that it was caused by this module and not by one added earlier.

The first decision that must be made when coding algorithms is what programming language to use, which obviously depends on the languages available to the programmer and those that he or she is able to use. Also, the problem may have characteristics that make one language more suitable than another. For example, if the problem requires scientific computing with extended precision and/or complex numbers, FORTRAN may be the most suitable language. Problems that involve extensive file manipulation and report generation may perhaps best be done with COBOL. Structured algorithms, especially those developed as a collection of subalgorithms in a top-down manner, can best be implemented in a structured language such as Pascal, Modula-2, or Ada.

Regardless of the language in which they are written, *programs must be correct, readable, and understandable*. Correctness is obviously the most important property. No matter what other qualities a program has—it is well structured, is well documented, looks nice, and so on—it is worthless if it does not produce correct results. Testing and validation are thus important steps in software development and are reviewed in more detail in the next section.

It is often difficult for beginning programmers to appreciate the importance of the other program characteristics and of developing good programming habits that lead to the design of programs that are readable and understandable. They have difficulty because programs developed in an academic environment are often quite different from those developed in real-world situations, in which program style and form are critical. Student programs are usually quite small (usually less than a few hundred lines of code); are executed and modified only a few times (almost never, once they have been handed in); are rarely examined in detail by anyone other than the student and the instructor; and are not developed within the context of budget restraints. Real-world systems, on the other hand, may be very large (several thousand lines of code); are developed by teams of programmers; are commonly used for long periods of time and thus require maintenance if they are to be kept current and correct; and are often maintained by someone other than the original programmer. As hardware costs continue to decrease and programmer costs increase, the importance of reducing programming and maintenance costs, and the corresponding importance of writing programs that can be easily read and understood by others, continues to increase.

A number of programming practices contribute to the development of correct, readable, and understandable software. Because good programming habits are essential, we shall review some of these guidelines once again. One principle is that *programs should be well structured*. The following guidelines are helpful in this regard:

- *Use a top-down approach when developing a program for a complex problem.* Divide the problem into simpler subproblems, and write individual procedures and functions to solve these subproblems. These subprograms should be relatively short and as self-contained as possible.
- *Use the basic control structures when developing each program module.* Any program unit can be written using only the sequential (**begin . . . end**), selection (**if, case**), and repetition (**while, repeat, for**) structures. These structures should be combined to form nested blocks of code that are entered only at the top and exited only at the bottom.
- *Use local variables within subprograms.* Variables used only within a subprogram should be declared within that subprogram.
- *Use parameters to pass information to and from subprograms.* Avoid using **global variables** to share information between subprograms because it destroys their independence. It can be difficult to determine the value of a global variable at some point in the program because it may have been changed by any of the program units.
- *To protect parameters that should not be modified by a subprogram, declare them to be value parameters rather than variable parameters.* Otherwise, the subprogram may unexpectedly change the value of an actual parameter in some other program unit. One exception in Pascal is that parameters of file type must be variable parameters, since as-

signment of one file to another is not allowed. Another common exception is for arrays; declaring them to be variable parameters saves memory and makes it unnecessary to copy the elements of the actual array into the formal array.

● *Use variable "status" parameters to signal error conditions or other special conditions encountered during execution of a subprogram.* For example, a procedure for searching a list should return a value for a boolean parameter that indicates whether the search was successful; it might also return a list-empty indicator. A procedure to insert an item into a list might return a value for the parameter *ListFull,* and a delete procedure might return a value for *ListEmpty.*

● *Use constant identifiers to improve readability, flexibility, and portability.* For example, the following statement violates what has been termed the "Houdini principle" because it allows "magic numbers" to arise suddenly without explanation:

$$PopChange := (0.1758 - 0.1257) * Population;$$

The numbers 0.1758 and 0.1257 should be replaced by constant identifiers (or variables whose values are read or assigned during execution), as in

```
const
    BirthRate = 0.1758;
    DeathRate = 0.1257;
        .
        .
        .
    PopChange := (BirthRate - DeathRate) * Population;
```

The second assignment statement is more readable than the first. Also, if these numbers must be changed, one need only change the definitions of *BirthRate* and *DeathRate* in the constant section rather than conduct an exhaustive search of the program to locate all their occurrences. Similarly, using a predefined constant identifier such as *maxint* rather than some machine-dependent constant such as 32767 increases the portability of the program.

● *Strive for simplicity and clarity.* Clever programming tricks intended only to demonstrate the programmer's ingenuity or to produce code that executes only slightly more efficiently should be avoided.

A second principle is that *each program should be documented.* In particular:

● *Each program should include opening documentation.* Comments should be included at the beginning of the program to explain what it does, how it works, any special algorithms it implements, and so on and may also include a summary of the problem's specification, assumptions, and other items of information such as the name of the programmer, the date the program was written, when it was last modified, and references to books and manuals that give additional information about the program. In addition, it is a good practice to explain the use of each identifier declared in the **const** and **var** declaration sections.

- *Each subprogram should be documented in a manner similar to the main program.* In particular, it should include a summary of the specification of the subproblem for which it was developed.
- *Comments should be used to explain key program segments and/or segments whose purpose or design is not obvious.* However, don't clutter the program with needless comments, as in

$$Count := Count + 1; (* \text{ Increment } Count *)$$

- *Use meaningful identifiers.* For example,

$$Wages := HoursWorked * HourlyRate;$$

is clearer than

$$W := H * R;$$

Don't use "skimpy" abbreviations just to save a few keystrokes when entering the program. Also, follow what has been called the "Shirley Temple principle" and avoid "cute" identifiers, as in

$$BaconBroughtHome := SlaveLabor * LessThanImWorth;$$

A third principle has to do with a program's appearance: *A program should be aesthetic; it should be formatted in a style that enhances its readability.* In particular, the following are some guidelines for good programming style:

- *Put each statement on a separate line.*
- *Use uppercase and lowercase letters in a way that contributes to the program's readability.* For example, use upper case for reserved words; use lower case for standard identifiers; capitalize the first letter of each user-defined identifier and the first letter of each part of a "compound" identifier, as in *TotalHonorPoints*.
- *Use spaces between the items in a statement to make it more readable,* for example, before and after each operator ($+$, $-$, $<$, $:=$, etc.).
- *Insert a blank line before each section of the program and wherever appropriate in a sequence of statements to set off blocks of statements.*
- *When a statement is continued from one line to another, indent the continuation line(s).*
- *Adhere rigorously to alignment and indentation guidelines to emphasize the relationship between reserved words, clauses, and statements that comprise control structures, program sections, and so on.*

1.4 Validation, Verification, and Testing

Errors may occur in any of the phases of the software development life cycle. For example, the specifications may not accurately reflect information given in the problem or the customer's needs and/or desires; the algorithms may contain logical errors; and the program units may not be coded or integrated correctly. The detection and correction of errors is an important part of software development and is known as validation and verification. *Validation* is concerned with checking that the documents, program modules, and the like that are produced match the problem's specification. *Verification* refers to checking that these products are correct and complete and that they are consistent with one another and with those of the preceding phases. Validation is sometimes described as answering the question "Are we building the right product?" and verification as answering the question "Are we building the product right?"

Since errors may occur at each phase of the development process, different kinds of tests are required to detect them: *unit tests* in which each program unit is tested individually, *integration tests* that check that these units have been combined correctly, and *system tests* that test to see whether the overall system functions correctly. These correspond to the various phases of the software life cycle, as indicated by the following diagram of the "V" Life Cycle Model:[1]

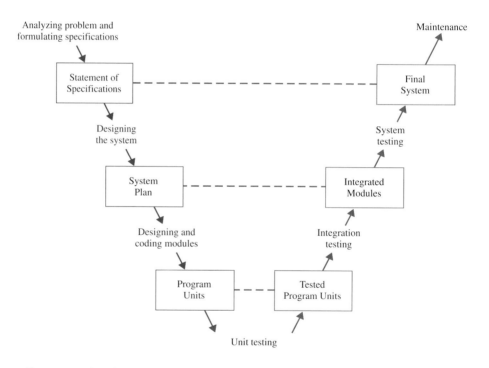

System testing is obviously related to the first phase, as described in Section 1.1, where we noted that the specification document serves as a benchmark against which the correctness and performance of the final system are measured. Integration tests are considered in the case study in Section 1.6,

---

[1] Additional information about the "V" Life Cycle Model and about software testing can be found in Dorothy Graham, *Software Test and Debug: Techniques and Tools* (Manchester, England: A National Computing Centre Limited Technical Report, 1989).

where we illustrate top-down design and top-down testing. In Section 4.2 we illustrate a different kind of testing known as ***bottom-up testing.*** In this section we restrict our attention to some of the techniques used in unit testing, probably the most rigorous and time-consuming of the various kinds of testing. It is surely the most fundamental and important kind of testing, since incorrectness of an individual module implies incorrectness of the larger system of which it is a part.

The specification document for the original problem serves as a standard for validating the system as a whole. Similarly, specifications of the subproblems obtained in the top–down design process are needed as standards against which the individual modules are tested. Each of these specifications should include at least a description of

1. The function or purpose of the module.
2. Items input to the module (from input devices).
3. Items *accepted* from other modules.
4. Items output by the module (to output devices).
5. Items *returned* to other modules.

When a correctness proof of the module is required, the specifications must also include ***preconditions*** and ***postconditions*** that describe the state of processing before and after the module is executed. These assertions are usually stated using formal mathematical and logical notation. Thus, although these concepts are introduced briefly in Chapter 6, correctness proofs and formal statements of pre- and postconditions are better left to more advanced courses in computer science. When it is appropriate in the examples of this text, we will include informal descriptions of pre- and postconditions in the descriptions of the module's input/accepted items and output/returned items, respectively.

Only in the rarest cases is the first attempt at writing a program free of errors. ***Syntax errors*** (caused by incorrect punctuation, misspelled reserved words, and so on) and ***run-time errors*** such as division by zero and integer overflow that occur during execution are usually quite easy to detect and correct, since system-generated error messages can help locate and explain these errors. ***Logical errors***, however, are far more difficult to detect and locate, because the program executes but does not produce the correct results. These errors may be due to inaccurate coding of an algorithm or in the design of the algorithm itself.

There are many kinds of tests that can be used to locate errors. One common classification of testing techniques is into black-box tests and white-box tests. In a ***black-box*** or ***functional test*** of a program unit, the outputs produced for various inputs are checked for correctness without considering the structure of the module itself. That is, the module is viewed as a black box that accepts inputs and produces outputs, but the inner workings of the box are not visible. In a ***white-box*** (***clear-box, glass-box***) or ***structural test***, the performance of a module is tested by examining its internal structure. Test data is carefully selected so that the various parts of the program unit are exercised.

To illustrate some of the testing techniques that can be used to detect logical errors, consider a module to perform a binary search for some item in an ordered list stored in an array.

The specification for this module is:

Specification for Binary Search

FUNCTION: Module is to perform a binary search of an array for a specified item, and if found, determine its position in the array.

INPUT: None

ACCEPTS: An array having n elements ordered in ascending order, and a value *Item* having the same type as the array components.

OUTPUT: None

RETURNS: *Found* and *Mid* where *Found* is true and *Mid* is the position of *Item* if the search is successful; otherwise *Found* is false.

Eighty percent of all beginning programmers will not write a binary search algorithm correctly. One common attempt is

BINARY SEARCH ALGORITHM (∗ INCORRECT VERSION ∗)

1. Set *Found* equal to false.
2. Set *First* equal to 1.
3. Set *Last* equal to n.
4. While *First* ≤ *Last* and not *Found* do the following:
    a. Calculate *Mid* = (*First* + *Last*) / 2.
    b. If *Item* < A[*Mid*] then
        Set *Last* equal to *Mid*.
       Else if *Item* > A[*Mid*] then
        Set *First* equal to *Mid*.
       Else
        Set *Found* equal to true.

A Pascal procedure that implements this algorithm is

```
procedure BinarySearch (var A : NumberArray; n : integer;
                             Item : ElementType;
                             var Found : boolean; var Mid : integer);
```

```
(∗ INCORRECT PROCEDURE
    Accepts: Item and an array A having n items, arranged in
             ascending order.
    Function: Performs a binary search of A for Item.
    Returns: Found and Mid where Found is true and Mid is the
             position of Item if the search is successful;
             otherwise Found is false. ∗)
```

```
var
    First,                    (* First and last positions in sublist *)
    Last : integer;           (* currently being searched *)
begin (* BinarySearch *)
    Found := false;
    First := 1;
    Last := n;
    while (First <= Last) and not Found do
        begin
            Mid := (First + Last) div 2;
            if Item < A[Mid] then
                Last := Mid
            else if Item > A[Mid] then
                First := Mid
            else
                Found := true
        end (* while *)
end (* BinarySearch *);
```

Note that as suggested in the documentation guidelines of Section 1.3, we have included a summary of the specification for binary search within the opening documentation of procedure *BinarySearch*.

This procedure might be tested using a black-box approach with $n = 7$ and the following array A of integers:

$$A[1] = 45$$

$$A[2] = 64$$

$$A[3] = 68$$

$$A[4] = 77$$

$$A[5] = 84$$

$$A[6] = 90$$

$$A[7] = 96$$

A search for *Item* $= 77$ returns the values *true* for *Found* and 4 for *Mid*, which is the location of 77 in the array. Testing with *Item* $= 90$ and *Item* $= 64$ also yields correct results. If the value 76 is used for *Item*, *Found* is returned as *false*, indicating that the item is not in the array. These tests might lead one to conclude that this procedure is correct. Experienced programmers know, however, that special cases must always be considered when selecting test data, since it is often these cases that cause a program unit to malfunction. For example, in processing lists like that in this problem, one special case that must be tested is searching at the ends of the list. For procedure *BinarySearch*, therefore, we should test it with values of 45 and 96 for *Item* as well as with values less than 45 and values greater than 96. For *Item* $= 45$, the procedure returns *Found* $=$ *true* and *Mid* $= 1$, as it should. A search for *Item* $= 96$

fails, however; the search procedure did not terminate and it was necessary for the programmer to terminate execution using a ''break'' key on the keyboard.

White-box testing would also detect an error, because in this approach, we choose data to test the various paths that execution can follow. For example, one set of data should test a path in which the first condition *Item* < *A*[*Mid*] in the **if** statement is true on each iteration so that the first alternative *Last* := *Mid* is always selected. Using values less than or equal to 45 will cause execution to follow this path. Similarly, values greater than or equal to 96 will cause execution to follow a path in which the second condition *Item* > *A*[*Mid*] in the **if** statement is true on each iteration so that the second alternative *First* := *Mid* is always selected.

Once an error has been detected, various techniques can be used to locate the error. One approach is to trace the execution of a program segment by inserting temporary output statements to display values of key variables at various stages of program execution. For example, inserting the statements

> *writeln* ('DEBUG: At top of while loop in BinarySearch');
> *writeln* ('First = ', *First*:1, ', Last = ', *Last* :1, ', Mid = ', *Mid*:1);

after the statement that assigns a value to *Mid* at the beginning of the while loop in the preceding procedure *BinarySearch* results in the following output in a search for 96:

```
DEBUG:  At top of while loop in BinarySearch
First = 1, Last = 7, Mid = 4
DEBUG:  At top of while loop in BinarySearch
First = 4, Last = 7, Mid = 5
DEBUG:  At top of while loop in BinarySearch
First = 5, Last = 7, Mid = 6
DEBUG:  At top of while loop in BinarySearch
First = 6, Last = 7, Mid = 6
DEBUG:  At top of while loop in BinarySearch
First = 6, Last = 7, Mid = 6
DEBUG:  At top of while loop in BinarySearch
First = 6, Last = 7, Mid = 6
                  .
                  .
                  .
```

One must be careful, however, to put such temporary output statements in places that are helpful in locating the source of the error and not to use so many of these statements that the volume of output hinders the search for the error.

One can also manually trace an algorithm or program segment by working through it step by step, recording the values of certain key variables in a ***trace table.*** This technique is known as ***desk checking*** the algorithm/program segment. For example, tracing the while loop in the binary search algorithm using the preceding array *A* with *Item* = 96, recording the values of *First, Last,* and

Mid, gives the following trace table:

Step	First	Last	Mid
Initially	1	7	—
4a	1	7	4
4b	4	7	4
4a	4	7	5
4b	4	7	5
4a	5	7	6
4b	5	7	6
4a	6	7	6
4b	6	7	6
4a	6	7	6
4b	6	7	6
4a	6	7	6
4b	6	7	6
.	.	.	.
.	.	.	.
.	.	.	.

Either manual or automatic tracing of this procedure reveals that when *Item* = 96, the last array element, *First* eventually becomes 6, *Last* becomes 7, and *Mid* is then always computed as 6, so that *First* and *Last* never change. Because the algorithm does locate each of the other array elements, the beginning programmer might "patch" it by treating this special case separately and inserting the statement

if *Item* = *A*[*n*] **then**
   begin
     Mid := *n*;
     Found := *true*
   end;

before the while loop. The procedure now correctly locates each of the array elements, but it is still not correct, as searching for any item greater than *A*[7] still will result in an infinite loop.

Attempting to fix program units with "quick and dirty" patches like this is almost always a bad idea because it fails to address the real source of the problem and thus makes the program unnecessarily complicated and "messy." The real source of difficulty in the preceding example is not that the last element of the array requires special consideration but that the updating of *First* and *Last* within the while loop is not correct. If *Item* < *A*[*Mid*], then the part of the array *preceding* location *Mid*, that is, *A*[*First*], . . . , *A*[*Mid* − 1], should be searched, not *A*[*First*], . . . , *A*[*Mid*]. Thus, in this case, *Last* should be set equal to *Mid* − 1, not *Mid*. Similarly, if *Item* > *A*[*Mid*], then *First* should be set equal to *Mid* + 1 rather than *Mid*.

Once an error has been found, the program unit must be corrected and tested again. This cycle of testing and correcting may have to be repeated many times before one can be reasonably confident that the module is correct. It must be realized, however, that it is almost never possible to test a program unit with every possible set of test data. No matter how much testing has been done, more can always be done. Thus, testing is never finished; it is only stopped. No matter how extensively a module is tested, there is no guarantee that all the errors have been found. Obscure ''bugs'' will often remain and will not be detected until some time later, perhaps after the software has been released for public use. As these bugs turn up, the cycle of testing and correction must be repeated and a ''fix'' or ''patch'' or a new release sent to the users.

In some applications such as defense systems and spacecraft guidance systems, program errors are more than just a nuisance and cannot be tolerated. In such cases, relying on the results of test runs may not be sufficient because *testing can only show the presence of errors, not their absence.* It may be necessary to give a deductive proof that the program is correct and that it will *always* produce the correct results (assuming no system malfunction). Correctness proofs are considered in Chapter 6.

1.5 System Maintenance

Once a program or system of programs has been validated and verified, it begins its useful life and will, in many cases, be used for several years. It is likely, however, that it will require some modification. As we noted in the previous section, some software systems, especially large ones developed for complex projects, will often have obscure bugs that were not detected during testing and that will surface after the software is released for public use. One important aspect of system maintenance is fixing such flaws in the software.

It may also be necessary to enhance the software by improving its performance, by adding new features, and so on. Other modifications may be required because of changes in the computer hardware and/or the system software such as the operating system. External factors such as changes in government rules and regulations or changes in the organizational structure of the company may also force software modification. These changes are easier to make in systems that are developed in a modular manner with well-structured modules than in poorly designed systems because the changes can often be made by modifying only a few of the modules or by adding new modules.

Software maintenance is a major component of the life cycle of software. Studies have shown that in recent years more than 50 percent of computer center budgets and more than 50 percent of programmer time have been devoted to software maintenance and that worldwide, billions and perhaps trillions of dollars have been spent on software maintenance. A major factor that has contributed to this high cost in money and time is that many programs and systems were originally written with poor structure, documentation, and style. This problem is complicated by the fact that maintenance must often be done by someone not involved in the original design. Thus it is mandatory that programmers do their utmost to design programs and systems of programs that are readable, well documented, and well structured so they are easy to understand and modify and are thus easier to maintain than is much of the software developed in the past.

1.6 Case Study: The Financial Aid Problem

To illustrate the ideas and techniques reviewed in the preceding sections, we will develop a program to solve the financial aid problem introduced in Section 1.1. Recall that the statement of the problem as posed by the vice-president of scholarships and financial aid was quite vague, stating only that accurate records of all students currently receiving financial aid must be maintained and that regular reports must be submitted to the FFAO (Federal Financial Aid Office).

The first step in solving this problem is to formulate a precise specification for it, in particular, to identify the input and the output of the problem. After consultation with the scholarships and financial aid staff, we might formulate the following specification:

Input
1. A disk file of student records, each containing a student's number, name, GPA, credits, and financial aid received.
2. The identification numbers of several students, entered from the keyboard.

Output
1. The records of specified students, displayed on the user's screen.
2. A file of student records, some of which are updated by changes to a student's cumulative grade point average (gpa) and/or credits and/or amount of financial aid.
3. A printed report showing the current (updated) information—student number, name, GPA, credits, and financial aid—for all students.

Using top-down design to develop a program to solve this problem, we begin by identifying the three main tasks needed to solve it, describing them in fairly general terms:

1. An initialization task in which the student information in the file stored on disk is copied into main memory so that it can be processed.
2. A processing task that processes this information to produce the required output.
3. A wrap-up task in which the updated information is copied back into the disk file where it can be saved for later processing.

It is helpful to display these tasks and their relationship to one another in a *structure diagram* like the following:

Typically, one or more of these first-level tasks are still quite complex and so must be divided into subtasks. In this example, the description of the task *ProcessRecords* is very general, and further analysis shows that this task consists of servicing the three main types of requests identified earlier:

1. Retrieve the record for a given student.
2. Update the information in a student's record.
3. Generate a report displaying information for all students.

These subtasks are displayed in the second level of the following refined structure diagram:

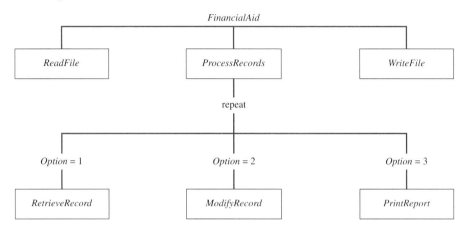

These subtasks may require further division into still smaller subtasks, producing additional levels of refinement, for example:

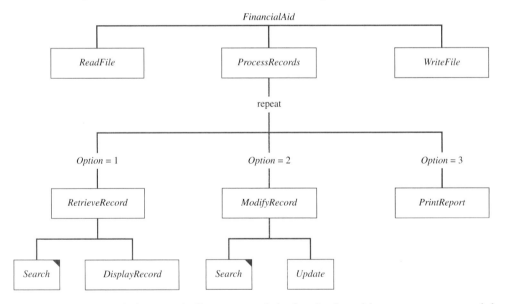

(The shaded corner indicates a module that is shared by two or more modules. This process continues until each subtask is sufficiently simple that designing a module for it is quite easy and straightforward.

As we noted in Section 1.1, another important component of the design plan is the selection of data structures for organizing the data. The input data consists of information about students receiving financial aid at Dispatch University. For each student, this information consists of his or her student number, name, grade point average, current credits, and amount of financial aid received. Since these five items of information are related (they all pertain to one student) but are of different types (integer, string, real, real, integer), it seems natural to organize this information into a record. These records are stored on a disk, and thus the input data is organized as a *file of records*. The basic processing operations that must be performed on this data are

1. Retrieve the information for a particular student, given the student's number.
2. Modify a student's record by updating the grade point average, current credits, or amount of financial aid.
3. Traverse the collection of records so that a report can be generated and also so that an updated file of records can be created.

Both the first two basic operations, retrieval and modification, require searching the collection of records to locate a particular record. One possibility would be to use a *sequential file* and to search it from its beginning each time a record must be retrieved or modified. In the case of modification, we would copy the records into another file as they are examined until the desired record is located, write the updated record for that student into the new file, and then copy the remainder of the original file into the new file. The contents of this new file would then be copied back into the original file so more searches could be performed. File input/output is slow, however, so if a large number of retrievals and/or modifications are to be performed, the response time may not be acceptable.

Another possibility would be to use a *direct access file,* in which a given record can be located directly without processing all those that precede it, and this record in the file can then be read and/or written; thus modification of a record in the file can be carried out "in place" without an excessive amount of file input/output. However, some programming languages—standard Pascal, in particular—do not support direct access files.

A third alternative would be to make direct access to the records possible by first copying them from the file into an array (or into several arrays), assuming of course that the number of records is not so large that they cannot be stored in main memory. Because storing data in and retrieving data from main memory is considerably faster than for secondary memory, this would appear to be the most attractive option and is the one we adopt in this example. Thus we will use the following data structures to organize the data of this problem:

Data Structures

1. Records: student records, each of which contains a student's number, name, GPA, credits, and financial aid.
2. File: a file containing student records input to the program.
3. Array of records: an array of student records.
4. File: the file of updated student records output by the program.

We turn now to formulating more detailed descriptions of the processing to be carried out by each of the required modules. The main part of the program will call three separate subprograms to perform the three top-level tasks.

MAIN MODULE

Specification

INPUT: A disk file of student records, each containing a student's number, name, GPA, credits, and financial aid.
Identification numbers of several students, entered from the keyboard.

FUNCTION: Reads student records from the input file into an array and allows the user to process these records. After processing is done, copies the updated list of records into a new file.

OUTPUT: The records of specified students, displayed on the user's screen.
A file of updated student records, in some of which there have been changes to a student's cumulative GPA and/or credits and/or amount of financial aid.
A printed report showing the updated records.

Algorithm

1. Use the subprogram *ReadFile* to copy the records from a given input file into an array.
2. If this file load was not successful then
   Display an unsuccessful load message.
   Else do the following:
   a. Call the subprogram *ProcessRecords* to carry out processing as requested by the user.
   b. After processing is completed, use subprogram *WriteFile* to copy the array of updated records back into the file.

FIRST-LEVEL MODULES

ReadFile

Specification

Input: A file of student records.
Function: Reads and counts records and stores them in the array *Student*.
Returns: The array *Student*, the number *NumRecs* of records read, and *ArrayFull*, which is true if there are too many records to store in the array.

Algorithm

1. Open the file for input.
2. Initialize a counter *NumRecs* to 0, and a boolean variable *ArrayFull* to false.

3. While not end of file and not *ArrayFull* do the following:
    If *NumRecs* < *ArrayLimit* then:
       a. Increment *NumRecs* by 1.
       b. Read a record from the file into location *NumRecs* of the
          array *Student*.
    Else
       Set *ArrayFull* to true to signal that the file load was not suc-
       cessful.

ProcessRecords

Specification

Accepts: Array *Student* having *NumRecs* student records.
Input: An *Option* from the user, which indicates the type of
                processing selected by the user.
Function: Allows the user to process any of the records in *Student*
                by retrieving a record, modifying it, or printing a listing of
                the records.
Returns: Updated array *Student*.

Algorithm

1. Get the first *Option*—R(etrieve), M(odify), P(rint report), or Q(uit).
2. While *Option* ≠ 'Q' do the following:
    a. If option selected is legal, then call an appropriate subprogram
       to carry out the required action:
          'R' : *RetrieveRecord*;
          'M' : *ModifyRecord*;
          'P' : *PrintReport*;
    b. Get the next *Option*.

WriteFile

Specification

Accepts: Array *Student* having *NumRecs* student records.
Function: Copys *Student* into a file.
Output: A file containing the records in *Student*.

Algorithm

1. Open the file for output.
2. For an index *i* ranging from 1 to *NumRecs* do the following:
    Write the *i*th element of array *Student* into the file.

SECOND-LEVEL MODULES

RetrieveRecord

Specification

Accepts: Array *Student* having *NumRecs* student records and a student number entered by the user.

Function: Searches *Student* for a record containing the student number and if found, displays this record.

Output: Student's record or a ''Not Found'' message.

Algorithm

1. Enter student's number.
2. Call subprogram *Search* to search array *Student* for a record containing this number.
3. If student's record is found then
      Call subprogram *DisplayRecord* to display it.
   Else
      Display a 'Not Found' message.

ModifyRecord

Specification

Accepts: Array *Student* having *NumRecs* student records.

Input: A student number entered by the user.

Function: Searches *Student* for a record containing the student number and if found, allows the user to update this record.

Returns: Updated array *Student*

Output: A ''Not Found'' message if student record is not found.

Algorithm

1. Enter student's number.
2. Call subprogram *Search* to search array *Student* for a record containing this number.
3. If student's record is found then
      Call subprogram *UpdateRecord* to update it.
   Else
      Display a 'Not Found' message.

PrintReport

Specification

Accepts: Array *Student* having *NumRecs* student records.

Function: Displays the records in *Student*.

Output: A report showing the student records.

Algorithm

1. Print headings for the report.
2. For an index i ranging from 1 to *NumRecs* do the following:
   Display the ith record in array *Student*.

THIRD-LEVEL MODULES

Search

A standard binary search algorithm that every programmer should have in his or her toolbox.

DisplayRecord

Specification

Accepts: A student's record.
Function: Displays the contents of this record.
Output: Specially-formatted display of the fields in the record.

Algorithm

A custom-designed output procedure to display the fields in a student's record in an acceptable format.

Update

Specification

Accepts: A student's record
Input: A *SubOption* entered by the user, which indicates the kind of updating to be done.
Function: Updates the student's record by changing the student's credits, GPA, or financial aid.
Returns: Updated student record.

Algorithm

1. Get the first *SubOption*—C(redits change), G(PA change), or F(inancial aid change), or D(one updating).
2. While *SubOption* $\neq$ 'D' do the following:
   a. Read a new value for current credits, grade point average, or financial aid in this record according to whether *SubOption* is C, G, or F.
   b. Get the next *SubOption*.

This design plan must now be implemented by coding and testing these modules and integrating the resulting program units into a program. To illustrate, a first version of the program to solve the financial aid problem is shown in Figure 1.2. Here only one of the first-level modules, namely *ReadFile*, has been implemented as a procedure. The other first-level modules are represented by **program stubs**; *ProcessRecords* produces a temporary printout of the number of records and the student numbers in the first and last records of the array as a check that *ReadFile* has performed correctly; *WriteFile* simply displays a message indicating that it has been called. This makes it possible to do **top–down testing** of the main program unit and the procedure *ReadFile*.

```
PROGRAM FinancialAid (input, StuFile, output, NewStuFile);

(**********************************************************************

    Input (file):      A file StuFile of student records, each containing
                       a student's number, name, GPA, credits, and
                       financial aid received.
    Input (keyboard):  Identification numbers of several students.
    Function:          Reads student records from StuFile into array
                       Student and allows the user to process these
                       records.  After processing is done, copies the
                       updated list of records into a new file NewStuFile.
    Output (screen):   Records of specified student.
                       Report showing the updated records.
    Output (file):     A file NewStufile of student records, some of
                       which are updated by changes to a student's
                       cumulative GPA and/or credits and/or amount of
                       financial aid.

**********************************************************************)

CONST
    StringLimit = 20;        (* limit on length of name string *)
    ArrayLimit = 100;        (* limit on number of student records *)

TYPE
    StringType = PACKED ARRAY[1..StringLimit] OF char;
    StudentRecord = RECORD
                        Number : integer;
                        Name : StringType;
                        GPA,
                        Credits : real;
                        FinAid : integer
                    END;
    ArrayOfRecords = ARRAY[1..ArrayLimit] OF StudentRecord;

VAR
    StuFile,                 (* original file of student records *)
    NewStuFile : text;       (* updated file of student records *)
    Student : ArrayOfRecords; (* array of student records *)
    NumRecs : integer;       (* number of records *)
    ArrayFull : boolean;     (* signals if array becomes full *)
```

Figure 1.2

Figure 1.2 (cont.)

```
PROCEDURE ReadFile (VAR StuFile : Text; VAR Student : ArrayOfRecords;
                    Limit : integer; VAR NumRecs : integer;
                    VAR ArrayFull : boolean);

   (*********************************************************************

      Input (file):   File Stufile of student records.
      Function:       Reads and counts records and stores them in the
                      array Student.
      Output (param): Array Student, number NumRecs of records read,
                      and boolean value ArrayFull, which is true if
                      the array cannot hold all of the records.

      ******************************************************************)

   VAR
      i : integer;           (* index *)

   BEGIN (* ReadFile *)
      reset (StuFile);
      NumRecs := 0;
      ArrayFull := false;
      WHILE NOT eof(StuFile) AND NOT ArrayFull DO
         IF NumRecs < Limit THEN
            BEGIN
               NumRecs := NumRecs + 1;
               WITH Student[NumRecs] DO
                  BEGIN
                     read (StuFile, Number);
                     FOR i := 1 TO StringLimit DO
                        IF NOT eoln(StuFile) THEN
                           read (StuFile, Name[i])
                        ELSE
                           Name[i] := ' ';
                     readln (StuFile);
                     readln (StuFile, GPA, Credits, FinAid)
                  END (* WITH *)
            END (* IF *)
         ELSE
            ArrayFull := true
   END (* ReadFile *);

PROCEDURE ProcessRecords (VAR Student : ArrayOfRecords; NumRecs : integer);

   (*********************************************************************

      Input (param):  Array Student and number NumRecs of records in
                      the array.
      Function:       Allows the user to process any of the records in
                      Student by retrieving a record, modifying it, or
                      printing a list of the updated records.
      Output (param): Updated array Student.

      ******************************************************************)

   BEGIN (* ProcessRecords *)
      writeln ('***** In ProcessRecords *****');
      writeln (NumRecs:1, ' records read');
      writeln ('Student numbers in first and last records:');
      writeln (Student[1].Number, Student[NumRecs].Number)
   END (* ProcessRecords *);
```

Figure 1.2 (cont.)

```
PROCEDURE WriteFile (VAR Student : ArrayOfRecords; NumRecs : integer;
                     VAR NewStuFile : text);

   (*********************************************************************

      Input (param):  Array Student and number NumRecs of records
                      in the array.
      Function:       Copies Student into the file NewStuFile.
      Output (file):  The file NewStuFile of updated student records.

    ********************************************************************)

   BEGIN (* WriteFile *)
      writeln ('***** In WriteFile *****')
   END (* WriteFile *);

BEGIN (* main program *)
   ReadFile (StuFile, Student, ArrayLimit, NumRecs, ArrayFull);
   IF ArrayFull THEN
      writeln ('Error in reading student records from file')
   ELSE
      BEGIN
         ProcessRecords (Student, NumRecs);
         WriteFile (Student, NumRecs, NewStuFile)
      END (* ELSE *)
END (* main program *).
```

Listing of StuFile used in sample run:

```
12345Smith, John
3.35 22.0 5000
12349Doe, Mary Jane
2.94 16.5 2500
12355Jones, Fred A.
2.00 28.5 6250
```

Sample run:

```
***** In ProcessRecords *****
3 records read
Student numbers in first and last records:
    12345     12355
***** In WriteFile *****
```

The sample run shows the output produced for one set of data. Additional testing indicates that procedure *ReadFile* and the main program appear to be working correctly. Thus one might now begin developing the next first-level algorithm *ProcessRecords*. It might be coded as shown in Figure 1.3, where the second-level procedures *RetrieveRecord, ModifyRecord,* and *PrintReport* are program stubs that simply signal their execution.

```
PROGRAM FinancialAid (input, StuFile, output, NewStuFile);

(*********************************************************************

      Input (file):       A file StuFile of student records, each containing
                          a student's number, name, GPA, credits, and
                          financial aid received.
      Input (keyboard):   Identification numbers of several students.
      Function:           Reads student records from StuFile into array
                          Student and allows the user to process these
                          records.  After processing is done, copies the
                          updated list of records into a new file NewStuFile.
      Output (screen):    Records of specified student.
                          Report showing the updated records.
      Output (file):      A file NewStufile of student records, some of
                          which are updated by changes to a student's
                          cumulative GPA and/or credits and/or amount of
                          financial aid.

********************************************************************)

CONST
    StringLimit = 20;          (* limit on length of name string *)
    ArrayLimit = 100;          (* limit on number of student records *)

TYPE
    StringType = PACKED ARRAY[1..StringLimit] OF char;
    StudentRecord = RECORD
                        Number : integer;
                        Name : StringType;
                        GPA,
                        Credits : real;
                        FinAid : integer
                    END;
    ArrayOfRecords = ARRAY[1..ArrayLimit] OF StudentRecord;

VAR
    StuFile,                    (* original file of student records *)
    NewStuFile : text;          (* updated file of student records *)
    Student : ArrayOfRecords;   (* array of student records *)
    NumRecs : integer;          (* number of records *)
    ArrayFull : boolean;        (* signals if array becomes full *)
```

Figure 1.3

Figure 1.3 (cont.)

```
PROCEDURE ReadFile (VAR StuFile : Text; VAR Student : ArrayOfRecords;
                    Limit : integer; VAR NumRecs : integer;
                    VAR ArrayFull : boolean);

   (*******************************************************************

      Input (file):   File Stufile of student records.
      Function:       Reads and counts records and stores them in the
                      array Student.
      Output (param): Array Student, number NumRecs of records read,
                      and boolean value ArrayFull, which is true if
                      the array cannot hold all of the records.

   *******************************************************************)

   VAR
      i : integer;            (* index *)

   BEGIN (* ReadFile *)
      reset (StuFile);
      NumRecs := 0;
      ArrayFull := false;
      WHILE NOT eof(StuFile) AND NOT ArrayFull DO
         IF NumRecs < Limit THEN
            BEGIN
               NumRecs := NumRecs + 1;
               WITH Student[NumRecs] DO
                  BEGIN
                     read (StuFile, Number);
                     FOR i := 1 TO StringLimit DO
                        IF NOT eoln(StuFile) THEN
                           read (StuFile, Name[i])
                        ELSE
                           Name[i] := ' ';
                     readln (StuFile);
                     readln (StuFile, GPA, Credits, FinAid)
                  END (* WITH *)
            END (* IF *)
         ELSE
            ArrayFull := true
   END (* ReadFile *);

PROCEDURE ProcessRecords (VAR Student : ArrayOfRecords; NumRecs : integer);

   (*******************************************************************

      Input (param):  Array Student and number NumRecs of records in
                      the array.
      Function:       Allows the user to process any of the records in
                      Student by retrieving a record, modifying it, or
                      printing a list of the updated records.
      Output (param): Updated array Student.

   *******************************************************************)

   VAR
      Option : char;       (* User option *)
```

Figure 1.3 (cont.)

```
PROCEDURE RetrieveRecord (VAR Student : ArrayOfRecords;
                              NumRecs : integer);

   (*******************************************************************

      Input (param):    Array Student and number NumRecs of records
                        in the array.
      Input (keyboard): Student number Snumb entered by user.
      Function:         Searches Student for a record containing
                        Snumb, and if found, displays this record.
      Output (screen):  Student's record or a "not found" message.

   *******************************************************************)

   BEGIN (* RetrieveRecord *)
      writeln ('*** In RetrieveRecord ***')
   END (* RetrieveRecord *);

PROCEDURE ModifyRecord (VAR Student : ArrayOfRecords; NumRecs : integer);

   (*******************************************************************

      Input (param):    Array Student and number NumRecs of records
                        in the array.
      Input (keyboard): Student number Snumb entered by user.
      Function:         Searches Student for a record containing
                        Snumb, and if found, allows the user to
                        update this record.
      Output (param):   Updated array Student.
      Output (screen):  A "not found" message if student record
                        is not found.

   *******************************************************************)

   BEGIN (* ModifyRecord *)
      writeln ('*** In ModifyRecord ***')
   END (* ModifyRecord *);

PROCEDURE PrintReport (VAR Student : ArrayOfRecords; NumRecs : integer);

   (*******************************************************************

      Input (param):    Array Student and number NumRecs of records
                        in the array.
      Function:         Displays the records in Student.
      Output (screen):  A report showing the student records.

   *******************************************************************)

   BEGIN (* PrintReport *)
      writeln ('*** In PrintReport ***')
   END (* PrintReport *);
```

Figure 1.3 (cont.)

```
BEGIN (* ProcessRecords *)
   write ('Option:  R(etrieve), M(odify), P(rint list), Q(uit)?  ');
   readln (Option);
   WHILE NOT (Option IN ['Q', 'q']) DO
      BEGIN
         IF Option IN ['R','r','M','m','P','p'] THEN
            CASE Option OF
               'R','r': RetrieveRecord (Student, NumRecs);
               'M','m': ModifyRecord (Student, NumRecs);
               'P','p': PrintReport (Student, NumRecs)
            END (* CASE *)
         ELSE
            writeln (Option, ' is not a legal option');
         write ('Option:  R(etrieve), M(odify), P(rint list)',
               'Q(uit)?  ');
         readln (Option)
      END (* WHILE *)
END (* ProcessRecords *);


PROCEDURE WriteFile (VAR Student : ArrayOfRecords; NumRecs : integer;
                     VAR NewStuFile : text);

   (******************************************************************

      Input (param): Array Student and number NumRecs of records
                     in the array.
      Function:      Copies Student into the file NewStuFile.
      Output (file): The file NewStuFile of updated student records.

    *****************************************************************)

   VAR
      i : integer;    (* index *)

   BEGIN (* WriteFile *)
      writeln ('***** In WriteFile *****')
   END (* WriteFile *);

BEGIN (* main program *)
   ReadFile (StuFile, Student, ArrayLimit, NumRecs, ArrayFull);
   IF ArrayFull THEN
      writeln ('Error in reading student records from file')
   ELSE
      BEGIN
         ProcessRecords (Student, NumRecs);
         WriteFile (Student, NumRecs, NewStuFile)
      END (* ELSE *)
END (* main program *).
```

Listing of StuFile used in sample run:

```
12345Smith, John
3.35 22.0 5000
12349Doe, Mary Jane
2.94 16.5 2500
12355Jones, Fred A.
2.00 28.5 6250
```

Figure 1.3 (cont.)

Sample run:

```
Option:  R(etrieve), M(odify), P(rint list), Q(uit)?  R
*** In RetrieveRecord ***
Option:  R(etrieve), M(odify), P(rint list), Q(uit)?  N
N is not a legal option
Option:  R(etrieve), M(odify), P(rint list), Q(uit)?  M
*** In ModifyRecord ***
Option:  R(etrieve), M(odify), P(rint list), Q(uit)?  P
*** In PrintReport ***
Option:  R(etrieve), M(odify), P(rint list), Q(uit)?  Q
***** In WriteFile *****
```

This process of developing subprograms and integrating them with program units already developed continues until eventually the complete program in Figure 1.4 results. Once a program unit has been developed, tested, and integrated with the others, it normally will not require any changes when other subprograms are added later. Also, when an error is detected, one does not usually have to search through the whole program to find its cause, since it will usually be in one of the new subprograms being added to the program.

```
PROGRAM FinancialAid (input, StuFile, output, NewStuFile);

(******************************************************************

    Input (file):       A file StuFile of student records, each containing
                        a student's number, name, GPA, credits, and
                        financial aid received.
    Input (keyboard):   Identification numbers of several students.
    Function:           Reads student records from StuFile into array
                        Student and allows the user to process these
                        records.  After processing is done, copies the
                        updated list of records into a new file NewStuFile.
    Output (screen):    Records of specified student.
                        Report showing the updated records.
    Output (file):      A file NewStufile of student records, some of
                        which are updated by changes to a student's
                        cumulative GPA and/or credits and/or amount of
                        financial aid.

******************************************************************)

CONST
    StringLimit = 20;       (* limit on length of name string *)
    ArrayLimit = 100;       (* limit on number of student records *)
```

Figure 1.4

Figure 1.4 (cont.)

```
TYPE
   StringType = PACKED ARRAY[1..StringLimit] OF char;
   StudentRecord = RECORD
                      Number : integer;
                      Name : StringType;
                      GPA,
                      Credits : real;
                      FinAid : integer
                   END;
   ArrayOfRecords = ARRAY[1..ArrayLimit] OF StudentRecord;

VAR
   StuFile,                   (* original file of student records *)
   NewStuFile : text;         (* updated file of student records *)
   Student : ArrayOfRecords;  (* array of student records *)
   NumRecs : integer;         (* number of records *)
   ArrayFull : boolean;       (* signals if array becomes full *)

      PROCEDURE ReadFile (VAR StuFile : Text; VAR Student : ArrayOfRecords;
                   Limit : integer; VAR NumRecs : integer;
                   VAR ArrayFull : boolean);

   (*********************************************************************

   Input (file):   File Stufile of student records.
   Function:       Reads and counts records and stores them in the
                   array Student.
   Output (param): Array Student, number NumRecs of records read,
                   and boolean value ArrayFull, which is true if
                   the array cannot hold all of the records.

   *********************************************************************)

   VAR
      i : integer;            (* index *)

   BEGIN (* ReadFile *)
      reset (StuFile);
      NumRecs := 0;
      ArrayFull := false;
      WHILE NOT eof(StuFile) AND NOT ArrayFull DO
         IF NumRecs < Limit THEN
            BEGIN
               NumRecs := NumRecs + 1;
               WITH Student[NumRecs] DO
                  BEGIN
                     read (StuFile, Number);
                     FOR i := 1 TO StringLimit DO
                        IF NOT eoln(StuFile) THEN
                           read (StuFile, Name[i])
                        ELSE
                           Name[i] := ' ';
                     readln (StuFile);
                     readln (StuFile, GPA, Credits, FinAid)
                  END (* WITH *)
            END (* IF *)
         ELSE
            ArrayFull := true
   END (* ReadFile *);
```

Figure 1.4 (cont.)

```
PROCEDURE ProcessRecords (VAR Student : ArrayOfRecords; NumRecs : integer);

   (*****************************************************************

      Input (param):   Array Student and number NumRecs of records in
                       the array.
      Function:        Allows the user to process any of the records in
                       Student by retrieving a record, modifying it, or
                       printing a list of the updated records.
      Output (param):  Updated array Student.

   *****************************************************************)

   VAR
      Option : char;        (* User option *)

   PROCEDURE Search (VAR Student : ArrayOfRecords; NumRecs : integer;
                     Snumb : integer; VAR Found : boolean;
                     VAR Location : integer);

      (**************************************************************

         Input (param):   Array Student, number NumRecs of records in the
                          array, and student number Snumb.
         Function:        Performs a binary search of Student for a record
                          containing Snumb, and if found, determines its
                          position in the array.
         Output (param):  Found and Location, where Found is set to true
                          and Location to the position of the record
                          containing Snumb if the search is successful;
                          otherwise, Found is false.

      **************************************************************)

      VAR
         First,              (* first item in sublist being searched *)
         Last,               (* last item in sublist *)
         Middle : integer;   (* middle item in sublist *)

      BEGIN (* Search *)
         First := 1;
         Last := NumRecs;
         Found := false;
         WHILE (First <= Last) AND (NOT Found) DO
            BEGIN
               Middle := (First + Last) DIV 2;
               IF Snumb < Student[Middle].Number THEN
                  Last := Middle - 1    (* item in first half of sublist *)
               ELSE IF Snumb > Student[Middle].Number THEN
                  First := Middle + 1   (* item in last half of sublist *)
               ELSE
                  BEGIN
                     Found := true;      (* item found *)
                     Location := Middle
                  END (* IF *)
            END (* WHILE *)
      END (* Search *);
```

Figure 1.4 (cont.)

```
PROCEDURE DisplayRecord (StuRec: StudentRecord);

   (**********************************************************************

      Input (param):   Student record StuRec.
      Function:        Displays the contents of StuRec.
      Output (screen): Specially-formatted display of the fields
                       of StuRec.

   **********************************************************************)

   BEGIN (* DisplayRecord *)
      WITH StuRec DO
         BEGIN
            writeln (Name);
            writeln ('GPA  - - - - - - - - -', GPA:8:2);
            writeln ('Credits  - - - - - - -', Credits:8:1);
            writeln ('Financial Aid  - - - $', FinAid:8)
         END (* WITH *);
      writeln
   END (* DisplayRecord *);

PROCEDURE RetrieveRecord (VAR Student : ArrayOfRecords;
                          NumRecs : integer);

   (**********************************************************************

      Input (param):     Array Student and number NumRecs of records
                         in the array.
      Input (keyboard):  Student number Snumb entered by user.
      Function:          Searches Student for a record containing
                         Snumb, and if found, displays this record.
      Output (screen):   Student's record or a "not found" message.

   **********************************************************************)

   VAR
      Snumb,                  (* student number in record to retrieve *)
      Location : integer;     (* location of record in array Student *)
      Found : boolean;        (* indicates if search is successful *)

   BEGIN (* RetrieveRecord *)
      write ('Enter Student''s number:  ');
      readln (Snumb);
      Search (Student, NumRecs, Snumb, Found, Location);
      IF Found THEN
         DisplayRecord (Student[Location])
      ELSE
         writeln ('*** Student ', Snumb:1, ' not found ***')
   END (* RetrieveRecord *);
```

Figure 1.4 (cont.)

```
PROCEDURE ModifyRecord (VAR Student : ArrayOfRecords; NumRecs : integer);

   (*****************************************************************

      Input (param):    Array Student and number NumRecs of records
                        in the array.
      Input (keyboard): Student number Snumb entered by user.
      Function:         Searches Student for a record containing
                        Snumb, and if found, allows the user to
                        update this record.
      Output (param):   Updated array Student.
      Output (screen):  A "not found" message if student record
                        is not found.

   *****************************************************************)


VAR
   Snumb,                 (* student number in record to modify *)
   Location : integer;    (* location of record in array Student *)
   Found : boolean;       (* indicates if search is successful *)

PROCEDURE Update (VAR StuRec : StudentRecord);

   (*****************************************************************

      Input (param):    A student's record StuRec.
      Input (keyboard): A SubOption entered by user, which
                        indicates the kind of updating to be done.
      Function:         Updates StuRec by changing the student's
                        credits, GPA, or financial aid.
      Output (param):   Updated student record StuRec.

   *****************************************************************)


VAR
   SubOption : char; (* option from submenu for updating *)
```

Figure 1.4 (cont.)

```
    BEGIN (* Update *)
       write ('Option:  G(pa), C(redits), F(in. aid), D(one)?  ');
       readln (SubOption);
       WHILE NOT (SubOption IN ['D', 'd']) DO
          BEGIN
             IF SubOption IN ['C','c','G','g','F','f'] THEN
                CASE SubOption OF
                   'C','c': BEGIN
                               write ('Enter new credits:  ');
                               readln (StuRec.Credits)
                            END (* 'C', c' *);
                   'G','g': BEGIN
                               write ('Enter new GPA:  ');
                               readln (StuRec.GPA)
                            END (* 'G', g' *);
                   'F','f': BEGIN
                               write ('Enter new financial aid:  ');
                               readln (StuRec.FinAid)
                            END (* 'F', f' *)
                END (* CASE *)
             ELSE
                writeln (SubOption, ' is not a legal option');
             write ('Option:  G(pa), C(redits), F(in. aid)',
                    'D(one)?  ');
             readln (SubOption)
          END (* WHILE *)
    END (* Update *);

BEGIN (* ModifyRecord *)
    write ('Enter Student''s number:  ');
    readln (Snumb);
    Search (Student, NumRecs, Snumb, Found, Location);
    IF Found THEN
       Update (Student[Location])
    ELSE
       writeln ('*** Student ', Snumb:1, ' not found ***')
END (* ModifyRecord *);

PROCEDURE PrintReport (VAR Student : ArrayOfRecords; NumRecs : integer);

    (******************************************************************

    Input (param):    Array Student and number NumRecs of records
                      in the array.
    Function:         Displays the records in Student.
    Output (screen):  A report showing the student records.

    ******************************************************************)

    VAR
       i : integer;      (* index *)
```

Figure 1.4 (cont.)

```
   BEGIN (* PrintReport *)
      writeln;
      writeln ('Number      Name              GPA  Credits  Fin. Aid');
      writeln ('======      ====              ====  =======  ========');
      FOR i := 1 TO NumRecs DO
         WITH Student[i] DO
            writeln (Number:5, '   ', Name, GPA:4:2, Credits:8:1,
                     FinAid:10);
      writeln
   END (* PrintReport *);

BEGIN (* ProcessRecords *)
   write ('Option:  R(etrieve), M(odify), P(rint list), Q(uit)?  ');
   readln (Option);
   WHILE NOT (Option IN ['Q', 'q']) DO
      BEGIN
         IF Option IN ['R','r','M','m','P','p'] THEN
            CASE Option OF
               'R','r': RetrieveRecord (Student, NumRecs);
               'M','m': ModifyRecord (Student, NumRecs);
               'P','p': PrintReport (Student, NumRecs)
            END (* CASE *)
         ELSE
            writeln (Option, ' is not a legal option');
         write ('Option:  R(etrieve), M(odify), P(rint list)',
                ' Q(uit)?  ');
         readln (Option)
      END (* WHILE *)
END (* ProcessRecords *);

PROCEDURE WriteFile (VAR Student : ArrayOfRecords; NumRecs : integer;
                     VAR NewStuFile : text);

(***********************************************************************

   Input (param): Array Student and number NumRecs of records
                  in the array.
   Function:      Copies Student into the file NewStuFile.
   Output (file): The file NewStuFile of updated student records.

***********************************************************************)

VAR
   i : integer;    (* index *)

BEGIN (* WriteFile *)
   rewrite (NewStuFile);
   FOR i := 1 TO NumRecs DO
      WITH Student[i] DO
         BEGIN
            writeln (NewStuFile, Number:5, Name);
            writeln (NewStuFile, GPA:4:2, Credits:5:1, FinAid:5)
         END (* WITH *)
END (* WriteFile *);
```

Figure 1.4 (cont.)

```
BEGIN (* main program *)
   ReadFile (StuFile, Student, ArrayLimit, NumRecs, ArrayFull);
   IF ArrayFull THEN
      writeln ('Error in reading student records from file')
   ELSE
      BEGIN
         ProcessRecords (Student, NumRecs);
         WriteFile (Student, NumRecs, NewStuFile)
      END (* ELSE *)
END (* main program *).
```

Listing of StuFile used in sample run:

```
12345Smith, John
3.35 22.0 5000
12349Doe, Mary Jane
2.94 16.5 2500
12355Jones, Fred A.
2.00 28.5 6250
```

Sample run:

```
Option:  R(etrieve), M(odify), P(rint list), Q(uit)?  R
Enter Student's number:  12349
Doe, Mary Jane
GPA  - - - - - - - - -    2.94
Credits  - - - - - - -    16.5
Financial Aid  - - - $    2500

Option:  R(etrieve), M(odify), P(rint list), Q(uit)?  M
Enter Student's number:  12344
*** Student 12344 not found ***
Option:  R(etrieve), M(odify), P(rint list), Q(uit)?  M
Enter Student's number:  12345
Option:  G(pa), C(redits), F(in. aid), D(one)?  G
Enter new GPA:  3.6
Option:  G(pa), C(redits), F(in. aid), D(one)?  F
Enter new financial aid:  7000
Option:  G(pa), C(redits), F(in. aid), D(one)?  D
Option:  R(etrieve), M(odify), P(rint list), Q(uit)?  P

Number     Name          GPA   Credits  Fin. Aid
======     ====          ====  =======  ========
12345   Smith, John      3.60   22.0      7000
12349   Doe, Mary Jane   2.94   16.5      2500
12355   Jones, Fred A.   2.00   28.5      6250

Option:  R(etrieve), M(odify), P(rint list), Q(uit)?  Q
```

Figure 1.4 (cont.)

Listing of updated NewStuFile produced:

```
12345Smith, John
3.60 22.0 7000
12349Doe, Mary Jane
2.94 16.5 2500
12355Jones, Fred A.
2.00 28.5 6250
```

Exercises

1. List and briefly describe the five phases of the software life cycle.

2. What are some of the ways in which problems in introductory programming courses differ from real-world problems?

3. What are structured data types? Give some examples from Pascal.

4. Give some examples of user-defined data structures.

5. Define an algorithm, naming and describing the properties it must possess.

6. What is pseudocode?

7. Name and describe the three control structures used in developing structured algorithms.

8. Describe the top-down approach to algorithm design.

9. What are some of the ways in which student programs differ from real-world programs?

10. Name three kinds of programming errors and give examples of each. When during program development is each likely to be detected?

11. Name and briefly describe the two main types of unit testing.

12. What are some situations in which program maintenance may be required?

13. Write the following unstructured program segment in structured form (but different from those given in Exercises 14 and 15):

(∗ Search the entries of the $n \times n$ matrix *Mat* in rowwise order for an entry equal to *Item* ∗)

```
      Row := 0;
10:  Col := 0;
      Row := Row + 1;
20:  Col := Col + 1;
      if Col <= n then goto 30;
      goto 10;
30:  if Row <= n then goto 40;
      goto 60;
40:  if Mat[Row, Col] = Item then goto 50;
      goto 20;
50:  writeln ('Item found');
      goto 70;
60:  writeln ('Item not found');
70:
```

14. Although the following program segment is structured, it is not a correct solution to Exercise 13.

(∗ Search the entries of the $n \times n$ matrix *Mat* in rowwise order for an entry equal to *Item* ∗)

```
for Row := 1 to n do
  for Col := 1 to n do
    if Mat[Row, Col] = Item then
      Found := true
    else
      Found := false;
if Found then
  writeln ('Item found')
else
  writeln ('Item not found');
```

(a) Write a program that incorporates this program segment and then perform black-box testing of it, beginning with the matrix

$$Mat = \begin{bmatrix} 45 & 77 & 93 \\ 78 & 79 & 85 \\ 72 & 96 & 77 \end{bmatrix}$$

and

$$Item = 77$$

as the first set of test data. Produce enough output to show that your testing has turned up an error.

(b) Use program tracing to determine what is wrong with this program segment.

15. The following program segment is correct, but it is not a good solution to Exercise 13. Why not? (Consider its efficiency.)

     (∗ Search the entries of the $n \times n$ matrix *Mat* in rowwise order for an entry equal to *Item* ∗)

```
Found := false ;
for Row := 1 to n do
   for Col := 1 to n do
      if Mat[Row, Col] = Item then
         Found := true;
if Found then
   writeln ('Item found')
else
   writeln ('Item not found');
```

16. The following procedure performs a linear search of a list L of length LL for the item *It*, returning $F = 0$ or 1 depending on whether or not *It* is found. Many principles of good programming are violated. Describe some of these and rewrite the procedure in an acceptable format:

```
procedure LS;
(∗ Search L for It ∗)
label 1,2,3; var i:integer;
begin
F:=0; i:=1; 1: if L[i]=It then
goto 2; if i>=LL then goto
3;(∗ADD 1 TO i∗)i:=i+1;goto 1;
2:F:=1;3:end;
```

2

Introduction to Data Structures and Abstract Data Types

The second phase of the software life cycle described in Chapter 1 is system design, which includes the selection of data structures and the design of algorithms, and the main purpose of this text is to explore these two topics in detail. The data to be processed by a program must be organized using some structure that reflects the relationships among the data items and that allows the data to be processed efficiently. As we have already noted, the selection of data structures to store these data items and the design of algorithms to perform the processing cannot be separated; they must be done in parallel.

Because these data structures and algorithms must be implemented in some programming language, they must be designed to take advantage of the features of that language. This means that where possible, they should be based on the predefined data types, operations, and functions available in the language. In this chapter we define and illustrate data structures and their implementations and describe how some of the predefined Pascal data types are implemented.

2.1 Data Structures, Abstract Data Types, and Implementations

To illustrate the process of organizing and structuring data in a problem, let us consider the following example. Suppose that Trans-Fryslan Airlines operates a single ten-passenger airplane. TFA would like to modernize its operations and, as a first step, needs a program that will determine for each flight which seats are unoccupied so that they can be assigned.

In this problem, it is clear that the input information is a collection of ten seats and, for each seat, some indication of whether it is occupied. We must be able to perform the following operations: (1) examine the collection of seats to determine which of them are unoccupied, (2) reserve a seat, and (3) cancel a seat assignment. To perform these operations, it is convenient to think of the seats as organized in a list.

After organizing the data as a list of ten seats and identifying the basic operations to be performed, we can consider possible ways to implement this structure. A variety of implementations are possible. For example, we might define an enumerated type

type
    SeatStatus = (Occupied, Unoccupied);

and represent the list of seats by ten simple variables of type *SeatStatus*:

var
    Seat1, Seat2, . . . , Seat10 : SeatStatus;

Although this is a simple representation of the list of seats, the algorithms to perform the required operations are somewhat awkward. For example, the algorithm to scan the list of seats and to produce a listing of those seats that are unoccupied might be as follows:

ALGORITHM TO LIST UNOCCUPIED SEATS

1. If *Seat1 = Unoccupied* then
    Display 1.
2. If *Seat2 = Unoccupied* then
    Display 2.
3. If *Seat3 = Unoccupied* then
    Display 3.
        .
        .
        .
10. If *Seat10 = Unoccupied* then
    Display 10.

An algorithm for reserving a seat would be even more awkward and, in fact, is completely unreasonable!

ALGORITHM TO RESERVE A SEAT

1. Set *Done* to false.
2. If *Seat1 = Unoccupied* then do the following:
    a. Display 'Do you wish to assign Seat #1?'.
    b. Read *Response* from user.
    c. If *Response = 'Y'* then do the following:
        i. Set *Seat1* equal to *Occupied*.
        ii. Set *Done* equal to true.
3. If not *Done* and *Seat2 = Unoccupied* then do the following:
    a. Display 'Do you wish to assign Seat #2?'.
    b. Read *Response* from user.
    c. If *Response = 'Y'* then to the following:
        i. Set *Seat2* equal to *Occupied*.
        ii. Set *Done* equal to true.
        .
        .
        .

An algorithm for canceling a seat assignment would be equally unreasonable.

Pascal procedures could be written to implement these algorithms, but they would be clumsy. They would be inflexible and difficult to modify and would become even more awkward if TFA replaced its ten-seat airliner with a larger aircraft having more seats.

These difficulties certainly suggest that it may be appropriate to consider other ways to represent the data of this problem. One alternative is to represent the list of seats as an array whose elements are of type *SeatStatus*:

const
   MaxSeats = 10; (∗ upper limit on the number of seats ∗)

type
   SeatStatus = (*Occupied, Unoccupied*);
   SeatList = **array**[1..*MaxSeats*] **of** *SeatStatus*;

var
   Seat : *SeatList*;

Because the elements of an array can be easily accessed by using an indexed variable, the algorithms to implement the required operations are much simpler:

ALGORITHM TO LIST UNOCCUPIED SEATS

1. For *Number* ranging from 1 to *MaxSeats* do the following:
    If *Seat*[*Number*] = *Unoccupied* then
       Display *Number.*

ALGORITHM TO RESERVE A SEAT

1. Read *Number* of seat to be reserved.
2. If *Seat*[*Number*] = *Unoccupied* then
       Set *Seat*[*Number*] equal to *Occupied.*
    Else
       Display a message that the seat having this *Number* has already been assigned.

The algorithm for canceling a seat assignment is similar to that for reserving a seat.

Although this is a very simple example, it does illustrate several general concepts. One is that solving a problem involves the manipulation of data and an important part of the solution is the careful organization of the data. This requires that we identify the collection of data items and possible relationships among them and the basic operations that must be performed on these data items. Such a collection with these operations and relations is called an ***abstract data structure*** (or simply ***data structure***) or an ***abstract data type*** (commonly abbreviated as ***ADT***). In this example, the data structure consists of a list of seats or some representation of them (for example, a seating chart of the plane), together with the basic operations: (1) scan the list to determine which seats are occupied, and (2) change a seat's status from unoccupied to occupied or from occupied to unoccupied.

The terms *abstract data structure* and *abstract data type* are often used interchangeably. However, the term *data structure* is more appropriate when data is being studied at a logical or conceptual level, independent of any programming considerations. The term *abstract data type* is appropriate when the structure is being viewed as an object to be processed in a program. In both cases, the word *abstract* refers to the fact that the data and the basic operations and relations defined on it are being studied independently of any implementation.

An ***implementation*** of a data structure consists of **storage structures** to store the data items and ***algorithms*** for the basic operations and relations. In the preceding example, two implementations are given. In the first, the storage structure consists of ten simple variables, and in the second implementation, it is an array. In both cases, algorithms for the basic operations are given, but those in the second implementation are considerably easier than those in the first.

This idea of ***data abstraction***, in which the definition of the data structure is separated from its implementation, is an important concept that is a natural part of a top-down approach to software development. It makes it possible to study and use the structure without being concerned about the details of its implementation. In fact, this is usually the approach used for predefined data types such as *integer*, *real*, and *char* and arrays; a programmer uses these data types without knowing how they are implemented. Nevertheless, these data types can be used more effectively and efficiently if the programmer has some understanding of the implementation used. Consequently, in the next several sections we review the predefined data types of Pascal and examine some of their implementations. The data types provided in Pascal and the relationship between them are summarized in the following diagram:

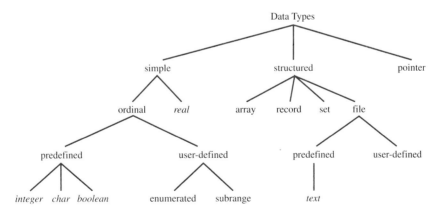

2.2 Simple Data Types

As we indicated in the preceding section, problem solving invariably involves manipulating some kind of data. In its most basic form, data values (as well as instructions) are encoded in the memory of a computer as sequences of 0s and 1s. This is because the devices that make up a computer's memory are two-state devices and hence are ideally suited for storing information that is coded using only two symbols. If one of the states is interpreted as 0 and the other as 1, then a natural scheme for representing information is one that uses only the two binary digits, or **bits**, 0 and 1. The two-state devices used in computer memory are organized into groups called **bytes**, each of which consists of eight bits. These bytes are in turn organized into **words**, usually with two or four bytes (sixteen or thirty-two bits) per word. These memory units—bits, bytes, and words—are the basic storage structures for all simple data types and indeed, for all data stored in a computer. In **word-addressable** computers, the words are numbered, and the number associated with a word is called its **address**. In **byte-addressable** computers, bytes rather than words are assigned addresses. In either case, each *memory cell* (a byte or a word) can be accessed by means of its address.

Basic data types such as *integer*, *real*, *char*, and *boolean* in Pascal are called **simple data types** because a value of one of these types is atomic; that is, it consists of a single entity that cannot be subdivided. Each can be viewed as an abstract data type because it consists of a collection of values and one or more basic operations and relations defined on these values. Their implementations use the basic memory cells as storage structures, and the algorithms for the basic operations and relations are implemented by the hardware and/or software of the computer system. In this section we examine the implementations of these Pascal simple data types.

Integer Data. The set of integers is $\{\ldots, -3, -2, -1, 0, 1, 2, 3, \ldots\}$. The number system that we are accustomed to using to represent such values is a **decimal** or **base-ten number system**, which uses the digits 0, 1, 2, 3, 4, 5, 6, 7, 8, and 9. The significance of these digits in a numeral depends on the positions they occupy in that numeral. For example, in the numeral 427, the digit 4 is interpreted as 4 hundreds, the digit 2 as 2 tens, and the digit 7 as 7 ones. Thus, the numeral 427 represents the number four-hundred twenty-seven and can be written in **expanded form** as

$$4 \cdot 100 + 2 \cdot 10 + 7 \cdot 1$$

or

$$4 \cdot 10^2 + 2 \cdot 10^1 + 7 \cdot 10^0$$

The digits that appear in the various positions of the base-ten numeral thus represent coefficients of powers of 10.

Similar number systems can be designed with numbers other than 10 as a base. The **base-two number system** uses 2 as the base and has only two digits, 0 and 1. As in a decimal system, the significance of a bit in a base-two numeral is determined by its position in that numeral. For example, the base-two numeral 101 can be written in expanded form (in decimal notation) as

$$1 \cdot 2^2 + 0 \cdot 2^1 + 1 \cdot 2^0$$

that is, the base-two numeral 101 has the decimal value

$$4 + 0 + 1 = 5$$

Thus the integer 5 can be stored in a 16-bit memory word as

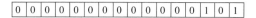

Similarly, the integer 427 can be written in base-two as 110101011 and can be stored as

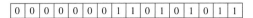

Most schemes for representing integers use one bit to indicate the sign of a number. One simple way to do this is to set the leftmost bit to 1 if the number is negative, 0 if it is not, and to use the remaining bits to store the magnitude of the number, using the base-two representation described earlier. This representation is called the *sign-magnitude* representation for integers. For example, the 8-bit sign-magnitude representation of 6 is

$$6 \rightarrow 00000110$$

sign bit

and the sign-magnitude representation of -6 is

$$-6 \rightarrow 10000110$$
$\uparrow$
sign bit

Although this is a very simple scheme for representing integers, the algorithms for the basic arithmetic operations are not as easy as they are in some other representations. In particular, addition of integers with opposite signs is rather difficult.

One scheme commonly used to represent integers for which the algorithms for the basic operations are simpler is called *two's complement* notation. In this scheme, the nonnegative integers are represented as in the sign-magnitude notation. The representation of a negative integer $-n$ is obtained by first finding the base-two representation for n, complementing it (that is, changing each 0 to 1 and each 1 to 0), and then adding 1 to the result. Thus the two's complement representation of -6 using a string of sixteen bits is obtained as follows:

1. Represent 6 as a 16-bit base-two number:

$$0000000000000110$$

2. Complement this bit string:

$$1111111111111001$$

3. Add 1:

$$1111111111111010$$

The integer -6 can thus be stored in a 16-bit memory word as

Since 2^n different patterns can be formed with n bits, it follows that there are 2^n different integers that can be represented by a string of n bits. For

example, using $n = 16$ bits, we can represent $2^{16} = 65536$ different integers. If the two's complement scheme is used, the integers in the range from -32768 through 32767 can be represented as follows:

Two's Complement	Decimal
1000000000000000	-32768
1000000000000001	-32767
1000000000000010	-32766
1000000000000011	-32765
.	.
.	.
.	.
1111111111111101	-3
1111111111111110	-2
1111111111111111	-1
0000000000000000	0
0000000000000001	1
0000000000000010	2
0000000000000011	3
.	.
.	.
.	.
0111111111111101	32765
0111111111111110	32766
0111111111111111	32767

Note that the leftmost bit of the two's complement representation of each of the negative integers -32768 through -1 is 1, whereas the leftmost bit of the two's complement representation of the nonnegative integers 0 through 32767 is 0. Thus the leftmost bit is the sign bit, with 0 indicating a nonnegative value and 1 indicating a negative value.

The algorithms to implement the usual arithmetic operations on integers represented using two's complement notation are similar to the familiar algorithms for carrying out these operations on base-ten numbers. The basic addition and multiplication tables are

+	0	1
0	0	1
1	1	10

$\times$	0	1
0	0	0
1	0	1

Thus, for example, the sum $5 + 7$ is calculated by adding, bit by bit, the base-two representations of these numbers, carrying when necessary:

$$
\begin{array}{r}
111 \longleftarrow \text{carry bits} \\
0000000000000101 \\
+\ 0000000000000111 \\
\hline
0000000000001100
\end{array}
$$

Similarly, the sum $5 + (-6)$ is calculated as

$$
\begin{array}{r}
0000000000000101 \\
+\ 1111111111111010 \\
\hline
1111111111111111
\end{array}
$$

which yields the two's complement representation of -1. Comparison of two integers in two's complement notation is somewhat awkward, however, since the representation of negative integers seems to indicate that these integers are greater than the positive integers.

Another useful scheme for representing integers is *excess* or ***biased notation.*** In this scheme, the representation of an integer as a string of n bits is formed by adding the *bias* 2^{n-1} to the integer and representing the result in base-two. Thus, the 8-bit biased representation of -6 is obtained as follows:

1. Add the bias $2^7 = 128$ to -6, giving 122.
2. Represent the result in base-two notation:

$$01111010$$

The integers in the range from -8 through 7 can be represented using four bits (and thus a bias of $2^3 = 8$) as follows:

Biased	Decimal
0000	-8
0001	-7
0010	-6
0011	-5
0100	-4
0101	-3
0110	-2
0111	-1
1000	0
1001	1
1010	2
1011	3
1100	4
1101	5
1110	6
1111	7

Note that the leftmost bit is again a sign bit, with 0 indicating a negative value and 1 a nonnegative value.

Although algorithms for the basic arithmetic operations are more complicated in this scheme than in the two's complement scheme, two integers can be compared more easily. This is one reason that this biased representation is typically used for the exponent in the floating point representation of real numbers, to be described momentarily.

The details of how integers are represented internally are usually of little concern to the programmer because they are automatically handled by the computer. One aspect that is important, however, is that the word size limits the range of integers that can be stored. The largest integer that can be stored in a 16-bit word is $2^{15} - 1 = 32767$, and in a 32-bit word, $2^{31} - 1 = 2147483647$. An attempt to store an integer greater than the maximum allowed will result in the loss of some of the bits of its binary representation, a phenomenon known as *overflow*. This limitation may be partially overcome by using more than one word to store an integer. Although this approach enlarges the range of integers that can be stored, it does not resolve the problem of overflow, as the range of representable integers is still finite. Thus the integer type in Pascal is not a perfect representation of the mathematical concept of integer because in mathematics, the set of integers is infinite.

Real Data. In a decimal numeral representing a fraction, the digits to the right of the decimal point are also coefficients of powers of 10. In this case, however, the exponents are negative integers. For example, the numeral 0.317 can be written in expanded form as

$$3 \cdot 10^{-1} + 1 \cdot 10^{-2} + 7 \cdot 10^{-3}$$

The point in a base-two numeral representing a fraction is called a *binary point*, and the positions to the right of the binary point represent negative powers of the base 2. For example, the expanded form of 110.101 is

$$1 \cdot 2^2 + 1 \cdot 2^1 + 0 \cdot 2^0 + 1 \cdot 2^{-1} + 0 \cdot 2^{-2} + 1 \cdot 2^{-3}$$

and thus it has the decimal value

$$4 + 2 + 0 + \frac{1}{2} + \frac{0}{4} + \frac{1}{8} = 6.625$$

There are a number of schemes used to store real numbers as bit strings, but nearly all of them use a *scientific* or *floating point* form. For example, the base-two representation

$$110.101$$

of the real value 6.625 is equivalent to

$$0.110101 \times 2^3$$

Typically, one part of a memory word (or words) is used to store a fixed number of bits of the *mantissa* or *fractional part* 0.110101 in *normalized* form—that is, so that the first bit is nonzero (unless the value is 0)—and another part to store the *exponent* 3. For example, suppose this value is stored in a 32-bit memory cell in which the first twenty-four bits store the mantissa, and the last eight bits store the exponent. If two's complement representation is used for the mantissa and biased notation is used for the exponent, 6.625 can be stored as

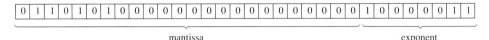

Thus we see that the *overflow* problem discussed in connection with integer representation will also occur in the storage of a real number when the exponent is too large; a negative exponent that is too small will result in *underflow*.

Another problem occurs when the mantissa requires more than the allotted number of bits. For example, the base-two representation of 0.7 is

$$0.10110011001100110\ldots$$

where the block 0110 is repeated indefinitely. Since only a finite number of these bits can be stored, the stored value is not exactly 0.7. For example, if only the first twenty-four bits are stored and all the remaining bits are truncated, the stored representation of 0.7 will be

$$0.101100110011001100110011001$$

which has the decimal value 0.6999999284744263. If the binary representation is rounded to 24 bits, then the stored representation of 0.7 will be

$$0.101100110011001100110011010$$

which has the decimal value 0.7000000476837159. In either case, the stored value is not exactly 0.7. This error, called *roundoff error* (in both cases), can be reduced, but not eliminated, by using a larger number of bits to store the mantissa.

This approximation error may be compounded when real numbers are combined in arithmetic expressions. To illustrate, consider adding the three real numbers 0.4104, 1.0, and 0.2204; for simplicity, assume that the computations are done using decimal representation with four-digit precision. The normalized floating point representations of these values are 0.4104×10^0, 0.1000×10^1, and 0.2204×10^0. The first step in the addition of two values is to "align the decimal point" by increasing the smaller of the two exponents and shifting the mantissa. Thus, the sum of the first two values is obtained by adding 0.0410×10^1 and 0.1000×10^1, which gives 0.1410×10^1. Adding the third number again requires adjusting the exponent and shifting the mantissa, 0.0220×10^1, and the final result is 0.1630×10^1, or 1.630. On the other hand, if the two smaller values are added first, giving 0.6308×10^0, and then the larger number is added, the result is 0.1631×10^1, or 1.631 (assuming rounding). In a long chain of such calculations, these small errors can accumulate so that the error in the final result may be very large. This example also illustrates that two real quantities that are algebraically equal, such as $(A + B) + C$ and $(A + C) + B$, may have computed values that are not equal. Consequently, some care must be taken when comparing two real values with the relational operators $=$ and $<>$.

It should now be clear that, as with integers, only a finite range of real numbers can be stored because of the limited number of bits allotted to the exponent. Unlike integers, however, not all real numbers within this range can be stored because of the limit on the number of bits in the mantissa. In fact, only a finite subset of these real numbers can be stored exactly, and this means that there are infinitely many real numbers that cannot be stored exactly.

Character Data. Computers store and process not only numeric data but also character data and other nonnumeric information. The schemes used for storing character data are based on the assignment of a numeric code to each of the characters in the character set. Several standard coding schemes have been devised, such as ASCII (American Standard Code for Information Interchange) and EBCDIC (Extended Binary Coded Decimal Interchange Code). A complete table of ASCII and EBCDIC codes for all characters is given in Appendix B.

Characters are represented internally by these binary codes, which are stored in bytes. For example, the character string HI can be stored in a 16-bit word with the code for H in the first byte and the code for I in the second byte; with ASCII code, the result is:

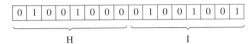

The most common operation involving character values is comparison to determine whether two characters are equal or whether one is less than another. This comparison is carried out using the integer codes that represent the characters. The two characters are equal if their codes are equal, and one character is less than the other if the code of the first is less than the code of the second. The ordering defined in this way is called the *collating sequence* for the character set.

Boolean Data.   There are only two boolean values, true and false, which can be represented by a single bit, with 0 representing false and 1 representing true. In some systems, boolean values are stored one per byte or one per word, with a bit string of all zeros representing false and any other bit string representing true.

Three boolean operations are defined in Pascal: **and, or,** and **not.** Because a boolean expression of the form p **and** q is true only in the case that p and q both are true, the bit operation that implements **and** is defined by the following table:

and	0	1
0	0	0
1	0	1

Similarly, a boolean expression of the form p **or** q is false only in the case that p and q both are false, and so the corresponding bit operation is defined by

or	0	1
0	0	1
1	1	1

The boolean operation **not** is implemented simply by bit complementation.

Summary. We have seen that each of the predefined Pascal data types *integer*, *real*, *char*, and *boolean* can be represented by bit strings. It is the *interpretation* of a bit string and the operations that may be applied to it that determine the data type of the value represented by that bit string. A given bit string may represent an integer, real, character, or boolean value, depending on the interpretation used. For example, the bit string

$$0\ 1\ 0\ 0\ 1\ 0\ 0\ 1\ 0\ 1\ 0\ 1\ 0\ 0\ 0\ 1$$

can be interpreted as the integer value

$$2^{14} + 2^{11} + 2^{8} + 2^{6} + 2^{4} + 2^{0} = 18769$$

or as the real value (using an 11-bit mantissa and a biased 5-bit exponent)

$$\left(\frac{1}{2} + \frac{1}{16} + \frac{1}{128} + \frac{1}{512}\right) \times 2^{1} = 1.154453124$$

or (if ASCII code is used) as the pair of characters

IQ

or (if boolean values are stored one per 16-bit word) as the single boolean value

true

or (if each boolean value is stored in one byte) as the pair of boolean values

true, true

or (if each boolean value is stored in one bit) as a sequence of sixteen boolean values

false, true, false, false, true, . . . , true

It might even be interpreted as a machine-language instruction in which the first eight bits represent the opcode $01001001_2 = 73$ of some operation to be applied to the data value stored in the memory cell whose address $01010001_2 = 81$ is given by the last eight bits.[1]

Exercises

1. Find the integer (base-ten value) represented by each of the following bit strings of length 16, assuming a sign-magnitude representation:

   (a) 0100000001000000   (b) 0110111001101111
   (c) 1011111111111110   (d) 1100000000000001
   (e) 1001100110011001   (f) 1010101010101010

2. Find the integer represented by each of the bit strings in Exercise 1, assuming two's complement representation.

[1] When writing numerals in bases other than ten, the number base is sometimes written as a subscript to avoid confusion.

3. Find the integer represented by each of the bit strings in Exercise 1, assuming biased notation.

4. Find the real value represented by each of the bit strings in Exercise 1, assuming that the leftmost eleven bits represent the mantissa in two's complement notation and the rightmost five bits represent the exponent in biased notation.

5. Indicate how each of the bit strings in Exercise 1 can be interpreted as (i) a boolean value, (ii) a pair of boolean values, or (iii) a sequence of sixteen boolean values.

6. Interpret each of the bit strings in (a) and (b) of Exercise 1 as a pair of characters assuming (i) ASCII and (ii) EBCDIC representation.

7. Another useful and important number system in computer science is an *octal* number system which uses a base of 8 and the digits 0, 1, 2, 3, 4, 5, 6, and 7. In the octal representation of a positive integer such as 1703_8, the digits represent coefficients of powers of 8. Thus this numeral is an abbreviation for the expanded form

$$(1 \times 8^3) + (7 \times 8^2) + (0 \times 8^1) + (3 \times 8^0)$$

which has the decimal value

$$512 + 448 + 0 + 3 = 963$$

Find the decimal value represented by each of the following octal numerals:

(a) 321_8	**(b)** 2607_8	**(c)** 100000_8
(d) 7777_8	**(e)** 6.6_8	**(f)** 432.234_8

8. Besides an octal system (see Exercise 7), a *hexadecimal* number system is also useful. This is a base-sixteen system that uses the digits 0, 1, 2, 3, 4, 5, 6, 7, 8, 9, A (ten), B (eleven), C (twelve), D (thirteen), E (fourteen), and F (fifteen). The hexadecimal numeral $7E3_{16}$ has the expanded form

$$(7 \times 16^2) + (14 \times 16^1) + (3 \times 16^0)$$

which has the decimal value

$$1792 + 224 + 3 = 2019$$

Find the decimal value represented by each of the following hexadecimal numerals:

(a) 45_{16}	**(b)** $3A0_{16}$	**(c)** ABC_{16}
(d) FFF_{16}	**(e)** $7.C_{16}$	**(f)** $FE.DC_{16}$

9. Conversion from octal to binary (base-two) is easy; we need only replace each octal digit by its 3-bit binary equivalent. For example to convert 714_8 to binary, replace 7 by 111, 1 by 001, and 4 by 100, to obtain 111001100_2. Convert each of the octal numerals in Exercise 7 to binary numerals.

10. Imitating the conversion scheme in Exercise 9, convert each of the hexadecimal numerals in Exercise 8 to binary numerals.

11. To convert a binary numeral to octal, group the digits in groups of three, starting from the binary point (or from the right end if there is none), and replace each group with the corresponding octal digit. For example,

$$11110101_2 = (11\ 110\ 101)_2 = 365_8$$

Convert each of the following binary numerals to octal numerals:

(a) 101010
(b) 1011
(c) 10000000000
(d) 0111111111111111111
(e) 11.1
(f) 10101.10101

12. Imitating the conversion scheme in Exercise 11, convert each of the binary numerals given there to hexadecimal numerals.

13. One method for finding the ***base-b representation*** of a positive integer represented in base-ten notation is to divide the number by b repeatedly until a quotient of zero results. The successive remainders are the digits from right to left of the base-b representation. For example, the base-two representation of 26 is 11010_2, as the following computation shows:

$$
\begin{array}{r}
0\ \text{R}\ 1 \\
2\overline{)1}\ \text{R}\ 1 \\
2\overline{)3}\ \text{R}\ 0 \\
2\overline{)6}\ \text{R}\ 1 \\
2\overline{)13}\ \text{R}\ 0 \\
2\overline{)26}
\end{array}
$$

Convert each of the following base-10 numerals to base- (i) two; (ii) eight; (iii) sixteen:

(a) 99   (b) 2571   (c) 5280

14. To convert a decimal fraction to its base-b equivalent, repeatedly multiply the fractional part of the number by b. The integer parts are the digits from left to right of the base-b representation. For example, the decimal numeral .6875 corresponds to the base-two numeral $.1011_2$,

as the following computation shows:

$$
\begin{array}{c|l}
 & .6875 \\
 & \times\ 2 \\
\hline
1 & .375 \\
 & \times\ 2 \\
\hline
0 & .75 \\
 & \times 2 \\
\hline
1 & .5 \\
 & \times 2 \\
\hline
1 & .0 \\
\end{array}
$$

Convert the following base-10 numerals to base (i) two, (ii) eight, (iii) sixteen:

(a) .5   **(b)** .6875   **(c)** 13.828125

15. As noted in the text, even though the base-ten representation of a fraction may terminate, its representation in some other base need not terminate; for example,

$$0.7 = (0.10110011001100110011 \cdots)_2 = 0.1\overline{0110}_2$$

where the "overline" in the last notation indicates that the bit string 0110 is repeated indefinitely.

$$
\begin{array}{c|l}
 & .7 \\
 & \times\ 2 \\
\hline
1 & .4 \leftarrow \\
 & \times\ 2 \\
\hline
0 & .8 \\
 & \times\ 2 \\
\hline
1 & .6 \\
 & \times\ 2 \\
\hline
1 & .2 \\
 & \times\ 2 \\
\hline
0 & .4 \\
\end{array}
$$

Convert the following base-ten numerals to base (i) two; (ii) eight; (iii) sixteen:

(a) 0.6   **(b)** 0.05   **(c)** $0.\overline{3} = 0.33333 \cdots = 1/3$

16. Find the 16-bit two's complement representation for each of the following integers:

     (a) 99   **(b)** 5280   **(c)** 255
     (d) -255 **(e)** 1024   **(f)** -1024

17. Assuming that the leftmost eleven bits of a 16-bit word are used to store a mantissa in two's complement notation and the rightmost five bits store the exponent in biased notation, indicate how each of the following real numbers will be stored if extra bits in the mantissa are (i) truncated or (ii) rounded:

(a) 0.625	**(b)** 25.625	**(c)** 14.78125
(d) 0.015625	**(e)** 0.1	**(f)** 2.01

18. Indicate how each of the following character strings would be stored in two-byte words using ASCII:

(a) BE	**(b)** be	**(c)** ABLE
(d) Mr. Doe	**(e)** 1234	**(f)** 12.34

19. Write Pascal procedures to add and multiply nonnegative integers in base-two. Use these procedures in a program that reads two bit strings representing nonnegative integers, calls these procedures to find their sum and product, and then displays the corresponding bit strings.

20. The "repeated division" method for converting from base ten to base b described in Exercise 13 generates the base-b digits in reverse order, from right to left. Describe a data structure that can be used to store these digits as they are generated so that they can be displayed in correct order when the conversion is complete.

21. Write a program to carry out the conversion described in Exercise 20 for $0 \le b \le 10$.

22. Proceed as in Exercise 21, but for $0 \le b \le 16$. (Use A, B, C, D, E, and F for digits as necessary.)

23. Proceed as in Exercise 21, but for $b = 26$; use as "digits" A for 1, B for 2, . . . , Y for 25, and Z for 0.

2.3 Arrays

In addition to simple data types, most high-level programming languages also provide **structured data types.** Values of variables of these types are collections of data items. In this section we consider the most common of these data types, the array.

As a data structure, an **array** may be defined as a finite sequence or ordered collection of elements, all of the same type, for which the basic operation is direct access to each position in the array so that the element in this position can be retrieved or a data item can be stored in this position. Thus an array has a specific fixed number of elements, also called *components*, and these are ordered so that there is a first element, a second element, and so on. All the array elements must be of the same type; thus we might have an array of integers, an array of characters, or even an array of arrays. An array is therefore an appropriate data structure to consider for organizing *homogeneous* data collections, that is, those in which all the data items are of the same type, and especially those collections whose sizes remain fairly constant and in which there is an order associated with the data items.

Direct or *random access* means that each array element can be accessed simply by specifying its location in the array, so that the time required to access each element in the array is the same for all elements, regardless of their positions in the array. For example, in an array of 100 elements, the time required to access the seventy-fifth element is the same as that for the fifth. This is quite different from a *sequential access* structure in which one can access an element only by first processing all those that precede it. Clearly, in this case, the time required to access the seventy-fifth element would be considerably greater than that needed to access the fifth.

In most high-level languages, an array is denoted by a variable whose value is the collection of elements that comprise the array. A particular element of the array is then accessed by attaching to the array name one or more *indices* (also called *subscripts*) that specify the position of that element in the array. If only one index is used, the array is said to be *one-dimensional*; arrays involving more than one index are called *multidimensional* arrays.

One-Dimensional Arrays. An array declaration must specify two features of the array: the type of the array elements and the index type. Declarations of one-dimensional arrays in Pascal have the general form

array[*index-type*] **of** *element-type*

where *index-type* specifies the type of values for the index and may be any ordinal type; *element-type* specifies the type of the array elements and may be any type. For example, an array A to store a collection of twenty integers can be declared by

const
    ArrayLimit = 20;

type
    NumberArray = **array**[1..*ArrayLimit*] **of** *integer*;

var
    A : *NumberArray*;

This array declaration instructs the compiler to reserve a block of memory cells (words or bytes according to whether the computer is word addressable or byte addressable) that is large enough to store the elements of the array. The address of the first memory cell used to store the elements is called the *base address* of the array, denoted base(A), and the address of any other array element can be calculated in terms of this base address. For example, if an integer can be stored in a single memory cell, then the address of the cell in which the fifth element $A[5]$ of A is stored is base(A) + 4; and in general, as the following diagram indicates, $A[i]$ is stored in location

$$\text{base}(A) + (i - 1)$$

When an array element is to be accessed, the computer first performs this *address translation.* The bit string stored in the cell whose address is calculated is then retrieved and interpreted as an integer, since the array declaration specifies that the data type of each element of *A* is *integer.*

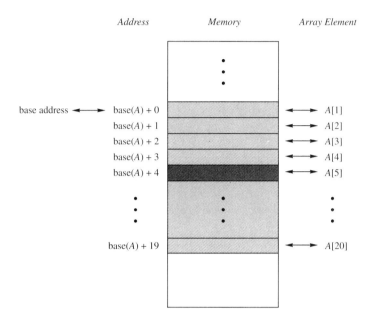

As another example, consider the array *Alpha* declared by

type
    RealArray = **array**[− 3..3] **of** *real*;

var
    Alpha : *RealArray*;

and suppose that each real value requires two memory cells for storage. The fifth array element *Alpha*[1] is then stored in memory cells base(*Alpha*) + 8 and base(*Alpha*) + 9. Since the data type of the elements of *Alpha* is declared as *real*, the bit string formed by concatenating the bit strings in these two locations is interpreted as a real number when a reference is made to *Alpha*[1].

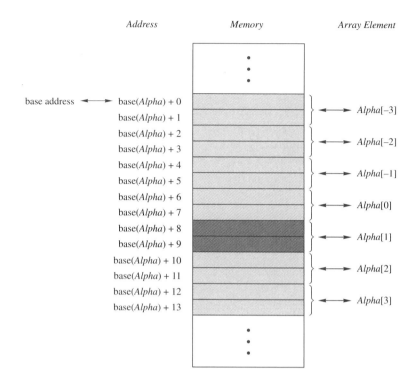

In general, if *n* memory cells are required to store each element of an array *A*, the *i*th array element is stored in the block of *n* memory locations beginning at the cell with address base(A) + (i − 1)n. This means that if the indices of *A* are integers ranging from *l* through *u*, the address of the memory cell where $A[k]$ begins is

$$base(A) + (k - l)n$$

since $A[k]$ is in position $i = k - l + 1$ of the array.

The address translation we have considered thus far has been for arrays whose index type is some subrange of integers, but it can easily be modified for arrays whose index type is some other ordinal type. For example, suppose that array *Count* is declared by

type
   FrequencyArray = **array**['A'..'Z'] **of** *integer*;

var
   Count : *FrequencyArray*;
   Ch : *char*;

and that each element of *Count* can be stored in one memory cell. Then the position of *Count*[*Ch*] is

$$i = ord(Ch) - ord('A') + 1$$

and thus is stored in the memory cell whose address is

$$\text{base}(Count) + i - 1 = \text{base}(Count) + ord(Ch) - ord(\text{'A'})$$

String Processing. One important use of arrays in Pascal is to store a string of characters such as a name or an address. The element type of the array is *char*, and each array element is a single character in the string. For example, a one-dimensional array *Name* having five elements of character type might be used to store the string SMITH; *Name*[1] would have the value 'S', *Name*[2] the value 'M', and so on.

The commonly used coding schemes ASCII and EBCDIC require only eight bits (one byte) to store a single character. Some Pascal compilers, however, allocate one cell for each variable. Because the values assigned to such variables require only eight bits for storage, this is an inefficient use of memory in word-addressable machines. For example, in a 32-bit word machine, only eight bits in each word are used to store a character, and thus three fourths of each word is wasted. Memory utilization in such machines can be improved by using **packed arrays** in which several characters are stored in a single word. (Similarly, since a boolean value can be represented by a single bit, it may also be possible to pack several elements of an array of type *boolean* into a single word.)

In byte-addressable machines, the address translation required to access elements of packed arrays of characters is the same as for unpacked arrays, but for word-addressable machines it is more complex. To illustrate, consider the packed array *P* declared by

```
const
  StringLimit = 40;

type
  String = packed array[1..StringLimit] of char;

var
  P : String;
```

Declaring *P* to be a packed array allows, but does not require, the compiler to pack several characters into a single memory word. Suppose that for this example, four characters are packed in each memory word. The array elements *P*[1], *P*[2], *P*[3], and *P*[4] are then stored in the four bytes of the memory word with address base(*P*); *P*[5], *P*[6], *P*[7], and *P*[8] are stored in the four bytes of word base(*P*) + 1; and so on.

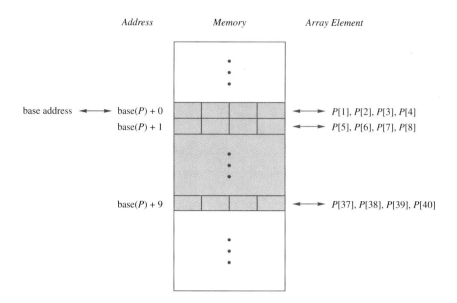

In general, array element $P[i]$ is stored in one of the bytes of the word with address

$$\text{base}(P) + (i - 1) \textbf{ div } 4$$

The number of the byte in which it is stored is given by

$$1 + (i - 1) \textbf{ mod } 4$$

For example, $P[39]$ is stored in byte

$$1 + (39 - 1) \textbf{ mod } 4 = 3$$

of the memory word whose address is

$$\text{base}(P) + (39 - 1) \textbf{ div } 4 = \text{base}(P) + 9$$

and the bit string stored in this byte is interpreted as a character when $P[39]$ is referenced.

As this illustration shows, accessing elements in packed arrays may be more complicated than for unpacked arrays because the address translation formulas may be more complex and it may be necessary to extract and interpret a part of a memory cell. Consequently, processing packed arrays may take more time than processing unpacked arrays does, which is one reason that some Pascal compilers restrict the operations that may be performed on packed arrays.

Multidimensional Arrays.   Most high-level languages also support arrays that have more than one dimension. Two-dimensional arrays are particularly useful when the data being processed can be arranged in rows and columns. Similarly, a three-dimensional array is appropriate when the data can be arranged in rows, columns, and ranks. When several characteristics are associated with the data, still higher dimensions may be appropriate, with each dimension corresponding to one of these characteristics.

To illustrate the use of two-dimensional arrays, consider the problem of recording and processing the daily sales of four different items at each of three different stores. These sales figures can be arranged naturally in a table having four rows and three columns

	Store		
Item	1	2	3
1	15	20	7
2	5	0	3
3	12	14	29
4	1	1	2

and a two-dimensional array is therefore an appropriate data structure to use to store these values. Such an array can be declared in Pascal as follows:

const
    MaxItems = 4;
    MaxStores = 3;

type
    SalesTable = **array**[1..*MaxItems*, 1..*MaxStores*] **of** *integer*;

var
    SalesTab : *SalesTable*;

The doubly-indexed variable *SalesTab*[3, 2] can then be used to access the number of sales (14) of item 3 (row 3) at store 2 (column 2).

Now suppose that the sales figures are collected for a six-day week so that six such tables are collected:

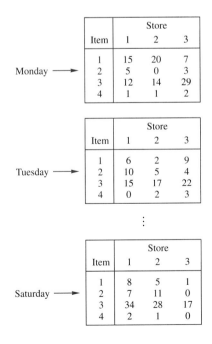

A three-dimensional array *Sales* declared by

const
    MaxItems = 4;
    MaxStores = 3;

type
    Days = (*Monday, Tuesday, Wednesday, Thursday, Friday, Saturday*);
    ListOfSalesTables =
                 array[*Days*, 1..*MaxItems*, 1..*MaxStores*] **of** *integer*;

var
    Sales : *ListOfSalesTables*;

might be used to store and organize these seventy-two sales figures. Access to the array element in the table for Monday, third row, and second column—that is, to the number representing sales (14) on Monday of item 3 at store 2—is provided by the triply-indexed variable *Sales*[*Monday*, 3, 2].

As an illustration of an array with more than three dimensions, consider the five-dimensional array *Inv* declared by

type
    Make = (*Chrysler, Dodge, Plymouth*);
    Style = (*TwoDoor, FourDoor, StationWagon, Van*);
    Color = (*blue, green, brown, red, yellow, gray*);
    Year = 1980..1992;
    ModelCode = 1..5;
    InventoryArray =
                 array[*Make, Style, Color, Year, ModelCode*] **of** *integer*;

var
    Inv : *InventoryArray*;

Such an array might be used in a program to maintain an inventory at an automobile dealership; thus

    Inv[*Chrysler, TwoDoor, red,* 1990, 4] :=
                       Inv[*Chrysler, TwoDoor, red,* 1990, 4] − 1;

could record the sale of one red two-door Model-4 1990 Chrysler.

Unlike some other high-level languages, Pascal does not limit the number of dimensions that an array may have. For any positive integer *n*, an *n*-dimensional array can be defined with a declaration of the form

    array[*index-type-1, index-type-2, . . . , index-type-n*] **of** *element-type*

where *index-type-i* specifies the type of the *i*th index and may be any ordinal type.

An alternative approach to multidimensional arrays is to define them as **arrays of arrays**, that is, arrays whose elements are arrays. For example, in

Pascal, the array declaration

> **type**
>   *SalesTable* = **array**[1..*MaxItems*, 1..*MaxStores*] **of** *integer*;

used to declare the two-dimensional array *SalesTab* earlier could equivalently be given as an array-of-arrays declaration:

> **type**
>   *StoreList* = **array**[1..*MaxStores*] **of** *integer*;
>   *SalesTable* = **array**[1..*MaxItems*] **of** *StoreList*;

or

> **type**
>   *SalesTable* = **array**[1..*MaxItems*] **of array**[1..*MaxStores*] **of** *integer*;

In any case, *SalesTab* can be viewed as an array whose elements are one-dimensional arrays. For example, *SalesTab*[3] is a one-dimensional array whose value is the third row of the sales table

12	14	29

and either *SalesTab*[3][2] or *SalesTab*[3, 2] refers to the second entry (14) in this array.

Similarly, the three-dimensional array *Sales* declared using

> **type**
>   *Days* = (*Monday, Tuesday, Wednesday, Thursday, Friday, Saturday*);
>   *ListOfSalesTables* =
>   **array**[*Days*, 1..*MaxItems*, 1..*MaxStores*] **of** *integer*;

can equivalently be declared using

> **type**
>   *Days* = (*Monday, Tuesday, Wednesday, Thursday, Friday, Saturday*);
>   *StoreList* = **array**[1..*MaxStores*] **of** *integer*;
>   *SalesTable* = **array**[1..*MaxItems*] **of** *StoreList*;
>   *ListOfSalesTables* = **array**[*Days*] **of** *SalesTable*;

In either case, *Sales*[*Tuesday*] refers to the sales table for Tuesday:

Item	Store 1	2	3
1	6	2	9
2	10	5	4
3	15	17	22
4	0	2	3

*Sales[Tuesday][*1] or *Sales[Tuesday,* 1] is the list of sales on Tuesday of item 1:

And any of *Sales[Tuesday][*1][3], *Sales[Tuesday,* 1, 3], *Sales[Tuesday][*1, 3], and *Sales[Tuesday,* 1][3] refers to the sales on Tuesday of item 1 at store 3:

$$\boxed{9}$$

The implementation of multidimensional arrays is somewhat more complicated than is that for one-dimensional arrays. Memory is organized as a sequence of memory cells and thus is one dimensional in nature. Consequently we must determine how to use a one-dimensional structure to store a higher-dimensional one.

To illustrate, suppose that M is a 3×4 array of integers declared by

type
    Table = **array**[1..3, 1..4] **of** *integer*;

var
    M : *Table*;

or equivalently,

type
    Row = **array**[1..4] **of** *integer*;
    Matrix = **array**[1..3] **of** *Row*;

var
    M : *Matrix*;

in which the following table is to be stored:

$$\begin{bmatrix} 37 & 45 & 82 & 75 \\ 61 & 50 & 0 & 27 \\ 17 & 9 & 62 & 91 \end{bmatrix}$$

If an integer can be stored in a single memory cell, then this array declaration instructs the compiler to reserve twelve consecutive memory locations to store the array elements. These elements might be stored in ***rowwise*** order (also called ***row major*** order), with the first four cells beginning at base(M) used to store the elements in the first row of M, the next four cells for the second row, and so on.

Address Memory Array Element

Address	Memory	Array Element
	⋮	
base(M) + 0	37	$M[1,1]$
base(M) + 1	45	$M[1,2]$
base(M) + 2	82	$M[1,3]$
base(M) + 3	75	$M[1,4]$
base(M) + 4	61	$M[2,1]$
base(M) + 5	50	$M[2,2]$
base(M) + 6	0	$M[2,3]$
base(M) + 7	27	$M[2,4]$
base(M) + 8	17	$M[3,1]$
base(M) + 9	9	$M[3,2]$
base(M) + 10	62	$M[3,3]$
base(M) + 11	91	$M[3,4]$
	⋮	

It also is possible to store the elements in **columnwise** (or **column major**) order, with the first three cells storing the elements in the first column of M, the next three cells storing the elements in the second column, and so on.

Address	Memory	Array Element
	⋮	
base(M) + 0	37	$M[1,1]$
base(M) + 1	61	$M[2,1]$
base(M) + 2	17	$M[3,1]$
base(M) + 3	45	$M[1,2]$
base(M) + 4	50	$M[2,2]$
base(M) + 5	9	$M[3,2]$
base(M) + 6	82	$M[1,3]$
base(M) + 7	0	$M[2,3]$
base(M) + 8	62	$M[3,3]$
base(M) + 9	75	$M[1,4]$
base(M) + 10	27	$M[2,4]$
base(M) + 11	91	$M[3,4]$
	⋮	

In either case, an address translation must be carried out to determine the memory cell in which a given array element $M[i, j]$ is stored.

The formulas for this address translation can be derived from those given earlier for one-dimensional arrays if a two-dimensional array is viewed as a one-dimensional array whose elements are also one-dimensional arrays. To see this, suppose that rowwise storage is used for M. M can be viewed as a one-dimensional array having three elements (the rows of M), each of which requires four memory cells for storage. Thus, by the address translation formula for one-dimensional arrays, the ith row of M, $M[i]$, is stored beginning at the cell with address

$$\text{base}(M[i]) = \text{base}(M) + 4(i - 1)$$

Since this ith row of M is itself a one-dimensional array with base address $\text{base}(M[i])$, the jth element in this row, $M[i, j]$, is stored in memory cell

$$\text{base}(M[i]) + (j - 1)$$

that is, $M[i, j]$ is stored in cell

$$\text{base}(M) + 4(i - 1) + (j - 1)$$

In general, consider rowwise storage of a two-dimensional array M declared using an array declaration of the form

    array$[l_1..u_1, l_2..u_2]$ **of** *element-type*

where l_1, u_1, l_2, and u_2 are integers, and suppose that each array element requires n memory cells for storage. Each row of M has $m = u_2 - l_2 + 1$ elements, each of which requires n cells for storage so that $\bar{n} = m \cdot n$ cells are needed to store one row of M. Since M is a one-dimensional array whose elements are these rows, the address translation formulas of the preceding section give the beginning address of the ith row of M, $M[i]$, as

$$\text{base}(M[i]) = \text{base}(M) + (i - l_1)\bar{n} = \text{base}(M) + (i - l_1)mn$$

Because this row of M is itself a one-dimensional array with base address $\text{base}(M[i])$, where each element requires n cells for storage, we find, using these same formulas, that the jth element of this row, $M[i, j]$, is stored in the n consecutive cells beginning at

$$\text{base}(M[i]) + (j - l_2)n = \text{base}(M) + (i - l_1)mn + (j - l_2)n$$
$$= \text{base}(M) + [(i - l_1)m + (j - l_2)]n$$

Similarly, the address translation formulas for one- and two-dimensional arrays can be used to derive formulas for three-dimensional arrays if they are viewed as one-dimensional arrays whose elements are two-dimensional arrays (or as two-dimensional arrays whose elements are one-dimensional arrays). For example, consider the three-dimensional array B declared by

    type
        ThreeDimArray = **array**$[1..3, 0..3, 2..4]$ **of** *real*;

    var
        B : *ThreeDimArray*;

or equivalently,

type
   TwoDimArray = **array**[0..3, 2..4] **of** *real*;
   ThreeDimArray = **array**[1..3] **of** *TwoDimArray*;

var
   B : *ThreeDimArray*;

B can thus be viewed as a one-dimensional array having three elements, *B*[1], *B*[2], and *B*[3], each of which is a two-dimensional array with twelve elements.

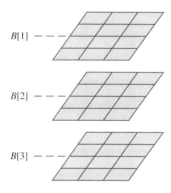

If each real number requires two memory cells of storage, twenty-four cells will be needed to store each of the tables *B*[1], *B*[2], and *B*[3]. Thus, *B*[*i*] is stored beginning at the cell with address

$$\text{base}(B[i]) = \text{base}(B) + 24(i - 1)$$

Since each *B*[*i*] is a two-dimensional array, the address translation formulas for two-dimensional arrays give as the beginning address for *B*[*i*, *j*, *k*]

$$\text{base}(B[i]) + 6(j - 0) + 2(k - 2)$$
$$= \text{base}(B) + 24(i - 1) + 6(j - 0) + 2(k - 2)$$

In general, for a three-dimensional array *B* declared with an array declaration of the form

$$\textbf{array}[l_1..u_1, l_2..u_2, l_3..u_3] \textbf{ of } \textit{element-type}$$

where each element requires *n* cells of storage, the beginning address of *B*[*i*, *j*, *k*] using this storage scheme will be

$$\text{base}(B) + [(i - l_1)m_2 m_3 + (j - l_2)m_3 + (k - l_3)]n$$

where $m_2 = u_2 - l_2 + 1$ and $m_3 = u_3 - l_3 + 1$. Address translation formulas for arrays having more than three dimensions can be derived similarly, but their complexity increases as the number of dimensions increases.

Exercises

1. Assume that values of type *integer* and *char* are stored in one memory cell, reals require two memory cells, values of type T require ten memory cells, strings are packed two characters per cell, and type *Days* is as defined in this section.

   (a) Find how many memory cells are required for an array A of the specified type:

      (i) **array**[1..10] **of** *real*
     (ii) **array**[−5..5] **of** *char*
    (iii) **array**[*Day*] **of** *T*
    (iv) **array**['A'..'Z'] **of** *integer*
     (v) **packed array**[1..8] **of** *char*

   (b) Assuming the declarations in part (a), find where each of the following elements of A is stored:

      (i) $A[4]$ and $A[10]$
     (ii) $A[-3]$ and $A[4]$
    (iii) $A[Thursday]$ and $A[Saturday]$
    (iv) $A['B']$ and $A['X']$
     (v) $A[5]$ and $A[6]$

2. Assuming the storage requirements and array declarations of a one-dimensional array A given in Exercise 1, indicate with diagrams like those in the text where each element of A is stored if the base address of A is b. Also, give the general address translation formula for $A[i]$.

3. Assuming the storage requirements given in Exercise 1, find where the indicated elements of a two-dimensional array M of the specified type are stored if the base address of M is 100 and storage is rowwise.

   (a) **array**[0..3, 1..10] **of** *real*; $M[0, 9]$ and $M[3, 3]$
   (b) **array**[2..9, −3..3] **of** *integer*; $M[5, -1]$ and $M[3, 3]$
   (c) **array**[*Monday..Friday*, 1..6] **of** *T*; $M[Tuesday, 4]$ and $M[Friday, 3]$
   (d) **packed array**[0..4, 1..5] **of** *char*; $M[2, 4]$ and $M[3, 3]$
   (e) **array**['A'..'J', 1..5] **of** *real*; $M['F', 1]$ and $M['C', 3]$
   (f) **array**['W'..'Z', −3..4] **of** *T*; $M['X', -1]$ and $M['Y', 3]$

4. Repeat Exercise 3, but for columnwise storage.

5. In the text, a general address translation formula for $M[i, j]$ was derived for a two-dimensional array M of type *Table* = **array**[1..3, 1..4] **of** *integer*, assuming rowwise storage and that integers can be stored in one memory cell. Find the corresponding formula if the array elements are stored columnwise.

6. Find the general address translation formula for $M[i, j]$, where M is a two-dimensional array of type

   array$[l_1..u_1, l_2..u_2]$ **of** *element-type*

   assuming columnwise storage.

7. In the text, a general address translation formula for $B[i, j, k]$ was derived for a three-dimensional array B of type *ThreeDimArray* = **array**$[1..3, 0..3, 2..4]$ **of** *real* by viewing B as a one-dimensional array whose elements were two-dimensional arrays. Alternatively, we could have viewed B as a two-dimensional array whose elements are one-dimensional arrays, that is, as though *ThreeDimArray* were defined by

   type
       OneDimArray = **array**$[2..4]$ **of** *real*;
       ThreeDimArray = **array**$[1..3, 0..3]$ **of** *OneDimArray*;

   Derive the address translation formula for $B[i, j, k]$ in this case, assuming that real values require two memory cells for storage.

8. Derive the address translation formula for $F[i, j, k, l]$ where F is a four-dimensional array of type

   array$[l_1..u_1, l_2..u_2, l_3..u_3, l_4..u_4]$ **of** *element-type*

   by viewing F as a one-dimensional array indexed by $l_1..u_1$ of three-dimensional arrays indexed by $l_2..u_2, l_3..u_3, l_4..u_4$. Assume that three-dimensional arrays are allocated storage as described in the text.

9. Give one possible address translation formula for an element $H[i_1, i_2, \ldots, i_q]$ of a q-dimensional array of type

   array$[l_1..u_1, l_2..u_2, l_3..u_3, \ldots, l_q..u_q]$ **of** *element-type*

   assuming that each element requires n memory cells for storage.

10. A *lower triangular* matrix M is a square matrix in which the only positions that may contain nonzero entries are on and below the main diagonal from the upper left corner to the lower right corner; all entries above this diagonal are zero:

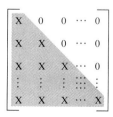

   That is, M is a two-dimensional array in which $M[i, j] = 0$ if $i < j$. Memory would be utilized more efficiently if instead of storing all the entries of M, only those on and below the diagonal were stored. Derive an address translation formula in this case for $M[i, j]$ where $i \geq j$, assuming that each entry of M can be stored in one memory cell and rowwise storage is used beginning at the word with address b.

11. Proceed as in Exercise 10 but for an *upper triangular* matrix M, in which the only positions that may contain nonzero entries are on and above the diagonal; all entries below this diagonal are zero:

$$
\begin{bmatrix}
X & X & X & \cdots & X \\
0 & X & X & \cdots & X \\
0 & 0 & X & \cdots & X \\
\vdots & \vdots & \vdots & \ddots & \vdots \\
0 & 0 & 0 & \cdots & X
\end{bmatrix}
$$

12. A *tridiagonal* matrix is a square matrix M in which the only positions where nonzero entries may appear is in the "band" consisting of locations on the diagonal, immediately above the diagonal (on the "superdiagonal") and immediately below it (on the "subdiagonal"); all entries not in this band are zero:

$$
\begin{bmatrix}
X & X & 0 & 0 & \cdots & 0 & 0 \\
X & X & X & 0 & \cdots & 0 & 0 \\
0 & X & X & X & \cdots & 0 & 0 \\
0 & 0 & X & X & \cdots & 0 & 0 \\
\cdot & \cdot & \cdot & \cdot & \cdots & \cdot & \cdot \\
\cdot & \cdot & \cdot & \cdot & \cdots & \cdot & \cdot \\
\cdot & \cdot & \cdot & \cdot & \cdots & \cdot & \cdot \\
0 & 0 & 0 & 0 & \cdots & X & X
\end{bmatrix}
$$

that is, $M[i, j] = 0$ if $|i - j| \geq 1$. Devise an efficient storage scheme for such matrices, and derive an address translation formula.

13. Letter grades are sometimes assigned to numeric scores by using the grading scheme commonly known as **grading on the curve**. In this scheme, a letter grade is assigned to a numeric score according to the following table:

x = Numeric Score	Letter Grade
$x < m - \dfrac{3}{2}\sigma$	F
$m - \dfrac{3}{2}\sigma \le x < m - \dfrac{1}{2}\sigma$	D
$m - \dfrac{1}{2}\sigma \le x < m + \dfrac{1}{2}\sigma$	C
$m + \dfrac{1}{2}\sigma \le x < m + \dfrac{3}{2}\sigma$	B
$m + \dfrac{3}{2}\sigma \le x$	A

Here m is the mean score and σ is the standard deviation; for a set of n numbers $x_1, x_2, \ldots, x_n$, these are defined as follows:

$$m = \frac{1}{n}\sum_{i=1}^{n} x_i \qquad \sigma = \sqrt{\frac{1}{n}\sum_{i=1}^{n}(x_i - m)^2}$$

Write a program to read a list of real numbers representing numeric scores, calculate their mean and standard deviation, and then determine and display the letter grade corresponding to each numeric score.

14. Peter the postman became bored one night and to break the monotony of the night shift, he carried out the following experiment with a row of mailboxes in the post office. These mailboxes were numbered 1 through 150, and beginning with mailbox 2, he opened the doors of all the even-numbered mailboxes. Next, beginning with mailbox 3, he went to every third mail box, opening its door if it were closed, and closing it if it were open. Then he repeated this procedure with every fourth mailbox, then every fifth mailbox, and so on. When he finished, he was surprised at the distribution of closed mailboxes. Write a program to determine which mailboxes these were.

15. Write a program to add two large integers of length up to 300 digits. One approach is to treat each number as a list, each of whose elements is a block of digits of that number. For example, the integer 179,534,672,198 might be stored with $Block[1] = 198$, $Block[2] = 672$, $Block[3] = 534$, $Block[4] = 179$. Then add two integers (lists), element by element, carrying from one element to the next when necessary.

16. Proceeding as in Exercise 15, write a program to multiply two large integers of length up to 300 digits.

17. A demographic study of the metropolitan area around Dogpatch divided it into three regions—urban, suburban, and exurban—and

published the following table showing the annual migration from one region to another (the numbers represent percentages):

	Urban	Suburban	Exurban
Urban	1.1	0.3	0.7
Suburban	0.1	1.2	0.3
Exurban	0.2	0.6	1.3

For example, 0.3 percent of the urbanites (0.003 times the current population) move to the suburbs each year. The diagonal entries represent internal growth rates. Using a two-dimensional array with an enumerated type for the indices to store this table, write a program to determine the population of each region after 10, 20, 30, 40, and 50 years. Assume that the initial populations of the urban, suburban, and exurban regions are 2.1 million, 1.4 million, and 0.9 million, respectively.

18. If A and B are two $m \times n$ matrices, their **sum** is defined as follows: If A_{ij} and B_{ij} are the entries in the ith row and jth column of A and B, respectively, then $A_{ij} + B_{ij}$ is the entry in the ith row and jth column of their sum, which will also be an $m \times n$ matrix. Write a program to read two $m \times n$ matrices, display them, and calculate and display their sum.

19. The product of an $m \times n$ matrix A with an $n \times p$ matrix B is the $m \times p$ matrix $C = A * B$ whose entry C_{ij} in the ith row and jth column is given by

$$C_{ij} = \text{the sum of the products of the entries in row } i \text{ of } A$$
$$\text{with the entries in column } j \text{ of } B$$

$$= A_{i1} * B_{1j} + A_{i2} * B_{2j} + \cdots + A_{in} * B_{nj}$$

Write a program that will read two matrices A and B, display them, and calculate and display their product (or a message indicating that it is not defined).

20. A **magic square** is an $n \times n$ matrix in which each of the integers 1, 2, 3, ... , n^2 appears exactly once and all column sums, row sums, and diagonal sums are equal. For example, the following is a 5 × 5 magic square in which all the rows, columns, and diagonals add up to 65:

17	24	1	8	15
23	5	7	14	16
4	6	13	20	22
10	12	19	21	3
11	18	25	2	9

The following is a procedure for constructing an $n \times n$ magic square for any odd integer n. Place 1 in the middle of the top row. Then after integer k has been placed, move up one row and one column to the right to place the next integer $k + 1$, unless one of the following occurs:

- If a move takes you above the top row in the jth column, move to the bottom of the jth column and place $k + 1$ there.
- If a move takes you outside to the right of the square in the ith row, place $k + 1$ in the ith row at the left side.
- If a move takes you to an already filled square or if you move out of the square at the upper right-hand corner, place $k + 1$ immediately below k.

Write a program to construct an $n \times n$ magic square for any odd value of n.

21. Suppose that each of the four edges of a thin square metal plate is maintained at a constant temperature and that we wish to determine the steady-state temperature at each interior point of the plate. To do this, we divide the plate into squares (the corners of which are called *nodes*) and find the temperature at each interior node by averaging the four neighboring temperatures; that is, if T_{ij} denotes the old temperature at the node in row i and column j, then

$$\frac{T_{i-1,j} + T_{i,j-1} + T_{i,j+1} + T_{i+1,j}}{4}$$

will be the new temperature.

   To model the plate, we can use a two-dimensional array, with each array element representing the temperature at one of the nodes. Write a program that first reads the four constant temperatures (possibly different) along the edges of the plate, and some guess of the temperature at the interior points, and uses these values to initialize the elements of the array. Then determine the steady-state temperature at each interior node by repeatedly averaging the temperatures at its four neighbors, as just described. Repeat this procedure until the new temperature at each interior node differs from the old temperature at that node by no more than some specified small amount. Then print the array and the number of iterations used to produce the final result. (It may also be of interest to print the array at each stage of the iteration.)

22. The game of *Life*, invented by the mathematician John H. Conway, is intended to model life in a society of organisms. Consider a rectangular array of cells, each of which may contain an organism. If the array is viewed as extending indefinitely in both directions, then each cell has eight neighbors, the eight cells surrounding it. In each gen-

eration, births and deaths occur according to the following rules:

- An organism is born in any empty cell having exactly three neighbors.
- An organism dies from isolation if it has fewer than two neighbors.
- An organism dies from overcrowding if it has more than three neighbors.
- All other organisms survive.

To illustrate, the following shows the first five generations of a particular configuration of organisms:

Write a program to play the game of *Life* and investigate the patterns produced by various initial configurations. Some configurations die off rather rapidly; others repeat after a certain number of generations; others change shape and size and may move across the array; and still others may produce ''gliders'' that detach themselves from the society and sail off into space.

2.4 Records in Pascal

Like an array, a ***record*** is a finite sequence of elements; however, these elements, called the ***fields*** of the record, may be of different types. As for arrays, the basic operation is direct access to each element in the record.

The declaration of this structured data type in Pascal specifies the name of the record and the type of each of its fields. It has the form

> **record**
>   *field-list*
> **end**

where a simple form of *field-list* is

> *list-1* : *type-1*;
> *list-2* : *type-2*;
>   .
>   .
>   .
> *list-n* : *type-n*

Each *list-i* is a single identifier or a list of identifiers that name the fields of the record, and *type-i* specifies the type of each of these fields.

To illustrate, records maintained for users of a computer system might contain a user identification number, a password, a resource limit, and the resources used to date. Such records could be declared by

```
type
   String = packed array[1..10] of char;
   UserRecord = record
                   IdNumber : integer;
                   Password : String;
                   ResourceLimit,
                   ResourcesUsed : real
                end;

var
   User : UserRecord;
```

The variable *User* may have as a value any record of type *UserRecord*. The first field of the record is of type *integer* and is named with the field identifier *IdNumber*; the second field is of type *String* and has the name *Password*; and both the third and fourth fields, named *ResourceLimit* and *ResourcesUsed*, are of type *real*. A typical value for *User* might be pictured as follows:

IdNumber	Password	ResourceLimit	ResourcesUsed
12345	EPSILON	100.00	37.45

Each field of a record can be accessed directly by using a **_field-designated variable_**, or simply **_fielded variable_**, of the form

record-name.field-name

Thus, *User.IdNumber* specifies the first field of the value of record variable *User* and can be assigned a value by the statement

User.IdNumber := 12345;

or

readln (User.IdNumber);

Similarly, *User.Password*, *User.ResourceLimit*, and *User.ResourcesUsed* refer to the second, third, and fourth fields. The statement

writeln (User.Password);

displays the value of *User.Password* and

if *User.ResourcesUsed* > *User.ResourceLimit* **then**
   writeln ('*** Resource limit exceeded ***');

displays the message *** Resource limit exceeded *** if the value of *User.ResourcesUsed* exceeds the value of value of *User.ResourceLimit*.

The fields that comprise a record may be of any data type; in particular, they may be other records. For example, the declarations

```
type
    String8 = packed array[1..8] of char;
    String20 = packed array[1..20] of char;
    DirectoryListing = record
                    Name, Street, CityAndState : String20;
                    PhoneNumber : integer
                end;
    Date = record
                Month : String8;
                Day : 1..31;
                Year : 1900..2000
            end;
    PersonalInfo = record
                    Ident : DirectoryListing;
                    Birth : Date;
                    CumGPA,
                    Credits : real
                end;

var
    Student : PersonalInfo;
```

specify that values of *Student* are records with four fields, the first of which is itself a record with four fields, and the second of which is a record with three fields. The fields within such a ***nested*** or ***hierarchical record*** can be accessed by simply affixing a second field identifier to the name of the larger record. Thus, *Student.Ident.Name* refers to the first field in the inner record.

Because using fielded variables for each of a record's fields may be quite cumbersome, Pascal provides an option that makes it unnecessary to write the record name each time that a field within that record is referenced. This is accomplished by using a **with** statement of the form

```
with record-name do
    statement
```

The specified record name is automatically combined with each field identifier in the statement qualified by the **with** clause to form a complete fielded variable. Thus the statement

```
with User do
    write (IdNumber:5, ResourceLimit:8:2, ResourcesUsed:8:2);
```

attaches the record name *User* to the field identifiers *IdNumber*, *ResourceLimit*, and *ResourcesUsed* to form the fielded variables *User.IdNumber*, *User.ResourceLimit*, and *User.ResourcesUsed*. It is thus equivalent to the statement

```
write (User.IdNumber:5, User.ResourceLimit:8:2,
        User.ResourcesUsed:8:2);
```

Identifiers in a **with** statement that are not field identifiers in the specified record are not combined with the record name but are treated in the usual way. Thus, in the statement

> **with** *User* **do**
>   *write* (*IdNumber*:5, *ResourcesUsed*:8:2, *ResourcesLeft*:8:2);

the identifier *ResourcesLeft* is not a field identifier in the record *User* and hence is not modified by the **with** statement. This statement is equivalent, therefore, to

> *write* (*User.IdNumber*:5, *User.ResourceUsed*:8:2, *ResourcesLeft*:8:2);

An extended form of the **with** statement allows several record names to be listed:

> **with** *record-name-1*, *record-name-2*, . . . , *record-name-n* **do**
>   *statement*

This form is equivalent to

> **with** *record-name-1* **do**
>   **with** *record-name-2* **do**
>   .
>   .
>   .
>   **with** *record-name-n* **do**
>   *statement*

For example, the statements

> *writeln* (*Student.Ident.Name*);
> *writeln* ('Birthday: ', *Student.Birth.Month*, *Student.Birth.Day*:3,
>   ', ', *Student.Birth.Year*:5, ' Age = ', *Age*:1);
> *writeln* ('Cumulative GPA = ', *Student.CumGPA*:4:2);

can be written

> **with** *Student* **do**
>   **begin**
>   **with** *Ident* **do**
>   *writeln* (*Name*);
>   **with** *Birth* **do**
>   *writeln* ('Birthday: ', *Month*, *Day*:3, ', ', *Year*:5,
>   ' Age = ', *Age* :1);
>   *writeln* ('Cumulative GPA = ', *CumGPA*:4:2)
>   **end** (* **with** *);

or simply

```
with Student, Ident, Birth do
  begin
    writeln (Name);
    writeln ('Birthday: ', Month, Day:3, ', ', Year:5,
             ' Age = ', Age:1);
    writeln ('Cumulative GPA = ', CumGPA:4:2)
  end (* with *);
```

An assignment statement of the form

$$record\text{-}variable\text{-}1 := record\text{-}variable\text{-}2$$

can be used to copy the fields of one record into another record. In this case the two record variables must have the **same type.**[2]

The examples of records considered thus far have consisted of a fixed number of fields, each of which has a fixed type. It is also possible to declare **variant records** in which some of the fields are fixed but the number and types of other fields may vary, so that a record may have a *fixed part* and a *variant part.* The number and types of the fields in the fixed part do not change during program execution, but those in the variant part may change in number and/or in type.

To illustrate variant records, consider computer-user records described by

```
UserRecord1 = record
                IdNumber : integer;
                Password : String;
                ResourceLimit,
                ResourcesUsed : real;
                Department : char
              end;
```

---

[2] The same rule applies to arrays and sets. For two structures to have the same type means that they must be declared by the same type identifier or by equivalent type identifiers. Two type identifiers are equivalent if their definitions can be traced back to a common type identifier. For example, consider the following record type declarations:

```
type
  Arecord = record
              X, Y : real
            end;
  Brecord = Arecord;
  Crecord = Arecord;
  Drecord = Brecord;
  Erecord = record
              X, Y : real
            end;
```

Type identifiers *Brecord* and *Crecord* are equivalent to *Arecord*, since they are synonyms for the type identifier *Arecord*. Similarly, *Drecord* is a synonym for *Brecord* and is therefore equivalent to *Brecord*. Type identifiers *Arecord, Brecord, Crecord,* and *Drecord* all are equivalent because their definitions can be traced back to a common type *identifier* (*Arecord*). It is important to note, however, that even though the definitions of *Arecord* and *Erecord* are identical, these type identifiers are not equivalent because they are not defined using a common type *identifier*.

where *String* is defined as **packed array**[1..10] **of** *char*. Such records are appropriate for the support staff who use the computer system at an engineering laboratory. For research personnel, records might have the following structure:

> *UserRecord2* = **record**
> > *IdNumber* : *integer*;
> > *Password* : *String*;
> > *Account* : *integer*;
> > *SecurityClearance* : 1..10
> > **end**;

and for administrators, an appropriate record structure might be

> *UserRecord3* = **record**
> > *IdNumber* : *integer*;
> > *Password* : *String*;
> > *Division* : *char*
> > **end**;

All of these record structures can be incorporated into a single record by using a record with a variant part:

> *UserRecord* = **record**
> > *IdNumber* : *integer*;
> > *Password* : *String*;
> > **case** *UserCode* : *char* **of**
> > > 'S' : (∗ support staff ∗)
> > > > (*ResourceLimit*,
> > > > *ResourcesUsed* : *real*;
> > > > *Department* : *char*);
> > >
> > > 'R' : (∗ research personnel ∗)
> > > > (*Account* : *integer*;
> > > > *SecurityClearance* : 1..10);
> > >
> > > 'A' : (∗ administration ∗)
> > > > (*Division* : *char*)
> > **end**;

This record has a fixed part consisting of the fields *IdNumber*, *Password*, and *UserCode* that is the same for all values of type *UserRecord*. In addition to these fields, some values have *ResourceLimit*, *ResourcesUsed*, and *Department* fields; others have *Account* and *SecurityClearance* fields; and still others have only a *Division* field. If *UserCode* has the value S, the fields *ResourceLimit*, *ResourcesUsed*, and *Department* are in effect; if *UserCode* has the value R, the fields *Account* and *SecurityClearance* are in effect; and if the value of *UserCode* is A, the field *Division* is in effect.

The field *UserCode* in this record is called a **tag field**. The values it may have are used to label the variant fields of the record and to determine the structure of a particular value of type *UserRecord*. Thus, if the value of *UserCode* is S, which labels the variant for a member of the support staff, the structure of the record is the same (except for the extra tag field) as one of type *UserRecord1*. If the value of *UserCode* is R, which labels the variant for research personnel, the structure of the record is essentially that of type *UserRecord2* . Finally, if the value of *UserCode* is A, which labels the variant for an administrator, the structure is basically the same as that of type *UserRecord3*.

In a variant record, several tag field values may label the same variant field list. For example, suppose that research personnel are classified according to their areas of specialization and these areas are coded as C, D, E, and M, so that the code for these employees may be any of these letters rather than simply R. In this situation an appropriate record declaration might be

> *UserRecord* = **record**
> > *IdNumber* : *integer*;
> > *Password* : *String*;
> > **case** *UserCode* : *char* **of**
> > > 'S': (∗ support staff ∗)
> > > > (*ResourceLimit*,
> > > > *ResourcesUsed* : *real*;
> > > > *Department* : *char*);
> >
> > > 'C', 'D',
> > > 'E', 'M': (∗ research personnel ∗)
> > > > (*Account* : *integer*;
> > > > *SecurityClearance* : 1..10);
> >
> > > 'A': (∗ administration ∗)
> > > > (*Division* : *char*)
> > **end**;

It is also permissible for tag field values to label empty variant field lists. To illustrate, suppose that in addition to support staff, researchers, and administrators, records of computer use are maintained for several other groups of individuals who are not currently on the payroll, for example, student interns, visiting researchers, and people on leave. These groups could be individually coded, I, V, and L, and so on, and an empty variant field used for them:

> *UserRecord* = **record**
> > *IdNumber* : *integer*;
> > *Password* : *String*;
> > **case** *UserCode* : *char* **of**
> > > 'S': (∗ support staff ∗)
> > > > (*ResourceLimit*,
> > > > *ResourcesUsed* : *real*;
> > > > *Department* : *char*);

'C', 'D',
'E', 'M': (* research personnel *)
 (*Account* : *integer*;
  SecurityClearance : 1..10);

'A': (* administration *)
 (*Division* : *char*);

'I','V','L': (* currently not on payroll *)
 (* no additional information stored *)
end;

The general form of a record structure is

record
 field-list
end

where each *field-list* has one of the following forms:

fixed-part   *fixed-part*;   *variant-part*
         variant-part

Here *fixed-part* has the form described in preceding sections:

list-1 : *type-1*;
list-2 : *type-2*;
 .
 .
 .
list-n : *type-n*;

where each *list-i* is a single identifier or a list of identifiers, separated by commas, that names the fields of the record, and *type-i* specifies the type of each of these fields. The *variant-part* has the form

case *tag-field* : *tag-type* **of**
 tag-list-1 : (*variant-1*);
 tag-list-2 : (*variant-2*);
 .
 .
 .
 tag-list-n : (*variant-n*)

where each *variant-i* is a field list of the form just described; thus the syntax of each *variant-i* is the same as for a record, but parentheses are used to enclose it rather than the reserved words **begin** and **end**. The type of the *tag-field* may be any ordinal type, and each of the possible values of the tag field variable must appear in exactly one *tag-list-i*.

Note that a record may have both a fixed part and a variant part, only a fixed part, or only a variant part. It might also be noted that the tag field identifier, but not its type identifier, may be omitted. In this case, access to the items in a variant field list is still possible; but because no tag field identifier is used, the tag field itself cannot be accessed. Such records might be used when it is possible to determine by some other means which variant is in effect, for example, when the first fifty records all use the same variant and the remaining fifty records involve some other variant. Omitting the tag field identifier, however, can easily lead to subtle errors and should normally be avoided. Finally, records may be packed so as to permit the compiler to minimize the amount of storage required for a record.

2.5 Example: Information Retrieval

Records are frequently used in problems involving the storage and retrieval of information, because in many such applications, not all the items of information are of the same type. Typically, one of the fields in the record serves as a *key field*, which uniquely identifies the record.

To illustrate, suppose that a file contains records for computer usage by the three kinds of users described earlier: support staff (S), research personnel (R), and administrators (A):

```
11395
DINGALING
S 500.00 329.74 A
12274
SANTACLAUS
R 1135 17
12556
HELLOTHERE
S 300.00 53.25 C
12690
SECRET
AC
13007
BINGO
R 225 9
13234
XXYYZZ
S 400.00 399.55 B
       .
       .
       .
```

Each record contains the computer user's id number (which serves as a key field), password, and user code, together with other information determined by the user code. The program in Figure 2.1 is an information retrieval program similar to that in Figure 1.4. It calls the procedure *ReadFile* that reads these records from the file, using procedure *ReadRecord*, counts them, and stores them in the array *User*, whose elements are variant records of type *UserRecord*. We assume that the records in this file have been sorted so that the id numbers are in ascending order. Thus the array *User* will also be sorted so that the procedure *BinarySearch* can be used to locate the record for a given user. If this record is found, the procedure *DisplayRecord* is called to display the information in it. The program thus has the following structure:

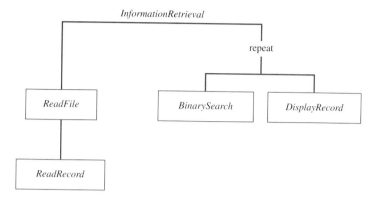

```
PROGRAM InfoRetrieval (input, output, UsageFile);

(*********************************************************************

    Input (file):      A file UsageFile of computer usage records, sorted
                       so that id numbers are in ascending order.
    Input (keyboard):  Identification numbers of several users.
    Function:          Reads computer usage records from UsageFile into
                       an array of variant records and allows information
                       about a given user to be retrieved.
    Output (screen):   Records of specified users.

********************************************************************)

    CONST
        StringLimit = 10;      (* maximum number of characters in strings *)
        ArrayLimit = 100;      (* limit on size of array *)

    TYPE
        String = PACKED ARRAY[1..StringLimit] OF CHAR;
        UserRecord = RECORD
                        IdNumber : integer;
                        Password : String;
                        CASE UserCode : CHAR OF
                            'S' : (* support staff *)
                                    (ResourceLimit,
                                     ResourcesUsed : real;
                                     Department : char);

                            'R' : (* research personnel *)
                                    (Account : integer;
                                     SecurityClearance : 1..10);

                            'A' : (* administrator *)
                                    (Division : char)
                     END;
        ArrayOfRecords = ARRAY[1..ArrayLimit] OF UserRecord;
```

Figure 2.1

Figure 2.1 (cont.)

```
    VAR
        User : ArrayOfRecords;   (* array of user records *)
        Count,                   (* number of records *)
        Location,                (* location of specified record in the
                                    array *)
        IdSought : integer;      (* id number of user to be searched for *)
        Found : boolean;         (* indicates if record is found *)
        UsageFile : text;        (* file of computer usage information *)

    PROCEDURE ReadFile (VAR UsageFile : text; VAR User : ArrayOfRecords;
                        VAR Count : integer);

(**********************************************************************

    Input (file):     File UsageFile of computer records.
    Function:         Reads and counts records and stores them in the
                      array User.
    Output (param):   Array User and number Count of records read.
    Output (screen):  "Array-full" message if there are too many
                      records in the file.

**********************************************************************)

    VAR
        UserRec : UserRecord;    (* a computer-usage record *)

    PROCEDURE ReadRecord (VAR UsageFile : text;
                          VAR UserRec : UserRecord);

    (**********************************************************************

        Input (file param): File UsageFile of computer records.
        Function:           Reads one record UserRec from UsageFile.
        Output (param):     UserRec.

    **********************************************************************)

    BEGIN (* ReadRecord *)
        WITH UserRec DO
            BEGIN
                readln (UsageFile, IdNumber);
                readln (UsageFile, Password);
                read (UsageFile, UserCode);
                    CASE UserCode OF
                        'S' : (* support staff *)
                              BEGIN
                                  readln (UsageFile, ResourceLimit,
                                          ResourcesUsed);
                                  readln (UsageFile, Department)
                              END;
```

Figure 2.1 (cont.)

```
                    'R' : (* research personnel *)
                       readln (UsageFile, Account,
                              SecurityClearance);

                    'A' : (* administration *)
                       readln (UsageFile, Division)
                END (* CASE *)
             END (* WITH *)
      END (* ReadRecord *);

   BEGIN (* ReadFile *)
      reset (UsageFile);
      Count := 0;
      ReadRecord (UsageFile, UserRec);
      WHILE NOT eof(UsageFile) AND (Count <= ArrayLimit) DO
         BEGIN
            Count := Count + 1;
            IF Count > ArrayLimit THEN
               writeln ('*** Too many records ***')
            ELSE
               User[Count] := UserRec;
            ReadRecord (UsageFile, UserRec)
         END (* WHILE *)
   END (* ReadFile *);

PROCEDURE BinarySearch (VAR User : ArrayOfRecords;
                        n, IdSought : integer;
                        VAR Location : integer; VAR Found : boolean);

(***********************************************************************

   Input (param):   An id number IdSought and array User of n computer
                    records, arranged in order by id numbers.
   Function:        Performs a binary search of User for a record
                    containing IdSought.
   Output (param):  Found and Location, where Found is true and
                    Location is the position of this record if the
                    search is successful; otherwise Found is false.

 ***********************************************************************)

      VAR
         First, Last : integer; (* first and last positions of
                                   the sublist being searched *)
      BEGIN (* BinarySearch *)
         First := 1;
         Last := n;
         Found := false;
         WHILE (First <= Last) AND NOT Found DO
            BEGIN
               Location := (First + Last) DIV 2;
               WITH User[Location] DO
                  IF IdSought < IdNumber THEN
                     Last := Location - 1
                  ELSE IF IdSought > IdNumber THEN
                     First := Location + 1
                  ELSE
                     Found := TRUE
            END (* WHILE *)
      END (* BinarySearch *);
```

Figure 2.1 (cont.)

```
     PROCEDURE DisplayRecord (UserRec : UserRecord);

     (*********************************************************************

         Input (param):    A computer usage record UserRec.
         Function:         Displays the contents of UserRec.
         Output (screen): Specially-formatted output of the fields of the
                          variant record UserRec.

     *******************************************************************)

     BEGIN (* DisplayRecord *)
        WITH UserRec DO
           BEGIN
              writeln ('Password:  ', Password);
              CASE UserCode OF
                 'S' : BEGIN
                          writeln ('*** Support staff ***');
                          writeln ('Resource Limit . .', ResourceLimit:8:2);
                          writeln ('Resources Used . .', ResourcesUsed:8:2);
                          writeln ('Department . . . . . . . ', Department);
                       END;

                 'R' : BEGIN
                          writeln ('*** Research personnel ***');
                          writeln ('Account   . . . . .', Account:8);
                          writeln ('Sec. Clearance . .', SecurityClearance:8);
                       END;

                 'A' : BEGIN
                          writeln ('*** Administration ***');
                          writeln ('Division . . . . . . . . ', Division)
                       END
              END (* CASE *)
           END (* WITH *)
     END (* DisplayRecord *);

BEGIN (* main program *)
   ReadFile (UsageFile, User, Count);
   writeln ('Enter 0 for user-id to quit.');
   writeln;
   write ('User''s id-number?  ');
   readln (IdSought);
   WHILE IdSought <> 0 DO
      BEGIN
         BinarySearch (User, Count, IdSought, Location, Found);
         IF Found THEN
            DisplayRecord (User[Location])
         ELSE
            writeln ('User''s record not found');
         writeln;
         write ('User''s id-number?  ');
         readln (IdSought)
      END (* WHILE *)
END (* main program *).
```

Figure 2.1 (cont.)

Listing of USAGEFILE used in sample run:

```
11395
DINGALING
S 500.00 329.74
A
12274
SANTACLAUS
R 1135 7
12556
HELLOTHERE
S 300.00 53.25
C
12690
SECRET
AC
13007
BINGO
R 225 9
13234
XXYYZZ
S 400.00 399.55
B
```

Sample run:

```
Enter 0 for user-id to quit.

User's id-number?  11395
Password:  DINGALING
*** Support staff ***
Resource Limit . .  500.00
Resources Used . .  329.74
Department . . . . . . . A

User's id-number?  12699
User's record not found

User's id-number?  12690
Password:  SECRET
*** Administration ***
Division . . . . . . . . C

User's id-number?  13007
Password:  BINGO
*** Research personnel ***
Account  . . . . .    225
Sec. Clearance . .      9

User's id-number?  0
```

Exercises

1. For each of the following, design a record structure to store the given information, writing appropriate type declarations for the records:

(a) Time in civilian format (hours, minutes, seconds, and an A.M./P.M. indicator).

(b) Time in military format (*xx.yy* where $0 \le xx \le 23, 0 \le yy \le 59$).

(c) Length measured in yards, feet, and inches.

(d) Angles measured in degrees, minutes, and seconds.

(e) Cards in a deck of playing cards.

(f) Listings in a telephone directory.

(g) Description of an automobile (make, model, style, color, and the like).

(h) Description of a book in a library's card catalogue (author, publisher, and the like).

(i) Teams in a baseball league (name, won–lost record, and the like).

(j) Position of a checker on a checker board.

2. For each of the following, design a variant record structure to store the given information, writing appropriate type declarations for the records:

(a) Time in either civilian or military format (see Exercise 1) as specified by the tag field in the record.

(b) Information about a person: name, birthday, age, sex, social security number, height, weight, hair color, eye color, marital status, and, if married, number of children.

(c) Statistics about a baseball player: name; age; birth date; position (pitcher, catcher, infielder, outfielder); for a pitcher: won–lost record, earned-run average, number of strikeouts, and number of walks; if a starting pitcher, number of complete games; and if a relief pitcher, number of innings pitched and number of saves; for the other positions, batting average; slugging average; bats right, left, or is a switch hitter; fielding percentage; also, for an infielder: the positions he can play; for a catcher, whether he can catch a knuckleball.

(d) Weather statistics: date; city and state, province, or country; time of day; temperature; barometric pressure; weather conditions (clear skies, partly cloudy, cloudy, stormy); if cloudy conditions prevail, cloud level and type of clouds; for partly cloudy, percentage of cloud cover; for stormy conditions, snow depth if it is snowing, amount of rainfall if it is rainy, size of hail if it is hailing.

3. The file *UsersFile* (see Appendix E) consists of records of computer users, each of which contains a user's id number (integer), name (string of length 30 in the form Last Name, First Name), password (5-character string), resource limit (integer), and resources used to date (real). At the end of each month, a report is produced that shows the status of each user's account. Write a program to read these records and print a report like the following that shows the status of each user's account.

The three asterisks indicate that the user has already used 90 percent or more of the resources available to him or her:

```
              USER ACCOUNTS - 6/30/91

                                 RESOURCE    RESOURCES
      USER NAME         USER-ID     LIMIT       USED
      =========         =======   ========    =========
      MILTGEN, JOSEPH   100101       $750     $380.81
      SMALL, ISAAC      100102       $650     $598.84***
         .                 .           .          .
         .                 .           .          .
         .                 .           .          .
```

4. Consider the master file *StudentFile* containing permanent student records and the update file *StudentUpdate* containing current information for each student (see Appendix E). Each record in *StudentFile* consists of a student's number (integer), last name (15-character string), first name (10-character string), middle initial (character), hometown (25-character string), phone number (7-character string), sex (character), class level (1-digit integer), major (4-character string), total credits earned to date (integer), and cumulative GPA (real). Each record in *StudentUpdate* contains a student's number and a list of five course records, each consisting of a course name (7-character string), a letter grade (2-character string), and the number of course credits (integer). The records in each file are arranged so that the student numbers are in ascending order. Write a program that reads the information for each student from these files, storing it in appropriate record structures, and produces an updated grade report of the form:

```
      GRADE REPORT - Semester #2
           5/31/91

      Dispatch University

   10103 JAMES    L. JOHNSON

   COURSE        CREDITS        GRADE
   ======        =======        =====
   CPSC152          3            B+
   ENGL100          3            C
   ENGR131          4            B+
   MATH161          5            A-
   P E 100          2            D

   Cumulative Credits: 33
   Semester GPA: 2.22
   Cumulative GPA: 2.64
```

(To calculate the semester GPA: Multiply the credits by the numeric grade—A $= 4.0$, A$- = 3.7$, B$+ = 3.3$, B $= 3.0, \ldots,$ D$- = 0.7$, F $= 0.0$—for each course to find the number of honor points earned for that course; sum these to find the total number of new honor points; then divide the total number of new honor points by the total number of new credits. To update the cumulative GPA, first calculate the number of old honor points = old credits times old cumulative GPA; add the new honor points; and then divide this total by the updated total number of credits.)

5. The ***point-slope*** equation of a line having slope m and passing through the point P with coordinates (x_1, y_1) is

$$y - y_1 = m(x - x_1)$$

   (a) Write a record description for a line, given its slope and a point on the line.
   (b) Write a program that reads the slope of a line and the coordinates of a point on the line and that then

   (i) Finds the point-slope equation of the line.
   (ii) Finds the slope-intercept equation of the line

$$y = mx + b$$

   where m is the slope of the line and b is its y intercept.

   (c) Write a program to read the point and slope information of two lines and determine whether they intersect or are parallel. If they intersect, find the point of intersection and also determine whether they are perpendicular.

6. A ***complex number*** has the form $a + bi$, where a and b are real numbers and $i^2 = -1$. The four basic arithmetic operations for complex numbers are defined as follows:

$$\text{addition: } (a + bi) + (c + di) = (a + c) + (b + d)i$$

$$\text{subtraction: } (a + bi) - (c + di) = (a - c) + (b - d)i$$

$$\text{multiplication: } (a + bi) * (c + di) = (ac - bd) + (ad + bc)i$$

$$\text{division: } \frac{a + bi}{c + di} = \frac{ac + bd}{c^2 + d^2} + \frac{bc - ad}{c^2 + d^2} i,$$

$$\text{provided } c^2 + d^2 \neq 0.$$

Write a program to read two complex numbers and a symbol for one of these operations and to perform the indicated operation. Use a record to represent complex numbers, and use procedures to implement the operations.

7. A ***rational number*** is of the form a/b, where a and b are integers with $b \neq 0$. Write a program to do rational number arithmetic, representing each rational number as a record with a numerator field and a denominator field. The program should read and display all rational numbers in the format a/b, or simply a if the denominator is 1. The following examples illustrate the menu of commands that the user should be allowed to enter:

Input	Output	Comments
3/8 + 1/6	13/24	$a/b + c/d = (ad + bc)/bd$ reduced to lowest terms.
3/8 − 1/6	5/24	$a/b − c/d = (ad − bc)/bd$ reduced to lowest terms.
3/8 * 1/6	1/16	$a/b * c/d = ac/bd$ reduced to lowest terms.
3/8 / 1/6	9/4	$a/b / c/d = ad/bc$ reduced to lowest terms.
3/8 I	8/3	Invert a/b.
8/3 M	2 + 2/3	Write a/b as a mixed fraction.
6/8 R	3/4	Reduce a/b to lowest terms.
6/8 G	2	Greatest common divisor of numerator and denominator.
1/6 L 3/8	24	Least common denominator of a/b and c/d.
1/6 < 3/8	true	$a/b < c/d$?
1/6 <= 3/8	true	$a/b \le c/d$?
1/6 > 3/8	false	$a/b > c/d$?
1/6 >= 3/8	false	$a/b \ge c/d$?
3/8 = 9/24	true	$a/b = c/d$?
2/3X + 2 = 4/5	X = −9/5	Solution of linear equation $(a/b)X + c/d = e/f$.

8. Write a declaration of a record having only a variant part for four geometric figures: a circle, a square, a rectangle, and a triangle. For a circle, the record should store its radius; for a square, the length of a side; for a rectangle, the length of two adjacent sides; and for a triangle, the lengths of the three sides. Then write a program that reads one of the letters C (circle), S (square), R (rectangle), T (triangle), and the appropriate numeric quantity or quantities for a figure of that type and then calculates its area. For example, the input R 7.2 3.5 represents a rectangle with length 7.2 and width 3.5, and T 3 4 6.1 represents a triangle having sides of lengths 3, 4, and 6.1. (For a triangle, the area can be found with *Hero's formula:*

$$area = \sqrt{s(s − a)(s − b)(s − c)}$$

where a, b, and c are the lengths of the sides and s is one half the perimeter.)

9. Modify the program of Figure 2.1 by making it a menu-driven program that allows at least the following options:

GET: Get the records from *UsageFile* and store them in the array *User*.

INS: Insert the record for a new user, keeping the array sorted so the name fields are in alphabetical order.

RET: Retrieve and display the record for a specified user.

UPD: Update the information in the record for a specified user.

DEL: Delete the record for some user.

LIS: List the records (or perhaps selected items in the records) in order. This option should allow suboptions
U—to list for all users
S—to list for only support staff
R—to list for only research personnel
A—to list for only administration

SAV: Copy the records from the array into a permanent file.

2.6 Implementation of Records

We have seen that to store an array, sufficient memory is allocated to store all the array elements and that each array reference involves two steps: First, an address translation must be performed to locate the memory cell(s) in which that array element is stored, and second, the bit string stored there must be interpreted in the manner prescribed by the type specification for the array elements in the array declaration. Similarly, the implementation of a record structure also requires sufficient memory to store all of the fields that comprise the record. Address translation is again required to determine the location in which a particular field is stored, but this address translation is slightly more complex than for arrays because different fields usually require a different number of cells for storage. Also, unlike arrays, different interpretations of the bit strings are usually required for different fields, since the fields within a record need not be of the same type.

To illustrate, consider the record declaration for *UserRecord* of the preceding section:

```
type
  String = packed array[1..10] of char;
  UserRecord = record
                  IdNumber : integer;
                  Password : String;
                  ResourceLimit,
                  ResourcesUsed : real
                end;

var
  User : UserRecord;
```

and suppose that integers can be stored in one memory cell, real values require two cells, and values of type *String* require five memory cells. This record declaration instructs the compiler to reserve a block of ten memory cells to store such a record; the address of the first cell, as for arrays, is called the **base address.** The field *User.IdNumber* is then stored in the cell with address base(*User*); *User.Password* is stored in cells base(*User*) + 1 through base(*User*) + 5; *User.ResourceLimit*, in cells base(*User*) + 6 and base(*User*) + 7; and *User.ResourcesUsed*, in cells base(*User*) + 8 and base(*User*) + 9:

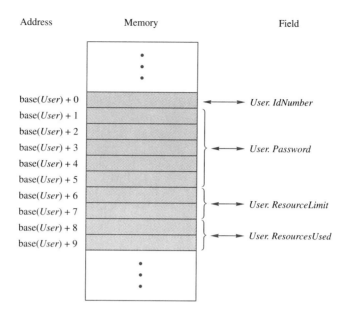

When one of these fields is accessed, the bit string stored in the associated cell or cells is interpreted according to the type specified for that field in the record declaration.

In general, for a record R with fields F_1 of type T_1, F_2 of type T_2, ... , F_r of type T_r, which require n_1, n_2, ... , n_r cells for storage, respectively, the field $R.F_i$ is stored in the block of r words beginning with

$$\text{base}(R) + \sum_{j=1}^{i-1} n_j = \text{base}(R) + n_1 + n_2 + \cdots + n_{i-1}$$

and the bit string stored in this block is interpreted as a value of data type T_i.

For a variant record, sufficient memory is ordinarily allocated to store the fixed part together with the largest variant. When a field in the fixed part is referenced, the address translation and interpretation are as just described. When a field within the variant part is referenced, the address translation and interpretation are carried out using the declaration for that variant part. To illustrate, consider the record declaration

```
type
    String6 = packed array[1..6] of char;
    RecordType = record
                    A : String6;
                    B : integer;
                    case T : integer of
                        1 : (C1 : String6; C2 : integer;
                             C3 : boolean; C4 : integer);
                        2 : (D1 : boolean; D2 : String6; D3 : integer);
                        3 : ( )
                 end;
```

var
   R : *RecordType*;

and suppose that in some word-addressable machine, characters can be packed two per word and that integer and boolean values require one word for storage. Since the fixed part of this record structure requires four memory words, the tag field requires one word, and the first variant, which is the largest, requires six words for storage, a block of eleven memory words would be allocated for R. If one of the other variants is in effect, this same block is used to store the record. The following diagram illustrates this storage scheme and indicates the locations of the fields in different variants in the block of memory cells allocated for R.

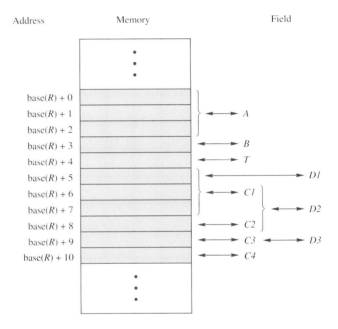

Now suppose that a value is assigned to R using the second variant:

with R **do**
   begin
      $A :=$ 'ABCDEF';
      $B :=$ 16392;
      $T :=$ 2;
      $D1 :=$ *true*;
      $D2 :=$ 'GHIJKL';
      $D3 :=$ 0
   end (∗ **with** ∗);

The bit strings stored in the eleven memory cells allocated to R might then be as follows:

base(R) + 0	0100000101000010
base(R) + 1	0100001101000100
base(R) + 2	0100010101000110
base(R) + 3	0100000000001000
base(R) + 4	0000000000000010
base(R) + 5	0000000000000001
base(R) + 6	0100011101001000
base(R) + 7	0100100101001010
base(R) + 8	0100101101001100
base(R) + 9	0000000000000000
base(R) + 10	0000000000001111	◀—— "Garbage"

The last word in this block has been indicated as containing "garbage" because the bit string shown was not stored there by this assignment of a value to R; it is a carryover from some previous computation when this memory word was used, perhaps in a reference to R using the first (largest) variant.

If now $R.D3$ is referenced, the address base(R) + 3 + 1 + 1 + 1 + 3 = base(R) + 9 is calculated, and the bit string 0000000000000000 stored in this memory word is interpreted as the integer 0. Similarly, if $R.D2[3]$ is referenced, the beginning address base(R) + 3 + 1 + 1 + 1 = base(R) + 6 of the field $R.D2$ is computed; the location of the third element of this packed array is determined to be the first byte of word base(R) + 6 + 1 = base(R) + 7 (using the address translation formulas of Section 2.3); and the bit string 01001001 stored in this byte is interpreted as the character I.

If a reference is made to a field in a variant different from that used to assign a value to a record variable, the address translation and interpretation appropriate to the referenced field are carried out. Thus if $R.C1[5]$ is referenced, its location, the first byte of word (base(R) + 3 + 1 + 1) + 2 = base(R) + 7, is computed, and the bit string stored in this byte is interpreted as the character I. A reference to $R.C3$ locates the memory word base(R) + 9, and the bit string composed of all zeros that is stored there is interpreted as the boolean value *false*, even though it was created as a representation of the integer constant 0 when this value was assigned to $R.D3$. Had the value 6 been assigned to $R.D3$ so that this memory word stored 0000000000000110, a reference to $R.C3$ would produce the boolean value *false* if only the rightmost bit were used, the boolean value *true* if any nonzero bit string represented true, or an error if interpretation were not possible.

Exercises

1. Suppose that integers are stored in one memory cell; real values require two cells for storage; values of type *char* require an entire cell and strings of characters are packed two characters per word. Give diagrams

like those in the text showing where each field of the following record types would be stored:

(a) *Date* = **record**
                Month : **packed array**[1..8]of *char*;
                Day : 1..31;
                Year : 1900..2000
        end

(b) *Point* = **record**
                X, Y : *real*
        end;

(c) *StudentRecord* = **record**
                Snumb : *integer*;
                Name : **packed array**[1..16] **of** *char*;
                Scores : **record**
                        Homework, Tests, Exam : *real*
                  end;
                FinalNumScore : *real*;
                LetterGrade : *char*
        end;

(d) *ClassRecord* = **record**
                Snumb : *integer*;
                Name : **packed array**[1..16] **of** *char*;
                Sex : *char*;
                TestScore : **array**[1..5] **of** *integer*
        end;

(e) A record of type *UserRecord* as defined in Figure 2.1.

(f) *Transaction* = **record**
                CustomerName : **packed array**[1..20] **of** *char*;
                Number : *integer*;
                TransDate : **record**
                        Month, Day, Year : *integer*
                  end;
                case *TransType* : *char* **of**
                'D', 'W': (*Amount* : *real*);
                    'L' : (*LoanNumber* : *integer*;
                      Payment, Interest,
                      NewBalance : *real*);
                    'T': (*TransferAccount* : *integer*;
                      AmountOfTransfer : *real*;
                      Code : *char*)
                  'V': ( )
        end;

2. Consider the student records in the financial aid program of Figure 1.4. Suppose that Pascal did not provide records as a predefined structured data type. Write a program that reads such records and stores them in *parallel arrays*, one containing the students' names, another their student numbers, and so on. Then implement the *Retrieve* option.

3. Describe how an array of variant records might be implemented in
Pascal if it did not provide records as a predefined data type. Illustrate
using the records of type *UserRecord* in the program of Figure 2.1 and
write procedures *BinarySearch* and *DisplayRecord* in this implementation.

2.7 Sets in Pascal

In mathematics and computer science, the term ***set*** refers to an unordered collection of objects called the ***elements*** or ***members*** of the set. A set is commonly
denoted by listing the elements enclosed in braces, { and }. For example, the
set of decimal digits contains the elements 0, 1, 2, 3, 4, 5, 6, 7, 8, and 9 and is
denoted {0, 1, 2, 3, 4, 5, 6, 7, 8, 9}. The set of uppercase letters is
{A, B, C, ... , Z}. The set of even prime numbers {2} contains the single
element 2; and the set of even prime numbers greater than 2 is the empty set,
denoted $\emptyset$ or { }, that is, the set containing no elements.

In a problem involving sets, the elements are selected from some given
set called the ***universal set*** for that problem. For example, if the set of vowels
or the set {X, Y, Z} is being considered, the universal set might be the set of
all letters. If the universal set is the set of names of months of the year, then
one might use the set of summer months {June, July, August}; the set of
months whose names do not contain the letter *r* {May, June, July, August}; or
the set of all months having fewer than 30 days {February}.

The basic relation in defining a set is the ***membership*** relation. Given a
set S and any object x in the universal set, one must be able to determine that
x belongs to S, denoted by $x \in S$, or that it does not belong to S, denoted by
$x \notin S$.

Three basic set operations are intersection, union, and set difference. The
intersection of two sets S and T, denoted in mathematics by $S \cap T$, is the set
of elements that are in both sets. The ***union*** of S and T, $S \cup T$, is the set of
elements that are in S or in T or in both. The set ***difference***, $S - T$, consists
of those elements of S that are not in T. The following ***Venn diagrams*** illustrate
these basic set operations:

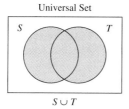
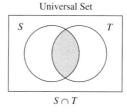
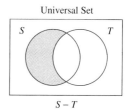

Viewed as a data structure, a set is an unordered collection of objects on
which are defined the basic operations of membership, union, intersection, and
difference. Since the elements of a set are not ordered, it does not make sense
to speak of a first element, a second element, and so on. For example, the set
{1, 3, 5, 7, 9} is the same as the set {3, 1, 9, 5, 7} or {9, 5, 7, 3, 1}. Thus,
unlike the elements in an array, the elements of a set are not directly accessible.

Sets differ from records in two important ways. Data items stored in a record are directly accessible and may be of different types. In Pascal, however, the elements of a set must be of the same type, and as we have noted, they are not directly accessible.

In this section we describe how sets can be processed using the predefined structured data type **set** in Pascal and certain predefined set relations and operations.

Set Declarations. In Pascal, all of the elements of a set must be of the same type, called the *base type* of the set, which must be an ordinal type; thus sets of real numbers or sets of arrays are not allowed. A *set declaration* has the form

> **set of** *base-type*

and specifies the type of elements in a universal set consisting of all elements of the given base type. Most Pascal compilers also impose additional restrictions on sets, such as a limit on the number of elements that a set may have. This limit usually excludes *integer* as a base type and may also exclude *char*. In these cases, subranges of integers and/or subranges of characters must be used.

To illustrate, consider the declarations

> **type**
>   *Digits* = 0..9;
>   *Months* = (*January, February, March, April, May, June, July,*
>   *August, September, October, November, December*);
>   *DigitSet* = **set of** *Digits*;
>   *BinarySet* = **set of** 0..1;
>   *MonthSet* = **set of** *Months*;
>   *CapLetterSet* = **set of** 'A'..'Z';
>   *MonthArray* = **array**[1..4] **of** *MonthSet*;

These declarations establish four universal sets: {0, 1, 2, 3, 4, 5, 6, 7, 8, 9}, {0, 1}, {*January, February, March, . . . , December*} and {'A', 'B', . . . , 'Z'}. Sets whose elements are selected from one of these universal sets may then be used in the program by declaring set variables to be one of these set types; for example,

> **var**
>   *Numbers, Evens, Odds* : *DigitSet*;
>   *Bits* : *BinarySet*;
>   *Winter* : *MonthSet*;
>   *Vowels, Consonants* : *CapLetterSet*;
>   *Season* : *MonthArray*;

The set variables *Numbers, Evens,* and *Odds* may have as values any sets of elements chosen from 0, 1, 2, . . . , 9; *Bits* may have as a value any set with elements selected from 0, 1; *Winter* and any element of the array *Season* may have as values any set of elements selected from *January, February, . . . , December*; and the variables *Vowels* and *Consonants* may have values that are sets of uppercase letters.

Set Values. A *set value* in Pascal has the form

[*element-list*]

where *element-list* is a list (possibly empty) of constants, variables, or expressions separated by commas; it is enclosed in brackets, [and]. The elements in this list must be of the same type (which must be an ordinal type), and consecutive values may be indicated by subrange notation. Thus, for the base types just defined,

[0, 2, 4, 6, 8]

is a valid set constant that might be the value of *Evens*. Since sets are unordered, this same set could be denoted [4, 0, 8, 2, 6] or [8, 6, 4, 2, 0]. If *Dig* has the value 4, then

[*Dig* − 4, *Dig* **div** 2, *Dig*, 6, 2 ∗ *Dig*]

is another representation of this same set value. The set constant

[0, 1, 2, 3, 4]

can be expressed by using subrange notation as

[0..4]

or

[*Dig* − 4 .. *Dig*]

The value of the set variable *Winter* might be the set constant

[*December, January .. March*]

but it could not be ['D', 'J', 'F', 'M'] because the base type of this set constant is not compatible with the base type of *Winter*.

The *empty set* is denoted in Pascal by the set constant

[ ]

and may be assigned to a set variable of any base type. Thus [ ] could be the value of both *Numbers* and *Winter*, even though these set variables have different base types.

Set Assignment. To assign a value to a variable of set type, an assignment statement of the form

$$set\text{-}variable := set\text{-}value$$

may be used. The base type of *set-value* must be compatible with the base type of *set-variable*. Thus, for the base types defined earlier, the statement

$$Evens := [0, 2, 4, 6, 8]$$

is a valid assignment statement and assigns the set constant [0, 2, 4, 6, 8] to the set variable *Evens*.

Set Relations. The test for set membership is implemented in Pascal by the relational operator **in.** Boolean expressions used to test set membership have the form

$$element \textbf{ in } set$$

where *set* is a set constant, a set variable, or a set expression, and the type of *element* and the base type of *set* are compatible. For example, if $N = 4$,

    2 **in** *Evens*
    3 **in** *Evens*
    $N + 1$ **in** *Evens*

are valid boolean expressions and have the values true, false, and false, respectively.

Sometimes it is necessary to determine whether all of the elements of some set *set1* are also members of another set *set2*, that is, to determine whether *set1* is a **subset** of *set2*. This can be done in Pascal by using the relational operators $<=$ and $>=$ to construct boolean expressions of the form

$$set1 <= set2$$

or equivalently,

$$set2 >= set1$$

where *set1* and *set2* are set constants, variables, or expressions with compatible base types. These expressions are true if *set1* is a subset of *set2* and are false otherwise. For example, if *Evens* has the value [0, 2, 4, 6, 8], then the value of the boolean expression

$$[2, 6] <= Evens$$

is true.

Two sets are said to be **equal** if they contain exactly the same elements. Set equality can be checked in Pascal with a boolean expression of the form

$$set1 \ = \ set2$$

where again *set1* and *set2* must have compatible base types. The relational operator $<>$ may also be used,

$$set1 \ <> \ set2$$

and is equivalent to the boolean expression **not** (*set1* $=$ *set2*).

Set Operations. In addition to the relational operations **in**, $<=$, $>=$, $=$, and $<>$, there are three binary set operations that are used to combine two sets to form another set. These are the operations of union, intersection, and difference. The ***union*** of *set1* and *set2* is denoted by a set expression of the form

$$set1 \ + \ set2$$

and the ***intersection*** of *set1* and *set2* by

$$set1 \ * \ set2$$

The ***set difference***

$$set1 \ - \ set2$$

is the set of elements that are in *set1* but not in *set2*. For each of these set expressions, the base types of *set1* and *set2* must be compatible.

When a set expression contains two or more of these operators, it is evaluated according to the following priorities:

```
*        ←——————  high priority
+, −  ←——————  low priority
```

Thus in the expression

$$[2, 3, 5] \ + \ [2, 4, 7] \ * \ [2, 4, 6, 8]$$

the intersection operation is performed first, giving the set $[2, 4]$, and then

$$[2, 3, 5] \ + \ [2, 4]$$

is evaluated, yielding

$$[2, 3, 4, 5]$$

Operations having the same priority are evaluated in the order in which they appear in the expression, from left to right. Parentheses may be used in the usual way to alter the standard order of evaluation.

Input/Output of Sets. To construct a set by reading its elements, we first initialize it to the empty set and then read each element and add it to the set. This process is described in the following algorithm:

ALGORITHM TO CONSTRUCT A SET

(* Input:	Elements of a set.
Function:	Construct a set S by repeatedly reading an element x of S and adding it to S.
Returns:	The set S. *)

1. Initialize S to the empty set.
2. While there is more data, do the following:
   a. Read a value for a variable x whose type is the base type of S.
   b. Add x to S.

In Pascal, an element x can be added to a set S by applying the union operation to S and the singleton set $[x]$:

$$S := S + [x]$$

To display the elements of a set, we can use the following algorithm:

ALGORITHM TO DISPLAY A SET

(* Input:	A set S.
Function:	Display set S by repeatedly finding an element x of S, displaying it, and removing it from S.
Output:	Elements of the set S.
Note:	The set S is destroyed since it is reduced to the empty set. *)

1. Let x be a variable whose type is the base type of S and initialize x to the first element of this base type.
2. While S is not empty, do the following:
   a. While x is not in S, replace x with its successor.
   b. Display x.
   c. Remove x from S.

In Pascal, an element x can be removed from a set S, as required in step 2c, by applying the difference operation to S and the singleton set $[x]$:

$$S := S - [x]$$

If the set to be displayed with this algorithm is to be preserved, it should first be copied into some temporary set

$$TempSet := S;$$

whose elements are then displayed.

EXAMPLE: Planning a Trip. Sets are useful in applications in which the order of the data items being processed is not important. For example, a tourist planning a trip to Europe has a set of cities that she wishes to visit, but the order in which she visits them is not important. Since a large number of tours are available, a program that examines a file to find all the tours that would satisfy the tourist's requirements would be very helpful to a travel agent. Such a program is given in Figure 2.2. It displays a numbered list of cities from which the user selects the numbers of those cities to be visited; these numbers are stored in the set *RequestedCities*. A file containing the itineraries of various tours is then opened and read. For each tour, the set *TourCities* containing the numbers of the cities visited on that tour is constructed. The program then checks if the set *RequestedCities* is a subset of the set *TourCities*, and if so, it displays the number of the tour and the set of cities it visits.

```
PROGRAM TourPlanner (input, output, TourFile);

(*******************************************************************

    Input (file):      A file TourFile containing tour numbers and the
                       numbers of cities visited on these tours.
    Input (keyboard):  A set of numbers of cities the user wishes to
                       visit.
    Function:          Finds all tours that visit the cities requested
                       by the user.
    Output (screen):   A list of numbers and names of available cities,
                       the names of the cities selected by the user,
                       and a list of all tours that visit these cities.

*******************************************************************)

CONST
    StringLimit = 10;
    MaxCities = 50;

TYPE
    String = PACKED ARRAY[1..StringLimit] OF char;
    ArrayOfNames = ARRAY[1..MaxCities] OF String;
    SetOfNumbers = SET OF 1..MaxCities;

VAR
    City : ArrayOfNames;            (* array of city names *)
    TourNumber,                     (* tour number *)
    NumCities : integer;            (* total number of cities on all tours *)
    TourFile : text;                (* text file containing tour info *)
    CitySet,                        (* some set of cities *)
    RequestedCities,                (* set of cities requested by user *)
    TourCities : SetOfNumbers;      (* set of cities visited on a tour *)
    Response : char;                (* user's response *)

PROCEDURE ConstructCityList (VAR City : ArrayOfNames;
                             VAR NumCities : integer);
```

Figure 2.2

Figure 2.2 (cont.)

```
(*********************************************************************

    Input:              None.
    Function:           Initializes the array City of NumCities city
                        names.
    Output (param):     The array City and NumCities.


********************************************************************)

BEGIN (* ConstructCityList *)
   City[1] := 'Amsterdam ';      City[2] := 'Berlin    ';
   City[3] := 'Brussels  ';      City[4] := 'Cologne   ';
   City[5] := 'Innsbruck ';      City[6] := 'Rome      ';
   City[7] := 'Paris     ';      City[8] := 'Salzburg  ';
   City[9] := 'Venice    ';      City[10] := 'Zurich    ';
   NumCities := 10
END (* ConstructCityList *);

PROCEDURE PrintCities (City : ArrayOfNames; NumCities : integer);

   (********************************************************************

       Input (param):    The array City of NumCities names.
       Function:         Displays the city names.
       Output (screen):  List of city names in City.


   *******************************************************************)

   VAR
      i : integer;      (* index *)

   BEGIN (* PrintCities *)
      writeln ('Number    City');
      writeln ('======    ====');
      FOR i := 1 TO NumCities DO
         writeln (i:4, '    ',City[i])
   END (* PrintCities *);

PROCEDURE ReadCitySet (VAR InfoFile : text; VAR CitySet : SetOfNumbers);

   (********************************************************************

       Input (file param): A file InfoFile from which numbers of cities
                           are to be read.
       Function:           Reads numbers of cities from TourFile and
                           constructs a set CitySet containing these
                           numbers.
       Output (param):     The set CitySet.


   *******************************************************************)

   VAR
      CityNum : integer;    (* number read and added to CitySet *)
```

Figure 2.2 (cont.)

```
   BEGIN (* ReadCitySet *)
      CitySet := [];
      read (InfoFile, CityNum);
      WHILE CityNum <> 0 DO
         BEGIN
            CitySet := CitySet + [CityNum];
            read (InfoFile, CityNum)
         END (* WHILE *);
      readln (InfoFile)
   END (* ReadCitySet *);

PROCEDURE PrintCitySet (CitySet : SetOfNumbers;
                        City : ArrayOfNames);

   (**********************************************************************

      Input (param):   A set CitySet of city numbers and array City
                       of  names of available cities.
      Function:        Displays the names of the cities in CitySet.
      Output (screen): List of names of cities in CitySet.

   **********************************************************************)

   VAR
      CityNum : integer;   (* number of a city in CitySet *)

   BEGIN (* PrintCitySet *)
      CityNum := 1;
      WHILE CitySet <> [] DO
         BEGIN
            WHILE NOT (CityNum IN CitySet) DO
               CityNum := CityNum + 1;
            writeln (City[CityNum]);
            CitySet := CitySet - [CityNum]
         END (* WHILE *)
   END (* PrintCitySet *);

BEGIN (* main program *)
   ConstructCityList (City, NumCities);
   writeln ('Here is a list of European cities visited on our tours:');
   PrintCities (City, NumCities);
   writeln;
   RequestedCities := [];
   REPEAT
      writeln ('Enter the numbers of the cities you wish to visit ',
               '(0 to stop)');
      ReadCitySet (input, CitySet);
      RequestedCities := RequestedCities + CitySet;
      writeln ('Here are the cities you selected:');
      PrintCitySet (RequestedCities, City);
      write ('Do you wish to add more cities (Y or N)? ');
      readln (Response)
   UNTIL NOT (Response IN ['y', 'Y']);
```

Figure 2.2 (cont.)

```
    (* Now find all tours that visit these cities *)
    reset (TourFile);
    WHILE NOT eof(TourFile) DO
        BEGIN
            read (TourFile, TourNumber);
            ReadCitySet (TourFile, TourCities);
            IF RequestedCities <= TourCities THEN
                BEGIN
                    writeln ('Cities on Tour ', TourNumber:1, ' are:');
                    PrintCitySet (TourCities, City)
                END (* IF *);
            writeln
        END (* WHILE *)
END (* main program *).
```

Listing of TourFile used in sample run:

```
1 5 8 3 7 4 2 6 0
2 1 2 3 4 5 6 7 8 9 10 0
3 3 4 5 0
4 1 8 6 4 3 2 0
5 5 6 7 8 9 10 0
```

Sample run:

```
Here is a list of European cities visited on our tours:
Number    City
======    ====
     1    Amsterdam
     2    Berlin
     3    Brussels
     4    Cologne
     5    Innsbruck
     6    Rome
     7    Paris
     8    Salzburg
     9    Venice
    10    Zurich
```

Figure 2.2 (cont.)

```
Enter the numbers of the cities you wish to visit (0 to stop)
2 3 0
Here are the cities you selected:
Berlin
Brussels
Do you wish to add more cities (Y or N)? Y
Enter the numbers of the cities you wish to visit (0 to stop)
4 5 0
Here are the cities you selected:
Berlin
Brussels
Cologne
Innsbruck
Do you wish to add more cities (Y or N)? N
Cities on Tour 1 are:
Berlin
Brussels
Cologne
Innsbruck
Rome
Paris
Salzburg

Cities on Tour 2 are:
Amsterdam
Berlin
Brussels
Cologne
Innsbruck
Rome
Paris
Salzburg
Venice
Zurich
```

2.8 Application of Sets: Finite State Automata and Lexical Analyzers.

Compilers are programs whose function is to translate a source program written in some high-level language such as Pascal into an object program in machine code. This object program is then executed by the computer.

The basic parts of a compiler are summarized in the following diagram:

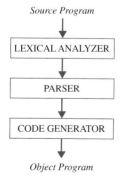

The input to a compiler is a stream of characters that comprise the source program. Before the translation can actually be carried out, this stream of characters must be broken up into meaningful groups, such as identifiers, reserved words, constants, and operators. These units are called **tokens**, and the part of the compiler that recognizes these tokens is called the **lexical analyzer**. For example, for a program segment such as

```
BEGIN
    I :=    IFI + 256;
    IF I<NUM THEN
        I := I+NUM
END
```

or as a "stream" of characters

```
BEGIN·ƀƀƀIƀ:=ƀƀƀƀIFIƀ+ƀ256;·ƀƀƀIFƀI<NUMƀTHEN·
ƀƀƀƀƀƀIƀ:=ƀI+NUM·END·
```

(where ƀ is a blank and · is an end-of-line mark), the lexical analyzer must identify the following tokens:

`BEGIN`	reserved word
`I`	identifier
`:=`	assignment operator
`IFI`	identifier
`+`	addition operator
`256`	integer constant
`;`	semicolon
`IF`	reserved word
`I`	identifier
`<`	relational operator
`NUM`	identifier
`THEN`	reserved word
`I`	identifier
`:=`	assignment operator
`I`	identifier
`+`	arithmetic operator
`NUM`	identifier
`END`	reserved word

It is then the task of the **parser** to group these tokens together to form the basic **syntactic structures** of the language as determined by the syntax rules. For example, it must recognize that the three consecutive tokens

identifier	*relational-operator*	*integer-constant*
↓	↓	↓
I	<	500

can be grouped together to form a valid boolean expression, that the three consecutive tokens

form a valid arithmetic expression, that

constitutes an assignment statement and then that

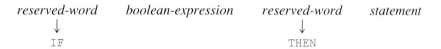

forms a valid **if** statement. The complete *parse tree* constructed during the compilation of this **if** statement is

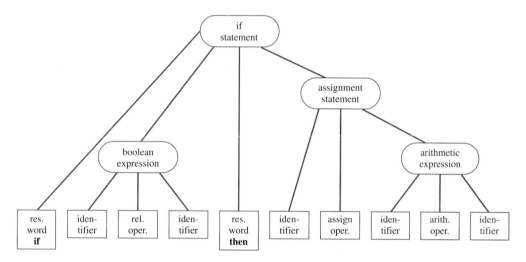

Later phases of the compiling process then generate the machine code for this **if** statement.

When designing a lexical analyzer to recognize various tokens, one can begin by designing a **finite state automaton,** also called a **finite state machine,** to recognize each token. A finite state automaton consists of a finite number of states together with a function that defines transitions from one state to another, depending on the current machine state and the current input character. One state is designated as the *initial state* since it is the state in which the automaton begins processing an input string of characters. If the machine is in one of the special states called *accepting states* after an input string is processed, then that string is said to be *recognized* or *accepted* by the automaton. For example, a finite state automaton to recognize bit strings that contain 01 is

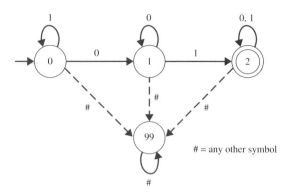

Here, the arrow pointing to state 0 indicates that this is the initial state. The automaton begins processing input symbols in state 0 and makes transitions from one state to another state or remains in the current state, as specified by the labels on the arrows.

To illustrate, consider the input string 0011. The finite state automaton begins in state 0, and because the first input symbol is 0, it transfers to state 1. Since the next input symbol is a 0, it remains in state 1. However, the third symbol is a 1, which causes a transition to state 2. The final symbol is a 1 and does not cause a state change. The end of the input string has now been reached, and because the automaton is in an accept state, as indicated by the double circle, we say that it accepts the string 0011. It is easy to see that any bit string containing 01 will be processed in a similar manner and lead to the accept state and that only such strings will cause the automaton to terminate in state 2. For example, the string 11000 is not accepted, since the automaton will be in state 1 after processing this string and state 1 is not an accept state. The bit string 100201 also is not accepted, since the "illegal" symbol 2 causes a transition from state 1 to state 99, which is not an accept state.

State 99 is a "reject" or "dead" state; once it is entered, it is never exited. The transitions to this state are shown as dashed lines, since the existence of such a state is usually assumed and transitions are not drawn in the diagram. For any state and any input symbol for which no transition is specified, it is assumed that the transition is to such a reject state. Thus, the finite state automaton is usually drawn as

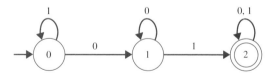

Similarly, the following finite state automaton recognizes bit strings ending in 00 or 11:

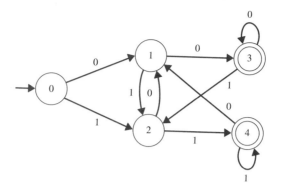

and a finite state automaton to recognize Pascal identifiers is

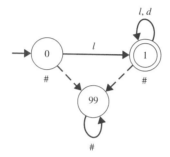

where *l* denotes a letter and *d* denotes a digit.

To illustrate how a finite state automaton can be used to aid the design of lexical analyzers, we consider the problem of recognizing Pascal integer constants. A finite state automaton that does this is

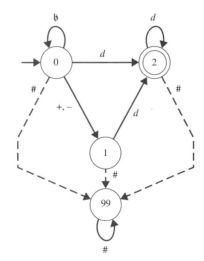

where *d* denotes one of the digits 0, 1, . . . , 9, b̸ denotes a blank, and state 2 is the only accepting state. The machine begins in state 0, and if the first input symbol is a blank, it stays in state 0, "gobbling up" leading blanks; if it is + or −, it goes to state 1; if it is a digit, it goes to state 2; otherwise, the input character is not valid, and thus the string does not represent a valid integer.

Writing program statements that simulate such a finite state automaton is straightforward. The program in Figure 2.3 illustrates this. It reads a string of characters and determines whether it represents a valid Pascal integer. The part of the program highlighted in color implements the preceding finite state automaton.

```
PROGRAM LexicalAnalyzer (input, output);

(*****************************************************************

    Input (keyboard):  A sequence of characters.
    Function:          Determines if the sequence of characters
                       represents a valid Pascal integer.
    Output (screen):   Message indicating whether input represents a
                       valid integer.
    Note:              This program simulates a finite state automaton
                       for recognizing integer constants.

******************************************************************)

CONST
    MaxState = 99;            (* largest state number *)
    DeadState = MaxState;     (* dead (reject) state *)

TYPE
    CharacterSet = SET OF char;
    StateSet = SET OF 0..MaxState;

VAR
    Digits : CharacterSet;       (* set of delimiters *)
    AcceptStates : StateSet;     (* set of accept states *)
    State : 0..MaxState;         (* current state *)
    EndOfToken : boolean;        (* signals end of token being checked *)
    Symbol,                      (* current input symbol *)
    Response : char;             (* user response *)
```

Figure 2.3

Figure 2.3 (cont.)

```
BEGIN
    Digits := ['0'..'9'];
    AcceptStates := [2];
    REPEAT
        (* begin in initial state *)
        State := 0;
        write ('Enter the string to be checked: ');
        WHILE NOT eoln  DO
            BEGIN
                read (Symbol);
                CASE State OF
                        0 : IF Symbol = ' ' THEN
                                State := 0
                            ELSE IF Symbol IN ['+', '-'] THEN
                                State := 1
                            ELSE IF Symbol IN Digits THEN
                                State := 2
                            ELSE
                                State:= DeadState;
                      1,2 : IF Symbol IN Digits THEN
                                State := 2
                            ELSE
                                State:= DeadState;
                DeadState : (* stay in dead state *)
                END (* CASE *)
            END (* WHILE *);
        IF State IN AcceptStates THEN
            writeln ('Valid integer')
        ELSE
            writeln ('Not a valid integer');
        readln;
        writeln;
        write ('More data (Y or N)? ');
        readln (Response)
    UNTIL NOT (Response IN ['y', 'Y'])
END.
```

Sample run:

```
Enter the string to be checked: 1234
Valid integer

More data (Y or N)? Y
Enter the string to be checked: -1
Valid integer

More data (Y or N)? Y
Enter the string to be checked: +9999
Valid integer

More data (Y or N)? Y
Enter the string to be checked: 123+4
Not a valid integer

More data (Y or N)? Y
Enter the string to be checked: abccdef
Not a valid integer

More data (Y or N)? N
```

Exercises

1. Suppose that *A*, *B*, *C*, and *D* are Pascal set variables whose values are assigned by

   $A := [2, 4..8, 11];$
   $B := [1..7, 11, 12];$
   $C := [1, 3, 5, 7, 9];$
   $D := [5..9];$

   and calculate the following:

   (a) $A * B + C$ **(b)** $A * (B + C)$
   (c) $A * (B - C)$ **(d)** $B - C$
   (e) $C - B$ **(f)** $(A - B) - C$
   (g) $A - (B - C)$ **(h)** $D - [\ ]$
   (i) $[\ ] - D$ **(j)** $A + B + C + D$
   (k) $A * B * C * D$ **(l)** $A * B - C * D$
   (m) $(A - (B + C)) * D$ **(n)** $A + B - A * B$
   (o) $A * B - (A + B)$ **(p)** $B - (B - C)$
   (q) $A - B - C - D$ **(r)** $((A * A) + A) - A$

2. Write appropriate declarations for the following set variables and statements to assign to each the specified value:

   (a) *Evens:* The set of all even integers from 1 through *N* and *Odd:* the set of all odd integers in the range from 1 through *N*, for some integer *N*.
   (b) *OneModThree:* the set of all numbers of the form $3k + 1$ in the range from 1 through *N* for some integer *N*, where *k* is an integer.
   (c) *EvenPrimes:* the set of all even primes. (A **prime number** is an integer *n* greater than 1 whose only divisors are 1 and *n* itself.)
   (d) *LargeEvenPrimes:* the set of all even primes greater than 3.
   (e) *LargeFactors:* the set of all numbers in the range 1 through 99 that are not divisible by 2, 3, 5, or 7.
   (f) *Divisors:* the set of all divisors of a given integer *Number*.
   (g) *JMonths:* the set of months whose names begin with the letter ''J'' (assuming the base type *MonthSet* given in the text).
   (h) *UMonths:* the set of months whose names begin with the letter ''U'' (assuming the base type *MonthSet* given in the text).
   (i) *Vowels:* the set of all vowels; and *Consonants:* the set of all consonants.
   (j) *WeekDays:* the set of all weekdays.
   (k) *FaceCards:* the set of all face cards in a suit; and *NumberCards:* the set of all number cards in a suit.

3. The **complement** *A'* of a subset *A* of the universal set *U* is defined by

   $$A' = \{x \in U \mid x \notin A\}$$

   (a) Write a procedure that returns the complement of a set *A*, assuming that the *First* and *Last* elements in this base type are passed as parameters to this procedure.

(b) Suppose that $+$ and $*$ are predefined set operations but that $-$ is not. Rewriting the procedure in (a) if necessary (so it does not use $-$), explain how it could be used to calculate $A - B$.

4. Write a function to calculate the ***cardinal number*** of a set, that is, the number of elements in the set.

5. Write a program to find the set of all vowels and the set of all consonants that appear in a given line of text.

6. Write a program to find all letters that are not present in a given line of text and display them in alphabetical order.

7. Write a program to read two lines of text and find all characters that appear in both lines.

8. The following algorithm describes a method for finding prime numbers developed by the Greek mathematician Eratosthenes (c. 276– c. 194 B.C.) and known as the ***Sieve method of Eratosthenes***:

ALGORITHM FOR THE SIEVE METHOD
OF ERATOSTHENES

(* Input: An integer n.
  Function: To construct a set *Sieve* of all primes in the
             range 2 through n.
  Returns: The set *Sieve*. *)

1. Initialize the set *Sieve* to contain the integers 2 through n.
2. Select the smallest element *Prime* in *Sieve*.
3. While $Prime^2 \leq n$, do the following:
    a. Remove from *Sieve* all elements of the form $Prime * k$ for $k > 1$.
    b. Replace *Prime* with the smallest element in *Sieve* that is greater than *Prime*.

The following diagram illustrates this algorithm for $n = 30$.

Sieve

[2,3,4,5,6,7,8,9,10,11,12,13,14,15,16,17,18,19,20,21,22,23,24,25,26,27,28,29,30]

↓

$Prime = 2$

↓

[2,3,5,7,9,11,13,15,17,19,21,23,25,27,29]

↓

$Prime = 3$

↓

[2,3,5,7,11,13,17,19,23,25,29]

↓

$Prime = 5$

↓

[2,3,5,7,11,13,17,19,23,29]

↓

$Prime = 7$; terminate since $Prime^2 > 30$

Write a program using sets and this sieve method to find prime numbers.

9. In many versions of Pascal, the size of a set is limited to small subranges of ordinal types, and the program developed in Exercise 8 can be used only to find small sets of prime numbers. An alternative data structure is an array *Sieve* of sets, *Sieve*[0], *Sieve*[1], *Sieve*[2], . . . , whose elements are integers in the range 0 through 99 (or some other small subrange of integers). Each element of *Sieve*[1] must be interpreted as 100 plus its value, each element of *Sieve*[2] as 200 plus its value, and so on. Write a program that uses an array of sets in this manner and the Sieve Method of Eratosthenes to find all primes in the range 2 through *n* for large values of *n*.

10. Suppose that the components of an inventory file are records whose fields are the following:

> Stock number: a string consisting of three letters followed by three digits.
> Item name: a 25-character string.
> Number currently in stock: an integer.
> Unit price: a real value.

Write a program in which the user enters a set of letters and that then displays the records in this file of all parts whose stock numbers begin with one of these letters.

11. Design a finite state automaton to recognize bit strings:

   (a) containing 00 or 11.
   (b) containing an even number of 1's.
   (c) containing an even number of 0's and an even number of 1's.
   (d) in which *n* **mod** 3 $= 1$ where *n* is the number of 1's.

12. A real number in Pascal has one of the forms *m.n*, $+m.n$, or $-m.n$, where *m* and *n* are sequences of digits; or it may be expressed in exponential form *x*E*e*, *x*E$+e$, *x*E$-e$, where *x* is an integer or a real number not in exponential form and *e* is a nonnegative integer. Write a program that accepts a string of characters and then checks to see if it represents a valid real constant.

13. Write a program for a lexical analyzer to process assignment statements of the form *identifier* $:=$ *string-constant*. Have it recognize the following tokens: identifier, assignment operator $(:=)$, and string constant.

14. Write a program for a lexical analyzer to process assignment statements of the form *identifier* $:=$ *set-value*. Have it recognize the following tokens: identifier, set constant, set operation $(+, *, -)$, and assignment operator $(:=)$.

2.9 Implementation of Sets

In Section 2.2 we observed that each of the four Pascal predefined simple data types—*integer*, *real*, *char*, and *boolean*—can be represented by bit strings and that different data types can be viewed simply as different interpretations of these bit strings. Other interpretations of bit strings are also possible, and in this section we show how a bit string can be used to represent a set.

Sets whose elements are selected from a *finite* universal set can be represented in computer memory by bit strings in which the number of bits is equal to the number of elements in this universal set. Each bit corresponds to exactly one element of the universal set. A given set is then represented by a bit string in which the bits corresponding to the elements of that set are 1 and all other bits are 0.

To illustrate, suppose the universal set is the set of uppercase letters. Then any set of uppercase letters can be represented by a string of twenty-six bits, with the first bit corresponding to the letter A, the second bit corresponding to the letter B, and so on. Thus, the set of vowels can be represented by the bit string

```
1 0 0 0 1 0 0 0 1 0 0 0 0 0 1 0 0 0 0 0 1 0 0 0 0 0
| | | | | | | | | | | | | | | | | | | | | | | | | |
A B C D E F G H I J K L M N O P Q R S T U V W X Y Z
```

and the empty set by

```
0 0 0 0 0 0 0 0 0 0 0 0 0 0 0 0 0 0 0 0 0 0 0 0 0 0
```

The bit operations corresponding to the boolean operations **and**, **or**, and **not** described in Section 2.2 can be used to implement the basic set operations of intersection, union, and difference. Applying the **and** operation bitwise to the bit strings representing two sets yields a bit string representing the intersection of these sets. For example, consider the sets $S = \{A, B, C, D\}$ and $T = \{A, C, E, G, I\}$, where the universal set is the set of uppercase letters. The 26-bit string representations of these sets are as follows:

```
S: 1 1 1 1 0 0 0 0 0 0 0 0 0 0 0 0 0 0 0 0 0 0 0 0 0 0
T: 1 0 1 0 1 0 1 0 1 0 0 0 0 0 0 0 0 0 0 0 0 0 0 0 0 0
   | | | | | | | | | | | | | | | | | | | | | | | | | |
   A B C D E F G H I J K L M N O P Q R S T U V W X Y Z
```

Performing the **and** operation bitwise gives the bit string

```
1 0 1 0 0 0 0 0 0 0 0 0 0 0 0 0 0 0 0 0 0 0 0 0 0 0
| | | | | | | | | | | | | | | | | | | | | | | | | |
A B C D E F G H I J K L M N O P Q R S T U V W X Y Z
```

which represents the set $\{A, C\}$, the intersection of S and T.

Bitwise application of the **or** operation to the bit strings representing two sets S and T yields the representation of $S \cup T$. For the preceding sets, this gives the bit string

which represents {A, B, C, D, E, G, I}, the union of S and T.

Complementing each bit in the representation of a set T gives a bit string representing T', the **complement** of T, that is, the set of elements of the universal set that are not in T. Applying the **and** operation to the bit string for a set S and the string for T' yields a bit string for $S \cap T'$, which is clearly equal to $S - T$. For the preceding sets, bitwise complementation of the string for T gives

0 1 0 1 0 1 0 1 0 1 0 1 1 1 1 1 1 1 1 1 1 1 1 1 1 1

and performing bitwise **and** with S gives

which represents $S - T = \{B, D\}$.

Exercises

1. Assuming a universal set with base type 0..19, give the bit string representations of the following sets:

   (a) The set of odd integers.
   (b) The set of prime integers.
   (c) The intersection of the set of prime integers and the set of even integers.
   (d) The union of the set of prime integers and the set of odd integers.
   (e) The set of odd integers that are not prime integers.
   (f) The set of integers divisible by 1.
   (g) The set of integers not divisible by 1.

2. An alternative method for implementing a set S is to imitate the bit string implementation by using a boolean array S where $S[i]$ is true if the element i is in S and is false otherwise. Using this implementation, write procedures for the basic set operations of union, intersection, and set difference and boolean-valued functions for the set relations of subset and equality.

3. The implementation of sets as boolean arrays described in Exercise 2 can be extended to universal sets whose elements are not ordinal types, provided that the elements are fixed in some specific order, and $S[i]$ is then true or false according to whether or not the ith element of this ordered universal set is in S. Consider the universal set $U = \{0.0, 0.1, 0.2, \ldots, 9.9, 10.0\}$ consisting of all real numbers in the range 0

through 10 that can be expressed in decimal form with one digit to the right of the decimal point, and assume that these real numbers are fixed in increasing order. Describe how each of the following sets would be represented:

(a) $\{x \in U \mid 3 \le x \le 4\}$ **(b)** $\{x \in U \mid 3x - 1.1 = 4.7\}$

(c) $\{x \in U \mid x < 8.8\}$ **(d)** $\{x \in U \mid x^2 - 5x + 6 = 0\}$

4. Proceed as in Exercise 3 but for a universal set consisting of a set of names (strings) Alan, Alice, Barb, Ben, Bob, Carl, Cora, Dick, Don, Dora, Dot, Fred, arranged in alphabetical order. Show how the following sets would be represented:

   (a) Set of names that begin with B.
   (b) Set of names that begin with E.
   (c) Set of names that begin with D and have fewer than three letters.
   (d) Set of names that have fewer than six letters.

5. Write a program using the implementation of sets as boolean arrays described in Exercises 2 and 3 to find prime numbers using the Sieve Method of Eratosthenes (see Exercise 8 of Section 2.8).

6. Write a program like that described in Exercise 10 of Section 2.8 but have the user enter a set of three-letter strings and display the records of all parts whose stock numbers begin with one of these three-letter combinations. Use the implementation of sets as boolean arrays described in Exercises 2 and 3.

3

Strings

Some data structures such as arrays and records are implemented directly with the corresponding predefined data types provided in the programming language being used. For such structures the programmer usually need not be concerned with the details of the storage structures and algorithms used in their implementations because these are handled by the compiler and other system software. In many applications, however, new data types must be designed and implemented by the programmer. In these cases, the implementation can usually be done most efficiently by using data types that have previously been defined and implemented. The remaining chapters of this text describe some of the more common of these "higher-level" data structures.

In this chapter we consider the string data type that is useful in processing sequences of characters such as words and sentences in text-editing and word-processing applications. The string data type is a predefined type in many programming languages such as BASIC, FORTRAN 77, SNOBOL, and some versions of Pascal. This is not the case for standard Pascal, however, and thus we also consider how strings can be implemented using the structures that standard Pascal provides.

3.1 Strings as Abstract Data Types

A *string* is a finite sequence of characters drawn from some given character set. The basic operations on strings depend on the particular application, but in most text-editing and word-processing applications, they include the following:

Length:	The number of characters in a string.
Concat(enate):	Strings are concatenated by joining them together.
Copy:	Copy a substring from a given string.
Position:	Locate one string within another.
Insert:	Insert one string into another.
Delete:	Delete part of a string.

To illustrate these basic operations, suppose that *str1* is the string 'ABCBCD' and *str2* is 'FG3'. Then the length of *str1* is 6 and the length of *str2* is 3. The concatenation of *str1* with *str2* is

'ABCBCDFG3'

and the concatenation of *str2* with *str1* is

'FG3ABCBCD'

Copying the substring of *str1* of length 3 beginning at position 2 gives

'BCB'

and the position or index of 'BC' in *str1* is 2. The position of *str2* in *str1* is defined to be 0 to indicate that *str2* does not appear in *str1*.

The preparation of textual material such as letters, books, and computer programs often involves the insertion, deletion, and replacement of parts of the text. The software of most computer systems includes an **editor** that makes it easy to carry out these operations. These and other text-editing operations are often implemented using the basic string operations, as illustrated in the program in Figure 3.1. This program assumes the availability of a string type *String* and string-processing functions and procedures that implement the basic string operations. (See Section 3.2 for descriptions of these functions and procedures.) It also assumes the availability of a procedure *ReadString* for reading a value for a string variable, and it uses the standard Pascal output procedures *write* and *writeln* to display strings. The definitions and declarations needed to use the type *String* and these functions and procedures have been collected in three files that must be inserted at appropriate points in the program. In this example we assume that a special compiler directive #include can be used for this. Most Pascal compilers provide such a directive for inserting files into a program, although it may have a different format such as %include *file-name*, %insert *file-name*, (**$i *file-name* *), or {$i *file-name*}.

```
PROGRAM TextEditor (input, output, TextFile, EditedFile);

(*********************************************************************

    Input (file):       A text file TextFile
    Input (keyboard):   Edit commands entered by the user.
    Function:           Performs several basic text-editing operations on
                        lines of text read from TextFile; after editing
                        has been completed, each line is written to a
                        new file EditedFile.  Text-editing commands
                        include the following:
                        Insert   : insert a substring in a line
                        Delete   : delete a substring from a line
                        Replace  : replace one substring in a line with
                                   another
                        Length   : determine the length of a line
                        Position : find the position of a substring in
                                   a line
                        NewLine  : get next line of text
                        Quit     : quit editing
    Output (screen):    A menu of editing commands, unedited and edited
                        lines of text.
    Output (file):      Text file EditedFile

    Note:               Certain constant and type definitions together
                        with functions and procedures for the basic
                        string operations must be inserted into the
                        declaration part.  The compiler directive
                        #include inserts these items from the three
                        files STRING-CONST, STRING-TYPE, and STRING-OPS.

*********************************************************************)

CONST
#include 'STRING-CONST'      (* StringLimit *)

TYPE
#include 'STRING-TYPE'       (* StringType *)

VAR
    TextFile,                        (* file of original text *)
    EditedFile : text;               (* file of edited text *)
    Line : String;                   (* line of text to be edited *)
    Command : char;                  (* editing command *)
    Str1, Str2, Str3 : String;       (* strings used in editing *)
    Position,                        (* position of a string in Line *)
    Len : integer;                   (* length of some string *)

#include 'STRING-OPS'        (* Length, Pos, Concat, Copy *)
                             (* Delete, Insert, ReadString *)
```

Figure 3.1

Figure 3.1 (cont.)

```
PROCEDURE PrintCommands;

  (*******************************************************************

     Input:               None.
     Function:            Displays a menu of editing commands.
     Output (screen):     Menu of editing commands.

  ******************************************************************)

  BEGIN (* PrintCommands *)
    writeln ('Editing commands are:');
    writeln ('     I(nsert)    : insert a substring');
    writeln ('     D(elete)    : delete a substring');
    writeln ('     R(eplace)   : replace one substring with another');
    writeln ('     L(ength)    : determine the length of current line');
    writeln ('     P(osition)  : find position of a substring');
    writeln ('     N(ewLine)   : get next line of text');
    writeln ('     Q(uit)      : quit editing')
  END (* PrintCommands *);

PROCEDURE Replace (Sub1, Sub2 : String; VAR Str : String);

  (*******************************************************************

     Input (param):   Strings Sub1 and Sub2
     Function:        Replaces substring Sub1 with string Sub2 in
                      string Str.
     Output (param):  String Str.
     Note:            Uses functions Length and Pos and procedures
                      Copy and Concatenate.

  ******************************************************************)

  VAR
    Position,         (* position where replacement to be made *)
    Len : integer;    (* length of replacement string *)

  BEGIN (* Replace *)
    Len := Length(Sub1);
    Position := Pos(Sub1, Len, Str, Length(Str));
    IF Position > 0 THEN
      BEGIN
        Delete (Str, Position, Len);
        Insert (Sub2, Length(Sub2), Str, Position)
      END (* IF *)
  END (* Replace *);
```

Figure 3.1 (cont.)

```
BEGIN(* main program *)
   reset (TextFile);
   rewrite (EditedFile);
   PrintCommands;
   writeln ('Enter a 1-character editing command following the prompt >');
   writeln;
   ReadString (TextFile, Line);
   writeln (Line);
   REPEAT
      write ('>');
      readln (Command);
      IF Command IN ['D','I','L','N','P','Q','R',
                     'd','i','l','n','p','q','r'] THEN
         CASE Command OF
            'L','l' : writeln ('Length = ', Length(Line):1);
            'P','p' : BEGIN
                         write ('Position of?  ');
                         ReadString (input, Str1);
                         writeln ('     is ', pos(Str1, Length(Str1),
                                       Line, Length(Line)))
                      END (* Position *);
            'I','i' : BEGIN
                         write ('Insert what?  ');
                         ReadString (input, Str1);
                         write (' At position?  ');
                         readln (Position);
                         Insert (Str1, Length(Str1), Line, Position);
                         writeln (Line)
                      END (* Insert *);
            'D','d' : BEGIN
                         write ('Delete where?  ');
                         readln (Position);
                         write ('How many characters?  ');
                         readln (Len);
                         Delete (Line, Position, Len);
                         writeln (Line)
                      END (* Delete *);
            'R','r' : BEGIN
                         write ('Replace what?  ');
                         ReadString (input, Str1);
                         write ('   With what?  ');
                         ReadString (input, Str2);
                         Replace (Str1, Str2, Line);
                         writeln (Line)
                      END (* Replace *);
            'N','n' : BEGIN
                         writeln (EditedFile, Line);
                         IF NOT eof(TextFile) THEN
                            BEGIN
                               writeln ('Next Line:');
                               ReadString (TextFile, Line);
                               writeln (Line)
                            END (* IF *)
                         ELSE
                            Command := 'Q'
                      END (* NewLine *);
```

Figure 3.1 (cont.)

```
             'Q','q' : BEGIN
                           writeln (EditedFile, Line);
                           WHILE NOT eof(TextFile) DO
                               BEGIN
                                   ReadString (TextFile, Line);
                                   writeln (EditedFile, Line)
                               END (* WHILE *);
                       END (* Quit *)
           END (* CASE *)
       ELSE
           BEGIN
               writeln;
               writeln ('*** Illegal command ***');
               PrintCommands;
               writeln (Line)
           END (* ELSE *)
   UNTIL (Command IN ['Q','q']);
   writeln (EditedFile, Line);
   WHILE NOT eof(TextFile) DO
       BEGIN
           ReadString (TextFile, Line);
           writeln (EditedFile, Line)
       END (* WHILE *);
   writeln;
   writeln ('*** Editing complete ***')
END (* main program *).
```

Listing of TextFile used in sample run:

```
Foursscore and five years ago, our mothers
brought forth on continent
a new nation conceived in liberty and and dedicated
to the preposition that all men
are created equal.
```

Sample run:

```
Editing commands are:
     I(nsert)    : insert a substring
     D(elete)    : delete a substring
     R(eplace)   : replace one substring with another
     L(ength)    : determine the length of current line
     P(osition)  : find position of a substring
     N(ewLine)   : get next line of text
     Q(uit)      : quit editing
Enter a 1-character editing command following the prompt >
```

Figure 3.1 (cont.)

```
Foursscore and five years ago, our mothers
>D
Delete where?  5
How many characters?  1
Fourscore and five years ago, our mothers
>R
Replace what?  five
   With what?  seven
Fourscore and seven years ago, our mothers
>R
Replace what?  mo
   With what?  fa
Fourscore and seven years ago, our fathers
>N
Next Line:
brought forth on continent
>P
Position of?  con
      is           18
>I
Insert what?  this
 At position?  17
brought forth on this continent
>N
Next Line:
a new nation conceived in liberty and and dedicated
>P
Position of?  and
      is           35
>D
Delete where?  35
How many characters?  4
a new nation conceived in liberty and dedicated
>N
Next Line:
to the preposition that all men
>R
Replace what?  pre
   With what?  pro
to the proposition that all men
>N
Next Line:
are created equal.
>Q

*** Editing complete ***
```

Listing of EditedFile produced:

```
Fourscore and seven years ago, our fathers
brought forth on this continent
a new nation conceived in liberty and dedicated
to the proposition that all men
are created equal.
```

The following specification serves as a formal definition of strings as an abstract data type (ADT):

ADT String

Collection of Data Elements

Finite sequences of characters drawn from a given character set.

Basic Operations

Length

    ACCEPTS: String *str*.

    FUNCTION: Determine the length of a string *str*, which is the number of characters in it.

    RETURNS: Length of *str*.

Concat:

    ACCEPTS: Strings *str1* and *str2*.

    FUNCTION: Concatenate *str1* with *str2* by appending *str2* to *str1*.

    RETURNS: String obtained by concatenating *str1* with *str2*.

Copy:

    ACCEPTS: String *str*, and two integers *p* and *n*.

    FUNCTION: Copy a substring of length *n* from *str*, beginning at position *p*.

    RETURNS: Substring of *str*.

Position:

    ACCEPTS: Strings *str1* and *str2*.

    FUNCTION: Determine the index of *str1* in *str2*, which is the starting position of the first occurrence (if any) of *str1* in *str2*.

    RETURNS: Index of *str1* in *str2*.

Insert:

    ACCEPTS: Strings *str1* and *str2* and integer *p*.

    FUNCTION: Inserts *str1* into *str2* at position *p*.

    RETURNS: String obtained by inserting *str1* into *str2*.

Delete:

    ACCEPTS: String *str*, and two integers *p* and *n*.

    FUNCTION: Removes *n* characters from *str* beginning at position *p*.

    RETURNS: String obtained by removing characters from *str*.

Although many versions of Pascal provide a predefined string data type, this is not the case with standard Pascal. In the next section we describe how strings can be implemented in standard Pascal, and in Section 3.3 we describe the predefined string data type of Turbo Pascal and some other versions of Pascal.

3.2   A String Package for Standard Pascal

Recall that implementing a data structure requires (1) choosing appropriate
storage structures to store the data items and (2) designing algorithms to carry
out the basic operations and relations. Thus we begin our implementation of
the string data type by describing an appropriate storage structure.

STORAGE STRUCTURE

Because strings are finite sequences of characters, it seems natural to use
arrays of characters to store strings. And because several characters can be
packed into a single memory word in most computer systems, memory will be
used more efficiently if packed arrays are used. Thus strings are most often
implemented in standard Pascal using declarations of the form

> **const**
>   *StringLimit* = . . . ; (* maximum length allowed for strings *)
>
> **type**
>   *String* = **packed array**[1 . . *StringLimit*] **of** *char*;
>
> **var**
>   *Name* : *String*;

Although using packed arrays of characters as storage structures for strings
is the most common implementation of strings in standard Pascal, there are
several problems associated with this implementation. One is that the size of
an array is fixed, and consequently, the length of a string that can be stored is
limited by this fixed size. Also, some memory is wasted because not all of the
array positions are needed to store the characters in short strings; unused array
locations are usually filled with blanks.

The usual operations that may be performed on arrays may also be applied
to packed arrays.[1] For example, one packed array may be assigned to another
packed array of the same type (see footnote 2 in Section 2.4). In the case of
strings implemented as packed arrays of characters, string constants are treated
as packed arrays with index type 1..*L*, where *L* is the number of characters in
the string constant. Thus the assignment statement

> *Name* := 'John Doe';

would be legal only if *StringLimit* were 8. This means, however, that an assignment statement such as

> *Name* := 'J. Doe';

in which the string value has fewer than eight characters, would not be allowed.
The string value must be padded with blanks to make its length equal to the

---

[1] One exception is that a component of a packed array may not be an actual parameter in a
procedure or function reference that corresponds to a variable formal parameter.

length specified for the variable to which it is being assigned:

Name := 'J. Doe̸b̸';

As abstract data types, strings are dynamic structures and do not have fixed lengths. In this array-based implementation of strings, therefore, the operation of string assignment is not implemented perfectly.

Certain array operations can be used with packed arrays of characters that cannot be used with unpacked arrays. In particular, the value of a string variable such as *Name* can be displayed by simply including it in the output list of a *write* or *writeln* statement such as

writeln ('Name is ', *Name*);

Many Pascal compilers also allow a value to be read for a string variable by using the variable name in a *readln* statement such as

readln (*Name*);

or

readln (*TextFile*, *Name*);

In this case, the characters are read and stored in the packed array until either the array is full or an end-of-line character is read, which then causes blank filling to occur. Because this feature is not part of standard Pascal, it is necessary in some versions to design a procedure like the following for reading strings:

procedure *ReadString* (**var** *TextFile* : *text*; **var** *Str* : *String*);

```
(* Accepts:   File parameter TextFile.
   Function:  Read characters into string variable Str from TextFile until
              an end of line is encountered or the upper limit StringLimit
              on the length of Str is reached. Any positions for which no
              characters are read will be filled with blanks.
   Returns:   String Str. *)

var
   i : integer; (* index *)

begin (* ReadString *)
   for i := 1 to StringLimit do
      if not eoln(TextFile) then
         read (TextFile, Str[i])
      else
         Str[i] := ' ';
   readln (TextFile)
end (* ReadString *);
```

Strings stored as packed arrays of characters may be compared with the relational operators $=$, $<$, $>$, $<=$, $>=$, and $<>$, provided that they have the same length. A character-by-character comparison is carried out using the numeric codes (for example, ASCII) of the characters in the string.

The second part of an implementation of an abstract data type is a collection of algorithms or subprograms to carry out the basic operations. Thus we turn now to developing functions and procedures for the six basic string operations.

ALGORITHMS FOR BASIC OPERATIONS

Length. Padding strings with blanks makes it difficult to implement the length operation for strings because trailing blanks that are part of the string cannot be distinguished from those that are used to fill unused array positions. This problem can be solved by simply ignoring trailing blanks in a string, by placing a special end-of-string mark in the array after the last character in the string, or by modifying the storage structure so that both the length of the string and the characters in the string are stored.

If trailing blanks are ignored, the length operation can be easily implemented by the following Pascal function:

function *Length(Str : String) : integer*;

(* Accepts: String *Str*.
   Function: Determine the length of a string *str*, which is the number
              of characters in it..
   Returns: Length of *Str.* *)

   var
     i : integer;   (* index *)
     EndOfString : boolean;   (* signals end of string *)

   begin (* *Length* *)
     i := *StringLimit*;
     EndOfString := *false*;
     while ($i > 0$) **and not** *EndOfString* **do**
       if *Str[i]* = ' ' **then**
         i := *i* − 1
       else
         EndOfString := *true*;
     Length := *i*
   end (* *Length* *);

Concatenation. If the sum of the lengths of the two strings to be concatenated does not exceed the maximum string length allowed, the characters in the first string followed by those in the second string are copied into a third string. The following procedure implements this concatenation operation:

   procedure *Concat (Str1 : String; Num1 : integer;*
                      Str2 : String; Num2 : integer;
                      var *Str3 : String*);

(* Accepts: Strings *Str1* and *Str2* and integers *Num1* and *Num2*.

Function: Concatenate *Str1* having *Num1* characters with *Str2* having *Num2* characters by appending *Str2* to *Str1*.

Returns: String *Str3* obtained by concatenating *Str1* with *Str2*. *)

var
   i : *integer*;   (* index *)

begin (* *Concat* *)
   if (*Num1* + *Num2*) <= *StringLimit* **then**
      begin
         (* copy *Str1* to *Str3*; blanks used to pad *Str1*
            are also used to pad *Str3* *)
         Str3 := *Str1*;
         (* copy the *Num2* characters of *Str2* into *Str3*
            beginning at position *Num1* + 1 *)
         for *i* := 1 **to** *Num2* **do**
            Str3[*i* + *Num1*] := *Str2*[*i*]
      end (* **if** *)
   else
      writeln ('Strings too long to be concatenated')
end (* *Concat* *);

Copy. A procedure to implement the copy operation is as follows:

procedure *Copy* (*Str* : *String*; *p*, *n* : *integer*; **var** *Substr* : *String*);

(* Accepts: String *Str* and integers *p* and *n*.

Function: Copy a substring of length *n* from *Str*, beginning at position *p*.

Returns: Substring *Substr*. *)

var
   i,   (* index *)
   Last : *integer*;   (* position of last character to copy *)

begin (* *Copy* *)
   Last := *p* + *n* − 1;
   if *Last* <= *StringLimit* **then**
      begin
         (* copy required characters from *Str* into *Substr*
            and pad *Substr* with blanks *)
         for *i* := 1 **to** *n* **do**
            Substr[*i*] := *Str*[*p* + *i* − 1];
         for *i* := *n* + 1 **to** *StringLimit* **do**
            Substr[*i*] := ' '
      end (* **if** *)
   else
      writeln ('Index out of range')
end (* *Copy* *);

Position. The position or index operation determines the starting location of the first occurrence of one string in a second string, or it gives the value 0 if the first string does not appear in the second string. As an illustration of a "brute force" implementation of this operation, suppose we wish to find the index of *Str1* = 'abcabd' in *Str2* = 'abcabcabdabba'. The search for *Str1* in *Str2* begins at the first position of each. The first five characters match, but a mismatch occurs when the sixth characters are compared:

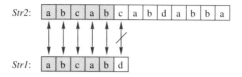

We then backtrack and start the search over again at the second character in *Str2*:

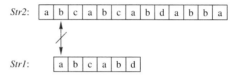

A mismatch occurs immediately, so we must backtrack again and restart the search with the third character in *Str2*:

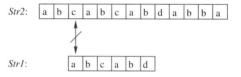

Once again a mismatch occurs, so we must backtrack again and restart at the fourth character in *Str2*:

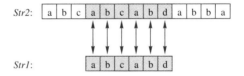

Now the six characters in *Str1* match the corresponding characters in positions 4 through 9 in *Str2*, and thus the index of *Str1* in *Str2* is 4.

The following function implements this brute force approach. (A more efficient algorithm is described in Section 3.6.)

> **function** *Pos(Str1* : *String*; *Num1* : *integer*;
> *Str2* : *String*; *Num2* : *integer*) : *integer*;
>
> (∗ Accepts: Strings *Str1* and *Str2* and integers *Num1* and *Num2*.
>   Function: Determine the index of *Str1* having *Num1* characters in
>   *Str2* having *Num2* characters.
>   Returns: Index of *Str1* in *Str2*. ∗)

```
    var
        i,                          (* index running through Str1 *)
        j,                          (* index running through Str2 *)
        Index : integer;            (* beginning position of Str1 in Str2 *)
    begin (* Pos *)
        Index := 1;
        i := 1;
        j := 1;
        while (i <= Num1) and (j <= Num2) do
            if Str1[i] = Str2[j] then (* continue matching *)
                begin
                    i := i + 1;
                    j := j + 1
                end (* if *)
            else (* backtrack and start over at next position in Str2 *)
                begin
                    Index := Index + 1;
                    j := Index;
                    i := 1
                end (* else *);
        if i > Num1 then        (* Str1 found in Str2 *)
            Pos := Index
        else                    (* Str1 not found in Str2 *)
            Pos := 0
    end (* Pos *);
```

Insert. The insert operation modifies a string by inserting another string into it at some specified position. For example, inserting *Str1* = 'XY' into the string *Str2* = 'abc' at position 3 changes *Str2* to 'abXYc'; and inserting it at position 1 changes *Str2* to 'XYabc'. Insertion at a position greater than the length of *Str2* is not permitted; the concatenation operation can be used to do this.

The following procedure implements this operation:

procedure *Insert* (*Str1* : *String*; *Num1* : *integer*;
                  var *Str2* : *String*; *Position* : *integer*);

(* Accepts: Strings *Str1* and *Str2* and integers *Num1* and *Position*.
    Function: Insert *Str1* having *Num1* characters in *Str2* at the specified
                 Position.
    Returns: Modified string *Str2*.
    Note: Uses function *Length* and procedures *Copy* and *Concat*. *)

```
    var
        First, Last : String;       (* first and last parts of Str2 *)
        FSize, LSize : integer      (* sizes of First, Last *)
```

```
begin (* Insert *)
  if (Position > 0) and (Position <= Length (Str2)) then
    begin
      FSize := Position - 1;
      LSize := Length(Str2) - FSize;
      Copy (Str2, 1, FSize, First);
      Copy (Str2, Position, LSize, Last);
      Concat (First, FSize, Str1, Num1, First);
      Concat (First, FSize + Num1, Last LSize, Str2)
    end (* if *)
  else
    writeln ('Position to insert negative or too large')
end (* Insert *);
```

Delete. The delete operation modifies a string by deleting from it a substring of some specified length at some specified position. For example, deleting the substring of length 3 at position 2 from Str = 'compute' changes Str into 'cute'. Deleting characters beyond the end of the string, that is, characters in positions greater than the length of the string, is not allowed.

The following procedure implements the delete operation:

```
procedure Delete (var Str : String; Position, Size : integer);

(* Accepts:   String Str and integers Position and Size.
   Function: Delete a substring of the specified Size from string Str
             beginning at a specified Position.
   Returns:  Modified string Str.
   Note:     Uses function Length and procedures Copy and Concat. *)

var
  First, Last : String;        (* first and last parts of Str *)
  FSize, LSize,                (* sizes of First, Last *)
  Len : integer;               (* length of Str *)

begin (* Delete *)
  Len := Length(Str);
  if (Position > 0) and (Size >= 0) and
     (Size <= Len - Position + 1) then
    begin
      FSize := Position - 1;
      Copy (Str, 1, FSize, First);
      Position := Position + Size;
      LSize := Len - Position + 1;
      Copy (Str, Position, LSize, Last);
      Concat (First, FSize, Last, LSize, Str)
    end (* if *)
  else
    writeln ('Starting position or size negative or substring too long')
end (* Delete *);
```

Other Implementations. As noted earlier, trailing blanks can be allowed in strings if some special end-of-string mark is placed in the array after the last character in the string. This is the technique used in the Modula-2 and C languages to implement strings; the ***null*** character with ASCII code 0 is placed at the end of each string. Procedures for the basic string operations in this type of implementation are left as exercises.

Another implementation that permits trailing blanks uses a record for the storage structure. This record contains two fields, one to store the length of a string and the other to store the characters that make up the string:

> **const**
>   *StringLimit* = . . . ; (* maximum length allowed for strings *)
>
> **type**
>   *String* = **record**
>   *Length* : 0..*StringLimit*;
>   *Character* : **packed array**[1..*StringLimit*] **of** *char*
>   **end**;

This is the implementation of strings used in several versions of Pascal such as THINK Pascal™ and Dr. Pascal®.

For this implementation of strings, the procedure *ReadString*, given earlier, for reading a value for a string variable, should be modified as follows:

> **procedure** *ReadString* (**var** *TextFile* : *text*; **var** *Str* : *String*);
>
> (* Accepts: File parameter *TextFile*.
>   Function: Read characters into string variable *Str* from *TextFile* until
>   an end of line is encountered or the upper limit *StringLimit*
>   on the length of *Str* is reached. Any positions for which no
>   characters are read will be filled with blanks.
>   Returns: String *Str*. *)
>
> **var**
>   *i* : *integer*; (* index *)
>
> **begin** (* *ReadString* *)
>   *i* := 0;
>   **while** (*i* < *StringLimit*) **and not** *eoln* (*TextFile*) **do**
>   **begin**
>   *i* := *i* + 1;
>   *read* (*TextFile*, *Str.Character*[*i*])
>   **end** (* **while** *);
>   *Str.Length* := *i*;
>   **for** *i* := *Str.Length* + 1 **to** *StringLimit* **do**
>   *Str.Character*[*i*] := ' ';
>   *readln* (*TextFile*)
> **end** (* *ReadString* *);

The length operation is then implemented trivially, since it consists of simply accessing the length field. Implementations of the concatenation, copy, and index operations are simple modifications of the preceding procedures *Concat* and *Copy* and the function *Pos*. For example, the procedure *Concat* can be modified as follows:

procedure *Concat* (*Str1*, *Str2* : *String*; **var** *Str3* : *String*)

(∗ Accepts: Strings *Str1* and *Str2*.
   Function: Concatenate *Str1* with *Str2* by appending *Str2* to *Str1*.
   Returns: String *Str3* obtained by concatenating *Str1* with *Str2*. ∗)

var
   Num1, *Num2*, *i* : *integer*; (∗ number of characters in *Str1*, *Str2* ∗)

begin (∗ *Concat* ∗)
   Num1 := *Str1.Length*;
   Num2 := *Str2.Length*;
   if (*Num1* + *Num2*) <= *StringLimit* **then**
     begin
      (∗ set length field of *Str2* ∗)
      Str3.Length := *Num1* + *Num2*;
      (∗ copy *Str1* to *Str3* into character field of *Str3* ∗)
      Str3.Character := *Str1.Character*;
      (∗ copy the *Num2* characters of *Str2* into this character field of
        Str3 beginning at position *Num1* + 1 ∗)
      for *i* := 1 **to** *Num2* **do**
        Str3.Character[*i* + *Num1*] := *Str2.Character*[*i*]
     end (∗ **if** ∗)
   else
     writeln ('Strings too long to be concatenated')
   end (∗ *Concat* ∗);

A similar implementation that stores both the length of the string and the characters of the string uses a zero-based packed array as the basic storage structure:

const
   StringLimit = . . . ; (∗ maximum length allowed for strings ∗)

type
   String = **packed array**[0..*StringLimit*] **of** *char*;

var
   Name : *String*;

and stores *chr*(*len*) in position 0, where *len* is the length of the string. This is the approach used to implement strings in Turbo Pascal, as described in the next section.

To illustrate, suppose that the string 'John Doe' is to be stored in *Name*. The eight characters comprising the string would be stored in locations 1, 2, . . . , 8 of *Name*, and *Name*[0] would be assigned the value *chr*(8), the character whose numeric code is 8. (In ASCII, this is the nonprinting control character for a backspace.) Note that storing *chr(len)* imposes an upper limit on the length of a string, since the *chr* function is defined only over a certain subrange of integers, usually 0..255. Procedures for the basic string operations in this implementation are also left as exercises.

In the program in Figure 3.1 and in the following chapters we assume that a package consisting of the constant and type definitions for implementing a string type together with the functions and procedures for the basic string operations is available and that these declarations and definitions can be inserted at appropriate points in any program that requires the string data type. As we indicated in the preceding section, in most Pascal compilers, this can easily be done by using a special directive like #include *file-name* (or %include *file-name* or %insert *file-name* or (*$i *file-name* *) or {$I *file-name*}) for copying files into a program as it is being compiled.[2] Thus in our examples, we place the directive

   #include 'STRING-CONST'

in the constant section of a program, where STRING-CONST is the name of a file that contains the definition

   StringLimit = 80;

This directive then causes this definition to be inserted into the constant section at compile time. We put the directive

   #include 'STRING-TYPE'

at the beginning of the type section to copy the type definition

   String = **packed array**[1..*StringLimit*] **of** *char*;

into the program at this point. The directive

   #include 'STRING-OPS'

is placed at the beginning of the subprogram section to copy in the functions *Length* and *Pos* and the procedures *Concat, Copy, Delete, Insert,* and *Read-String* from the file STRING-OPS. In those versions of Pascal that allow several declaration parts, a single file containing constant, type, and subprogram sections having all of these definitions and declarations can be inserted into the program.

---

[2] If your compiler does not provide such a directive, you need only copy these files, using an editor, into the source program at the designated points.

Exercises

1. As described in the text, one implementation of strings uses a packed array as a storage structure and uses a special end-of-string mark after the last character in the string.

    (a) Write procedures/functions for the basic string operations in this implementation.

    (b) Modify *ReadString* for this implementation.

    (c) Write a procedure *PrintString* to display a string in this implementation.

2. Write procedures for the position, copy, insert and delete operations for the record implementation of strings described in the text.

3. Using the packed array implementation of strings in which trailing blanks are ignored, write a program that reads a string of digits, possibly preceded by + or −, and converts this string to the integer value it represents. Be sure that your program checks that the string is well formed, that is, that it represents a valid integer.

4. Proceed as in Exercise 3, but for strings representing real numbers in either decimal or scientific form.

5. A string is said to be a ***palindrome*** if it does not change when the order of characters in the string is reversed. For example,

    MADAM
    45811854
    ABLE WAS I ERE I SAW ELBA

are palindromes. Using the record implementation of a string, write a program to read a string and determine whether it is a palindrome.

6. Using any of the implementations of strings described in this section, write a program that accepts two strings and determines whether one string is an ***anagram*** of the other, that is, whether one string is a permutation of the characters in the other string. For example, *dear* and *dare* are anagrams of *read*.

7. Each of the implementations of strings described in the text wastes space in those applications using strings whose lengths vary considerably. An alternative implementation is to establish some "work space" array *Storage* of characters to store the characters of strings to be processed and to represent each string as a record whose fields are indices *Start* and *Length* that specify where in *Storage* the string is stored. For example, if S is a string variable with $S.Start = 11$ and $S.Length = 8$, the string of characters for S, 'JOHN DOE', can be found in positions 11 through $11 + 8 − 1 = 18$ of *Storage*:

Storage: | F | R | E | D | | S | M | I | T | H | J | O | H | N | | D | O | E | | | | • • • | |

Using this implementation of strings, write procedures/functions to

(a) Display the string of characters corresponding to a string variable *S*.

(b) Implement the length operation.

(c) Implement the position operation.

(d) Implement the copy operation.

8. For the string implementation described in Exercise 7, the work space must be managed in some appropriate way. Devise a scheme for doing this and then write procedures to

   (a) Read a string of characters, store them in *Storage*, and return the appropriate record for a string variable.

   (b) Implement the concatenate operation.

9. Write a program that reads a Pascal program and strips all comments from it.

10. Write a program that analyzes text contained in a file by finding the number of nonblank characters, number of nonblank lines, number of words, and number of sentences and that calculates the average number of characters per word and the average number of words per sentence.

11. Write a simple ***text-formatting*** program that reads a text file and produces another text file in which blank lines are removed, multiple blanks are replaced with a single blank, and no lines are longer than some given length. Put as many words as possible on the same line. You will have to break some lines of the given file, but do not break any words.

12. Extend the text-formatting program of Exercise 11 to right-justify each line except the last in the new text file by adding evenly distributed blanks in lines where necessary.

13. (Project) Some text formatters allow command lines to be placed within the unformatted text. These command lines might have forms like the following:

.P *m n*	Insert *m* blank lines before each paragraph and indent each paragraph *n* spaces.
.W *n*	Set the page width (line length) to *n*.
.L *n*	Set the page length (number of lines per page) to *n*.
.I *n*	Indent all lines following this command line by *n* spaces.
.U	Undent all following lines by the amount specified in the last indent command.

    Extend the program of Exercises 11 and 12 to implement command lines.

14. (Project) A ***pretty-printer*** is a special kind of text formatter that reads a text file containing a program and then prints it in a "pretty" format. For example, a pretty-printer for Pascal programs might insert blank lines between subprograms and indent and align statements within statements such as **if** statements, compound statements, type declarations, and variable declarations to produce a format similar to that used in this text's sample programs. Write a pretty-print program for Pascal programs to indent and align statements in a pleasing format.

3.3 The Predefined Data Type *string* in Turbo and Other Pascals

As we noted in Section 3.1, several versions of Pascal provide a predefined string data type along with the functions and procedures for the basic string operations. For example, in Turbo Pascal, *string*[20] can be used to declare the type of a string variable of maximum length 20; this same declaration can be used in THINK Pascal™. In Dr. Pascal® the brackets are replaced by parentheses: *string*(20); and in VAX Pascal, one can use **varying**[20] **of** *char*. Both Turbo Pascal and THINK Pascal provide functions *Length, Concat, Copy,* and *Pos* and procedures *Insert* and *Delete* for processing strings. VAX Pascal and Dr. Pascal provide a concatenation operator (+), functions *Length, Index* (equivalent to *Pos*), and *Substr* (equivalent to *Copy*). Although we focus in this section on the string data type of Turbo Pascal, the differences between this implementation of strings and those in other versions of Pascal are rather small.

Type Declarations. In Turbo Pascal, the predefined type identifier *string* can be used to declare string variables in declarations of the form

> *list-of-variables* : *string*[*limit*];

where *limit* is a constant that specifies the maximum number of characters in a value for the string variables. This length specifier may be omitted so that the declaration has the form

> *list-of-variables* : *string*;

This declaration assumes a default maximum string length of 255 and is therefore equivalent to a declaration of the form

> *list-of-variables* : *string*[255];

For example, the declarations

> **const**
>   *StringLimit* = 8;
>
> **var**
>   *Name* : *string*[*StringLimit*];
>   *Department* : *string*[20];
>   *Sentence* : *string*;

specify that *Name* is a string variable whose values will be strings containing at most 8 characters, *Department* is a string variable whose values will have at most 20 characters, and *Sentence* is a string variable whose value may be any string containing 255 or fewer characters. In any case, the value of a string variable may be an **empty string** consisting of no characters and denoted by the string constant '', a pair of consecutive single quotes.

When the compiler encounters a string declaration of the form

string-variable : *string*[*L*];

it associates an array named *string-variable* of type *char* indexed 0..*L* with *string-variable* and uses this array to store the value of *string-variable*. If there are *n* characters in this value ($n \leq L$), they are stored in positions 1, 2, ..., *n* of this array. Position 0 stores the character whose ASCII code is the length *n* of this value.

For example, the declaration

var
    Department : *string*[20];

associates with *Department* an array named *Department* of type *char* with index type 0..20. The assignment statement

    Department := 'Accounting';

then stores the characters of this string in locations 1, 2, ..., 10 of the array:

i	0	1	2	3	4	5	6	7	8	9	10	11	12	13	14	15	16	17	18	19	20
Department[*i*]	↓	A	c	c	o	u	n	t	i	n	g	?	?	?	?	?	?	?	?	?	?

The question marks in locations 11, 12, ..., 20 indicate unused locations in the array. The character ↓ in position 0 represents the line feed character whose ASCII code is 10, the length of the string. Thus *ord*(*Department*[0]) is the length of the string assigned to *Department*.

Because an array is used to store a string, an indexed variable may be used to access the individual characters in the string. For example, *Department*[1] is the letter 'A' and *Department*[9] is the letter 'n'. The for loop

    for *i* := 3 **to** 10 **do**
      write (*Department*[*i*]);

or equivalently,

    for *i* := 3 **to** *ord*(*Department*[0]) **do**
      write (*Department*[*i*]);

displays the rightmost characters in the value of *Department*, beginning at position 3:

```
counting
```

Assignment.   An assignment statement may be used to assign a value to a string variable:

> *string-var* := *expr*

Here *expr* may be a constant, variable, or expression of any string type or of type *char* or a packed array of characters. For example, the statement

> *Name* := 'John Doe';

assigns the string 'John Doe' to *Name*. The length of the value being assigned may be less than the declared length of the string variable. For example,

> *Name* := 'J. Doe';

assigns the string 'J. Doe' to *Name*, and its length becomes 6. Thus we see that strings in Turbo Pascal are dynamic structures and that this is therefore a better implementation of the abstract data type string than is the array-based implementation described in the preceding section. However, it is not a completely faithful implementation, because it limits the maximum length that a string may have. If the length of the value being assigned is greater than the declared length of the variable, the value is truncated to the size of the variable, and the leftmost characters are assigned; thus, the statement

> *Name* := 'Thomas Jefferson';

assigns the value 'Thomas J' to *Name*.

Input/Output.   In Turbo Pascal, strings can be read from a text file using procedure *readln* and written to text files using procedures *write* and *writeln*. When a value is read for a string variable, the characters are read, beginning at the current position of the data pointer and continuing until an end-of-line mark or the end-of-file mark is encountered. If the length of the resulting string is greater than the declared length of the string variable, the string is truncated and only the leftmost characters are retained.

Comparison.   Two values of string type may be compared with the relational operators <, >, =, <=, >=, and <>. If the two strings have different lengths, they are compared as though the shorter string were padded with blanks to make its length the same as the longer string.

Length.   A reference to the prefined *length* function has the form

> *length*(*str*)

and returns the current length of *str*. Note that *length(str)* returns the same value as

   ord(str[0])

Concatenation. Turbo Pascal provides both a concatenation operation and a concatenation function *concat*. The concatenation operation is denoted by +. Thus,

   'Pasc' + 'al'

produces the string 'Pascal'. A reference to the function *concat* has the form

   concat(str-1, str-2, . . . , str-n)

and returns the string formed by concatenating *str-1, str-2, . . . , str-n* in this order. For example, if *FirstName* and *LastName* are of type *string* and have the values

   FirstName := 'THOMAS';
   LastName := 'JEFFERSON';

then the function reference

   *concat(FirstName, '***', LastName)*

returns the value

   THOMAS***JEFFERSON

Note that *concat(str-1, str-2, . . . , str-n)* has the same value as an expression of the form

   str-1 + str-2 + . . . + str-n

Copy. The function *copy* is referenced with an expression of the form

   copy(str, index, size)

and returns a substring of the specified *size* from the string *str*, beginning at position *index*. For example, the function reference

   copy(LastName, 2, 5)

returns the value

   EFFER

and

$$copy(LastName, 7, length(LastName) - 6)$$

returns the value

   SON

In some versions of Pascal like VAX Pascal and Dr. Pascal, this function is named *substr*. It may also be possible, as in Dr. Pascal, to specify a substring consisting of characters in positions *first* through *last* by attaching a substring designator of the form [*first..last*] to a string variable.

Position.   A reference to the function *pos* has the form

   pos(str-1, str-2)

and returns the starting location of the first occurrence of *str-1* in *str-2* or the value 0 if *str-1* does not appear in *str-2*. For example,

   pos('SO', LastName)

has the value 7, and

   pos('E', LastName)

has the value 2, whereas

   pos('so', LastName)

has the value 0. In some versions of Pascal, like VAX Pascal and Dr. Pascal, this function is named *index*, and the roles of the two parameters may be reversed.

Insert.   The insert operation is implemented in Turbo Pascal by the procedure *insert*, which is referenced with a statement of the form

   insert (str-1, str-2, position)

and modifies the string variable *str-2* by inserting the value of the string expression *str-1* at the specified *position*. For example,

   insert (' P', LastName, 5)

changes the value of *LastName* from JEFFERSON to

   JEFF PERSON

THINK Pascal also provides the function *include*; *include(str-1, str-2, p)* returns the string obtained by inserting *str-1* into *str-2* at position *p*. In VAX Pascal, the function reference *Pad(s, c, l)* returns the string of length *l* obtained by padding *s* with the fill character *c*.

Delete.   A reference to the procedure *delete* has the form

> *delete (str, position, size)*

This procedure modifies the string variable *str* by removing a substring of the specified *size*, starting at the specified *position*. For example,

> *delete (FirstName, 5, 2)*

changes the value of *FirstName* from THOMAS to

> THOM

THINK Pascal also provides the function *omit*; *omit(s, p, n)* returns the string obtained by removing from *s* the *n* characters beginning at position *p*. In Dr. Pascal the function reference *Trim(s)* returns the string obtained by stripping all trailing blanks from *s*.

Other String-processing Procedures.   Those versions of Pascal that provide a predefined string data type typically provide other special string-processing functions and procedures. For example, Turbo Pascal provides the procedures *Str* and *Val. Str (x, s)* converts the value of the numeric expression *x* (which may have output format descriptors of the form :*w* or :*w*:*d* attached) to a string of characters and assigns this string to the string variable *s*. *Val (s, x, ec)* converts the string expression *s* to the corresponding numeric value, if possible, and assigns this value to *x*. If the conversion is successful, error code *ec* is assigned the value 0; otherwise, it is assigned the position of the first character in the string that prevented the conversion.

VAX Pascal provides functions *Bin, Hex, Oct,* and *Pad. Bin(x, l, d)* returns the binary representation of any type expression *x* in a string of length *l* with *d* significant digits; similarly, *Hex(x, l, d)* and *Oct(x, l, d)* return hexadecimal and octal representations, respectively.

3.4   Data Abstraction and Information Hiding

We have already noted that a programmer can effectively use predefined data types such as arrays, records, and sets without knowing the details of their implementation. This is possible because data structures are defined at an *abstract* or *logical* level, separated from their actual physical implementation, the details of which are handled by the system hardware and software and are hidden from the user. This separation of the logical structure from implementation details is known as ***data abstraction*** and is an important concept for user-defined data types as well.

Such data abstraction is a natural part of the top-down approach to program development. It makes it possible for the programmer to concentrate on organizing and processing the data at a logical level without worrying about how the data items will actually be stored or how the basic operations will be performed. This data abstraction is illustrated in the text-editing example in Figure 3.1 where we assumed the existence of a string data type with its basic operations of length, position, concatenate, copy, insert, and delete. If the programming language being used does provide this data structure, usually the programmer is not concerned with how it is implemented. But even if it is not provided in the programming language, the programmer has at least postponed consideration of the implementation details so that he or she is not distracted by them at the higher levels of program development.

A second benefit of separating an abstract data type (ADT) from its implementation is that this makes it possible to change the implementation of the structure with little or no change in the programs that use this ADT. In the case of predefined data types, changes in the system hardware or software that provide the physical implementations should not affect the use of these data types at the logical level. Similarly, changes in implementations of user-defined data structures should require little or no change in programs in which they are used.

To illustrate, suppose that we are developing the text-editing program of Figure 3.1 using a compiler that provides a #include directive for loading the contents of specified files into the source program. As we noted in Section 3.1, we might put the constant definition

> **const**
>   *StringLimit* = 80;

in a file named STRING-CONST, the type definition

> **type**
>   *String* = **packed array**[1..*StringLimit*] **of** *char*;

in a file named STRING-TYPE, and the string functions and procedures described in Section 3.2 in a file named STRING-OPS and then use three #include directives as illustrated in Figure 3.1 to insert the contents of these files into the program at compile time:

```
PROGRAM TextEditor (input, output, TextFile, EditedFile);

(**********************************************
                      .
                      .
                      .
  **********************************************)

CONST
#include 'STRING-CONST'

TYPE
#include 'STRING-TYPE '
```

```
VAR
   TextFile,          (* file of original text *)
     .
     .
     .
   Len : integer;   (* length of some string *)
#include 'STRING-OPS'

PROCEDURE PrintCommands;
     .
     .
     .
BEGIN (* main program *)
     .
     .
     .
END (* main program *).
```

If we wish to improve the performance of this program by replacing the brute force algorithm used for the position operation with a more efficient algorithm like that in Section 3.6, we need only replace the function *Pos* in the file STRING-OPS with the function that implements the more efficient algorithm; no changes in the program are required.

In some versions of Pascal, such as Turbo Pascal and THINK Pascal, these constant, type, function, and procedure definitions can be placed in a separately compiled *unit* (as described in Section 4.3). These items can then be imported from that unit into any program. Some versions of Pascal such as VAX Pascal and other programming languages such as Modula-2 and Ada provide *modules* and *packages* for this purpose.

A third benefit of data abstraction is that it makes it possible to hide the implementation details. This *information hiding* encourages the programmer to use the data type correctly, that is, to use only the properties and operations given in its logical definition. For example, if it is not known whether the storage structure used for a string is an array, a programmer will not be tempted to display a reversed string with the statement

> **for** i = *length*(Str) **downto** 1 **do**
>   *write*(Str[i]);

It is important to avoid such improper uses of data types because they are implementation dependent, and changes in the implementation may cause programs containing such abuses to fail. Also, such programs are less *portable* than those that use data types correctly, since the implementations of these structures vary from one system to another.

In summary, the *interface* between a user and a data type should be at a logical level where the basic operations of the type are visible to the user but the implementation details are hidden as much as possible. For the reasons cited in this section, *it is important that the distinction between a date type as an abstract or logical entity and its actual physical implementation be maintained and enforced.*

3.5 Data Encryption

The basic string operations length, position, concatenate, copy, insert, and delete introduced in the preceding sections are the operations most useful in text-editing applications. There are, however, some important kinds of string processing that require other basic operations. In this section we consider one such application, data encryption, and the basic operations of **substitution** and **permutation** that are important in this application.

Encryption refers to the coding of information in order to keep it secret. Encryption is accomplished by transforming the string of characters comprising the information to produce a new string that is a coded form of the information. This is called a **cryptogram** or **ciphertext** and may be safely stored or transmitted. At a later time it can be deciphered by reversing the encrypting process to recover the original information, which is called **plaintext.**

Data encryption has been used to send secret military and political messages from the days of Julius Caesar to the present. Recent applications include the Washington–Moscow hotline, electronic funds transfer, electronic mail, database security, and many other situations in which the transmission of secret data is crucial. Less profound applications have included Captain Midnight secret decoder rings that could be obtained in the 1950s for twenty-five cents and two Ovaltine labels, puzzles appearing in the daily newspaper, and a number of other frivolous applications. In this section we describe some encryption schemes ranging from the Caesar cipher scheme of the first century B.C. to the Data Encryption Standard and the public key encryption schemes of the twentieth century.

The simplest encryption schemes are based on the string operation of **substitution,** in which the plaintext string is traversed and each character is replaced by some other character according to a fixed rule. For example, the *Caesar cipher* scheme consists of replacing each letter by the letter that appears k positions later in the alphabet for some integer k. (The alphabet is thought of as being arranged in a circle, with A following Z.) In the original Caesar cipher, k was 3, so that each occurrence of A in the plaintext was replaced by D, each B by E, . . . , each Y by B, and each Z by C. For example, using the character set

A B C D E F G H I J K L M N O P Q R S T U V W X Y Z

we would encrypt the string 'IDESOFMARCH' as follows:

To decode the message, the receiver uses the same **key** k and recovers the plaintext by applying the inverse transformation, that is, by traversing the ciphertext string and replacing each character by the character k positions earlier in the alphabet. This is obviously not a very secure scheme, since it is possible to ''break the code'' by simply trying the twenty-six possible values for the key k.

An improved substitution operation is to use a ***keyword*** to specify several different displacements of letters rather than the single offset k of the Caesar cipher. In this ***Vignère cipher*** scheme, the same keyword is added character by character to the plaintext string, where each character is represented by its position in the character set and addition is carried out mod 26. For example, suppose the character set and positions of characters are given by

Position	0	1	2	3	4	5	6	7	8	9	10	11	12
Character	A	B	C	D	E	F	G	H	I	J	K	L	M

13	14	15	16	17	18	19	20	21	22	23	24	25
N	O	P	Q	R	S	T	U	V	W	X	Y	Z

and that the keyword is DAGGER. The plaintext IDESOFMARCH is then encrypted as follows:

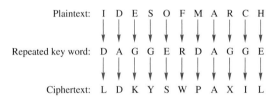

Again, the receiver must know the key and recovers the plaintext by subtracting the characters in this keyword from those in the ciphertext.

A different substitution operation is to use a ***substitution table,*** for example:

Original character:	A	B	C	D	E	F	G	H	I	J	K	L	M
Substitute character:	Q	W	E	R	T	Y	U	I	O	P	A	S	D

N	O	P	Q	R	S	T	U	V	W	X	Y	Z
F	G	H	J	K	L	Z	X	C	V	B	N	M

The string IDESOFMARCH would then be encoded as follows:

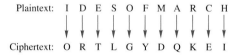

To decode the ciphertext string, the receiver must again know the key, that is, the substitution table.

Since there are 26! (approximately 10^{28}) possible substitution tables, this scheme is considerably more secure than the simple Caesar cipher scheme. Experienced cryptographers can easily break the code, however, by analyzing frequency counts of certain letters and combinations of letters.

Another basic string operation in some encryption schemes is ***permutation,*** in which the characters in the plaintext or in blocks of the plaintext are rearranged. For example, we might divide the plaintext string into blocks (substrings) of size 3 and permute the characters in each block as follows:

Original position: 1 2 3

Permuted position: 3 1 2

Thus the message IDESOFMARCH is encrypted (after the addition of a randomly selected character X so that the string length is a multiple of the block length)

Plaintext: I D E S O F M A R C H X

Ciphertext: D E I O F S A R M H X C

To decode the ciphertext string, the receiver must know the key permutation and its inverse:

Original position: 1 2 3
Permuted position: 2 3 1

Data Encryption Standard. Most modern encryption schemes use both of these techniques, by combining several substitution and permutation operations. Perhaps the best known is the ***Data Encryption Standard (DES)*** developed in the early 1970s by the federal government and the IBM corporation. The scheme is described in *Federal Information Processing Standards Publication 46* (FIPS Pub 46)[3] and is outlined in Figure 3.2, which is a diagram from this government publication.

The input is a bit string of length 64 representing a block of characters in the plaintext string (for example, the concatenation of the ASCII codes of eight characters), and the output is a 64-bit string which is the ciphertext. The encryption is carried out as a series of permutations and substitutions. The substitution operations used are similar to those in earlier examples: Some are obtained by the addition of keywords, and others use a substitution table.

The first operation applied to the 64-bit input string is an initial permutation (*IP*) given by the following table:

				IP			
58	50	42	34	26	18	10	2
60	52	44	36	28	20	12	4
62	54	46	38	30	22	14	6
64	56	48	40	32	24	16	8
57	49	41	33	25	17	9	1
59	51	43	35	27	19	11	3
61	53	45	37	29	21	13	5
63	55	47	39	31	23	15	7

---

[3] Copies of this publication can be obtained from the National Institute of Standards and Technology of the U.S. Department of Commerce.

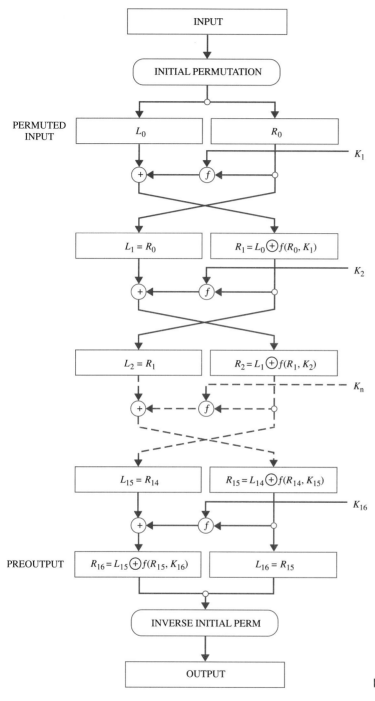

Figure 3.2 DES encryption.

For example, the first bit in the permuted result is the fifty-eighth bit in the original string; the second bit is the fiftieth; and so on. This permuted string is then split into two 32-bit substrings: a left substring, denoted by L_0 in the diagram in Figure 3.2, and a right substring, denoted by R_0. A ***cipher function*** denoted by f uses substitutions and a key K_1 to transform R_0 into a new 32-bit string denoted by $f(R_0, K_1)$. This string is then added to L_0 using bit-by-bit addition modulo 2 (that is, they are combined using the exclusive or operation $\oplus$) to produce the right substring R_1 at the next stage. The original R_0 becomes the left substring L_1.

This basic sequence of operations is performed sixteen times with sixteen different key strings $K_1, \ldots, K_{16}$, except that no "crossover" is performed at the last stage. These operations produce a 64-bit string $R_{16}L_{16}$ labeled "PREOUTPUT" in the diagram. The inverse of the initial permutation (IP^{-1}) is then applied to this preoutput string to yield the final ciphertext.

IP^{-1}							
40	8	48	16	56	24	64	32
39	7	47	15	55	23	63	31
38	6	46	14	54	22	62	30
37	5	45	13	53	21	61	29
36	4	44	12	52	20	60	28
35	3	43	11	51	19	59	27
34	2	42	10	50	18	58	26
33	1	41	9	49	17	57	25

The details of the operation f are shown in Figure 3.3. The right substring denoted by R is first expanded into a 48-bit string using the following bit-

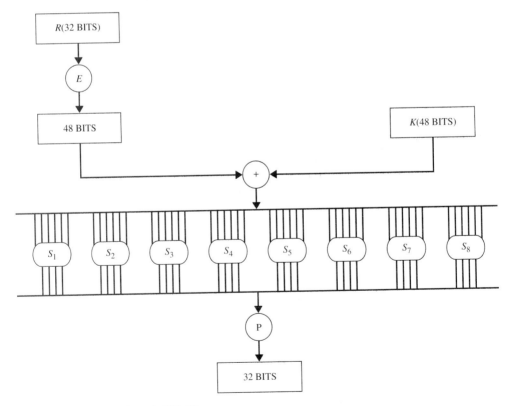

Figure 3.3   Calculation of $f(R, K)$.

selection table E:

			E		
32	1	2	3	4	5
4	5	6	7	8	9
8	9	10	11	12	13
12	13	14	15	16	17
16	17	18	19	20	21
20	21	22	23	24	25
24	25	26	27	28	29
28	29	30	31	32	1

Thus the first 6-bit block consists of bits 32, 1, 2, 3, 4, and 5 of R; the second block consists of bits 4, 5, 6, 7, 8, and 9; and so on. A substitution operation is then applied to this 48-bit string by combining it with a 48-bit key string K using the exclusive or operation. Another substitution using a different table is then applied to each of the 6-bit blocks to produce 4-bit blocks so that the final result is again a 32-bit string. For example, the substitution table for S_1 is

									S_1							
							Column Number									
Row No.	0	1	2	3	4	5	6	7	8	9	10	11	12	13	14	15
0	14	4	13	1	2	15	11	8	3	10	6	12	5	9	0	7
1	0	15	7	4	14	2	13	1	10	6	12	11	9	5	3	8
2	4	1	14	8	13	6	2	11	15	12	9	7	3	10	5	0
3	15	12	8	2	4	9	1	7	5	11	3	14	10	0	6	13

To illustrate how it is used, suppose that the first 6-bit block is 101000. The binary numeral 10 consisting of the first and last bits determines a row in this table, namely, row 2, and the middle four bits 0100 determine a column, namely, column 4. The 4-bit binary representation 1101 of the entry 13 in the second row and the fourth column of this table is the replacement for this 6-bit block. Similar substitution tables $S_2, \ldots, S_8$ are used to transform the other seven 6-bit blocks.

One final permutation P is applied to the resulting 32-bit string to yield $f(R, K)$:

		p	
16	7	20	21
29	12	28	17
1	15	23	26
5	18	31	10
2	8	24	14
32	27	3	9
19	13	30	6
22	11	4	25

The sixteen different keys used in DES are extracted in a carefully pre-scribed way from a single 64-bit key. Thus the user need supply only one key string to be used for encryption and decryption, rather than sixteen different keys. The algorithm for decrypting ciphertext is the same as that for encryption, except that the sixteen keys are applied in reverse order.

The National Institute of Standards and Technology (formerly the National Bureau of Standards) adopted DES as the "standard" encryption scheme for sensitive federal documents. It has been the subject of some controversy, how-ever, because of questions about whether the 48-bit keys used in the substitu-tions are long enough and the substitution keys are sophisticated enough to provide the necessary security.

Public Key Encryption. Each of the encryption schemes considered thus far requires that both the sender and the receiver know the key or keys used in encrypting the plaintext. This means that although the cryptogram may be transmitted through some public channel such as a telephone line that is not secure, the keys must be transmitted in some secure manner, for example, by a courier. This problem of maintaining secrecy of the key is compounded when it must be shared by several persons.

Recently developed encryption schemes eliminate this problem by using two keys, one for encryption and one for decryption. These schemes are called *public key encryption schemes* because the encryption key is not kept secret. The keys used in these systems have the following properties:

1. For each encryption key there is exactly one corresponding decryption key, and it is distinct from the encryption key.
2. There are many such pairs of keys, and they are relatively easy to compute.
3. It is almost impossible to determine the decryption key if one knows only the encryption key.
4. The encryption key is made public by the receiver to all those who will transmit messages to him or her, but only the receiver knows the decryption key.

In 1978, Rivest, Shamir, and Adelman proposed one method of imple-menting a public key encryption scheme.[4] The public key is a pair (e, n) of integers, and one encrypts a message string M by first dividing M into blocks $M_1, M_2, \ldots, M_k$ and converting each block M_i of characters to an integer P_i in the range 0 through $n - 1$ (for example, by concatenating the ASCII codes of the characters). M is then encrypted by raising each block to the power e and reducing modulo n:

$$\text{Plaintext: } M = M_1 M_2 \cdots M_k \rightarrow P_1 P_2 \cdots P_k$$

$$\text{Ciphertext: } C = C_1 C_2 \cdots C_k, C_i = P_i^e \bmod n$$

The cipher text C is decrypted by raising each block C_i to the power d and reducing modulo n, where d is a secret decryption key. Clearly, to recover the plaintext, we need

$$P_i = C_i^d \bmod n = (P_i^e)^d \bmod n = P_i^{e \cdot d} \bmod n$$

[4] R. L. Rivest, A. Shamir, and L. Adelman. A method for obtaining digital signatures and public-key cryptosystems, *Communications of the ACM* 21, 2 (February 1978): 120–126.

for each block P_i. Thus e and d must be chosen so that

$$x^{e \cdot d} \bmod n = x$$

for each nonnegative integer x.

The following algorithms summarize this Rivest–Shamir–Adelman (RSA) public key encryption system:

RSA ENCRYPTION ALGORITHM

(* Accepts: Plaintext M.
    Function: Encrypt M using public encryption code (e, n) to produce
              ciphertext C.
    Returns: Ciphertext C. *)

1. Pad M with some randomly selected character if necessary so that *length*(M) is a multiple of *BlockLength*.
2. Calculate *NumberOfBlocks* = *length*(M) / *BlockLength*.
3. Initialize index j to 1.
4. For $i = 1$ to *NumberOfBlocks*, do the following:
    a. Extract the substring M_i from M consisting of the *BlockLength* characters beginning at position j.
    b. Convert M_i to numeric form to give P_i.
    c. Calculate $C_i = P_i^e \bmod n$.
    d. Increment j by *BlockLength*.

RSA DECRYPTION ALGORITHM

(* Accepts: Ciphertext C.
    Function: Decrypt ciphertext consisting of numeric blocks C_i, $i =$
              $1, \ldots,$ *NumberOfBlocks*, using secret decryption key d.
    Returns: Plaintext M. *)

1. Initialize M to the empty string.
2. For $i = 1$ to *NumberOfBlocks*, do the following:
    a. Calculate $P_i = C_i^d \bmod n$.
    b. Convert P_i to a string of characters M_i.
    c. Concatenate M_i onto M.

To illustrate, suppose that (17, 2773) is the public encryption code and that characters are converted to numeric values using the following table:

Character:	A	B	C	D	E	F	G	H	I	J	K	L	M
Code:	00	01	02	03	04	05	06	07	08	09	10	11	12

Character:	N	O	P	Q	R	S	T	U	V	W	X	Y	Z
Code:	13	14	15	16	17	18	19	20	21	22	23	24	25

To encrypt a string such as $M = $ 'IDESOFMARCH' using the RSA algorithm, we divide M into 2-character blocks $M_1, M_2, M_3, M_4, M_5, M_6$ (after appending the randomly selected character X) and represent each block M_i as an integer P_i in the range 0 through $2773 - 1 = 2772$ by concatenating the numeric codes of the characters that comprise the block:

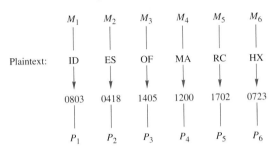

Each of these blocks is then encrypted by calculating $C_i = P_i^{17}$ mod 2773:

Ciphertext:	0779	1983	2641	1444	0052	0802
	C_1	C_2	C_3	C_4	C_5	C_6

For this encryption key, the corresponding decrypting key is $d = 157$. Thus, we decrypt the ciphertext by calculating C_i^{157} **mod** 2773 for each block C_i. For the preceding ciphertext this gives

Decrypted ciphertext: 0803 0418 1405 1200 1702 0723

which is the numeric form of the original message.

Two points in the preceding discussion of the RSA encryption scheme require further explanation: (1) How are n, e, and d chosen? (2) How can the exponentiation be performed efficiently?

The number n is the product of two large "random" primes p and q,

$$n = p \cdot q$$

In the preceding example, we used the small primes 47 and 59 to simplify the computations, but Rivest, Shamir, and Adelman suggest that p and q have at least one hundred digits. The decrypting key d is then selected to be some large random integer that is relatively prime to both $p - 1$ and $q - 1$, that is, one that has no factors in common with either number. In our example, $d = 157$ has this property. The number e is then selected to have the property that

$$e \cdot d \text{ mod } ((p - 1) \cdot (q - 1)) \text{ is equal to 1}$$

A result from number theory then guarantees that e and d will have the required property described earlier, namely, that

$$P_i^{e \cdot d} \text{ mod } n = P_i$$

for each block P_i.

We can efficiently carry out the exponentiations required in encryption and decryption by repeatedly squaring and multiplying, as follows:

EXPONENTIATION ALGORITHM

(* Input: Integers x, k, and n.
   Function: Calculate $y = x^k$ mod n.
   Returns: y *)

1. Find the base-2 representation $b_t \ldots b_1 b_0$ of the exponent k.
2. Initialize y to 1.
3. For $i = t$ down to 0, do the following:
     a. Set $y = y^2$ mod n.
     b. If $b_i = 1$ then
             Set $y = (y * x)$ mod n.

Recall that the encrypting key (e, n) is a public key, so that no attempt is made to keep it secret. The decrypting key d is a private key, however, and so must be kept secret. To break this code, one would need to be able to determine the value of d from the values of n and e. Because of the manner in which d and e are selected, this is possible if n can be factored into a product of primes. The security of the RSA encryption scheme is based on the difficulty of determining the prime factors of a large integer. Even with the best factorization algorithms known today, this is a prohibitively time-consuming task. A study of a few years ago gave the following table displaying some estimated times, assuming that each operation required one microsecond:

Number of Digits in Number Being Factored	Time
50	4 hours
75	104 days
100	74 years
200	4 billion years
300	5×10^{15} years
500	4×10^{25} years

Although the research on factorization continues, no efficient algorithms have been found that significantly reduce the times in the preceding table. Improved algorithms and the use of high-speed computers have made factorization possible in less time than the table shows, but not significantly less for large numbers. This public key encryption scheme thus appears (so far) to be quite secure and is being endorsed by a growing number of major computer vendors; and the adoption of some public key encryption scheme is being considered by the National Institute of Standards and Technology.

Exercises

1. A pure permutation encryption scheme is very insecure. Explain why by describing how an encryption scheme that merely permutes the bits in an n-bit string can easily be cracked by studying how certain basic bit strings are encrypted. Illustrate for $n = 4$.

2. Consider a simplified DES scheme that encrypts messages using the DES approach pictured in Figure 3.2 but with only two keys, K_1 and K_2, instead of sixteen keys, $K_1, \ldots, K_{16}$, and that in the calculation of $f(R, K)$ pictured in Figure 3.3 uses the same substitution table S_1 for each of the 6-bit blocks instead of eight different tables $S_1, \ldots, S_8$. Encrypt the string 'AARDVARK' using this simplified DES scheme with keys $K_1 = $ 'ABCDEF' and $K_2 = $ 'SECRET' and assuming that strings are converted into bit strings by replacing each character by its binary ASCII code.

3. Using the character codes 00, 01, ... , 25 given in the text:

   (a) Find the RSA ciphertext produced by the key $(e, n) = (5, 2881)$ for the plaintext 'PUBLIC'.

   (b) Verify that $d = 1109$ is a decrypting key for the RSA scheme in (a).

4. If the RSA ciphertext produced by key $(e, n) = (13, 2537)$ is 0095 and the character codes 00, 01, ... , 25 given in the text are used, find the plaintext.

5. A public key encryption scheme can be used to provide positive identification of the sender of a message by incorporating a **digital signature** into it. To illustrate, suppose that Al wishes to send a message M to Bob. Al first "signs" M by encrypting it using his secret decrypting key, which we might indicate by

$$S = D_{Al}(M)$$

He then encrypts S using Bob's public encryption key and sends the result to Bob:

$$M' = E_{Bob}(S)$$

Bob first decrypts the ciphertext M' with his secret decrypting key to obtain the signature S

$$D_{Bob}(M') = D_{Bob}(E_{Bob}(S)) = S$$

and then extracts the message M by using Al's public encryption key:

$$E_{Al}(S) = E_{Al}(D_{Al}(M)) = M$$

Bob's pair (M, S) is similar to a paper document that Al signed, since only Al could have created S. For the message $M = $ "HI" and using the character codes 00, 01, ... , 25 given in the text, find M' if Al and Bob have published RSA encryption keys (3, 1081) and (1243, 1829), respectively.

6. Write a program to implement the Caesar cipher scheme.

7. Write a program to implement the Vignère cipher scheme.

8. Write a program to encrypt and decrypt a message by using a substitution table.

9. Write a program to encrypt and decrypt a message by using a permutation scheme.

10. Write a program to encrypt and decrypt messages using the simplified DES scheme described in Exercise 2.

11. Write a procedure or function to implement the algorithm given in the text for calculating $y = x^k \bmod n$ by repeated squaring and multiplication.

12. Use the subprogram of Exercise 11 in a program that implements the RSA scheme (with integer values in the range allowed by your version of Pascal).

13. A simple "probabilistic" algorithm for testing whether a number is prime that is similar to that recommended for finding the large primes needed in the RSA scheme is based on the following result discovered by the mathematician Fermat: If n is a prime, then $x^{n-1} \bmod n = 1$ for all positive integers less than n. Thus, to test whether a given number n is prime, one might proceed as follows: Randomly select a positive integer $x < n$, and compute $y = x^{n-1} \bmod n$. If $y \neq 1$, n is not prime; but if $y = 1$, n *may be* prime and further testing is required, so we repeat the test with another value of x. If $y = 1$ for many different values of x, n is *probably* prime. Write a program that uses this method of testing primality.

3.6 Pattern Matching

In Section 3.2 we presented algorithms for some of the basic string operations, but as we noted, the brute force algorithm for the position operation, which finds the index of one string in another, is not the best possible. Because the index operation is a special case of the more general pattern-matching problem that occurs in many applications, such as text editing and text processing, a good deal of work has gone into designing more efficient algorithms. In this section we describe one such algorithm, called the *Knuth-Morris-Pratt algorithm.*

To review the brute force method and to discover how it can be improved, consider again the example of finding the first occurrence of the pattern 'abcabd' in the line of text 'abcabcabdabba':

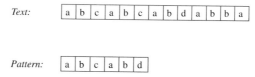

Text: | a | b | c | a | b | c | a | b | d | a | b | b | a |

Pattern: | a | b | c | a | b | d |

We begin matching characters in *Pattern* with those in *Text* and find that the first five characters match, but that the next characters do not:

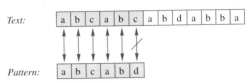

When such a mismatch occurs, we must backtrack to the beginning of *Pattern*, shift one position to the right in *Text*, and start the search over again:

This time a mismatch occurs immediately, and so we backtrack once more to the beginning of *Pattern*, shift another position to the right in *Text*, and try again:

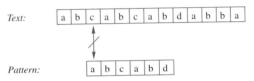

Another mismatch of the first characters occurs, so we backtrack and shift once again:

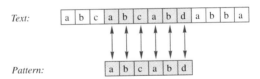

On the next search, all of the characters in *Pattern* match the corresponding characters in *Text*, and thus the pattern has been located in the line of text.

In this example, only three backtracks were required, and two of these required backing up only one character. The situation may be much worse, however. To illustrate, suppose that the text to be searched consists of one hundred characters, each of which is the same, and the pattern consists of forty-nine of these same characters followed by a different character, for example,

In beginning our search for *Pattern* in *Text*, we find that the first forty-nine characters match but that the last character in *Pattern* does not match the corresponding character in *Text*:

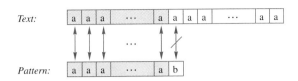

We must therefore backtrack to the beginning of *Pattern*, shift one position to the right in *Text*, and repeat the search. As before, we make forty-nine successful comparisons of characters in *Pattern* with characters in *Text* before a mismatch occurs:

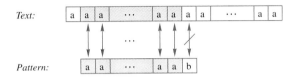

This same thing happens again and again until eventually we reach the end of *Text* and are able to determine that *Pattern* is not found in *Text*. After each unsuccessful scan, we must backtrack from the last character of *Pattern* way back to the first character and restart the search one position to the right in *Text*.

The source of inefficiency in this algorithm is the backtracking required whenever a mismatch occurs. To illustrate how it can be avoided, consider again the first example in which *Pattern* = 'abcabd' and *Text* = 'abcabcab-dabba':

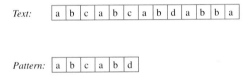

In the first scan, we find that $Pattern[1] = Text[1]$, $Pattern[2] = Text[2]$, $Pattern[3] = Text[3]$, $Pattern[4] = Text[4]$, and $Pattern[5] = Text[5]$, but $Pattern[6] \neq Text[6]$:

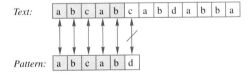

Examining *Pattern*, we see that $Pattern[1] \neq Pattern[2]$; thus $Pattern[1]$ cannot possibly match $Text[2]$ because $Pattern[2]$ did. Similarly, since $Pattern[1]$ is different from $Pattern[3]$, which matched $Text[3]$, neither can $Pattern[1]$ match $Text[3]$. Consequently, we can immediately "slide" *Pattern* three positions to the right, eliminating the backtracks to positions 2 and 3 in *Text*. Moreover, examining the part of *Pattern* that has matched a substring of *Text*,

abcab

we see that we need not check *Pattern*[1] and *Pattern*[2] again, since they are the same as *Pattern*[4] and *Pattern*[5], respectively, which have already matched characters in *Text*:

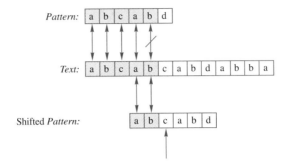

This partial match means that we can continue our search at position 6 in *Text* and position 3 in *Pattern*; no backtracking to examine characters before that in the position where a mismatch occurred is necessary at all!

Now consider the general problem of finding the index of a pattern $p_1 p_2 \ldots p_m$ in a text $t_1 t_2 \ldots t_n$, and suppose that these strings are stored in the arrays *Pattern* and *Text* so that $Pattern[i] = p_i$ and $Text[j] = t_j$. Also suppose that in attempting to locate *Pattern* in *Text* we have come to a point where the first $i - 1$ characters in *Pattern* have matched characters in *Text*, but a mismatch occurs when *Pattern*[i] is compared with *Text*[j]:

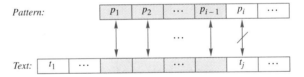

To avoid backtracking, we must shift *Pattern* to the right so that the search can continue with *Text*[j] and *Pattern*[k], for some $k < i$:

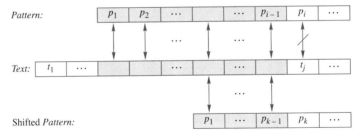

It is clear from this diagram that in order to do this, the first $k - 1$ characters of *Pattern* must be identical to the $k - 1$ characters that precede *Pattern*[i] and that *Pattern*[k] must be different from *Pattern*[i] so that *Pattern*[k] has a chance of matching *Text*[j]:

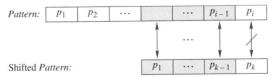

Let us denote this value k by *Next*[i]. Thus, as we have just observed, *Next*[i] is the position in *Pattern* at which the search can continue by comparing *Pattern*[*Next*[i]] with the character *Text*[j] that did not match *Pattern*[i]; that is, we slide *Pattern* to the right to align *Pattern*[*Next*[i]] with *Text*[j] and continue searching at this point. If no such k exists, we take *Next*[i] = 0 to indicate that the search is to resume with *Pattern*[1] and *Text*[$j + 1$]. (In this case, we can think of sliding *Pattern* to the right to align the nonexistent character in position 0 with *Text*[j] and resume the search.)

KNUTH–MORRIS–PRATT PATTERN MATCHING ALGORITHM

(* Input: Strings *Text* and *Pattern* and integers m and n.
  Function: Determine the *Index* of a pattern in a text string. The pattern is stored in positions 1 through m of the array *Pattern*, and the text is stored in positions 1 through n of the array *Text*.
  Returns: *Index* *)

1. Initialize each of *Index*, i, and j to 1.
  (* *Index* is the beginning position of the substring of *Text* being compared with *Pattern*, and indices i and j run through *Pattern* and *Text*, respectively. *)
2. While $i \le m$ and $j \le n$ do the following:
  If *Pattern*[i] = *Text*[j] then   (* match *)
    Increment each of i and j by 1.
  Else do the following: (* mismatch *)
    a. (* Slide *Pattern* to the right the appropriate distance *)
      Add $i - $ *Next*[i] to *Index*.
    b. (* Determine where the search is to continue *)
      If *Next*[i] > 0 then
        Set i equal to *Next*[i].
      Else
        Set i equal to 1 and increment j by 1.
3. If $i > m$ then *Index* is the index of *Pattern* in *Text*; otherwise, *Pattern* does not appear in *Text*.

To illustrate, consider the following pattern

Pattern = abcaababc

and assume that the we are given the following table of *Next* values for this pattern:

i	1	2	3	4	5	6	7	8	9
Pattern[i]	a	b	c	a	a	b	a	b	c
Next[i]	0	1	1	0	2	1	3	1	1

Now suppose that we wish to determine the index of *Pattern* in

$$Text = \text{aabcbabcaabcaababcba}$$

Initially, *Index, i,* and *j* are 1. Both *Text*[1] and *Pattern*[1] are 'a', and so both *i* and *j* are incremented to 2. A mismatch now occurs:

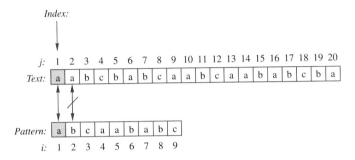

Since *Next*[2] = 1, *Index* is set to *Index* + (2 − *Next*[2]) = *Index* + (2 − 1) = 2; *i* is set to *Next*[2] = 1; *j* retains the value 2; and the search continues by comparing *Pattern*[*Next*[2]] = *Pattern*[1] with *Text*[2]. The next mismatch occurs when *i* = 4 and *j* = 5:

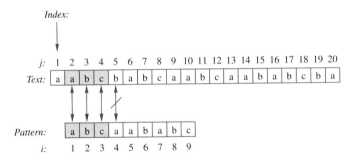

Since *Next*[4] = 0, *Index* is set to *Index* + (4 − (0)) = 6; *i* is set to 1; and *j* is incremented to 6. The search then resumes by comparing *Pattern*[1] with *Text*[6], and continues until the next mismatch, when *j* = 12 and *i* = 7:

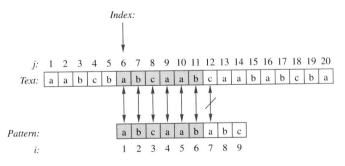

Next[7] = 3, so *Index* is updated to *Index* + (7 − 3) = 10; *i* is set equal to *Next*[7] = 3; *j* remains at 12; and the search resumes by comparing *Pattern*[3] with *Text*[12]. This search locates a substring of *Text* that matches *Pattern*

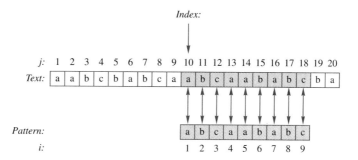

so the algorithm terminates with *Index* = 10 as the index of *Pattern* in *Text*.

To complete our discussion of the Knuth–Morris–Pratt algorithm, we must describe how the table of *Next* values is computed. Recall that *Next*[i] is the length *k* of the longest prefix *Pattern*[1], *Pattern*[2], . . . , *Pattern*[k] of *Pattern* that matches the *k* − 1 characters preceding *Pattern*[i] but that *Pattern*[k] ≠ *Pattern*[i]. For example, consider again the pattern 'abcaababc':

i	1	2	3	4	5	6	7	8	9
Pattern[i]	a	b	c	a	a	b	a	b	c

Next[7] = 3, since the characters a, b in positions 1 and 2 match those in positions 5 and 6, and *Pattern*[3] = 'c' is different from *Pattern*[7] = 'a'. The following diagram shows this matching prefix and suffix in abcaaba and that the characters that follow these in positions 3 and 7 do not match:

This property of *Pattern* guarantees that if a mismatch occurs in comparing some character in *Text* with *Pattern*[7], the search can continue by comparing *Pattern*[*Next*[7]] = *Pattern*[3] with this character:

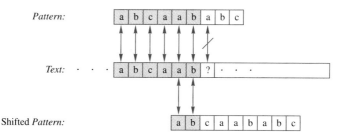

The determination that *Next*[5] = 2 is similar to that for *Next*[7]. The following diagram shows the matching prefix and suffix in abcaa and that *Pattern*[2] ≠ *Pattern*[5]:

The calculation of *Next*[6] requires a bit more care. In looking for a matching prefix and suffix in abcaa, we find one of length 1, that is, *Pattern*[1] = *Pattern*[5]; however, the characters that follow these matching substrings, *Pattern*[2] and *Pattern*[6], are not different. Thus *Next*[6] is not 2. Since an empty prefix always matches an empty suffix and since *Pattern*[1] = 'a' differs from *Pattern*[6] = 'b', we obtain *Next*[6] = 1:

By similar analyses, the remaining values of the *Next* table can be verified.

An algorithm for calculating *Next* values using this method is essentially the same as the pattern-matching algorithm except that the pattern is matched against itself. To see this, consider again a general pattern $p_1p_2 \ldots p_m$. Clearly *Next*[1] must have the value 0, since there are no characters that precede *Pattern*[1]. Now, if *Next*[1], . . . , *Next*[*j* − 1] have been determined, these values can be used to calculate *Next*[*j*], as follows: We "slide" a copy of *Pattern* across itself until we find a prefix (possibly empty) that matches the characters preceding *Pattern*[*j*]:

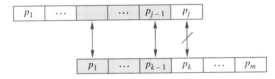

If this prefix has length $k-1$ (possibly 0) and *Pattern*[*k*] ≠ *Pattern*[*j*], then *Next*[*j*] = *k* by definition. However, if *Pattern*[*k*] = *Pattern*[*j*], then clearly *Next*[*j*] has the same value as *Next*[*k*], which has already been calculated. This method of calculating *Next* values is used in the following algorithm:

ALGORITHM FOR *Next* TABLE

(∗ Input: String *Pattern* and integer *m*.
   Function: Compute *Next* values for a pattern stored in positions 1
              through *m* of the array *Pattern*.
   Returns: The array *Next*. ∗)

1. Initialize *Next*[1] to 0, *k* to 0, and *j* to 1.
2. While *j* < *m*, do the following:
   a. Set *PrefixFound* to false.
   b. While (*k* > 0) and not *PrefixFound* do the following:
        If *Pattern*[*k*] ≠ *Pattern*[*j*] then
            Set *k* equal to *Next*[*k*].
        Else
            Set *PrefixFound* to true.
   c. Increment *k* and *j* by 1.
   d. If *Pattern*[*j*] = *Pattern*[*k*] then
        Set *Next*[*j*] equal to *Next*[*k*].
      Else
        Set *Next*[*j*] equal to *k*.

To illustrate, consider the pattern used earlier:

Pattern = abcaababc

The following table traces the execution of this algorithm as it calculates the *Next* table for this pattern:

Instruction	*PrefixFound*	k	j	*Next* Value Computed
Initially		0	1	$Next[1] = 0$
2a	false	0	1	
2b	false	0	1	
2c	false	1	2	
2d	false	1	2	$Next[2] = 1$
2a	false	1	2	
2b	false	$Next[1] = 0$	2	
2c	false	1	3	
2d	false	1	3	$Next[3] = 1$
2a	false	1	3	
2b	false	$Next[1] = 0$	3	
2c	false	1	4	
2d	false	1	4	$Next[4] = Next[1] = 0$
2a	false	1	4	
2b	true	1	4	
2c	true	2	5	
2d	true	2	5	$Next[5] = 2$
2a	false	2	5	
2b	false	$Next[2] = 1$	5	
	true	1	5	
2c	true	2	6	
2d	true	2	6	$Next[6] = Next[2] = 1$
2a	false	2	6	
2b	true	2	6	
2c	true	3	7	
2d	true	3	7	$Next[7] = 3$
2a	false	3	7	
2b	false	$Next[3] = 1$	7	
	true	1	7	
2c	true	2	8	
2d	true	2	8	$Next[8] = Next[2] = 1$
2a	false	2	8	
2b	true	2	8	
2c	true	3	9	
2d	true	3	9	$Next[9] = Next[3] = 1$

The Knuth–Morris–Pratt solution to the pattern-matching problem has an interesting history. A theorem proved by S. A. Cook in 1970 states that any problem that can be solved using an abstract model of a computer called a ***pushdown automaton*** can be solved in time proportional to the size of the problem using an actual computer (more precisely, using a random access machine). In particular, this theorem implies the existence of an algorithm for solving the pattern-matching problem in time proportional to $m + n$, where m and n are the maximum indices in arrays that store the pattern and text, respectively. Donald Knuth and Vaughn R. Pratt painstakingly reconstructed the proof of Cook's theorem and so constructed the pattern-matching algorithm described in this section. At approximately the same time, James H. Morris, Jr. constructed essentially the same algorithm while considering the practical problem of designing a text editor. Thus we see that not all algorithms are discovered by a "flash of insight" and that theoretical computer science does indeed sometimes lead to practical applications.

Exercises

1. Compute *Next* tables for the following patterns:

   (a) A B R A C A D A B R A   (b) A A A A A
   (c) M I S S I S S I P P I   (d) I S S I S S I P P I
   (e) B A B B A B A B   (f) 1 0 1 0 0 1 1
   (g) 1 0 0 1 0 1 1 1   (h) 1 0 0 1 0 0 1 0 0 1

2. Construct tables tracing the action of the *Next* table algorithm for the patterns in Exercise 1.

3. Write a program to implement a CHANGE editor command that is used in the form

   CHANGE(*string1, string2, string3*)

   to replace the first occurrence (if there is one) of *string2* in *string1* by *string3*. Use the Knuth–Morris–Pratt method to determine the index of *string2* in *string1*.

4. Write a program that generates a random bit string *Text* of some specified length, say 1000, and a shorter random bit string *Pattern* of length 10 or so, and then uses the Knuth–Morris–Pratt method to locate all occurrences of *Pattern* in *Text*. (See footnote 2 in Section 5.2 if your version of Pascal does not provide a random number generator.)

5. Many versions of Pascal provide some function or procedure that returns the elapsed CPU time since execution of the program began. If we use it to determine a value *Time1* before some subprogram P is referenced and then use it again to determine a value *Time2* after the execution of P is complete, then *Time2* − *Time1* will measure the execution time of P. If such a timing function/procedure is available in your version of Pascal, use it in a program that implements the index operation, first using the brute force approach and then using the Knuth–Morris–Pratt scheme, and compare the computing times of these two implementations. You might generate test strings *Text* and *Pattern* randomly, as suggested in Exercise 4.

4

Stacks

An implementation of a data structure consists of storage structures to store the data items and algorithms for the basic operations and relations. As we have seen, there may be several different implementations, and some are better than others. The idea of **data abstraction,** in which the definition of a data structure is separated from its implementation, is an important concept because it makes it possible to study and use the structure without being concerned about the details of its implementation.

In the preceding chapter we considered the string data type and its implementation using an array to store the characters that comprise the string. There are several other simple but important data structures that can be implemented using arrays as the basic storage structure, and in this chapter we consider one such data structure, the stack, and some of its applications. This structure is often implemented using an array because most programming languages provide a predefined array data type, and such an implementation is therefore quite easy. In this chapter we also discuss the strengths and weaknesses of such an array-based implementation.

4.1 Introduction to Stacks

Consider the following problems:

PROBLEM 1:
Data items are stored in computer memory using a binary representation. In particular, positive integers are commonly stored using the base-two representation described in Section 2.2. This means that the base-ten representation of an integer that appears in a program or in a data file must be converted to a base-two representation. One algorithm for carrying out this conversion uses repeated division by 2, with the successive remainders giving the binary digits in the base-two representation from right to left. For example, the base-two

representation of 26 is 11010, as the following computation shows:

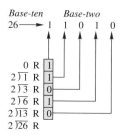

What data structure should be used to keep track of these remainders?

PROBLEM 2:

One task that must be performed by a compiler is to scan an arithmetic expression containing parentheses to determine whether these parentheses balance, that is, if each left parenthesis has exactly one matching right parenthesis later in the expression. What data structure will facilitate this syntax checking?

PROBLEM 3:

A program is to be written to simulate a certain card game. One aspect of this simulation is to maintain a discard pile. On any turn, a player may discard a single card from his hand to the top of this pile, or he may retrieve the top card from this discard pile. What data structure is needed to model this discard pile?

PROBLEM 4:

A program is to be written to model a railroad switching yard. One part of the switching network consists of a main track and a siding onto which cars may be shunted and removed at any time:

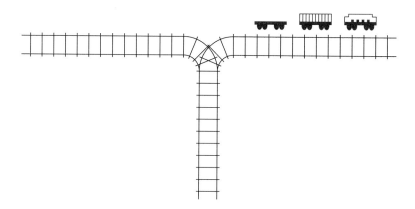

What data structure can be used to model the operation of this siding?

Each of these problems involves a collection of related data items: a sequence of remainders in Problem 1, a collection of left and right parentheses in Problem 2, a deck of cards in Problem 3, and a set of railroad cars in Problem 4. From the diagram in Problem 1, we note that the bits that comprise the base-two representation of 26 have been generated in reverse order, from right to left, and that the remainders must therefore be stored in some structure so they can later be displayed in the usual left-to-right order. To solve Problem 2, we must scan the expression and store each left parenthesis until a right parenthesis is encountered. The right parenthesis matches the last left parenthesis that was stored, and thus that left parenthesis is removed from storage and the scan is continued. In Problem 3, the basic operations are adding a card to and removing a card from the top of the discard pile. In Problem 4, the basic operations are pushing a car onto the siding or removing the last car previously placed on the siding.

In each case we need a "last-generated-first-displayed," "last-stored-first-removed," "last-discarded-first-removed," "last-pushed-onto-first-removed" structure. To illustrate this data structure, we focus on Problem 1. To display the base-two representation of an integer like 26 in the usual left-to-right sequence, we must "stack up" the remainders generated during the repeated division by 2, as illustrated in the diagram in Problem 1. When the division process terminates, we can retrieve the bits from this stack of remainders in the required "last-in-first-out" order.

Assuming that an ADT for this stack structure is available, we are led to the following algorithm to convert from base-ten to base-two and to display the result:

BASE-CONVERSION ALGORITHM

(* Accepts: Positive integer *Number*.
   Function: Convert *Number* from base-ten to base-two.
   Output: The base-two representation of *Number*. *)

1. Create an empty stack to hold the remainders.
2. While *Number* $\neq$ 0 do the following:
   a. Calculate the *Remainder* that results when *Number* is divided by 2.
   b. Put *Remainder* on the top of the stack of remainders.
   c. Replace *Number* by the integer quotient of *Number* divided by 2.
3. While the stack of remainders is not empty do the following:
   a. Remove the *Remainder* from the top of the stack of remainders.
   b. Display *Remainder*.

The following diagram traces this algorithm for the integer 26:

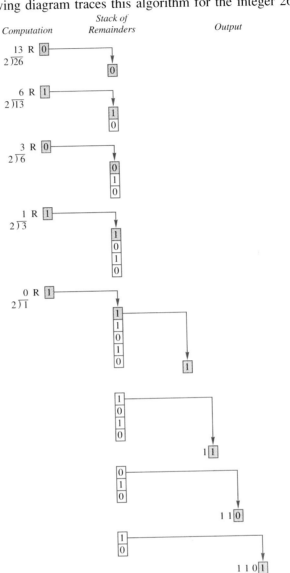

This type of last-in-first-out processing occurs in a wide variety of applications, and consequently, a data structure that embodies this idea is very useful. This *last-in-first-out* (*LIFO*) data structure is called a *stack.* It consists of a list or sequence of data items in which all insertions and deletions are made at one end, called the *top* of the stack. More precisely, the basic operations for a stack include

1. Create an empty stack.
2. Determine whether a stack is empty.
3. Retrieve and remove the element at the top of the stack.

4. Insert a new element at the top of the stack.

The operation of retrieving and removing the top element of a stack is usually called a *pop* operation and the operation of inserting a new element at the top of stack is called *push*. The reason for this terminology is that the structure functions in the same manner as does a spring-loaded stack of plates or trays used in a cafeteria:

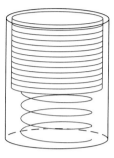

One adds plates to the stack by *pushing* them onto the *top* of the stack. When a plate is removed from the top of the stack, the spring causes the next plate to *pop* up.

A formal specification for the abstract data type stack is:

ADT Stack

Collection of Data Elements:

An ordered collection of data items which can be accessed at only one location, called the *top* of the stack.

Basic Operations:

CreateStack:
    FUNCTION: Creates an empty stack.
    RETURNS: An empty stack.

EmptyStack:
    ACCEPTS: A stack.
    FUNCTION: Checks if the stack is empty.
    RETURNS: True if the stack is empty, and false otherwise.

Pop:
    ACCEPTS: A stack.
    FUNCTION: Retrieves and removes the element at the top of the stack.
    RETURNS: Top element of the stack and the modified stack.

Push:
    ACCEPTS: A stack and a data item.
    FUNCTION: Inserts the data item at the top of the stack.
    RETURNS: The modified stack.

If we assume that this ADT has been implemented so that procedures *CreateStack*, *Pop*, and *Push* referenced with statements of the form

> *CreateStack* (*Stack*);   (∗ creates an empty stack ∗)
> *Pop* (*Stack*, *Item*);   (∗ pops *Item* from *Stack*, assuming the stack is
>   nonempty ∗)
> *Push* (*Stack*, *Item*);   (∗ pushes *Item* onto *Stack* ∗)

and a boolean function *EmptyStack* referenced by

> *EmptyStack*(*Stack*)   (∗ determines if stack is empty ∗)

implement the basic stack operations, then a program segment to implement the base conversion algorithm is easy to write:

> *CreateStack* (*StackOfRemainders*);
> **while** *Number* $<>$ 0 **do**
>   **begin**
>   *Remainder* := *Number* **mod** 2;
>   *Push* (*StackOfRemainders*, *Remainder*);
>   *Number* := *Number* **div** 2
>   **end** (∗ **while** ∗);
> *write* ('Base-two representation: ');
> **while not** *EmptyStack*(*StackOfRemainders*) **do**
>   **begin**
>   *Pop* (*StackOfRemainders*, *Remainder*);
>   *write* (*Remainder*:1)
>   **end** (∗ **while** ∗);
> *writeln*;

Once again we have an illustration of one of the benefits of data abstraction, that is, of separating the definition of a data structure at a logical or abstract level from its actual physical implementation. Regarding a stack as an abstract data type allows us to use it in a solution of the base-conversion problem without being distracted by implementation details. Now, however, we switch from our role as an ADT user to that of an ADT implementer as we consider in the next section how arrays and records can be used to implement stacks in Pascal. In Chapter 8 we consider a linked implementation.

4.2 Implementing Stacks with Arrays and Records; A Stacks Package

The first step in implementing a stack data structure is to select a storage structure to store the stack elements. Because a stack is a sequence of data items, we might use an array to store these items, with each stack element occupying one position in the array and position 1 serving as the top of the stack. For example, in the base-two conversion problem of the preceding section, if the first three remainders 0, 1, and 0 have already been pushed onto the stack, the stack might be pictured as follows:

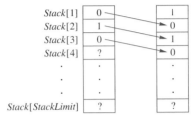

Pushing the next remainder 1 onto the stack requires shifting the elements in array positions 1, 2, and 3 to positions 2, 3, and 4, respectively, so that 1 can be stored in the first position:

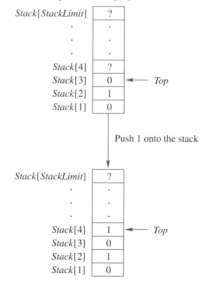

Similarly, when an item is popped from the stack, the array elements must all be shifted up by one, so that the top item is in position 1.

The shifting of array elements in this implementation is time-consuming, but it can easily be avoided. Rather than thinking of a spring-loaded stack of plates, we think of a stack of books on a table. We can add and remove books at the top of this stack without ever moving any of the other books in the stack! For a spring-loaded stack of plates, the top of the stack is fixed, and so the bottom plate (and therefore all of the other plates) move when we add or remove a plate at the top of the stack. For a stack of books, however, only the top moves when we add or remove a book; the bottom of the stack stays fixed (as do all of the other books). To model this view of a stack, we need only "flip the array over," fixing position 1 at the bottom of the stack, and let the stack grow toward position *StackLimit,* using a variable *Top* to keep track of the top of the stack, and then push and pop at this location:

In this implementation, the storage structure for a stack consists of an array that stores the stack elements and a variable *Top* that stores the position of the top element in the stack. This structure suggests using a record as the storage structure:

const
    StackLimit = . . .; (∗ maximum size of the stack ∗)

type
    StackElementType = . . .; (∗ type of elements in the stack ∗)
    StackArray = **array**[1..*StackLimit*] **of** *StackElementType*;
    StackType = **record**
                    Top : 0..*StackLimit*;
                    Element : *StackArray*
        end;

To complete this implementation of a stack, procedures or functions must be written to perform the basic stack operations. The operation of creating an empty stack consists simply of setting *Stack.Top* to 0, and a stack will be empty when the boolean expression *Stack.Top* = 0 is true.

An algorithm for the pop operation is

Pop

(∗ Algorithm to pop *Item* from the top of *Stack*. ∗)

1. Check if the stack is empty.
2. If it is not empty then
    a. Set *Item* equal to the element *Stack.Element*[*Stack.Top*] at the top of the stack.
    b. Decrement *Stack.Top* by 1.
  Otherwise
  Signal that an error (stack empty) has occurred.

And an algorithm for the push operation is

Push

(∗ Algorithm to push *Item* onto the *Stack*. ∗)

1. Check if the stack is full by checking if *Stack.Top* is equal to the array limit.
2. If it is not then
    a. Increment *Stack.Top* by 1.
    b. Set the element *Stack.Element*[*Stack.Top*] equal to *Item*.
  Otherwise
  Signal that an error (stack full) has occurred.

It is important to note that the possibility of a stack-empty condition is inherent in the definition of a stack and does not arise because of the way the stack is implemented. However, a stack-full condition is not inherent in this data structure, as there is theoretically no limit on the number of elements that a stack may have. Any implementation of a stack that uses an array to store the stack elements will thus not be a completely faithful representation because an array has a fixed size, which places an upper limit on the size of the stack. This implementation requires, therefore, that the push algorithm include a check to determine if the stack is full before we attempt to push an element onto it. In Chapter 8 we consider an alternative implementation using linked lists which does not impose an a priori size limit and that thus implements stacks more faithfully.

Since stacks are useful in solving many different problems, it would be convenient to have a stack data type. In some programming languages (such as Modula-2 and Ada) and in some versions of Pascal (such as Turbo), one can, in effect, extend the language to include this abstract data type by designing a *module* or *unit* that encapsulates the declarations needed to define this type and the procedures and functions to implement its basic operations and relations. The ADT stack can then be used in a program simply by importing the necessary items from this module or unit. It can be used *abstractly*, that is, independently of its implementation details, which remain hidden in this module or unit.

Although standard Pascal does not provide such modules and units (as yet), it is nevertheless convenient to have available the following package of declarations for defining a stack data type and procedures and functions that implement these basic stack operations:

(* **Package for the ADT Stack** *)

const
   StackLimit = . . .; (* limit on stack size *)

type
   StackElementType = . . .; (* type of stack elements *)
   StackArray = **array**[1..*StackLimit*] **of** *StackElementType*;
   StackType = **record**
                     Top : 0..*StackLimit*;
                     Element : *StackArray*
                  end;

var
   StackError : *boolean*; (* signals if an error occurred while attempting
                        to carry out some stack operation. *)

procedure *CreateStack* (**var** *Stack* : *StackType*);

   (* Function: Creates an empty stack.
      Returns: Empty *Stack*. *)

   begin (* *CreateStack* *)
      Stack.Top := 0;
      StackError := *false*
   end (* *CreateStack* *);

```
function EmptyStack(Stack : StackType) : boolean;

    (* Accepts:   Stack.
       Function:  Checks if Stack is empty.
       Returns:   True if Stack is empty, false otherwise *)

    begin (* EmptyStack *)
        EmptyStack := (Stack.Top = 0);
        StackError := false
    end (* EmptyStack *);

procedure Pop (var Stack : StackType; var Item : StackElementType);

    (* Accepts:   Stack.
       Function:  Pops Item from the top of Stack or sets StackError
                  to true if Stack is empty.
       Returns:   Item and modified Stack
       Output:    "Stack-empty" message if Stack is empty. *)

    begin (* Pop *)
        StackError := EmptyStack(Stack);
        if not StackError then
            with Stack do
                begin
                    Item := Element[Top];
                    Top := Top - 1
                end (* with *)
        else
            writeln ('*** Attempt to pop from an empty stack ***')
    end (* Pop *);

procedure Push (var Stack : StackType; Item : StackElementType);

    (* Accepts:   Stack and Item.
       Function:  Pushes Item onto Stack or sets StackError to true
                  if Stack is full.
       Returns:   Modified Stack.
       Output:    "Stack-full" message if Stack is full *)

    begin (* Push *)
        StackError := (Stack.Top = StackLimit);
        if not StackError then
            with Stack do
                begin
                    Top := Top + 1;
                    Element[Top] := Item
                end (* with *)
        else
            writeln ('*** Attempt to push onto a full stack ***')
    end (* Push *);
```

Before this new ADT can be used in applications, it must be thoroughly tested. This can be done with ***bottom-up testing*** using a *command-driven ADT tester* that allows the user to perform each of the basic operations individually and to observe its effect. A command-driven tester for the ADT stack should therefore allow the user to perform each of the basic operations *CreateStack, EmptyStack, Push,* and *Pop*. To observe the effects of these operations it is helpful to add a procedure to display the contents of the stack. Figure 4.1 shows such an ADT tester. It uses the special compiler directive #include to copy files containing the declarations and definitions from the stack package into the program at compile time. In this example, the file 'STACK-CONST' contains the definition of the constant *StackLimit* = 3, and the directive #include 'STACK-CONST' inserts this definition into the constant section at compile time. The directive #include 'STACK-TYPE' copies the definitions of the types *StackArray* and *StackType* from the file 'STACK-TYPE' into the type section, and #include 'STACK-VAR' inserts the declaration of the variable *StackError* into the variable section. The directive #include 'STACK-OPS' copies the definitions of procedures *CreateStack, Pop,* and *Push* and the function *EmptyStack* from file 'STACK-OPS' into the subprogram section.

```
PROGRAM TestStack (input, output);

(********************************************************************

   Input (keyboard):  Commands entered by the user.
   Function:          Program to test the package for the ADT stack.
   Output (screen):   List of commands and messages describing the
                      effects of each command.

   Note:              Certain constant, type, variable, function and
                      procedure declarations from the stack ADT
                      package must be inserted into the declaration
                      part.  The compiler directive #include inserts
                      these items from the four files STACK-CONST,
                      STACK-TYPE, STACK-VAR, and STACK-OPS.

********************************************************************)
CONST
#include 'STACK-CONST'

TYPE
   StackElementType = integer;
#include 'STACK-TYPE'    (* StackArray, StackType *)

VAR
#include 'STACK-VAR'     (* StackError *)
   S : StackType;        (* Stack of integers *)
   Com1, Com2 : char;    (* First 2 characters of command *)

#include 'STACK-OPS'     (* CreateStack, EmptyStack, Push, Pop *)
```

Figure 4.1

Figure 4.1 (cont.)

```
PROCEDURE ShowCommands;

   (*****************************************************************

      Function:        List the available commands.
      Output (screen): List of commands.

   *****************************************************************)

   BEGIN (* Show Commands *)
      writeln ('Use the following commands to test the ADT stack.');
      writeln ('C ---- create an stack');
      writeln ('D ---- dump the stack, top to bottom');
      writeln ('E ---- test whether a stack is empty');
      writeln ('F ---- check if operation failed -- show StackError');
      writeln ('H ---- print this list of commands');
      writeln ('PO --- pop an element from the stack');
      writeln ('PU --- push an item onto the stack');
      writeln ('Q ---- quit testing');
      writeln
   END (* ShowCommands *);

FUNCTION UpCase(Ch : char) : char;

   (*****************************************************************

      Input (param):   Character Ch.
      Function:        Convert Ch to uppercase.
      Output (UpCase): Returns uppercase equivalent of Ch.
      Note:            Assumes ASCII representation.

   *****************************************************************)

   BEGIN
      IF Ch IN ['a'..'z'] THEN
         UpCase := chr(ord(Ch) - 32)
      ELSE
         UpCase := Ch
   END (* UpCase *);

PROCEDURE DoCreateStack (VAR S : StackType);

   (*****************************************************************

      Input:           None.
      Function:        Test the procedure CreateStack.
      Output (param):  Empty stack S.
      Output (screen): "Stack-created" message.

   *****************************************************************)

   BEGIN (* DoCreateStack *)
      CreateStack (S);
      writeln ('--> Stack created')
   END (* DoCreateStack *);
```

Figure 4.1 (cont.)

```
PROCEDURE DoEmptyStack (S : StackType);

    (********************************************************************

        Input (param):   Stack S.
        Function:        Test the function EmptyStack.
        Output (screen): Value of EmptyStack(S).

    ********************************************************************)

    BEGIN (* DoEmptyStack *)
        writeln ('--> StackEmpty? ', EmptyStack(S))
    END (* DoEmptyStack *);

PROCEDURE DoStackError;

    (********************************************************************

        Input:           None.
        Function:        Check the value of StackError.
        Output (screen): Value of StackError.

    ********************************************************************)

    BEGIN (* DoStackError *)
        writeln ('--> Value of StackError is ', StackError)
    END (* DoStackError *);

PROCEDURE DoPopStack (VAR S : StackType);

    (********************************************************************

        Input (param):   Stack S.
        Function:        Test the procedure Pop.
        Output (screen): Item popped from S, unless an error occurs.
        Output (param):  Modified stack S.

    ********************************************************************)

    VAR
        Item : StackElementType;    (* Element popped from stack *)

    BEGIN (* DoPopStack *)
        Pop (S, Item);
        IF NOT StackError THEN
            writeln ('--> Element popped: ', Item)
    END (* DoPopStack *);
```

Figure 4.1 (cont.)

```
PROCEDURE DoPushStack (VAR S : StackType);

    (*****************************************************************

        Input (param):    Stack S.
        Input (keyboard): Item entered by the user.
        Function:         Test the procedure Push.
        Output (screen):  Item, unless an error occurs.
        Output (param):   Modified stack S.

    *****************************************************************)

    VAR
        Item : StackElementType;    (* Item to push onto stack *)

    BEGIN (* DoPushStack *)
        write ('Item to push? ');
        read (Item);
        Push (S, Item);
        IF NOT StackError THEN
            writeln ('--> ', Item, ' pushed')
    END (* DoPushStack *);

PROCEDURE DumpStack (S : StackType);

    (*****************************************************************

        Input (param):    Stack S.
        Function:         Display stack contents.
        Output (screen): A listing of the elements in S.

    *****************************************************************)

    VAR
        Item : StackElementType;            (* A stack element *)

    BEGIN (* DumpStack *)
        writeln ('--> Stack contents:');
        WHILE NOT EmptyStack (S) DO
            BEGIN
                Pop (S, Item);
                writeln (Item)
            END (* WHILE *)
    END (* DumpStack *);
```

Figure 4.1 (cont.)

```
BEGIN
   ShowCommands;
   REPEAT
      write ('Command? ');
      read (Com1);
      Com1 := UpCase(Com1);
      IF Com1 IN ['C', 'D', 'E', 'F', 'H', 'P', 'Q'] THEN
         CASE Com1 OF
            'C' : DoCreateStack (S);
            'D' : DumpStack (S);
            'E' : DoEmptyStack (S);
            'F' : DoStackError;
            'H' : ShowCommands;
            'P' : BEGIN  (* Pop and Push *)
                     read (Com2);
                     Com2 := UpCase(Com2);
                     IF Com2 = 'O' THEN
                        DoPopStack (S)
                     ELSE IF Com2 = 'U' THEN
                        DoPushStack (S)
                     ELSE
                        writeln ('*** Illegal command: ', Com1, Com2)
                  END (* Pop & Push *);
            'Q' : writeln ('--> End of test')
         END (* CASE *)
      ELSE
         writeln ('*** Illegal command: ', Com1);
      readln
   UNTIL Com1 = 'Q'
END (* main program *).
```

Sample run:

```
Use the following commands to test the ADT stack.
C ---- create an stack
D ---- dump the stack, top to bottom
E ---- test whether a stack is empty
F ---- check if operation failed -- show StackError
H ---- print this list of commands
PO --- pop an element from the stack
PU --- push an item onto the stack
Q ---- quit testing

Command? C
--> Stack created
Command? E
--> StackEmpty? true
Command? PU
Item to push? 2
-->          2 pushed
```

Figure 4.1 (cont.)

```
Command? PO
--> Element popped:              2
Command? E
--> StackEmpty? true
Command? PU
Item to push? 1
-->            1 pushed
Command? E
--> StackEmpty? false
Command? PU
Item to push? 2
-->            2 pushed
Command? PU
Item to push? 3
-->            3 pushed
Command? PU
Item to push? 4
*** Attempt to push onto a full stack ***
Command? F
--> Value of StackError is true
Command? D
--> Stack contents:
          3
          2
          1
Command? PO
--> Element popped:              3
Command? PO
--> Element popped:              2
Command? PO
--> Element popped:              1
Command? PO
*** Attempt to pop from an empty stack ***
Command? F
--> Value of StackError is true
Command? E
--> StackEmpty? true
Command? Q

--> End of test
```

Once the stack package has been tested, the ADT stack can then be used as a new data type in programs, simply by including the definitions and declarations from the package. Figure 4.2 shows such a program, which uses the new stack data type to solve the base-ten to base-two conversion problem described in the preceding section.

```
PROGRAM BaseTenToBaseTwo (input, output);

(*******************************************************************

   Input (keyboard): A positive integer in base-ten notation and a
                     user response.
   Function:         Calculates the base-two representation of a
                     positive integer.
   Output (screen):  Base-two representation of input integer.

   Note:             Certain constant, type, variable, function and
                     procedure declarations from the stack ADT
                     package must be inserted into the declaration
                     part.  The compiler directive #include inserts
                     these items from the four files STACK-CONST,
                     STACK-TYPE, STACK-VAR, and STACK-OPS.

*******************************************************************)

CONST
#include 'STACK-CONST'             (* StackLimit *)

TYPE
   StackElementType = integer;
#include 'STACK-TYPE'              (* StackArray, StackType *)
                                ,
VAR
#include 'STACK-VAR'               (* StackError *)
   Number,                         (* the number to be converted *)
   Remainder : integer;            (* remainder when Number is divided by 2 *)
   StackOfRemainders : StackType;  (* stack of remainders *)
   Response : char;                (* user response *)

#include 'STACK-OPS'               (* CreateStack, EmptyStack, Push, Pop *)

BEGIN (* main program *)
   REPEAT
      write ('Enter positive integer to convert:  ');
      readln (Number);
      CreateStack (StackOfRemainders);
      WHILE Number <> 0 DO
         BEGIN
            Remainder := Number MOD 2;
            Push (StackOfRemainders, Remainder);
            Number := Number DIV 2
         END (* WHILE *);
         write ('Base-two representation:  ');
      WHILE NOT EmptyStack(StackOfRemainders) DO
         BEGIN
            Pop (StackOfRemainders, Remainder);
            write (Remainder:1)
         END (* WHILE *);
      writeln; writeln;
      write ('More (Y or N)?  ');
      readln (Response)
   UNTIL NOT (Response IN ['Y', 'y'])
END (* main program *).
```

Figure 4.2

Figure 4.2 (cont.)

Sample run:

```
Enter positive integer to convert:  2
Base-two representation:  10

More (Y or N)?  Y
Enter positive integer to convert:  127
Base-two representation:  1111111

More (Y or N)?  Y
Enter positive integer to convert:  128
Base-two representation:  10000000

More (Y or N)?  N
```

4.3   Implementing ADTs in Turbo Pascal with Units; *StackADT*

As noted in the preceding section, some languages such as Modula-2, Ada, and Turbo Pascal provide modules or units that can be used to implement abstract data types. In this section we illustrate the use of units in Turbo Pascal by developing a unit *StackADT* to implement the ADT stack described in the preceding sections. In Chapter 14 another implementation of the ADT stack is given that uses *objects*, which are the basic building blocks of the programming paradigm known as *Object-Oriented Programming* (*OOP*).

In Turbo Pascal we can combine all of the constant, type, and variable definitions and declarations and the stack-processing procedures and function from the stacks package of the preceding section into a single *unit*:

(∗ **Unit for the ADT Stack** ∗)

unit *StackADT*;

    (∗ Function: Defines the ADT stack using the array-based implementation of stacks.

        Exports: The type *StackType* for stacks whose elements are of type *StackElementType*; procedures *CreateStack*, *Pop*, and *Push* and boolean-valued function *EmptyStack*, which implement the basic stack operations; variable *StackError*, is assigned the value true if an error occurs while attempting to carry out push or pop. ∗)

interface

   const
     StackLimit = . . .; (∗ limit on stack size ∗)

type
  StackElementType = . . .; (∗ type of stack elements ∗)
  StackArray = **array**[1..*StackLimit*] **of** *StackElementType*;
  StackType = **record**
          Top : 0..*StackLimit*;
          Element : *StackArray*
      end;

var
  StackError : *boolean*; (∗ signals if an error occurred while
                 attempting to carry out some stack
                 operation ∗)

procedure *CreateStack* (**var** *Stack* : *StackType*);

  (∗ Function: Creates an empty stack.
      Returns: Empty *Stack.* ∗)

function *EmptyStack*(*Stack* : *StackType*) : *boolean*;

  (∗ Accepts: *Stack.*
      Function: Checks if *Stack* is empty.
      Returns: True if *Stack* is empty, false otherwise ∗)

procedure *Pop* (**var** *Stack* : *StackType*;
               var *Item* : *StackElementType*);

  (∗ Accepts: *Stack.*
      Function: Pops *Item* from the top of *Stack* or sets *StackError*
                to true if *Stack* is empty.
      Returns: *Item* and modified *Stack.*
      Output: ''Stack-empty'' message if *Stack* is empty. ∗)

procedure *Push* (**var** *Stack* : *StackType*; *Item* : *StackElementType*);

  (∗ Accepts: *Stack* and *Item.*
      Function: Pushes *Item* onto *Stack* or sets *StackError*
                to true if *Stack* is full.
      Returns: Modified *Stack.*
      Output: ''Stack-full'' message if *Stack* is full. ∗)

implementation

procedure *CreateStack* (**var** *Stack* : *StackType*);

  (∗ Procedure to create an empty stack ∗)

  begin (∗ *CreateStack* ∗)
    Stack.Top := 0;
    StackError := *false*
  end (∗ *CreateStack* ∗);

function *EmptyStack* (*Stack* : *StackType*) : *boolean*;

  (∗ Returns true if *Stack* is empty, false otherwise ∗)

```
    begin (* EmptyStack *)
      EmptyStack := (Stack.Top = 0);
      StackError := false
    end (* EmptyStack *);

  procedure Pop (var Stack : StackType;
                     var Item : StackElementType);

    (* Procedure to pop Item from the top of Stack, assuming that the
       stack is nonempty *)

    begin (* Pop *)
      StackError := EmptyStack(Stack);
      if not StackError then
        with Stack do
          begin
            Item := Element[Top];
            Top := Top - 1
          end (* with *)
      else
        writeln ('*** Attempt to pop from an empty stack ***')
    end (* Pop *);

  procedure Push (var Stack : StackType; Item : StackElementType);

    (* Procedure to push Item onto Stack, assuming
       that the stack is not full *)

    begin (* Push *)
      StackError := (Stack.Top = StackLimit);
      if not StackError then
        with Stack do
          begin
            Top := Top + 1;
            Element [Top] := Item
          end (* with *)
      else
        writeln ('*** Attempt to push onto a full stack ***')
    end (* Push *);

  end (* StackADT *).
```

Here the **unit heading**

  unit *StackADT*;

names the unit. (The name of the actual disk file in which a unit is stored must consist of the first eight characters of the unit name followed by the extension .PAS; for this unit, therefore, the disk file would be named STACKADT.PAS. This file must also be compiled to create the object file STACKADT.TPU.)

The **interface part** of a unit begins with the reserved word **interface** and may contain a uses clause (described later) to import items from other units and a declaration part. The constant, type, and variable (and label) sections have the usual forms, but subprogram sections contain only headings of the procedures and functions defined in the unit.

The *implementation part* of a unit consists of the reserved word **implementation** followed by an optional uses clause, a declaration part, and an initialization part. However, the items imported into or defined in this implementation part are local to it and are *not* available to programs or other units. The subprogram sections in the declaration part contain the complete procedure and function definitions for the procedures and functions given in the interface part. The *initialization part* may be trivial, consisting simply of the reserved word **end**, as in this example, or it may have the same form as the statement part of a program. In the second case, the statements in this initialization part are executed before those in any program or other unit in which this unit is used.

After a unit has been compiled, the constants, types, procedures, and function defined in its interface part can then be imported into and used in any program by simply inserting a *uses clause* after the program heading, as shown in the program in Figure 4.3. This program is the Turbo Pascal equivalent of that in Figure 4.2 for the base-ten to base-two conversion problem described in Section 4.1.

```
PROGRAM BaseTenToBaseTwo (input, output);

(**********************************************************************

   Input (keyboard):  A positive integer in base-ten notation and a user
                      response.
   Function:          Calculates the base-two representation of a
                      positive integer.
   Output (screen):   Base-two representation of input integer.

   Note:              Imports the type identifier StackType, the
                      variable StackError, and function EmptyStack,
                      and procedures CreateStack, Push, and Pop from
                      the unit StackADT .

**********************************************************************)

USES StackADT

VAR
   Number,                       (* the number to be converted *)
   Remainder : integer;          (* remainder when Number is divided by 2 *)
   StackOfRemainders : StackType; (* stack of remainders *)
   Response : char;              (* user response *)
```

Figure 4.3

Figure 4.3 (cont.)

```
BEGIN (* main program *)
   REPEAT
      write ('Enter positive integer to convert:  ');
      readln (Number);
      CreateStack (StackOfRemainders);
      WHILE Number <> 0 DO
         BEGIN
            Remainder := Number MOD 2;
            Push (StackOfRemainders, Remainder);
            Number := Number DIV 2
         END (* WHILE *);
         write ('Base-two representation:  ');
      WHILE NOT EmptyStack(StackOfRemainders) DO
         BEGIN
            Pop (StackOfRemainders, Remainder);
            write (Remainder:1)
         END (* WHILE *);
      writeln; writeln;
      write ('More (Y or N)?  ');
      readln (Response)
   UNTIL NOT (Response IN ['Y', 'y'])
END (* main program *).
```

Sample run:

```
Enter positive integer to convert:  2
Base-two representation:  10

More (Y or N)?  Y
Enter positive integer to convert:  127
Base-two representation:  1111111

More (Y or N)?  Y
Enter positive integer to convert:  128
Base-two representation:  10000000

More (Y or N)?  N
```

As this example demonstrates, units in Turbo Pascal (and modules in Modula-2 and packages in Ada) provide a better method of encapsulating an ADT than does the approach described in the preceding section for standard Pascal. Not only is it much easier and "cleaner" to import items into a program and use them, but better data abstraction is provided by separating a unit into an interface part and an implementation part. Because all the information that one needs to know to use the ADT defined in a unit is given in the interface part, the implementation details can be "hidden" in the implementation part. (In Modula-2, this implementation part is in a completely separate module whose contents need never be published.) *Such **information hiding** makes it possible to use the unit without being concerned about these implementation details.* For example, one can use the unit *StackADT* without being concerned with the details of the actual storage structure or with the actual procedures and functions used to implement the basic operations. *Information hiding also encourages correct usage of an ADT.* For example, if it is not known that an array is used to store the stack elements, users of this unit will not attempt to access the bottom of the stack by examining the element in the first position of the array.

Another benefit of using units (and modules in Modula-2 and packages in Ada) to define ADTs is that they can be compiled independently. *Separate or independent compilation makes it possible to change the implementation part and recompile only the unit; programs that use the unit need not be changed or recompiled.* For example, if procedures *Pop* and *Push* in the implementation part of the unit *StackADT* (but not their headings in the interface part) were changed, then only the unit itself would require recompilation. However, if the interface part of a unit or the definition part of a module is changed, then the unit or module and all programs that use it must be recompiled.

In addition to facilitating the task of defining new ADTs and making them available to programs whenever needed, *units (modules and packages) also introduce another level of modularity into software design.* Subprograms that perform related tasks in a system can be grouped together into independent units, which is especially useful in large programming projects. Separate units can be developed and tested independently, perhaps by different programmers or teams of programmers, and then integrated into the total system. The interface parts of these units provide a well-defined interface between them, their developers, and their users.

Exercises

1. Assume that S is of type *StackType* as implemented in Section 4.2, *StackElementType* is *integer*, *StackLimit* is 5, and I, J, and K are integer variables. Give the value of *S.Top* and the contents of *S.Element* after each of the following independent code segments, or indicate why an error occurs:

   (a) *CreateStack* (S);
   Push (S, 10);
   Push (S, 22);
   Push (S, 37);
   Pop (S, J);
   Pop (S, K);
   Push (S, J + K);

   (b) *CreateStack* (S);
   Push (S, 10);
   Push (S, 9);
   Push (S, 8);
   while not *EmptyStack*(S) **do**
      Pop (S, K);

   (c) *CreateStack* (S);
   for $I := 1$ **to** 6 **do**
      Push (S, 10 ∗ I);

   (d) *Push* (S, 1);
   Push (S, 2);
   Pop (S, J);

2. Although a stack cannot, in theory, become full, the array-based implementation of stacks used in this chapter requires that an upper limit *StackLimit* be placed on the maximum size that a stack may have. Write a boolean function *FullStack* that has a stack as a parameter

and returns true or false according to whether or not the array used to store the stack elements is full.

3. Write a procedure *GetTopElement* that returns the top element of its *StackType* parameter but that does not delete it from the stack. If *GetTopElement* is called for an empty stack, an appropriate error message should be displayed.

   (a) Write *GetTopElement* at the application level. That is, you may use only *Push, Pop, CreateStack,* and *EmptyStack* to access the top element, if there is one.

   (b) Write *GetTopElement* at the implementation level. That is, you may directly access the storage structure in order to access the top element.

4. Proceed as in Exercise 3 but design a procedure *GetBottomElement* to retrieve the bottom stack element, leaving the stack empty.

5. Proceed as in Exercise 4, but leave the stack contents unchanged.

6. Proceed as in Exercise 3, but design a procedure *GetNthElement* to retrieve the nth stack element, leaving the stack without its top n elements.

7. Proceed as in Exercise 6, but leave the stack contents unchanged.

8. Consider the following railroad switching network:

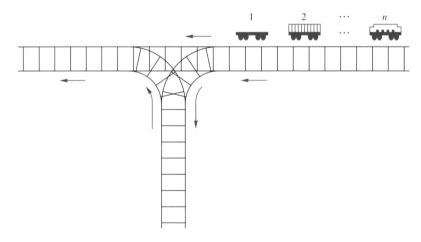

   Railroad cars numbered 1, 2, ... , n on the right track are to be permuted and moved along on the left track. As described in Problem 4 of Section 4.1, a car may be moved directly onto the left track, or it may be shunted onto the siding to be removed at a later time and placed on the left track. The siding thus operates like a stack, a push operation moving a car from the right track onto the siding and a pop operation moving the "top" car from the siding onto the left track.

(a) For $n = 3$, find all possible permutations of cars that can be obtained (on the left track) by a sequence of these operations. For example, push 1, push 2, move 3, pop 2, pop 1 arranges them in the order 3, 2, 1. Are any permutations not possible?

(b) Find all possible permutations for $n = 4$. What permutations (if any) are not possible?

(c) Repeat (b) for $n = 5$.

(d) *Challenge*: In general, what permutations of the sequence 1, 2, ..., n can be obtained when a stack is used in this manner?

9. Suppose that some application requires using two stacks whose elements are of the same type. A natural implementation of such a two-stack data structure would be to use two arrays and two top pointers. Explain why this may not be a spacewise efficient implementation.

10. A better implementation of a two-stack data structure than that described in Exercise 9 is to use a single array for the storage structure and let the stacks grow toward each other:

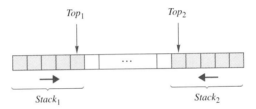

Write appropriate declarations for this implementation, and write procedures/functions for the basic stack operations in which the number of the stack to be processed, 1 or 2, is passed as a parameter. The subprogram implementing the push operation should not fail because of a stack-full condition until *all* locations in the storage array have been used.

11. Storing more than two stacks in a single one-dimensional array in such a way that no stack-full condition occurs for any of the stacks until all the array elements have been used cannot be done as efficiently as in Exercise 10 because some of the array elements will have to be shifted. Nevertheless, design such an implementation for n stacks, $n > 2$. Write the appropriate declarations and write procedures/functions for the basic stack operations in which the stack number is passed as a parameter. (*Hint:* You might partition the storage array into n equal subarrays, one for each stack, and use two arrays of "pointers," *Bottom* and *Top*, to keep track of where the bottoms and the tops of the stacks are located in the storage array. When one of these stacks becomes full, search to find the nearest empty location(s) in the array, and then move stacks as necessary to enlarge the storage space for this stack.)

12. Empirical evidence suggests that any program that comes close to using all available space will eventually run out of space. Conse-

quently, shifting stacks around in an array as described in Exercise 11 so that all possible array locations are used seems rather futile. Redesign the implementation so that no push operations are attempted if there are fewer than *LowerLimit* unused locations left in the array.

13. Use the ADT stack in a program that solves Problem 1 in Section 4.1. It should read a string, one character at a time, and determine whether the string contains balanced parentheses, that is, for each left parenthesis (if there are any) there is exactly one matching right parenthesis later in the string.

14. For a given integer $n > 1$, the smallest integer $d > 1$ that divides n is a prime factor. We can find the prime factorization of n if we find d and then replace n by the quotient of n divided by d, repeating this until n becomes 1. Write a program that determines the prime factorization of n in this manner but that displays the prime factors in descending order. For example, for $n = 3960$, your program should produce

$$11 * 5 * 3 * 3 * 2 * 2 * 2$$

15. A program is to be written to find a path from one point in a maze to another.

    (a) Describe how a two-dimensional array could be used to model the maze.
    (b) Describe how a stack could be used in an algorithm for finding a path.
    (c) Write the program.

4.4 Application of Stacks: Reverse Polish Notation

The task of a compiler is to generate the machine instructions required to carry out the instructions of the source program written in a high-level language. One part of this task is to generate machine instructions for evaluating arithmetic expressions like that in the assignment statement

$$X := A * B + C$$

The compiler must generate machine instructions like the following:

1. LOA *A*:   Retrieve the value of *A* from the memory location where it is stored and load it into the accumulator register.
2. MUL *B*:   Retrieve the value of *B* and multiply the value in the accumulator register by it.
3. ADD *C*:   Retrieve the value of *C* and add it to the value in the accumulator register.
4. STO *X*:   Store the value in the accumulator register in the memory location associated with *X*.

In most programing languages, arithmetic expressions are written in **infix** notation like $A * B + C$, in which the symbol for each binary operation is placed between the operands. Many compilers first transform these infix expressions into **postfix** notation (or prefix notation described in the exercises), in which the operator follows the operands, and then generates machine instructions to evaluate postfix expressions. This two-step process is used because the transformation from infix to postfix is straightforward, and postfix expressions are, in general, easier to evaluate mechanically than are infix expressions.

When infix notation is used for arithmetic expressions, parentheses are often needed to indicate the order in which operations are to be carried out. For example, parentheses are placed in the expression $2 * (3 + 4)$ to indicate that the addition is to be performed before the multiplication. If the parentheses were omitted, giving $2 * 3 + 4$, the standard priority rules would dictate that the multiplication is to be performed before the addition.

In the early 1950s, the Polish logician Jan Lukasiewicz observed that parentheses are not necessary in postfix notation, also called **Reverse Polish Notation (RPN)**. For example, the infix expression $2 * (3 + 4)$ can be written in RPN as

$$2\ 3\ 4\ +\ *$$

As an illustration of how RPN expressions are evaluated, consider the expression

$$1\ 5\ +\ 8\ 4\ 1\ -\ -\ *$$

which corresponds to the infix expression $(1 + 5) * (8 - (4 - 1))$. This expression is scanned from left to right until an operator is found. At that point, the last two preceding operands are combined using this operator. For our example, the first operator encountered is $+$, and its operands are 1 and 5, as indicated by the underline in the following:

$$\underline{1\ 5\ +}\ 8\ 4\ 1\ -\ -\ *$$

Replacing this subexpression with its value 6 yields the reduced RPN expression

$$6\ 8\ 4\ 1\ -\ -\ *$$

Resuming the left-to-right scan, we next encounter the operator $-$ and determine its two operands:

$$6\ 8\ \underline{4\ 1\ -}\ -\ *$$

Applying this operator then yields

$$6\ 8\ 3\ -\ *$$

The next operator encountered is another $-$, and its operands are 8 and 3:

$$6\ \underline{8\ 3\ -}\ *$$

Evaluating this difference gives

$$6\ 5\ *$$

The final operator is *

$$6\ 5\ *$$

and the value 30 is obtained for this expression.

This method of evaluating an RPN expression requires that the operands be stored until an operator is encountered in the left-to-right scan. At this point, the last two operands must be retrieved and combined using this operation. This suggests that a last-in-first-out structure—that is, a stack—should be used to store the operands. Each time an operand is encountered, it is pushed onto the stack. Then, when an operator is encountered, the top two values are popped from the stack; the operation is applied to them; and the result is pushed back onto the stack. The following algorithm summarizes this procedure:

ALGORITHM TO EVALUATE RPN EXPRESSIONS

(* Accepts: An RPN expression.
   Function: Evaluate the expression.
   Output: The value of the RPN expression.
   Note: Uses a stack to store operands. *)

1. Initialize an empty stack.
2. Repeat the following until the end of the expression is encountered:
   a. Get the next token (constant, variable, arithmetic operator) in the RPN expression.
   b. If the token is an operand, push it onto the stack. If it is an operator, then do the following:
      (i) Pop the top two values from the stack. (If the stack does not contain two items, an error due to a malformed RPN expression has occurred, and evaluation is terminated.)
      (ii) Apply the operation to these two values.
      (iii) Push the resulting value back onto the stack.
3. When the end of the expression is encountered, its value is on top of the stack (and, in fact, must be the only value in the stack).

Figure 4.4 illustrates the application of this algorithm to the RPN expression

$$2\ 4\ *\ 9\ 5\ +\ -$$

The up arrow (↑) indicates the current token.

As an illustration of how a stack is also used in the conversion from infix to RPN, consider the infix expression

$$7\ +\ 2\ *\ 3$$

In a left-to-right scan of this expression, 7 is encountered and may be immediately displayed. Next, the operator + is encountered, but as its right operand has not yet been displayed, it must be stored and thus is pushed onto a stack of operators:

Output　　Stack

7　　　| + |

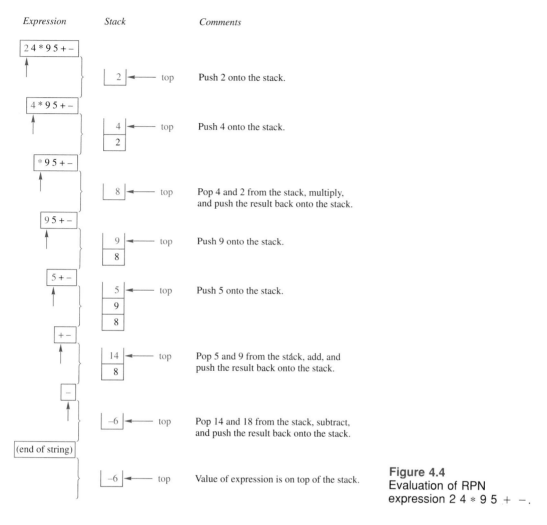

Figure 4.4
Evaluation of RPN
expression 2 4 * 9 5 + −.

Next, the operand 2 is encountered and displayed. At this point, it must be determined whether 2 is the right operand for the preceding operator + or is the left operand for the next operator. We determine this by comparing the operator + on the top of the stack with the next operator *. Since * has higher priority than +, the preceding operand 2 that was displayed is the left operand for *; thus we push * onto the stack and search for its right operand:

Output   Stack

7 2

The operand 3 is encountered next and displayed. Since the end of the expression has now been reached, the right operand for the operator * on the top of the stack has been found, and so * can now be popped and displayed:

Output   Stack

7 2 3 * | + |

The end of the expression also signals that the right operand for the remaining operator + in the stack has been found, and so it too can be popped and displayed, yielding the RPN expression

$$7 \ 2 \ 3 * +$$

Parentheses within infix expressions present no real difficulties. A left parenthesis indicates the beginning of a subexpression, and when encountered, it is pushed onto the stack. When a right parenthesis is encountered, operators are popped from the stack until the matching left parenthesis rises to the top. At this point, the subexpression originally enclosed by the parentheses has been converted to RPN, so the parentheses may be discarded and the conversion continues. All of this is contained in the following algorithm:

ALGORITHM TO CONVERT AN INFIX EXPRESSION TO RPN

(* Accepts: An infix expression.
     Function: Convert the expression to RPN.
     Output: The RPN expression.
     Note: Uses a stack to store operators. *)

1. Initialize an empty stack of operators.
2. While no error has occurred and the end of the infix expression has not been reached, do the following:
   a. Get the next input *Token* (constant, variable, arithmetic operator, left parenthesis, right parenthesis) in the infix expression.
   b. If *Token* is

   (i) a left parenthesis: Push it onto the stack.

   (ii) a right parenthesis: Pop and display stack elements until a left parenthesis is popped, but do not display it. (It is an error if the stack becomes empty with no left parenthesis found.)

   (iii) an operator: If the stack is empty or *Token* has a higher priority than the top stack element, push *Token* onto the stack. Otherwise, pop and display the top stack element; then repeat the comparison of *Token* with the new top stack item.

   Note: A left parenthesis in the stack is assumed to have a lower priority than that of operators.

   (iv) an operand: Display it.

3. When the end of the infix expression is reached, pop and display stack items until the stack is empty.

Figure 4.5 illustrates this algorithm for the infix expression

$$7 * 8 - (2 + 3)$$

An up arrow (↑) has been used to indicate the current input symbol and the symbol displayed by the algorithm.

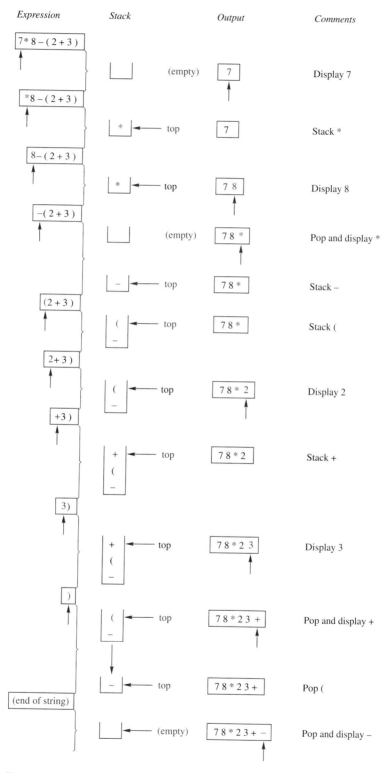

Figure 4.5 Converting infix expression 7 ∗ 8 − (2 + 3) to RPN.

The program in Figure 4.6 implements this algorithm for converting an infix expression to RPN using the ADT stack, as described in Section 4.2. It uses the procedures *CreateStack*, *Pop*, and *Push* and the function *EmptyStack* to maintain the stack of operators. It assumes that the input is a valid infix expression and does very little checking that it is well formed. The problem of checking the syntax of an infix expression is considered in the parsing example of Section 6.2.

```
PROGRAM InfixToRPN (input, output);

(**********************************************************************

   Input (keyboard): An infix expression and user responses.
   Function:         Converts the infix expression to Reverse Polish
                     Notation.
   Output (screen):  The RPN expression.

   Note:             Certain constant, type, variable, function and
                     procedure declarations from the stack ADT
                     package must be inserted into the declaration
                     part.  The compiler directive #include inserts
                     these items from the four files STACK-CONST,
                     STACK-TYPE, STACK-VAR, and STACK-OPS.

   **********************************************************************)

(* Insert USES ADTStack and remove #include directives for Turbo Pascal *)

CONST
#include 'STACK-CONST'            (* StackLimit *)
   MaxExpression = 80;           (* limit on expression length *)
   EndMark = ';';               (* marks end of infix expression *)

TYPE
   StackElementType = char;
#include 'STACK-TYPE'             (* StackArray, StackType *)
   Expression = PACKED ARRAY[1..MaxExpression] OF char;
   CharacterSet = SET OF char;

VAR
#include 'STACK-VAR'              (* StackError *)
   Exp : Expression;            (* infix expression *)
   OperatorSet : CharacterSet;  (* set of operators *)
   i : integer;                 (* index *)
   Response : char;             (* user response *)

#include 'STACK-OPS'             (* CreateStack, EmptyStack, Push, Pop *)
```

Figure 4.6

Figure 4.6 (cont.)

```
PROCEDURE ConvertToRPN (Exp : Expression; OperatorSet : CharacterSet);

    (*************************************************************

        Input (param):    Infix expression Exp and the set OperatorSet
                          of operators.
        Function:         Convert Exp to RPN.
        Output (screen):  RPN Expression and/or error messages.
        Note:             Uses procedures Priority, ProcessRightParen,
                          ProcessOperator, and stack-processing
                          functions and procedures.

    *************************************************************)


    VAR
        OpStack : StackType;     (* stack of operators *)
        i : integer;            (* index *)
        Token : char;           (* a character in the expression *)
        Error : boolean;        (* signals error in expression *)

    FUNCTION Priority (Operator : char) : integer;

        (*************************************************************

            Input (param):    The character Operator
            Function:         Find the priority of Operator, an
                              arithmetic operator or (.
            Output (Priority): Returns priority (0 - 2) of Operator.

        *************************************************************)


        BEGIN  (* Priority *)
            CASE Operator OF
                '('       : Priority := 0;
                '+', '-' : Priority := 1;
                '*', '/' : Priority := 2
            END (* CASE *)
        END (* Priority *);
```

Figure 4.6 (cont.)

```
PROCEDURE ProcessRightParen (VAR OpStack : StackType;
                            VAR Error : boolean);

    (*********************************************************************

        Input (param):     The stack OpStack.
        Function:          Pop and display operators from OpStack until
                           a left parenthesis is on top of the stack;
                           it too is popped, but not displayed.
        Output (param):    Modified stack OpStack, and Error, which is
                           true if the stack becomes empty with no left
                           parenthesis being found.
        Output (screen):   Arithmetic operators popped from OpStack.
        Note:              Uses stack procedures EmptyStack and Pop.

    *********************************************************************)


    VAR
        TopToken : char;       (* token at top of stack *)

    BEGIN
        REPEAT
            Error := EmptyStack(OpStack);
            IF NOT Error THEN
                BEGIN
                    Pop (OpStack, TopToken);
                    IF TopToken <> '(' THEN
                        write (TopToken:2)
                END   (* IF *)
        UNTIL (TopToken = '(') OR Error
    END   (* ProcessRightParen *);

PROCEDURE ProcessOperator (Operator : char; VAR OpStack : StackType);

    (*********************************************************************

        Input (param):     A character denoting an arithmetic Operator,
                           and a stack OpStack of operators.
        Function:          Process an arithmetic operator. Operators are
                           popped from OpStack until the stack becomes
                           empty or an operator appears on the top of the
                           stack whose priority is less than or equal to
                           that of the Operator. Operator is then pushed
                           onto the stack.
        Output (param):    Modified stack OpStack.
        Output (screen):   Arithmetic operators popped from OpStack.
        Note:              Uses stack procedures EmptyStack, Pop, and
                           Push.

    *********************************************************************)


    VAR
        TopOperator : char;      (* operator on top of stack *)
        DonePopping : boolean;   (* signals when stack-popping is
                                    completed *)
```

Figure 4.6 (cont.)

```
      BEGIN
         DonePopping := false;
         REPEAT
            IF EmptyStack(OpStack) THEN
               DonePopping := true
            ELSE
               BEGIN
                  Pop (OpStack, TopOperator);
                  IF (Priority(Operator) <= Priority(TopOperator)) THEN
                     write (TopOperator : 2)
                  ELSE
                     BEGIN
                        Push (OpStack, TopOperator);
                        DonePopping := true
                     END  (* ELSE *)
               END  (* ELSE *)
         UNTIL DonePopping;
         Push (OpStack, Operator)
      END  (* ProcessOperator *);

   BEGIN (* ConvertToRPN *)

      (* Initialize an empty stack *)
      CreateStack (OpStack);
      Error := false;

      (* Begin the conversion to RPN *)
      i := 1;
      Token := Exp [1];

      WHILE (Token <> EndMark) AND NOT Error DO
         BEGIN
            IF Token IN ([' ', '(', ')'] + OperatorSet) THEN
               CASE Token OF
                     ' ' : (* skip blanks *)
                           (* do nothing *);

                     '(' : (* left parenthesis *)
                           Push (OpStack, Token);

                     ')' : (* right parenthesis *)
                           ProcessRightParen (OpStack, Error);

                  '+', '-',
                  '*', '/' : (* arithmetic operator *)
                           ProcessOperator (Token, Opstack)
               END  (* CASE *)

            ELSE            (* operand *)
                           write (Token : 2);

            (* Now get next Token and process it *)
            i := i + 1;
            Token := Exp[i]
         END  (* WHILE *);
```

Figure 4.6 (cont.)

```
        (* Pop and display operators on the stack *)
        WHILE NOT EmptyStack(OpStack) AND NOT Error DO
           BEGIN
               Pop (OpStack, Token);
               IF Token <> '(' THEN
                   write (Token:2)
               ELSE
                   Error := true
           END  (* WHILE *);
        IF Error THEN
           writeln (' <<< Error in infix expression >>>')
        ELSE
           writeln
     END  (* ConvertToRPN *);

BEGIN (* main program *)

   (* Initialize set of arithmetic operators *)
   OperatorSet := ['+', '-', '*', '/'];

   (* Read infix expression *)
   writeln ('NOTE:  Enter ', EndMark,
            ' at the end of each infix expression.');
   writeln;
   REPEAT
      write ('Infix Expression?  ');
      i := 0;
      REPEAT
         i := i + 1;
         read (Exp[i])
      UNTIL Exp[i] = EndMark;
      readln;
      write ('RPN Expression is ');

      ConvertToRPN (Exp, OperatorSet);

      writeln;
      write ('More (Y or N)?  ');
      readln (Response)
   UNTIL NOT (Response IN ['Y', 'y'])
END (* main program *).
```

Sample run:

```
NOTE:  Enter ; at the end of each infix expression.

Infix Expression?  A + B;
RPN Expression is  A B +

More (Y or N)?  Y
Infix Expression?  A - B - C;
RPN Expression is  A B - C -

More (Y or N)?  Y
Infix Expression?  A - (B - C);
RPN Expression is  A B C - -
```

Figure 4.6 (cont.)

```
More (Y or N)?  Y
Infix Expression?  ((A + 5)/B - 2)*C;
RPN Expression is  A 5 + B / 2 - C *

More (Y or N)?  Y
Infix Expression?  (A + B));
RPN Expression is  A B + <<< Error in infix expression >>>

More (Y or N)?  Y
Infix Expression?  ((A + B);
RPN Expression is  A B + <<< Error in infix expression >>>

More (Y or N)?  N
```

Exercises

1. Suppose that $A = 7.0$, $B = 4.0$, $C = 3.0$, and $D = -2.0$. Evaluate the following RPN expressions:

    (a) $A\ B\ +\ C\ /\ D\ *$
    (b) $A\ B\ C\ +\ /\ D\ *$
    (c) $A\ B\ C\ D\ +\ /\ *$
    (d) $A\ B\ +\ C\ +\ D\ +$
    (e) $A\ B\ +\ C\ D\ +\ +$
    (f) $A\ B\ C\ +\ +\ D\ +$
    (g) $A\ B\ C\ D\ +\ +\ +$
    (h) $A\ B\ -\ C\ -\ D\ -$
    (i) $A\ B\ -\ C\ D\ -\ -$
    (j) $A\ B\ C\ -\ -\ D\ -$
    (k) $A\ B\ C\ D\ -\ -\ -$

2. For each of the following RPN expressions trace the algorithm for evaluating RPN expressions by showing the contents of the stack immediately before each of the tokens marked with a caret is read. Also, give the value of the RPN expression.

    (a) 32 5 3 + / 5 *
                ^ ^
    (b) 2 17 − 5 / 3 *
                ^ ^
    (c) 19 7 15 5 − − −
                ^ ^ ^

3. Convert the following infix expressions to RPN:

    (a) $A * B + C - D$
    (b) $A + B / C + D$
    (c) $(A + B) / C + D$
    (d) $A + B / (C + D)$
    (e) $(A + B) / (C + D)$
    (f) $(A - B) * (C - (D + E))$
    (g) $(((A - B) - C) - D) - E$
    (h) $A - (B - (C - (D - E)))$

4. For each of the following infix expressions trace the algorithm for converting infix to RPN by showing both the stack and the accumulated output immediately before each of the tokens marked with a caret is read. Also, show the final RPN expression.

    (a) $A + B / C - D$
              ^ ^ ^
    (b) $(A + B) / C - D + E$
                ^   ^
    (c) $A + B / (C - D) - E$
                ^   ^ ^
    (d) $A + B / (C - D) * E$
                ^   ^ ^

   (e) $A + B / ((C - D) * E) - F$

5. Convert the following RPN expressions to infix notation:

   (a) $A\ B\ C\ +\ -\ D\ *$ **(b)** $A\ B\ +\ C\ D\ -\ *$
   (c) $A\ B\ C\ D\ +\ -\ *$ **(d)** $A\ B\ +\ C\ -\ D\ E\ *\ /$
   (e) $A\ B\ /\ C\ /\ D\ /$ **(f)** $A\ B\ /\ C\ D\ /\ /$
   (g) $A\ B\ C\ /\ D\ /\ /$ **(h)** $A\ B\ C\ D\ /\ /\ /$

6. The symbol $-$ cannot be used for the unary minus operation in prefix or postfix notation because ambiguous expressions result. For example, 5 3 $-$ $-$ can be interpreted as either $5 - (-3) = 8$ or $-(5 - 3) = -2$. Suppose instead that $\sim$ is used for unary minus.

   (a) Evaluate the following RPN expressions if $A = 7$, $B = 5$, and $C = 3$:

      (i) $A \sim B\ C\ +\ -$ (ii) $A\ B \sim C\ +\ -$
      (iii) $A\ B\ C \sim +\ -$ (iv) $A\ B\ C\ +\ \sim\ -$
      (v) $A\ B\ C\ +\ -\ \sim$ (vi) $A\ B\ C\ -\ -\ \sim\sim\sim$

   (b) Convert the following infix expressions to RPN:

      (i) $A * (B + \sim C)$ (ii) $\sim(A + B / (C - D))$
      (iii) $(\sim A) * (\sim B)$ (iv) $\sim(A - (\sim B * (C + \sim D)))$

7. Convert the following logical expressions to RPN:

   (a) A **and** B **or** C
   (b) A **and** $(B$ **or not** $C)$
   (c) **not** $(A$ **and** $B)$
   (d) $(A$ **or** $B)$ **and** $(C$ **or** $(D$ **and not** $E))$
   (e) $(A = B)$ **or** $(C = D)$
   (f) $((A < 3)$ **and** $(A > 9))$ **or not** $(A > 0)$
   (g) $((B * B - 4 * A * C) >= 0)$ **and** $((A > 0)$ **or** $(A < 0))$

8. An alternative to postfix notation is **prefix** notation, in which the symbol for each operation precedes the operands. For example, the infix expression $2 * 3 + 4$ would be written in prefix notation as $+ * 2\ 3\ 4$, and $2 * (3 + 4)$ would be written as $* 2 + 3\ 4$. Convert each of the infix expressions in Exercise 3 to prefix notation.

9. Suppose that $A = 7.0$, $B = 4.0$, $C = 3.0$, and $D = -2.0$. Evaluate the following prefix expressions (see Exercise 8):

   (a) $* A / + B\ C\ D$ **(b)** $* / + A\ B\ C\ D$
   (c) $- A - B - C\ D$ **(d)** $- - A\ B - C\ D$
   (e) $- A - - B\ C\ D$ **(f)** $- - - A\ B\ C\ D$
   (g) $+ A\ B * - C\ D$ **(h)** $+ + * A\ B - C\ D$

10. Convert the following prefix expressions to infix notation (see Exercise 8):

(a) $* + A\ B\ - C\ D$	**(b)** $+ * A\ B\ - C\ D$
(c) $- - A\ B\ - C\ D$	**(d)** $- - A\ - B\ C\ D$
(e) $- - - A\ B\ C\ D$	**(f)** $/ + * A\ B\ - C\ D\ E$
(g) $/ + * A\ B\ C\ - D\ E$	**(h)** $/ + A\ * B\ C\ - D\ E$

11. Modify the program *InfixToRPN* in Figure 4.6 so that it provides tracing information similar to that in Figure 4.1. To make the output more manageable, you may simplify it to something like the following trace for the expression $7 * 8 - (2 + 3)$; (where ; is the end-of-string mark):

```
Token      Output       Stack (bottom to top)
-----      ------       ---------------------
  7          7          empty
  *                       *
  8          8          *
  -                     *
                          -
  (                       - (
  2          2            - (
  +                       - ( +
  3          3            - ( +
  )          +          -
  ;          -          empty
```

12. Modify the program *InfixToRPN* in Figure 4.6 to detect and report infix expressions that are improperly formed.

13. The algorithm given in the text for converting from infix to RPN assumes *left associativity;* that is, when two or more consecutive operators of the same priority occur, they are to be evaluated from left to right; for example, $6 - 3 - 1$ is evaluated as $(6 - 3) - 1$ and not as $6 - (3 - 1)$. **Right associativity,** however, is usually used for the exponentiation operator; for example, in FORTRAN 77, exponentiation is denoted by $**$, and the expression $2 ** 3 ** 4$ is evaluated as $2 ** (3 ** 4) = 2^{(3^4)} = 2^{81}$, not as $(2 ** 3) ** 4 = (2^3)^4 = 8^4$. Extend the algorithm in the text to allow $**$ as an additional binary operator with highest priority. *Hint*: One approach is to use two different priorities for each operator, one for when it is in the infix expression and the other for when it is in a stack.

14. Extend the program in Figure 4.6 so that it can also convert infix expressions that contain the binary operators **div** and **mod** in addition to $+$, $-$, and $*$.

15. Proceed as in Exercise 14, but also allow the exponent operator $**$ (see Exercise 13).

16. Proceed as in Exercise 14 or 15, but also allow the unary operator $\sim$ (see Exercise 6.

17. Write a program to implement the algorithm for evaluating RPN expressions that involve only single-digit integers and the integer operations $+$, $-$, $*$, and / (**div**). Each RPN expression will be terminated by a semicolon, and a period will signal the end of input. The following is a possible program "shell":

```
program RPNEvaluator (input, output);

const
  StringLimit = 80;
  EndOfExpression = ';';
  EndOfInput = '.';

type
  String = packed array[1..StringLimit] of char;

var
  RPNExp : String;
  Value : integer;

function ExpValue (* you supply this *)

begin (* main program *)
  writeln ('End each RPN expression with ', End Of Expression);
  writeln ('Enter ', EndOfInput, ' to stop.');
  writeln ('Enter RPN expression:');
  readln (RPNExp);
  whileRPNExp[1] <> EndOfInput do
    begin
      Value := ExpValue(RPNExp);
      writeln(RPNExp, ' = ', Value);
      writeln;
      writeln ('Enter RPN expression:');
      readln (RPNExp)
    end (* while *)
end (* main program *).
```

To trace the action of RPN evaluation, print each token as it is encountered, and display the action of each *Push, Pop,* and *CreateStack* operation. For example, the output of your program should resemble the following for the RPN expression 9 2 1 $+$ / 4 $*$;

```
Create stack
Token = 9      Push 9
Token = 2      Push 2
Token = 1      Push 1
Token = +      Pop 1      Pop 2      Push 3
Token = /      Pop 3      Pop 9      Push 3
Token = 4      Push 4
Token = *      Pop 4      Pop 3      Push 12
Token = ;      Pop 12
```

18. Modify the RPN evaluation program of Exercise 17 to detect and report RPN expressions that are not well formed.

19. Modify the RPN evaluation program of Exercise 17 to

   (a) Process RPN expressions that contain the integer operators $+$, $-$, $*$, **div**, and **mod**.

   (b) Also allow RPN expressions that contain the unary operator $\sim$ (see Exercise 16).

   (c) Allow integers with more than one digit.

20. Modify the RPN evaluation program of Exercise 17 so that it generates machine instructions in assembly code for evaluating the expression using one accumulator register and the following instructions:

LOA X — Place the value of X in the accumulator register.
STO X — Store the contents of the accumulator register into variable X.
ADD X — Add the value of X to the contents of the accumulator register.
SUB X — Subtract the value of X from the contents of the accumulator register.
MUL X — Multiply the contents of the accumulator register by the value of X.
DIV X — Divide the contents of the accumulator register by the value of X.

For example, the postfix expression $A\ B\ C\ +*\ D\ E\ *-$ should give the following sequence of instructions:

LOA B
ADD C
STO $TEMP1$
LOA A
MUL $TEMP1$
STO $TEMP2$
LOA D
MUL E
STO $TEMP3$
LOA $TEMP2$
SUB $TEMP3$
STO $TEMP4$

where each $TEMPi$ is a temporary variable.

21. Write a program that converts a postfix expression to the corresponding fully parenthesized infix expression. For example, $A\ B\ +$ and $A\ B\ +\ C\ D\ -\ *$ should give $(A\ +\ B)$ and $((A\ +\ B)\ *\ (C\ -\ D))$, respectively.

5

Queues

In the preceding chapter, we defined stacks, considered array-based implementations of stacks in some detail, and looked at several of their applications. In this chapter we consider another data structure, the *queue*, that is similar to the stack and that has at least as many applications as stacks have. Queues are also often implemented using arrays as the basic storage structures, but as we will discover, a bit more effort is required to construct an efficient array-based implementation of queue than it was for a stack. The chapter closes with a simulation of an information/reservations center in which an ''on-hold'' queue is used to store incoming telephone calls.

5.1 Introduction

According to Webster, a *queue* is a ''waiting line,'' such as a line of persons waiting to check out at a supermarket, a line of vehicles at a toll booth, a queue of planes waiting to land at an airport, or a queue of jobs in a computer system waiting for some output device such as a printer. In each of these examples, the items are serviced in the order in which they arrive; that is, the first item in the queue is the first to be served. Thus, whereas a stack is a Last-In-First-Out (LIFO) structure, a queue is a *First-In-First-Out* (*FIFO*) or *First-Come-First-Served* (*FCFS*) structure.

As a data structure, a queue is a special kind of list in which the basic insert and delete operations are restricted to the ends of the list. Unlike stacks, in which elements are popped and pushed only at one end of the list, items are removed from a queue at one end, called the *front* or *head* of the queue, and elements are added only at the other end, called the *rear* or *tail*. Other basic operations are creating an empty queue and determining if a queue is empty. More formally, the abstract data type queue can be specified as follows:

ADT Queue

Collection of Data Elements:

An ordered collection of data items with the property that items can be removed only at one end, called the *front* of the queue, and items can be added only at the other end, called the *rear* of the queue.

Basic Operations:

CreateQ:
FUNCTION:	Creates an empty queue.
RETURNS:	A queue.

EmptyQ:
ACCEPTS:	A queue.
FUNCTION:	Checks if the queue is empty.
RETURNS:	True if the queue is empty, and false otherwise.

RemoveQ:
ACCEPTS:	A queue.
FUNCTION:	Retrieves and removes the element at the front of the queue.
RETURNS:	Element at the front of the queue and the modified queue.

AddQ:
ACCEPTS:	A queue and a data item.
FUNCTION:	Inserts the data item at the rear of the queue.
RETURNS:	The modified queue.

A queue is obviously an appropriate data structure for storing items that must be processed in the order in which they are generated. As a simple example, suppose that a program is to be designed to provide drill-and-practice exercises in elementary arithmetic. More precisely, suppose that these exercises are problems involving the addition of randomly generated integers. If a student answers correctly, another problem is generated; but if he or she answers incorrectly, the problem is stored so that it can be asked again at the end of the session. It seems natural to present these incorrectly answered problems in the same order in which they were presented initially, and a queue is therefore an appropriate data structure for storing these exercises.

If we assume that a package or unit for the ADT queue has been developed which defines a data type *QueueType* that can be used to declare a queue *WrongQueue* of problem records of the form

record
   Addend1,
    Addend2 : *0..NumberLimit*
end;

and procedures *CreateQ*, *AddQ*, and *RemoveQ* and the boolean function *EmptyQ* that implement the basic queue operations, then statements like the following can be used to generate a problem and add it to *WrongQueue* if it is answered incorrectly:

```
CreateQ (WrongQueue);
      .
      .
      .
Problem.Addend1 := RandomInt(0, NumberLimit);
Problem.Addend2 := RandomInt(0, NumberLimit);
Ask (Problem, Correct, 1);
if not Correct then
    AddQ (WrongQueue, Problem);
```

Here, *RandomInt* is a function that generates random integers in a specified range. Procedure *Ask* displays an addition problem to the student, reads an answer, and returns the value true or false for the boolean parameter *Correct* to indicate if the answer was correct; the parameter 1 is the number of times the problem has been asked. Statements such as the following can then be used to repeat problems that were answered incorrectly:

```
while not EmptyQ(WrongQueue) do
    begin
        RemoveQ (WrongQueue, Problem);
        Ask (Problem, Correct, 2);
        if not Correct then
            Wrong := Wrong + 1
    end (* while *);
```

Queues are also commonly used to model waiting lines that arise in the operation of computer systems. These queues are formed whenever more than one process requires a particular resource, such as a printer, a disk drive, or the central processing unit. As processes request a particular resource, they are placed in a queue to wait for service by that resource. For example, several personal computers may be sharing the same printer, and a ***print queue*** is used to schedule output requests in a first-come-first-served manner. If some process requests the printer and the printer is free, it is immediately allocated to this process. While this output is being printed, other processes may request the printer. They are placed in a queue to wait their turns. When the output from the current process terminates, the printer is released from that process and is allocated to the first process in the queue.

Another important use of queues in computing systems is for ***input/output buffering***. The transfer of information from an input device or to an output device is a relatively slow operation, and if the processing of a program must be suspended while data is transferred, program execution is slowed dramatically. One common solution to this problem uses sections of main memory known as **buffers** and transfers data between the program and these buffers rather than between the program and the input/output device directly.[1]

In particular, consider the problem in which data processed by a program must be read from a disk file. This information is transferred from the disk file to an input buffer in main memory while the central processing unit (CPU) is performing some other task. When data is required by the program, the next value(s) stored in this buffer is retrieved. While this value is being processed, additional data values can be transferred from the disk file to the buffer. Clearly, the buffer must be organized as a first-in-first-out structure, that is, as a queue. A queue-empty condition indicates that the input buffer is empty and program execution is suspended while the operating system loads more data into the buffer. Of course, such a buffer has a limited size, and thus a queue-full condition must also be used to signal when it is full and no more data is to be transferred from the disk file to the buffer.

The insert and delete operations for a queue are restricted so that insertions are performed at only one end and deletions at the other. In some applications, however, insertions and deletions must be made at both ends. To model these situations, a double-ended queue, abbreviated to **deque** (pronounced "deck"), is the data structure that should be used (but it could as well be called a "dack" for "double-ended stack"). For example, in the case of interactive input, the user can insert data into the input buffer by entering it from the keyboard. But the user may also be able to delete information by depressing a "delete" or "rubout" key. A deque might therefore be a more appropriate data structure for modeling this situation; or because data values are only removed and not inserted at the other end, a better model might be a queue-stack hybrid, sometimes called a **scroll** (although more colorful names might be "queue-and-a-half," "heque," or "quack").

Another data structure related to the queue is the so-called **priority queue.** In this structure, a certain priority is associated with each data item, and these items are to be stored in such a way that those with higher priority are removed from the queue and serviced before those of lower priority. Within this structure, the scheduling of items of equal priority is not specified. Priority queues, together with deques and scrolls, are considered in more detail in the exercises at the end of the next section and in Section 10.2.

5.2 Implementation of Queues with Arrays and Records

Because a queue resembles a stack in many ways, we might imitate the array-based implementation of a stack considered in Chapter 4 to construct an array-based implementation of a queue. Thus we might use an array to store the elements of the queue and maintain two variables: *Front* to record the position in the array of the element that can be removed, that is, the first queue element; and *Rear* to record the position in the array at which an element can be added,

---

[1] In Pascal, the contents of the buffer associated with *file-variable* are accessible by use of the **file buffer variable** or **file window** *file-variable*↑.

that is, the position following the last queue element. An element is then removed from the queue by retrieving the array element at position *Front* and
then incrementing *Front* by 1. An item is added to the queue by storing it at
position *Rear* of the array, provided that *Rear* does not exceed some maximum
size *QueueLimit* allowed for the array, and then incrementing *Rear* by 1.

   The difficulty with this implementation is that elements "shift to the right"
in the array, so that eventually all the array elements may have to be shifted
back to the beginning positions. For example, consider a queue for which
QueueLimit = 5 and whose elements are integers. The sequence of operations
AddQ 70, *AddQ* 80, *AddQ* 50 produces the following configuration:

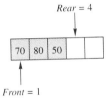

Now suppose that two elements are removed:

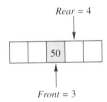

and that 90 and 60 are then added:

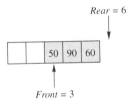

Before another item can be inserted into the queue, the elements in the array
must be shifted back to the beginning of the array:

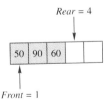

   This shifting of array elements can be avoided if we think of the array as
circular, with the first element following the last. This can be done by indexing
the array beginning with 0, and incrementing *Front* and *Rear* using addition
modulo *QueueLimit*. For the sequence of operations just considered, this im-

plementation yields the following configurations:

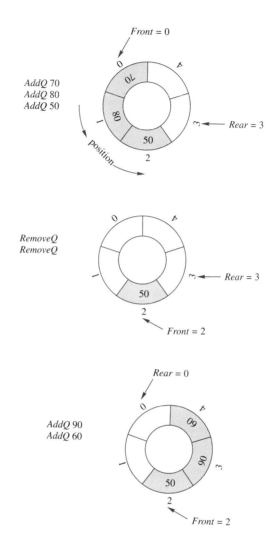

Another insertion is now possible without our having to move any array elements; we simply store the item in position *Rear* = 0.

Now consider the basic operation *EmptyQ* to determine if a queue is empty. If the queue contains a single element, it is in position *Front* of the array, and *Rear* is the vacant position following it. If this element is deleted, *Front* is incremented by 1 so that *Front* and *Rear* have the same value. Thus, to determine if a queue is empty, we need only check the condition *Front* = *Rear*. Initially, *CreateQ* will set *Front* and *Rear* both equal to 0.

Just as the array implementation for a stack introduced the possibility of a stack-full condition, the implementation of a queue raises the possibility of a queue-full condition. To see how this condition can be detected, suppose that the array is almost full, with only one empty location remaining:

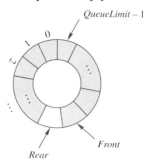

If an item were stored in this location, *Rear* would be incremented by 1 and thus would have the same value as *Front*. However, the condition *Front* = *Rear* indicates that the queue is empty. Thus, we could not distinguish between an empty queue and a full queue if this location were used to store an element. But we can avoid this difficulty if we maintain one empty position in the array. The condition indicating that a queue is full then becomes (*Rear* + 1) **mod** *QueueLimit* = *Front*.

In summary, to implement a queue, we can use for the storage structure a record consisting of a circular array to store the queue elements and fields *Front* and *Rear* to record the position of the front element and the position following the last element, respectively:

> **const**
>   *QueueLimit* = . . . ;   (∗ maximum size of queue ∗)
>   *MaxIndex* = . . . ;   (∗ upper limit on array index
>   = *QueueLimit* − 1 ∗)
>
> **type**
>   *QueueElementType* = . . . ;   (∗ type of elements in the queue ∗)
>   *QueueArray* = **array**[0..*MaxIndex*] **of** *QueueElementType*;
>   *QueueType* = **record**
>   *Front, Rear* : 0..*MaxIndex*;
>   *Element* : *QueueArray*
>   **end**;
>
> **var**
>   *QueueError* : *boolean*; (∗ signals if last queue operation was
>   unsuccessful ∗)
>   *Queue* : *QueueType*;

The operation of creating an empty queue consists simply of setting both of the fields *Front* and *Rear* of *Queue* to 0 (or to any other value in 0..*MaxIndex*), and a queue will be empty when the boolean expression *Queue.Front* = *Queue.Rear* is true. An algorithm for the *AddQ* operation is

AddQ

(∗ Algorithm to add *Item* at the rear of *Queue*, assuming that the array is not full. ∗)

1. Set *NewRear* equal to (*Queue.Rear* + 1) **mod** *QueueLimit*.
2. If *NewRear* ≠ *Queue.Front*, then do the following:
   a. Set *QueueError* to false.
   b. Set *Queue.Element*[*Queue.Rear*] equal to *Item*.
   c. Set *Queue.Rear* equal to *NewRear*.

   Otherwise:
   Signal that a queue error (queue full) occurred
   and set *QueueError* to true.

And an algorithm for the *RemoveQ* operation is

RemoveQ

(∗ Algorithm to retrieve *Item* and delete it from the front of *Queue*,
assuming that the array is not empty ∗)

If the queue is not empty then do the following:
   a. Set *QueueError* to false.
   b. Set *Item* equal to the element *Queue.Element*[*Queue.Front*] at
      the front of the queue.
   c. Set *Queue.Front* equal to (*Queue.Front* + 1) **mod** *QueueLimit*.

Otherwise:
   Signal that a queue error (queue empty) occurred
   and set *QueueError* to true.

The program in Figure 5.1 solves the drill-and-practice problem considered
in the preceding section. It assumes that a system-provided random number
generator is available for which a function reference *Random* with no parameters returns a random real number in the range 0 to 1 and that procedure
Randomize initializes this generator.[2] It also assumes the existence of a package

---

[2] Turbo Pascal provides such a function *Random* and procedure *Randomize*. *Random* has the
additional property that a function reference *Random(k)* with *k* an integer returns a random integer in
the range of 0 to *k*. If no such random number generator is available in your version of Pascal, the
following can be used. Details of this and other techniques for generating random numbers can be
found in Donald Knuth, *The Art of Computer Programming: Seminumerical Algorithms*, vol. 2 (Reading, Mass.: Addison-Wesley, 1981).

```
function Random : real;
```

   (∗ This function generates a random real number in the interval from 0 to 1. It uses the
   global variable *Seed*, which is initialized by the user and should be an odd positive
   integer; thereafter, it is the random integer generated on the preceding reference to
   Random.
   Note: The constant 65536 used in this function is appropriate for a machine having 32-bit
   words. For a machine having *M*-bit words, it should be replaced by the value of 2 to the
   power *M*/2. ∗)

```
const
   Modulus = 65536;
   Multiplier = 25173;
   Addend = 13849;

begin (* Random *)
   Seed := (Multiplier * Seed + Addend) mod Modulus;
   Random := Seed / Modulus
end (* Random *);
```

(*continued on next page*)

or unit to implement the ADT queue from which the type *QueueType*, the boolean variable *QueueError*, procedures *CreateQ*, *AddQ*, and *RemoveQ* and the boolean-valued function *EmptyQ* can be obtained. (The development of these subprograms is left as an exercise.) In the program shown here, the directive #include 'QUEUE-CONST' inserts definitions of the constants *QueueLimit* and *MaxIndex* into the constant section; #include 'QUEUE-TYPE' inserts definitions of *QueueArray* and *QueueType* into the type section; #include 'QUEUE-VAR' inserts a declaration of *QueueError* into the variable section; and #include 'QUEUE-OPS' inserts the procedures and function for the basic queue operations into the subprogram section.

```
PROGRAM DrillAndPractice (input, output);

(*******************************************************************

   Input (keyboard): Number of problems to generate, student's
                     answers to problems.
   Function:         Generates random drill-and-practice addition
                     problems.  Problems that are answered
                     incorrectly on the first attempt are queued
                     and asked again at the end of the session.
   Output (screen):  Messages, problems, correct answers, number
                     of problems answerd correctly.
   Note:             Program assumes the availability of a system
                     function Random to generate random numbers and
                     a procedure Randomize to initialize it.  Also,
                     certain constant, type, variable, function and
                     procedure declarations from the queue ADT
                     package must be inserted into the declaration
                     part.  The compiler directive #include inserts
                     these items from the four files QUEUE-CONST,
                     QUEUE-TYPE, QUEUE-VAR, and QUEUE-OPS.

   ****************************************************************)

(* For Turbo Pascal, insert USES QueueADT and remove the
   #include directives *)

CONST
   NumberLimit = 99;              (* upper limit on size of numbers *)
#include 'QUEUE-CONST'            (* QueueLimit, MaxIndex *)
```

Figure 5.1

(*continued*)

```
procedure Randomize;

   (* Procedure to initialize the random number generator *)

   begin
      write ('Enter any odd integer: ');
      readln (Seed)
   end (* Randomize *);
```

Figure 5.1 (cont.)

```
TYPE
   ProblemRecord = RECORD
                      Addend1,
                      Addend2 : 0..NumberLimit
                   END;
   QueueElementType = ProblemRecord;
#include 'QUEUE-TYPE'            (* QueueArray and QueueType *)

VAR
#include 'QUEUE-VAR'             (* QueueError *)
   WrongQueue : QueueType;       (* queue of problems answered wrong *)
   Correct : boolean;            (* indicates if answer correct or not *)
   Problem : ProblemRecord;      (* an addition problem *)
   NumProblems,                  (* number of problems asked *)
   Count,                        (* index *)
   Wrong : integer;              (* number gotten wrong -- on both tries *)

#include 'QUEUE-OPS'            (* CreateQ, EmptyQ, AddQ, RemoveQ *)

FUNCTION RandomInt (First, Last : integer) : integer;

   (*********************************************************************

      Input (param):       Integers First and Last, which specify a range
                           of integers.
      Function:            Calculates a random integer in the range First
                           through Last.
      Output (RandomInt):  Returns a random integer in First..Last.

   *********************************************************************)

   BEGIN (* RandomInt *)
      RandomInt := First + trunc((Last - First + 1) * Random)
   END (* RandomInt *);

PROCEDURE Ask (Problem : ProblemRecord; VAR Correct : boolean;
               RoundNum : integer);

   (*********************************************************************

      Input (param):       Problem to be asked and the number RoundNum of
                           times it has been asked.
      Input (keyboard):    Student's answer to problem.
      Function:            Displays an addition Problem, reads student's
                           answer, checks if it is correct.  If
                           RoundNum = 2, correct answer is displayed if
                           student answers incorrectly.
      Output (param):      Returns true or false for Correct according to
                           whether or not student's answer is correct, and
                           updated value of RoundNum.
      Output (screen):     Problem, message, and correct answer if Roundnum
                           is 2.

   *********************************************************************)

   VAR
      Answer,           (* student's answer *)
      Sum : integer; (* correct sum *)
```

Figure 5.1 (cont.)

```
   BEGIN (* Ask *)
      writeln;
      WITH Problem DO
         BEGIN
            write (Addend1:1, ' + ', Addend2:1, ' = ');
            readln (Answer);
            Sum := Addend1 + Addend2
         END (* WITH *);
      Correct := (Answer = Sum);
      IF Correct THEN
         writeln ('Correct!')
      ELSE IF RoundNum = 2 THEN
         writeln ('Wrong -- correct answer is ', Sum:1)
      ELSE
         writeln ('Wrong.')
   END (* Ask *);

BEGIN (* main program *)
   (* Initialize queue and random number generator *)
   CreateQ (WrongQueue);
   Randomize;

   (* Carry out the practice drill *)
   write ('How many problems would you like?  ');
   readln (NumProblems);
   FOR Count := 1 to NumProblems DO
      BEGIN
         Problem.Addend1 := RandomInt(0, NumberLimit);
         Problem.Addend2 := RandomInt(0, NumberLimit);
         Ask (Problem, Correct, 1);
         IF NOT Correct THEN
            AddQ (WrongQueue, Problem)
      END  (* FOR *);

   (* Now reask any problems student missed *)
   writeln;
   writeln ('If you got any problems wrong, you will now be given');
   writeln ('a second chance to answer them correctly.');
   writeln;
   IF QueueError THEN
      writeln ('Some problems were lost because of queue overflow');
   Wrong := 0;
   WHILE NOT EmptyQ(WrongQueue) DO
      BEGIN
         RemoveQ (WrongQueue, Problem);
         Ask (Problem, Correct, 2);
         IF NOT Correct THEN
            Wrong := Wrong + 1
      END (* WHILE *);
   writeln;
   writeln ('You answered ', Wrong:1, ' problems incorrectly')
END (* main program *).
```

Figure 5.1 (cont.)

Sample run:

```
How many problems would you like?   5

35 + 47 = 82
Correct!

43 + 30 = 73
Correct!

6 + 5 = 11
Correct!

25 + 99 = 26
Wrong.

30 + 72 = 102
Correct!

If you got any problems wrong, you will now be given
a second chance to answer them correctly.


25 + 99 = 126
Wrong -- correct answer is 124

You answered 1 problems incorrectly
```

Exercises

1. Assume that Q is a queue implemented as described in this section, $QueueElementType = char$, $QueueLimit = 5$, ch is a character variable, and i is an integer variable. Show the values of $Q.Front$ and $Q.Rear$ and the contents of $Q.Element$ after each of the following independent program segments has been executed, or indicate why an error has occurred.

   (a) *CreateQ (Q);*
       AddQ (Q, 'A');
       AddQ (Q, 'B');
       AddQ (Q, 'C');
       RemoveQ (Q, ch);
       AddQ (Q, ch);

   (b) *CreateQ (Q);*
       AddQ (Q, 'X');
       AddQ (Q, 'Y');
       AddQ (Q, 'Z');
       while not *EmptyQ(Q)* **do**
         RemoveQ (Q, ch);

   (c) *CreateQ (Q);*
       ch := 'M';
       for $i := 1$ **to** 3 **do**
         begin
           AddQ (Q, ch);
           AddQ (Q, succ(ch));
           RemoveQ (Q, ch)
         end;

   (d) *AddQ (Q, 'A');*
       AddQ (Q, 'B');
       RemoveQ (Q, ch);

2. Although a queue, like a stack, cannot (in theory) become full, the array-based implementation of queues requires an upper limit *QueueLimit* on the size of the array that stores the elements of the queue. Complete the definition of the following boolean function *FullQ*:

> **function** *FullQ(Q : QueueType)* : *boolean*;
> (* Accepts: A queue *Q*.
>   Function: Determines if *Q* is full.
>   Returns: True if *Q* is full and false otherwise. *)

3. (a) Complete the following definition of the function *QSize* using only the application-level queue operations *CreateQ, EmptyQ, AddQ,* and *RemoveQ*:

> **function** *QSize(***var** *Q : QueueType)* : *integer*;
> (* Accepts: A queue *Q*.
>   Function: Determines the number of elements in *Q*.
>   Returns: The number of elements in *Q*. *)

Be careful! *Q* is a variable parameter.

   (b) Proceed as in (a) but with *Q* as a value parameter.
   (c) Discuss the advantages and disadvantages of the two versions of *QSize*.
   (d) Complete either definition of *QSize* at the implementation level. That is, you may use information contained in the record and the array used to store the queue.
   (e) Which version of *QSize* do you prefer? Discuss.

4. Write the following procedure *DumpQ* at both the application level and the implementation level. (See Exercise 3 for a description of application level and implementation level.)

> **procedure** *DumpQ (Q : QueueType)*;
> (* Accepts: A queue *Q*.
>   Function: Displays the contents of *Q* from front to rear,
>   without altering *Q*.
>   Output: A list of the elements in *Q*. *)

5. Write a procedure at (i) the application level and (ii) the implementation level to retrieve the element at the front of a queue, but do not delete it from the queue. (See Exercise 3 for a description of application level and implementation level.)

6. Proceed as in Exercise 5 but design procedures to

   (a) Retrieve the element at the rear of a queue, leaving the queue empty.
   (b) Retrieve the element at the rear of a queue, leaving the queue contents unchanged.

7. Proceed as in Exercise 5 but design procedures to

   (a) Retrieve the nth queue element, leaving the queue without its first n elements.

   (b) Retrieve the nth queue element, leaving the queue contents unchanged.

8. Using the basic queue and stack operations, give an algorithm to reverse the elements in a queue.

9. In Problem 4 of Section 4.1 and in Exercise 8 of Section 4.3 we considered a railroad switching network that could be modeled with a stack. Now consider the following network:

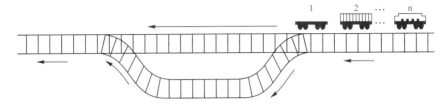

Again, railroad cars numbered 1, 2, . . . , n on the right track are to be permuted and moved along on the left track. As the diagram suggests, a car may be moved directly onto the left track, or it may be shunted onto the siding (which acts like a queue), to be removed at a later time and placed on the left track.

   (a) For $n = 3$, find all possible permutations of cars that can be obtained (on the left track) by a sequence of these operations. For example, *AddQ* 1, *AddQ* 2, *Move* 3, *RemoveQ*, *RemoveQ* arranges them in the order 3, 1, 2. Are any permutations not possible?

   (b) Find all possible permutations for $n = 4$. What permutations (if any) are not possible?

   (c) Repeat (b) for $n = 5$.

   (d) *Challenge*: In general, what permutations of the sequence 1, 2, . . . , n can be obtained by using a queue in this manner?

10. Develop a package or unit for the ADT queue whose elements are of type *QueueElementType* using the array-based implementation described in this section. It should define the type *QueueType*, procedures *CreateQ*, *AddQ*, and *RemoveQ*, and function *EmptyQ* to implement the basic queue operations, and boolean variable *QueueError* that signals whether an error occurred during the last queue operation attempted.

11. Carry out bottom-up testing of the queue package or unit developed in Exercise 10 by writing a command-driven ADT tester similar to that for stacks in Section 4.3. It should allow the user to select from the following menu of commands:

A *item*   Add *item* to the queue.
C   Create a queue.
D   Dump the contents of the queue (as described in Exercise 4).
E   Check if the queue is empty.
F   Failed? Check if the previous queue operation failed.
H   Help: Print a list of commands and a brief explanation of each.
R   Remove and display the front element of the queue.
S   Print the size of the queue (see Exercise 3).
X   Exit the tester.

Execute your program with a sequence of commands that thoroughly tests your queue package/unit.

12. An alternative implementation of a queue using a circular array that does not require keeping an empty slot between the front and the rear elements to distinguish between a queue-full and a queue-empty condition is to add an integer field *Count* to the records of type *QueueType*, which stores the number of elements currently in the queue. Write functions and/or procedures for the basic queue operations in this implementation.

13. Proceed as in Exercise 12, but use a boolean field *Full* instead of the integer field *Count*. It should be set to true only when the queue becomes full; it should be false otherwise.

14. In Exercise 9 of Section 4.3 we described an efficient implementation of a two-stack data structure that uses a single array for the storage structure. Describe a similar implementation of a two-queue data structure.

15. Imitating the implementation of a queue using a circular array, construct an implementation of a deque. Write appropriate declarations and subprograms to implement the basic operations (create an empty deque, check if the deque is empty, add at the front, add at the rear, remove at the front, remove at the rear).

16. If some location in the middle of a deque is held fixed, then the two halves of the deque behave like stacks. Devise an implementation of a deque based on this observation.

17. Construct an implementation of a scroll, giving appropriate declarations and subprograms to implement the basic operations.

18. Explain why stacks and queues are special cases of a priority queue.

19. Modify the implementation of a queue given in the text for a priority queue. Items should be stored in a single array, and two "pointers"

should be maintained, one for the front of the queue and the other for the rear. Write appropriate declarations and subprograms for the basic operations. You may assume that a function *Priority* that returns the priority of a given item is provided.

20. If the priorities of items are integers in some range 1..*p*, then one could use *p* different arrays to implement a priority queue, one for each queue of items having equal priority. Construct such an implementation, giving appropriate declarations and subprograms for the basic operations.

21. If the priorities of the items are not uniformly distributed, the implementation of a priority queue considered in Exercise 20 may be very inefficient. An alternative is to use a single array, as in Exercise 19, and *p* + 1 pointers, one to the front of the priority queue and one to the rear of each of the ''internal'' queues of items having equal priority. Construct such an implementation.

22. Write a memory-recall program that generates a random sequence of letters and/or digits, displays them to the user one at a time for a second or so, and then asks the user to reproduce the sequence. Use a queue to store the sequence of characters. (*Hint*: If your version of Pascal does not provide a ''time'' procedure or function, a ***busy–wait loop*** of the form

   for *i* := 1 **to** *n* **do** (* nothing *);

   might be used.)

23. Write a program that reads a string of characters, pushing each character onto a stack as it is read and simultaneously adding it to a queue. When the end of the string is encountered, the program should use the basic stack and queue operations to determine if the string is a palindrome (see Exercise 5 of Section 3.2).

24. In text-editing and word-processing packages, one formatting convention sometimes used to indicate that a piece of text is a footnote or an endnote is to mark it with some special delimiters such as { and }. When the text is formatted for output, these notes are not printed as normal text but are stored in a queue for later output. Write a program that reads a document containing endnotes indicated in this manner, collects them in a queue, and prints them at the end of the document.

5.3 Application of Queues: Information Center Simulation

As we noted in the preceding section, queues may be used to model waiting lines. Almost all waiting lines are dynamic; that is, their lengths change over time, growing as new items arrive and are added to the queues, shrinking as items are removed from the queues and serviced. The term *simulation* refers to modeling such a dynamic process and using this model to study the behavior or the process. The behavior of some *deterministic* processes can be modeled with an equation or a set of equations. For queues, however, it is normally not known in advance exactly when there will be a new arrival or exactly how much time will be required to service a specified item. Thus, the behavior of a queue often involves randomness, and a program that simulates such behavior must also incorporate randomness.

As an illustration, we consider the operation of an information/reservation center that services calls made by customers to a toll-free number, such as one provided by an airline or a rental car company. When a call arrives at this center, it is serviced immediately if the agent is available, but if the agent is busy, the call is placed on hold in a queue to be serviced later. A program is to be written that simulates the operation of such an information center and computes several statistics to measure its performance.

Problem Analysis and Specification

The overall simulation should proceed as follows: A simulated clock is initialized to 0 and then repeatedly advanced by 1 (minute) until it is equal to some given time limit (minutes). On each "tick" of the clock, a check is made to determine if service has been completed for the current call, and if so, a new call is taken from the queue of calls that are waiting for service (if there are any), and its simulated service is initiated. A check is also made to determine if a new call has arrived. If it has, its arrival time is recorded, its service time is determined and recorded, and it is placed on the queue for processing in a first-come-first-served manner when the agent becomes available. When the specified time limit has been reached, no new calls are accepted, but service continues until all the calls in the on-hold queue have been processed.

When the simulation is complete, statistics such as the number of calls processed and the average waiting time for each call that measure the performance of the information center must be reported. Also, during peak hours, some incoming calls may be rejected—because there is no room for them in the queue—and it may be useful to know the number of times that this occurs. These three statistics will constitute the output of this simulation:

- Number of calls processed.
- Average waiting time per call.
- Number of calls rejected.

Other statistics, such as the average queue length and the average turnaround time, are described in the exercises.

As we noted earlier, the simulation is to run for a specified period of time, and thus one input item must be a time limit. Since it is necessary to stimulate the arrival and service of calls, information about arrival rates and service times is also needed. Thus the input will be

- Arrival rate of calls.
- Distribution of service times.
- Time limit.

Data Structures

The three input items arrival rate, service times, and time limit are the basic parameters that govern the simulation; it is thus convenient to store these in a record:

SimParameters = **record**
                    ArrivalRate : *real*;
                    ServicePerc : **array**[1..*NumLimits*] **of** *real*;
                    TimeLimit : *integer*
         end;

Here *ArrivalRate* is the probability that a call will arrive in a given minute. For example, if the average time between calls is five minutes, then the arrival rate is $1/5 = 0.2$ calls per minute. The array *ServicePerc* will record information regarding service time:

ServicePerc[1] = % of calls serviced in 1 minute or less;
ServicePerc[2] = % of calls serviced in 2 minutes or less;
              .
              .
              .

TimeLimit is the specified time limit for the simulation.

For this simulation, the basic object is a call to the information center, and such calls are characterized by the time at which they arrive, the amount of time required to service the call, and the time when the service of that call is completed. A record is thus an appropriate data structure to use for simulated calls:

CallRecord = **record**
                   TimeOfArrival,
                   ServiceTime,
                   TimeOfCompletion : *integer*
        end;

The final data structure needed is a queue *OnHold* of call records used to store calls that must be placed on hold because the agent is unavailable when the call arrives. The element type of this queue thus is

QueueElementType = *CallRecord*;

Design Plan

We identify three main tasks that the program must perform. The first level of our design plan will thus consist of three modules:

First-Level Modules

GetSimParameters:

Function:	Gets the simulation parameters.
Returns:	A record of type *SimParameters*.

Simulate:

Accepts:	A record of type *SimParameters*.
Function:	Carries out the simulation.
Returns:	Total number of calls, total waiting time, and number of calls rejected.

PrintReport:

Accepts:	Total number of calls, total waiting time, and number of calls rejected.
Function:	Calculates and reports simulation statistics.
Output:	Number of calls, average waiting time, and number of calls rejected.

GetSimParameters will ask the user to enter the arrival rate, a distribution of service times, and a time limit for the simulation, and these will be stored in a record of type *SimParameters*. For the service times, the user will enter the percentage of calls that can be serviced in one minute or less, the percentage of calls requiring more than one minute but at most two minutes, and similar percentages for the other categories. These percentages are accumulated and stored in the array *ServicePerc*. This array will be used to determine a service time for each call.

Since *PrintReport* is straightforward, the only other module that requires some additional explanation is *Simulate*. In the analysis and specification of this problem we described how this simulation is to be carried out. This description is summarized in the following algorithm:

(∗ Algorithm for *Simulate* ∗)

1. Initialize the clock, the on-hold queue, and other simulation variables.
2. While the clock has not reached the specified time limit:
    a. Advance the clock one time unit.
    b. Continue service of the current call or begin service of a call on the on-hold queue (if there are any such calls).
    c. Check for arrival of a new call.
3. While calls remain in the on-hold queue:
    a. Advance the clock.
    b. Remove the call at the front of the queue and service it.

We see that there are three main subtasks that *Simulate* must perform, and we thus identify three second-level modules:

Second-Level Modules

Initialize:

Function:	Initializes simulation variables and a random number generator.

Returns: An empty queue *OnHold*; the value 0 for *NumCalls*, *WaitingTime*, *Rejected*, and *Clock*; the value false for the boolean variable *InService*, indicating that no call is currently being serviced.

Service:
Accepts: A *Call*, *Clock*, *WaitingTime*, and *InService*.
Function: Continues service of the current *Call* or begins service of a call in the *OnHold* queue.
Returns: Updated values of *Call*, *Clock*, *WaitingTime*, and *InService*.

CheckForNewCall:
Accepts: *Clock*, *Rejected*, the *SimParams* record, and the *OnHold* queue.
Function: Checks if a new call has arrived and if so, places it on the *OnHold* queue, if possible; otherwise, updates the number of calls *Rejected*.
Returns: Updated values of *Rejected*, *NumCalls*, and *OnHold*.

The module *Initialize* is straightforward. An algorithm for *Service* is

(∗ Algorithm for *Service* ∗)

1. If *Inservice* (∗ a call is being serviced ∗)
   If *Clock* = *Call.TimeOfCompletion*
     Set *InService* to false. (∗ Service of current *Call* completed ∗)
2. If not *Inservice* (∗ no call is being serviced ∗)
   If *OnHold* queue is not empty
     a. Remove a *Call* from *OnHold*.
     b. Set *Call.TimeOfCompletion* equal to *Clock* + *Call.ServiceTime*.
     c. Update *WaitingTime* by adding *Clock* − *Call.TimeOfArrival* (∗ the time *Call* was in *OnHold* ∗).
     d. Set *InService* to true (∗ place *Call* in service ∗)

The module *CheckForNewCall* checks if a new call has arrived and if so, attempts to place it on the *OnHold* queue. To determine whether or not a call has arrived in a particular minute, we generate a random number between 0 and 1, and if this number is less than *SimParams.ArrivalRate*, we say that a call has arrived during this minute:

The numbers produced by a random number generator are assumed to be uniformly distributed over the interval from 0 to 1. Consequently, if many such numbers are generated, we expect approximately 20 percent of them to be in the subinterval (0, 0.2). In terms of our simulation, this means that the probability that a call arrives in a given minute should be approximately 0.2, as desired.

When a new call arrives, its arrival time and the time required to service the call must be recorded. The service time is determined by using the array *ServicePerc*. For example, suppose the array *ServicePerc* contains the values 0.50, 0.75, 0.90, 0.97, and 1.00. We generate a random number in the interval (0, 1); the subinterval (0, 0.50], (0.50, 0.75], (0.75, 0.90], (0.90, 0.97], (0.97, 1.00) in which it falls then determines the service time for the call:

The following algorithm for *CheckForNewCall* summarizes all of this:

(* Algorithm for *CheckForNewCall* *)

1. Generate a random number *R*.
2. If *R* < *SimParams.ArrivalRate* (* new call has arrived *)
   a. Set *NewCall.TimeOfArrival* equal to *Clock*.
   b. Increment *NumCalls* by 1.

   (* Determine its service time *)
   c. Generate a new random number *R*.
   d. Set *i* to 1.
   e. While *R* > *SimParams.ServicePerc*[*i*]
        Increment *i* by 1.
   f. Set *NewCall.ServiceTime* equal to *i*.

   g. Add *Call* to the *OnHold* queue.
   h. If *QueueError* (* queue is full *)
        Increment *Rejected* by 1.

The following diagram summarizes the overall structure of this design:

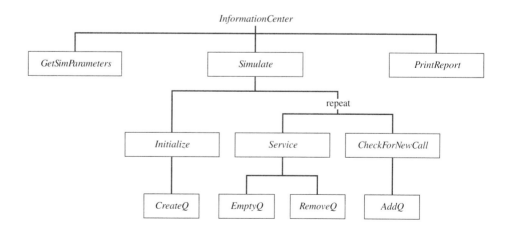

The program in Figure 5.2 is based on this design plan. It assumes the availability of a queue-processing package and a random number generator as described in the preceding section.

```
PROGRAM InformationCenter (input, output);

(*******************************************************************

    Input (keyboard): Arrival rate of calls, distribution of service
                      times, and time limit for simulation.
    Function:         Simulates the operation of an information/
                      reservation center that services telephone
                      calls.
    Output (screen):  The number of calls processed, the average
                      waiting time for each call, and the number of
                      calls rejected because the "on-hold" queue
                      was full.
    Note:             Program assumes the availability of a system
                      function Random to generate random numbers and
                      a procedure Randomize to initialize it.  Also,
                      certain constant, type, variable, function and
                      procedure declarations from the queue ADT
                      package must be inserted into the declaration
                      part.  The compiler directive #include inserts
                      these items from the four files QUEUE-CONST,
                      QUEUE-TYPE, QUEUE-VAR, and QUEUE-OPS.

*******************************************************************)

(* For Turbo Pascal, insert USES ADTQueue and remove the
   #include directives. *)

CONST
   NumLimits = 5;            (* maximum # of service time categories *)
#include 'QUEUE-CONST'    (* QueueLimit, MaxIndex *)

TYPE
   SimParameters = RECORD
                      ArrivalRate : real;
                      ServicePerc : ARRAY[1..NumLimits] of real;
                      TimeLimit : integer
                   END;
   CallRecord = RECORD
                   TimeOfArrival,
                   ServiceTime,
                   TimeOfCompletion : integer
                END;
   QueueElementType = CallRecord;
#include 'QUEUE-TYPE'              (* QueueArray, QueueType *)
```

Figure 5.2

Figure 5.2 (cont.)

```
VAR
#include 'QUEUE-VAR'           (* QueueError *)
   SimParams : SimParameters; (* parameters needed in the simulation *)
   NumCalls,                  (* total # of calls during simulation *)
   WaitingTime,               (* total wait time for all calls *)
   Rejected : integer;        (* # of calls rejected *)

#include 'QUEUE-OPS'           (* CreateQ, EmptyQ, AddQ, RemoveQ *)

PROCEDURE GetSimParameters (VAR SimParams: SimParameters);

   (***************************************************************

      Input (keyboard): Arrival rate, percentages for service times,
                        and time limit for simulation.
      Function:         Gets the simulation parameters.
      Output (param):   Returns the record SimParams that stores
                        these simulation parameters.

   ***************************************************************)

   VAR
      i : integer;   (* index *)
      Perc,          (* percentage *)
      Sum : real;    (* sum of percentages *)

   BEGIN (* GetSimParameters *)
      write ('Enter arrival rate:  ');
      readln (SimParams.ArrivalRate);
      writeln ('Enter percent (in decimal form) of calls serviced in ');
      Sum := 0;
      FOR i := 1 TO NumLimits - 1 DO
         BEGIN
            write (i:5, ' min. or less:  ');
            readln (Perc);
            Sum := Sum + Perc;
            SimParams.ServicePerc[i] := Sum
         END (* FOR *);
      Simparams.ServicePerc[NumLimits] := 1;
      write ('Enter # of minutes to run simulation:  ');
      readln (SimParams.TimeLimit)
   END (* GetSimParameters *);
```

Figure 5.2 (cont.)

```
PROCEDURE Simulate (SimParams : SimParameters;
                    VAR NumCalls, WaitingTime, Rejected : integer);

   (*********************************************************************

      Input (param):   The record SimParams of simulation parameters.
      Function:        Carries out the simulation.
      Output (param):  Returns total number NumCalls of calls, the
                       total WaitingTime, and the number of calls
                       Rejected.

   *********************************************************************)

   VAR
      Clock : integer;        (* simulated clock -- time in minutes *)
      OnHold : QueueType;     (* queue of calls put on hold *)
      InService : boolean;    (* indicates if a call is being serviced *)
      Call : CallRecord;      (* call being serviced *)

   PROCEDURE Initialize (VAR OnHold : QueueType;
                         VAR Clock, NumCalls, WaitingTime,
                             Rejected : integer;
                         VAR InService : boolean);

      (*********************************************************************

         Input:           None.
         Function:        Initialize simulation variables and a random
                          number generator.
         Output (param):  Returns empty queue OnHold, 0 for NumCalls,
                          WaitingTime, Rejected, and Clock; false for
                          InService.
         Note:            Assumes a system procedure Randomize to
                          initialize the random number generator.

      *********************************************************************)

      BEGIN (* Initialize *)
         CreateQ (OnHold);
         InService := false;
         NumCalls := 0;
         WaitingTime := 0;
         Rejected := 0;
         Clock := 0;
         Randomize
      END (* Initialize *);
```

Figure 5.2 (cont.)

```
PROCEDURE Service (VAR Call : CallRecord; Clock : integer;
                   VAR WaitingTime : integer;
                   VAR InService : boolean);

   (*******************************************************************

      Input (param):   Call, Clock, total WaitingTime, and InService.
      Function:        Continue service of the current Call or begin
                       service of a call in the OnHold queue
      Output (param):  Updated values of Call, Clock, WaitingTime, and
                       Inservice.

   *******************************************************************)

   BEGIN (* Service *)
      IF InService THEN
         IF Clock = Call.TimeOfCompletion THEN
            InService := false;

      (* If service complete, begin serving a new call *)
      IF NOT InService THEN
         IF NOT EmptyQ(OnHold) THEN
            BEGIN
               RemoveQ (OnHold, Call);
               Call.TimeOfCompletion := Clock + Call.ServiceTime;
               WaitingTime := WaitingTime +
                              Clock - Call.TimeOfArrival;
               InService := true
            END (* IF *)
   END (* Service *);

PROCEDURE CheckForNewCall (SimParams : SimParameters;
                           Clock : integer;
                           VAR NumCalls: integer;
                           VAR OnHold : QueueType;
                           VAR Rejected : integer);

   (*******************************************************************

      Input (param):   The SimParams record, Clock, OnHold queue, and
                       number of calls Rejected.
      Function:        Checks if a new call has arrived and if so,
                       places it on the OnHold queue, if possible;
                       otherwise, updates the number of calls Rejected.
      Output (param):  Updated values of Rejected and OnHold.
      Note:            Assumes a system function Random for generating
                       random real numbers.

   *******************************************************************)

   VAR
      R : real;              (* random number *)
      i : integer;           (* index *)
      NewCall : CallRecord;  (* new call *)
```

Figure 5.2 (cont.)

```
    BEGIN (* CheckForNewCall *)
        R := Random;
        IF R < SimParams.ArrivalRate THEN
            BEGIN
                (* New call has arrived; record it's
                   time of arrival and count it *)
                NewCall.TimeOfArrival := Clock;
                NumCalls := NumCalls + 1;

                (* and generate a service time for it *)
                R := Random;
                i := 1;
                WHILE R > SimParams.ServicePerc[i] DO
                    i := i + 1;
                NewCall.ServiceTime := i;

                (* and then add it to the OnHold queue *)
                AddQ (OnHold, NewCall);
                IF QueueError THEN
                    Rejected := Rejected + 1
            END (* IF *)
    END (* CheckForNewCall *);

BEGIN (* Simulate *)
    Initialize (OnHold, Clock, NumCalls, WaitingTime,
                Rejected, InService);
    WHILE Clock < SimParams.TimeLimit DO
        BEGIN
            (* Tick the clock *)
            Clock := Clock + 1;

            (* Service the current call *)
            Service (Call, Clock, WaitingTime, InService);

            (* Check for arrival of new call *)
            CheckForNewCall(SimParams, Clock, NumCalls, OnHold, Rejected)
        END (* WHILE *);

    (* Service any calls remaining in OnHold queue *)
    WHILE InService DO
        BEGIN
            Clock := Clock + 1;
            Service (Call, Clock, WaitingTime, InService)
        END (* WHILE *)
END (* Simulate *);
```

Figure 5.2 (cont.)

```
PROCEDURE PrintReport (NumCalls, WaitingTime, Rejected : integer);

   (***********************************************************************

      Input (param):    Total number NumCalls of calls, total
                        WaitingTime, and the number of calls Rejected.
      Function:         Calculates and reports simulation statistics.
      Output (screen):  Number of calls, average waiting time, and the
                        number of calls rejected.


   ***********************************************************************)

   BEGIN (* PrintReport *)
      writeln ('Number of calls processed: ', NumCalls:6);
      writeln ('Ave. waiting time per call:', WaitingTime/NumCalls:6:2);
      writeln ('Number of calls rejected:  ', Rejected:6)
   END (* PrintReport *);

BEGIN (* main program *)
   GetSimParameters (SimParams);
   Simulate (SimParams, NumCalls, WaitingTime, Rejected);
   PrintReport (NumCalls, WaitingTime, Rejected)
END (* main program *).
```

Sample runs:

```
Enter arrival rate:  0.2
Enter percent (in decimal form) of calls serviced in
    1 min. or less:  0.2
    2 min. or less:  0.5
    3 min. or less:  0.2
    4 min. or less:  0.1
Enter # of minutes to run simulation:  500
Number of calls processed:    114
Ave. waiting time per call:  1.60
Number of calls rejected:      0


Enter arrival rate:  0.3
Enter percent (in decimal form) of calls serviced in
    1 min. or less:  0.1
    2 min. or less:  0.2
    3 min. or less:  0.4
    4 min. or less:  0.25
Enter # of minutes to run simulation:  500
*** Attempt to add to a full  queue ***
*** Attempt to add to a full  queue ***
*** Attempt to add to a full  queue ***
*** Attempt to add to a full  queue ***
*** Attempt to add to a full  queue ***
*** Attempt to add to a full  queue ***
*** Attempt to add to a full  queue ***
*** Attempt to add to a full  queue ***
Number of calls processed:    152
Ave. waiting time per call:  5.84
Number of calls rejected:      8
```

Exercises

1. Modify the program in Figure 5.2 so that it also calculates the average turnaround time. The turnaround time for a given call is the difference between the time when service for that call is completed and the time the call arrived.

2. Modify the program in Figure 5.2 so that it also calculates the average queue length. If n minutes are simulated and $L_1, L_2, \ldots, L_n$ are the lengths of the on-hold queue at times $1, 2, \ldots, n$, respectively, then the average queue length is $(L_1 + L_2 + \cdots + L_n)/n$.

3. Modify the program in Figure 5.2 so that several agents are available to service calls. Investigate the behavior of various queue statistics as the number of agents varies.

4. Suppose that in addition to the simulation parameters given in the text, another is the percentage of calls that cannot be serviced by the agent but must be transferred to the manager. In addition to the other random information generated for each call, also generate randomly an indicator of whether or not it can be serviced by the agent. If it cannot, it should be added to a *ManagerQueue*, and a new service time should be generated for it. Modify the program in Figure 5.2 to simulate this information center, and calculate various statistics like those in the text and in Exercises 1 and 2 for each call, for each queue, and so on.

5. (Project) Suppose that a certain airport has one runway, that each airplane takes *LandingTime* minutes to land and *TakeOffTime* minutes to take off, and that on the average, *TakeOffRate* planes take off and *LandingRate* planes land each hour. Assume that the planes arrive at random instants of time. (Delays make the assumption of randomness quite reasonable.) There are two types of queues: a queue of airplanes waiting to land and a queue of airplanes waiting to take off. Because it is more expensive to keep a plane airborne than to have one waiting on the ground, we assume that the airplanes in the landing queue have priority over those in the takeoff queue.

    Write a program to simulate this airport's operation. You might assume a simulated clock that advances in one-minute intervals. For each minute, generate two random numbers: If the first is less than *LandingRate* / 60, a ''landing arrival'' has occurred and is added to the landing queue; and if the second is less than *TakeOffRate* / 60, a ''takeoff arrival'' has occurred and is added to the takeoff queue. Next, check whether the runway is free. If it is, first check whether the landing queue is nonempty, and if so, allow the first airplane to land; otherwise, consider the takeoff queue. Have the program calculate the average queue length and the average time that an airplane spends in a queue. You might also investigate the effect of varying arrival and departure rates to simulate the prime and slack times of day, or what happens if the amount of time to land or take off is increased or decreased.

6. (Project) Suppose that in a certain computer system, jobs submitted for execution are assigned a priority from 1 through 10. Jobs with the highest priorities are executed first, and those of equal priority are executed on a first-come-first-served basis. The operating system maintains a priority queue of *job control blocks,* each of which is a record storing certain information about a particular job, such as its priority, a job identifier, its time of arrival, and the expected execution time. Using one of the implementations of a priority queue described in Exercises 19–21 of Section 5.2, write a program to simulate the operation of this system. It should read or generate randomly a sequence of job control blocks containing at least the four items of information just given (ordered according to time of arrival), storing them in a priority queue until they can be executed. A simulated clock can be advanced by the expected execution time for a job to simulate its execution. Your program should calculate the turnaround time for each job (see Exercise 1), the average turnaround time, and any other statistics you care to use to measure the performance of the system (average wait time, amount of time the CPU is idle between jobs, and so on). You may assume *nonpreemptive* scheduling, in which the execution of a given job is not preempted by the arrival of a job of higher priority.

6

Algorithms
and Recursion

Two important parts of system design, the second phase of the software development process described in Chapter 1, are the selection of data structures and the design of algorithms. In the preceding chapters we have focused primarily on data structures and abstract data types, including arrays, records, sets, strings, stacks, and queues. In this chapter we turn our attention to a more careful study of algorithms.

In our discussion of validation and verification in Chapter 1, we noted that in some applications, logical errors,cannot be tolerated. In these situations it is necessary to prove that the algorithms are correct and in this chapter, we describe some of the techniques of formal verification. Moreover, for a given problem, there may be several different algorithms for performing the same task, and in these situations, it is important that we be able to compare their performance. Thus, we also consider more carefully the analysis of algorithms and introduce some techniques for measuring their efficiency.

The algorithms we have considered thus far and the procedures and functions that implement them all have been nonrecursive; that is, they do not reference themselves, either directly or indirectly. There are some problems, however, for which the most appropriate algorithms are recursive. Thus in this chapter we begin by reviewing recursion and how recursive subprograms are written in Pascal, and we illustrate recursion with several examples. We also consider how to prove recursive algorithms to be correct and how to compare their efficiency with that of nonrecursive algorithms. Finally, we discuss the role of stacks in supporting recursion.

6.1 Recursion

We have seen several examples of functions and procedures that reference other functions and/or procedures. In some programming languages, such as Pascal, a subprogram may also reference itself, a phenomenon known as *recursion*, and in this section we review how recursion, both *direct* and *indirect*, is supported in Pascal.

To illustrate the basic idea of recursion, we consider the problem of calculating x^n, where x is a real value and n is a nonnegative integer. The first definition of x^n that one learns is usually an iterative (nonrecursive) one:

$$x^n = \underbrace{x \times x \times \cdots \times x}_{n \ x\text{'s}}$$

and later one learns that x^0 is defined to be 1. (For convenience, we assume here that x^0 is 1 also when x is 0, although in this case, it is usually left undefined.)

In calculating a sequence of consecutive powers of some number, however, it would be foolish to calculate each one using this definition, that is, to multiply the number by itself the required number of times; for example,

$$3^0 = 1$$
$$3^1 = 3$$
$$3^2 = 3 \times 3 = 9$$
$$3^3 = 3 \times 3 \times 3 = 27$$
$$3^4 = 3 \times 3 \times 3 \times 3 = 81$$
$$3^5 = 3 \times 3 \times 3 \times 3 \times 3 = 243$$

It is clear that once some power of 3 has been calculated, it can be used to calculate the next power; for example, given the value of $3^3 = 27$, we can use this value to calculate

$$3^4 = 3 \times 3^3 = 3 \times 27 = 81$$

and this value to calculate

$$3^5 = 3 \times 3^4 = 3 \times 81 = 243$$

and so on. Indeed, to calculate any power of 3, we only need to know the value of 3^0,

$$3^0 = 1$$

and the fundamental relation between one power of 3 and the next:

$$3^n = 3 \times 3^{n-1}$$

This approach to calculating powers leads to the following recursive definition of the power function:

$$x^0 = 1$$

$$\text{For } n > 0, \ x^n = x \times x^{n-1}$$

Another classic example of a function that can be calculated recursively is the factorial function. The first definition of the factorial $n!$ of a nonnegative integer n that one usually learns is

$$n! = 1 \times 2 \times \cdots \times n, \quad \text{for } n > 0$$

and that 0! is 1. Thus, for example,

$$0! = 1$$
$$1! = 1$$
$$2! = 1 \times 2 = 2$$
$$3! = 1 \times 2 \times 3 = 6$$
$$4! = 1 \times 2 \times 3 \times 4 = 24$$
$$5! = 1 \times 2 \times 3 \times 4 \times 5 = 120$$

Once again the value of this function for a given integer can be used to calculate the value for the next integer. For example, to calculate 5!, we can simply multiply the value of 4! by 5:

$$5! = 4! \times 5 = 24 \times 5 = 120$$

Similarly, we can use 5! to calculate 6!,

$$6! = 5! \times 6 = 120 \times 6 = 720$$

and so on. We need only know the value of 0!,

$$0! = 1$$

and the fundamental relation between one factorial and the next:

$$n! = n \times (n - 1)!$$

This suggests the following recursive definition of $n!$:

$$0! = 1$$
$$\text{For } n > 0, n! = n \times (n - 1)!$$

In general, a function is said to be **defined recursively** if its definition consists of two parts:

1. An **anchor** or **base case**, in which the value of the function is specified for one or more values of the parameter(s).
2. An **inductive** or **recursive step**, in which the function's value for the current value of the parameter(s) is defined in terms of previously defined function values and/or parameter values.

We have seen two examples of such recursive definitions of functions, the power function

$x^0 = 1$ (the anchor or base case)
For $n > 0, x^n = x \times x^{n-1}$ (the inductive or recursive step)

and the factorial function

$0! = 1$ (the anchor or base case)
For $n > 0, n! = n \times (n - 1)!$ (the inductive or recursive step)

In each definition, the first statement specifies a particular value of the function, and the second statement defines its value for n in terms of its value for $n - 1$.

As we noted in these examples, such recursive definitions are useful in calculating function values $f(n)$ for a sequence of consecutive values of n. Using them to calculate any one particular value, however, requires computing earlier values. For example, consider using the recursive definition of the power function to calculate 3^5. We must first calculate 3^4, because 3^5 is defined as the product of 3 and 3^4. But to calculate 3^4 we must calculate 3^3 because 3^4 is defined as 3×3^3. And to calculate 3^3, we must apply the inductive step of the definition again, $3^3 = 3 \times 3^2$, then again to find 3^2, which is defined as $3^2 = 3 \times 3^1$, and once again to find $3^1 = 3 \times 3^0$. Now we have finally reached the anchor case:

$$3^5 = 3 \times 3^4$$
$$\downarrow$$
$$3^4 = 3 \times 3^3$$
$$\downarrow$$
$$3^3 = 3 \times 3^2$$
$$\downarrow$$
$$3^2 = 3 \times 3^1$$
$$\downarrow$$
$$3^1 = 3 \times 3^0$$
$$\downarrow$$
$$3^0 = 1$$

Since the value of 3^0 is given, we can now backtrack to find the value of 3^1,

$$3^5 = 3 \times 3^4$$
$$\downarrow$$
$$3^4 = 3 \times 3^3$$
$$\downarrow$$
$$3^3 = 3 \times 3^2$$
$$\downarrow$$
$$3^2 = 3 \times 3^1$$
$$\downarrow$$
$$3^1 = 3 \times 3^0 = 3 \times 1 = 3$$
$$\downarrow \qquad \nearrow$$
$$3^0 = 1$$

then backtrack again to find the value of 3^2,

$$3^5 = 3 \times 3^4$$
$$\downarrow$$
$$3^4 = 3 \times 3^3$$
$$\downarrow$$
$$3^3 = 3 \times 3^2$$
$$\downarrow$$
$$3^2 = 3 \times 3^1 = 3 \times 3 = 9$$
$$\downarrow \qquad \leftarrow$$
$$3^1 = 3 \times 3^0 = 3 \times 1 = 3$$
$$\downarrow \qquad \nearrow$$
$$3^0 = 1$$

and so on until we eventually obtain the value 243 for 3^5:

$$3^5 = 3 \times 3^4 = 3 \times 81 = 243$$
$$3^4 = 3 \times 3^3 = 3 \times 27 = 81$$
$$3^3 = 3 \times 3^2 = 3 \times 9 = 27$$
$$3^2 = 3 \times 3^1 = 3 \times 3 = 9$$
$$3^1 = 3 \times 3^0 = 3 \times 1 = 3$$
$$3^0 = 1$$

As this example demonstrates, calculating function values by hand using recursive definitions may require considerable bookkeeping to record information at the various levels of the recursive evaluation so that after the anchor case is reached, this information can be used to backtrack from one level to the preceding one. Fortunately, most modern high-level languages, including Pascal, allow recursive functions and/or procedures, and the computer automatically does all of the necessary bookkeeping and backtracking.

To illustrate, consider the power function again. The recursive definition of this function can be implemented as a recursive function in Pascal in a straightforward manner:

function *Power*(*x* : *real*; *n* : *integer*) : *real*;

(* Accepts: Real number *x* and integer $n \geq 0$.
   Function: Computes x^n recursively.
   Returns: x^n. *)

begin (* *Power* *)
  if *n* $=$ 0 **then**   (* anchor *)
    Power := 1
  else
    Power := *x* * *Power*(*x*, *n* $-$ 1)   (* inductive step *)
end (* *Power* *);

When this function is referenced, the inductive step is applied repeatedly until the anchor case is reached. For example, when the reference *Power*(3.0, 5) is made to calculate 3.0^5, the inductive step generates another reference *Power*(3.0, 4). The inductive step in this second reference to *Power* then generates another reference *Power*(3.0, 3), which in turn generates another reference *Power*(3.0, 2), then another, *Power*(3.0, 1), and finally the reference *Power*(3.0, 0). Because the anchor condition is now satisfied, no additional references are generated.

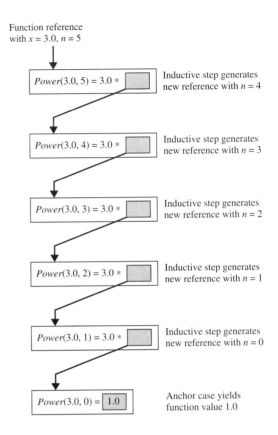

The value 1.0 is returned for *Power*(3.0, 0) which is then used to calculate the value of *Power*(3.0, 1), and so on until the value 243.0 is eventually returned as the value for the original function reference *Power*(3.0, 5):

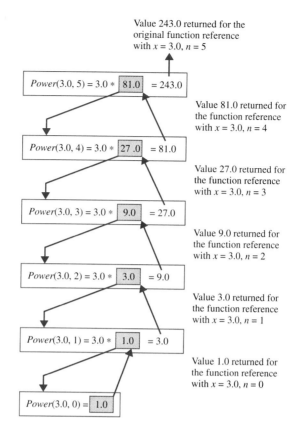

Value 243.0 returned for the original function reference with $x = 3.0, n = 5$

$Power(3.0, 5) = 3.0 * \boxed{81.0} = 243.0$

Value 81.0 returned for the function reference with $x = 3.0, n = 4$

$Power(3.0, 4) = 3.0 * \boxed{27.0} = 81.0$

Value 27.0 returned for the function reference with $x = 3.0, n = 3$

$Power(3.0, 3) = 3.0 * \boxed{9.0} = 27.0$

Value 9.0 returned for the function reference with $x = 3.0, n = 2$

$Power(3.0, 2) = 3.0 * \boxed{3.0} = 9.0$

Value 3.0 returned for the function reference with $x = 3.0, n = 1$

$Power(3.0, 1) = 3.0 * \boxed{1.0} = 3.0$

Value 1.0 returned for the function reference with $x = 3.0, n = 0$

$Power(3.0, 0) = \boxed{1.0}$

The recursive definition of the factorial function is also easily implemented as a recursive function in Pascal. Writing this function and tracing its execution, as we did for the function *Power*, are left as an exercise.

Each execution of the inductive step in the definitions of the power function and the factorial function generates only one reference to the function itself, but recursive definitions of other functions may require more than one such reference. To illustrate, consider the sequence of **Fibonacci numbers**,

$$1, 1, 2, 3, 5, 8, 13, 21, 24, 34, 53, \ldots$$

which begins with two 1's and in which each number thereafter is the sum of the two preceding numbers. This infinite sequence is defined recursively by

$$f_1 = 1$$
$$f_2 = 1$$
$$\text{For } n > 2, \ f_n = f_{n-1} + f_{n-2}$$

where f_n denotes the nth term in the sequence. This definition leads naturally to the following recursive function:

function *Fib*(*n* : *integer*) : *integer*;

(* Accepts: Positive integer *n*.
    Function: Computes *n*th Fibonacci number recursively.
    Returns: *n*th Fibonacci number. *)

    begin (* *Fib* *)
      if $n <= 2$ **then**   (* anchor *)
        Fib := 1
      else
        Fib := *Fib*(*n* − 1) + *Fib*(*n* − 2)   (* inductive step *)
    end (* *Fib* *);

If the function reference *Fib*(5) is made to obtain the fifth Fibonacci number, the inductive step

    else
      Fib := *Fib*(*n* − 1) + *Fib*(*n* − 2)

immediately generates the reference *Fib*(4) with parameter $5 - 1 = 4$:

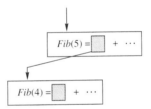

This generates another function reference *Fib*(3), which in turn generates the reference *Fib*(2):

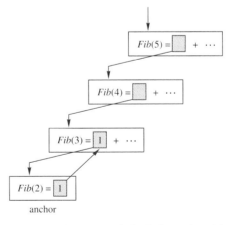

Because the anchor condition is now satisfied, the value 1 is returned for *Fib*(2), and the second reference *Fib*(1) needed to calculate *Fib*(3) is generated:

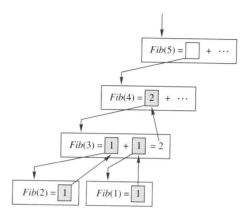

Here again, the value 1 is returned, and the function reference $Fib(3)$ is completed so that the value $1 + 1 = 2$ is returned. The first term in the sum for the reference $Fib(4)$ thus has been calculated, and the reference $Fib(2)$ is generated to determine the second term. This process continues until eventually the value 5 is returned for $Fib(5)$:

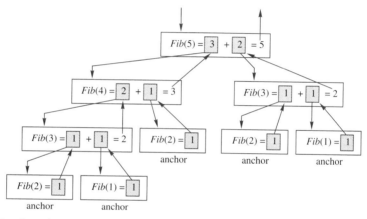

Note the function references with the same parameter in this ***recursion tree***; there are three references with parameter 1, three with parameter 2, and two with parameter 3. These multiple references suggest that this is not the most efficient way to calculate Fibonacci numbers; an inefficiency that is confirmed by comparing the computing time of this recursive Fibonacci function with a nonrecursive version in the next section.

In Pascal, procedures as well as functions may be recursive. For example, consider the binary search algorithm, which was described in the preceding section. Although the algorithm given there is an iterative one, the approach of the binary search method is recursive. If the (sub)list we are currently examining is empty, the item for which we are searching is obviously not in the (sub)list, and so we can stop searching (anchor condition 1). If the (sub)list is not empty, we examine its middle element, and if this is the item for which we are searching, we are finished (anchor condition 2). Otherwise, either the sublist of items preceding this middle item or the sublist of items following it is searched *in the same manner* (inductive step).

A recursive procedure for binary search is therefore quite simple:

procedure *RecBinarySearch* (**var** *A* : *ArrayType*; *First, Last* : *integer*;
                                    Item : *ElementType*; **var** *Found* : *boolean*;
                                    var *Loc* : *integer*);

(* Accepts: A list of elements in ascending order stored in array *A*,
             integers *First* and *Last*, and *Item* of the same type as the
             array elements.
   Function: Recursively search sub(list) *A*[*First*], . . . , *A*[*Last*] for *Item*
             using a binary search.
   Returns: *Found* = *true* and *Loc* = position of *Item* if the search is
             successful; otherwise, *Found* is false. *)

begin (* *RecBinarySearch* *)
  if *First* > *Last* **then**   (* anchor 1—empty sublist *)
    Found := *false*
  else   (* inductive step *)
   begin
    Loc := (*First* + *Last*) **div** 2;
    if *Item* < *A*[*Loc*] **then**   (* recursively search first half *)
      RecBinarySearch (*A, First, Loc* − 1, *Found, Loc*)
    else if *Item* > *A*[*Loc*] **then**   (* recursively search last half *)
      RecBinarySearch (*A, Loc* + 1, *Last, Found, Loc*)
    else   (* anchor 2—*Item* found *)
      Found := *true*
   end (* **else** *)
end (* *RecBinarySearch* *);

To illustrate the action of this procedure, suppose that the list 11, 22, 33, 44, 55, 66, 77, 88, 99 is stored in positions 1 through 9 of array A and that we wish to search this list for the number 66. We begin with the procedure reference statement

RecBinarySearch (*A*, 1, 9, 66, *ItemFound, Position*)

The procedure calculates *Loc* = 5, and since 66 > *A*[5] = 55, the second part of the inductive step generates another reference,

RecBinarySearch (*A*, 6, 9, 66, *ItemFound, Position*):

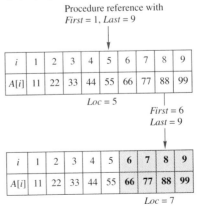

Since the sublist is nonempty, this procedure call calculates $Loc = 7$, and since $66 < A[7] = 77$, the first part of the inductive step generates another function reference with $First = 6$ and $Last = 6$:

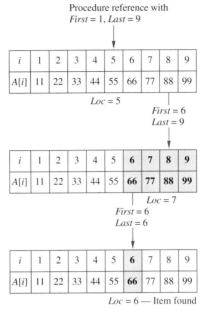

The sublist being searched still has one element, and so in this third procedure reference, the value $Loc = 6$ is calculated, and since $A[6] = 66$ is the desired item, the second anchor condition assigns the value *true* to *Found*. This third execution of *RecBinarySearch* then terminates and returns the values *Found* = *true* and $Loc = 6$ to the second procedure reference. This second execution likewise terminates and returns these same values to the first execution of *RecBinarySearch*. The original reference to this procedure is thus completed, and the value *true* is returned to the actual parameter *ItemFound* and the value 6 to the actual parameter *Position*:

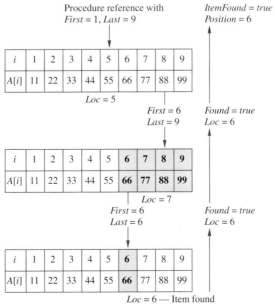

Developing recursive algorithms is difficult for many beginning programmers. Practice, practice, and more practice seems to be the only way to develop the ability to think recursively. Consequently, we give one more example of a recursive algorithm here, and more will be given in subsequent chapters.

An integer is said to be a *palindrome* if its value does not change when its digits are reversed; that is, the number reads the same from left to right as it does from right to left. For example, 1, 33, 5665, and 123454321 are palindromes. Now, suppose we wish to develop a boolean-valued function that checks if a given positive integer is a palindrome, returning *true* if it is and *false* otherwise.

Thinking nonrecursively, we might begin by trying to decompose the number into its separate digits, then put them together in reverse order, and finally check if this reversed number is equal to the original number. A similar approach would be to decompose the number into its separate digits, pushing each one onto a stack. Because of a stack's LIFO property, when these digits are popped from the stack, they will appear in the opposite order from that in the original number, and so we can check if the number's reversal is the same as the number. Another nonrecursive approach might be to convert the number into a string of characters stored in an array and then to scan this array from both ends, checking to see if the digits match.

A more straightforward solution to the problem is a recursive one and is obtained simply by analyzing how one would solve this problem by hand. In checking a number like

$$8504058$$

most people first check the first and last digits and, if they agree, cross them out (perhaps only mentally) and consider the number that remains:

$$\cancel{8}\ 50705\ \cancel{8}$$

The resulting number 50705 is then checked *in the same way*, which is a recursive approach to the problem. After two more applications of this inductive step of checking and truncating the first and last digits,

$$\cancel{5}\ 070\ \cancel{5}$$
$$\cancel{0}\ 7\ \cancel{0}$$

a one-digit number results:

$$7$$

and this obviously is a palindrome (anchor case 1). If the original number had an even number of digits, then at this last step, no digits would remain and the number would be a palindrome. If at any point along the way, the first and last digits did not match (anchor case 2), we would stop checking, since the number obviously is not a palindrome.

This leads to the following recursive algorithm:

RECURSIVE PALINDROME CHECKER

(* Accepts: Nonnegative integers *Number* and *NumDigits,* the number
of digits in *Number.*
Function: Recursively checks if *Number* is a palindrome.
Returns: True if *Number* is a palindrome, and *false* otherwise. *)

1. If *NumDigits* ≤ 1 then   (* anchor case 1 *)
   Return the value true.

   (* Otherwise check if the first and last digits match, and if not, return
   the value false *)

2. Divide Number by $10^{NumDigits - 1}$ to obtain *FirstDigit.*
3. Set *LastDigit* equal to *Number* **mod** 10.
4. If *FirstDigit* ≠ *LastDigit* then   (* anchor case 2 *)
   Return the value false.

   (* Otherwise, the first and last digits match, so more digits must be
   checked—inductive step *)

5. Apply the algorithm recursively to *Number* with *FirstDigit* and
   LastDigit removed, that is, to *Number* **mod** $10^{NumberDigits - 1}$ **mod** 10,
   and *NumDigits* − 2.

Implementing this algorithm as a recursive function is straightforward and is
left as an exercise.

The examples of recursion given thus far have illustrated ***direct recursion;***
that is, the functions and procedures have referenced themselves directly. ***Indirect recursion*** occurs when a subprogram references other subprograms, and
some chain of subprogram references eventually results in a reference to the
first subprogram again. For example, function *A* may reference function *B,*
which references procedure *C,* which references *A* again. Since Pascal requires
that a subprogram be defined before it is referenced, *B* would have to be defined
before *A* because *A* references *B,* and *C* must be defined before *B* because *B*
references *C.* However, since *C* references *A, A* would have to be defined before
C. Thus it would seem that indirect recursion is not possible in Pascal programs.

To permit indirect recursions without violating the rule that subprograms
must be defined before they are referenced, Pascal allows ***dummy definitions***
of functions and procedures in addition to "actual" definitions. A dummy
definition consists of only the subprogram heading followed by the reserved
word **forward,** which is a directive that indicates to the compiler that the actual
definition appears later in the subprogram section of the program. The definitions of the aforementioned subprograms *A, B,* and *C* then have the following
form:

function *A*(*formal-parameter-list*) : *result-type*; **forward**;
   (∗ Dummy definition of *A* ∗)

procedure *C* (*formal-parameter-list*);

        ⋮

   (∗ Actual definition of *C* ∗)

        ⋮

function *B*(*formal-parameter-list*) : *result-type*;

        ⋮

   (∗ Actual definition of *B* ∗)

        ⋮

function *A*;

        ⋮

   (∗ Actual definition of *A* ∗)

        ⋮

Note that in the actual definition of function *A*, the formal parameter list and the result type are omitted in the function heading. Indirect recursion is illustrated in the parsing example of the next section.

Exercises

1. Assuming ASCII representation of characters, consider the following procedure:

```
procedure P (ch: char);
  begin (* P *)
    if ('A' <= ch) and (ch <= 'H') then
      begin
        P (pred(ch));
        write (ch)
      end
    else
      writeln
  end (* P *);
```

   (a) What output is produced by each of the following procedure calls?
   (i) *P* ('C')   (ii) *P* ('G')   (iii) *P* ('3')
   (b) If *pred* is replaced by *succ* in the procedure, what output will be produced by the procedure calls in (a)?

(c) If the *write* statement and the recursive call to *P* are interchanged, what output will be produced by the calls in (a)?

(d) If a copy of the *write* statement is inserted before the recursive call to *P*, what output will be produced by the calls in (a)?

2. Given the following function *F* and assuming ASCII representation of characters, use the method illustrated in this section to trace the sequence of function calls and returns in evaluating *F*('a', 'e') and *F*('h', 'c').

```
function F(chl, ch2 : char) : integer;
   begin (* F *)
      if chl > ch2 then
         F := 0
      else if succ(chl) = ch2 then
         F := 1
      else
         F := F(succ(chl), pred(ch2)) + 2
   end (* F *);
```

3. Assuming ASCII representation of characters, consider the following procedure:

```
procedure Q (ch : char; n : integer);
   begin (* Q *)
      if n <= 0 then
         writeln
      else
         begin
            Q (pred(ch), n − 1);
            write (ch);
            Q (succ(ch), n − 1)
         end
   end (* Q *);
```

(a) What output is produced by the procedure call *Q* ('M', 4)? (*Hint:* First try *Q* ('M', 2), then *Q* ('M', 3).)

(b) How many letters are output by the call *Q* ('M', 10)?

(c) If the *write* statement is moved before the first recursive call to *Q*, what output will be produced by *Q* ('M', 4)?

4. Determine what is calculated by the following recursive functions, where the type identifier *Cardinal* is defined as 0..*maxint*:

(a)
```
function F(n : Cardinal) : Cardinal;
   begin (* F *)
      if n = 0 then
         F := 0
      else
         F := n * F(n − 1)
   end (* F *);
```

(b) **function** $F(x : real; n : Cardinal) : real;$
    begin (∗ F ∗)
      if $n = 0$ **then**
        $F := 0$
      else
        $F := x + F(x, n - 1)$
    end (∗ F ∗);

(c) **function** $F(n : Cardinal) : Cardinal;$
    begin (∗ F ∗)
      if $n < 2$ **then**
        $F := 0$
      else
        $F := 1 + F(n \textbf{ div } 2)$
    end (∗ F ∗);

(d) **function** $F(n : Cardinal) : Cardinal;$
    begin (∗ F ∗)
      if $n = 0$ **then**
        $F := 0$
      else
        $F := F(n \textbf{ div } 10) + n \textbf{ mod } 10$
    end (∗ F ∗);

(e) **function** $F(n : integer) : Cardinal;$
    begin (∗ F ∗)
      if $n < 0$ **then**
        $F := F(-n)$
      else if $n < 10$ **then**
        $F := n$
      else
        $F := F(n \textbf{ div } 10)$
    end (∗ F ∗);

5. Write nonrecursive versions of the functions in Exercise 4.

6. Write a recursive procedure to display the digits of any nonzero integer in reverse order.

7. Given the declarations

    const
      $ArrayMax = $ (∗ user defined ∗);

    type
      $Element = $ (∗ user defined ∗);
      $ArrayType = $ **array**$[1..ArrayMax]$ **of** $Element;$

write recursive versions of the following procedures and functions:

(a) **procedure** *ReverseArray* (**var** *A* : *ArrayType*;
> *First, Last* : *integer*);
(* Reverse the contents of *A*[*First..Last*]. *)

(b) **function** *SumArray*(*A* : *ArrayType*; *n* : *integer*) : *integer*;
(* Return the sum of *A*[1], . . . , *A*[*n*]. *)

(c) **function** *Location*(*A* : *ArrayType*; *First, Last* : *integer*;
> *El* : *Element*) : *integer*;

> (* Return the location of *El* in *A*[*First..Last*].
> If not found, return 0. *)

8. Using the basic string operations length, concatenate, substring, and index (see Section 3.1), develop a recursive algorithm for reversing a string.

9. Proceed as in Exercise 8, but develop a nonrecursive algorithm.

10. Write a test driver for one of the functions in Exercise 4. Add output statements to the function to trace its actions as it executes. For example, the trace displayed for *F*(19) for the function *F* in part (c) should have a form like

```
F(19) = 1 + F(9)
   F(9) = 1 + F(4)
      F(4) = 1 + F(2)
         F(2) = 1 + F(1)
            F(1) returns 0
         F(2) returns 1
      F(4) returns 2
   F(9) returns 3
F(19) returns 4
```

where the indentation level reflects the depth of the recursion. (*Hint*: This can be accomplished by using a global variable *Level* that is incremented when the function is entered and decremented when it is exited.)

11. Write a test driver for the procedure *Reverse* of Exercise 6, and add output statements to the procedure to trace its actions as it executes. For example, the trace displayed for *Reverse*(9254) might have a form like

```
Reverse (9254): Output 4, then call Reverse(925).
   Reverse (925): Output 5, then call Reverse(92).
      Reverse (92): Output 2, then call Reverse(9).
         Reverse (9): Output 9, then call Reverse(0).
            Reverse (0) returns.
         Reverse (9) returns.
      Reverse (92) returns.
   Reverse (925) returns.
Reverse (9254) returns.
```

where the indentation level reflects the depth of the recursion. (See the hint in Exercise 10.)

12. **(a)** Write a recursive function that implements the algorithm in this section for determining if a number is a palindrome.
    (b) Use the function of part (a) in a program that checks if several numbers are palindromes.

13. **(a)** Write a recursive function that returns the number of digits in a nonnegative integer.
    (b) Write a program to test the function of part (a).

14. Proceed as in Exercise 13, but write a nonrecursive function.

15. The **greatest common divisor** of two integers a and b, GCD(a, b), not both of which are zero, is the largest positive integer that divides both a and b. The **Euclidean algorithm** for finding this greatest common divisor of a and b is as follows: Divide a by b to obtain the integer quotient q and the remainder r, so that $a = bq + r$ (if $b = 0$, GCD(a,b) = a). Then GCD(a,b) = GCD(b,r). Replace a with b and b with r and repeat this procedure. Because the remainders are decreasing, eventually a remainder of 0 will result. The last nonzero remainder is GCD(a,b). For example,

$$
\begin{array}{ll}
1260 = 198 \cdot 6 + 72 & \text{GCD}(1260, 198) = \text{GCD}(198, 72) \\
198 = 72 \cdot 2 + 54 & \qquad\qquad\qquad\;\; = \text{GCD}(72, 54) \\
72 = 54 \cdot 1 + 18 & \qquad\qquad\qquad\;\; = \text{GCD}(54, 18) \\
54 = 18 \cdot 3 + 0 & \qquad\qquad\qquad\;\; = 18
\end{array}
$$

(*Note*: If either a or b is negative, replace them with their absolute values in this algorithm.)

(a) Write a recursive greatest common divisor function.
(b) Write a program that uses the function of part (a) to find the greatest common divisors of several pairs of numbers.

16. Proceed as in Exercise 15, but write a nonrecursive function.

17. **Binomial coefficients** can be defined recursively as follows:

$$
\left.
\begin{array}{l}
\dbinom{n}{0} = 1 \\[2ex]
\dbinom{n}{n} = 1
\end{array}
\right\} \text{(anchor)}
$$

For $0 < k < n$, $\dbinom{n}{k} = \dbinom{n-1}{k-1} + \dbinom{n-1}{k}$ (inductive step)

(a) Write a recursive function or procedure to calculate binomial coefficients.

(b) Draw a recursion tree like that in this section showing the subprogram references and returns involved in calculating the binomial coefficient $\binom{4}{2}$.

(c) Use your recursive subprogram in a program that reads values for n and k and displays the value of $\binom{n}{k}$, using the subprogram to obtain this value.

18. Binomial coefficients can also be defined as follows:

$$\binom{n}{k} = \frac{n!}{k!(n-k)!}$$

(a) Write a nonrecursive function or procedure for calculating binomial coefficients using this definition.

(b) If possible with your version of Pascal, write a program to compare the computing time of this nonrecursive subprogram for calculating binomial coefficients with the recursive subprogram developed in Exercise 17. (See Exercise 5 of Section 3.4.)

19. (a) Write a recursive procedure that prints a nonnegative integer with commas in the correct locations. For example, it should print 20131 as 20,131.

(b) Write a program to test the procedure of part (a).

20. Consider a square grid, some of whose cells are empty and others contain an asterisk. Define two asterisks to be *contiguous* if they are adjacent to each other in the same row or in the same column. Now suppose we define a *blob* as follows:

(a) A blob contains at least one asterisk.

(b) If an asterisk is in a blob, then so is any asterisk that is contiguous to it.

(c) If a blob has more than two asterisks, then each asterisk in it is contiguous to at least one other asterisk in the blob.

For example, there are four blobs in the partial grid

seven blobs in

and only one in

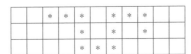

Write a program that uses a recursive function or procedure to count the number of blobs in a square grid. Input to the program should consist of the locations of the asterisks in the grid, and the program should display the grid and the blob count.

21. Consider a network of streets laid out in a rectangular grid, for example,

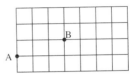

In a *northeast path* from one point in the grid to another, one may walk only to the north (up) and to the east (right). For example, there are four northeast paths from A to B in the preceding grid:

Write a program that uses a recursive function or procedure to count the number of northeast paths from one point to another in a rectangular grid.

22. In Sections 4.1 and 4.2 we considered the problem of converting an integer from base-ten to base-two and we used a stack to store the binary digits so that they could be displayed in correct order. Write a recursive procedure to accomplish this conversion without using a stack.

23. Write a recursive procedure to find the prime factorization of an integer, and display these prime factors in descending order. (See Exercise 11 of Section 4.3.)

24. Develop a recursive procedure to generate all of the $n!$ permutations of the set $\{1, 2, \ldots, n\}$. (*Hint*: The permutations of $\{1, 2, \ldots, k\}$ can be obtained by considering each permutation of $\{1, 2, \ldots, k-1\}$ as an ordered list and inserting k into each of the k possible positions in this list, including at the front and at the rear.) For example, the permutations of $\{1, 2\}$ are $(1, 2)$ and $(2, 1)$. Inserting 3 into each of the three possible positions of the first permutation yields the permutations $(3, 1, 2)$, $(1, 3, 2)$, and $(1, 2, 3)$ of $\{1, 2, 3\}$, and using the second permutation gives $(3, 2, 1)$, $(2, 3, 1)$, and $(2, 1, 3)$. Write a program to test your procedure.

6.2 Examples of Recursion: Towers of Hanoi; Parsing

Towers of Hanoi. The Towers of Hanoi problem is a classic example of a problem for which a recursive algorithm is especially appropriate. It can be

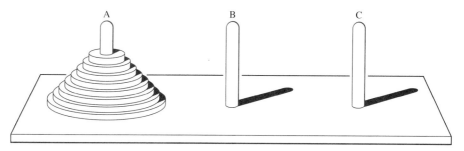

Figure 6.1

solved easily using recursion, but a nonrecursive solution is quite difficult. The problem is to solve the puzzle shown in Figure 6.1, in which one must move the disks from the left peg to the right peg according to the following rules:

1. When a disk is moved, it must be placed on one of the three pegs.
2. Only one disk may be moved at a time, and it must be the top disk on one of the pegs.
3. A larger disk may never be placed on top of a smaller one.

Legend has it that the priests in the Temple of Bramah were given a puzzle consisting of a golden platform with three golden needles on which were placed sixty-four golden disks. Time was to end when they had successfully finished moving the disks to another needle, following the preceding rules. (*Query*: If the priests moved one disk per second and began their work in the year 0, when would time come to an end?)

Novices usually find the puzzle easy to solve for a small number of disks, but they have more difficulty as the number of disks grows to seven, eight, and beyond. To a computer scientist, however, the Towers of Hanoi puzzle is easy:

> If there is one disk, move it from Peg A to Peg C; thus the puzzle can be solved for $n = 1$ disk.

Assuming that a solution exists for $n - 1$ disks, a solution for n disks can easily be obtained recursively:

1. Move the topmost $n - 1$ disks from Peg A to Peg B, using C as an auxiliary peg.
2. Move the large disk remaining on Peg A to Peg C.
3. Move the $n - 1$ disks from Peg B to Peg C, using Peg A as an auxiliary peg.

This scheme is implemented by the following recursive procedure:

procedure *Move* (*n : integer*; *StartPeg, AuxPeg, EndPeg : char*);

(∗ Accepts: Positive integer *n* and three characters representing pegs of the Towers of Hanoi puzzle: *StartPeg, AuxPeg,* and *EndPeg.*

Function: Moves *n* disks from *StartPeg* to *EndPeg* using *AuxPeg* as
            an auxiliary peg.
Output: A sequence of moves that solves the puzzle. *)

begin (* *Move* *)
  if *n* = 1 **then**
    writeln ('Move disk from ', *StartPeg*, 'to ', *EndPeg*)
  else
    begin
      (* Move *n* − 1 disks from *StartPeg* to *AuxPeg*
         using *EndPeg* *)
      Move (*n* − 1, *StartPeg*, *EndPeg*, *AuxPeg*);

      (* Move disk from *StartPeg* to *EndPeg* *)
      Move (1, *StartPeg*, ' ', *EndPeg*);

      (* Move *n* − 1 disks from *AuxPeg* to *EndPeg*
         using *StartPeg* *)
      Move (*n* − 1, *AuxPeg*, *StartPeg*, *EndPeg*)
    end (* *else* *)
end (* *Move* *);

The program in Figure 6.2 uses this procedure to solve the problem.

```
PROGRAM TowersOfHanoi (input, output);

(***********************************************************

   Input (keyboard):  Number of disks.
   Function:          Solves the Towers of Hanoi puzzle
                      recursively, using procedure Move.
   Output (screen):   Sequence of moves that solves the
                      puzzle.

***********************************************************)

CONST
   Peg1 = 'A';
   Peg2 = 'B';
   Peg3 = 'C';

VAR
   NumDisks : integer;      (* number of disks *)
```

Figure 6.2

Figure 6.2 (cont.)

```
PROCEDURE Move (n : integer; StartPeg, AuxPeg, EndPeg : char);

   (*************************************************************

      Input (param):   Number n of disks and three characters
                       representing pegs:  StartPeg, AuxPeg,
                       and EndPeg.
      Function:        Moves n disks from StartPeg to EndPeg
                       using AuxPeg as an auxiliary peg.
      Output (screen): Instructions for moving the disks.

   *************************************************************)

   BEGIN (* Move *)
     IF n = 1 THEN
        writeln ('Move disk from ', StartPeg, ' to ', EndPeg)
     ELSE
        BEGIN
           (* Move n-1 disks from StartPeg to AuxPeg using EndPeg *)

           Move (n - 1, StartPeg, EndPeg, AuxPeg);

           (* Move disk from StartPeg to EndPeg *)

           Move (1, StartPeg, ' ', EndPeg);

           (* Move n-1 disks from AuxPeg to EndPeg using StartPeg *)

           Move (n - 1, AuxPeg, StartPeg, EndPeg)
        END (* ELSE *)
   END (* Move *);

BEGIN (* main program *)
   write ('# of disks:  ');
   readln (NumDisks);
   Move (NumDisks, Peg1, Peg2, Peg3);
END (* main program *).
```

Sample run:

```
# of disks:  4
Move disk from A to B
Move disk from A to C
Move disk from B to C
Move disk from A to B
Move disk from C to A
Move disk from C to B
Move disk from A to B
Move disk from A to C
Move disk from B to C
Move disk from B to A
Move disk from C to A
Move disk from B to C
Move disk from A to B
Move disk from A to C
Move disk from B to C
```

Parsing. All the examples of recursion that we have given thus far have used direct recursion. To illustrate indirect recursion, in which some chain of procedure references eventually results in a reference to the first procedure in this chain, we consider the compiler problem of processing arithmetic expressions. In particular, we consider the specific problem of parsing arithmetic expressions, that is, determining whether they are well formed and, if so, what their structure is.

The **syntax rules** of a language specify how basic constructs such as assignment statements and expressions are formed. Thus, an arithmetic expression is well formed if it is formed according to the syntax rules for generating arithmetic expressions. These syntax rules are commonly stated as **substitution rules**, or **productions**. For the simplified arithmetic expressions considered in the preceding section, the rules might be the following:

(1) *expression* → *term* + *term* | *term* − *term* | *term*
(2) *term* → *factor* * *factor* | *factor* / *factor* | *factor*
(3) *factor* → (*expression*) | *letter* | *digit*

Here the vertical bar (|) is used to separate the various alternatives. For example, the third syntax rule specifies that a factor may be a left parenthesis followed by an expression followed by a right parenthesis, or it may be a single letter or a single digit.

To show how these syntax rules are used in parsing an arithmetic expression, consider the expression 2 * (3 + 4). According to the first syntax rule, an expression can be a term, and by the second rule, a term may have the form *factor* * *factor*. These substitutions can be displayed by the following partially developed **parse tree** for this expression:

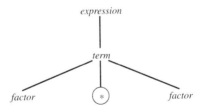

By the third syntax rule, a factor may be a digit; in particular, it may be the digit 2;

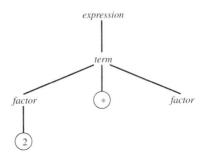

and the second alternative of the third syntax rule specifies that a factor may be an expression enclosed in parentheses:

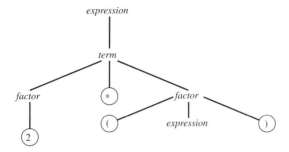

Continued application of these syntax rules produces the following complete parse tree, which shows how 2 ∗ (3 + 4) can be generated according to the syntax rules and thus demonstrates that it is a legal expression:

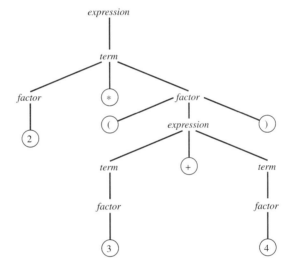

It is clear that these syntax rules for expressions involve indirect recursion. For example, an expression may be a term, which may be a factor, which may be a parenthesized expression, thus defining an expression indirectly in terms of itself.

The program in Figure 6.3 for parsing these simplified arithmetic expressions uses the three procedures *CheckForExpression*, *CheckForTerm*, and *CheckForFactor*, which are derived directly from the corresponding syntax rules. For example, consider the procedure *CheckForExpression*. According to the first syntax rule, an expression may have one of the three forms

term + *term*
term − *term*
term

In each case, it must begin with a term, and so the first action in this procedure is a call to *CheckForTerm*.

If *CheckForTerm* identifies a valid term and returns the value true for *Valid*, then the procedure *CheckForExpression* must examine the next symbol to determine which of these three forms is applicable, and so it calls *GetChar*. If this symbol is + or −, *CheckForTerm* must then be called to check for one of the first two forms for an expression; *CheckForExpression* then returns the value true or false for parameter *Valid* to the main program according to whether *CheckForTerm* returns the value true or false. If the symbol is not + or −, then an expression of the last form has been identified, and the procedure must "back up" one symbol before resuming the parse.

The following table traces the action of these three procedures in parsing the first expression *A* + *B* used in the sample run:

Active Procedure	Position	Symbol	Valid	Action
Main program	0			Call *CheckForExpression.*
CheckForExpression	0			Call *CheckForTerm.*
CheckForTerm	0			Call *CheckForFactor.*
CheckForFactor	0			Call *GetChar* to get next symbol.
	1	A		*GetChar* increments *Position* and returns *Symbol* = 'A'.
	1	A		Else clause sets *Valid* to true and execution returns to *CheckForTerm.*
CheckForTerm	1	A	*true*	Call *GetChar* to get next symbol.
	2	+	*true*	"Unget" symbol because it is not * or /, and return to *CheckForExpression.*
CheckForExpression	1	A	*true*	Call *GetChar* to get next symbol.
	2	+	*true*	Since *Symbol* is in [' + ',' − '], call *CheckForTerm.*
CheckForTerm	2	+	*true*	Call *CheckForFactor.*
CheckForFactor	2	+	*true*	Call *GetChar* to get next symbol.
	3	B	*true*	*GetChar* increments *Position* and returns *Symbol* = 'B'.
	3	B	*true*	Else clause sets *Valid* to true and execution returns to *CheckForTerm.*
CheckForTerm	3	B	*true*	Call *GetChar* to get next symbol.
	4	$	*true*	"Unget" symbol because it is not * or /, and return to *CheckForExpression.*
CheckForExpression	3	B	*true*	Return to main program.
Main Program	3	B	*true*	Because the value *true* is returned for *ValidExpression* and *Position* = 3, signaling a complete parse, print a message indicating a valid expression.

For the second expression *A* + *B*) in the sample run, the same trace table would result except that when execution returns to the main program, *Position* = 3, so the end of the string *Expr* has not been reached, indicating an unsuccessful parse.

```
PROGRAM ExpressionParser (input, output);

(******************************************************************

    Input (keyboard): Strings representing arithmetic expressions and
                      user responses used to control repetition.
    Function:         Parses simplified arithmetic expressions given
                      by the syntax rules:
             expression --> term + term | term - term | term
             term --> factor * factor | factor / factor | factor
             factor --> ( expression) | letter | digit
    Output (screen):  Messages indicating valid or invalid arithmetic
                      expressions.


********************************************************************)

(* In Turbo Pascal, remove the #include directives and replace
   ReadString with readln. *)

CONST
#include 'STRING-CONST'
   EndMark = ';';

TYPE
#include 'STRING-TYPE'              (* String *)

VAR
   Expr : String;                   (* expression to be parsed *)
   Position  : integer;             (* position of next character in Expr *)
   ValidExpression : boolean;       (* signals if well-formed expression
                                       found *)

   Response : char;                 (* user response to control repetition *)

#include 'STRING-OPS'              (* ReadString, Length *)

PROCEDURE GetChar(Expr : String; VAR Position : integer;
                  VAR NextSymbol : char);

    (*************************************************************

    Input (param):   String Expr and a Position in this string.
    Function:        Gets the next nonblank symbol NextSymbol in
                     expression Expr after the current Position.
    Output (param):  Updated values of Position and NextSymbol.


    *************************************************************)

   BEGIN (* GetChar *)
      Position := Position + 1;
      WHILE (Expr[Position] = ' ') DO
         Position := Position + 1;
      NextSymbol := Expr[Position]
   END (* GetChar *);
```

Figure 6.3

Figure 6.3 (cont.)

```
PROCEDURE CheckForExpression (Expr: String;
                             VAR Position : integer;
                             VAR Valid : boolean); FORWARD;

    (*****************************************************************

       Input (param):   String Expr and a Position in the string.
       Function:        Checks if there is a valid arithmetic
                        expression in Expr beginning at the current
                        Position.
       Output (param):  Returns updated value of Position and true
                        for Valid if there is a valid expression in
                        Expr at Position, false otherwise.

       NOTE:            This is a dummy definition of
                        CheckForExpression; the actual definition
                        appears later.

    *****************************************************************)

PROCEDURE CheckForFactor (Expr : String;
                          VAR Position : integer; VAR Valid : boolean);

    (*****************************************************************

       Input (param):  String Expr and a Position in this string.
       Function:       Checks if there is a valid factor in Expr
                       beginning at the current Position.
       Output (param): Returns updated value of Position and true
                       for Valid if there is a valid factor in
                       Expr at Position, false otherwise.

    *****************************************************************)

VAR
    Symbol : char;              (* symbol in Expr *)

BEGIN (* CheckForFactor *)
    GetChar (Expr, Position, Symbol);
    IF Symbol = '(' THEN
       BEGIN
          CheckForExpression (Expr, Position, Valid);
          IF Valid THEN
             BEGIN
                GetChar (Expr, Position, Symbol);
                IF Symbol <> ')' THEN
                   Valid := false
             END (* IF Valid *)
       END (* IF Left Paren *)
    ELSE
       Valid := Symbol IN ['A'..'Z', 'a'..'z', '0'..'9']
END (* CheckForFactor *);
```

Figure 6.3 (cont.)

```
PROCEDURE CheckForTerm (Expr : String;
                       VAR Position : integer; VAR Valid : boolean);

    (*****************************************************************

    Input (param):   String Expr and a Position in this string.
    Function:        Checks if there is a valid term in Expr
                     beginning at the current Position.
    Output (param):  Returns updated value of Position and true
                     for Valid if there is a valid term in
                     Expr at Position, false otherwise.

    *****************************************************************)

    VAR
        Symbol : char;              (* symbol in Expr *)

    BEGIN (* CheckForTerm *)
        CheckForFactor (Expr, Position, Valid);
        IF Valid THEN
            BEGIN
                GetChar (Expr, Position, Symbol);
                IF Symbol IN ['*', '/'] THEN
                    CheckForFactor(Expr, Position, Valid)
                ELSE
                    (* "Unget" a character *)
                    Position := Position - 1
            END (* IF *)
    END (* CheckForTerm *);

PROCEDURE CheckForExpression;

    (*****************************************************************

    This is the actual definition of CheckForExpression.
    Input (param):   String Expr and a Position in the string.
    Function:        Checks if there is a valid arithmetic
                     expression in Expr beginning at the current
                     Position.
    Output (param):  Returns updated value of Position and true
                     for Valid if there is a valid expression in
                     Expr at Position, false otherwise.

    *****************************************************************)

    VAR
        Symbol : char;              (* symbol in Expr *)
```

Figure 6.3 (cont.)

```
   BEGIN (* CheckForExpression *)
      CheckForTerm (Expr, Position, Valid);
      IF Valid THEN
         BEGIN
            GetChar (Expr, Position, Symbol);
            IF Symbol IN ['+', '-'] THEN
               CheckForTerm(Expr, Position, Valid)
            ELSE
               (* "Unget" a character *)
               Position := Position - 1
         END (* IF *)
   END (* CheckForExpression *);

BEGIN (* main program *)
   REPEAT
      writeln ('Enter arithmetic expression (end with ', EndMark, ')');
      ReadString (input, Expr);

      (* Parse the expression *)
      Position := 0;
      CheckForExpression (Expr, Position, ValidExpression);
      IF ValidExpression AND (Position = Length(Expr) - 1) THEN
         writeln ('Valid Expression')
      ELSE
         writeln ('Not a Valid Expression');
      writeln;
      write ('More (Y or N)?  ');
      readln (Response)
   UNTIL NOT (Response in ['Y', 'y'])
END (* main program *).
```

Sample run:

```
Enter arithmetic expression (end with ;)
A+B;
Valid Expression

More (Y or N)?  Y
Enter arithmetic expression (end with ;)
A+B);
Not a Valid Expression

More (Y or N)?  Y
Enter arithmetic expression (end with ;)
A*B;
Valid Expression

More (Y or N)?  Y
Enter arithmetic expression (end with ;)
(((((1)))));
Valid Expression
```

Figure 6.3 (cont.)

```
More (Y or N)?  Y
Enter arithmetic expression (end with ;)
((A+B) - C;
Not a Valid Expression

More (Y or N)?  Y
Enter arithmetic expression (end with ;)
(((A + B) * 2) - (C*D)) * 5;
Valid Expression

More (Y or N)?  Y
Enter arithmetic expression (end with ;)
A * + B;
Not a Valid Expression

More (Y or N)?  N
```

Exercises

1. Trace the execution of *Move* (4, 'A' , 'B' , 'C') far enough to produce the first five moves. Does your answer agree with the program output in Figure 6.2? Do the same for *Move* (5, 'A', 'B , 'C').

2. Modify the program in Figure 6.2 so that it displays a picture of each move rather than a verbal description.

3. Draw parse trees for the following expressions:

   (a) $A * B$ (b) $(A * B)$
   (c) $(((1)))$ (d) $(A * B) * C$
   (e) $A * (B * C)$ (f) $(((A + B) * 2) - (C * D)) * 5$

4. Construct trace tables like those in the text for parses of the following expressions:

   (a) $A * B$ (b) $(A * B)$
   (c) $(A - B) - C$ (d) $A - (B - C)$

5. Syntax rules for simplified boolean expressions might be the following:

   > *bexpression* → *bterm* **or** *bterm* | *bterm*
   > *bterm* → *bfactor* **and** *bfactor* | *bfactor*
   > *bfactor* → **not** *bfactor* | (*bexpression*) | *letter* | true | false

   Write a program that parses such boolean expressions. In the input string, you may simplify matters by using the symbols |, &, and ~ for **or**, **and**, and **not**, respectively.

6. Assuming the syntax rules of Exercise 5, draw parse trees for the following simplified boolean expressions:

(a) not *Y* **and** (*Z* **or** false)   **(b)** *X* **or** *Y* **and** *Z*

(c) false **or** *X* **or** true   **(d) not** (*X* **or** *Y*)

7. By adding the production

   AssignmentStatement → *letter* := *expression*

at the beginning of the list of syntax rules for simplified expressions in this section, we obtain a list of syntax rules for simplified assignment statements. Extend the program of Figure 6.3 so that it will parse such assignment statements.

8. Write a program that reads lines of input, each of which is a (perhaps invalid) Pascal statement, and that strips each line of all valid Pascal comments. However, the structure of your program is restricted as follows:

(a) The only repetition structure allowed is a "while not eof" loop for reading the input; all other repetition must be carried out by using recursion.

(b) The characters must be read one at a time, and looking ahead at the next character in the input buffer is not allowed.

Execute your program with at least the following lines of input

```
Distance := Rate * Time
Wages := ((*** regular ***) Hours * Rate (* hourly *));
writeln ('(*** DISPATCH UNIVERSITY ***)');
Temp(*erature*) := ((* Centigrade *)Deg(*rees*)*1.0);
Temp( *erature*) := (((((* zero *) 0 )))));
```

The output produced by your program for this input should be

```
Distance := Rate * Time
Wages := ( Hours * Rate );
writeln ('(*** DISPATCH UNIVERSITY ***)');
Temp := (Deg*1.0);
Temp( *erature*) := (((( 0 ))));
```

9. Strings consisting of balanced parentheses can be generated by the productions

   pstring → (*pstring*) *pstring* | () *pstring* | (*pstring*) | ()

Draw parse trees for the following strings of balanced parentheses:

(a) ()()()   **(b)** ((()))   **(c)** ()(()())()

10. Write a program that reads a string consisting of only parentheses and that determines whether the parentheses are balanced, as specified by the syntax rules in Exercise 9.

11. Proceed as in Exercise 10, but design the program to read any string, ignoring all characters other than parentheses.

6.3 Proving Algorithms Correct

In our discussion of program verification and validation in Chapter 1, we noted that in some applications such as defense systems and spacecraft guidance systems, program errors cannot be tolerated. In such situations, simply running a program or system of programs with various sets of test data is not sufficient because *testing can show only the presence of errors, not their absence.* Instead, a deductive proof must be given that guarantees that the program is correct and will *always* produce the correct results (assuming no system malfunction). In this section we describe some of the techniques used in such correctness proofs.

To prove that an algorithm for solving a given problem is correct, we must prove deductively that the steps of the algorithm correctly process the input given in the problem's specification so that the required output is obtained. Thus a ***proof of correctness*** of an algorithm $\mathscr{A}$ begins with an **assertion** (assumption) I about its input data, also called a ***precondition***, and an assertion (conclusion) O about its output, also called a ***postcondition***. It then provides a logical argument demonstrating that O follows from I; that is, it is a proof of the theorem

$I \Rightarrow O$ (''I implies O'')
Theorem: Given precondition I.
 After $\mathscr{A}$ is executed, the postcondition O holds.

To illustrate, consider the following algorithm to find the mean of a set of numbers stored in an array:

ALGORITHM TO CALCULATE MEAN

(* Accepts: An integer $n \geq 1$ and an array $X[1], \ldots, X[n]$ of real numbers.
  Function: Finds the mean of n real numbers.
  Returns: The mean of $X[1], \ldots, X[n]$. *)

1. Initialize *Sum* to 0.
2. Initialize index variable i to 0.
3. While $i < n$ do the following:
    a. Increment i by 1.
    b. Add $X[i]$ to *Sum*.
4. Calculate and return *Mean* = *Sum* / n.

Here the input assertion might be stated as

  I: Input consists of an integer $n \geq 1$ and an array X of n real numbers.

and the output assertion as

  O: The algorithm terminates, and when it does, the value of the variable *Mean* is the mean (average) of $X[1], \ldots, X[n]$.

To demonstrate that the postcondition O follows from the precondition I, one usually introduces, at several points in the algorithm, intermediate assertions about the state of processing when execution reaches these points. For the preceding algorithm we might use an additional intermediate assertion at the bottom of the while loop that will be true each time execution reaches this point. Such an assertion is called a *loop invariant*:

I: Input consists of an integer $n \geq 1$ and an array X of n real numbers.

1. Initialize *Sum* to 0.
2. Initialize index variable i to 0.
3. While $i < n$ do the following:
   a. Increment i by 1.
   b. Add $X[i]$ to *Sum*.

A: The value of i is the number of times execution has reached this point, and *Sum* is the sum of the first i elements of array X.

4. Calculate and return *Mean* $=$ *Sum* $/ n$.

O: The algorithm terminates, and when it does, the value of the variable *Mean* is the mean (average) of $X[1], \ldots, X[n]$.

The proof then consists of showing that assertion A follows from the input assertion I and then showing that the output assertion O follows from A.

Mathematical induction can be used to establish the loop invariant A. To see this, suppose we let k denote the number of times that execution has reached the bottom of the loop, and let i_k and Sum_k denote the values of i and *Sum*, respectively, at this time. When $k = 1$, that is, on the first pass through the loop, the value of i will be 1, since it was initially 0 (Step 2) and has been incremented by 1 (Step 3a). *Sum* will be equal to $X[1]$, since it was initially 0 (Step 1), i has the value 1, and $X[i]$ has been added to *Sum* (Step 3b). Thus i and *Sum* have the values asserted in A when $k = 1$.

Now assume that when execution reaches the bottom of the loop for the kth time, the loop invariant A holds

$$i_k = k \text{ and } Sum_k = X[1] + \cdots + X[k]$$

We must prove that A is also true when execution continues through the loop for the $k+1$-st time, that is,

$$i_{k+1} = k + 1 \text{ and } Sum_{k+1} = X[1] + \cdots + X[k+1]$$

On this $k+1$-st pass through the loop, the value of i will be incremented by 1 so that

$$\begin{aligned} i_{k+1} &= i_k + 1 \text{ (Step 3a)} \\ &= k + 1 \text{ (Induction assumption)} \end{aligned}$$

thus i will have the correct value; also,

$$\begin{aligned} Sum_{k+1} &= Sum_k + X[k+1] \text{ (Step 3b)} \\ &= X[1] + \cdots + X[k] + X[k+1] \text{ (Induction assumption)} \end{aligned}$$

It now follows by induction that each time execution reaches the bottom of the loop, i and *Sum* will have the values asserted in the loop invariant A. In particular, after the nth pass through the loop, *Sum* will equal $X[1] + \cdots + X[n]$, and i will become equal to n.

Since i will thus eventually have the value n, the boolean expression $i < n$ that controls repetition will become false, and the while loop will terminate. Execution will then continue with statement 4 in the algorithm. This statement correctly calculates the mean of the array elements, and execution will reach the end of the algorithm. Thus the output assertion is established, and the correctness proof is complete; that is, we have proved:

Theorem
  Given an integer $n > 1$ and an array X of n real numbers.
  When Algorithm to Calculate Mean is executed, it terminates, and when it does, *Mean* is the mean of $X[1], \ldots, X[n]$.

Mathematical induction is also used to prove the correctness of recursive algorithms, since by its very nature, recursion involves an inductive step. As an illustration, consider the recursive power function of Section 6.1:

function *Power*(x : *real*; n : *integer*) : *real*;

(* Accepts: Real number x and nonnegative integer n.
    Function: Calculate x^n.
    Returns: x^n. *)

  begin (* *Power* *)
    if $n = 0$ **then**   (* anchor *)
      Power := 1.0
    else
      Power := x * *Power*(x, $n - 1$)   (* inductive step *)
  end (* *Power* *);

Here the input and output assertions are

  I: Input consists of a real number x and a nonnegative integer n.
  O: Execution of the function terminates, and when it does, the value returned by the function is x^n.

We can use mathematical induction on n to show that the output assertion O follows from the input assertion I. If n is 0, the anchor statement

  Power := 1.0

is executed immediately, so that execution terminates and the correct value 1.0 is returned for x^0. Now assume that for $n = k$, execution terminates and returns the correct value for x^n. When it is referenced with $n = k + 1$, the inductive step

  Power := x * *Power*(x, $n - 1$)

is executed. The value of $n - 1$ is k, and thus by the induction assumption, the function reference $Power(x, n - 1)$ terminates and returns the correct value of x^k. It follows that the function reference with $n = k + 1$ terminates and returns the value $x * x^k = x^{k+1}$, which is the correct value of x^n. We have thus established that in all cases, the output assertion follows from the input assertion.

These examples of correctness proof have been rather informal. They could be formalized, however, by using some special notation to state the assertions (such as the predicate calculus or some other formal notation) and a formal deductive system that spells out the rules that can be used to reason from one assertion to the next. For example, a rule governing an assignment statement S of the form $v := e$ might be stated symbolically as

$$P \xrightarrow{\ S\ } \{Q = P(v, e)\}$$

an abbreviation for "If precondition P holds before an assignment statement S of the form $v := e$ is executed, then the postcondition Q is obtained from P by replacing each occurrence of the variable v by the expression e." Such formalization is necessary in the design of mechanized "theorem provers," and we leave it to more advanced courses in theoretical computer science where it more properly belongs.

Also, these proofs were quite simple in that only one intermediate assertion A was used in the first example and none in the second. The form of the first proof thus was

$$I \Rightarrow A \Rightarrow O$$

that is, the input assertion I implies the intermediate assertion A, and A implies the output assertion O. For more complex algorithms it is usually necessary to introduce several intermediate assertions $A_1, A_2, \ldots, A_n$. The algorithm/program is broken down into small segments, each having one of the A_i (or I) as a precondition and A_{i+1} (or O) as a postcondition:

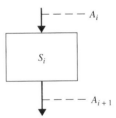

One must show that A_{i+1} follows logically from A_i for each $i = 1, \ldots, n - 1$ and thus the structure of the correctness proof is

$$I \Rightarrow A_1 \Rightarrow A_2 \Rightarrow \cdots \Rightarrow A_n \Rightarrow O$$

If one of these program segments is or contains a selection structure, there may be many paths that execution may follow from A_i to A_{i+1}, and because it is necessary to examine *all* such paths, the correctness proof can become quite complex.

Algorithm/program unit verification is an important part of program development, and ideally, the correctness of each program unit should be formally proved. In practice, however, the time and effort required to write out carefully and completely all the details of a correctness proof of a complicated algorithm are usually prohibitive. Nevertheless, it is still a good programming practice to formulate the major assertions that would be used in a correctness proof and then "walk through" the algorithm/program unit, tracing each possible execution path, following the pattern of a deductive proof. This is a more formal and systematic way of desk checking that every good programmer uses in testing algorithms and programs. Although it does not ensure that the algorithm/program unit is absolutely correct, it does increase one's understanding of the algorithm/program unit and one's confidence in its correctness, and it may uncover logical errors that might otherwise go undetected. As programmers gain experience, it is important that they accumulate *toolboxes* of constructs and algorithms whose correctness has already been established and that can therefore be used with confidence.

Exercises

1. Consider the following algorithm with precondition I, intermediate assertion A, and postcondition O:

ScanAndCount

(* Accepts: Integer $n \geq 1$, an array X of n real numbers, and a real number *Cutoff.*

Function: Finds and displays a *Count* of the elements in X that exceed *Cutoff.*

Output: *Count.* *)

I: Input consists of an integer $n \geq 1$, an array X of n real numbers, and a real number *Cutoff.*

1. Initialize *Count* to 0.
2. Initialize i to 0.
3. While $i < n$ do the following:
   a. Increment i by 1.
   b. If $X[i] > Cutoff$ then
       Add 1 to *Count.*

A: The value of i is the number of times execution has reached this point, and *Count* is the number of array elements among $X[1], \ldots X[i]$ that are greater than *Cutoff.*

4. Display *Count.*

O: The algorithm terminates, and when it does, the value of the variable *Count* is the number of elements in array X that are greater than *Cutoff.*

Using the given input, intermediate, and output assertions, prove the correctness of this algorithm. Note that on each pass through the loop there are two possible paths that execution may follow.

2. Write a nonrecursive version of procedure *Power* and prove its correctness.

3. Give an algorithm that finds and returns the largest element in an array X of n elements, and prove its correctness.

4. Write a recursive function for calculating $n!$, the factorial of n (see Section 6.1), and prove its correctness.

5. Use mathematical induction to prove that the minimum number of moves required to solve the Towers of Hanoi puzzle with n disks is $2^n - 1$. (See Section 6.2.)

6.4 Algorithm Efficiency

An algorithm's efficiency is usually measured according to two criteria. The first is *space utilization*, the amount of memory required to store the data, and the second is *time efficiency*, the amount of time required to process the data. Unfortunately, it is usually not possible to minimize both the space and the time requirements. Algorithms that require the least memory are often slower than those that use more memory. Thus the programmer is usually faced with a trade-off between space efficiency and time efficiency. An algorithm's time efficiency is usually considered the more important of the two, and in this section we consider how it can be measured.

The execution time of an algorithm is influenced by several factors. Obviously, one factor is the size of the input, since the number of input items usually affects the time required to process these items. For example, the time it takes to sort a list of items surely depends on the number of items in the list. Thus the execution time T of an algorithm must be expressed as a function $T(n)$ of the size n of the input.

The kind of instructions and the speed with which the machine can execute them also influence execution time. These factors, however, depend on the particular computer being used; consequently, we cannot expect to express meaningfully the value of $T(n)$ in real time units such as seconds. Instead, $T(n)$ will be an approximate count of the number of instructions executed.

Another factor that influences computing time is the quality of the source code that implements the algorithm and the quality of the machine code generated from this source code by a compiler. Some languages are better suited than others for certain algorithms; some programmers write better programs than others; and some compilers generate more efficient code than others. This means, in particular, that $T(n)$ cannot be computed as the number of machine instructions executed, and thus it is taken to be the number of times the instructions in the *algorithm* are executed.

As an example, consider the algorithm of the preceding section for finding the mean of a set of n numbers stored in an array. (The statements have been numbered for easy reference.)

ALGORITHM TO CALCULATE MEAN

(∗ Accepts: An integer $n \geq 1$ and an array $X[1], \dots, X[n]$ of real
numbers.
Function: Finds the mean of n real numbers.
Returns: The mean of $X[1], \dots, X[n]$. ∗)

1. Initialize *Sum* to 0.
2. Initialize index variable i to 0.
3. While $i < n$ do the following:
4.   a. Increment i by 1.
5.   b. Add $X[i]$ to *Sum*.
6. Calculate and return *Mean* = *Sum* / n.

Statements 1 and 2 each are executed one time. Statements 4 and 5, which comprise the body of the while loop, are executed n times, and statement 3, which controls repetition, is executed $n + 1$ times, since one additional check is required to determine that the control variable i is no longer less than the value n. After repetition terminates, statement 6 is then executed one time. This analysis is summarized in the following table:

Statement	# of times executed
1	1
2	1
3	$n + 1$
4	n
5	n
6	1
Total:	$3n + 4$

Thus we see that the computing time for this algorithm is given by

$$T(n) = 3n + 4$$

As the number n of inputs increases, the value of this expression for $T(n)$ grows at a rate proportional to n, and so we say that $T(n)$ has "order of magnitude n," which is usually denoted using the "big Oh notation" as

$$T(n) = O(n)$$

In general, the computing time $T(n)$ of an algorithm is said to have **order of magnitude** $f(n)$, denoted

$$T(n) = O(f(n))$$

if there is some constant C such that

$$T(n) \leq C \cdot f(n) \text{ for all sufficiently large values of } n$$

That is, $T(n)$ is bounded above by some constant times $f(n)$ for all values of n from some point on. The **computational complexity** of the algorithm is said to be O($f(n)$). For example, the complexity of the preceding algorithm is O(n), since the computing time was found to be

$$T(n) = 3n + 4$$

and since

$$3n + 4 \leq 3n + n \text{ for } n \geq 4$$

we see that

$$T(n) \leq 4n \text{ for all } n \geq 4$$

Thus, taking $f(n) = n$ and $C = 4$, we may write

$$T(n) = O(n)$$

Of course, it would also be correct to write $T(n) = O(5280n)$ or $T(n) = O(4n + 5)$ or $T(n) = O(3.1416n + 2.71828)$, but we prefer a *simple* function like n, n^2, or $\log_2 n$ to express an algorithm's complexity. Also, $T(n) = O(n)$ obviously implies that $T(n) = O(n^2)$ as well as $T(n) = O(n^{5/2})$ or $T(n) = O(2^n)$, and in general $T(n) = O(g(n))$ if $g(n) \geq n$ for all n from some point on; but the smaller the function $g(n)$ is, the more information it will provide about the computing time $T(n)$.

In this example, the computing time depends only on the size of the input. In other problems, however, it may depend on the arrangement of the input items as well. For example, it may take less time to sort a list of items that are nearly in order initially than to sort a list in which the items are in reverse order. We might then attempt to measure T in the **worst case** or in the **best case**, or we might attempt to compute the **average** value of T over all possible cases. The best-case performance of an algorithm is usually not very informative, and the average performance is usually more difficult to determine than the worst-case performance is. Consequently, $T(n)$ is frequently taken as a measure of the algorithm's performance in the worst case.

As an illustration, consider the following sorting algorithm. (Again, we have numbered the statements for easy reference.)

SIMPLE SELECTION SORTING ALGORITHM

(∗ Accepts: Integer n and an array $X[1], \ldots, X[n]$.
       Function: Uses selection sort to sort the elements of X into ascending
              order.
       Returns: X sorted so $X[1] \leq X[2] \leq \ldots X[n]$. ∗)

1. For $i = 1$ to $n - 1$ do the following:

   (∗ On the ith pass, first find the smallest element in the
       sublist $X[i], \ldots, X[n]$. ∗)

2.   a. Set *SmallPos* equal to i.
3.   b. Set *Smallest* equal to $X[SmallPos]$.
4.   c. For $j = i + 1$ to n do the following:
5.   If $X[j] < Smallest$ then (∗ smaller element found ∗)
6.   i. Set *SmallPos* equal to j.

7.   ii. Set *Smallest* equal to $X[SmallPos]$.

(* Now interchange this smallest element with the element at the beginning of this sublist. *)

8.   d. Set $X[SmallPos]$ equal to $X[i]$.
9.   e. Set $X[i]$ equal to *Smallest*.

Statement 1 is executed n times (for i ranging from 1 through the value $n - 1$, which causes termination), and statements 2, 3, 8, and 9 each are executed $n - 1$ times, once on each pass through the outer loop. On the first pass through this loop with $i = 1$, statement 4 is executed n times; statement 5 is executed $n - 1$ times, and assuming a worst case (when the items are in descending order) so are statements 6 and 7. On the second pass with $i = 2$, statement 4 is executed $n - 1$ times, statements 5, 6, and 7 $n - 2$ times, and so on. Thus statement 4 is executed a total of $n + (n - 1) + \cdots + 2$ times, and statements 5, 6, and 7 each are executed a total of $(n - 1) + (n - 2) + \cdots + 1$ times. These sums are equal to $n(n + 1)/2 - 1$ and $n(n - 1)/2$, respectively[1]; thus the total computing time is given by

$$T(n) = n + 4(n - 1) + \frac{n(n + 1)}{2} - 1 + 3\left(\frac{n(n - 1)}{2}\right)$$

which simplifies to

$$T(n) = 2n^2 + 4n - 5$$

Since $n \leq n^2$ for all $n \geq 0$, we see that

$$2n^2 + 4n - 5 \leq 2n^2 + 4n^2 = 6n^2$$

and hence that

$$T(n) \leq 6n^2 \text{ for all } n \geq 0$$

Thus taking $f(n) = n^2$ and $C = 6$ in the definition of big Oh notation, we may write

$$T(n) = O(n^2)$$

The big Oh notation gives an approximate measure of the computing time of an algorithm for a large number of inputs. If two algorithms for performing the same task have different complexities, the algorithm with the lower-order computing time is usually preferable. For example, if the computing time $T_1(n)$ of Algorithm 1 is $O(n)$ and the computing time $T_2(n)$ for Algorithm 2 is $O(n^2)$, then Algorithm 1 is usually considered better than Algorithm 2, since it will perform more efficiently for large values of n. It must be noted, however, that for small values of n, Algorithm 2 might well outperform Algorithm 1. For example, suppose that $T_1(n) = 10n$ and $T_2(n) = 0.1n^2$. Since $10n > 0.1n^2$ for values of n up to 100, we see that

$$T_1(n) < T_2(n) \text{ only for } n > 100$$

---

[1] Here we have used the summation formula

$$\sum_{i=1}^{n} i = \frac{n(n + 1)}{2}$$

Thus Algorithm 2 is more efficient than Algorithm 1 only for inputs of size greater than 100.

To illustrate, consider the problem of searching an array of n elements $A[1], \ldots, A[n]$ to determine whether a specified value *Item* appears in this list and, if so, to determine its location. A simple algorithm for performing this search is **linear search**, in which we start at the beginning of the list and examine successive elements until either *Item* is found or we reach the end of the list.

LINEAR SEARCH ALGORITHM

(* Accepts: A list of n elements stored in array A and *Item* of the same type as the array elements.
Function: Performs a linear search of the list $A[1], \ldots, A[n]$.
Returns: *Found* = *true* and *Loc* = position of *Item* if the search is successful; otherwise, *Found* is false. *)

1. Set *Found* equal to false.
2. Set *Loc* equal to 1.
3. While *Loc* $\leq n$ and not *Found* do the following:
4.   If *Item* = $A[Loc]$ then   (* *Item* found *)
5.   Set *Found* to true.
6.   Else   (* keep searching *)
           Increment *Loc* by 1.

The worst case is obviously that in which *Item* is not in the list, and in this case, we find the computing time $T_L(n)$ for the linear search algorithm as follows:

Statement	# of Times Executed
1	1
2	1
3	$n + 1$
4	n
5	0
6	n

Thus $T_L(n) = 3n + 3$ so that

$$T_L(n) = O(n)$$

since $3n + 3 \leq 4n$ for all $n \geq 3$.

If the list being searched has previously been sorted so that the elements are in ascending order, a **binary search** can be used instead of a linear search. To locate *Item* in such a list, the element $A[Loc]$ in the middle of the list is examined. There are three possibilities:

Item $< A[Loc]$: Search the first half of the list.
Item $> A[Loc]$: Search the last half of the list.
Item $= A[Loc]$: Search is successful.

We continue this halving process until either *Item* is located or the sublist to search becomes empty. The following algorithm gives the details:

BINARY SEARCH ALGORITHM

(* Accepts: A list of *n* elements in ascending order stored in array *A* and *Item* of the same type as the array elements.

  Function: Performs a binary search of the list $A[1], \ldots, A[n]$.

  Returns: *Found* = *true* and *Loc* = position of *Item* if the search is successful; otherwise, *Found* is false. *)

1. Set *Found* equal to false.
2. Set *First* equal to 1.
3. Set *Last* equal to *n*.
4. While *First* ≤ *Last* and not *Found* do the following:
5.   Calculate *Loc* = (*First* + *Last*) / 2.
6.   If *Item* < *A*[*Loc*] then
7.   Set *Last* equal to *Loc* − 1.   (* search first half *)
8.   Else if *Item* > *A*[*Loc*] then
9.   Set *First* equal to *Loc* + 1.   (* search last half *)
10.   Else
           Set *Found* equal to true.   (* *Item* found *)

In this algorithm, statements 1, 2, and 3 are clearly executed exactly once, and to calculate the worst case computing time $T_B(n)$, we must determine the number of times the loop composed of statements 4 through 10 is executed. Each pass through this loop reduces by at least one-half the size of the sublist still to be searched. The last pass occurs when the sublist reaches size one. Thus the total number of iterations of this loop is 1 plus the number *k* of passes required to produce a sublist of size one. Since the size of the sublist after *k* passes is at most $n / 2^k$, we must have

$$\frac{n}{2^k} < 2$$

that is,

$$n < 2^{k+1}$$

or equivalently,

$$\log_2 n < k + 1$$

The required number of passes, therefore, is the smallest integer that satisfies this inequality, that is, the integer part of $\log_2 n$. Thus, in the worst case, when *Item* is greater than each of $A[1], \ldots, A[n]$, statement 4 is executed no more than $2 + \log_2 n$ times, statements 5, 6, 8, and 9 no more than $1 + \log_2 n$ times, and statements 7 and 10 zero times. The total computing time, therefore, is no more than $9 + 5 \log_2 n$, so that

$$T_B(n) = O(\log_2 n)$$

Since the complexity of linear search is O(*n*) and that of binary search is O($\log_2 n$), it is clear that binary search will be more efficient than linear search for large lists. For small lists, however, linear search may—and in fact, does—outperform binary search. Empirical studies indicate that linear search is more efficient than binary search for lists of up to twenty elements.

In addition to $O(\log_2 n)$, $O(n)$, and $O(n^2)$, other computing times that frequently arise in algorithm analysis are $O(1)$, $O(\log_2\log_2 n)$, $O(n\log_2 n)$, $O(n^3)$, and $O(2^n)$. $O(1)$ denotes a *constant* computing time, that is, one that does not depend on the size of the input. A computing time of $O(n)$ is said to be *linear*; $O(n^2)$ is called *quadratic*; $O(n^3)$ is called *cubic*; and $O(2^n)$ is called *exponential*. The following table displays the values of these computing functions for several values of n:

$\log_2\log_2 n$	$\log_2 n$	n	$n\log_2 n$	n^2	n^3	2^n
—	0	1	0	1	1	2
0	1	2	2	4	8	4
1	2	4	8	16	64	16
1.58	3	8	24	64	512	256
2	4	16	64	256	4096	65536
2.32	5	32	160	1024	32768	4294967296
2.6	6	64	384	4096	2.6×10^5	1.85×10^{19}
3	8	256	2.05×10^3	6.55×10^4	1.68×10^7	1.16×10^{77}
3.32	10	1024	1.02×10^4	1.05×10^6	1.07×10^9	1.8×10^{308}
4.32	20	1048576	2.1×10^7	1.1×10^{12}	1.15×10^{18}	6.7×10^{315652}

Graphs of these functions are shown in Figure 6.4.

It should be clear from the preceding table and graphs that algorithms with exponential complexity are practical only for solving problems in which the number of inputs is small. To emphasize this, suppose that each instruction in some algorithm can be executed in one microsecond. The following table shows the time required to execute $f(n)$ instructions for the common complexity functions f with $n = 256$ inputs:

Function	Time
$\log_2\log_2 n$	3 microseconds
$\log_2 n$	8 microseconds
n	.25 milliseconds
$n\log_2 n$	2 milliseconds
n^2	65 milliseconds
n^3	17 seconds
2^n	3.7×10^{61} centuries

All the algorithms for which we have determined the computing times have thus far been nonrecursive algorithms. The computing time $T(n)$ of a recursive algorithm is naturally given by a *recurrence relation*, which expresses the computing time for inputs of size n in terms of smaller-sized inputs.

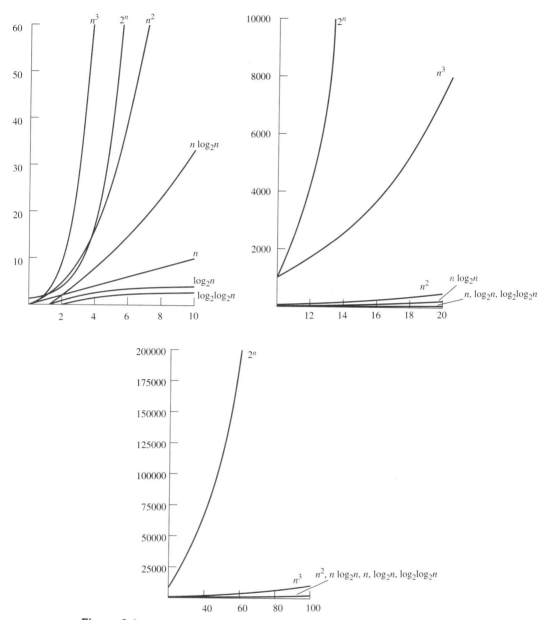

Figure 6.4

To illustrate, consider again the recursive function *Power* of Section 6.1:

function *Power*(*x* : *real*; *n* : *integer*) : *real*;

(* Accepts: Real number *x* and integer $n \geq 0$.
   Function: Computes x^n recursively.
   Returns: x^n. *)

   begin (* *Power* *)
     if $n = 0$ **then**   (* anchor *)
      Power := 1
     else
      Power := *x* * *Power*(*x*, *n* − 1)   (* inductive step *)
   end (* *Power* *);

When *Power* is referenced with $n > 0$, the boolean expression

$$n = 0$$

is first evaluated, and since it is false, the inductive statement

$$Power := x * Power(x, n - 1)$$

is executed. The total computing time is thus 2 plus the time required to compute *Power*(*x*, *n* − 1). Thus $T(n)$ is given by the recurrence relation

$$T(n) = 2 + T(n - 1)$$

Similarly, if $n - 1 > 0$,

$$T(n - 1) = 2 + T(n - 2)$$

and combining these gives

$$T(n) = 2 + 2 + T(n - 2)$$

Continuing this process, we eventually obtain

$$T(n) = 2 + 2 + \cdots + 2 + T(0)$$

The time $T(0)$ to compute x^0 is clearly 2, since the boolean expression $n = 0$ is evaluated and the anchor statement

$$Power := 1.0$$

is executed. Thus we have

$$T(n) = 2(n + 1)$$

so that

$$T(n) = O(n)$$

As we described in Section 6.1, the power function may also be defined iteratively as

$$x^0 = 1$$

$$x^n = \underbrace{x \times x \times \cdots \times x}_{n \; x\text{'s}}, \text{ for } n > 0$$

and this definition leads to the following nonrecursive function:

function *NRPower*(*x* : *real*; *n* : *integer*) : *real*;

(* Accepts: Real number *x* and integer *n* ≥ 0.
    Function: Computes x^n nonrecursively.
    Returns: x^n. *)

  var
    i : *integer*;   (* loop index *)
    Prod : *real*;   (* the product $x * x * \cdots * x$ *)

  begin (* *NRPower* *)
    Prod := 1;
    for *i* := 1 **to** *n* **do**
      Prod := *Prod* * *x*;
    NRPower := *Prod*
  end (* *NRPower* *);

The computing time of this function is easily computed as

$$T_{NR}(n) = O(n)$$

Although the computational complexity of the recursive and nonrecursive functions is the same, the overhead in implementing recursion (as described in the next section) does produce some inefficiency. Consequently, in cases such as this, in which both a recursive algorithm and a nonrecursive one can be developed with little difference in effort, the nonrecursive solution is usually preferred.

In some cases, the computing time of a recursive algorithm to solve a problem may be much greater than that of a nonrecursive algorithm for the same problem. This is especially true of those like the recursive function *Fib* for calculating Fibonacci numbers in Section 6.1, in which the inductive step requires more than one reference to the function itself:

function *Fib*(*n* : *integer*) : *integer*;

(* Accepts: Positive integer *n*.
    Function: Computes *n*th Fibonacci number recursively.
    Returns: *n*th Fibonacci number. *)

  begin (* *Fib* *)
    if *n* <= 2 **then**   (* anchor *)
      Fib := 1
    else
      Fib := *Fib*(*n* − 1) + *Fib*(*n* − 2)   (* inductive step *)
  end (* *Fib* *);

We noted that multiple function references with the same parameter indicate that this is not a particularly efficient method of calculating Fibonacci numbers. Indeed, it is extremely inefficient!

To find the computing time of this function *Fib*, we observe that for

$n > 2$, the boolean expression $n <= 2$ is checked, the anchor step is skipped, and the inductive step is executed. The computing time is thus given by the recurrence relation

$$T(n) = 2 + T(n - 1) + T(n - 2)$$

for $n > 2$. Since this recurrence relation is not especially easy to solve to obtain an explicit formula for $T(n)$, we will use it instead to obtain a lower bound for $T(n)$ that grows exponentially with n and thus show that $T(n)$ grows exponentially.

This recurrence relation holds for all integers n greater than 2, and thus if $n > 3$ (so that $n - 1$ is greater than 2), we may apply it to $n - 1$ to say that

$$T(n - 1) = 2 + T(n - 2) + T(n - 3)$$

Substituting this in the original relation gives

$$T(n) = 4 + 2T(n - 2) + T(n - 3) \text{ for } n > 3$$

and thus

$$T(n) > 2T(n - 2) \text{ for } n > 3$$

If $n > 5$ so that $n - 2 > 3$, we may apply this inequality to $n - 2$ and obtain

$$T(n) > 2T(n - 2) > 4T(n - 4)$$

Continuing in this matter, we obtain

$$T(n) > 2T(n - 2) > 4T(n - 4) > \cdots > 2^{(n-2)/2}T(2) \text{ if } n \text{ is even}$$

or

$$T(n) > 2T(n - 2) > 4T(n - 4) > \cdots > 2^{(n-1)/2}T(1) \text{ if } n \text{ is odd}$$

and since $T(2) = T(1) = 2$, we conclude in either case that

$$T(n) > 2^{n/2} = (2^{1/2})^n = (\sqrt{2})^n > (1.4)^n \text{ for } n > 2$$

The recursive function *Fib* thus has computing time that is at least exponential. In fact, it can be shown that

$$T(n) = O\left(\left(\frac{1 + \sqrt{5}}{2}\right)^n\right)$$

where $\dfrac{1 + \sqrt{5}}{2} = 1.618034 \cdots$ is the **golden ratio** approached by ratios of consecutive Fibonacci numbers.[2]

---

[2] The sequence of ratios of consecutive Fibonacci numbers:

$$\frac{1}{1} = 1$$

$$\frac{2}{1} = 2$$

$$\frac{3}{2} = 1.5$$

(continued on next page)

In contrast, the computing time of the following nonrecursive Fibonacci function is easily seen to grow linearly with n; that is,

$$T_{NR}(n) = O(n)$$

function *NRFib*(n : *integer*) : *integer*;

```
(* Accepts:  Positive integer n.
   Function: Computes nth Fibonacci number nonrecursively.
   Returns:  nth Fibonacci number. *)

var
    Fib1, Fib2, Fib3,      (* 3 consecutive Fibonacci numbers *)
    i : integer;           (* index *)

begin (* NRFib *)
    Fib1 := 1;
    Fib2 := 1;
    for i := 3 to n do
        begin
            Fib3 := Fib1 + Fib2;
            Fib1 := Fib2;
            Fib2 := Fib3
        end (* for *);
    NRFib := Fib2
end (* NRFib *);
```

On one machine, the time required to compute *NRFib*(n) for $n \leq 30$ was less than three milliseconds, whereas the time to compute *Fib*(n) was much greater, as shown by the following table (time is in milliseconds):

n	10	15	20	22	24	26	28	30
Time	6	69	784	2054	5465	14121	36921	96494

Quite obviously, the nonrecursive function *NRFib* is preferable to the recursive function *Fib*.

(*continued*)

$$\frac{5}{3} = 1.6666\cdots$$

$$\frac{8}{5} = 1.6$$

$$\frac{13}{8} = 1.61825$$

$$\cdot$$
$$\cdot$$
$$\cdot$$
$$\downarrow$$

$$\frac{1 + \sqrt{5}}{2} = 1.618034\cdots$$

In summary, calculating powers and finding Fibonacci numbers are examples of problems that can be solved with nearly equal ease using either a nonrecursive or a recursive algorithm. For reasons that will become apparent in the next section, nonrecursive functions and procedures usually (but not always) execute more rapidly and use memory more efficiently than do the corresponding recursive subprograms. Thus, if the problem can be solved recursively or nonrecursively with little difference in effort, it is usually better to use the nonrecursive version.

For many problems, however, it is more natural and straightforward to give a recursive algorithm for solving the problem. Two examples are the Towers of Hanoi and parsing problems described in Section 6.2. Other examples will arise in later chapters when we consider data structures that are defined recursively. For such problems, it is often not obvious how the nonrecursive functions and/or procedures used to implement the basic algorithms should be formulated. A good deal of effort may be required to develop them, and the results are often much less readable and understandable than are the recursive versions. In such cases, the simplicity and elegance of the recursive subprograms more than compensate for any inefficiency they may have. Unless these subprograms are to be executed a large number of times and it can be demonstrated that the corresponding nonrecursive formulations are more efficient, the extra effort required to develop the nonrecursive versions is not warranted.

Exercises

1. Which of the orders of magnitude given in this section is the best O notation to describe the following computing times?

   (a) $T(n) = n^3 + 100n \cdot \log_2 n + 5000$
   (b) $T(n) = 2^n + n^{99} + 7$
   (c) $T(n) = \dfrac{n^2 - 1}{n + 1} + 8 \log_2 n$
   (d) $T(n) = 1 + 2 + 4 + \cdots + 2^{n-1}$

2. Give an example of an algorithm with complexity O(1).

3. Explain why if $T(n) = O(n)$ then it is also correct to say $T(n) = O(n^2)$.

4. For each of the following segments, determine which of the orders of magnitude given in this section is the best O notation to use to express the worst-case computing time as a function of n:

   (a) (* Calculate mean *)
       $n := 0$;
       $Sum := 0$;
       $readln\ (x)$;
       while $x <> -999$ **do**

```
        begin
           n := n + 1;
           Sum := Sum + x;
           readln (x)
        end (* while *);
        Mean := Sum / n;
```

(b) (* Matrix addition *)
```
    for i := 1 to n do
       for j := 1 to n do
          C[i, j] := A[i, j] + B[i, j];
```

(c) (* Matrix multiplication *)
```
    for i := 1 to n do
       for j := 1 to n do
          begin
             C[i, j] := 0;
             for k := 1 to n do
                C[i, j] := C[i, j] + A[i, k] * B[k, j]
          end (* for j *);
```

(d) (* Bubble sort *)
```
    for i := 1 to n - 1 do
       begin
          for j := i to n - 1 do
             if X[j] > X[j + 1] then
                begin
                   Temp := X[j];
                   X[j] := X[j + 1];
                   X[j + 1] := Temp
                end (* if *)
       end (* for *);
```

(e)
```
    while n ≥ 1 do
       n := n div 2;
```

(f)
```
    x := 1;
    for i := 1 to n - 1 do
       begin
          for j := 1 to x do
             writeln (j);
          x := 2 * x
       end (* for *);
```

5. Write a recurrence relation for the computing time of procedure *Move* in the program *TowersOfHanoi* in Figure 6.1 and solve it to find this computing time.

6.5   Implementing Recursion

Whenever execution of a program or subprogram begins, a set of memory locations called an ***activation record*** is created for it. If execution is interrupted by a reference to another (or the same) subprogram, the values of the subprogram's local variables, parameters, the return address, and so on are stored in this activation record. When execution of this program unit resumes, its activation record is used to restore these items to what they were before the interruption.

Suppose, for example, that program A references procedure B, which, in turn, references procedure C. When A is initiated, its activation record is created. When A references B so that B becomes active, its activation record is also created. Similarly, when B references C, C becomes the active procedure, and its activation record is created. When execution of C terminates and control is passed back to B so that it becomes active again, the values in its activation record are the values of its parameters and local variables at the time B was interrupted; thus these values are the ones needed to resume execution of B. Likewise, when B terminates and A is reactivated, its activation record is needed to restore the values being used before its interruption. In each case, the fact that the last (sub)program interrupted is the first one to be reactivated suggests that a stack can be used to store the addresses of the activation records so that they can be retrieved in a last-in-first-out order.

As an example, consider the recursive function of Section 6.1 for calculating powers:

> **function** *Power*(*x* : *real*; *n* : *integer*) : *real*;
>   **begin** (∗ *Power* ∗)
>   **if** *n* = 0 **then**
>   *Power* := 1.0
>   **else**
> (∗ A ∗)   *Power* := *x* ∗ *Power*(*x*, *n* − 1)
>   **end** (∗ *Power* ∗);

and a reference to it in an assignment statement:

> **begin** (∗ program *PowerDemo* ∗)
>   .
>   .
>   .
> (∗ B ∗)   *z* := *Power*(2.0, 3);
>   .
>   .
>   .
> **end** (∗ *PowerDemo* ∗).

Here we have indicated as A and B the return addresses, that is, the locations of the instructions where execution is to resume when the program or procedure is reactivated.

When execution of the main program is initialized, its activation record is created. This record is used to store the values of variables, actual parameters, return addresses, and so on during the time the program is active. When execution of the main program is interrupted by the function reference *Power*(2.0, 3), the parameters 2.0 and 3 and the return address B (plus other items of information) are stored in the activation record, and this record is pushed onto a stack.

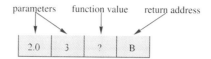

2.0	3	?	B

The function *Power* now becomes active, and an activation record is created for it. When the statement

$$Power := x * Power(x, n - 1)$$

is encountered, the execution of *Power* is interrupted. The actual parameters 2.0 and 2 for this function reference with parameters $x = 2.0$ and $n - 1 = 3 - 1 = 2$ and the return address A (and other items of information) are stored in the activation record, and this record is pushed onto the stack of activation records.

	2.0	2	?	A
Second reference to *Power* ($x = 2.0, n = 2$):	2.0	3	?	B

Since this is a new reference to *Power*, another activation record is created, and when this reference is interrupted by the reference *Power*(2.0, 1), this activation record is pushed onto the stack:

	2.0	1	?	A
Third reference to *Power* ($x = 2.0, n = 1$):	2.0	2	?	A
	2.0	3	?	B

The reference *Power*(2.0, 1) results in the creation of yet another activation record, and when its execution is interrupted, this time by the reference *Power*(2.0, 0), this activation record is pushed onto the stack:

	2.0	0	?	A
Fourth reference to *Power* ($x = 2.0, n = 0$):	2.0	1	?	A
	2.0	2	?	A
	2.0	3	?	B

Execution of *Power* with parameters 2.0 and 0 terminates with no interruptions and calculates the value 1.0 for *Power*(2.0, 0). The activation record for this reference is then popped from the stack, and the execution resumes at the statement specified by the return address in it:

First return from *Power*:

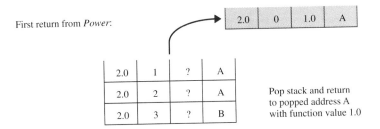

2.0	1	?	A
2.0	2	?	A
2.0	3	?	B

Pop stack and return
to popped address A
with function value 1.0

Execution of the preceding reference to *Power* with parameters 2.0 and 1 then resumes and terminates without interruption, so that its activation record is popped from the stack, the value 2.0 is returned, and the previous reference with parameters 2.0 and 2 is reactivated at statement A:

Second return from *Power*:

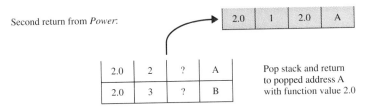

| 2.0 | 2 | ? | A |
| 2.0 | 3 | ? | B |

Pop stack and return
to popped address A
with function value 2.0

This process continues until the value 8.0 is computed for the original reference *Power*(2.0, 3), and execution of the main program is resumed at the statement specified by the return address *B* in its activation record.

Third return from *Power*:

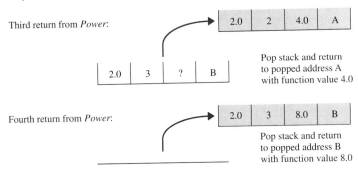

| 2.0 | 3 | ? | B |

Pop stack and return
to popped address A
with function value 4.0

Fourth return from *Power*:

Pop stack and return
to popped address B
with function value 8.0

7

Lists

Stacks and queues, considered in the preceding chapters, are special kinds of lists. Each of these data structures is a sequence of data items, and the basic operations are insertion and deletion. For these structures, however, insertion and deletion are restricted to the ends of the list. But no such limitations are imposed on a general list, as items may be inserted and/or deleted at any point in the list. In this chapter we consider in more detail these general lists and several possible implementations.

7.1 Sequential Storage Implementation of Lists

Lists of various kinds are common in everyday life. There are grocery lists, dean's lists, class lists, appointment lists, mailing lists, lists of seats (on TransFryslan Airlines), and even lists of lists like this one! The features that these examples have in common are abstracted to motivate the following definition of a list.

As a data structure, a *list* is a finite sequence (possibly empty) of elements. Although the basic operations performed on lists vary with each application, they usually include the following:

1. Create an empty list.
2. Determine whether a list is empty.
3. Traverse the list or a portion of it, accessing and processing the elements in order (for example, to display the elements of the list or to search the list for some item).
4. Insert a new element into the list.
5. Delete an element from the list.

A formal specification for the data type list with these operations is

ADT List

Collection of Data Elements

An ordered collection of data items.

Basic Operations

CreateList:
FUNCTION:	Creates an empty list.
RETURNS:	An empty list.

EmptyList:
ACCEPTS:	A list.
FUNCTION:	Checks if the list is empty.
RETURNS:	True if the list is empty, and false otherwise.

Traverse:
ACCEPTS:	A list.
FUNCTION:	Traverses the list (or perhaps only partially), accessing and processing the elements in order.
OUTPUT/RETURNS:	Depends on the kind of processing.

Insert:
ACCEPTS:	A list, a data item, and a position in the list.
FUNCTION:	Inserts the data item into the list at the specified position.
RETURNS:	The modified list.

Delete:
ACCEPTS:	A list and a position in the list.
FUNCTION:	Deletes the element in the specified position from the list.
RETURNS:	The modified list.

Because lists, like stacks and queues, are sequences of data items, it would seem natural once again to use an array as the basic storage structure. This is indeed a common method of implementing lists and is the one that we used earlier. It is characterized by the fact that successive list elements are stored in a sequence of consecutive array locations: the first list element in location 1 of the array, the second list element in location 2, and so on:

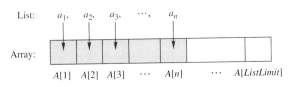

We will refer to this implementation of a list as the **_sequential storage_** implementation.

It is also convenient to use an auxiliary variable to maintain a count of the number of items currently in the list. Thus we are led to declarations like the following:

const
  ListLimit = . . .;   (* maximum size of the list *)

type
  ListElementType = . . .; (* type of elements in the list *)
  ListArray = **array**[1..*ListLimit*] **of** *ListElementType*;
  ListType = **record**
       Size : 0..*ListLimit*;
       Element : *ListArray*
    end;

Implementing the first three basic list operations is then easy. For example, given these declarations, if *List* is of type *ListType*, the assignment statement

  List.Size := 0

can be used to create an empty list, and the assignment statement

  EmptyList := (*List.Size* = 0)

can be used to assign the value *true* or *false* to the boolean variable or function name *EmptyList* according to whether or not *List* is empty. Lists are easily traversed using a loop in which the array index varies. For example, to display all the elements in *List*, we might use

  for *i* := 1 **to** *List.Size* **do**
   writeln (*List.Element*[*i*])

Implementing the insertion operation is somewhat more complicated. For example, suppose we wish to insert the new value 56 after the element 48 in the list of integers

    23, 25, 34, 48, 61, 79, 82, 89, 91, 99

to produce the new list

    23, 25, 34, 48, 56, 61, 79, 82, 89, 91, 99

Since the definition of a list as a data structure imposes no limit on the size of the list, such an insertion is always possible theoretically. In this sequential storage implementation, however, the fixed size of the array used as the basic storage structure limits the size of the list. This means that it may not be possible to insert a new item into a list because there is no room in the array for it. Thus, in addition to the constant and type definitions given earlier and the procedures and functions for the basic list operations, a package (or unit) for the ADT list should contain a boolean variable *ListError* (like *StackError* in the package for the ADT stack) which signals if an error occurred while attempting to carry out some list operation.

Another complication arises from the fact that in this implementation, list elements are stored in consecutive positions of the array. Consequently, in order to insert a new item, it usually is necessary to move array elements to make room for it. For example, for the insertion operation just described, the array elements in positions 5 through 10 must first be shifted into positions 6 through 11 before the new element can be inserted at position 5:

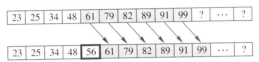

Thus a procedure for insertion must first check whether the array is full and, if it is not, carry out the necessary shifting of array elements before the new item is placed in the array. If the array is full, insertion is obviously impossible and some other action is required. In the following procedure, the action taken is similar to that for stacks and queues, namely, to display a list-full message and assign *true* to *ListError*.

```
procedure Insert (var List : ListType;
                  Item : ListElementType; Pos : integer);

(* Accepts:  A List, a position Pos, and a data Item.
   Function: Insert Item into List after the element in position Pos
             (Pos = 0 for insertion at the beginning of the list).
   Returns:  Modified List and ListError, which is true if insertion is
             not possible and is false otherwise.
   Output:   Error message if insertion fails. *)

var
   i : integer; (* array index *)

begin (* Insert *)
   if List.Size = ListLimit then
      begin
         writeln ('*** Attempt to insert into a full list ***');
         ListError := true
      end (* if *)
   else
      with List do
      begin
         ListError := false;
         (* Shift array elements right to make room for Item *)
         for i := Size downto Pos + 1 do
            Element[i + 1] := Element[i];
         (* Insert Item at position Pos + 1 and increase list size *)
         Element[Pos + 1] := Item;
         Size := Size + 1
      end (* with *)
end (* Insert *);
```

The efficiency of procedure *Insert* obviously depends on the number of array elements that must be shifted to make room for the new element, that is, on the number of times that the body of the for loop is executed. In the worst case, the new item must be inserted at the beginning of the list, which requires shifting all of the array elements. In the average case, one half of the array elements must be shifted to make room for a new item. Thus, for a list of size *n*, it follows that both the worst-case and the average-case computing times for procedure *Insert* are O(*n*). The best case occurs when the new item is inserted at the end of the list. Because no array elements need to be shifted in this case (so the body of the for loop is never executed), the computing time does not depend on the size of the list. Insertions can be carried out in constant time, so the best-case computing time of *Insert* is O(1).

If the order in which the elements appear in a list is not important, then new items can be inserted at any convenient location in the list; in particular, they may always be inserted at the end of the list. For such lists, therefore, insertions can always be carried out in constant time. Note that for these lists, the insertion operation is nothing more than the push operation for stacks described in Chapter 4.

Implementing the deletion operation also requires shifting array elements if list elements are to be stored in consecutive array locations. For example, to delete the second item in the list

$$23, 25, 34, 48, 56, 61, 79, 82, 89, 91, 99$$

we must shift the array elements in positions 3 through 11 into locations 2 through 10 to "close the gap" in the array:

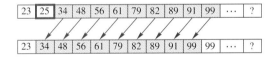

procedure *Delete* (**var** *List* : *ListType*; *Pos* : *integer*);

   (∗ Accepts: A *List* and a position *Pos* in the list.
        Function: Deletes from *List* the element at position *Pos*.
        Returns: Modified *List* and *ListError*, which is true if deletion is
                not possible and is false otherwise.
        Output: Error message if deletion fails. ∗)

   var
     i : *integer*;   (∗ array index ∗)

   begin (∗ *Delete* ∗)
     if *EmptyList*(*List*) **then**
       begin
         writeln ('∗∗∗ Attempt to delete from an empty list ∗∗∗');
         ListError := *true*
       end (∗ **if** ∗)

    else
        with *List* **do**
            begin
                ListError := *false*;
                (* Decrease list size by 1 and close the gap *)
                Size := *Size* − 1;
                for *i* := *Pos* **to** *Size* **do**
                    Element[*i*] := *Element*[*i* + 1]
            end (* **with** *)
    end (* *Delete* *);

The computing time of this procedure is easily seen to be the same as that of procedure *Insert*, $O(n)$ in the worst and average cases and $O(1)$ in the best case.

Because insertion and deletion in this sequential storage implementation may require shifting many array elements, these operations may be quite slow. Thus, although this implementation is adequate for **static lists,** it may not be appropriate for **dynamic lists** in which a large number of insertions and deletions are performed. In applications in which it is necessary to insert and/or delete items at any position in the list, a better implementation is to use a linked list, as described in the following sections.

Exercises

1. Explain why the best-, worst-, and average-case computing times of procedure *Delete* are $O(1)$, $O(n)$, and $O(n)$, respectively.

2. Suppose we modify the sequential storage implementation to allow "holes" in the array; that is, the list elements need not be stored in consecutive array locations, but only stored in order. When a list element is deleted, we simply store some special value in that array location to indicate that it does not contain a list element. (For example, for a list of test scores, we might use a negative value.)

   (a) Write a procedure to traverse a list of test scores stored in an array in this manner and calculate the mean score.
   (b) Modify procedure *Delete* for this implementation, and determine its computing time.
   (c) Modify procedure *Insert* for this implementation and determine its computing time.

3. A **polynomial of degree n** has the form

$$a_0 + a_1x + a_2x^2 + \cdots + a_nx^n$$

   where $a_0, a_1, \ldots, a_n$ are numeric constants called the **coefficients** of the polynomial and $a_n \neq 0$. For example,

$$1 + 3x - 7x^3 + 5x^4$$

is a polynomial of degree 4 with integer coefficients 1, 3, 0, -7, and 5. One common implementation of a polynomial stores the degree of the polynomial and the list of coefficients. Thus we might use a record consisting of an integer field for the degree and an array for the list of coefficients.

(a) Write appropriate declarations for this implementation of polynomials.

(b) Write a procedure to read information about a polynomial and construct such a representation.

(c) Write a procedure to implement the operation of polynomial addition. Determine its complexity.

(d) Write a procedure to implement the operation of polynomial multiplication. Determine its complexity.

(e) Use your declarations and procedures in a menu-driven program for processing polynomials. Options on the menu should include polynomial addition, polynomial multiplication, printing a polynomial using the usual mathematical format with x^n written as $x \uparrow n$ or $x^\wedge n$, and evaluation of a polynomial for a given value of the variable.

4. The Cawker City Candy Company maintains two warehouses, one in Chicago and one in Detroit, each of which stocks at most twenty-five different items. Write a program that first reads the product numbers of items stored in the Chicago warehouse and stores them in an array *Chicago*, and then repeats this for the items stored in the Detroit warehouse, storing these product numbers in an array *Detroit*. The program should then find and display the ***intersection*** of these two lists of numbers, that is, the collection of product numbers common to both lists. Do not assume that the lists have the same number of elements.

5. Repeat Exercise 4, but find and display the ***union*** of the two lists, that is, the collection of product numbers that are elements of at least one of the lists.

7.2 Introduction to Linked Lists

A list is a sequence of data items, which means that there is an order associated with the elements in the list: It has a first element, a second element, and so on. Thus any implementation of this data structure must incorporate a method for specifying this order. In the sequential storage implementation considered in the preceding section, this ordering of list elements was given *implicitly* by the natural ordering of the array elements, since the first element was stored in the first position of the array, the second list element in the second position, and so on. It was this implicit specification of the ordering of the list elements that necessitated shifting them in the array each time an element was inserted or deleted. In this section we begin consideration of an alternative implementation of lists in which the ordering of the list elements is given *explicitly*.

In any structure used to store the elements of a list, it must be possible to perform at least the following operations if the ordering of the list elements is to be preserved:

1. Locate the first element.
2. Given the location of any list element, determine the location of its successor.

As we have seen, in the sequential storage implementation the ordering is given implicitly by the indices of the array: The first list element is stored in array location 1, and the successor of the element in location i is found in location $i + 1$ of the array.

One structure for storing the elements of a list in which the ordering is given explicitly is called a ***linked list.*** It consists of a collection of elements called ***nodes,*** each of which stores two items of information: (1) an element of the list and (2) a ***link*** or ***pointer*** that indicates explicitly the location of the node containing the successor of this list element. Access to the node storing the first list element must also be maintained. For example, a linked list storing the list names

Brown, Jones, Smith

might be pictured as follows:

In this diagram, arrows represent links, and *List* points to the first node in the list. The *Data* part of each node stores one of the names in the list, and the dot in the last node having no arrow emanating from it represents a ***nil pointer*** and indicates that this list element has no successor. If p is a pointer to any of the nodes in such a linked list, we will denote the data portion of this node by *Data*(p) and the link part by *Next*(p). We will also assume that *NilValue* is a special value that can be assigned to p to indicate that it is a nil pointer, that is, that it does not point to any node.

We now consider how the five basic list operations given in the preceding section can be implemented in this setting. To create an empty list *List*, we assign *NilValue* to *List* to indicate that it does not point to any node:

List ●

We can then perform the second list operation, determining whether *List* is an empty list, simply by checking whether *List* has the value *NilValue*.

The third basic list operation is list traversal. To traverse a linked list like the preceding list of names, we begin by initializing some auxiliary pointer *CurrPtr* to point to the first node, and we process the list element 'Brown' stored in this node:

Initialize *CurrPtr* to *List*.
Process *Data*(*CurrPtr*).

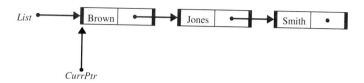

To move to the next node, we follow the link from the current node, setting *CurrPtr* equal to *Next(CurrPtr)*—analogous to incrementing an index by 1 in a sequential storage implementation—and process the name 'Jones' stored there:

> Set *CurrPtr* equal to *Next(CurrPtr)*.
> Process *Data(CurrPtr)*.

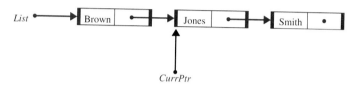

After processing the item stored in this node, we move to the next node and process the list element 'Smith' stored there:

> Set *CurrPtr* equal to *Next(CurrPtr)*.
> Process *Data(CurrPtr)*.

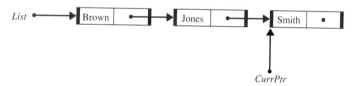

If we now attempt to move to the next node, *CurrPtr* becomes nil, signaling the end of the list:

> Set *CurrPtr* equal to *Next(CurrPtr)*.

In summary, a linked list can be traversed as follows:

ALGORITHM TO TRAVERSE A LINKED LIST

(* Accepts: A linked list with first node pointed to by *List*.
   Function: Traverses this linked list, processing each list
                element exactly once.
 Returns/Output: Depends on the kind of processing. *)

1. Initialize *CurrPtr* to *List*.
2. While *CurrPtr* ≠ *NilValue* do the following:
    a. Process *Data(CurrPtr)*.
    b. Set *CurrPtr* equal to *Next(CurrPtr)*.

Note that this algorithm is correct even for an empty list, since in this case *List* has the value *NilValue* and the while loop is bypassed.

The fourth and fifth basic list operations are insertion and deletion. In this section we illustrate these operations, leaving to later sections the general algorithms and the procedures for implementing them.

To insert a new data value into a linked list, we must first obtain a new node and store the value in its data part. We assume that there is a storage pool of available nodes and some mechanism for obtaining nodes from it as needed. More precisely, we assume that some procedure *GetNode* can be called with a statement of the form *GetNode (TempPtr)* to return a pointer *TempPtr* to such a node. The second step is to connect this new node to the existing list, and for this, there are two cases to consider: (1) insertion at the beginning of the list and (2) insertion after some element in the list.

To illustrate the first case, suppose we wish to insert the name 'Adams' at the beginning of the preceding linked list. We first obtain a new node temporarily pointed to by *TempPtr* and store the name 'Adams' in its data part:

GetNode (TempPtr)
Set Data(TempPtr) equal to 'Adams.'

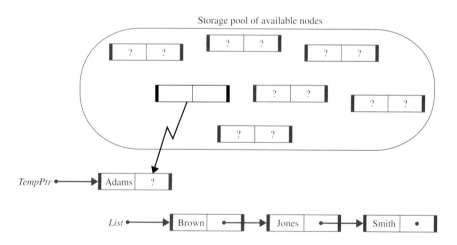

We then insert this node into the list by setting its link part to point to the first node in the list:

Set *Next(TempPtr)* equal to *List*.

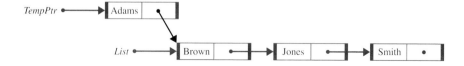

and then setting *List* to point to this new first node:

Set *List* equal to *TempPtr*.

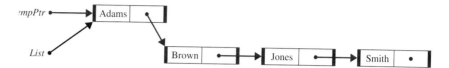

As an illustration of the second case, suppose that we wish to insert the name 'Lewis' after the node containing 'Jones' and that *PredPtr* is a pointer to this predecessor. We begin as before by obtaining a new node in which to store the name 'Lewis':

GetNode (*TempPtr*).
Set *Data*(*TempPtr*) equal to 'Lewis'.

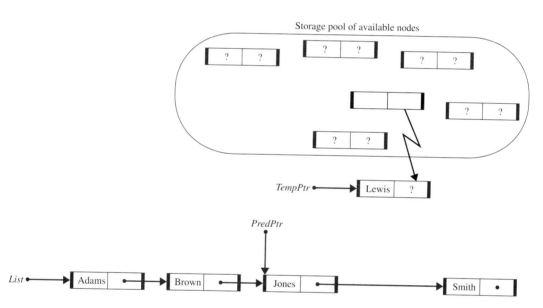

We insert it into the list by first setting its link part equal to *Next*(*PredPtr*) so that it points to its successor:

Set *Next*(*TempPtr*) equal to *Next*(*PredPtr*).

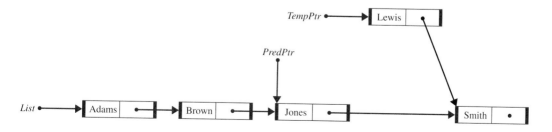

and then resetting the link part of the predecessor node to point to this new node:

Set *Next(PredPtr)* equal to *TempPtr*.

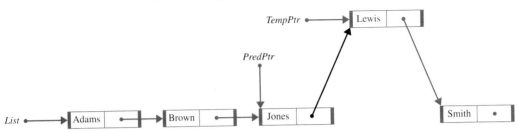

For deletion, there are also two cases to consider: (1) deleting the first element in the list and (2) deleting an element that has a predecessor. As an illustration of the first case, suppose we wish to delete the name 'Adams' from the preceding list. This case is easy and consists of simply resetting *List* to point to the second node in the list and then returning this node to the storage pool of available nodes by calling some procedure *ReleaseNode* that we assume is available for this purpose:

Set *TempPtr* equal to *List*.
Set *List* equal to *Next(List)*.
ReleaseNode (TempPtr).

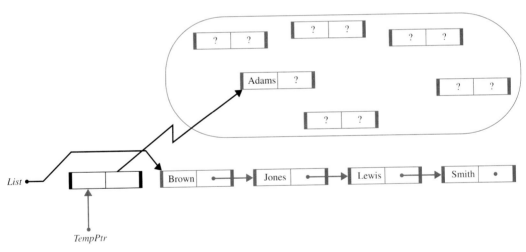

The second case is almost as easy as the first. For example, to delete the node containing 'Lewis' from the preceding list, we need only set the link of its predecessor to point to the node containing its successor (if there is one):

Set *TempPtr* equal to *Next(PredPtr)*.
Set *Next(PredPtr)* equal to *Next(TempPtr)*.
ReleaseNode (TempPtr).

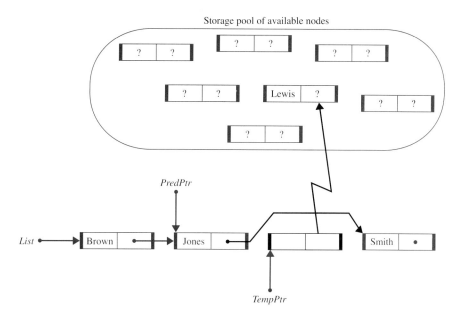

Storage pool of available nodes

As this discussion demonstrates, it is possible to insert and delete data items in a linked list without shifting array elements, as required in the sequential storage implementation. At this stage, however, we have described linked lists only abstractly, at a logical level, and have not considered an implementation for them. To implement linked lists, we need at least the following capabilities:

1. Some means of dividing memory into nodes, each having a data part and a link part, and some implementation of pointers.
2. Operations/functions to access the values stored in each node, that is, implementations of the operations we have denoted by $Data(p)$ and $Next(p)$, where p points to a node.
3. Some means of keeping track of the nodes in use and the available free nodes and of transferring nodes between those in use and the pool of free nodes.

Unfortunately, there are only a few programming languages (such as LISP, an acronym for LISt Processing) that provide linked lists as predefined data structures. In other languages, such as Pascal, it is necessary to implement linked lists using other data types. In the next section we show how they can be implemented using arrays of records and, in Section 7.4, how they can be implemented using the pointer data type in Pascal.

Exercises

In the following exercises you may assume that some procedure *GetNode* as described in the text may be used to obtain a new node from the storage pool of available nodes. You may also assume that a procedure reference of the form *ReleaseNode* (*Ptr*) returns the node pointed to by pointer *Ptr* to the storage pool.

1. Write an algorithm to count the nodes in a linked list with first node pointed to by *List*.

2. Write an algorithm to determine the average of a linked list of real numbers with first node pointed to by *List*.

3. Write an algorithm to append a node at the end of a linked list with first node pointed to by *List*.

4. Write an algorithm to determine whether the data items in a linked list with first node pointed to by *List* are in ascending order.

5. Determine the computing times of the algorithms in Exercises 1 through 4.

6. Write an algorithm to search a linked list with first node pointed to by *List* for a given item and if found, return a pointer to the predecessor of the node containing that item.

7. Write an algorithm to insert a new node into a linked list with first node pointed to by *List* after the nth node in this list for a given integer n.

8. Write an algorithm to delete the nth node in a linked list with first node pointed to by *List* where n is a given integer.

9. The **shuffle-merge** of two lists $X_1, X_2, \ldots, X_n$ and $Y_1, Y_2, \ldots, Y_m$ is the list

   $$Z = X_1, Y_1, X_2, Y_2, \ldots, X_n, Y_n, Y_{n+1}, \ldots, Y_m \text{ if } n < m$$

   or

   $$Z = X_1, Y_1, X_2, Y_2, \ldots, X_m, Y_m, X_{m+1}, \ldots, X_n \text{ if } n > m$$

   Write an algorithm to shuffle-merge two linked lists with first nodes pointed to by *List1* and *List2*, respectively. The items in these two lists should be copied to produce the new list; the original lists should not be destroyed.

10. Proceed as in Exercise 9 but do not copy the items. Just change links in the two lists (thus destroying the original lists) to produce the merged list.

11. Suppose the items stored in two linked lists are in ascending order. Write an algorithm to merge these two lists to yield a list with the items in ascending order.

12. Write an algorithm to reverse a linked list with first node pointed to by *List*. Do not copy the list elements; rather, reset links and pointers so that *List* points to the last node and all links between nodes are reversed.

7.3 An Array-Based Implementation of Linked Lists

We noted that a linked list is not a predefined data structure in most programming languages, and so the programmer is usually faced with the problem of implementing linked lists using other predefined structures. Because nearly every high-level language provides arrays, we first consider how arrays—and, in particular, arrays of records—can be used to implement linked lists.

Recall that the nodes in a linked list contain two parts: a data part that stores an element of the list and a link part that points to a node containing the successor of this list element or that is nil if this is the last element in the list. This suggests that each node may be represented as a record and the linked list as an array of records. Each record will contain two fields: a data field and a link field. The data field will be used to store a list element, and the link field will point to its successor by storing its index in the array. Thus, appropriate declarations for the array-based storage structure for linked lists are

```
const
    NumberOfNodes = ... ;              (* size of the storage pool *)
    NilValue = 0;                      (* special nil value *)

type
    ListElementType = ... ;            (* type of list elements *)
    PointerType = 0..NumberOfNodes;    (* type of pointers *)
    ListPointer = PointerType;
    NodeType = record
                    Data : ListElementType;
                    Next : ListPointer
               end;
    ArrayOfNodes = array[1..NumberOfNodes] of NodeType;
    LinkedListType = ListPointer;

var
    Node : ArrayOfNodes;               (* the storage pool *)
    FreePtr : PointerType;             (* pointer to first free node *)
```

To illustrate, consider again a linked list containing the names Brown, Jones, and Smith, in this order:

Here *List* is a variable of type *LinkedListType* and points to the first node by storing its location in *Node*, the storage pool. Suppose that *NumberOfNodes* is 10 so that the array *Node* established by the preceding declarations consists of ten records, each of which has a *Data* field for storing a name and a *Next* field for storing the location of its successor.[1] The nodes of the linked list can be stored in any three of these array locations, provided that the links are appropriately set and *List* is maintained as a pointer to the first node. For example, the first node might be stored in location 8 in this array, the second node in location 2, and the third in location 4. Thus, *List* would have the value 8, *Node*[8].*Data* would store the string 'Brown', and *Node*[8].*Next* would have the value 2. Similarly, we would have *Node*[2].*Data* = 'Jones' and *Node*[2].*Next* = 4. The last node would be stored in location 4 so that *Node*[4].*Data* would have the value 'Smith'. Since there is no successor for this node, the *Next* field must store a nil pointer to indicate this fact; that is, *Node*[4].*Next* must have a value that is not the index of any array location, and for this, the value 0 is a natural choice.

The following diagram displays the contents of the array *Node* and indicates how the *Next* fields connect these nodes. The question marks in some array locations indicate undetermined values because these nodes have not been used to store this linked list.

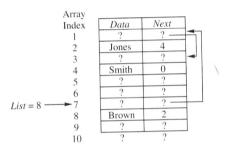

To traverse this list, displaying the names in order, we begin by finding the location of the first node by using the pointer *List*. Since *List* has the value 8, the first name displayed is 'Brown', stored in *Node*[8].*Data*. Following the link fields leads us to array location *Node*[8].*Next* = 2, where the name 'Jones' is stored in *Node*[2].*Data*, and then to location *Node*[2].*Next* = 4, where 'Smith' is stored. The nil value 0 for *Node*[4].*Next* signals that this is the last node in the list.

In general, to traverse any linked list we use the method given in the traversal algorithm of the preceding section:

1. Initialize *CurrPtr* to *List*.
2. While *CurrPtr* ≠ *NilValue* do the following:
   a. Process *Data*(*CurrPtr*).
   b. Set *CurrPtr* equal to *Next*(*CurrPtr*).

In the current array-based implementation of linked lists, these instructions are implemented by the following program segment; where *CurrPtr* is of type *ListPointer*:

---

[1] For languages that do not provide records, *Node* can be replaced by *parallel* arrays *Data* and *Next* so that *Data*[*i*] and *Next*[*i*] correspond to the fields *Node*[*i*].Data and *Node*[*i*].Next, respectively.

while *CurrPtr* <> *NilValue* (∗ 0 ∗) **do**
   begin
      (∗ Appropriate statements to process *Node[CurrPtr].Data* are
         inserted here ∗)
      CurrPtr := *Node[CurrPtr].Next*
   end (∗ **while** ∗)

Now suppose we wish to insert a new name into this list, for example, to insert 'Grant' after 'Brown'. We must first obtain a new node in which to store this name. Seven locations are available, namely, positions 1, 3, 5, 6, 7, 9, and 10 in the array. Let us assume for now that this storage pool of available nodes has been organized in such a way that a call to the procedure *GetNode* returns the index 10 as the location of an available node. The new name is then inserted into the list using the method described in the preceding section: *Node[10].Data* is set equal to 'Grant'; *Node[10].Next* is set equal to 2 so that it points to the successor of 'Brown'; and the link field *Node[8].Next* of the predecessor is set equal to 10:

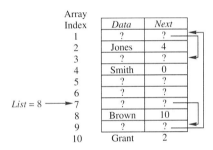

This example illustrates that the elements of the array *Node* are of two kinds. Some of the array locations—namely, 2, 4, 8, and 10—are used to store nodes of the linked list. The others represent unused "free" nodes that are available for storing new items as they are inserted into the list. We have described in detail how the nodes used to store list elements are organized, and we must now consider how to structure the storage pool of available nodes.

One simple way to organize this pool of free nodes is as a linked list. In this case, the contents of the data parts of these nodes are irrelevant, and the link fields serve simply to link these nodes together. Initially, all nodes are available and thus must be linked together to form the storage pool. One natural way to do this is to let the first node point to the second, the second to the third, and so on. The link field of the last node will be nil, and a pointer *FreePtr* is set equal to 1 to provide access to the first node in this storage pool.

InitializeStoragePool

(∗ Accepts: An array *Node* of *NumberOfNodes* records.
   Function: Initializes a storage pool *Node* as a linked list by linking
              the records together in order.
   Returns: Modified array *Node* and the index *FreePtr* of the first
              available node. ∗)

1. For i ranging from 1 to *NumberOfNodes* $-$ 1
     Set *Node[i].Next* equal to $i + 1$.
2. Set *Node[NumberOfNodes].Next* equal to 0 (∗ nil ∗).
3. Set *FreePtr* equal to 1.

	Array Index	Data	Next
FreePtr = 1 →	1	?	2
	2	?	3
	3	?	4
	4	?	5
	5	?	6
	6	?	7
	7	?	8
	8	?	9
	9	?	10
	10	?	0

A procedure call *GetNode* (*TempPtr*) returns the location of a free node by assigning to *TempPtr* the value of *FreePtr* and deleting that node from the free list by setting *FreePtr* equal to *Node[FreePtr].Next*.

GetNode

(∗ Accepts: The array *Node*, representing the storage pool.
    Function: Obtains a free node.
    Returns: Modified array *Node* and the index *P* of an available node. ∗)

1. Set *P* equal to *FreePtr*.
2. If *FreePtr* is not zero then
     Set *FreePtr* equal to *Node[FreePtr].Next*.
   Otherwise
     Signal that the storage pool is empty.

Thus, if 'Mills' is the first name to be inserted into a linked list, it will be stored in the first position of the array *Node*, because *FreePtr* has the value 1; *List* will be set equal to 1; and *FreePtr* will be set equal to 2.

	Array Index	Data	Next
List = 1 →	1	Mills	0
FreePtr = 2 →	2	?	3
	3	?	4
	4	?	5
	5	?	6
	6	?	7
	7	?	8
	8	?	9
	9	?	10
	10	?	0

If 'Baker' is the next name to be inserted, it will be stored in location 2 because this is the value of *FreePtr*, and *FreePtr* will be set equal to 3. If the list is to be maintained in alphabetical order, *List* will be set equal to 2;

Node[2].*Next* will be set equal to 1; and *Node*[1].*Next* will be set equal to 0 (nil).

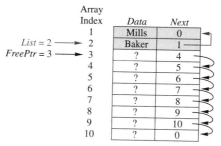

If 'Wells' is the next name inserted into the list, the following configuration will result:

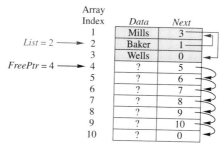

When a node is deleted from a linked list, it should be returned to the storage pool of free nodes so that it can be reused later to store some other list element. An algorithm for this procedure is

ReleaseNode

(* Accepts: The array *Node*, representing the storage pool, and an
                   index *P*.
     Function: Returns node pointed to by *P* to the storage pool.
     Returns: Modified array *Node*. *)

1. Set *Node*[*P*].*Next* equal to *FreePtr*.
2. Set *FreePtr* equal to *P*.

A procedure call *ReleaseNode* (*TempPtr*) simply inserts the node pointed to by *TempPtr* at the beginning of the free list by first setting *Node*[*TempPtr*].*Next* equal to *FreePtr* and then setting *FreePtr* equal to *TempPtr*. For example, deleting the name 'Mills' from the preceding linked list produces the following configuration:

Note that it is not necessary to actually remove the string 'Mills' from the data part of this node because changing the link of its predecessor has *logically* removed it from the linked list. This string 'Mills' will be overwritten when this node is used to store a new name.

A procedure that implements the basic list operation of creating an empty list is trivial; we need only assign the nil value to *List*.

> **procedure** *CreateList* (**var** *List* : *LinkedListType*);
>
> > (* Function: Creates an empty linked list.
> >   Returns: Pointer (nil) to an empty linked list. *)
>
> > **begin** (* *CreateList* *)
> >   *List* := *NilValue* (* 0 *)
> > **end** (* *CreateList* *)

A function that checks for an empty list is likewise simple:

> **function** *EmptyList*(*List* : *LinkedListType*): *boolean*;
>
> > (* Accepts: A pointer *List* to a linked list.
> >   Function: Checks if the list is empty.
> >   Returns: True if *List* is empty and false otherwise. *)
>
> > **begin** (* *EmptyList* *)
> >   *EmptyList* := (*List* = *NilValue*) (* 0 *)
> > **end** (* *EmptyList* *)

The procedure *LinkedTraversal* given earlier implements the basic operation of traversing a list. The insertion and deletion operations are considered in more detail in Section 7.7 and procedures for these operations in this array-based implementation are left as exercises.

As a simple illustration of the use of linked lists, consider the problem of reversing the characters in a string. To solve this problem, we first call procedure *CreateList* to create an empty list for storing characters. A sequence of characters is then read and stored in this linked list. As each character is read, it is added to the beginning of the list. When the end of the string is encountered, procedure *LinkedTraverse* is used to traverse the list and display the characters. Because the last characters read are at the beginning of the list, they are displayed in reverse order.

The program in Figure 7.1 uses this approach to solve the string reversal problem. In addition to procedures *CreateList* and *LinkedTraverse*, it uses procedure *AddToList* to add elements at the beginning of the list in the manner described in the preceding section. It assumes the availability of a package of memory-management constant, type, and variable declarations and procedures, from which the constant *NilValue*, the type *PointerType*, and the procedures *InitializeStoragePool*, *GetNode*, and *ReleaseNode* can be obtained and used in the program. (The #include directives insert these items at the appropriate points.) All of these items were described in this section, and the actual design of this package is left as an exercise.

```
PROGRAM Reverse (input, output);

(*********************************************************************

    Input (keyboard): A string of characters.
    Function:         Reverses the string.  As each character is read,
                      it is stored at the beginning of a linked list.
                      This list is then traversed and the characters
                      displayed.
    Output (screen):  Reversed string.

*********************************************************************)

CONST
#include 'STORAGE-CONST'    (* NilValue *)
   EndMark = '$';           (* signals end of string *)

TYPE
   ListElementType = char;
#include 'STORAGE-TYPE'     (* PointerType *)
   ListPointer = PointerType;
   LinkedListType = ListPointer;

VAR
#include 'STORAGE-VAR'      (* Node, FreePtr *)
   List : LinkedListType;   (* pointer to first node in linked list *)
   Ch : char;               (* current character being processed *)

#include 'STORAGE-OPS' (* InitializeStoragePool, GetNode, ReleaseNode *)

PROCEDURE CreateList (VAR List : LinkedListType);

   (********************************************************************

      Input:             None.
      Function:          Creates an empty linked List.
      Output (param):    Nil pointer List.

   ********************************************************************)

   BEGIN (* CreateList *)
      List := NilPtr
   END (* CreateList *);
```

Figure 7.1

Figure 7.1 (*cont.*)

```
PROCEDURE AddToList (VAR List : LinkedListType; Item : ListElementType);

    (*******************************************************************

    Input (param):   A linked list with first node pointed to by List
                     and a data Item.
    Function:        Adds Item at the front of the linked list.
    Output (param):  Modified linked list with new first node
                     pointed to by List.

    *******************************************************************)

    VAR
        TempPtr : ListPointer;    (* pointer to new node *)

    BEGIN (* AddToList *)
        GetNode (TempPtr);
        Node[TempPtr].Data := Item;
        Node[TempPtr].Next := List;
        List := TempPtr
    END (* AddToList *);

PROCEDURE LinkedTraverse (List : LinkedListType);

    (*******************************************************************

    Input (param):   A linked list with first node pointed to by List.
    Function:        Traverses the linked list, processing each data
                     item exactly once.
    Output (screen): Data items stored in the list.

    *******************************************************************)

    VAR
        CurrPtr : ListPointer;        (* pointer to current node
                                         being processed *)
    BEGIN (* LinkedTraverse *)
        CurrPtr:= List;
        WHILE CurrPtr <> NilPtr DO
          BEGIN
            write (Node[CurrPtr].Data);
            CurrPtr:= Node[CurrPtr].Next
          END (* WHILE *);
        writeln
    END (* LinkedTraverse *);
```

Figure 7.1 (*cont.*)

```
BEGIN (* main program *)
   InitializeStoragePool;
   CreateList (List);
   writeln ('Enter the string, using ', EndMark, ' to signal its end:');
   read (Ch);
   WHILE Ch <> EndMark DO
      BEGIN
         AddToList (List, Ch);
         read (Ch)
      END (* WHILE *);
   readln;
   writeln ('Reversed string is:');
   LinkedTraverse (List)
END (* main program *).
```

Sample runs:

```
Enter the string, using $ to signal its end:
SHE SELLS SEASHELLS BY THE SEASHORE$
Reversed string is:
EROHSAES EHT YB SLLEHSAES SLLES EHS


Enter the string, using $ to signal its end:
ABLE WAS I ERE I SAW ELBA$
Reversed string is:
ABLE WAS I ERE I SAW ELBA
```

Exercises

1. An ordered linked list of characters has been constructed using the array-based implementation described in this section. The following diagram shows the current contents of the array that stores the elements of the linked list and the storage pool of available nodes:

Array Index	Data	Next	
1	J	4	
2	Z	7	
3	C	1	
4	P	0	
5	B	3	*List* = 5
6	M	2	*FreePtr* = 6
7	K	8	
8	Q	9	
9	?	10	
10	?	0	

(a) List the elements of this ordered list.

(b) List the nodes in the storage pool in the order in which they are linked together.

2. Assuming the contents of the array pictured in Exercise 1, show the contents of the array after the operation Insert F.

3. Proceed as in Exercise 2 but for the operation Delete J.

4. Proceed as in Exercise 2 but for the following sequence of operations: Delete J, Delete P, Delete C, Delete B.

5. Proceed as in Exercise 2 but for the following sequence of operations: Insert A, Delete P, Insert K, Delete C.

6. Assuming the array-based implementation in this section, write

   (a) a nonrecursive function
   (b) a recursive function

   to count the nodes in a linked list.

7. Assuming the array-based implementation in this section, write a

   (a) a nonrecursive boolean-valued function
   (b) a recursive boolean-valued function

   that determines whether the data items in a linked list are arranged in ascending order.

8. Assuming the array-based implementation in this section, write

   (a) a nonrecursive function
   (b) a recursive function

   that returns a pointer to the last node in a linked list.

9. Assuming the array-based implementation in this section, write a function or procedure to reverse a linked list in the manner described in Exercise 12 of Section 7.2.

10. Write the memory management package or unit described in this section and used in the program of Figure 7.1. This package/unit should initialize a storage pool of available nodes stored in the array *Node*, define the constant *NilPtr*, the type *PointerType*, the variable *FreePtr* and the array variable *Node*, and the procedures *InitializeStoragePool*, *GetNode*, and *ReleaseNode*.

11. A limited number of tickets for the Frisian Folk Singers concert go on sale tomorrow, and ticket orders are to be filled in the order in which they are received. Write a program that reads the names and addresses of the persons ordering tickets together with the number of tickets requested and stores these in a linked list. The program should then produce a list of names, addresses, and number of tickets for orders that can be filled.

12. Modify the program in Exercise 11 so that multiple requests from the same person are not allowed.

7.4 Pointers and Dynamic Memory Allocation/Deallocation in Pascal

The definition of a list as an abstract data type imposes no limit on the number of elements that a list may have. Consequently, any implementation of a list like that in the preceding section that uses an array as the basic storage structure cannot be faithful because the size of an array is fixed at compile time and cannot be changed during program execution. A faithful implementation would require the ability to allocate and deallocate the memory locations for nodes dynamically during program execution without specifying some upper limit on the size of the storage pool before execution. This capability is provided in Pascal by the predefined procedures *new* and *dispose* that are used in conjunction with pointer types. In this section we show how they can be used to provide a (nearly) faithful implementation of a linked list.

The predefined Pascal procedure *new* is used to allocate memory locations during program execution. When it is called, it returns the address of a memory location in which a data value can be stored. To reference this memory location so that data may be stored in it or retrieved from it, a special kind of variable called a ***pointer variable***, or simply a ***pointer***, is provided whose value is the address of a memory location.

The type of a pointer variable used to reference the memory location storing some data value must be specified by

$\uparrow$*type-identifier*   or $\wedge$*type-identifier*

where *type-identifier* specifies the type of the data value. The pointer is said to be ***bound*** to this type, as it may not be used to reference memory locations storing values of some other data type. For example, if the data values are strings, then a pointer to a memory location that may be used to store a string might be declared by

type
  .
  .
  .
    PointerType = $\uparrow$*StringType*;

var
    StringPtr : *PointerType*;

This pointer variable *StringPtr* is bound to the type *StringType* and may be used only to reference memory locations in which values of this type can be stored.

The procedure *new* may be used during program execution to acquire such memory locations. This procedure is called with a statement of the form

     new (pointer)

which assigns the address of a memory location to *pointer*.[2] Thus the statement

     new (StringPtr);

assigns to *StringPtr* a memory address, say 1005:

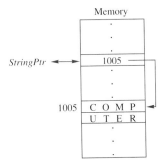

This is the address of a memory location where a string such as 'COMPUTER' can be stored. (In this case, it may, in fact, be the address of the first word in a block of consecutive memory locations in which the characters of the string are stored.) We say that *StringPtr* "points" to this memory location, and we picture this as we have done for pointers before, using a diagram

     StringPtr ●⟶ COMPUTER

Because this area of memory can be used to store values of type *StringType*, it is a variable, but it has no name! Such variables are thus sometimes called **anonymous variables,** and pointers can be said to point to anonymous variables. Since these variables come into existence during program execution and may later cease to exist, we shall instead refer to them as **dynamic variables.**

Each call to the procedure *new* acquires a new memory location and assigns its address to the specified pointer. Thus, if *TempPtr* is also of type *PointerType*, the statement

     new (TempPtr)

acquires a new memory location pointed to by *TempPtr*:

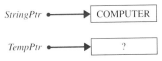

___

[2] An alternative form of reference to the procedure *new* may be used for data items that are variant records. This alternative form allows the system to allocate memory locations more efficiently and is described in Appendix F.

Pascal provides the special pointer constant **nil** for those situations in which it is necessary to assign a value to a pointer variable that indicates that it does not point to any memory location. This value may be assigned to a pointer of any type in an assignment statement of the form

pointer := **nil**

As we have done in the past, we will picture a nil pointer as simply a dot with no arrow emanating from it:

pointer ●

Because the values of pointers are addresses of memory locations, the operations that may be performed on them are limited: Only assignment and comparison using the relational operators = and <> are allowed. If *pointer1* and *pointer2* are bound to the same type, an assignment statement of the form

pointer1 := *pointer2*

assigns the value of *pointer2* to *pointer1* so that both point to the same memory location. The previous location (if any) pointed to by *pointer1* can no longer be accessed unless it is pointed to by some other pointer.

As an illustration, suppose that both *StringPtr* and *TempPtr* are pointer variables of type *PointerType* = ↑*StringType* and point to memory locations containing the strings 'COMPUTER' and 'SOFTWARE', respectively:

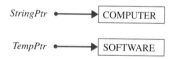

The assignment statement

TempPtr := *StringPtr*

assigns the memory address that is the value of *StringPtr* to *TempPtr* so that *TempPtr* points to the same memory location as does *StringPtr*:

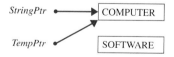

The string 'SOFTWARE' stored in the second location can no longer be accessed (unless it is pointed to by some other pointer of type *PointerType*).

The relational operators = and <> can be used to compare two pointers *bound to the same type* to determine if they both point to the same memory locations or both are nil. Thus the boolean expression

TempPtr = *StringPtr*

is valid and is true if and only if *TempPtr* and *StringPtr* point to the same memory location or both are nil. Similarly,

> *TempPtr* <> **nil**

is a valid boolean expression.

Pointers may also be used as parameters in functions and procedures. These parameters may be either value or variable parameters, but corresponding pointer parameters must be bound to the same type. The value of a function may also be a pointer (but see footnote 3).

The value of a nonil pointer is the *address* of the memory location to which it points, *not* the data item stored in this location. This data item can be accessed by appending the **dereferencing operator** ↑ or ∧ to the pointer:[3]

> *pointer*↑   or   *pointer*∧

If the pointer is nil or undefined, however, then there is no memory location associated with this variable, and so any attempt to use it is an error. At one point during program execution, there may be a particular memory location associated with it, and at a later time, no memory location or a different one may be associated with it. This differs from ordinary variables for which memory locations are allocated at compile time and this association remains fixed throughout the execution of the program.

To illustrate, suppose that pointer variable *StringPtr* has a nonnil value. Then *StringPtr*↑ is a variable of type *StringType* and may be used in the same manner as any other variable of this type. For example, a value can be assigned to it by an assignment statement

> *StringPtr*↑ := 'COMPUTER';

and its individual characters accessed as in

> **if** *StringPtr*↑[1] = 'A' **then**
>   *writeln* (*StringPtr*↑)
> **end** (* **if** *)

If, however, *StringPtr* is nil or undefined so that no memory location is associated with the dynamic variable *StringPtr*↑, an attempt to execute either of these statements is an error.

If both *TempPtr* and *StringPtr* have nonnil values, the statement

> *TempPtr*↑ := *StringPtr*↑;

is a valid assignment statement because both of the dynamic variables *TempPtr*↑ and *StringPtr*↑ exist and they have the same type *StringType*, since

---

[3] If *f* is a pointer-valued function, a function reference of the form *f*(*actual-parameters*)↑ is not permitted. The value of the function must first be assigned to the pointer variable, and this variable is used to access the contents of the memory location to which it points.

both *TempPtr* and *StringPtr* are bound to this type. This statement copies the contents of the memory location(s) pointed to by *StringPtr* into the location(s) pointed to by *TempPtr*:

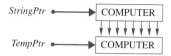

Note that this result is quite different from that produced by the assignment statement

$$TempPtr := StringPtr;$$

considered earlier, which causes *TempPtr* to point to the same memory location pointed to by *StringPtr*:

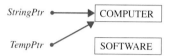

As another illustration of the difference between a pointer and a dereferenced pointer, consider the relational operators $=$ and $<>$. As we have noted, these operators can be used to determine whether two pointers bound to the same type point to the same memory location. Thus, the boolean expression

$$TempPtr = StringPtr$$

is true only if *TempPtr* and *StringPtr* point to the same memory location. This is not equivalent to the boolean expression

$$TempPtr\uparrow = StringPtr\uparrow$$

however, since this compares the string pointed to by *TempPtr* with the string pointed to by *StringPtr*. Obviously if *TempPtr* $=$ *StringPtr* is true and both pointer variables have nonnil values, then *TempPtr*$\uparrow$ $=$ *StringPtr*$\uparrow$ also is true; the string values of these two variables are identical since *TempPtr* and *StringPtr* point to the same memory location and thus to the same string. The converse is not true, however. The values of *TempPtr*$\uparrow$ and *StringPtr*$\uparrow$ may be equal but may be stored in different locations; that is, *TempPtr* and *StringPtr* point to different memory locations. It should also be emphasized that if one of the pointers *TempPtr* or *StringPtr* is nil, then the first boolean expression is valid, but the second is not.

If the memory location pointed to by a pointer is no longer needed, it may be released and made available for later allocation by calling the procedure *dispose* with a statement of the form

dispose (*pointer*)

This procedure frees the memory location pointed to by *pointer* and leaves *pointer* undefined.[4]

7.5 A Pointer-Based Implementation of Linked Lists in Pascal

As we suggested in the preceding section, pointers are used to implement a variety of linked structures. In this section we show how they are used to implement linked lists.

As in the array-based implementation of Section 7.3, the basic structure used to store the nodes of linked lists will be records containing two fields, *Data* and *Next*. The field *Data* will again be of a type that is appropriate for storing a list element, and the field *Next* will store a link that points to the successor of this element. However, unlike the array-based implementation, this link will be a Pascal pointer rather than an array index.

The appropriate declarations for this implementation of a linked list are

```
type
    ListElementType = ... ;         (* type of list elements *)
    ListPointer = ↑ListNode;        (* type of pointers to list nodes *)
    ListNode = record
                    Data : ListElementType;
                    Next : ListPointer
               end;
    LinkedListType = ListPointer;
```

Note that the definition of the type identifier *ListPointer* precedes the definition of *ListNode*. This is the only situation in Pascal in which it is permissible to use an identifier (*ListNode*) before it has been defined.

In this implementation of linked lists there is no need to be concerned about initializing and maintaining a storage pool of free nodes, as required in the array-based implementation. This is done automatically by the system, with the predefined Pascal procedures *new* and *dispose* playing the roles of *GetNode* and *ReleaseNode*, respectively.

The Pascal procedures and functions that carry out the basic list operations are straightforward implementations of the algorithms given earlier. Recall that the first basic operation is the creation of an empty list and that this is accomplished simply by assigning the special pointer value **nil** to a variable *List* of type *LinkedListType* that maintains access to the first node of the linked list:

> *List* := **nil**;

The second basic operation, checking if a list is empty, is then easily implemented by checking if *List* has the value **nil**:

> *EmptyList* := (*List* = **nil**);

---

[4] Just as there is an alternative form of reference to the procedure *new* that may be used for lcoations that store variant records, there is a similar alternative form for the procedure *dispose*. See Appendix F.

Lists are traversed as described before, by initializing a pointer *CurrPtr* to the first node and then advancing it through the list by following the link fields, processing the data stored in each node:

CurrPtr := *List*;
while *CurrPtr* <> **nil do**
   begin
      (∗ Appropriate statements to process *CurrPtr↑.Data* are inserted
        here ∗)
     CurrPtr := *CurrPtr↑.Next*
   end (∗ **while** ∗)

It should be clear that these Pascal pointer-based implementations of the basic list operations are simple restatements of those in the array-based implementation of linked lists. This is true of the other basic list operations as well, and these are described in the next section.

The program in Figure 7.2 is a simple illustration of this method of implementing lists. It is the same as the program in Figure 7.1 for reversing a string of characters except that the array-based implementation of the linked list used in the reversal is replaced with the Pascal pointer-based implementation.

```
PROGRAM Reverse (input, output);

(*********************************************************************

   Input (keyboard): A string of characters.
   Function:         Reverses the string.  As each character is read,
                     it is stored at the beginning of a linked list.
                     This list is then traversed and the characters
                     displayed.
   Output (screen):  Reversed string.

*******************************************************************)

CONST
   EndMark = '$';              (* signals end of string *)

TYPE
   ListElementType = char;
   ListPointer = ^ListNode;
   ListNode = RECORD
                 Data : ListElementType;
                 Next : ListPointer
              END;
   LinkedListType = ListPointer;

VAR
   List : LinkedListType;   (* pointer to first node in linked list *)
   Ch : char;               (* current character being processed *)
```

Figure 7.2

Figure 7.2 (*cont.*)

```
PROCEDURE CreateList (VAR List : LinkedListType);

   (************************************************************************

       Input:             None.
       Function:          Creates an empty linked List.
       Output (param):    Nil pointer List.

   ************************************************************************)

   BEGIN (* CreateList *)
      List := NIL
   END (* CreateList *);

PROCEDURE AddToList (VAR List : LinkedListType; Item : ListElementType );

   (************************************************************************

       Input (param):   A linked list with first node pointed to by List
                        and a data Item.
       Function:        Adds Item at the front of the linked list.
       Output (param):  Modified linked list with new first node
                        pointed to by List.

   ************************************************************************)

   VAR
      TempPtr : ListPointer;    (* pointer to new node *)

   BEGIN (* AddToList *)
      new (TempPtr);
      TempPtr^.Data := Item;
      TempPtr^.Next := List;
      List := TempPtr
   END (* AddToList *);

PROCEDURE LinkedTraverse (List : LinkedListType);

   (************************************************************************

       Input (param):   A linked list with first node pointed to by List.
       Function:        Traverses the linked list, processing each data
                        item exactly once.
       Output (screen): Data items stored in the list.

   ************************************************************************)

   VAR
      CurrPtr : ListPointer;      (* pointer to current node
                                     being processed *)
   BEGIN (* LinkedTraverse *)
      CurrPtr:= List;
      WHILE CurrPtr <> Nil DO
         BEGIN
            write (CurrPtr^.Data);
            CurrPtr:= CurrPtr^.Next
         END (* WHILE *);
      writeln
   END (* LinkedTraverse *);
```

Figure 7.2 (*cont.*)

```
BEGIN (* main program *)
   CreateList (List);
   writeln ('Enter the string, using ', EndMark, ' to signal its end:');
   read (Ch);
   WHILE Ch <> EndMark DO
      BEGIN
         AddToList (List, Ch);
         read (Ch)
      END (* WHILE *);
   readln;
   writeln ('Reversed string is:');
   LinkedTraverse (List)
END (* main program *).
```

Sample runs:

```
Enter the string, using $ to signal its end:
SHE SELLS SEASHELLS BY THE SEASHORE$
Reversed string is:
EROHSAES EHT YB SLLEHSAES SLLES EHS

Enter the string, using $ to signal its end:
abcdefghijklmnopqrstuvwxyz$
Reversed string is:
zyxwvutsrqponmlkjihgfedcba

Enter the string, using $ to signal its end:
ABLE WAS I ERE I SAW ELBA$
Reversed string is:
ABLE WAS I ERE I SAW ELBA
```

Exercises

1. Assume the following declarations:

   var
       X : *integer*;
       P1, P2 : $\uparrow$*integer*;
       Q1, Q2 : $\uparrow$*real*;

   What (if anything) is wrong with each of the following statements?

   (a) *writeln (P1)*;
   (b) *readln (P1$\uparrow$)*;
   (c) *P1 := Q1*;
   (d) *new (X)*;
   (e) **if** *P1$\uparrow$* = **nil then**
       Q1 := Q2;
   (f) **begin**
       P1$\uparrow$:= 17;
       new (P1)
       end

2. Assume the following declarations:

type
　　NumberPointer = ↑*NumberNode*;
　　NumberNode = **record**
　　　　　　　　　　　　Data : *integer*;
　　　　　　　　　　　　Next : *NumberPointer*
　　　　　　　　end;

var
　　P1, P2 : *NumberPointer*;
　　P3 : ↑*integer*;

and assume that the following three statements have already been executed:

　　new (*P1*);
　　new (*P2*);
　　new (*P3*);

Tell what will now be displayed by each of the following program segments or explain why an error occurs:

(a) *P1↑.Data* := 123;
　　P2↑.Data := 456;
　　P1↑.Next := *P2*;
　　writeln (*P1↑.Data*);
　　writeln (*P1↑.Next↑.Data*);

(b) *P1↑.Data* := 12;
　　P2↑.Data := 34;
　　P1 := *P2*;
　　writeln (*P1↑.Data*);
　　writeln (*P2↑.Data*);

(c) *P1↑.Data* := 123;
　　P2↑.Data := 456;
　　P1↑.Next := *P2*;
　　writeln (*P2↑.Data*);
　　writeln (*P2↑.Next↑.Data*);

(d) *P1↑.Data* := 12;
　　P2↑.Data := 34;
　　P3↑.Data := 34;
　　P1↑.Next := *P2*;
　　P2↑.Next := *P3*;
　　writeln (*P1↑.Data*);
　　writeln (*P2↑.Data*);
　　writeln (*P3↑.Data*);

(e) *P1↑.Data* := 111;
　　P2↑.Data := 222;

$P1\uparrow.Next := P2;$
$P2\uparrow.Next := P1;$
writeln $(P1\uparrow.Data, P2\uparrow.Data);$
writeln $(P1\uparrow.Next\uparrow.Data);$
writeln $(P1\uparrow.Next\uparrow.Next\uparrow.Data);$

(f) $P1\uparrow.Data := 12;$
$P2\uparrow.Data := 34;$
$P1 := P2;$
$P2\uparrow.Next := P1;$
writeln $(P1\uparrow.Data);$
writeln $(P2\uparrow.Data);$
writeln $(P1\uparrow.Next\uparrow.Data);$
writeln $(P2\uparrow.Next\uparrow.Data);$

3. Given the following linked list and pointers *P1*, *P2*, *P3*, and *P4* of type
NumberPointer as defined in Exercise 2:

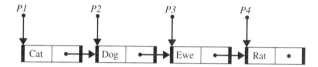

For each of the following, draw a similar diagram to show how this
configuration would change when the given program segment is executed or explain why an error occurs:

(a) $P1 := P2\uparrow.Next;$

(b) $P4 := P1;$

(c) $P4\uparrow.Data := P1\uparrow.Data;$

(d) $P4\uparrow.Next\uparrow.Data := P1\uparrow.Data;$

(e) $P2\uparrow.Next := P3\uparrow.Next;$

(f) $P4\uparrow.Next := P1;$

(g) $P1\uparrow.Next := P3\uparrow.Next;$
$P1 := P3;$

(h) $P1 := P3;$
$P1\uparrow.Next := P3\uparrow.Next;$

(i) $P4\uparrow.Next := P3\uparrow.Next;$
$P3\uparrow.Next := P2\uparrow.Next;$
$P2\uparrow.Next := P1\uparrow.Next;$

(**j**) *P4↑.Next* := *P3*;
    P4↑.Next↑.Next := *P2*;
    P4↑.Next↑.Next↑.Next := *P1*;
    P1 := **nil**;

4. Assuming the Pascal pointer-based implementation in this section, write

   (**a**) a nonrecursive function
   (**b**) a recursive function

   to count the nodes in a linked list.

5. Assuming the Pascal pointer-based implementation in this section, write

   (**a**) a nonrecursive function
   (**b**) a recursive function

   that determines whether the data items in a linked list are arranged in ascending order.

6. Assuming the Pascal pointer-based implementation in this section, write

   (**a**) a nonrecursive function
   (**b**) a recursive function

   that returns a pointer to the last node in a linked list.

7. Assuming the Pascal pointer-based implementation in this section, write a function or procedure to reverse a linked list in the manner described in Exercise 12 of Section 7.2.

8. In Exercise 11 of Section 7.3, a program is to be written to fill ticket orders for the Frisian Folk Singers concert in the order in which these orders are received. Write this program to read the names and addresses of persons ordering tickets together with the number of tickets requested, and stores these in a linked list, but use a Pascal pointer-based implementation for this list. The program is to produce a list of names, addresses, and number of tickets for orders that can be filled.

9. Modify the program in Exercise 8 so that multiple requests from the same person are not allowed.

7.6   A Package for the ADT Linked List

In Section 7.1 we defined the ADT list as a sequence of elements together with the basic operations of creating an empty list, checking if a list is empty, traversal, insertion, and deletion. And in Section 7.2 we saw that a linked implementation is better than a sequential storage implementation for dynamic lists. We have given algorithms for the first three operations on linked lists and have written the corresponding procedures, first in an array-based implementation and then in a pointer-based implementation. In this section we begin by developing algorithms for the basic operations of insertion and deletion for linked lists, thus completing the implementation of the ADT linked list.

In Section 7.2 we illustrated the insertion and deletion operations for linked lists by means of diagrams and examples. In these illustrations we assumed that we knew the location at which an item was to be inserted or deleted; we did not discuss how this location was determined. Here we use the same approach. We first develop algorithms and procedures for insertion and deletion, assuming that the locations at which these operations are to be performed is known. Then we will consider the problem of searching a linked list to locate a particular item or to find the location at which it should be inserted.

Recall that to insert an element into a linked list, we first obtain a new node temporarily accessed by some pointer *TempPtr* and store the item in the data part of this node. As we illustrated in Section 7.2, the second step is to connect this new node to the linked list, and there are two cases to consider here: (1) insertion at the beginning of the list and (2) insertion after a specified element in the list.

If the new node is to be inserted at the beginning of the list, we must first set its link field to point to the first node in the list:

Set *Next(TempPtr)* equal to *List.*

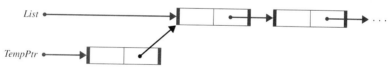

Next we reset the pointer to the former first node (if there was one) so that it points to this new first node:

Set *List* equal to *TempPtr.*

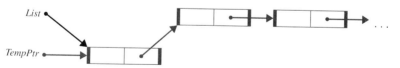

It is crucial that these operations be carried out in this order. For suppose that we first set *List* equal to *TempPtr*. Then setting *Next(TempPtr)* equal to *List* would simply cause the new node to point to itself, and access to the rest of the original list would be lost:

Set *List* equal to *TempPtr.*
Set *Next(TempPtr)* equal to *List.*

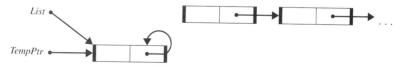

For the second case, suppose that the new node is to be inserted after the node pointed to by *PredPtr*. In this case, we first set the pointer in the link field of the new node to point to the successor of the node pointed to by *PredPtr* (if there is one):

Set *Next(TempPtr)* equal to *Next(PredPtr)*.

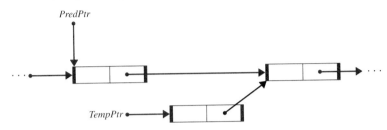

We then set the pointer in the link field of the node pointed to by *PredPtr* to point to the new node, because it is the new successor of the node pointed to by *PredPtr* :

Set *Next(PredPtr)* equal to *TempPtr*.

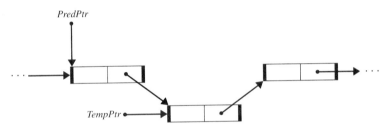

Again, it is important to carry out these operations in this order so that access to part of the list is not lost.

In summary, insertion into a linked list is performed by the following algorithm:

ALGORITHM FOR INSERTION INTO A LINKED LIST

(∗ Accepts: A linked list with first node pointed to by *List*, a data
                       Item, and a pointer *PredPtr*.
     Function: Inserts a node containing *Item* into the linked list following
                       the node pointed to by *PredPtr*, or at the front of the list
                       if *PredPtr* is nil.
     Returns: Modified linked list with first node pointed to by *List* ∗)

1. Get a node pointed to by *TempPtr*.
2. Set *Data(TempPtr)* equal to *Item*.
3. If *PredPtr* = nil then do the following:
     (∗ Insert *Item* at beginning of list ∗)
     a. Set *Next(TempPtr)* equal to *List*.
     b. Set *List* equal to *TempPtr*.

Else do the following:
(* There is a predecessor *)
a. Set *Next(TempPtr)* equal to *Next(PredPtr)*.
b. Set *Next(PredPtr)* equal to *TempPtr*.

When developing algorithms to implement the basic operations of a data structure, it is important to verify that they work correctly in special cases. One special case for insertion that should be checked is insertion into an empty list. In this case, the new item will be the first node in the resulting one-node list, and so this case falls under the rubric ''Insert *Item* at beginning of list.'' Since *List* has the value nil for an empty list, the first operation sets *Next(TempPtr)* equal to nil, which is correct because the new node will have no successor. The second operation then correctly sets *List* to point to the first node in this new one-node list:

Set *Next(TempPtr)* equal to *List* (= nil).

Set *List* equal to *TempPtr*.

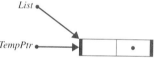

Another special case that should be checked is insertion at the end of a nonempty list. In this case, *Next(PredPtr)* is nil, and so the first instruction of a ''type-2'' insertion correctly sets to nil the link field *Next(TempPtr)* of the new node, indicating that this is the last node in the new list. The second instruction then sets the link field in what was formerly the last node to point to this new last node.

Set *Next(TempPtr)* equal to *Next(PredPtr)* (= nil).

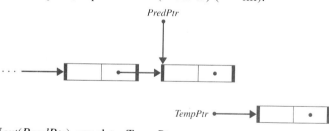

Set *Next(PredPtr)* equal to *TempPtr*.

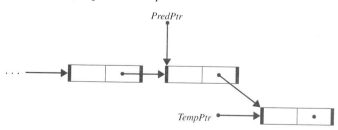

For deletion, suppose that *TempPtr* points to the node to be deleted. Once again there are two cases to consider: (1) deleting the first element in the list and (2) deleting an element that has a predecessor. We can delete the first element in a linked list by simply setting *List* to point to the second node in the list (or setting it to nil if there is none):

Set *List* equal to *Next(TempPtr)*.

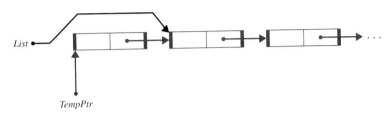

Note that in the special case of a one-node list, *Next(TempPtr)* is nil, and so *List* is correctly set to nil, as required for an empty list.

For the second kind of deletion, if *PredPtr* points to the predecessor of the node to be deleted, we need only set its link part to point to the successor of the node to be deleted (if there is one):

Set *Next(PredPtr)* equal to *Next(TempPtr)*.

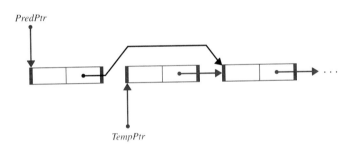

Note that in the special case in which the last node is being deleted, *Next(TempPtr)* is nil, and so *Next(PredPtr)* becomes nil. This is correct because the node pointed to by *PredPtr* becomes the new last node in the list.

The following algorithm implements the deletion operation for linked lists. Here we assume that a boolean variable *ListError* is used (like *StackError* for the ADT stack and *QueueError* for the ADT queue) to signal that an error has occurred if the operation fails.

ALGORITHM FOR DELETION FROM A LINKED LIST

(* Accepts: A linked list with first node pointed to by *List*, and a pointer *PredPtr*.

Function: Deletes the node from the linked list whose predecessor is pointed to by *PredPtr* or deletes the first node if *PredPtr* is nil, unless the list is empty.

Returns: Modified linked list with first node pointed to by *List*; *ListError* is true if the list was empty and is false otherwise.

Output: A list-empty message if the list was empty. ∗)

If the list is empty then
   Display a list-empty message and set *ListError* to true.

Else do the following:
1. Set *ListError* to false.
2. If *PredPtr* = nil then   (∗ deleting the first node ∗)
   a. Set *TempPtr* equal to *List*.
   b. Set *List* equal to *Next(TempPtr)*.

   Else do the following: (∗ node has a predecessor ∗)
   a. Set *TempPtr* equal to *Next(PredPtr)*.
   b. Set *Next(PredPtr)* equal to *Next(TempPtr)*.

3. Return the node pointed to by *TempPtr* to the storage pool of available free nodes.

The algorithms for insertion and deletion use a pointer to the predecessor of the item to be inserted or deleted (nil if there is no predecessor). If the elements need not be arranged in any particular order, so that it makes no difference where new items are inserted in the list, then we may as well insert them at the beginning of the list. For such unordered lists, the third step of the insertion algorithm simplifies to

3. Set *Next(TempPtr)* equal to *List*.
4. Set *List* equal to *TempPtr*.

Procedure *AddToList* in the programs of Figures 7.1 and 7.2 implements this simplified insertion algorithm. (Note that the insertion operation for such lists is precisely the push operation for stacks.)

To delete an item from a linked list, however, it is necessary to position the pointer *PredPtr*, given only the value of the item to be deleted. The following algorithm, which performs a linear search of a linked list, can be used:

ALGORITHM TO SEARCH A LINKED LIST

(∗ Accepts: A data *Item* and a linked list with first node pointed to by *List*.

Function: Performs a linear search of the linked list for a node containing *Item*.

Returns: If the search is successful, *Found* is true, *CurrPtr* points to the node containing *Item*, and *PredPtr* to its predecessor or is nil if there is none. *Found* is false for an unsuccessful search. ∗)

1. Initialize *CurrPtr* to *List*, *PredPtr* to nil, and *Found* to false.

2. While not *Found* and *CurrPtr* ≠ nil do the following:
   If *Data(CurrPtr)* = *Item* then
      Set *Found* equal to true.
   Else do the following:
      a. Set *PredPtr* equal to *CurrPtr*.
      b. Set *CurrPtr* equal to *Next(CurrPtr)*.

In an ***ordered*** or ***sorted list,*** the nodes are linked together in such a way that the items stored in the nodes are visited in ascending (or descending) order as the list is traversed. If the data part of a node is a record, then one of the fields in this record is designated as the ***key field***, and the ordering is based on the values that appear in this field. When a new item is inserted, it must be inserted in such a way that this ordering is maintained. Thus both the insertion algorithm and the deletion algorithm require a pointer *PredPtr* to the predecessor of the item being inserted or deleted (if there is one), and the following modified search algorithm can be used to position this pointer:

ALGORITHM TO SEARCH AN ORDERED LINKED LIST

(∗ Accepts: A data *Item* and an ordered linked list containing data
             items that are in ascending order with first node pointed to
             by *List*.

Function: Performs a linear search of the ordered linked list for the
           first node containing *Item* or for a position to insert a new
           node containing *Item*.

Returns: If the search is successful, *Found* is true, *CurrPtr* points
           to the node containing *Item*, and *PredPtr* to its predecessor
           or is nil if there is none. *Found* is false for an unsuccessful
           search. ∗)

1. Initialize *CurrPtr* to *List*, *PredPtr* to nil, and *Found* to false, and
   DoneSearching to false.
2. While not *DoneSearching* and *CurrPtr* ≠ nil do the following:
   If *Data(CurrPtr)* ≥ *Item* then
      a. Set *DoneSearching* equal to true.
      b. Set *Found* equal to true if *Data(CurrPtr)* = *Item*.
   Else do the following:
      a. Set *PredPtr* equal to *CurrPtr*.
      b. Set *CurrPtr* equal to *Next(CurrPtr)*.

Procedures to implement these algorithms for insertion, deletion, and searching are straightforward in both the array-based and the pointer-based implementations of linked lists. To illustrate, we now describe a package for the ADT linked list, using the pointer-based implementation. (The array-based version is left as an exercise.)

First of all, the package must contain type declarations to define the structure of the nodes and the pointers used to access these nodes and to link them together:

$ListPointer = \uparrow ListNode;$
$ListNode =$ **record**
                   $Data : ListElementType;$ (* defined by the user *)
                   $Next : ListPointer$
       end;
$LinkedListType = ListPointer;$

Here *ListElementType* is the type of the data items to be stored in the nodes of the linked list and must be defined by the user. It should also contain a boolean variable *ListError* that signals if an error occurred while attempting to carry out some list operation:

$ListError : boolean;$

The package must also contain procedures and functions to implement the basic list operations: creating an empty list, checking if a list is empty, traversal, searching, insertion, and deletion. Algorithms for these operations have been given in the preceding sections, and procedures and functions to implement these algorithms follow:

procedure *CreateList* (**var** *List* : *LinkedListType*);

  (* Function: Creates an empty linked *List*.
       Returns: Nil pointer *List* and *ListError* = false. *)

  begin (* *CreateList* *)
    List := **nil**;
    ListError := *false*
  end (* *CreateList* *);

function *EmptyList*(*List* : *LinkedListType*) : *boolean*;

  (* Accepts: A linked list with first node pointed to by *List*.
      Function: Checks if the list is empty.
      Returns: True if list is empty and false otherwise. *)

  begin (* *EmptyList* *)
    EmptyList := (*List* = **nil**);
    ListError := *false*
  end (* *EmptyList* *);

procedure *LinkedTraverse* (*List* : *LinkedListType*);

  (* Accepts: A linked list with first node pointed to by *List*.
      Function: Traverses the linked list, processing each data
                    item exactly once.
      Returns/Output: Depends on the kind of processing. *)

  var
    CurrPtr : *ListPointer*; (* pointer to current node being processed *)

```
begin (* LinkedTraverse *)
   CurrPtr := List;
   while CurrPtr <> nil do
      begin
         (* Appropriate statements to process CurrPtr↑.Data are
            inserted here *)
         CurrPtr := CurrPtr↑.Next
      end (* while *);
   ListError := false
end (* LinkedTraverse *);

procedure LinearSearch (List : LinkedListType; Item : ListElementType;
                        var PredPtr : ListPointer;
                        var Found : boolean);
```

(* Accepts: A data *Item* and a linked list with first node pointed to
             by *List*.
   Function: Performs a linear search of the (unordered) linked list
             for a node containing *Item*.
   Returns: If the search is successful, *Found* is true and *PredPtr*
             points to the predecessor of the node containing *Item* or
             is nil if there is none. *Found* is false for an unsuccessful
             search. *)

```
var
   CurrPtr : ListPointer; (* pointer to current node *)

begin (* LinearSearch *)
   CurrPtr := List;
   PredPtr := nil;
   Found := false;
   while not Found and (CurrPtr <> nil) do
      if CurrPtr↑.Data = Item then
         Found := true
      else
         begin
            PredPtr := CurrPtr;
            CurrPtr := CurrPtr↑.Next
         end (* else *);
   ListError := false
end (* LinearSearch *);

procedure OrderedLinearSearch (List : LinkedListType;
                               Item : ListElementType;
                               var PredPtr : ListPointer;
                               var Found : boolean);
```

(* Accepts: A data *Item* and an ordered linked list containing data
             items that are in ascending order with first node pointed
             to by *List*.
   Function: Performs a linear search of the ordered linked list for

the first node containing *Item* or for a position to insert
a new node containing *Item*.

Returns: If the search is successful, *Found* is true and *PredPtr*
points to the predecessor of the node containing *Item* or
is nil if there is none. *Found* is false for an unsuccessful
search. *)

var
   CurrPtr : *ListPointer*;   (* pointer to current node *)
   DoneSearching : *boolean*;   (* signals when search is complete *)

begin (* *OrderedLinearSearch* *)
   CurrPtr := *List*;
   PredPtr := **nil**;
   Found := *false*;
   DoneSearching := *false*;
   while not *DoneSearching* **and** (*CurrPtr* <> **nil**) **do**
     if *CurrPtr↑.Data* >= *Item* **then**
       begin
         DoneSearching := *true*;
         Found := (*CurrPtr↑.Data* = *Item*)
       end (* **if** *)
     else
       begin
         PredPtr := *CurrPtr*;
         CurrPtr := *CurrPtr↑.Next*
       end (* **else** *);
   ListError := *false*
   end (* *OrderedLinearSearch* *);

procedure *LinkedInsert* (**var** *List* : *LinkedListType*;
                      Item : *ListElementType*;
                      PredPtr: *ListPointer*);

(* Accepts: A linked list with first node pointed to by *List*, a data
Item, and a pointer *PredPtr*.

Function: Inserts a node containing *Item* into the linked list
following the node pointed to by *PredPtr*, or at the front
of the list if *PredPtr* is nil.

Returns: Modified linked list with first node pointed to by *List*. *)

var
   TempPtr : *ListPointer*;   (* points to new node to be inserted *)

begin (* *LinkedInsert* *)
   new (*TempPtr*);
   TempPtr↑.Data := *Item*;
   if *PredPtr* = **nil then**   (* insert at beginning of list *)
     begin
       TempPtr↑.Next := *List*;
       List := *TempPtr*
     end (* **if** *)

```
    else                        (* node has a predecessor *)
       begin
         TempPtr↑.Next : = PredPtr↑.Next;
         PredPtr↑.Next : = TempPtr
       end (* else *);
     ListError : = false
   end (* LinkedInsert *);
```

procedure *LinkedDelete* (**var** *List* : *LinkedListType*;
                                         PredPtr : *ListPointer*);

(* Accepts: A linked list with first node pointed to by *List*, and a
             pointer *PredPtr*.
   Function: Deletes the node from the linked list whose predecessor
             is pointed to by *PredPtr* or deletes the first node if
             PredPtr is nil, unless the list is empty.
   Returns: Modified linked list with first node pointed to by *List*;
             ListError is true if the list was empty and is false
             otherwise.
   Output: A list-empty message if the list was empty. *)

```
var
   TempPtr : ListPointer; (* points to node to be deleted *)

begin (* LinkedDelete *)
   if EmptyList(List) then
      begin
        writeln ('*** Attempt to delete from an empty list ***');
        ListError : = true
      end (* if *)
   else
      begin
        if PredPtr = nil then (* first node being deleted *)
           begin
             TempPtr : = List;
             List : = TempPtr↑.Next
           end (* if *)
        else (* node has a predecessor *)
           begin
             TempPtr : = PredPtr↑.Next;
             PredPtr↑.Next : = TempPtr↑.Next
           end (* else *);
        dispose (TempPtr);
        ListError : = false
      end (* else *)
   end (* LinkedDelete *);
```

In Turbo Pascal, this linked-list-processing package could be implemented
as a unit, and the preceding function and procedures would be placed in the

unit's implementation part:

unit *LinkedListADT*;

(∗ Function: Processes linked lists whose nodes store items of type
　　　　　　ListElementType.
　Exports:　The types *ListElementType*, *ListPointer*, and
　　　　　　LinkedListType; the boolean variable *ListError* which
　　　　　　signals if an error occurred while attempting to carry out
　　　　　　some list operation; the function *EmptyList*; and the
　　　　　　procedures *CreateList*, *LinkedTraverse*, *LinearSearch*,
　　　　　　OrderedLinearSearch, *LinkedInsert*, and *LinkedDelete* to
　　　　　　implement the basic list operations. ∗)

interface
　type
　　ListElementType = ... ;　　(∗ type of list elements ∗)
　　ListPointer = ↑*ListNode*;　　(∗ type of pointers to list nodes ∗)
　　ListNode = **record**
　　　　　　　　Data : *ListElementType*;
　　　　　　　　Next : *ListPointer*
　　　　　　end;
　　LinkedListType = *ListPointer*;

　var
　　ListError : *boolean*;

procedure *CreateList* (**var** *List* : *LinkedListType*);

　(∗ Function:　Creates an empty linked *List*.
　　Returns:　Nil pointer *List* and *ListError* = false. ∗)

function *EmptyList*(*List* : *LinkedListType*) : *boolean*;

　(∗ Accepts:　A linked list with first node pointed to by *List*.
　　Function:　Checks if the list is empty.
　　Returns:　True if list is empty and false otherwise. ∗)

procedure *LinkedTraverse* (*List* : *LinkedListType*);

　(∗ Accepts:　　　A linked list with first node pointed to by *List*.
　　Function:　　　Traverses the linked list, processing each data
　　　　　　　　　item exactly once.
　　Returns/Output: Depends on the kind of processing. ∗)

procedure *LinearSearch* (*List* : *LinkedListType*;
　　　　　　　　　　　　　Item : *ListElementType*;
　　　　　　　　　　　　　var *PredPtr* : *ListPointer*;
　　　　　　　　　　　　　var *Found* : *boolean*);

　(∗ Accepts:　A data *Item* and a linked list with first node pointed
　　　　　　　to by *List*.
　　Function:　Performs a linear search of the (unordered) linked list
　　　　　　　for a node containing *Item*.

Returns: If the search is successful, *Found* is true and *PredPtr*
points to the predecessor of the node containing *Item*
or is nil if there is none. *Found* is false for an
unsuccessful search. *)

procedure *OrderedLinearSearch* (*List* : *LinkedListType*;
Item : *ListElementType*;
var *PredPtr* : *ListPointer*;
var *Found* : *boolean*);

(∗ Accepts: A data *Item* and an ordered linked list containing data
items that are in ascending order with first node
pointed to by *List*.

Function: Performs a linear search of the ordered linked list for
the first node containing *Item* or for a position to
insert a new node containing *Item*.

Returns: If the search is successful, *Found* is true and *PredPtr*
points to the predecessor of the node containing *Item*
or is nil if there is none. *Found* is false for an
unsuccessful search. *)

procedure *LinkedInsert* (**var** *List* : *LinkedListType*;
Item : *ListElementType*;
PredPtr : *ListPointer*);

(∗ Accepts: A linked list with first node pointed to by *List*, a data
Item, and a pointer *PredPtr*.

Function: Inserts a node containing *Item* into linked list
following the node pointed to by *PredPtr*, or at the
front of the list if *PredPtr* is nil.

Returns: Modified linked list with first node pointed to by
List. *)

procedure *LinkedDelete* (**var** *List* : *LinkedListType*;
PredPtr : *ListPointer*);

(∗ Accepts: A linked list with first node pointed to by *List*, and a
pointer *PredPtr*.

Function: Deletes the node from a linked list whose predecessor
is pointed to by *PredPtr* or deletes the first node if
PredPtr is nil, unless the list is empty.

Returns: Modified linked list with first node pointed to by *List*;
ListError is true if the list was empty and is false
otherwise.

Output: A list-empty message if the list was empty. *)

implementation

.

.

.

end (∗ *LinkedListADT* ∗).

7.7 Application of Linked Lists: Text Concordance

A *text concordance* is an alphabetical listing of all the distinct words in a piece of text, and in this section we consider the problem of constructing such a concordance for a document stored in a file. Because the words in a concordance are arranged in alphabetical order, a concordance is an ordered list. To construct such a concordance, we begin with an empty list. As each word is read, it is inserted into this list in the appropriate place, provided that it does not appear in the list already. Obviously, it may be necessary to insert words at any point in this list, and thus a linked implementation is appropriate.

Each time a word is read from a document, this linked list must be searched sequentially, always beginning with the first node. For a large document, however, the concordance may grow so large that searching this single list is not efficient. In order to reduce the search time, we will use several smaller linked lists. In this problem, it seems natural to construct one list of words beginning with the letter 'A', another consisting of words beginning with 'B', and so on. Consequently, we will need a total of twenty-six pointers, one for each of these linked lists, and so we will use an array of pointers indexed by 'A'..'Z'. Thus, for the document

```
DEAR MARLIN:

THE AARDVARKS AND THE CAMELS WERE
MISTAKENLY SHIPPED TO THE AZORES.
SORRY ABOUT THAT.

SINCERELY,

JIM
```

the concordance will be stored in the following array of linked lists:

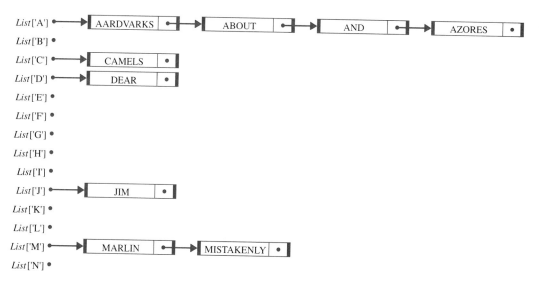

continued on next page

(Continued)

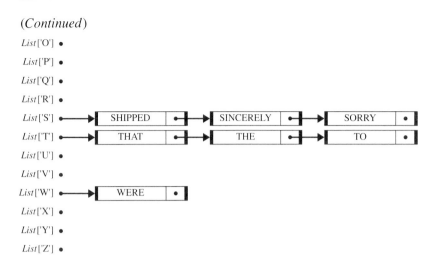

List['O'] •

List['P'] •

List['Q'] •

List['R'] •

List['S'] → SHIPPED → SINCERELY → SORRY •

List['T'] → THAT → THE → TO •

List['U'] •

List['V'] •

List['W'] → WERE •

List['X'] •

List['Y'] •

List['Z'] •

It can be displayed by simply traversing these twenty-six lists.

In summary, an algorithm for solving this text concordance problem is

ALGORITHM FOR CONSTRUCTING A TEXT CONCORDANCE

(* Input: A text file.

Function: Constructs a text concordance from a document stored in a
file. The concordance is stored in a data structure
composed of an array *List* of linked lists, where *List*[*Ch*]
is an ordered linked list of words beginning with the letter
Ch.

Output: A list of distinct words in the file. *)

1. For *Ch* ranging from 'A' to 'Z'
   Create an empty list *List*[*Ch*].
2. Open the file and get the first *Word*.
3. While there are more words to process, do the following:
   a. Search the list of words having the same first letter as *Word* to
      see if it already contains *Word*.
   b. Insert *Word* into this list if it is not already there.
   c. Get the next *Word*.
4. For *Ch* ranging from 'A' to 'Z' do the following:
   If *List*[*Ch*] is not empty then
      Traverse this list, displaying each word in it.

The program in Figure 7.3 implements this algorithm. It obtains the type
LinkedListType, the variable *ListError*, and the procedures *CreateList*, *Empty-
List*, *OrderedLinearSearch*, *LinkedInsert*, and *LinkedTraverse* from the package
for the ADT list described in the preceding section. Here, *ListElementType*
is defined to be a string type, and the statement *writeln* (*CurrPtr↑.Data*)
has been placed in the statement part of procedure *LinkedTraverse*.

```
PROGRAM TextConcordance (input, TextFile, output);

(*********************************************************************

    Input (file):    The file TextFile.
    Function:        Constructs a text concordance from a document
                     stored in a file.  The concordance is stored in
                     a data structure composed of an array List of
                     linked lists, where List[Ch] is an ordered linked
                     list of words beginning with the letter Ch.
    Output (screen): A list of distinct words in TextFile.


*********************************************************************)

CONST
   MaxWord = 15;    (* maximum length of words *)

TYPE
   WordType = PACKED ARRAY[1..MaxWord] OF char;
   ListElementType = WordType;
#include 'LINKEDLIST-TYPE'  (* LinkedListType, ListPointer *)
   ArrayOfLinkedLists = ARRAY['A'..'Z'] OF LinkedListType;

VAR
#include 'LINKEDLIST-VAR'      (* ListError *)
   PredPtr : ListPointer;      (* pointer to predecessor of a node *)
   TextFile : text;            (* text file containing document *)
   Word : WordType;            (* current word being processed *)
   List : ArrayOfLinkedLists;  (* pointers to lists of words *)
   Ch : char;                  (* index for the array List *)
   Found,                      (* indicates if search for word is successful *)
   MoreWords : boolean;        (* indicates if more words in TextFile *)

#include 'LINKEDLIST-OPS'      (* CreateList, EmptyList, LinkedTraverse *)
                               (* OrderedLinearSearch, LinkedInsert *)

PROCEDURE GetAWord (VAR TextFile : text; VAR Word : WordType;
                    VAR MoreWords : boolean);

    (*********************************************************************

    Input (file):   A file TextFile.
    Function:       Gets the next Word in TextFile.
    Output (param): Word and the boolean value MoreWords which is
                    false if there are no more words in the file,
                    true if there are.


    *********************************************************************)

    VAR
       Ch : char;        (* next character read from TextFile *)
       i : integer;      (* index *)
```

Figure 7.3

Figure 7.3 (*cont.*)

```
   BEGIN (* GetAWord *)
      (* Find first letter of next word *)
      MoreWords := false;
      WHILE NOT MoreWords AND NOT eof(TextFile) Do
         BEGIN
            read (TextFile, Ch);
            MoreWords := (Ch IN['A'..'Z']);
         END (* WHILE *);

      (* Find next word, if there is one *)
      IF MoreWords THEN
         BEGIN
            Word[1] := Ch;
            FOR i := 2 to MaxWord DO
               Word[i] := ' ';
            i := 1;
            IF NOT eof(TextFile) THEN
               read(TextFile, Ch);
            WHILE (Ch IN['A'..'Z']) AND NOT eof(TextFile) DO
               BEGIN
                  i := i + 1;
                  Word[i] := Ch;
                  read (TextFile, Ch)
               END (* WHILE *)
         END (* IF *)
   END (* GetAWord *);

BEGIN (* main program *)
   (* Initialization *)
   FOR Ch := 'A' TO 'Z' DO
      CreateList (List[Ch]);
   reset (TextFile);
   GetAWord (TextFile, Word, MoreWords);

   (* Construct the concordance *)
   WHILE MoreWords DO
      BEGIN
         OrderedLinearSearch  (List[Word[1]], Word, PredPtr, Found);
         IF NOT Found THEN
            LinkedInsert (List[Word[1]], Word, PredPtr);
         GetAWord (TextFile, Word, MoreWords)
      END (* WHILE *);

   (* Display the concordance *)
   FOR Ch := 'A' TO 'Z' DO
      IF NOT EmptyList(List[Ch]) THEN
         BEGIN
            writeln ('Words beginning with ', Ch, ':');
            LinkedTraverse (List[Ch]);
            writeln
         END (* IF *)
END (* main program *).
```

Figure 7.3 (*cont.*)

Listing of TextFile used in sample run:

```
DEAR MARLIN:

THE AARDVARKS AND THE CAMELS WERE
MISTAKENLY SHIPPED TO THE AZORES.
SORRY ABOUT THAT.

SINCERELY,

JIM
```

Sample run:

```
Words beginning with A:
   AARDVARKS
   ABOUT
   AND
   AZORES

Words beginning with C:
   CAMELS

Words beginning with D:
   DEAR

Words beginning with J:
   JIM

Words beginning with M:
   MARLIN
   MISTAKENLY

Words beginning with S:
   SHIPPED
   SINCERELY
   SORRY

Words beginning with T:
   THAT
   THE
   TO

Words beginning with W:
   WERE
```

Exercises

1. Implement the algorithms for

   (a) Insertion into a linked list
   (b) Deletion from a linked list
   (c) Searching a linked list
   (d) Searching an ordered linked list

   given in this section as procedures, using the array-based implementation of linked lists described in Section 7.3.

2. (a) Write a complete array-based version of the package or unit for the ADT list. It should obtain the necessary items from the storage package described in Section 7.3.
   (b) Modify the program of Figure 7.3 to use this package/unit.

3. Write a program to read the records from *StudentFile* (see Appendix E), and construct five linked lists of records, each of which contains a student's name, number, and cumulative grade point average (GPA), one list for each class. Each list is to be an ordered linked list in which the names are in alphabetical order. After the lists have been constructed, print each of them with appropriate headings.

4. (Project) Write a menu-driven program that allows at least the following options:

   GET: Read the records from *StudentFile* (see Appendix E), and store them in five linked lists, one for each class, with each list ordered so that the student numbers are in ascending order.
   INS: Insert the record for a new student, keeping the list sorted.
   RET: Retrieve and display the record for a specified student.
   UPD: Update the information in the record for a specified student.
   DEL: Delete the record for some student.
   LIS: List the records (or perhaps selected items in the records) in order. This option should allow suboptions:
       A: List for all students.
       C: List for only a specified class.
       G: List for students with GPAs above/below a specified value.
       M: List for a given major.
       S: List for a given sex.
   SAV: Save the updated list of records by writing them to *New-StudentFile*.

5. In addition to the words in a section of text, a concordance usually stores the numbers of selected pages on which there is a significant use of the word. Modify the program in Figure 7.3 so that the line numbers of the first ten or fewer references to a word are stored along with the

word itself. The program should display each word together with its references in ascending order.

6. Proceed as in Exercise 5, but modify the data structure used for the text concordance so that the numbers of *all* lines in which a word appears are stored.

7.8 List Lore and Pertinent Pointers About Pointers

In this chapter we discussed the list data type and two important kinds of implementation: sequential storage and linked storage. The sequential storage implementation is useful in a wide variety of list-processing problems, and in many applications it is preferable to the linked implementation. For example, many sorting and searching schemes require direct access to each list element, and this access is provided only in the sequential storage implementation. This implementation is also appropriate for lists whose maximum sizes can be estimated and whose actual sizes do not vary greatly during processing, especially those for which insertions and deletions are infrequent or are restricted to the ends of the lists.

As we have noted, however, the sequential storage implementation does have its weaknesses. It is possible to declare the array that stores the list elements to have exactly the right size only if the list is static, that is, if its size does not change. Otherwise we estimate the maximum size of the list and use this to declare the array size. However, if this estimate is too small, we run the risk of an error resulting from indices that are out of range, or we may lose some list elements because there is no room for them in the array. But if we make the array too large, then we may be wasting a considerable part of the memory allocated to the array. The other major weakness that we observed in Section 7.1 is the shifting of array elements required when items are inserted or deleted at points other than the ends of the list.

Dynamic lists whose sizes may vary greatly during processing and those for which items are frequently inserted and/or deleted anywhere in the list are generally best processed as linked lists. There are, however, certain drawbacks to this implementation as well. One is that only the first element in the list is directly accessible; the other elements are accessible only if those that precede them are first traversed. A second weakness is the additional memory required in this implementation. Memory must be allocated not only for the list elements but also for the links used to connect nodes to their successors.

The array-based implementation of a linked list does not have one of the important characteristics of a linked list—unlimited size—because the fixed size of the array limits the size of the storage pool. In the second implementation using Pascal pointers, the size of a list is limited only by the total memory available. It is, therefore, a more faithful implementation of linked lists and is the implementation that we will use for them and for other linked structures to be considered later.

Some words of warning are in order, however. Remember that the values of pointer variables are memory addressess, and therefore, the way in which pointers are used is quite different from the way in which other kinds of variables are manipulated. Using pointers correctly can be challenging not only to beginners but to experienced programmers as well. Pointers are used to create dynamic data structures such as linked lists, and algorithms for processing such structures are quite different from those for static data structures such as arrays. The following are some important things to remember when using pointer variables to implement linked structures in Pascal programs:

1. *Each pointer is bound to a fixed type.* It is the address of a memory location in which only a value of that type can be stored. This means that you cannot use pointer *P* at one place in the program to point to a memory location that stores an integer and, sometime later, to point to a memory location that stores a string.

2. *Only limited operations can be performed on pointers because they are memory addresses.* In particular:
   - A pointer *P* can be assigned a value in only the following ways:
     i. *new* (*P*)
     ii. *P* := **nil**
     iii. *P* := *Q* (∗ where *Q* is bound to the same type as *P* ∗)
   - No arithmetic operations can be performed on pointers.
   - Only = and <> can be used to compare pointers.
   - Pointers cannot be read or displayed.

3. *Don't confuse memory locations with the contents of memory locations.* If *P* is a pointer, its value is the address of a memory location; *P↑* refers to the contents of that location. *P* := *P* + 1 is not valid, but *P↑* := *P↑* + 1 may be (if *P* is bound to type integer or real); similarly, you cannot display the value of *P*, but you can perhaps display the value of *P↑*.

4. *You cannot access something that isn't there.* If pointer *P* is nil or undefined, then an attempt to use *P↑* is an error.

5. *Nil ≠ undefined.* A pointer becomes defined when it is assigned a memory address or the value **nil.** Assigning *P* the value **nil** is analogous to ''blanking out'' a character or string variable or ''zeroing out'' a numeric variable. (You might think of it as assigning a nonexistent address such as 0 to *P*.)

6. *Pay attention to special cases in processing linked structures, and be careful not to lose access to nodes.* In particular, remember the following ''programming proverbs'':
   - *Don't take a long walk off a short linked list.* It is an error if you attempt to process elements beyond the end of the list. As an illustration, consider the following incorrect attempts to search a linked list with first node pointed to by *List* for some *Item*:

     Attempt # 1:

     ```
     CurrPtr := List;
     while Curr↑.Data <> Item do
         CurrPtr := CurrPtr↑.Next;
     ```

     (∗ What happens if *Item* isn't in the list? ∗)

Attempt # 2:

CurrPtr := *List*;
while (*CurrPtr* <> **nil**) **and** (*CurrPtr*↑.*Data* <> *Item*) **do**
CurrPtr := *CurrPtr*↑.*Next*;

(∗ Unfortunately, standard Pascal permits the evaluation of boolean expressions in their entirety. Thus, if *Item* is not in the list, *CurrPtr* eventually becomes nil, but the second part of the boolean expression that controls repetition attempts to access the *Data* field of a nonexistent node. ∗)

Attempt # 3:

(∗ This time I'll make sure I don't fall off the end of the list by stopping if I find *Item* or reach a node whose link field is nil. ∗)
Found := *false*;
CurrPtr := *List*;
while not *Found* **and** (*CurrPtr*↑.*Next* <> **nil**) **do**
if *CurrPtr*↑.*Data* = *Item* **then**
Found := *true*
else
CurrPtr := *CurrPtr*↑.*Next*;

(∗ Almost, but there still are a few cases in which it fails. ∗)

Attempt # 4:

(∗ Now I see how to fix the last try! ∗)

Found := *false*;
CurrPtr := *List*;
repeat
if *CurrPtr*↑.*Data* = *Item* **then**
Found := *true*
else
CurrPtr := *CurrPtr*↑.*Next*
until *Found* **or** (*CurrPtr* = **nil**);

(∗ This is close, but there is still one case in which it fails. ∗)

- *You can't get water from an empty well.* Don't try to access elements in an empty list; this case usually requires special consideration. For example, if *List* is nil, then initializing *CurrPtr* to *List* and attempting to access *CurrPtr*↑.*Data* or *CurrPtr*↑.*Next* is an error. (Go back now and reconsider Attempts 3 and 4 if you didn't see when they might fail.)
- *Don't burn bridges before you cross them.* Be careful that you change links in the correct order, or you may lose access to a node or to many nodes! For example, in the following attempt to insert a new

node at the beginning of a linked list,

$$List := NewNodePtr;$$
$$NewNodePtr\uparrow.Next := List;$$

the statements are not in correct order. As soon as the first statement is executed, *List* points to the new node, and access to the remaining nodes in the list (those formerly pointed to by *List*) is lost. The second statement then simply sets the link field of the new node to point to itself:

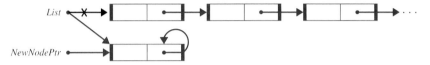

The correct sequence is first to connect the new node to the list and then to reset *List*:

$$NewNodePtr\uparrow.Next := List;$$
$$List := NewNodePtr;$$

8

Other Linked Structures

The "standard" linked lists considered in the preceding chapter are characterized by the following properties: (1) Only the first node is directly accessible, and (2) each node consists of a data part and a single link that connects this node to its successor (if there is one). They are, therefore, *linear structures* that must be processed sequentially in the order in which the nodes are linked together, from first to last.

In some applications, other kinds of list processing are required, and in these situations it may be convenient to allow other kinds of access and/or linkages. In this chapter we consider some of these variants of linked lists, such as linked stacks and queues, circular linked lists, symmetrically linked lists, and other multiply linked lists.

8.1 Linked Stacks and Queues

We have seen that implementations of lists that use arrays as the basic storage structures are not completely faithful because the fixed size of the array limits the size of the list. In particular, array-based implementations of stacks and queues like those considered in Chapters 4 and 5, are not perfect representations of these structures. In this section we show how these data structures can be implemented more faithfully as linked structures.

Recall that a stack is a list in which items can be accessed at only one end, called the *top*. Thus it seems natural to implement a stack using a linked list because, as we noted in the introduction, only the first node of a linked list is directly accessible. Using the Pascal pointer-based implementation of linked lists, we make the following declarations for a linked stack:

type
   StackElementType = ... ; (∗ type of elements in the stack ∗)
   StackPointer = ↑*StackNode*;
   StackNode = **record**
               Data : *StackElementType*;
               Next : *StackPointer*
        end;
   StackType = *StackPointer*;

var
   StackError : *boolean*;

A procedure to create an empty stack and a function to check for a stack-empty condition are basically the same as those for the corresponding operations for general linked lists described in the preceding chapter:

procedure *CreateStack* (**var** *Stack* : *StackType*);

   (∗ Function: Creates an empty stack.
     Returns: Empty *Stack*. ∗)

   begin (∗ *CreateStack* ∗)
     Stack := **nil**;
     StackError := *false*
   end (∗ *CreateStack* ∗);

function *EmptyStack*(*Stack* : *StackType*) : *boolean*;

   (∗ Accepts: *Stack*.
     Function: Checks if *Stack* is empty.
     Returns: True if *Stack* is empty, false otherwise. ∗)

   begin (∗ *EmptyStack* ∗)
     EmptyStack := (*Stack* = **nil**);
     StackError := *false*
   end (∗ *EmptyStack* ∗);

And since the pop operation for stacks is simply the deletion operation restricted to the beginning of the linked list, a procedure for it is a simplification of the procedure *LinkedDelete* for a general list:

procedure *Pop* (**var** *Stack* : *StackType*; **var** *Item* : *StackElementType*);

   (∗ Accepts: *Stack*.
     Function: Pops *Item* from the top of *Stack* or sets *StackError* to
              true if *Stack* is empty.
     Returns: *Item* and modified *Stack*.
     Output: ''Stack-empty'' message if *Stack* is empty.
     Note: *Stack* is a pointer to the node containing the top
           element. ∗)

   var
     TempPtr : *StackPointer*; (∗ temporary pointer to top node ∗)

```
      begin (* Pop *)
        if EmptyStack(Stack) then
          begin
            writeln ('*** Attempt to pop from an empty stack ***');
            StackError := true
          end (* if *)
        else
          begin
            Item := Stack↑.Data;
            TempPtr := Stack;
            Stack := Stack↑.Next;
            dispose (TempPtr);
            StackError := false
          end (* else *)
      end (* Pop *);
```

Similarly, a procedure that implements the push operation is a simple modification of the procedure *LinkedInsert*. It is basically the same as the procedure *AddToList* in the program of Figure 7.2.

```
      procedure Push (var Stack : StackType; Item : StackElementType);
```

    (* Accepts: *Stack* and *Item*.
         Function: Pushes *Item* onto *Stack*.
         Returns: Modified *Stack*.

         Note: *Stack* is a pointer to the node containing the top
                  element. *)

```
      var
        TempPtr : StackPointer; (* pointer to node for new element *)

      begin (* Push *)
        new (TempPtr);
        TempPtr↑.Data := Item;
        TempPtr↑.Next := Stack;
        Stack := TempPtr;
        StackError := false
      end (* Push *);
```

Note that unlike the procedure *Push* in the array-based implementation of a stack in Chapter 4, this procedure does not check for a stack-full condition. In the array-based implementation, the size of a stack is limited by the fixed size of the array, and consequently it is not possible to push a new item onto a stack when the array is full. The specification of a stack as an abstract data type, however, imposes no limit on the size of a stack, and so in theory, a stack can never become full. Because the size of a linked stack is limited only by the total memory available, this linked implementation is more faithful than the array-based implementation.

Like several other abstract data types that we have considered, the preceding definitions of the types *StackPointer, StackNode,* and *StackType,* the variable *StackError,* the function *EmptyStack,* and the procedures *CreateStack, Push,* and *Pop* can be combined into a package or unit for processing linked stacks. This package/unit is an alternative to the array-based implementation of stacks described in Section 4.2. In fact, any program that uses the array-based stack package can use this linked-stack package instead with no modifications of the program itself. For example, in the base-conversion program in Figure 4.2 we need only change the #include directives to copy the files containing the linked stack declarations, function, and procedures into the program. (The directive #include 'STACK-CONST' can be omitted, since the linked-stack package defines no constants.)

This example illustrates *one of the major benefits of data abstraction, that is, of separating the definition of an abstract data type as a logical structure from its implementation; the implementation can be changed without affecting programs that use the ADT.* If compiler directives are used to insert files that contain the definitions and declarations needed to implement the ADT, the contents of these files can be changed to reflect the new implementation, and no changes are required in the program.

A linked implementation of a queue is a simple extension of the linked implementation of stacks. Recall that a queue is a list in which items may be removed only at one end, called the *front* or *head,* and items may be inserted only at the other end, called the *rear* or *tail* of the queue. In a linked-list implementation of a queue, it seems natural to identify the first element in the list as the front of the queue. The deletion operation is then implemented in the same way that the pop operation is for a stack, but the insertion operation requires traversing the entire list to find the rear of the queue. This list traversal can be avoided if we adopt the approach of the array-based implementation in Chapter 5 and maintain two pointers, one to the first node (the front of the queue) and the other to the last node (the rear of the queue).

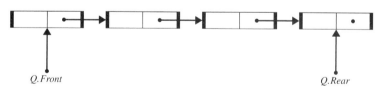

We are thus led to declarations of the form

type
   QueueElementType = . . . ;   (∗ type of elements in the queue ∗)
   QueuePointer = ↑*QueueNode*;
   QueueNode = **record**
               Data : *QueueElementType*;
               Next : *QueuePointer*
          end;
   QueueType = **record**
               Front,
               Rear : *QueuePointer*
          end;

var

    QueueError : *boolean*;

Procedures and functions that implement the basic queue operations are much like those for linked stacks and are left as exercises.

8.2 Other Variants of Singly Linked Lists

In the linked implementation of a queue described in the preceding section, two pointers are maintained, one to the front of the queue and the other to the rear. This modification of the standard linked list is convenient because the basic queue operations are performed at the ends of the list. In this section we consider other variants of linked lists that are appropriate for certain list applications and that make algorithms for some of the basic list operations simpler and more efficient.

Lists with Head Nodes. The first node in a standard linked list differs from the other nodes in that it does not have a predecessor. As we saw in Chapter 7, this means that two cases must be considered for some basic list operations such as insertion and deletion. This would not be necessary if we could ensure that every node that stores a list element will have a predecessor. And we can do this by simply introducing a dummy first node, called a **head node,** at the beginning of a linked list. No actual list element is stored in the data part of this head node; instead, it serves as a predecessor of the node that stores the actual first element because its link field points to this "real" first node. For example, the list of names Brown, Jones, and Smith can be stored in a linked list with a head node as follows:

In this implementation, every linked list is required to have a head node. In particular, an empty list has a head node:

To create an empty list, therefore, instead of simply initializing a pointer *List* to have the value nil, we must obtain a head node pointed to by *List* and set its link field to nil. In the Pascal pointer-based implementation of linked lists, the following two statements can be used:

    new (*List*);
    List↑.*Next* := **nil**;

Similarly, a function to check for a list-empty condition requires checking *List*↑.*Next* = **nil** rather than *List* = **nil**.

    In the creation of an empty list, a value (nil) has been assigned to the link part of the head node but the data part has been left undefined (as denoted by the question mark in the preceding diagrams). In some situations the data part of the head node might be used to store some information about the list. For example, if Brown, Jones, and Smith all are members of some organization, we might store the name of this organization in the head node:

The fact that every node in a linked list now has a predecessor simplifies algorithms for the insertion and deletion operations. For example, the insertion algorithm given in Section 7.6 for standard linked lists (without head nodes) simplifies to

ALGORITHM FOR INSERTION INTO A LINKED LIST WITH HEAD NODE

(* Accepts: A data *Item*, a linked list with head node pointed to by *List*, and a pointer *PredPtr*.

Function: Inserts a node containing *Item* into linked list following the node pointed to by *PredPtr*.

Returns: Modified linked list with head node pointed to by *List*. *)

1. Get a node pointed to by *TempPtr*.
2. Set *Data(TempPtr)* equal to *Item*.
3. Set *Next(TempPtr)* equal to *Next(PredPtr)*.
4. Set *Next(PredPtr)* equal to *TempPtr*.

The deletion algorithm simplifies in a similar manner.

Algorithms for traversing a standard linked list or a part of it can easily be modified for use with linked lists that have head nodes. Usually only instructions that initialize some auxiliary pointer to the first node in the list need to be altered. For example, in the traversal algorithm of Section 7.2, only the first instruction requires modification:

ALGORITHM TO TRAVERSE A LINKED LIST WITH HEAD NODE

(* Accepts: A linked list with first node pointed to by *List*.

Function: Traverses this linked list, processing each list element exactly once.

Returns/Output: Depends on the kind of processing. *)

1. Initialize *CurrPtr* to *Next(List)*.
2. While *CurrPtr* ≠ nil do the following:
   a. Process *Data(CurrPtr)*.
   b. Set *CurrPtr* equal to *Next(CurrPtr)*.

Circular Linked Lists.   We saw in Chapter 5 that a feasible implementation of a queue using an array to store the queue elements was obtained if we thought of the array as being circular, with the first element following the last. This suggests that an analogous *circular linked list* obtained by setting the link of the last node in a standard linear linked list to point to the first node might also be a useful data structure:

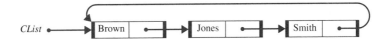

As this diagram illustrates, each node in a circular linked list has a predecessor (and a successor), provided that the list is nonempty. Consequently, as in the case of linked lists with head nodes, the algorithms for insertion and deletion do not require special consideration of nodes without predecessors. For example, an algorithm for inserting an item into a circular linked list is as follows:

ALGORITHM FOR INSERTION INTO A CIRCULAR LINKED LIST

(* Accepts: A data *Item*, a circular linked list with first node pointed
          to by *CList*, and a pointer *PredPtr*.
Function: Inserts a node containing *Item* into linked list following
          the node pointed to by *PredPtr* (if there is one).
Returns: Modified circular linked list with first node pointed to by
          CList. *)

1. Get a node pointed to by *TempPtr*.
2. Set *Data(TempPtr)* equal to *Item*.
3. If the list is empty then do the following:
    a. Set *Next(TempPtr)* equal to *TempPtr*.
    b. Set *CList* equal to *TempPtr*.
  Else do the following:
    a. Set *Next(TempPtr)* equal to *Next(PredPtr)*.
    b. Set *Next(PredPtr)* equal to *TempPtr*.

Note, however, that insertion into an empty list requires special consideration because in this case, the link in the one-node list that results must point to the node itself:

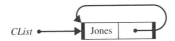

The deletion operation for a circular list is implemented by the following algorithm:

ALGORITHM FOR DELETION FROM A CIRCULAR LINKED LIST

(* Accepts: A circular linked list with first node pointed to by *CList*
          and a pointer *PredPtr*.
Function: Deletes from the linked list the node whose predecessor is
          pointed to by *PredPtr* (if there is one).
Returns: Modified circular linked list with first node pointed to by
          CList. *)

If the list is empty then
  Signal that a list-empty error occurred.

Else do the following:

1. Set *TempPtr* equal to *Next(PredPtr)*.
2. If *TempPtr* = *PredPtr* then   (* one-node list *)
       Set *CList* equal to nil.
      Else   (* list with more than one node *)
        Set *Next(PredPtr)* equal to *Next(TempPtr)*.
3. Return the node pointed to by *TempPtr* to the storage pool of available free nodes.

Notice that in addition to an empty list, a one-element list requires special treatment because, in this case, the list becomes empty after this node is deleted. This case is detected in the algorithm by checking if the node is its own predecessor, that is, that its link field points to itself.

Most other algorithms for standard linear linked lists also must be modified when applied to circular lists. To illustrate, consider again the general traversal algorithm given in Section 7.2:

ALGORITHM TO TRAVERSE A STANDARD LINKED LIST

(* Accepts: A linked list with first node pointed to by *List*.
   Function: Traverses the linked list, processing each data item exactly once.
   Returns/Output: Depends on the kind of processing. *)

1. Initialize *CurrPtr* to *List*.
2. While *CurrPtr* ≠ nil do the following:
      a. Process *Data(CurrPtr)*.
      b. Set *CurrPtr* equal to *Next(CurrPtr)*.

In this algorithm, the list traversal terminates when *CurrPtr* becomes nil, signaling that the last node has been processed.

For a circular linked list, the link in the last node points to the first node. Thus a naive attempt to modify this traversal algorithm for a circular list might produce the following:

(* INCORRECT attempt to traverse a circular linked list with first node pointed to by *CList*, processing each list element exactly once. *)

1. Initialize *CurrPtr* to *CList*.
2. While *CurrPtr* ≠ *CList* do the following:
      a. Process *Data(CurrPtr)*.
      b. Set *CurrPtr* equal to *Next(CurrPtr)*.

Here the expression *CurrPtr* ≠ *CList* is false immediately, and thus this algorithm correctly traverses only an empty list!

To obtain an algorithm that correctly traverses all circular linked lists, we can replace the while loop with a repeat loop, provided that we have made sure that the list is not empty:

ALGORITHM TO TRAVERSE A CIRCULAR LINKED LIST

(* Accepts: A circular linked list with first node pointed to by *CList*.

    Function: Traverses the circular linked list, processing each data item exactly once.

    Returns/Output: Depends on the kind of processing. *)

If the list is not empty, then do the following:

    1. Initialize *CurrPtr* to *CList*.
    2. Repeat the following steps:
        a. Process *Data(CurrPtr)*.
        b. Set *CurrPtr* equal to *Next(CurrPtr)*.
    Until *CurrPtr = CList*.

Another option is to use a circular linked list with a head node, for example,

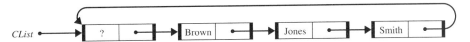

Both versions of the traversal algorithm for circular linked lists correctly traverse such lists if the initialization instruction is changed to

    1. Initialize *CurrPtr* to *Next(CList)*.

You should check these revised algorithms for circular lists like the preceding and for one-element lists such as

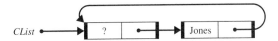

as well as empty lists that consist of only a head node that points to itself:

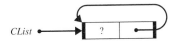

For some applications of circular linked lists, it is advantageous to maintain a pointer *CList* to the last node rather than the first; for example,

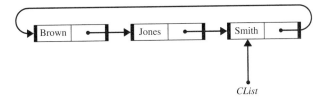

In this case we have direct access to the last node and almost direct access to the first node, since *Next(CList)* points to the first node in the list. This variation

is thus especially useful when it is necessary to access repeatedly the elements at the ends of the list. In particular, it is well suited for linked queues and deques.

Exercises

1. Beginning with an empty stack, draw a diagram of the linked stack that results when the following sequence of operations is performed: *Push* 'X', *Push* 'L', *Push* 'R', *Pop, Push* 'A', *Pop, Pop, Push* 'Q'.

2. Beginning with an empty queue, draw a diagram of the linked queue that results when the following sequence of operations is performed: *AddQ* 'X', *AddQ* 'L', *AddQ* 'R', *RemoveQ, AddQ* 'A', *RemoveQ, RemoveQ, AddQ* 'Q'.

3. Assuming a Pascal pointer-based implementation, write functions/procedures to implement the basic operations *CreateQ, EmptyQ, AddQ,* and *RemoveQ* for a linked queue.

4. In Section 5.1 a *priority queue* was described as a queuelike structure in which each item has a certain priority and is inserted in such a way that it will be removed before all those of lower priority. Assuming that such a priority queue is implemented as a linked list, write a procedure for the insertion operation.

5. (Project) Use the procedure of Exercise 4 together with functions/procedures for the other basic priority queue operations to develop a program to simulate the operation of a computer system as described in Exercise 6 of Section 5.3.

6. Write a procedure for deleting an item from a linked list with head node.

7. Write a procedure for searching a circular linked list for a given item.

8. Write a procedure for searching an ordered circular linked list for a given item.

9. Write an algorithm for locating the nth successor of an item in a circular linked list. (If the list has fewer than $n + 1$ items, there is no nth successor; otherwise, it is the nth item that follows the given item in the list.)

10. Write procedures/functions *CreateCList, CLInsert, CLDelete,* and *EmptyCList* for a circular linked list with a head node.

11. Redo Exercise 2 for a queue implemented as a circular linked list with a single pointer to the last node.

12. Write procedures for the basic operations *CreateQ*, *EmptyQ*, *AddQ*, and *RemoveQ* on a queue implemented as a circular linked list with a single pointer to the last node.

13. Repeat Exercise 12 for a deque.

14. The **shuffle-merge** operation on two lists was defined in Exercise 9 of Section 7.2. Write an algorithm to shuffle-merge two circularly linked lists. The items in the lists are to be copied to produce the new circularly linked lists; the original lists are not to be destroyed.

15. Proceed as in Exercise 14, but do not copy the items. Just change links in the two lists (thus destroying the original lists) to produce the merged list.

16. In implementations of linked lists in which the storage pool is maintained as a linked stack, as described in Section 7.3, it is possible to erase any circularly linked list in O(1)-time; that is, it is possible to return all of its nodes to the storage pool in constant time, independent of the size of the list. Give such an erase algorithm for a circularly linked list whose computing time is O(1); and show how it works using the following diagram:

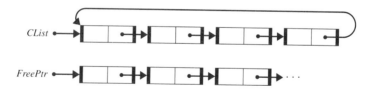

17. In the **Josephus problem**, a group of soldiers is surrounded by the enemy, and one soldier is to be selected to ride for help. The selection is made in the following manner: An integer *n* and a soldier are selected randomly. The soldiers are arranged in a circle and they count off, beginning with the randomly selected soldier. When the count reaches *n*, that soldier is removed from the circle, and the counting begins again with the next soldier. This process continues until only one soldier remains, who is the (un)fortunate one selected to ride for help. Write an algorithm to implement this selection strategy, assuming that a circular linked list is used to store the names (or numbers) of the soldiers.

18. Write a program to solve the Josephus problem described in Exercise 17. Use output statements to trace the selection process, showing the contents of the list at each stage.

19. Write a program that reads a string of characters, inserting each character as it is read into both a linked stack and a linked queue. When the end of the string is encountered, use basic stack and queue operations to determine whether the string is a palindrome (see Exercise 5 of Section 3.2).

8.3 Linked Implementations of Sets

Implementations of sets as bit strings, as described in Section 2.9, usually impose two limitations on the kinds of sets that can be processed. One restriction is that the size of the set is limited because the system allocates a fixed number of memory words and thus a fixed number of bits for any set. A second common restriction is that the elements in the universal set must be ordered so that the first element can be associated with the first bit in a bit string, the second element with the second bit, and so on. This is why the type of the elements of a set in Pascal must be some ordinal type; sets of real numbers, sets of strings, and sets of records are not allowed.

There are various alternatives to the bit-string implementation of sets, such as the array-based implementation described in Exercises 2 and 3 of Section 2.9. This implementation uses a boolean array S as the basic storage structure. The size of the array is the number of elements in the universal set, and each array component is associated with a unique element of the universal set. A particular subset S of the universal set is represented by setting $S[i]$ to true or false according to whether or not the ith element of the universal set belongs to S.

To illustrate, suppose that the universal set is

$$U = \{0, 1, 2, 3, 4, 5, 6, 7, 8, 9\}$$

Boolean arrays that represent subsets of U can then be indexed by 0..9. The subset of even integers,

$$\{0, 2, 4, 6, 8\}$$

is represented by an array *Even* whose elements are as follows:

i	*Even[i]*
0	*true*
1	*false*
2	*true*
3	*false*
4	*true*
5	*false*
6	*true*
7	*false*
8	*true*
9	*false*

The empty set is represented by an array *Empty*, all of whose elements are false:

i	*Empty*[*i*]
0	*false*
1	*false*
2	*false*
3	*false*
4	*false*
5	*false*
6	*false*
7	*false*
8	*false*
9	*false*

One obvious weakness of this implementation is that all sets, even those with only a few elements, are represented using arrays whose size is equal to the size of the universal set, which may be very large. It seems very inefficient to store all of the false entries in these arrays when a set is completely specified by the true entries. A second weakness is that as in the bit-string implementation, the elements of the universal set must be ordered because they must correspond to array positions.

An alternative approach that removes these deficiencies is to use a linked list to represent a set. For example, the set of even digits can be represented by the following linked list with head node

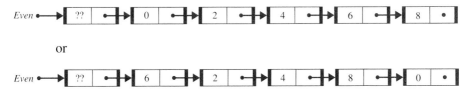

or

Even ── ?? ── 6 ── 2 ── 4 ── 8 ── 0 ── •

or by any other linked list that contains nodes storing the digits 0, 2, 4, 6, and 8 in some order. The empty set can be represented by

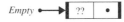

Of course, circular linked lists can also be used.

These linked lists can represent the set of even digits and the empty set for any universal set containing the even digits. In the array-based implementation, however, the array must change when the universal set changes. Note also that whereas the array-based implementation requires an ordered universal set, the linked implementation does not.

Because the order of the elements in these linked lists is not important, it is easy to construct this linked representation for a set. We can simply insert each element at the front of the list; that is, we can use the push operation for a linked stack. Beginning with an empty list that consists of only a head node, we repeatedly call the following procedure for each new set element:

```
procedure AddElement (var S : SetType; X : SetElementType);
```

(* Accepts: A set S and an element X.
   Function: Adds X to S.
   Returns: Modified set S.

   Note: Sets are implemented as linked lists with head nodes. *)

```
var
    TempPtr : SetPointer; (* pointer to new node for X *)

begin (* AddElement *)
    new (TempPtr);
    TempPtr↑.Element := X;
    TempPtr↑.Next := S↑.Next;
    S↑.Next := TempPtr
end (* AddElement *);
```

Here *SetType* and *SetPointer* are type identifiers defined by declarations of the form

```
type
    SetElementType = ... ;        (* type of elements for set *)
    SetPointer = ↑SetNode;
    SetNode = record
                    Element : SetElementType;
                    Next : SetPointer
              end;
    SetType = SetPointer;
```

The basic set operations can be implemented quite easily in this linked implementation. For example, the membership relation can be implemented by the following function *IsAMember*, which simply performs a linear search of the linked list representing the set:

```
function IsAMember(S : SetType; X : SetElementType) : boolean;
```

(* Accepts: A set S and an element X.
   Function: Checks if X is an element of set S.
   Returns: True if X is an element of S and false otherwise.

   Note: Sets are implemented as linked lists with head nodes. *)

```
var
    p : SetPointer;          (* auxiliary pointer to run through S *)
    Found : boolean;          (* indicates if X is found *)

begin (* IsAMember *)
    p := S↑.Next;
    Found := false;
    while not Found and (p <> nil) do
        if p↑.Element = X then
            Found := true
        else
            p := p↑.Next;
    IsAMember := Found
end (* IsAMember *);
```

The program in Figure 8.1 uses this linked implementation of sets. It determines the number of distinct users logged in to a particular computer system for some given period of time. User identifications (user-ids) are automatically entered into a log file each time they log in to the system. Because the same user may log in many times, this file may contain many duplicate user-ids. As the program reads each user-id from the file, it uses the function *IsAMember* to check whether it is an element of the set *Users* that contains the user-ids read thus far. If it is not, the user-id is added to the set using procedure *AddElement*, and a counter is incremented by 1. Note that the elements in the set *Users* are strings. Such a set cannot be constructed with the Pascal **set** data type, which requires an ordinal base type for all sets.

```
PROGRAM CountUsers (input, output, UserIdFile);

(*********************************************************************

    Input (file):    The text file UserIdFile.
    Function:        Determines the number of distinct users logged
                     into a computer system for a given period of time.
                     User-ids are read from UserIdFile, and each new
                     one is counted and added to the set Users of
                     user-ids already found in the file.
    Output (screen): Number of users logged in.

    Note:            The program uses a linked implementation of sets.

*********************************************************************)

CONST
#include 'STRING-CONST'

TYPE
#include 'STRING-TYPE' (* StringType *)
   SetElementType = String;
   SetPointer = ^SetNode;
   SetNode = RECORD
                Element : SetElementType;
                Next : SetPointer
             END;
   SetType = SetPointer;

VAR
   UserIdFile : text;    (* log file of user-ids *)
   UserId : String;      (* current user-id being processed *)
   Users : SetType;      (* set of user-ids found in UserIdFile *)
   NumUsers : integer;   (* count of distinct user-ids *)

#include 'STRING-OPS'  (* ReadString *)
```

Figure 8.1

Figure 8.1 (*cont.*)

```
FUNCTION EmptySet : SetType;

  (*******************************************************************

      Input:              None.
      Function:           Creates an empty set.
      Output (EmptySet):  Returns an empty set.

      Note:               Function returns a pointer to an empty list
                          consisting of only a head hode.  This is
                          the linked implementation of an empty set.

  *******************************************************************)

  VAR
     TempPtr : SetPointer;  (* temporary pointer *)

  BEGIN (* EmptySet *)
     new (TempPtr);
     TempPtr^.Next := NIL;
     EmptySet := TempPtr
  END (* EmptySet *);

FUNCTION IsAMember (S : SetType; X : SetElementType) : boolean;

  (*******************************************************************

      Input (param):      A set S and an element X.
      Function:           Checks if X is an element of set S.
      Output (IsAMember): Returns true if X is an element of S and
                          false otherwise.

      Note:               Sets are implemented as linked lists with
                          head nodes.
  *******************************************************************)

  VAR
     p : SetPointer;  (* auxiliary pointer to run through S *)
     Found : boolean; (* indicates if/when X is found *)

  BEGIN (* IsAMember *)
     p := S^.Next;
     Found := false;
     WHILE NOT Found AND (P <> NIL) DO
        IF p^.Element = X THEN
           Found := true
        ELSE
           p := p^.Next;
     IsAMember := Found
  END (* IsAMember *);
```

Figure 8.1 *(cont.)*

```
PROCEDURE AddElement (VAR S : SetType; X : SetElementType);

   (*******************************************************************

        Input (param):   A set S and an element X.
        Function:        Adds X to S.
        Output (param):  Modified set S.

     *****************************************************************)

     VAR
        TempPtr : SetPointer;   (* pointer to new node for X *)

     BEGIN (* AddElement *)
        new (TempPtr);
        TempPtr^.Element := X;
        TempPtr^.Next := S^.Next;
        S^.Next := TempPtr
     END (* AddElement *);

BEGIN (* main program *)
   reset (UserIdFile);
   Users := EmptySet;
   NumUsers := 0;
   WHILE NOT eof(UserIdFile) DO
      BEGIN
         ReadString (UserIdFile, UserId);
         IF NOT IsAMember(Users, UserId) THEN
            BEGIN
               NumUsers := NumUsers + 1;
               AddElement (Users, UserId)
            END (* IF *)
      END (* WHILE *);
   writeln ('Number of users who logged in:  ', NumUsers:1)
END (* main program *).
```

Listing of UserIdFile used in sample run:

```
S31416PI
S12345SL
S31416PI
S31313LN
S12345SL
S31416PI
S21718EX
S13331RC
S77777UP
S12345SL
S31416PI
S21718EX
S99099RR
S12345SL
S77777UP
S31313LN
S31416PI
```

Figure 8.1 (*cont.*)

Sample run:

```
Number of users who logged in:   7
```

The functions *EmptySet* and *IsAMember*, and the procedure *AddElement* implement three of the basic set operations and relations. Subprograms for the others are similar. For example, to form the union *AUB* of two sets *A* and *B* in this linked implementation, we first obtain a head node pointed to by *AUB* and then traverse *A*, copying each of its elements to *AUB* using procedure *AddElement*. Next we traverse *B* and use function *IsAMember* to determine which elements of *B* do not belong to *A* and add them to *AUB* using *Add-Element*. The following function implements set union in precisely this manner:

function *Union*(*A*, *B* : *SetType*) : *SetType*;

   (∗ Accepts: Sets *A* and *B*.
          Function: Computes the union of two sets *A* and *B*.
          Returns: Union of *A* and *B*.

          Note: Sets are implemented as linked lists with head nodes. ∗)

var
   ptr,   (∗ pointer to run through *A* and *B* ∗)
   AUB : *SetPointer*;   (∗ pointer to list for union of *A* and *B* ∗)

begin (∗ *Union* ∗)
   (∗ get head node for union ∗)
   new (*AUB*);
   AUB↑.Next := **nil**;

   (∗ copy *A* to *AUB* ∗)
   ptr := *A↑.Next*;
   while *ptr* <> **nil do**
     begin
       AddElement (*AUB*, *ptr↑.Element*);
        ptr := *ptr↑.Next*
     end (∗ **while** ∗);

   (∗ copy elements of *B* not in *A* to *AUB* ∗)
   ptr := *B↑.Next*;
   while *ptr* <> **nil do**
     begin
       if not *IsAMember*(*A*, *ptr↑.Element*) **then**
         AddElement (*AUB*, *ptr↑.Element*);
        ptr := *ptr↑.Next*
     end (∗ **while** ∗);

   Union := *AUB*
  end (∗ *Union* ∗);

Procedures for the other set operations and relations are similar to those given in this section and are left as exercises. These procedures can be collected in a package or unit for processing more general sets than those provided in Pascal.

Exercises

1. Determine the computing time of function *Union* for sets A and B having m and n elements, respectively.

2. Assuming the linked implementation of sets of this section, write a function for set intersection. Determine its computing time for sets A and B having m and n elements, respectively.

3. Proceed as in Exercise 2, but write a function to implement the operation of set difference.

4. Assuming the linked implementation of sets of this section, write a

   (a) nonrecursive boolean-valued function
   (b) recursive boolean-valued function

   Subset so that the function reference *Subset(A, B)* returns the value true if A is a subset of B and false otherwise.

5. Write a function *CardinalNumber* that returns the cardinal number (number of elements) of a set implemented as a linked list with a head node.

6. Suppose sets are maintained as ordered linked lists. Write an algorithm for set intersection that is more efficient than that in Exercise 2. It should have computing time $O(m + n)$.

7. Repeat Exercise 6 for set union.

8. The Cartesian product $A \times B$ of two sets A and B is the set of all ordered pairs (x, y) where $x \in A$ and $y \in B$. For example, if $A = \{1, 2\}$ and $B = \{a, b, c\}$, then

   $$A \times B = \{(1, a), (1, b), (1, c), (2, a), (2, b), (2, c)\}$$

   Write a function/procedure that accepts linked lists (with head nodes) representing sets A and B and returns a pointer to a linked list representing $A \times B$. Give appropriate type definitions for the case when A is some set of integers and B is some set of characters.

9. Write a procedure for the inverse of the operation in Exercise 8. It should accept a pointer to a linked list representing the Cartesian product $A \times B$ of two sets and should return pointers to the linked

lists for *A* and *B*. (This is commonly referred to as projecting onto the first/second component.)

10. Write a set-processing package or unit using the linked implementation of sets described in this section. It should define the type *SetType* and procedures and functions for the basic set operations: *Union, Intersection, Difference, IsAMember, Equal, Subset, AddElement,* and *EmptySet* and a procedure *Assign* that assigns a copy of a set to a set variable. Carry out bottom-up testing of the package using a command-driven ADT tester similar to that for stacks in Section 4.2.

11. Using the linked implementation of sets described in this section, write a program for finding prime numbers using the Sieve Method of Eratosthenes (see Exercise 8 of Sec. 2.8).

12. Using the linked implementation of sets described in this section, write a program that reads records from *StudentFile* (see Appendix E), constructs the set of all distinct majors, and displays this set.

13. Using the linked implementation of sets described in this section, write a program to simulate dealing hands of cards from a deck of cards. Use an array of sets to represent the various hands. (See footnote 2 in Section 5.2 for a description of a random number generator if your system does not provide one.)

8.4 Linked Implementation of Strings

The implementation of strings in Chapter 3 used packed arrays of characters as the basic storage structure. For example, the usual implementation in standard Pascal uses declarations of the form

    const
        StringLimit = ... ; (* maximum length allowed for strings *)

    type
        StringType = **packed array**[1..*StringLimit*] **of** *char*;

This implementation has the usual weaknesses of array-based implementations. In particular, it imposes a limit on the lengths of strings and does not allow efficient insertion and/or deletion of characters. Since strings are lists of characters, we might attempt to remedy these deficiencies by using a linked implementation.

An obvious way to change to a linked representation of strings is to replace the array of characters by a linked list in which each node stores a single character. For example, the string 'COMPUTE' can be stored in a linked list as

If we use a linked list like this as the storage structure for strings, determining the length of a string will require traversing the list to count the nodes. An alternative is to imitate the approach used in one of the array-based implementations of Chapter 3 and use a head node to store *chr(count)*, where *count* is the number of characters in the string. As we noted in Section 3.2, however, this imposes an upper limit on the length of a string, since the *chr* function is defined over only a small subrange of integers such as 0..255.

A better alternative is to imitate the preferred array-based implementation of Section 3.2 and use a record containing two fields, one to store the length of a string and the other to store a pointer to a linked list containing the characters that make up the string. Declarations for this implementation have the form

> **type**
>   *StringPointer* = ↑*StringNode*;
>   *StringNode* = **record**
>   *Ch* : *char*;
>   *Next* : *StringPointer*
>   **end**;
>   *StringType* = **record**
>   *Length* : 0..*maxint*;
>   *List* : *StringPointer*
>   **end**;

Algorithms for basic string operations in this linked implementation are not difficult. For example, two strings can be concatenated to form a third string using the following algorithm:

ALGORITHM FOR CONCATENATION

(* Accepts: Strings *Str1* and *Str2*.
     Function: Concatenates string *Str1* with string *Str2* to form the string
                 Str, where all strings are implemented as linked lists with
                 head nodes, with one character per node.
     Returns: String *Str*. *)

1. Set the length of *Str* equal to the sum of the lengths of *Str1* and *Str2*.
2. Get a head node for *Str*.
3. Traverse *Str1*, copying its nodes and attaching them to the end of the linked list for *Str*.
4. Traverse *Str2*, copying its nodes and attaching them to the end of the linked list for *Str*.
5. Set the link in the last node of *Str* to nil.

The following procedure implements this algorithm:

procedure *Concat* (*Str1*, *Str2* : *StringType*; **var** *Str* : *StringType*);

(∗ Accepts: Strings *Str1* and *Str2*.
  Function: Concatenates *Str1* and *Str2* to form string *Str*.
  Returns: String *Str*.

  Note: Strings are implemented as linked lists with head nodes,
      with one character per node. ∗)

var
  P, Q : *StringPointer*;   (∗ auxiliary pointers ∗)

begin (∗ *Concat* ∗)
  new (*Str.List*);
  Str.Length := *Str1.Length* + *Str2.Length*;
  Q := *Str.List*;
  P := *Str1.List*↑.*Next*;   (∗ First copy *Str1* into *Str*. ∗)
  while *P* <> **nil do**
    begin
      Attach (*P*↑.*Ch*, *Q*);
      P := *P*↑.*Next*
    end (∗ **while** ∗);
  P := *Str2.List*↑.*Next*;   (∗ Now copy *Str2* into *Str*. ∗)
  while *P* <> **nil do**
    begin
      Attach (*P*↑.*Ch*, *Q*);
      P := *P*↑.*Next*
    end (∗ **while** ∗);
  Q↑.*Next* := **nil**
end (∗ *Concat* ∗);

Here *Attach* is a procedure like the following that is used to attach nodes at the end of a linked list:

procedure *Attach* (*Character* : *char*; **var** *Last* : *StringPointer*);

(∗ Accepts: A *Character* and a pointer *Last*.
  Function: Creates a node containing *Character*, attaches it to a
      node pointed to by *Last*, and changes *Last* to point to
      this node.
  Returns: Modified pointer *Last*. ∗)

var
  TempPtr : *StringPointer*; (∗ pointer to a new node ∗)

begin (∗ *Attach* ∗)
  new (*TempPtr*);
  TempPtr↑.*Ch* := *Character*;
  TempPtr↑.*Next* := **nil**;
  Last↑.*Next* := *TempPtr*;
  Last := *TempPtr*
end (∗ *Attach* ∗);

This procedure *Attach* can also be used to develop a procedure *ReadString* for reading a string and constructing its linked representation. This procedure is used in the program of Figure 8.2, which is a revision of that in Figure 8.1 for counting users logged in to a computer system during a given period of time. This revised program uses the linked implementation of strings in place of the usual packed-array implementation. Note the function *EqualStrings* used to compare two linked strings. It first checks that the strings have the same length, and if so, it traverses each of the strings, comparing them character by character, returning *false* if a mismatch occurs and *true* otherwise.

```
PROGRAM CountUsers (input, output, UserIdFile);

(********************************************************************

    Input (file):    The text file UserIdFile.
    Function:        Determines the number of distinct users logged
                     into a computer system for a given period of time.
                     User-ids are read from UserIdFile, and each new
                     one is counted and added to the set Users of
                     user-ids already found in the file.
    Output (screen): Number of users logged in.

    Note:            The program uses linked implementations of sets
                     and strings.

********************************************************************)

TYPE
    StringPointer = ^StringNode;
    StringNode = RECORD
                     Ch : char;
                     Next : StringPointer
                 END;
    StringType = RECORD
                     Length : 0..maxint;
                     List : StringPointer
                 END;
    SetElementType = StringType;
    SetPointer = ^SetNode;
    SetNode = RECORD
                  Element : SetElementType;
                  Next : SetPointer
              END;
    SetType = SetPointer;

VAR
    UserIdFile : text;        (* log file of user-ids *)
    UserId : StringType;      (* current user-id being processed *)
    Users : SetType;          (* set of user-ids found in UserIdFile *)
    NumUsers : integer;       (* count of distinct user-ids *)
```

Figure 8.2

Figure 8.2 (*cont.*)

```
PROCEDURE ReadString (VAR TextFile : text; VAR Str : StringType);

   (****************************************************************


       Input (file):   TextFile.
       Function:       Reads a string Str of characters from TextFile
                       until an end-of-line mark is reached.
       Output (param): String Str.

       Note:           Characters are read and stored in a linked list
                       with head node pointed to by Str.  Procedure
                       Attach is used to attach nodes containing these
                       characters to the end of this linked list.

   ****************************************************************)

   VAR
      Character : char;       (* next character read from TextFile *)
      Last : StringPointer; (* pointer to last node in linked list *)

   PROCEDURE Attach (Character : char; VAR Last : StringPointer);

      (****************************************************************


          Input (param):  A Character and a pointer Last.
          Function:       Creates a node containing Character, attaches
                          it to a node pointed to by Last, and changes
                          Last to point to this node.
          Output (param): Modified pointer Last.

      ****************************************************************)

      VAR
         TempPtr : StringPointer;  (* pointer to new node *)

      BEGIN (* Attach *)
         new (TempPtr);
         TempPtr^.Ch := Character;
         TempPtr^.Next := NIL;
         Last^.Next := TempPtr;
         Last := TempPtr
      END (* Attach *);

   BEGIN (* ReadString *)
      Str.Length := 0;
      new (Str.List);
      Str.List^.Next := nil;
      Last := Str.List;
      WHILE NOT eoln(TextFile) DO
         BEGIN
            read (TextFile, Character);
            Str.Length := Str.Length + 1;
            Attach (Character, Last)
         END (* WHILE *);
      readln (TextFile)
   END (* ReadString *);
```

Figure 8.2 *(cont.)*

```
FUNCTION EqualStrings (A, B : StringType) : boolean;

  (*******************************************************************

        Input (param):          Strings A and B.
        Function:               Checks if A = B.
        Output (EqualStrings):  Returns true or false according to
                                whether or not strings A and B are the
                                same.

        Note:                   Strings are implemented as linked
                                lists with head nodes.

  *****************************************************************)

    VAR
        ptrA, ptrB : StringPointer; (* pointers to run through A and B *)
        Same : boolean;             (* signals if strings are same *)

    BEGIN (* EqualStrings *)
        Same := (A.Length = B.Length);
        ptrA := A.List^.Next;
        ptrB := B.List^.Next;
        WHILE Same AND (ptrA <> NIL) DO
            BEGIN
                IF ptrA^.Ch <> ptrB^.Ch THEN
                    Same := false
                ELSE
                    BEGIN
                        ptrA := ptrA^.Next;
                        ptrB := ptrB^.Next
                    END (* ELSE *)
            END (* WHILE *);
        EqualStrings := Same
    END (* EqualStrings *);

FUNCTION EmptySet : SetType;

  (*******************************************************************

        Input:             None.
        Function:          Creates an empty set.
        Output (EmptySet): Returns an empty set.

        Note:              Function returns a pointer to an empty list
                           consisting of only a head hode.  This is the
                           linked implementation of an empty set.

  *****************************************************************)

    VAR
        TempPtr : SetPointer;  (* temporary pointer *)
```

Figure 8.2 (*cont.*)

```
   BEGIN (* EmptySet *)
      new (TempPtr);
      TempPtr^.Next := NIL;
      EmptySet := TempPtr
   END (* EmptySet *);

FUNCTION IsAMember (S : SetType; X : SetElementType) : boolean;

   (*******************************************************************

      Input (param):      A set S and an element X.
      Function:           Checks if X is an element of set S.
      Output (IsAMember): Returns true if X is an element of S and
                          false otherwise.

      Note:               Sets are implemented as linked lists with
                          head nodes.
   *******************************************************************)

   VAR
      p : SetPointer;   (* auxiliary pointer to run through S *)
      Found : boolean; (* indicates if/when X is found *)

   BEGIN (* IsAMember *)
      p := S^.Next;
      Found := false;
      WHILE NOT Found AND (p <> NIL) DO
         IF EqualStrings(p^.Element, X) THEN
            Found := true
         ELSE
            p := p^.Next;
      IsAMember := Found
   END (* IsAMember *);

PROCEDURE AddElement (VAR S : SetType; X : SetElementType);

   (*******************************************************************

      Input (param):  A set S and an element X.
      Function:       Adds X to S.
      Output (param): Modified set S.


   *******************************************************************)

   VAR
      TempPtr : SetPointer;  (* pointer to new node for X *)

   BEGIN (* AddElement *)
      new (TempPtr);
      TempPtr^.Element := X;
      TempPtr^.Next := S^.Next;
      S^.Next := TempPtr
   END (* AddElement *);
```

Figure 8.2 (*cont.*)

```
BEGIN (* main program *)
   reset (UserIdFile);
   Users := EmptySet;
   NumUsers := 0;
   WHILE NOT eof(UserIdFile) DO
      BEGIN
         ReadString (UserIdFile, UserId);
         IF NOT IsAMember(Users, UserId) THEN
            BEGIN
               NumUsers := NumUsers + 1;
               AddElement (Users, UserId)
            END (* IF *)
      END (* WHILE *);
   writeln ('Number of users who logged in:  ', NumUsers:1)
END (* main program *).
```

Listing of UserIdFile used in sample run:

```
S31416PI
S12345SL
S31416PI
S31313LN
S12345SL
S31416PI
S21718EX
S13331RC
S77777UP
S12345SL
S31416PI
S21718EX
S99099RR
S12345SL
S77777UP
S31313LN
S31416PI
```

Sample run:

```
Number of users who logged in:   7
```

In a standard linear linked list, only the first node can be accessed directly, but some string operations may require fast access to other characters in the string. For example, to implement an append operation efficiently, we must be able to access the last character rapidly. But this is not possible if we maintain direct access only to the first node, since the entire list of characters must then be traversed each time to find the last node. One alternative is to maintain an auxiliary pointer to the last node, as in procedure *Concat*. Another alternative is to use a circular linked list with a pointer to the last node, as described in

Section 8.2. The following procedure *Append* uses this approach:

procedure *Append* (*Character* : char; **var** *Str* : *StringType*);

(* Accepts: A *Character* and a string *Str*.
    Function: Modifies string *Str* by appending *Character* to it. Strings
                 are implemented as circular linked lists with a pointer to
                 the last node.
    Returns: Modified string *Str*. *)

   var
     First : *StringPointer*;   (* pointer to first node *)

   begin (* *Append* *)
     First := *Str.List↑.Next*;
     Attach (*Character*, *Str.List*);
     Str.List↑.Next := *First*
   end (* *Append* *);

The following diagrams summarize the action of this procedure and *Attach* in
appending R to the string 'COMPUTE':

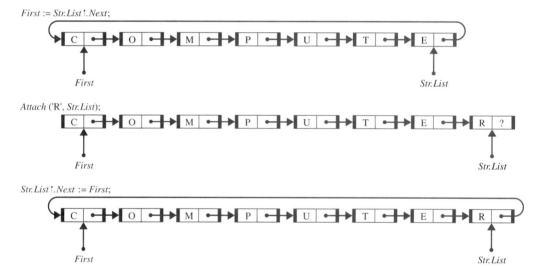

Exercises

1. Assuming the implementation of strings as linked lists with head
nodes described in this section, write a boolean-valued function *Precedes* for which a reference of the form *Precedes(string-1, string-2)*
returns the value true if *string-1* ≤ *string-2* and false otherwise.

2. Assuming the implementation of strings as linked lists with head
nodes described in this section, write procedures/functions for the
basic string operations:

   (a) length   **(b)** position   **(c)** copy

3. Assuming the implementation of strings as linked lists with head nodes described in this section, write a

   (a) nonrecursive procedure
   (b) recursive procedure
   to print a string.

4. Write a string-processing package or unit using the implementation of strings as linked lists with head nodes described in this section. In addition to procedures and functions for the basic string operations, it should also contain special input/output procedures *ReadString* and *WriteString* (see Exercise 3). Carry out bottom-up testing of the package using a command-driven ADT tester similar to that for stacks in Section 4.2.

5. Assuming a circular linked-list representation of strings, write procedures for the basic string operations:

   (a) length   (b) position   (c) copy   (d) concatenate

6. Assuming the implementation of strings as linked lists with head nodes described in this section, write a boolean-valued function that determines whether a string is a palindrome

   (a) using an auxiliary linked stack.
   (b) by constructing another string that is the reversal of the original string.
   (c) using recursion.

7. Write a recursive version of the function in Exercise 6 assuming a circular linked-list implementation of strings.

8. Write a program that reads a string, stores it in a linked list, prints it, and checks whether the string is a palindrome, using one of the functions in Exercise 6 or 7.

9. Write a program that reads names of the form First Middle Last and prints them in the format Last, F. M.. Use a linked-list implementation for all strings.

10. Extend the program in Exercise 9 to store these rearranged names in an array and sort them. Use the function in Exercise 1 to compare strings.

8.5 Linked Implementation of Sparse Polynomials

A *polynomial in one variable x*, $P(x)$, has the form

$$P(x) = a_0 + a_1 x + a_2 x^2 + \cdots + a_n x^n$$

where $a_0, a_1, a_2 \ldots , a_n$ are the *coefficients* of the polynomial. The *degree* of $P(x)$ is the largest power of x that appears in the polynomial with a nonzero coefficient; for example, the polynomial

$$P(x) = 5 + 7x - 8x^3 + 4x^5$$

has degree 5 and coefficients 5, 7, 0 -8, and 4. Constant polynomials such as $Q(x) = 3.78$ have degree 0, and the zero polynomial is also said to have degree 0.

A polynomial can be viewed as a list of coefficients

$$(a_0, a_1, a_2, \ldots, a_n)$$

and can be represented using any of the list implementations we have considered. For example, the polynomial $P(x) = 5 + 7x - 8x^3 + 4x^5$, which can also be written

$$P(x) = 5 + 7x + 0x^2 - 8x^3 + 0x^4 + 4x^5 \\ + 0x^6 + 0x^7 + 0x^8 + 0x^9 + 0x^{10}$$

can be identified with the list of coefficients

$$(5, 7, 0, -8, 0, 4, 0, 0, 0, 0, 0)$$

and this can be stored in an array P indexed 0..10:

i	0	1	2	3	4	5	6	7	8	9	10
$P[i]$	5	7	0	-8	0	4	0	0	0	0	0

If the degrees of the polynomials being processed do not vary too much from the upper limit imposed by the array size and do not have a large number of zero coefficients, this representation may be satisfactory. However, for *sparse* polynomials—that is, those that have only a few nonzero terms—this array implementation is not very efficient. For example, to store the polynomial

$$Q(x) = 5 + x^{99}$$

or equivalently,

$$Q(x) = 5 + 0x + 0x^2 + 0x^3 + \cdots + 0x^{98} + 1x^{99}$$

would require an array having 2 nonzero elements and 98 zero elements.

The obvious waste of memory caused by storing all of the zero coefficients can be eliminated if only the nonzero coefficients are stored. In such an implementation, however, it is clear that it would also be necessary to store the power of x that corresponds to each coefficient. Thus, rather than representing a polynomial by its list of coefficients, we might represent it as a list of coefficient–exponent pairs; for example,

$$P(x) = 5 + 7x - 8x^3 + 4x^5 \leftrightarrow ((5, 0), (7, 1), (-8, 3), (4, 5))$$

$$Q(x) = 5 + x^{99} \leftrightarrow ((5, 0), (1, 99))$$

Note that the pairs are ordered in such a way that the exponents are in increasing order.

Such lists can be implemented by arrays of records, each of which contains a coefficient field and an exponent field. However, the fixed array size again limits the size of the list and results in considerable waste of memory in applications in which the sizes of the lists—that is, the number of nonzero coefficients in the polynomials—varies considerably from this upper limit.

For this application, a linked-list implementation is appropriate. Each node will have the form

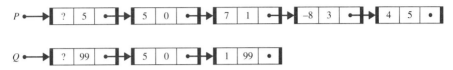

in which the three parts *Coef*, *Expo*, and *Next* store a nonzero coefficient, the corresponding exponent, and a pointer to the node representing the next term, respectively. For example, the preceding polynomials $P(x)$ and $Q(x)$ can be represented by the following linked lists with head nodes that store the polynomials' degrees in their *Expo* fields:

P →| ? | 5 |•|→| 5 | 0 |•|→| 7 | 1 |•|→| -8 | 3 |•|→| 4 | 5 |•|

Q →| ? | 99 |•|→| 5 | 0 |•|→| 1 | 99 |•|

and the zero polynomial by simply a head node:

Z →| ? | 0 |•|

For such linked polynomials we may use declarations of the following form:

```
type
    CoefType = real;      (* type of coefficients *)
    PolyPointer = ↑PolyNode;
    PolyNode = record
                     Coef : CoefType;
                     Expo : integer;
                     Next : PolyPointer
               end;
    PolynomialType = PolyPointer;
```

Of course, we could have used the "standard" node format of a *Data* field and a *Next* field by making the type of the *Data* field a record with a *Coef* field and an *Expo* field. This does not produce any real benefits, however, and would require double field designation to access these items, for example, $P↑.Data.Coef$ rather than simply $P↑.Coef$.

To illustrate how such linked polynomials are processed, we consider the operation of polynomial addition. For example, suppose we wish to add the following polynomials $A(x)$ and $B(x)$:

$$A(x) = 5 + 6x^3 + 2x^5 + x^7$$
$$B(x) = x^3 - 2x^5 + 13x^7 - 2x^8 + 26x^9$$

Recall that this sum is calculated by adding coefficients of terms that have matching powers of x. Thus, the sum of polynomials $A(x)$ and $B(x)$ is

$$C(x) = A(x) + B(x) = 5 + 7x^3 + 14x^7 - 2x^8 + 26x^9$$

Now consider the linked representations of these polynomials:

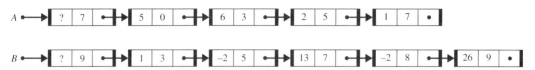

Since we have decided to use linked lists with head nodes, we begin by initializing C to point to a head node:

Three auxiliary pointers, *ptrA*, *ptrB*, and *ptrC*, will run through the lists A, B, and C, respectively; *ptrA* and *ptrB* will point to the current nodes being processed, and *ptrC* will point to the last node attached to C. Thus, *ptrA*, *ptrB*, and *ptrC* are initialized to $A\uparrow.Next$, $B\uparrow.Next$, and C, respectively:

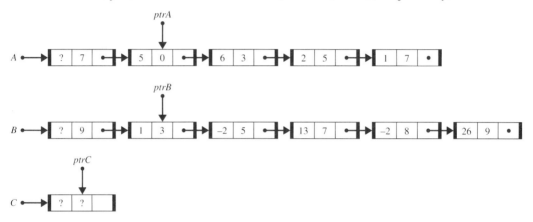

At each step of the computation, we compare the exponents in the nodes pointed to by *ptrA* and *ptrB*. If they are different, a node containing the smaller exponent and the corresponding coefficient is attached to C, and the pointer for this list and *ptrC* are advanced:

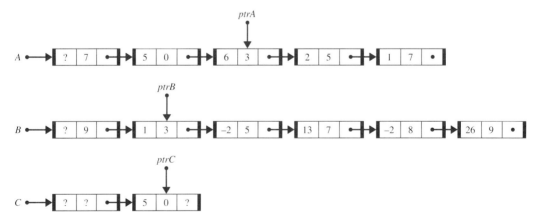

If the exponents in the nodes pointed to by *ptrA* and *ptrB* match, then the coefficients in these nodes are added. If this sum is not zero, a new node is created with its coefficient field equal to this sum and its exponent field equal to the common exponent, and this node is attached to C. Pointers for all three lists are then advanced:

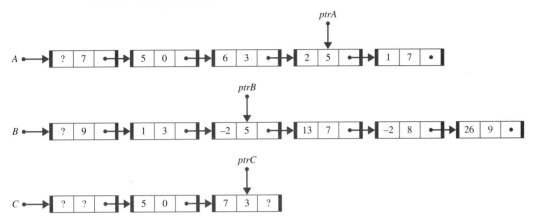

If the sum of the coefficients is zero, then $ptrA$ and $ptrB$ are simply advanced and no new node is attached to C :

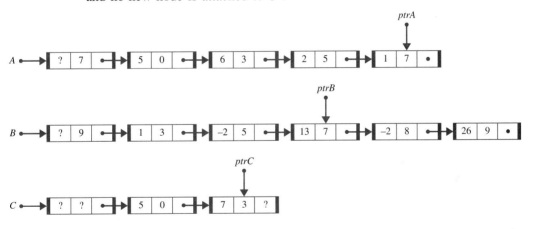

We continue in this manner until the end of A or B is reached, that is, until one of $ptrA$ or $ptrB$ becomes nil:

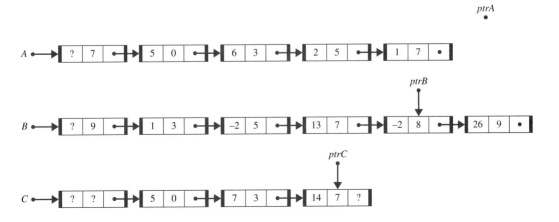

If the end of the other list has not been reached, we simply copy the remaining nodes in it, attaching each to C, and then set the link field in the last node of C to nil to complete the construction of the linked list C representing the sum $A(x) + B(x)$:

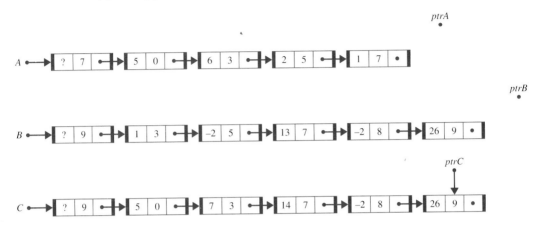

The following Pascal procedure implements this technique for adding linked polynomials:

procedure *LinkedPolyAdd* (*A, B* : *PolynomialType*;
                          var *C* : *PolynomialType*);

(* Accepts: Polynomials *A* and *B*.
  Function: Computes *C* = *A* + *B*.
  Returns: Polynomial *C*.

  Note: Polynomials are linked lists with head nodes. *)

var
   ptrA, ptrB, ptrC, TempPtr : *PolyPointer*;
   Sum : *CoefType*;
   Degree : *integer*;

begin (* *LinkedPolyAdd* *)
   ptrA := *A↑.Next*;
   ptrB := *B↑.Next*;
   new (*C*);
   ptrC := *C*;
   Degree := 0;
   while (*ptrA* <> **nil**) **and** (*ptrB* <> **nil**) **do**
      begin
         if *ptrA↑.Expo* < *ptrB↑.Expo* **then**   (* copy term from *A* *)
         begin
            Attach (*ptrA↑.Coef, ptrA↑.Expo, ptrC*);
            Degree := *ptrA↑.Expo*;
            ptrA := *ptrA↑.Next*
         end (* **if** *)

```
        else if ptrB↑.Expo < ptrA↑.Expo then  (* copy term from B *)
           begin
              Attach (ptrB↑.Coef, ptrB↑.Expo, ptrC);
              Degree := ptrB↑.Expo;
              ptrB := ptrB↑.Next
           end (* else if *)
        else                                    (* exponents match *)
           begin
              Sum := ptrA↑.Coef + ptrB↑.Coef;
              if Sum <> 0 then                  (* nonzero sum—put in C *)
                 begin
                    Attach (Sum, ptrA↑.Expo, ptrC);
                    Degree := ptrA↑.Expo
                 end (* if *);
              ptrA := ptrA↑.Next;
              ptrB := ptrB↑.Next
           end (* else *)
     end (* while *);

  (* Copy any remaining terms in A or B into C. *)

  if ptrA <> nil then
     TempPtr := ptrA
  else
     TempPtr := ptrB;
  while TempPtr <> nil do
     begin
        Attach (TempPtr↑.Coef, TempPtr↑.Expo, ptrC);
        Degree := TempPtr↑.Expo;
        TempPtr := TempPtr↑.Next
     end (* while *);
  ptrC↑.Next := nil;
  C↑.Expo := Degree
end (* LinkedPolyAdd *);
```

This procedure uses a procedure *Attach* similar to that used in the preceding section to create and attach new nodes to *C* as needed:

procedure *Attach* (*Co* : *CoefType*; *Ex* : *integer*; **var** *Last* : *PolyPointer*);

```
(* Accepts:   A coefficient Co, an exponent Ex, and a pointer Last.
   Function:  Creates a node containing Co and Ex, attaches it to a node
              pointed to by Last, and changes Last to point to this node.
   Returns:   Modified pointer Last. *)

var
   TempPtr : PolyPointer;     (* pointer to new node *)

begin (* Attach *)
   new (TempPtr);
   TempPtr↑.Coef := Co;
   TempPtr↑.Expo := Ex;
```

$TempPtr\uparrow.Next := $ **nil**;
$Last\uparrow.Next := TempPtr$;
$Last := TempPtr$
end (* *Attach* *);

The procedure for adding linked polynomials is more complex and less understandable than the corresponding procedure for the array-based implementation described at the beginning of this section, in which the ith coefficient is stored in the ith location of an array. In this case, two polynomials A and B can be added to produce C very simply:

for $i := 1$ **to** $MaxDegree$ **do**
$C[i] := A[i] + B[i]$;

Here $MaxDegree$ denotes the maximum degree of A and B.

Procedures for other basic polynomial operations, such as evaluation for a given value of x, multiplication, and so on, are likewise more complex in the linked implementation than in the array-based implementation. However, in applications in which the polynomials are sparse and of large degree, the memory saved will compensate for the increased complexity of the algorithms.

Exercises

1. Write a procedure that reads the nonzero coefficients and exponents of a polynomial, constructs the linked-list implementation of it, and returns a pointer to this linked list.

2. Write a procedure that prints a polynomial implemented as a linked list in the usual mathematical format except that x^n is written as $x\uparrow n$ or $x^{\wedge}n$.

3. Write a function that accepts a pointer to a linked list representing a polynomial $P(x)$ and a value a of x and returns $P(a)$, the value of $P(x)$ at $x = a$.

4. The ***derivative*** of a polynomial $P(x) = a_0 + a_1x + a_2x^2 + a_3x^3 + \cdots + a_nx^n$ of degree n is the polynomial $P'(x)$ of degree $n - 1$ defined by

$$P'(x) = a_1 + 2a_2x + 3a_3x^2 + \cdots + na_nx^{n-1}$$

Write a function that accepts a pointer to a linked list representing a polynomial and returns a pointer to a linked list that represents its derivative.

5. A ***root*** of a polynomial $P(x)$ is a number c for which $P(c) = 0$. The ***bisection method*** is one scheme that can be used to find an approximate root of $P(x)$ in some given interval $[a, b]$ where $P(a)$ and $P(b)$ have opposite signs (thus guaranteeing that $P(x)$ has a root in $[a, b]$). In this method, we begin by bisecting the interval $[a, b]$ and determining in

which half $P(x)$ changes sign, because P must have a root in that half of the interval. Now bisect this subinterval and determine in which half of this subinterval $P(x)$ changes sign. Repeating this process gives a sequence of smaller and smaller subintervals, each of which contains a root of $P(x)$, as pictured in the following diagram. The process can be terminated when a small subinterval—say, of length less than 0.0001—is obtained or $P(x)$ has the value 0 at one of the endpoints. Assuming a linked implementation of polynomials and using the procedures in Exercises 1 and 3, write a program that uses the bisection method to find a root of a given polynomial.

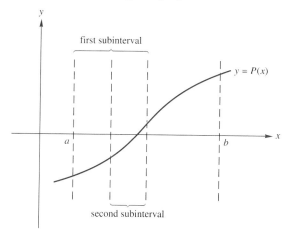

6. Another method for finding a root of a polynomial $P(x)$ is **Newton's method**. This method consists of taking an initial approximation x_1 and constructing a tangent line to the graph of $P(x)$ at that point. The point x_2 where this tangent line crosses the x axis is taken as the second approximation to the root. Then another tangent line is constructed at x_2, and the point x_3 where this tangent line crosses the x axis is the next approximation. The following diagram shows this process:

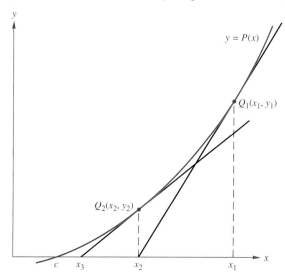

If c is an approximation to the root of $P(x)$, then the formula for obtaining the new approximation is

$$\text{new approximation} = c - \frac{P(c)}{P'(c)}$$

where $P'(x)$ is the derivative of $P(x)$. Assuming a linked implementation of polynomials and using the procedures in Exercises 1, 3, and 4, write a program to locate a root of a polynomial using Newton's method. The process should terminate when a value of $P(x)$ is sufficiently small in absolute value or when the number of iterations exceeds some upper limit. Display the sequence of successive approximations.

7. Use the procedures in Exercises 1 through 3 and those given in the text in a menu-driven program for processing polynomials. The menu of options should include (at least) reading a polynomial, printing a polynomial using the usual mathematical format described in Exercise 2, evaluating the polynomial for a given value of x, and polynomial addition.

8. Write a procedure to do polynomial multiplication, and determine its computing time.

9. Extend the menu of options in Exercise 7 to include

   (a) Calculating the derivative of a polynomial (see Exercise 4).
   (b) Finding a root of a polynomial.
   (c) Polynomial multiplication.

8.6 Hash Tables

The linear search and binary search algorithms considered in Chapter 6 locate an item in a list by a sequence of comparisons, in which the item being sought is repeatedly compared with the items in the list. On the average, linear search requires $O(n)$ comparisons for a collection of n items, whereas binary search requires $O(\log_2 n)$ comparisons. In some situations, these algorithms perform too slowly. For example, a *symbol table* constructed by a compiler stores identifiers and information about them. The speed with which this table can be constructed and searched is critical to the speed of compilation. A data structure known as a *hash table*, in which the location of an item is determined directly as a function of the item itself rather than by a sequence of trial-and-error comparisons, is commonly used to provide faster searching. Under ideal circumstances, the time required to locate an item in a hash table is $O(1)$; that is, it is constant and does not depend on the number of items stored.

As an illustration, supposed that up to 25 integers in the range 0 through 999 are to be stored in a hash table. This hash table can be implemented as an integer array *Table* indexed 0..999, in which each array element is initialized with some dummy value, such as -1. If we use each integer i in the data set as an index, that is, if we store *i* in *Table*[*i*], then to determine whether a particular integer *Number* has been stored, we need only check whether *Table*[*Number*] = *Number*. The function *h* defined by $h(i) = i$ that determines the location of an item *i* in the hash table is called a ***hash function.***

The hash function in this example works perfectly, since the time required to search the table for a given value is constant; only one location needs to be examined. This scheme is thus very time efficient, but it is surely not space efficient. Only 25 of the 1000 available locations are used to store items, leaving 975 unused locations; only 2.5 percent of the available space is used, and so 97.5 percent is wasted!

Because it is possible to store 25 values in 25 locations, we might try improving space utilization by using an array *Table* indexed 0..24. Obviously, the original hash function $h(i) = i$ can no longer be used. Instead we might use

$$h(i) = i \ \mathbf{mod} \ 25$$

since this function always produces an integer in the range 0 through 24. The integer 52 thus is stored in *Table*[2], since $h(52) = 52 \ \mathbf{mod} \ 25 = 2$. Similarly, 129, 500, 273, and 49 are stored in locations 4, 0, 23, and 24, respectively.

Hash table

Table[0]	500
Table[1]	−1
Table[2]	52
Table[3]	−1
Table[4]	129
Table[5]	−1
⋮	⋮
Table[23]	273
Table[24]	49

One difficulty, however, is that ***collisions*** may occur. For example, if 77 is to be stored, it should be placed at location $h(77) = 77 \ \mathbf{mod} \ 25 = 2$, but this location is already occupied by 52. In the same way, many other values may collide at a given position, for example, 2, 27, 102, and, in fact, all integers of the form $25k + 2$ "hash" to location 2.

Making the table size equal to the number of items to be stored, as in our first example, is usually not practical, but using any smaller table leaves open the possibility of collisions. In fact, even though the table is capable of storing considerably more items than necessary, collisions may be quite likely. For example, for a hash table with 365 locations in which 23 randomly selected items are to be stored, the probability that a collision will occur is greater than 0.5! (This is related to the birthday problem, whose solution states that in a room containing twenty-three people, there is a greater than 50 percent chance that two or more of them will have the same birthday.) Thus it is clearly unreasonable to expect a hashing scheme to prevent collisions completely. Instead, we must be satisfied with hash tables in which reasonably few collisions occur. Empirical studies suggest using tables whose sizes are approximately 1-1/2 to 2 times the number of items that must be stored.

One common approach for handling collisions, known as **chaining**, uses linked lists in much the same way that they are used in the text concordance problem of Section 7.7. In this scheme, the hash table is an array of pointers to linked lists that store items. To illustrate, suppose we wish to store a collection of names. We might use an array *Table* indexed 'A'..'Z' of pointers, initially nil, and the simple hash function *h(Name)* = the first letter in *Name*. Thus, for example, 'Adams, John' and 'Doe, Mary' are stored in nodes pointed to by *Table*['A'] and *Table*['D'], respectively.

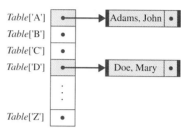

When a collision occurs, we simply insert the new item into the appropriate linked list. For example, since *h*('Davis, Joe') = *h*('Doe, Mary') = 'D', a collision occurs when we attempt to store the name 'Davis, Joe', and thus we add a new node containing this name to the linked list pointed to by *Table*['D']:

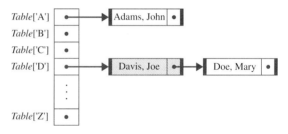

Searching such a hash table is straightforward. We simply apply the hash function to the item being sought and then use one of the search algorithms for linked lists.

The behavior of the hash function obviously affects the frequency of collisions. For example, the hash function *h(Name)* = *Name*[1] in the preceding example is not a good choice because some letters occur much more frequently than do others as first letters of names. Thus the linked list of names beginning with 'S' tends to be much longer than that containing names that begin with 'Z'. This clustering effect results in longer search times for S-names than for Z-names. A better hash function that distributes the names more uniformly throughout the hash table might be the "average" of the first and last letters in the name,

$$h(Name) = chr((ord(FirstLetter) + ord(LastLetter)) \textbf{ div } 2)$$

or one might use the "average" of all the letters. The hash function must not, however, be so complex that the time required to evaluate it makes the search time unacceptable.

An ideal hash function is one that is simple to evaluate and that scatters the items throughout the hash table, thus minimizing the probability of collisions. Although no single hashing method performs perfectly in all situations, a currently popular method known as ***random hashing*** uses a simple random number generation technique to scatter the items "randomly" throughout the hash table. The item is first transformed into a large random integer using a statement of the form

$$RandomInt := ((Multiplier * Item) + Addend) \textbf{ mod } Modulus$$

and this value is then reduced modulo the table size to determine the location of the item:

$$Location := RandomInt \textbf{ mod } TableSize;$$

(See footnote 2 in Section 5.2 for a discussion of appropriate values of *Multiplier*, *Addend*, and *Modulus*.) This hash function can be used with items other than integers if we first encode such items as integers; for example, a name might be encoded as the sum of the ASCII codes of some or all of its letters.

Exercises

1. Using a hash table with eleven locations and the hashing function $h(i) = i \textbf{ mod } 11$, show the hash table that results when the following integers are inserted in the order given: 26, 42, 5, 44, 92, 59, 40, 36, 12, 60, 80. Assume that collisions are resolved using chaining.

2. Suppose that the following character codes are used: 'A' = 1, 'B' = 2, . . . , 'Y' = 25, 'Z' = 26. Using a hash table with eleven locations and the hashing function $h(identifier) = average \textbf{ mod } 11$, where *average* is the average of the codes of the first and last letters in *identifier*, show the hash table that results when the following identifiers are inserted in the order given, assuming that collisions are resolved using chaining:

   BETA, RATE, FREQ, ALPHA, MEAN, SUM, NUM, BAR, WAGE, PAY, KAPPA

3. The method of ***double hashing*** for handling collisions is as follows: If item *i* collides with another table entry at location *a*, then apply a second hash function h_2 to the item to determine $k = h_2(i)$. Now examine the elements of the table in locations $a, a + k, a + 2k, \ldots$, reducing all these values mod *n* (*n* is the table size) until either the item is found or an empty slot is reached. In the latter case, the item is inserted at this location. Give the hash table that results using the numbers in Exercise 1, but using double hashing rather than chaining

to resolve collisions with the following secondary hash function:

$$h_2(i) = \begin{cases} 2i \text{ \bf mod } 11 & \text{if this is nonzero} \\ 1 & \text{otherwise} \end{cases}$$

4. Write a package or unit for the ADT *HashTable*, using the implementation described in this section. It should contain the necessary declarations and definitions, together with procedures and functions for the basic operations of creating a hash table, searching a hash table, and inserting an item into a hash table. Use random hashing for the hash function and chaining to resolve collisions.

5. Write a program that reads a collection of computer user-ids and passwords and stores them in a hash table. The program should then read two strings representing a user's id and password and then check if this is a legal user of the computer system by searching the hash table for this id and password.

6. Suppose that integers in the range 1 through 100 are to be stored in a hash table using the hashing function $h(i) = i \text{ \bf mod } TableSize$. Write a program that generates random integers in this range and inserts them into the hash table until a collision occurs. The program should carry out this experiment 100 times and calculate the average number of integers that can be inserted into the hash table before a collision occurs. Run the program with various values for *TableSize*.

8.7 Symmetrically Linked Lists; Large-Number Arithmetic

One characteristic of singly listed lists is that they are unidirectional, which means that it is possible to move easily from a node to its successor. Finding its predecessor, however, requires searching from the beginning of the list. In many applications, the need to locate the predecessor of an element arises just as often as does the need to locate its successor. In this section we consider how bidirectional lists can be constructed and processed, and we apply them to the problem of doing arithmetic with large integers.

Bidirectional lists can easily be constructed by using nodes that contain, in addition to a data part, two links: a forward link (*FLink*) pointing to the successor of the node and a backward link (*BLink*) pointing to its predecessor:

A linked list constructed from such nodes is usually called a ***symmetrically linked*** (or ***doubly linked***) list. As in the singly linked case, using head nodes for symmetrically linked lists eliminates some special cases (e.g., empty list and first node), and making the lists circular provides easy access to either end of the list. Thus we use head nodes for the symmetrically linked lists that we consider, and we assume they are circular, so that they have a structure like the following:

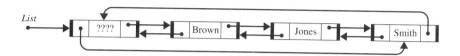

Symmetrically linked lists can be implemented using arrays of records (or parallel arrays) by a simple extension of the implementation described for singly linked lists, or they can be implemented using Pascal pointers. In this latter implementation, the following declarations might be used:

```
type
    SymmListElementType = ...; (* type of list elements *)
    SymmListPointer = ↑SymmListNode;
    SymmListNode = record
                       Data : SymmListElementType;
                       FLink, BLink : SymmListPointer
                   end;
    SymmLinkedListType = SymmListPointer;
```

Algorithms for the basic list operations are similar to those for the singly linked case, the main difference being the need to set some additional links. An empty symmetrically linked list is created by the following statements, where *List* is of type *SymmLinkedListType*:

```
new (List);
List↑.FLink := List;
List↑.BLink := List;
```

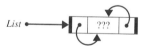

An empty-list condition can then be detected by using either of the boolean expressions $List↑.BLink = List$ or $List↑.FLink = List$.

Inserting a new node into a symmetrically linked list involves first setting its backward and forward links to point to its predecessor and successor, respectively, and then resetting the forward link of its predecessor and the backward link of its successor to point to this new node:

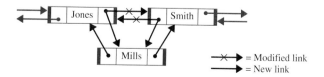

The following procedure implements this insertion operation:

procedure *SymmLinkedInsert* (**var** *List* : *SymmLinkedListType*;
Item : *SymmListElementType*;
PredPtr : *SymmListPointer*);

(* Accepts: A circular symmetrically linked list with head node
pointed to by *List*, a data *Item*, and a pointer *PredPtr*.
Function: Inserts a node containing *Item* into this list after the
node pointed to by *PredPtr*.
Returns: Modified circular symmetrically linked list with head
node pointed to by *List*. *)

var
TempPtr : *SymmListPointer*; (* pointer to new node *)

begin (* *SymmLinkedInsert* *)
new (*TempPtr*);
TempPtr↑.*Data* := *Item*;
TempPtr↑.*BLink* := *PredPtr*;
TempPtr↑.*FLink* := *PredPtr*↑.*FLink*;
PredPtr↑.*FLink* := *TempPtr*;
TempPtr↑.*FLink*↑.*BLink* := *TempPtr*
end (* *SymmLinkedInsert* *);

Note the last four statements, which set or reset the links as needed to connect
the new node to the list. It is important that these be done in the correct order.
You should study examples to see what happens if this order is changed.

A node can be deleted simply by resetting the forward link of its predecessor and the backward link of its successor to bypass the node:

A procedure that implements deletion is

procedure *SymmLinkedDelete* (**var** *List* : *SymmLinkedListType*;
CurrPtr : *SymmListPointer*);

(* Accepts: A circular symmetrically linked list with head node
pointed to by *List* and a pointer *CurrPtr*.
Function: Deletes the node pointed to by *CurrPtr*.
Returns: Modified circular symmetrically linked list with head
node pointed to by *List* and a pointer *CurrPtr*. *)

begin (* *SymmLinkedDelete* *)
CurrPtr↑.*BLink*↑.*FLink* := *CurrPtr*↑.*FLink*;
CurrPtr↑.*FLink*↑.*BLink* := *CurrPtr*↑.*BLink*;
dispose (*CurrPtr*)
end (* *SymmLinkedDelete* *);

As an application of symmetrically linked lists, we consider large-integer arithmetic. Recall that the size of a number that can be stored in computer memory is limited by the word size of the particular system being used. For example, the largest positive integer that can be stored in a 16-bit word with the usual binary representation described in Section 2.2 is $2^{15} - 1 = 32767$. In some applications (e.g., keeping track of the national debt), it obviously is necessary to process integers that are larger than this value.

The first step in solving the problem of how to compute with large integers is to select a data structure to represent these integers. Because the number of digits in these integers may vary considerably, a linked list seems appropriate. And because it is necessary to traverse this list in both directions, we use a symmetrically linked list. Each integer to be processed is stored in a separate linked list, with each node storing a three-digit integer corresponding to a block of three consecutive digits in the number. And for simplicity, we consider only nonnegative integers. For example, the integer 9,145,632,884 is represented by the symmetrically linked list

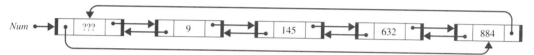

This linked representation of long integers is used in the program of Figure 8.3, which performs long-integer addition. The procedure *ReadLargeInt* reads a long integer in three-digit blocks, separated by blanks, and attaches a node containing the value of each of these three-digit blocks to the symmetrically linked list pointed to by *Num*. For example, suppose that the input data is

9 145 632 884

and that the first three blocks have already been read so that *Num* is the list

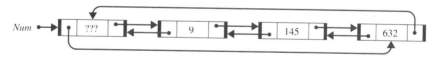

When the block 884 is read, a new node pointed to by *TempPtr* is created for it and is attached to the end of this list by setting the backward link in this new node to point to the last node in the list,

TempPtr↑.BLink := *Num↑.BLink*;

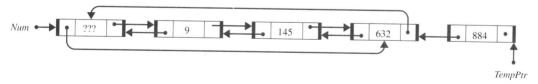

TempPtr

its forward link to point to the head node,

TempPtr↑.FLink := *Num*;

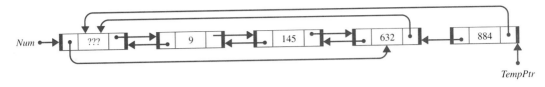

Num → ??? | 9 | 145 | 632 | 884 | *TempPtr*

and then setting the forward link in the last node and the backward link in the head node to point to this new node.

Num↑.BLink↑.FLink := TempPtr;
Num↑.BLink := TempPtr;

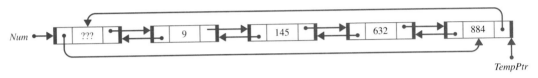

Num → ??? | 9 | 145 | 632 | 884 | *TempPtr*

The procedure *AddLargeInt* adds the two long integers, *Num1* and *Num2*. It traverses the symmetrically linked lists representing these two numbers, from right to left, adding the two three-digit integers in corresponding nodes and the carry digit from the preceding nodes to obtain a three-digit sum and a carry digit. A node is created to store this three-digit sum and is attached at the front of the list representing the sum of *Num1* and *Num2*. The following diagram shows the linked lists corresponding to the computation

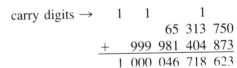

```
carry digits →   1   1       1
                     65 313 750
             +   999 981 404 873
             1 000 046 718 623
```

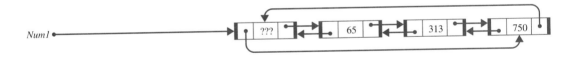

Num1 → ??? | 65 | 313 | 750

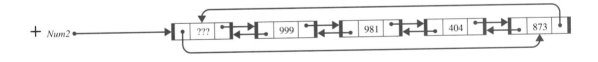

+ *Num2* → ??? | 999 | 981 | 404 | 873

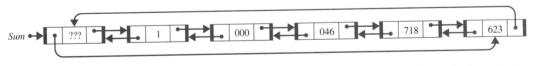

Sum → ??? | 1 | 000 | 046 | 718 | 623

After the sum has been calculated, the procedure *WriteLargeInt* is called to display the sum. It traverses a symmetrically linked list pointed to by *Num* from left to right, displaying the three digits corresponding to the value stored in each node.

```
PROGRAM LargeIntegerArithmetic (input, output);

(********************************************************************

    Input (keyboard):  Large integers.
    Function:          Reads large integers and finds their sum.
    Output (screen):   Sums of large integers.

    Note:              Integers are represented as symmetrically
                       linked lists with head nodes.

 *******************************************************************)

CONST
   BlockLength = 3; (* number of digits in blocks *)
   Limit = 1000;    (* 1 + largest integer having BlockLength digits *)

TYPE
   SymmListElementType = 0..Limit;
   SymmListPointer = ^ListNode;
   ListNode = RECORD
                 Data : SymmListElementType;
                 BLink, FLink : SymmListPointer
              END;
   SymmLinkedListType = SymmListPointer;
   LargeInteger = SymmLinkedListType;

VAR
   Num1, Num2,              (* pointers to two integers being added *)
   Sum : SymmLinkedListType; (* pointer to sum *)
   Response : char;          (* user response *)

PROCEDURE InsertFront (Item : SymmListElementType;
                       VAR List : SymmLinkedListType);

   (********************************************************************

       Input (param):  A data Item and a circular symmetrically linked
                       list with head node pointed to by List.
       Function:       Creates a node containing Item and inserts it at
                       the front of the list.
       Output (param): Modified circular symmetrically linked list with
                       head node pointed to by List.

    *******************************************************************)

   VAR
      TempPtr : SymmListPointer; (* pointer to new node *)
```

Figure 8.3

Figure 8.3 (*cont.*)

```
BEGIN (* InsertFront *)
   new (TempPtr);
   TempPtr^.Data := Item;
   TempPtr^.FLink := List^.FLink;
   TempPtr^.BLink := List;
   List^.FLink^.BLink := TempPtr;
   List^.FLink := TempPtr
END (* InsertFront *);

PROCEDURE ReadLargeInt (VAR Num : LargeInteger);

   (***********************************************************

      Input (keyboard): Blocks of integers.
      Function:         Reads a large integer in blocks of size
                        BlockLength.
      Output (param):   Returns the large integer Num.

      Note:             Blocks are read and stored in the nodes of a
                        circular symmetrically linked list with head
                        node pointed to by Num.

   ***********************************************************)

   VAR
      TempPtr : SymmListPointer;  (* pointer to new node *)

   BEGIN (* ReadLargeInt *)
      new (Num); (* set up head node *)
      Num^.FLink := Num;
      Num^.BLink := Num;
      WHILE NOT eoln DO
         BEGIN
            new (TempPtr);
            read (TempPtr^.Data);
            TempPtr^.BLink := Num^.BLink;
            TempPtr^.FLink := Num;
            Num^.BLink^.FLink := TempPtr;
            Num^.BLink := TempPtr
         END (* WHILE *);
      readln
   END (* ReadLargeInt *);
```

Figure 8.3 (*cont.*)

```
PROCEDURE AddLargeInt (Num1, Num2 : LargeInteger;
                       VAR Sum : LargeInteger);

(****************************************************************

     Input (param):   Large integers Num1 and Num2.
     Function:        Computes Sum = Num1 + Num2.
     Output (param):  Large integer Sum.

     Note:            Large integers are represented as circular
                      symmetrically linked lists with head nodes.

*****************************************************************)

   VAR
      p1, p2, p, Head : SymmListPointer; (* auxiliary pointers *)
      Carry,                             (* carry digit *)
      NodeSum : integer;                 (* sum of integers in list nodes *)

   BEGIN (* AddLargeInt *)
      p1 := Num1^.BLink;
      p2 := Num2^.BLink;
      Carry := 0;
      new (Sum); (* set up head node *)
      Sum^.FLink := Sum;
      Sum^.BLink := Sum;

      (* Add blocks in corresponding nodes of Num1 and Num2 *)

      WHILE (p1 <> Num1) AND (p2 <> Num2) DO
         BEGIN
            NodeSum := p1^.Data + p2^.Data + Carry;
            Carry := NodeSum DIV Limit;
            InsertFront (NodeSum MOD Limit, Sum);
            p1 := p1^.BLink;
            p2 := p2^.BLink;
         END (* WHILE *);

      (* Now continue with whichever integer is longer *)

      IF p1 = Num1 THEN (* continue with Num2 *)
         BEGIN
            p := p2;
            Head := Num2
         END (* IF *)
      ELSE                  (* continue with Num1 *)
         BEGIN
            p := p1;
            Head := Num1
         END (* ELSE *);

      WHILE p <> Head DO
         BEGIN
            NodeSum := p^.Data + Carry;
            Carry := NodeSum DIV Limit;
            InsertFront (NodeSum MOD Limit, Sum);
            p := p^.BLink
         END (* WHILE *);
      IF Carry > 0 THEN
         InsertFront (Carry, Sum)
   END (* AddLargeInt *);
```

Figure 8.3 (*cont.*)

```
PROCEDURE WriteLargeInt (Num : LargeInteger);

(*************************************************************

    Input (param):    Large integer Num.
    Function:         Displays Num.
    Output (screen):  Blocks of digits of Num.

    Note:             Large integers are represented as circular
                      symmetrically linked lists with head nodes, and
                      this procedure traverses a circular
                      symmetrically linked list for Num, displaying
                      the digits of the integers stored in each node.

*************************************************************)

    VAR
      p : SymmListPointer;        (* auxiliary pointer *)
      Block,                      (* a block of digits to be displayed *)
      PowerOfTen : SymmListElementType;
                                  (* power of 10 -- to split off digits *)

    BEGIN (* WriteLargeInt *)
      p := Num^.FLink;

      (* Print first block of digits *)

      IF p <> Num THEN
         BEGIN
            write (p^.Data:1, ' ');
            p := p^.FLink
         END (* IF *);

      (* Print remaining blocks, digit by digit *)

      WHILE p <> Num DO
         BEGIN
            Block := p^.Data;
            PowerOfTen := Limit DIV 10;
            WHILE PowerOfTen > 0 DO
               BEGIN
                  write (Block DIV PowerOfTen : 1);
                  Block := Block MOD PowerOfTen;
                  PowerOfTen := PowerOfTen DIV 10
               END (* WHILE *);
            write (' ');
            p := p^.FLink
         END (* WHILE *);
      writeln
    END (* WriteLargeInt *);
```

Figure 8.3 (*cont.*)

```
BEGIN (* main program *)
   writeln ('Enter two integers in blocks of size ', BlockLength:1);
   writeln ('separating these blocks by at least one space:');
   REPEAT
      writeln;
      write (' First #:  ');
      ReadLargeInt (Num1);
      write ('Second #:  ');
      ReadLargeInt (Num2);
      AddLargeInt (Num1, Num2, Sum);
      writeln;
      write ('  Sum is:  ');
      WriteLargeInt (Sum);
      writeln;
      write ('More (Y or N)?  ');
      readln (Response)
   UNTIL NOT (Response IN ['y', 'Y'])
END (* main *).
```

Sample run:

```
Enter two integers in blocks of size 3
separating these blocks by at least one space:

 First #:  1
Second #:  1

  Sum is:  2

More (Y or N)?  Y

 First #:     999 999 999 999 999 999 999 999
Second #:                                    1

  Sum is:  1 000 000 000 000 000 000 000 000

More (Y or N)?  Y

 First #:         65 313 750
Second #:     999 981 404 873

  Sum is:  1 000 046 718 623

More (Y or N)?  N
```

Exercises

1. Given the symmetrically linked list with the two pointers *P1* and *P2*

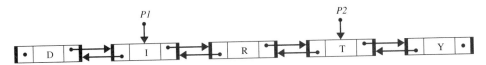

   Find the value of each of the following:

   (a) *P1↑.Data*
   (b) *P1↑.FLink↑.Data*
   (c) *P1↑.BLink↑.BLink*
   (d) *P1↑.FLink↑.FLink*
   (e) *P1↑.BLink↑.FLink*
   (f) *P2↑.BLink↑.BLink↑.Data*
   (g) *P2↑.BLink↑.BLink↑.BLink↑.BLink*
   (h) *P2↑.BLink↑.BLink↑.FLink↑.Data*

2. Using only pointer *P1* to access the symmetrically linked list in Exercise 1, write statements to

   (a) Display the contents of the nodes, in alphabetical order.
   (b) Replace 'D' by 'M' and 'R' by 'S'.
   (c) Delete the node containing 'T'.

3. Repeat Exercise 2, but using only pointer *P2* to access the list.

4. Repeat Exercise 1, but for the following circular symmetrically linked list:

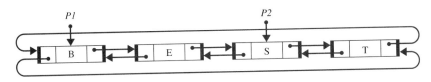

5. Using only pointer *P1* to access the circular symmetrically linked list in Exercise 4, write statements to

   (a) Display the contents of the nodes, in alphabetical order.
   (b) Insert a node containing 'L' after the node containing 'B' and replace 'E' with 'A'.
   (c) Delete the node containing 'T'.

6. Repeat Exercise 5, but using only pointer *P2* to access the list.

7. Assuming the linked implementation of long integers described in this section, write a boolean-valued function *LEQ* that determines if one long integer is less than or equal to another long integer.

8. What information might be stored in the head node of a linked list for a long integer so that a more efficient version of the less-than-or-equal-to function in Exercise 7 is possible?

9. Write a function *Difference* that subtracts nonnegative long integers; a function reference of the form *Difference*(A, B) where $A \geq B$ should return the value of $A - B$. (If $A < B$, no value need be returned.)

10. Using the functions in Exercises 7 and 9, modify the program in Figure 8.3 to process both positive and negative long integers. Use the head node in the linked list for a long integer to indicate the sign of the number.

11. The sequence of *Fibonacci numbers* begins with the integers

$$1, 1, 2, 3, 5, 8, 13, 21, 34, 55, 89, \ldots$$

where each number after the first two is the sum of the two preceding numbers. Write a program to calculate and display large Fibonacci numbers.

12. Write a function for multiplying long integers implemented as linked lists as described in the text.

13. Use the function in Exercise 12 in a program that calculates large factorials.

14. Write a package or unit for the ADT *LargeInteger*, using the linked representation of large integers described in this section. It should contain (at least) procedures for the basic operations of addition, subtraction (Exercise 9), multiplication (Exercise 12), comparison (Exercise 7), and procedures for reading, writing, and assigning large integer values. Carry out bottom-up testing of the package/unit using a command-driven ADT tester similar to that for stacks in Section 4.2.

15. Write a procedure for reversing a symmetrically linked list.

16. In a multiuser environment, jobs with various memory requirements are submitted to the computer system, and the operating system allocates a portion of memory to each job using some memory-management scheme. One popular scheme maintains a symmetrically linked list of records describing free memory blocks. When a memory request is received, this list is searched to locate the first available block that is large enough to satisfy the request. An appropriate portion of this block is allocated to the job, and any remaining portion remains on the free list.

Write a procedure to implement this *first-fit* memory-management scheme. Assume that the records in the free list contain the beginning address of an available block and its size, together with the links necessary to maintain a circular symmetrically linked list. Parameters for this procedure are a pointer to the first node in the free list and the size of the request. The procedure should return the address of the allocated block or an indication that the request cannot be satisfied.

17. Another common memory-allocation strategy is the ***best-fit*** scheme, in which the free list is scanned and the memory block that best fits the request is allocated. This block is either the first block whose size is equal to the request or the block whose size least exceeds the request. Rewrite the procedure in Exercise 16, using this best-fit scheme.

8.8 Other Multiply Linked Lists

We have seen that symmetrically linked lists are useful data structures in those applications in which it is necessary to move in either direction in a list. In this section we consider an assortment of other kinds of list processing in which linked lists whose nodes contain more than one link are useful. Such structures are usually considered in detail in advanced data structures courses and so are only previewed here.

Multiply Ordered Lists. In Chapter 7 we considered ordered lists in which the nodes were ordered so that the values in some key field of the data items stored in these nodes were in ascending order. In some applications, however, it is necessary to maintain a collection of records ordered in two or more different ways. For example, we might wish to have a collection of student records ordered by both name and id number.

One way to accomplish such multiple orderings is to maintain separate ordered linked lists, one for each of the desired orders. But this is obviously inefficient, especially for large records, because multiple copies of each record are required. A better approach is to use a single list in which multiple links are used to link the nodes together in the different orders. For example, to store a collection of records containing student names and id numbers, with the names in alphabetical order and the id numbers in ascending order, we might use the following multiply linked list having two links per node:

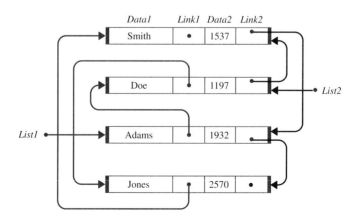

If this list is traversed and the data fields are displayed by using *List1* to point to the first node and following the pointers in the field *Link1*, the names will be in alphabetical order:

Adams	1932
Doe	1197
Jones	2570
Smith	1537

A traversal using *List2* to point to the first node and following the pointers in the field *Link2* gives the id numbers in ascending order:

Doe	1197
Smith	1537
Adams	1932
Jones	2570

This list is logically ordered, therefore, in two different ways.

Sparse Matrices. An *m* × *n matrix* is a rectangular array containing *m* rows and *n* columns. The usual storage structure for matrices is thus quite naturally a two-dimensional array, especially since arrays are provided in nearly every programming language.

In some applications, however (e.g., in solving differential equations), it is necessary to process very large matrices having few nonzero entries. Using a two-dimensional array to store all the entries (including zeros) of such *sparse matrices* is not very efficient. They can be stored more efficiently using a linked structure analogous to that for sparse polynomials described in Section 8.5.

One common linked implementation is to represent each row of the matrix as a linked list, storing only the nonzero entries in each row. In this scheme, the matrix is represented as an array of pointers $A[1], A[2], \ldots, A[m]$, one for each row of the matrix. Each array element $A[i]$ points to a linked list of nodes, each of which stores a nonzero entry in that row and the number of the column in which it appears, together with a link to the node for the next nonzero entry in that row:

For example, the 4 × 5 matrix

$$A = \begin{bmatrix} 9 & 0 & 0 & 8 & 0 \\ 7 & 0 & 0 & 0 & 0 \\ 0 & 0 & 0 & 0 & 0 \\ -1 & 6 & 0 & -8 & 0 \end{bmatrix}$$

can be represented by

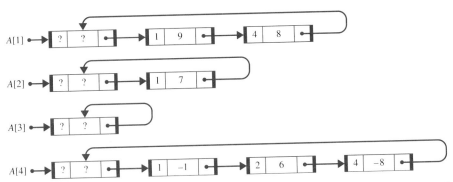

Although this is a useful linked storage structure for matrices, the size of the array limits the number of rows that such matrices may have. Moreover, for smaller matrices and/or those having a large number of rows with all zero entries, many of the elements in this array will be wasted.

An alternative implementation is to create a single linked list. Each node contains a row number, a column number, the nonzero entry in that row and column, and a link to the next node:

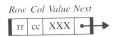

These nodes are usually arranged in the list so that traversing the list visits the entries of the matrix in rowwise order. For example, the preceding 4 × 5 matrix can be represented by the following circular linked list, which uses a head node to store the dimensions of the matrix:

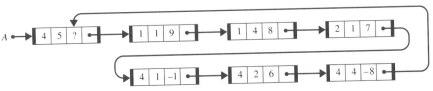

In this implementation, however, we lose direct access to each of the rows of the matrix. If rowwise processing is important to a particular application, such as the addition of matrices, it might be better to replace the array of pointers with a linked list of row head nodes, each of which contains a pointer to a nonempty row list. Each row head node will also contain the number of that row and a pointer to the next row head node, and these row head nodes are ordered so that the row numbers are in ascending order. In this implementation, the preceding 4 × 5 matrix might be represented by the following linked structure:

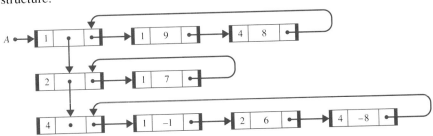

One drawback of all of these linked implementations is that it is difficult to process a matrix columnwise as required, for example, when multiplying two matrices. One linked structure that provides easy access to both the rows and the columns of a matrix is known as an ***orthogonal list.*** Each node stores a row number, a column number, and the nonzero entry in that row and column, and it appears in both a row list and a column list. This is accomplished by using two links in each node, one pointing to its successor in the row list and the other pointing to its successor in the column list:

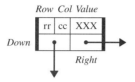

Usually each of the row lists and column lists is a circular list with a head node, and these head nodes are linked together to form circular lists with a master head node. For example, the orthogonal list representation of the preceding 4 × 5 matrix might be as shown in Figure 8.4.

Generalized Lists.   In nearly all of our examples of lists thus far, the list elements have been *atomic*, which means that they themselves are not lists. We considered, for example, lists of integers and lists of records. However, we just described a representation of sparse matrices that is a list of row lists. On several occasions, we also considered lists of strings, and a string is itself a list. In particular, in the program in Figure 8.3 we represented a set of strings as a linked list of strings and each string as a linked list of characters. In this

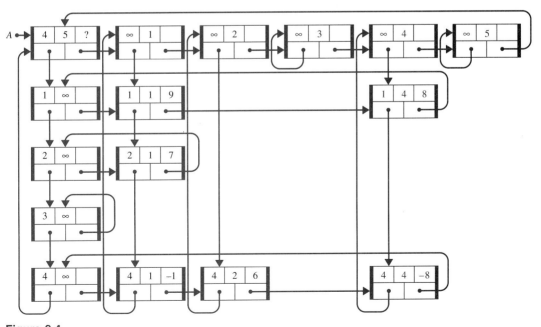

Figure 8.4

"linked list of linked lists" implementation, the set $S = \{AL, FRED, JOE\}$ would be represented as

Lists in which the elements are allowed to be lists are called **generalized lists.** As illustrations, consider the following examples of lists:

$$A = (4, 6)$$
$$B = ((4, 6), 8)$$
$$C = (((4)), 6)$$
$$D = (2, A, A)$$
$$E = (2, 4, E)$$

A is an ordinary list containing two atomic elements, the integers 4 and 6. B is also a list of two elements, but the first element $(4, 6)$ is itself a list with two elements. C is also a list with two elements; its first element is $((4))$, which is a list of one element (4), and this element is itself a list having one element, namely, the integer 4. D is a list with three elements in which the second and third are themselves lists. The list E also has three elements, but it differs dramatically from D in that it has itself as a member. Such lists are said to be **recursive lists.**

Generalized lists are commonly represented as linked lists in which the nodes have a tag field in addition to a data part and a link part:

This tag is used to indicate whether the data field stores an atom or a pointer to a list. It can be implemented as a single bit, with 0 indicating an atom and 1 indicating a pointer, or as a boolean variable, with false and true playing the roles of 0 and 1. Thus lists A, B, and C can be represented by the following linked lists:

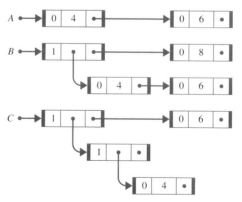

Of course, linked lists with head nodes, circular lists, and other variations may also be used.

Two implementations of D are possible. Because A is the list $(4, 6)$, we can think of D as the list

$$(2, (4, 6), (4, 6))$$

and represent it as

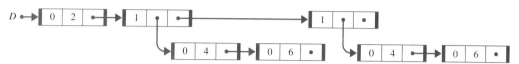

The second possibility is to allow **shared lists** and represent D and A as follows:

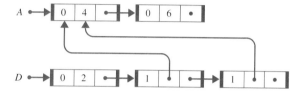

Note that in this case, modifying A also changes D.

The recursive list E can be represented as a circular linked structure:

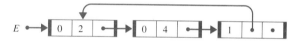

This is equivalent to the following infinite linked structure:

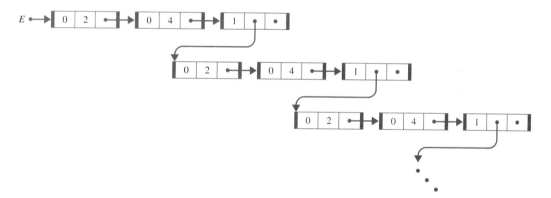

In Section 8.5 we described a linked implementation of polynomials in a single variable. Polynomials in more than one variable can be represented as generalized lists and can thus be implemented using linked structures similar to these. For example consider the polynomial $P(x,y)$ in two variables:

$$P(x,y) = 3 + 7x + 14y^2 + 25y^7 - 9x^2y^7 + 18x^6y^7$$

This can be written as a polynomial in y whose coefficients are polynomials in x:

$$P(x,y) = (3 + 7x) + 14y^2 + (25 - 9x^2 + 18x^6)y^7$$

If we use nodes of the form

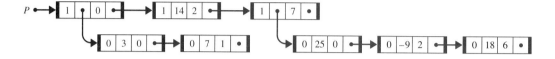

where *Tag* = 0 indicates that the field *Coef* stores a number and *Tag* = 1 indicates that it stores a pointer to a linked list representing a polynomial in *x*, we can represent the polynomial $P(x,y)$ as

Linked representations of generalized lists are used extensively in implementing the programming language LISP (LISt Processing). As an illustration, the assignment statement that would be written in Pascal as

$$Z := X + 3 * (-Y)$$

is written in LISP as

$$(setq\ Z\ (+\ X\ (*\ 3\ (-\ Y)\ )\ )\ )$$

This is, in fact, a list of three elements (without the separating commas we are accustomed to using). The first element is the key word *setq*, which denotes an assignment operator in LISP. The second element is a variable Z, to which a value is to be assigned. The third element is the list

$$(+\ X\ (*\ 3\ (-\ Y)\ )\ )$$

which corresponds to the Pascal expression $X + 3 * (-Y)$. This three-element list consists of the addition operator $+$, the variable X, and a list corresponding to the subexpression $3 * (-Y)$:

$$(*\ 3\ (-\ Y)\ )$$

Similarly, this list contains the multiplication operator $*$, the integer constant 3, and a two-element list corresponding to the subexpression $-Y$:

$$(-\ Y)$$

This list has the unary minus operator as its first element and the variable Y as its second element.

If we use nodes in which a tag value of 0 denotes atomic list elements, such as key words, variable names, and constants, and the tag value 1 denotes lists, this assignment statement can be represented by the following linked structure:

Assignment
statement

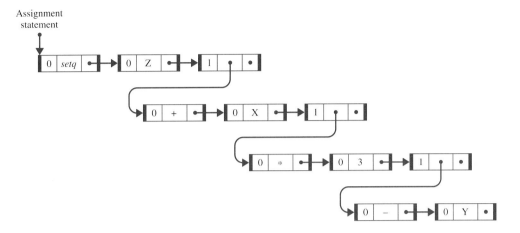

Looking Ahead. In this section we introduced several kinds of multiply linked structures and noted some of their applications. There are many other problems in which multiply linked structures can be used effectively. Several of these applications, including the study of trees and graphs, are considered in detail in later chapters.

Exercises

1. Write appropriate declarations for a multiply ordered linked list of names and id numbers like that described in the text.

2. Beginning with the multiply ordered linked list of names and id numbers pictured in the text, show the linked list that results from each of the following operations or sequence of operations:

   (a) Insert Brown with id number 2250.
   (b) Delete Smith with id number 1537.
   (c) Insert Zzyzk with id number 1025.
   (d) Insert Evans with id number 1620; insert Harris with id number 1750; and delete Adams with id number 1932.

3. Write a program to read the records from *StudentFile* (see Appendix E), and store them in a multiply ordered list with two link fields, in which one link is used to order the nodes so that the id numbers are in ascending order and another link orders the nodes so that the names are in alphabetical order. (Note that the records in *StudentFile* are already arranged in order of ascending id numbers.) Then search this list for a given student id or a given student name, and display the other information in the record.

4. Extend the program in Exercise 3 so that new records can be inserted or existing records can be deleted.

5. Suppose that the following sparse matrix is implemented by an array of pointers to row lists. Give a diagram of the resulting linked lists similar to that in the text.

$$A = \begin{bmatrix} 1 & 0 & 0 & 0 & 8 & 0 & 0 \\ -5 & -6 & 0 & 0 & 0 & 0 & 0 \\ 0 & 0 & 0 & 0 & 0 & 0 & 10 \\ 0 & 0 & 0 & 0 & 0 & 0 & 0 \\ 9 & 8 & 7 & 0 & 0 & 0 & 0 \end{bmatrix}$$

6. Repeat Exercise 5, but implement the matrix as a circular linked list having a head node that stores its dimensions.

7. Repeat Exercise 5, but implement the matrix as a linked list of head nodes containing pointers to linked row lists, as described in the text.

8. Repeat Exercise 5, but give an orthogonal list representation like that described in this section.

9. Write the declarations needed to store a sparse matrix of integers using the implementation in

   (a) Exercise 5   (b) Exercise 6   (c) Exercise 7   (d) Exercise 8

10. Write a procedure to add two sparse matrices, assuming the array of linked row lists implementation described in this section.

11. Repeat Exercise 10, but assume that each matrix is implemented as a circular linked list having a head node that stores its dimensions.

12. Repeat Exercise 10, but assume that each matrix is implemented as a linked list of head nodes containing pointers to linked row lists as described in the text.

13. Repeat Exercise 10, but assume that each matrix is implemented using an orthogonal list representation like that described in this section.

14. Write a program that reads the dimensions of a sparse matrix and its entries, that constructs one of the linked-list implementations described in this section, and that then prints the matrix in its usual tabular format.

15. Extend the program in Exercise 14 to read and calculate the sum of two matrices.

16. Give a diagram of the linked-list implementation of each of the following generalized lists:

    (a) (1, (2, 3))
    (b) ((1, 2), (3, 4), 5)

(c) $(1, (2, 3), ( ), 4)$ [$( )$ denotes an empty list.]

(d) $((1, (2, 3)), ((4)))$

17. Give a diagram of the linked-list implementation of the following polynomials in two variables:

    (a) $P(x,y) = 7 + 3xy + 5x^3y - 17y^2$

    (b) $P(x,y) = 6 - 5x + 4x^2 - 2x^3y^4 + 6x^5y^4 - x^9y^4 + y^8$

18. Describe how a polynomial $P(x,y,z)$ in three variables can be implemented as a linked list, and illustrate your implementation for the polynomial

$$P(x,y) = 6 - 5x + 4x^2 - 2x^3y^4 + 6x^5y^4z^3 - x^9y^4z^3 + y^8z^3 + z^7$$

9

Binary Trees

In the last sections of the preceding chapter we considered linked lists in which the nodes were connected by two or more links. For example, the nodes in symmetrically linked lists have two links, one pointing in the forward direction from a node to its successor and the other pointing backward from a node to its predecessor. The nodes in a multiply ordered linked list may have to be connected by several links, depending on how many logical orderings are desired. There are several other important multiply linked structures, and in this chapter we consider one of these, binary trees.

One important application of binary trees is to organize data in a linked structure so that it can be searched more efficiently than if it is stored in a linked list. Thus we begin by reviewing some of the search algorithms we have already considered. This will lead to the study of binary trees and, in particular, binary search trees. We also describe how binary trees are used in the construction of Huffman codes, which may be used for data compression. Other applications of binary trees and other kinds of trees are described in Chapter 12.

9.1 Review of Linear Search and Binary Search

In many applications, the collection of data items to be searched is organized as a list,

$$X_1, X_2, \ldots, X_n$$

This list is to be searched to determine whether one of the X_i's has a specified value. In practice, the list elements are often records, and the search is based on some key field in these records; that is, we search the list for a record X_i containing a specified value in its key field. In our review of the searching problem in this section, however, we assume for simplicity that the X_i's are simple items. The algorithms can easily be modified to handle the case of records.

The most straightforward searching scheme is *linear search,* in which we begin with the first list element and then search the list sequentially until we either find the specified item or reach the end of the list. An algorithm for linear search was given in Section 6.4 and for the array-based sequential storage implementation of lists, this algorithm is implemented by the following procedure:

> **procedure** *LinearSearch* (**var** *X* : *ListType*; *n* : *integer*;
> *Item* : *ListElementType*;
> **var** *Found* : *boolean*; **var** *Loc* : *integer*);

> (* Accepts: A list of *n* elements stored in array *X* and a data *Item*.
> Function: Performs a linear search of *X*[1], . . . , *X*[*n*] for *Item*.
> Returns: *Found* = true and *Loc* = position of *Item* if the search
> is successful; otherwise, *Found* is false. *)

> **begin** (* *LinearSearch* *)
> *Found* := *false*;
> *Loc* := 1;
> **while not** *Found* **and** (*Loc* <= *n*) **do**
> **if** *Item* = *X*[*Loc*] **then**
> *Found* := *true*
> **else**
> *Loc* := *Loc* + 1
> **end** (* *LinearSearch* *);

Here we assume that the type identifier *ListType* has been defined as an array of elements of some type *ListElementType* and with index type 1..*ListLimit* for some constant *ListLimit*.

A procedure to linearly search a linked list is similar. Instead of varying an index *Loc* over the positions of the array, we initialize a pointer *LocPtr* to the first node and advance it from one node to the next, following the links:

> **procedure** *LinkedLinearSearch* (*L* : *LinkedListType*; *Item* :
> *ListElementType*; **var** *Found* : *boolean*;
> **var** *LocPtr* : *ListPointer*);

> (* Accepts: A linked list with first node pointed to by *L* and a data
> *Item*.
> Function: Performs a linear search of this linked list for a node
> containing *Item*.
> Returns: *Found* = true and a pointer *LocPtr* to a node
> containing *Item* if the search is successful; otherwise,
> *Found* is false. *)

> **begin** (* *LinkedLinearSearch* *)
> *Found* := *false*;
> *LocPtr* := *L*;
> **while not** *Found* **and** (*LocPtr* <> **nil**) **do**
> **if** *Item* = *LocPtr*↑.*Data* **then**
> *Found* := *true*
> **else**
> *LocPtr* := *LocPtr*↑.*Next*
> **end** (* *LinkedLinearSearch* *);

Here we assume that the types *LinkedListType, ListPointer,* and *List-ElementType* are as defined in Chapter 7 for linked lists.

The worst case for linear search is obviously that in which the item for which we are searching is not in the list because, in this case, each of the n items in the list must be examined. The worst-case computing time for linear search is thus O(n).

If the list being searched is an ordered list, that is, if the elements are arranged in ascending (or descending) order, then it usually is possible to determine that a specified item is not in the list without examining every element of the list. As soon as a list element is encountered that is greater than (less than) the item, the search can be terminated. For example, when searching the list

$$10, 20, 30, 40, 50, 60, 70, 80, 90, 100$$

for the value 35, there is no need to search beyond the list element 40, because it—and therefore all the list elements that follow it—are greater than 35. This improved linear search algorithm for ordered lists is

LINEAR SEARCH FOR ORDERED LISTS

(* Accepts: An ordered list $X_1, \ldots, X_n$ with elements in ascending order and a data *Item*.

  Function: Performs a linear search of ordered list $X_1, \ldots, X_n$ for a specified *Item*.

  Returns: *Found* = true and *Loc* = position of *Item* if the search is successful; otherwise, *Found* is false. *)

1. Initialize *Found* and *DoneSearching* to false, *Loc* to 1.
2. While not *DoneSearching* do the following:
       If *Item* = X_{Loc} then
         Set *Found* and *DoneSearching* to true.
       Else if *Item* < X_{Loc} or *Loc* = n then
         Set *DoneSearching* to true.
       Else
         Increment *Loc* by 1.

If *Item* is in the range X_1 through X_n (and the possible values for it are uniformly distributed over this range), then on the average, $n/2$ comparisons of *Item* with the X_i are made before repetition terminates. But if *Item* is less than every X_i, the comparison of *Item* with X_{Loc} on the first pass through the while loop in this algorithm will immediately set *DoneSearching* to true, causing the loop to terminate. Thus, in many cases, linear search for ordered lists will require fewer comparisons than are needed for unordered lists. The worst-case computing time is still O(n), however, since n comparisons are required if *Item* > X_n.

An alternative scheme for searching an ordered list is **binary search,** also described in Section 6.4:

BINARY SEARCH

(∗ Accepts: An ordered list $X_1, \ldots, X_n$ with elements in ascending order and a data *Item*.

    Function: Performs a binary search of ordered list $X_1, \ldots, X_n$ for a specified *Item*.

    Returns: *Found* = true and *Loc* = position of *Item* if the search is successful; otherwise, *Found* is false. ∗)

1. Initialize *Found* to false, *First* to 1, and *Last* to n.
2. While not *Found* and *First* ≤ *Last* do the following:
   a. Calculate *Loc* = (*First* + *Last*) / 2.
   b. If *Item* < X_{Loc} then
       Set *Last* equal to *Loc* − 1.
      Else if *Item* > X_{Loc} then
       Set *First* equal to *Loc* + 1.
      Else
       Set *Found* to true.

Here the middle list element is examined first, and if it is not the desired item, the search continues with either the first half or the last half of the list. Thus, on each pass through the loop, the size of the sublist being searched is reduced by one half. We showed in some detail in Section 6.4 that it follows from this observation that the worst-case computing time for binary search is $O(\log_2 n)$. It is therefore more efficient than linear search for large n ($n \geq 20$, as indicated by empirical studies).

Although the preceding binary search algorithm is iterative, it is also natural to view binary search recursively, as noted in Chapter 6, because the basic idea at each stage is to examine the middle element of the (sub)list and, if it is not the desired item, then to search one of the two halves of the (sub)list *in exactly the same way.*

RECURSIVE BINARY SEARCH

(∗ Accepts: An ordered list $X_1, \ldots X_n$ with elements in ascending order and a data *Item*.

    Function: Searches the ordered list $X_1, \ldots X_n$ for *Item* using a recursive binary search.

    Returns: *Found* = true and *Loc* = position of *Item* if the search is successful; otherwise, *Found* is false. ∗)

1. Initialize *First* to 1 and *Last* to n.
2. If *First* > *Last* then   (∗ empty (sub)list ∗)
      Set *Found* to false.
   Else do the following:
   a. Calculate *Loc* = (*First* + *Last*) / 2.
   b. If *Item* < X_{Loc} then
       Apply the binary search algorithm with *Last* = *Loc* − 1.
      Else if *Item* > X_{Loc} then
       Apply the binary search algorithm with *First* = *Loc* + 1.
      Else
       Set *Found* to true.

Because the computing time of this recursive algorithm is $O(\log_2 n)$ and because it is no simpler than the iterative version, the guidelines given in Chapter 6 for choosing between recursive and iterative formulations of an algorithm suggest that we opt for the iterative version.

Although binary search usually outperforms linear search, it does require a sequential storage implementation so that list elements can be accessed directly. It is not appropriate for linked lists because locating the middle element would require traversing the sublist of elements that precede it. As the exercises ask you to show, this causes the worst-case computing time to become $O(n)$ for a list of size n.

It is possible, however, to store the elements of an ordered list in a linked structure that can be searched in a binarylike manner. To illustrate, consider the following ordered list of integers:

$$13, 28, 35, 49, 62, 66, 80$$

The first step in binary search requires examining the middle element in the list. Direct access to this element is possible if we maintain a pointer to the node storing it:

At the next stage, one of the two sublists, the left half or the right half, must be searched and must therefore be accessible from this node. This is possible if we maintain two pointers, one to each of these sublists. Since these sublists are searched in the same manner, these pointers should point to nodes containing the middle elements in these sublists:

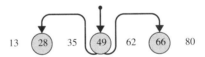

By the same reasoning, pointers from each of these "second-level" nodes are needed to access the middle elements in the sublists at the next stage:

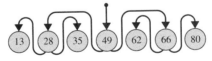

The resulting structure is usually drawn so that it has a treelike shape:

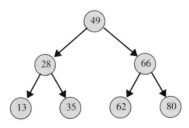

It is called a ***binary search tree*** and is a special kind of ***binary tree,*** which is the data structure studied in the rest of this chapter.

Exercises

1. Given the following array *Critters*:

i	1	2	3	4	5	6	7	8	9
Critters[*i*]	auk	bat	cow	eel	elk	fox	gnu	pig	rat

   Give the indices of the elements of *Critter* in the order that the components are examined during a binary search for

   (a) gnu   **(b)** eel   **(c)** fly   **(d)** ant   **(e)** yak

2. The performance of procedure *LinearSearch* can be improved slightly if the item being searched for is put at the end of the list (in position $n + 1$). This makes it possible to replace the compound boolean expression in the **while** statement by a simple one. Write this improved version of *LinearSearch.*

3. Write a recursive version of procedure

   (a) *LinearSearch*
   (b) *LinkedLinearSearch*

4. In many cases of list searching, certain items in the list are retrieved more frequently than others are. The performance of linear search in such cases improves if these frequently sought items are placed at the beginning of the list. One data structure that allows this is a ***self-organizing list***, in which list elements are rearranged so that frequently accessed items move to or toward the front of the list. Write a linear search procedure for such a self-organizing list using a ***move-to-the-front*** strategy in which the item being retrieved is moved to the front of the list. Assume that the list is implemented as

   (a) an array.
   (b) a linked list.

5. Proceed as in Exercise 4, but use a ***move-ahead-one*** strategy in which the item being retrieved is interchanged with its predecessor.

6. Linear search is not practical for large lists because the search time becomes unacceptably large. In a dictionary this problem is alleviated by providing thumb cutouts that allow direct access to the beginnings of sublists, which can then be searched. Imitating this approach, we might break a long list into a number of sublists and construct an ***index array*** of pointers to the beginnings of these sublists. Write a

program to read records from *StudentFile*, storing them in a linked list, and construct an array of pointers to sublists of names beginning with 'A', 'B', 'C', ... The program should then accept a name and retrieve the record for this student.

7. Linear search outperforms binary search for small lists. If possible with your version of Pascal, write a program to compare the computing times of linear search and binary search (see Exercise 5 of Section 3.6).

8. As noted in the text, binary search is not practical for linked lists because the worst-case computing time would be $O(n)$. Show that this is true by designing an algorithm to carry out a binary search of a linked list and analyzing its computing time.

9. In binary search, *probes* are always made at the middle of the (sub)list. In many situations, however, we have some idea of approximately where the item is located; for example, in searching a telephone directory for "Doe, John," we might estimate that this name is approximately 1/6 of the way through the list. This idea is the basis for **interpolation search**, in which probes of a sublist of size L are made at position $First + F * L$ for some fraction F (not necessarily 1/2). Write a procedure to implement interpolation search for an ordered list of integers using the fraction F given by

$$F = (Item - X_{First}) \textbf{ div } (X_{Last} - X_{First})$$

10. If possible with your version of Pascal, write a program to compare the computing times of

(a) linear search
(b) binary search
(c) interpolation search (see Exercise 9)

(See Exercise 5 of Section 3.6.)

9.2 Introduction to Binary Trees

We have seen that a linked list is a useful structure for processing dynamic lists whose maximum sizes are not known in advance and whose sizes change significantly because of repeated insertions and deletions. We noted in the preceding section that although binary search is not efficient for linked lists, it can be used for a *binary search tree*. This is a special kind of *binary tree*, which is a special instance of a more general structure called a *tree*.

A *tree* consists of a finite set of elements called *nodes*, or *vertices,* and a finite set of *directed arcs* that connect pairs of nodes. If the tree is nonempty, then one of the nodes, called the *root,* has no incoming arcs, but every other node in the tree can be reached from it by following a unique sequence of consecutive arcs.

Trees derive their names from the treelike diagrams that are used to picture them. For example,

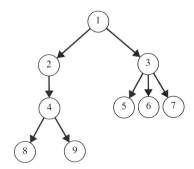

shows a tree having nine vertices in which vertex 1 is the root. As this diagram indicates, trees are usually drawn upside down, with the root at the top and the *leaves*—that is, vertices with no outgoing arcs—at the bottom. Nodes that are directly accessible from a given node (by using only one directed arc) are called the *children* of that node, and a node is said to be the *parent* of its children. For example, in the preceding tree, vertex 3 is the parent of vertices 5, 6, and 7, and these vertices are the children of vertex 3 and are called *siblings.*

Trees in which each node has at most two children are called *binary trees,* and as noted in the introduction to this chapter, they can be used to solve a variety of problems. They are especially useful in modeling processes in which some experiment or test with two possible outcomes (e.g., off or on, 0 or 1, false or true, down or up) is performed repeatedly. For example, the following tree might be used to represent the possible outcomes of flipping a coin three times:

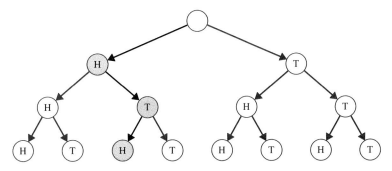

Each path from the root to one of the leaf nodes corresponds to a particular outcome, such as HTH, a head followed by a tail followed by another head, as highlighted in the diagram.

Similarly, a binary tree can be used in coding problems such as in encoding and decoding messages transmitted in Morse code, a scheme in which characters are represented as sequences of dots and dashes, as shown in the following table:

A · —	M — —	Y — · — —
B — · · ·	N — ·	Z — — · ·
C — · — ·	O — — —	1 · — — — —
D — · ·	P · — — ·	2 · · — — —
E ·	Q — — · —	3 · · · — —
F · · — ·	R · — ·	4 · · · · —
G — — ·	S · · ·	5 · · · · ·
H · · · ·	T —	6 — · · · ·
I · ·	U · · —	7 — — · · ·
J · — — —	V · · · —	8 — — — · ·
K — · —	W · — —	9 — — — — ·
L · — · ·	X — · · —	0 — — — — —

In this case, the nodes in a binary tree are used to represent the characters, and each arc from a node to its children is labeled with a dot or a dash, according to whether it leads to a left child or to a right child, respectively. Thus, part of the tree for Morse code is

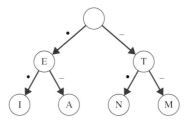

The sequence of dots and dashes labeling a path from the root to a particular node corresponds to the Morse code for that character; for example, · · is the code for I, and — · is the code for N. In Section 9.5 we use a similar tree to construct another kind of code known as *Huffman code*.

An array can be used to store binary trees. We simply number the nodes in the tree from the root down, numbering the nodes on each level from left to right,

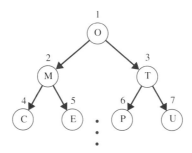

and store the contents of the ith node in the ith location of the array:

i	1	2	3	4	5	6	7	· · ·
$T[i]$	O	M	T	C	E	P	U	· · ·

This array-based implementation works very well for **complete** trees, in which each level of the tree is completely filled, except possibly the bottom level, and in this level, the nodes are in the leftmost positions. This completeness property guarantees that the data items will be stored in consecutive locations at the beginning of the array. It should be obvious, however, that this implementation may not be space efficient for other kinds of binary trees. For example, the tree

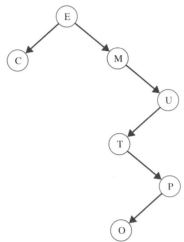

contains the same characters as the one before but requires fifty-eight array positions for storage:

i	1	2	3	4	5	6	7	8	9	10	11	12	13	14	15	16	17	18	19	20
$T[i]$	E	C	M				U							T						

21	22	23	24	25	26	27	28	29	30	31	32	33	34	35	36	37	38	39	40
								P											

41	42	43	44	45	46	47	48	49	50	51	52	53	54	55	56	57	58	$\cdots$
																	O	$\cdots$

To use space more efficiently and to provide additional flexibility, we instead implement binary trees as linked structures in which each node has two links, one pointing to the left child of that node (this link is nil if there is no left child) and the other pointing to the right child (if there is one). Any node in the tree can be accessed if we maintain a pointer to the root of the tree. Using records to represent the nodes, we make the following declarations for a binary tree:

```
type
    BinTreeElementType = . . . ;   (* type of data items stored in nodes *)
    BinTreePointer = ↑BinTreeNode;
    BinTreeNode = record
                    Data : BinTreeElementType;
                    LChild, RChild : BinTreePointer
                  end;
    BinaryTreeType = BinTreePointer;
```

The two link fields *LChild* and *RChild* in a node are pointers to nodes representing its left and right children, respectively,

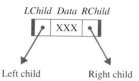

or are nil if the node does not have a left or right child. A leaf node is thus characterized by having nil values for both *LChild* and *RChild*:

The binary tree

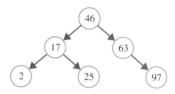

can thus be represented as the following linked tree of records:

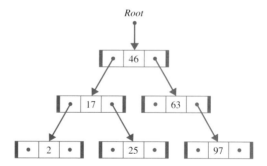

9.3   Binary Search Trees

In the binary tree considered at the end of the preceding section,

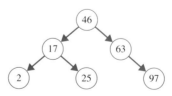

the value in each node is greater than the value in its left child (if there is one) and less than the value in its right child (if there is one). A binary tree having this property is called a ***binary search tree*** (***BST***) because, as we noted at the end of Section 9.1, it can be searched using an algorithm much like the binary search algorithm for lists. To illustrate, suppose we wish to search this BST for 25. We begin at the root, and since 25 is less than the value 46 in this root, we know that the desired value is located to the left of the root; that is, it must be in the left *subtree,* whose root is 17:

Now we continue the search by comparing 25 with the value in the root of this subtree. Since 25 > 17, we know that the right subtree should be searched:

Examining the value in the root of this one-node subtree locates the value 25.

Similarly, to search for the value 55, after comparing 55 with the value in the root, we are led to search its right subtree:

Now, because 55 < 63, if the desired value is in the tree, it will be in the left subtree. However, since this left subtree is empty, we conclude that the value 55 is not in the tree.

The following procedure *BSTSearch* incorporates these techniques for searching a binary search tree. The pointer *LocPtr* begins at the root of the BST and then is repeatedly replaced with the left or right link of the current node, according to whether the item for which we are searching is less than or greater than the value stored in this node. This process continues until either the desired item is found or *LocPtr* becomes nil, indicating an empty subtree, in which case the item is not in the tree. The procedure is designed to handle trees in which the data parts of the nodes are records; *Item* is compared with some key field in these nodes, and the outcome of this comparison is used to determine whether to descend to the left subtree or to the right subtree or to terminate the search because the item has been found.

> **procedure** *BSTSearch* (*Root : BinaryTreeType*; *KeyValue : KeyType*;
> **var** *Found : boolean*;
> **var** *LocPtr : BinTreePointer*);

> (* Accepts: BST with root pointed to by *Root* and a *KeyValue*.
> Function: Searches a BST for a node containing a specified
> *KeyValue* in its keyfield.
> Returns: *Found* is true and *LocPtr* points to a node containing
> *KeyValue* if the search is successful; otherwise, *Found*
> is false *)

```
begin (* BSTSearch *)
   LocPtr := Root;
   Found := false;
   while not Found and (LocPtr <> nil) do
      if KeyValue < LocPtr↑.Data.Key then
         LocPtr := LocPtr↑.LChild
      else if KeyValue > LocPtr↑.Data.Key then
         LocPtr := LocPtr↑.RChild
      else
         Found := true
end (* BSTSearch *);
```

As was the case for the binary search algorithm in Section 9.1, *BSTSearch* can be written either iteratively (as was done here) or recursively, with little difference of effort. The recursive version is left as an exercise.

A binary search tree can be constructed by repeatedly calling a procedure to insert elements into a BST that is initially empty (*Root* = **nil**). The method used to determine where an element is to be inserted is similar to that used to search the tree. In fact, we need only modify *BSTSearch* to maintain a pointer to the parent of the node currently being examined as we descend the tree, looking for a place to insert the item.

To illustrate, suppose that the following BST has already been constructed

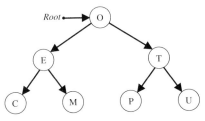

and we wish to insert the letter R. We begin at the root and compare 'R' with the letter there:

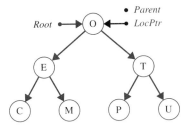

Since 'R' > 'O', we descend to the right subtree:

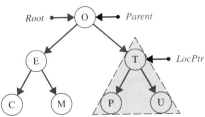

After comparing 'R' with 'T' stored in the root of this subtree pointed to by *LocPtr*, we descend to the left subtree, since 'R' < 'T':

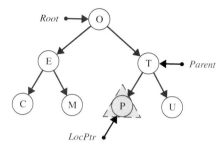

Since 'R' > 'P', we descend to the right subtree of this one-node subtree containing 'P':

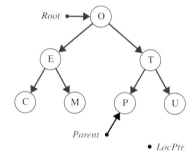

The fact that this right subtree is empty (*LocPtr* = **nil**) indicates that 'R' is not in the BST and should be inserted as a right child of its parent node:

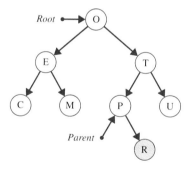

The following procedure uses this modified version of *BSTSearch* to locate where a given item is to be inserted (or is found). The pointer *Parent* that trails the search pointer *LocPtr* down the tree keeps track of the parent node so that the new node can be attached to the BST in the proper place.

procedure *BSTInsert* (**var** *Root* : *BinaryTreeType*;
　　　　　　　　Item : *BinTreeElementType*);

　(∗ Accepts:　BST with root pointed to by *Root* and a data *Item*.
　　Function:　Inserts *Item* into the BST.
　　Returns:　Modified BST with root pointed to by *Root*. ∗)

```
var
  LocPtr,                   (* search pointer *)
  Parent : BinTreePointer;  (* pointer to parent of current node *)
  Found : boolean;          (* indicates if Item already in BST *)

begin (* BSTInsert *)
  LocPtr := Root;
  Parent := nil;
  Found := false;
  while not Found and (LocPtr <> nil) do
    begin
      Parent := LocPtr;
      if Item.Key < LocPtr↑Data.Key then       (* descend left *)
        LocPtr := LocPtr↑.LChild
      else if Item.Key > LocPtr↑.Data.Key then  (* descend right *)
        LocPtr := LocPtr↑.RChild
      else                                       (* Item found *)
        Found := true
    end (* while *);
  if Found then
    writeln ('Item already in the tree')
  else
    begin
      new (LocPtr);                              (* get new node for Item *)
      with LocPtr↑ do
        begin
          Data := Item;
          LChild := nil;
          RChild := nil
        end (* with *);
      if Parent = nil then                       (* empty tree *)
        Root := LocPtr
      else
        with Parent↑ do
          if Item.Key < Data.Key then            (* insert to left of parent *)
            LChild := LocPtr
          else                                    (* insert to right of parent *)
            RChild := LocPtr
    end (* else *)
end (* BSTInsert*);
```

To illustrate the use of BSTs, consider the problem of organizing a collection of computer user-ids and passwords. Each time a user logs in to the system by entering his or her user-id and a secret password, the system must check this user-id and password to verify that this is a legitimate user. Because this user validation must be done many times each day, it is necessary to structure this information in such a way that it can be searched rapidly. Moreover, this must be a dynamic structure because new users are regularly added to the system. A BST is one possible candidate, and the program in Figure 9.1

uses a BST in which the data part of each node is a record with two fields, *UserId* and *Password*, the first of which is the key field on which searches are based. The program uses a package for processing such BSTs of user records. Among other items, this package defines the types *BinaryTreeType* and *BinTreePointer*; the procedure *CreateBST*, which creates an empty BST; the (modified) procedures *BSTInsert* and *BSTSearch* to construct and search this tree; and procedures for other basic tree operations, as described in the next section.

```
PROGRAM ValidateUsers1 (input, output, UsersFile);

(**********************************************************************

    Input (file):       The text file UsersFile.
    Input (keyboard):   User-ids and passwords.
    Function:           Validates computer user-ids and passwords.  A
                        list of valid ids and passwords is read from
                        UsersFile and is stored in a BST.  When user-ids
                        and passwords are entered during execution, this
                        BST is searched to determine whether they are
                        legal.
    Output (screen):    Messages indicating whether user-ids and
                        passwords are valid.

    Note:               Certain constant, type, variable, function and
                        procedure declarations from the packages for the
                        ADTs string and BST must be inserted into the
                        declaration part.  The compiler directive
                        #include inserts these items from the five files
                        STRING-CONST, STRING-TYPE, STRING-OPS, BST-TYPE,
                        and BST-OPS.

**********************************************************************)
CONST
#include 'STRING-CONST'       (* StringLimit *)

TYPE
#include 'STRING-TYPE'        (* String *)
   UserRecord = RECORD
                   Id,
                   Password : String
                END;
   BinTreeElementType = UserRecord;
   KeyType = String;
#include 'BST-TYPE'           (* BinTreePointer, BinaryTreeType *)
```

Figure 9.1

Figure 9.1 (*cont.*)

```
VAR
    UsersFile : text;            (* file of legal user-ids and passwords *)
    UserRec : UserRecord;        (* current user record being validated *)
    UserTree : BinaryTreeType;   (* BST of user records *)
    LocPtr : BinTreePointer;     (* pointer to a node in the BST *)
    Found,                       (* signals if search of BST was successful *)
    MoreUsers : boolean;         (* signals end of processing *)

#include 'STRING-OPS'            (* ReadString *)
#include 'BST-OPS'               (* CreateBST, BSTInsert, BSTSearch *)

PROCEDURE BuildTree (VAR UsersFile : text;
                     VAR UserTree : BinaryTreeType);

    (***********************************************************************

        Input (file):    The text file UsersFile.
        Function:        Constructs a BST of legal user records.
        Output (param): BST with root node pointed to by UserTree.

    ***********************************************************************)

    BEGIN  (* BuildTree *)
        CreateBST (UserTree);
        WHILE NOT eof(UsersFile) DO
            BEGIN
                ReadString (UsersFile, UserRec.Id);
                ReadString (UsersFile, UserRec.Password);
                BSTInsert (UserTree, UserRec)
            END  (* WHILE *)
    END  (* BuildTree *);

PROCEDURE Login (VAR UserRec : UserRecord; VAR MoreUsers : boolean);

    (***********************************************************************

        Input (keyboard): A user-id and a password.
        Function:         Reads the user-id and password fields of a
                          user record.
        Output (param):   The user record UserRec and the boolean value
                          MoreUsers, which is set to false if a special
                          QuitSignal is entered for the user-id and is
                          true otherwise.
    ***********************************************************************)

    CONST
        QuitSignal = 'QUIT    ';

    BEGIN (* Login *)
        write ('User-id?  ');
        ReadString (input, UserRec.Id);
        IF UserRec.Id = QuitSignal THEN
            MoreUsers := false
        ELSE
            BEGIN
                MoreUsers := true;
                write ('Password?  ');
                ReadString (input, UserRec.Password)
            END (* ELSE *)
    END (* Login *);
```

Figure 9.1 (*cont.*)

```
BEGIN (* main program *)
   reset (UsersFile);
   BuildTree (UsersFile, UserTree);

   (* Validate users *)
   Login (UserRec, MoreUsers);
   WHILE MoreUsers DO
      BEGIN
         BSTSearch (UserTree, UserRec.Id, Found, LocPtr);
         IF Found THEN
            IF LocPtr^.Data.Password = UserRec.Password THEN
               writeln ('Valid user')
            ELSE
               writeln ('*** Invalid Password ***')
         ELSE
            writeln ('*** Invalid User-Id ***');
         writeln;
         Login (UserRec, MoreUsers)
      END (* WHILE *)
END (* main program *).
```

Listing of UsersFile used in sample run:

```
S31416PI
CHERRY
S12345SL
CLAY
S31313LN
KANSAS
S21718EX
LOG
S13331RC
COLA
S77777UP
UNCOLA
S99099RR
RAILROAD
```

Sample run:

```
User-id?   S31416PI
Password?   CHERRY
Valid user

User-id?   S12345SL
Password?   SAND
*** Invalid Password ***

User-id?   S11111AB
Password?   ALPHA
*** Invalid User-Id ***

User-id?   QUIT
```

The order in which items are inserted into a BST determines the shape of the tree. For example, inserting the letters O, E, T, C, U, M, P into a BST of characters in this order gives the nicely *balanced* tree

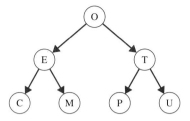

but inserting them in the order C, O, M, P, U, T, E yields the unbalanced tree

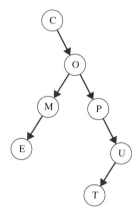

and inserting them in alphabetical order, C, E, M, O, P, T, U, causes the tree to degenerate into a linked list:

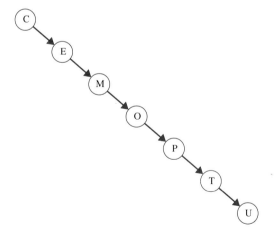

The time required to carry out most of the basic operations on a BST quite clearly depends on the "shape" of the tree. If it is balanced so that the left and right subtrees of each node contain approximately the same number of nodes, then as a search pointer moves down the tree from one level to the next, the size of the subtree to be examined is reduced by one half. Using an analysis like that used for binary search in Section 6.4, it is easy to show that the computing time for *BSTSearch* and *BSTInsert* is $O(\log_2 n)$ in this case. As the BST becomes increasingly unbalanced, however, the performance of these procedures deteriorates. For trees that degenerate into linked lists as in the last example, *BSTSearch* degenerates into linear search, so that the computing time is $O(n)$ for such BSTs.

It is usually not possible to determine a priori the optimal order in which to insert items into a BST, that is, to preorder the data items so that inserting them into a BST will result in a balanced tree. The usual solution is to rebalance the tree after each new element is inserted using rebalancing algorithms. One common rebalancing scheme is described in Chapter 12.

Exercises

1. Complete the binary tree for Morse code that was begun in this section.

2. For each of the following lists of letters, draw the BST that results when the letters are inserted in the order given:

   (a) A, C, R, E, S   (b) R, A, C, E, S
   (c) C, A, R, E, S   (d) S, C, A, R, E
   (e) C, O, R, N, F, L, A, K, E, S

3. Assuming the array-based implementation of binary trees described in Section 9.2, show the contents of arrays used to store the binary trees of Exercise 2.

4. Write a recursive version of procedure *BSTSearch*.

5. Complete the following procedure *GenerateBST* for generating a random binary search tree containing uppercase letters. (See footnote 2 in Section 5.2 regarding random number generation.)

   procedure *GenerateBST* (*n* : *integer*; **var** *R* : *BinaryTreeType*);

   (∗ Accept: An integer *n*.
       Function: Generates *n* random uppercase letters, prints each
                 one, and inserts each one into a BST.
       Returns: Binary tree with root pointed to by *R*. ∗)

6. Write a

   (a) nonrecursive function
   (b) recursive function

   BSTLevel that determines the *level* in a BST at which a specified item in the tree is located. The root of the BST is at level 0, its children are at level 1, and so on.

7. Test the function *BSTLevel* developed in Exercise 6. Use procedure *GenerateBST* of Exercise 5 to generate BSTs and then determine the level of 'A', 'B', . . . , 'Z' in each tree.

8. The worst-case number of comparisons in searching a BST is equal to its **depth**, that is, the number of levels in the tree. Write a recursive function *BSTDepth* to determine the depth of a BST.

9. Test the function *BSTDepth* developed in Exercise 8 by using the procedure *GenerateBST* of Exercise 5 to generate BSTs and then determine the depth of each tree.

10. In this section, binary search trees were implemented using Pascal pointers, but it also is possible to use an array-based implementation similar to that for linked lists described in Section 7.3. In this implementation, each node is represented as a record and the BST as an array of records. Each record contains three fields: a data field and two link fields that point to the left and the right child, respectively, by storing their indices in the array. Imitating the array-based implementation of linked lists in Section 7.3,

   (a) Write appropriate declarations for this array-based implementation of binary search trees.
   (b) Devise a scheme for maintaining a storage pool of available nodes, and write procedures *InitializeStoragePool*, *GetNode*, and *ReleaseNode* for maintaining this storage pool.

11. Assuming that an array of ten records constitutes the storage pool for an array-based implementation of a BST as described in Exercise 10, draw diagrams similar to those in Section 7.3 for the BSTs of Exercise 2.

12. Assuming the array-based implementation of BSTs in Exercise 10, write a procedure

   (a) *BSTSearch* for searching a BST.
   (b) *BSTInsert* for inserting an item into a BST.

9.4 Binary Trees as Recursive Data Structures

All the algorithms we developed in the preceding section for processing binary trees are iterative, but they can also be written recursively because a binary tree can be defined as a **recursive data structure** in a very natural way. As an illustration, consider the following binary tree:

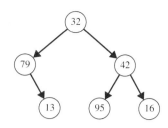

Its root node contains the integer 32 and has pointers to the nodes containing 79 and 42, each of which is itself the root of a binary **subtree**:

Left Subtree

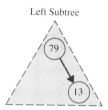

Right Subtree

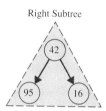

Now consider the left subtree. Its root node contains the integer 79 and has a right child but no left child. Nevertheless, we can still regard this node as having pointers to two binary subtrees, a left subtree and a right subtree, provided that we allow empty binary trees:

Left Subtree

Right Subtree

Both the left and right subtrees of the one-node tree containing 13 are thus empty binary trees. This leads to the following recursive definition of a binary tree:

RECURSIVE DEFINITION OF A BINARY TREE

A binary tree either

a. is empty ⟵ ———————————————— Anchor

or

b. consists of a node called the root, which has pointers to two disjoint binary subtrees called the **left subtree** and the **right subtree.** ⟵ ——— Inductive step

Because of the recursive nature of binary trees, many of the basic operations on them can be carried out most simply and elegantly using recursive algorithms. These algorithms are typically anchored by the special case of an empty binary tree, and the inductive step specifies how a binary tree is to be processed in terms of its root and either or both of its subtrees.

As an illustration, we first consider the operation of traversal, that is, moving through a binary tree like the preceding one, "visiting" each node exactly once. And suppose for now that the order in which the nodes are visited is not relevant. What is important is that we visit each node, not missing any, and that the information in each node is processed exactly once.

One simple recursive scheme is to traverse the binary tree as follows:

1. Visit the root and process its contents.
2. Now traverse the left subtree.
3. Then traverse the right subtree.

Thus, in our example, if we simply display a node's contents when we visit it, we begin by displaying the value 32 in the root of the binary tree. Next we must traverse the left subtree; after this traversal is finished, we then must traverse the right subtree; and when this traversal is completed, we will have traversed the entire binary tree.

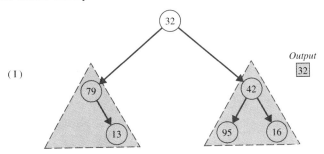

(I)

Output
32

Thus the problem has been reduced to the traversal of two smaller binary trees. We consider the left subtree and visit its root. Next we must traverse its left subtree and then its right subtree.

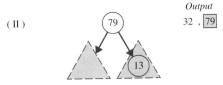

(II)

Output
32 , 79

The left subtree is empty, and so we have reached the anchor case of the recursive definition of a binary tree, and to complete the traversal algorithm, we must specify how an empty binary tree is to be traversed. But this is easy. We do nothing.

Because traversal of the empty left subtree is thus finished trivially, we turn to traversing the right subtree. We visit its root and then must traverse its left subtree followed by its right subtree:

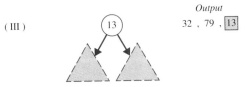

(III)

Output
32 , 79 , 13

As both subtrees are empty, no action is required to traverse them. Consequently, traversal of the binary tree in diagram III is complete, and since this was the right subtree of the tree in diagram II, traversal of this tree is also complete.

This means that we have finished traversing the left subtree of the root in the original binary tree in diagram I, and we finally are ready to begin traversing the right subtree. This traversal proceeds in a similar manner. We first visit its root, displaying the value 42 stored in it, then traverse its left subtree, and then its right subtree:

(IV)

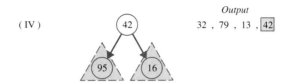

The left subtree consists of a single node with empty left and right subtrees and is traversed as described earlier for a one-node binary tree:

(V)

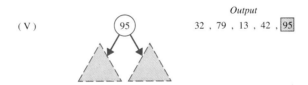

The right subtree is traversed in the same way:

(VI)

This completes the traversal of the binary tree in diagram IV and thus completes the traversal of the original tree in diagram I.

As this example demonstrates, traversing a binary tree recursively requires three basic steps, which we shall denote N, L, and R :

N: Visit a node.
L: Traverse the left subtree of a node.
R: Traverse the right subtree of a node.

We performed these steps in the order listed here, but in fact, there are six different orders in which they can be carried out:

LNR
NLR
LRN
NRL
RNL
RLN

For example, the ordering LNR corresponds to the following traversal algorithm:

If the binary tree is empty then   (* anchor *)
   Do nothing.
Else do the following: (* inductive step *)
   L: Traverse the left subtree.
   N: Visit the root.
   R: Traverse the right subtree.

For the preceding binary tree, this LNR traversal visits the nodes in the order 79, 13, 32, 95, 42, 16.

The first three orders, in which the left subtree is traversed before the right, are the most important of the six traversals and are commonly called by other names:

LNR ↔ Inorder
NLR ↔ Preorder
LRN ↔ Postorder

To see why these names are appropriate, consider the following *expression tree*, a binary tree used to represent the arithmetic expression

$$A - B * C + D$$

by representing each operand as a child of a parent node representing the corresponding operator:

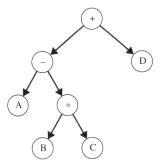

An *inorder* traversal of this expression tree produces the *infix* expression

$$A - B * C + D$$

A *preorder* traversal gives the *prefix* expression (see Exercise 8 in Section 4.4):

$$+ - A * B C D$$

And a *postorder* traversal yields the *postfix* (RPN) expression (see Section 4.4):

$$A \ B \ C \ * - D +$$

A recursive procedure to implement any of these traversal algorithms is easy. One need only attempt to write a correct nonrecursive version to appreciate the simple elegance of a procedure like the following:

procedure *Inorder* (*Root* : *BinaryTreeType*);

(* Accepts   A binary tree with root node pointed to by *Root*.
  Function: Performs an inorder traversal of the binary tree,
                              processing each node exactly once.
  Returns/Output: Depends on the type of processing. *)

begin (* *Inorder* *)
  if *Root* <> **nil then**
    begin
      Inorder (*Root*↑.*LChild*);   (* L operation *)
      (* Insert statements here to   (* N operation *)
         process *Root*↑.*Data* *)
      Inorder (*Root*↑.*RChild*)   (* R operation *)
    end (* **if** *)
   (* else
      do nothing *)
  end (* *Inorder* *);

Procedures for any of the other traversals are obtained by simply changing the order of the statements representing the L, N, and R operations. The following table traces the action of *Inorder* as it traverses the binary tree

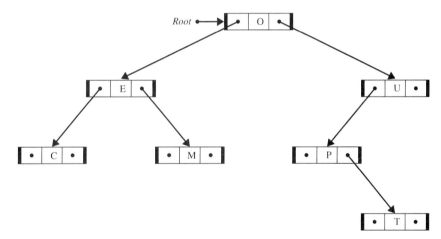

Contents of Current Node	Level in the Tree	Action	Output
O	1	Call *Inorder* with pointer to root (E) of left subtree.	
E	2	Call *Inorder* with pointer to root (C) of left subtree.	
C	3	Call *Inorder* with pointer (nil) to root of left subtree.	
none	4	None; return to parent node.	
C	3	Display contents of node.	C

Contents of Current Node	Level in the Tree	Action	Output
C	3	Call *Inorder* with pointer (nil) to root of right subtree.	
none	4	None; return to parent node.	
C	3	Return to parent node.	
E	2	Display contents of node.	E
E	2	Call *Inorder* with pointer to root (M) of right subtree.	
M	3	Call *Inorder* with pointer (nil) to root of left subtree.	
none	4	None; return to parent node.	
M	3	Display contents of node.	M
M	3	Call *Inorder* with pointer (nil) to root of right subtree.	
none	4	None; return to parent node.	
M	3	Return to parent node.	
E	2	Return to parent node.	
O	1	Display contents of node.	O
O	1	Call *Inorder* with pointer to root (U) of right subtree.	
U	2	Call *Inorder* with pointer to root (P) of left subtree.	
P	3	Call *Inorder* with pointer (nil) to root of left subtree.	
none	4	None; return to parent node.	
P	3	Display contents of node.	P
P	3	Call *Inorder* with pointer to root (T) of right subtree.	
T	4	Call *Inorder* with pointer (nil) to root of left subtree.	
none	5	None; return to parent node.	
T	4	Display contents of node.	T
T	4	Call *Inorder* with pointer (nil) to root of right subtree.	
none	5	None; return to parent node.	
T	4	Return to parent node.	
P	3	Return to parent node.	
U	2	Display contents of node.	U
U	2	Call *Inorder* with pointer (nil) to root of right subtree.	
none	3	None; return to parent node.	
U	2	Return to parent node.	
O	1	Terminate procedure; traversal complete.	

Notice that for this tree, an inorder traversal visits the nodes in alphabetical order,

C, E, M, O, P, T, U

The reason is that this binary tree is, in fact, a binary search tree, so that for each node, the value in the left child is less than the value in that node, which, in turn, is less than the value in the right child. This means that for each node, all of the values in the left subtree are smaller than the value in this node, which is less than all values in its right subtree. Because an inorder traversal is an LNR traversal, it follows that it must visit the nodes in ascending order.

Now that we have viewed binary trees, and BSTs in particular, as recursive data structures and have seen how easily traversal can be implemented by recursive procedures, we should reexamine the search and insert procedures considered in the preceding section. Recall that to search a BST we begin at the root. If it is the desired item, the search is finished; if the item we wish to find is less than the value in the root, we move down to the left subtree and search it; and if it is greater, we descend to the right subtree and search it. If the subtree we select is empty, we conclude that the item is not in the tree; otherwise, we search this subtree *in exactly the same manner* as we did the original tree. This means, therefore, that although we formulated our search procedure iteratively, we were, in fact, thinking recursively and could also have developed a recursive procedure like the following:

procedure *RecBSTSearch* (*Root* : *BinaryTreeType*; *KeyValue* : *KeyType*;
                          var *Found* : *boolean*;
                          var *LocPtr* : *BinTreePointer*);

(∗ Accepts: BST with root pointed to by *Root* and a *KeyValue*.
   Function: Recursively searches a BST for a node containing a
                specified *KeyValue* in its keyfield.
   Returns: *Found* is true and *LocPtr* points to a node containing
                KeyValue if the search is successful; otherwise, *Found*
                is false. ∗)

begin (∗ *RecBSTSearch* ∗)
  if *Root* = **nil** **then**   (∗ empty tree ∗)
    Found := *false*
  else   (∗ there is a nonempty tree to search ∗)
    if *KeyValue* < *Root*↑.*Data.Key* **then**   (∗ search left subtree ∗)
     RecBSTSearch (*Root*↑.*LChild*, *KeyValue*, *Found*, *LocPtr*)
    else if *KeyValue* > *Root*↑.*Data.Key* **then**
                              (∗ search right subtree ∗)
     RecBSTSearch (*Root*↑.*RChild*, *KeyValue*, *Found*, *LocPtr*)
    else   (∗ *KeyValue* found ∗)
      begin
        Found := *true*;
        LocPtr := *Root*
      end (∗ **else** ∗)
end (∗ *RecBSTSearch* ∗);

Because this procedure is not really more simple or understandable than the iterative version given in Section 9.2, in accord with the guidelines in Chapter 6 for choosing between a recursive and an iterative algorithm, we opt for the iterative version.

A recursive procedure for the insertion operation is, however, a bit easier than the iterative version. The obvious anchor is an empty BST, and we must specify how to insert an item into such a tree; otherwise, we can proceed recursively by inserting an item into the left subtree or the right subtree of the current node, according to whether the item is less than or greater than the value in this node.

procedure *RecBSTInsert* (**var** *Root* : *BinaryTreeType*;
                          Item : *BinTreeElementType*);

(∗ Accepts: BST with root pointed to by *Root* and a data *Item*.
  Function: Recursively inserts *Item* into the BST.
  Returns: Modified BST with root pointed to by *Root*. ∗)

```
begin (* RecBSTInsert *)
    if Root = nil then                          (* insert into empty tree *)
      begin
        new (Root);
        Root↑.Data := Item;
        Root↑.LChild := nil;
        Root↑.RChild := nil
      end (* if *)
    else                                        (* insert into: *)
      if Item.Key < Root↑.Data.Key then         (* left subtree *)
        RecBSTInsert (Root↑.LChild, Item)
      else if Item.Key > Root↑.Data.Key then    (* right subtree *)
        RecBSTInsert (Root↑.RChild, Item )
      else
        writeln ('Item already in the tree')
end (* RecBSTInsert *);
```

To delete a node x from a BST, we consider three cases:

1. x is a leaf.
2. x has one child.
3. x has two children.

The first case is easy. We simply set the appropriate pointer in x's parent to nil; this is the left or right pointer according to whether x is the left or the right child of its parent. For example, to delete the leaf node containing D in the following BST

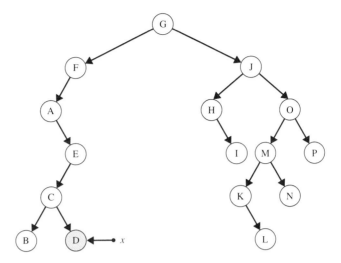

we can simply set the right pointer in its parent C to nil and then dispose of *x*:

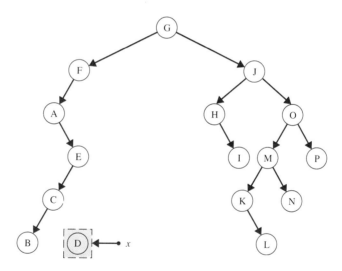

The second case, where the node *x* has exactly one child, is just as easy. Here we need only set the appropriate pointer in *x*'s parent to point to this child. For example, we can delete the node containing E in the BST of our example by simply setting the right pointer of its parent A to point to the node containing C and then dispose of *x*:

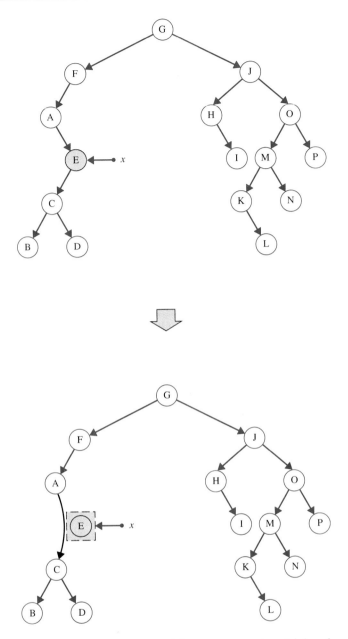

These two cases can be combined into one case in which x has at most one nonempty subtree. If the left pointer of x is nil, we set the appropriate pointer of x's parent to point to the right subtree of x (which may be empty—case 1); otherwise, we set it to point to the left subtree of x. The following statements handle both cases:

Subtree := $x\uparrow.LChild$;   (∗ pointer to a subtree of x ∗)
if *Subtree* = **nil then**
    Subtree := $x\uparrow.RChild$;

if *Parent* = **nil then**   (∗ root being deleted ∗)
  Root := *Subtree*
else if *Parent↑.LChild* = *x* **then**
  Parent↑.LChild := *Subtree*
else
  Parent↑.RChild := *Subtree*;

The third case, in which *x* has two children, can be reduced to one of the first two cases if we replace the value stored in node *x* by its inorder successor (or predecessor) and then delete this successor (predecessor). The inorder successor (predecessor) of the value stored in a given node of a BST is its successor (predecessor) in an inorder traversal of the BST.

To illustrate this case, consider again the following binary search tree, and suppose we wish to delete the node containing J:

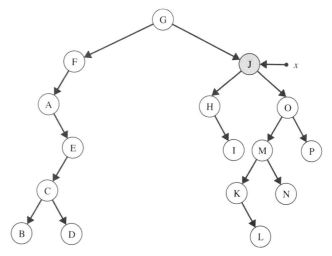

We can locate its inorder successor by starting at the right child of *x* and then descending left as far as possible. In our example, this inorder successor is the node containing K:

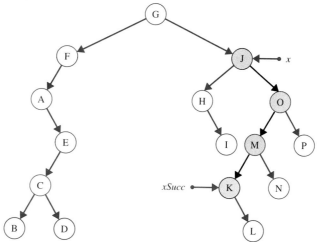

We replace the contents of x with this inorder successor:

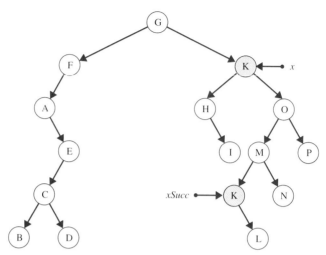

Now we need only delete the node pointed to by *XSucc*. We do this as described for cases 1 and 2, since this node will always have an empty left subtree (and perhaps an empty right subtree as well):

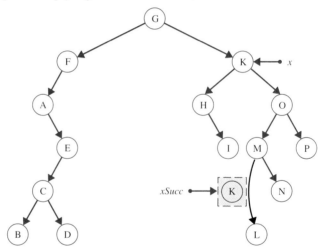

The following procedure implements the deletion operation for all cases, reducing case 3 to one of the first two cases, when necessary, in the manner we have just illustrated:

> **procedure** *BSTDelete* (**var** *Root* : *BinaryTreeType*;
>   *KeyValue* : *KeyType*);

> (∗ Accepts: A BST with root node pointed to by *Root* and a
>   *KeyValue*.
>   Function: Attempts to find a node in a BST containing *KeyValue*
>   in the keyfield of its data part and if successful, deletes
>   it from the BST.
>   Returns: Modified BST with root node pointed to by *Root*. ∗)

```
          var
            x,                        (* points to node containing KeyValue *)
            Parent,                   (* parent of x or xSucc *)
            xSucc,                    (* x's inorder successor *)
            Subtree : BinTreePointer; (* pointer to subtree of x *)
            Found : boolean;          (* true if KeyValue found *)
       begin (* BSTDelete *)
          BSTSearch2 (Root, KeyValue, Found, x, Parent);
          if not Found then
            writeln ('Item not in the binary search tree')
          else
            begin
              if (x↑.LChild <> nil) and (x↑.RChild <> nil) then
                begin                             (* node has two children *)
                  (* Find inorder successor and its parent *)
                  xSucc :=x↑.RChild;
                  Parent :=x;
                  while xSucc↑.LChild <> nil do    (* descend left *)
                    begin
                      Parent := xSucc;
                      xSucc := xSucc↑.LChild
                    end (* while *);
                  (* Move contents of xSucc to x and change x to point
                     to successor, which will be deleted. *)
                  x↑.Data := xSucc↑.Data;
                  x := xSucc
                end (* if node has 2 children *);

              (* Now proceed with case where node has 0 or 1 child. *)

              Subtree := x↑.LChild;
              if Subtree = nil then
                Subtree := x↑.RChild;
              if Parent = nil then                  (* root being deleted *)
                Root := Subtree
              else if Parent↑.LChild = x then       (* left child of parent *)
                Parent↑.LChild := Subtree
              else                                  (* right child of parent *)
                Parent↑.RChild := Subtree;
              dispose (x)
            end (* else *)
       end (* BSTDelete *)
```

This procedure uses the following modified form of the search procedure *BSTSearch* given in Section 9.3 to locate the node containing the item to be deleted and its parent:

```
procedure BSTSearch2 (Root : BinaryTreeType; KeyValue : KeyType ;
                      var Found : boolean;
                      var LocPtr, Parent : BinTreePointer);
```

(∗ Accepts: BST with root pointed to by *Root* and a *KeyValue*.
    Function: Searches a BST to locate a node containing *KeyValue* in
                  its keyfield and the parent of this node.
    Returns: *Found* is true, *LocPtr* points to a node containing
                  KeyValue and *Parent* points to the parent of this node,
                  if the search is successful; otherwise, *Found* is false. ∗)

begin (∗ *BSTSearch2* ∗)
    LocPtr := *Root*;   (∗ begin at the root ∗)
    Parent := **nil**;
    Found := *false*;
    while not *Found* **and** (*LocPtr* <> **nil**) **do**
        begin
            if *KeyValue* < *LocPtr*↑.*Data.Key* **then**
                begin   (∗ search left subtree∗)
                    Parent := *LocPtr*;
                    LocPtr := *LocPtr*↑.*LChild*
                end (∗ **if** ∗)
            else if *KeyValue* > *LocPtr*↑.*Data.Key* **then**
                begin   (∗ search right subtree ∗)
                    Parent := *LocPtr*;
                    LocPtr := *LocPtr*↑.*RChild*
                end (∗ **else if** ∗)
            else   (∗ *KeyValue* found ∗)
                Found := *true*
        end (∗ **while** ∗)
end (∗ *BSTSearch2* ∗);

It also is possible to design a recursive procedure for deletion from a
binary search tree. In this case, the necessary searching can be incorporated
into the deletion procedure. Note, however, that in the case that the node to be
deleted has two children, two descents into the the tree are made, the first to
find the node and the second to delete its successor node. (See Exercise 14 at
the end of this section.)

procedure *RecBSTDelete*(**var** *Root* : *BinaryTreeType*;
                                KeyValue : *KeyType*);

(∗ Accepts: A BST with root node pointed to by *Root* and a
                  KeyValue.
    Function: Recursively attempts to find a node in a BST containing
                  KeyValue in the keyfield of its data part and if
                  successful, deletes it from the BST.
    Returns: Modified BST with root node pointed to by *Root*. ∗)

var
    TempPtr : *BinTreePointer*;   (∗ auxiliary pointer ∗)

begin (* *RecBSTDelete* *)
   if *Root* = **nil then**   (* empty BST—item not found *)
    writeln('Item not in the binary search tree')
   else
    (* recursively search for the node containing *KeyValue* and
                                  delete it from the : *)
    if *KeyValue* < *Root*↑.*Data.Key* **then**   (* left subtree *)
      RecBSTDelete(*Root*↑.*LChild, KeyValue*)
    else if *KeyValue* > *Root*↑.*Data.Key* **then**   (* right subtree *)
      RecBSTDelete(*Root*↑.*RChild, KeyValue*)
    else   (* *KeyValue* found—delete node *)
     if *Root*↑.*LChild* = **nil then**
      begin
        TempPtr := *Root*↑.*RChild*;   (* no left child *)
        dispose(*Root*);
        Root := *TempPtr*
      end (* **if** *)
     else if *Root*↑.*RChild* = **nil then**
      begin
        TempPtr := *Root*↑.*LChild*;   (* left child, but no right *)
        dispose(*Root*);
        Root := *TempPtr*
      end (* **else if** *)
     else   (* two children *)
      begin
        (* find inorder successor *)
        TempPtr := *Root*↑.*RChild*;
        while *TempPtr*↑.*LChild* <> **nil do**
         TempPtr := *TempPtr*↑.*LChild*;

        (* Move contents of successor to the root of the subtree
          being examined and delete the successor node *)
        Root↑.*Data* := *TempPtr*↑.*Data*;
        RecBSTDelete (*Root*↑.*RChild, TempPtr*↑.*Data.Key*)
      end (* **else** *)
end (* *RecBSTDelete* *);

Exercises

1. For each of the following lists of Pascal reserved words,

    (a) Draw the binary search tree that is constructed when the words
        are inserted in the order given.
    (b) Perform inorder, preorder, and postorder traversals of the tree, and
        show the sequence of words that results in each case:

        (i) program, const, type, function, procedure, begin, end
        (ii) array, of, record, case, end, set, file
        (iii) div, mod, not, and, or, in, nil

(iv) **or, not, mod, in, div, and**
(v) **begin, end, if, then, else, case, while, do, repeat, until, for, to, downto, with**
(vi) **label, goto**

2. For each of the following, begin with the binary search tree

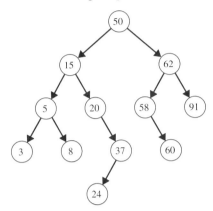

and show the BST that results after the operation or sequence of operations is performed:

(a) Insert 7.
(b) Insert 7, 1, 55, 29, and 19.
(c) Delete 8.
(d) Delete 8, 37, and 62.
(e) Insert 7, delete 8, insert 59, delete 60, insert 92, delete 50.

3. For the BST in Exercise 2, display the output produced by

(a) an inorder traversal.
(b) a preorder traversal.
(c) a postorder traversal.

4. Display the output produced by the following procedure for the BST of Exercise 2:

procedure *TraceInorder* (*Root* : *BinaryTreeType*);

```
begin (* TraceInorder *)
  if Root <> nil then
    begin
      write ('L');                        (* left *)
      TraceInorder (Root↑.LChild);
      writeln ('/', Root↑.Data.Key);
      write ('R');                        (* right *)
      TraceInorder (Root↑.RChild)
    end (* if *);
    write ('U')                           (* up *)
end (* TraceInorder *);
```

5. It is difficult to write a procedure to display a binary tree graphically, but it is easy to display enough information about a BST to reconstruct the tree. Write a procedure *DisplayPreOrder* that displays, in preorder, the key field of a node, its left child, and its right child. For example, the output of *DisplayPreorder* for the tree of Exercise 2 should be

Node.Key	LChild.Key	RChild.Key
========	==========	==========
50	15	62
15	5	20
5	3	8
3	-	-
.	.	.
.	.	.
.	.	.
58	-	60
60	-	-
91	-	-

6. For each of the following arithmetic expressions, draw a binary tree that represents the expression, and then use tree traversals to find the equivalent prefix and postfix expressions:

(a) $(A - B) - C$
(b) $A - (B - C)$
(c) $A / (B - (C - (D - (E - F))))$
(d) $((((A - B) - C) - D) - E) / F$
(e) $((A * (B + C)) / (D - (E + F))) * (G / (H / (I * J)))$

7. Assuming the array-based implementation of binary search trees described in Section 9.2, show the contents of an array used to store the BST in Exercise 2.

8. Repeat Exercise 7, but for the BSTs in Exercise 1.

9. Repeat Exercise 7, but for the BSTs in Exercise 6.

10. (a) A preorder traversal of a binary tree produced

   A D F G H K L P Q R W Z

   and an inorder traversal produced

   G F H K D L A W R Q P Z

   Draw the binary tree.

   (b) A postorder traversal of a binary tree produced

   F G H D A L P Q R Z W K

   and an inorder traversal gave the same result as in (a). Draw the binary tree.

   (c) Show by example that knowing the results of a preorder traversal and a postorder traversal of a binary tree does not uniquely determine the tree; that is, give an example of two different binary trees for which a preorder traversal of each gives the same result, and so does a postorder traversal.

11. **(a)** Write a recursive function *LeafCount* to count the leaves in a binary tree. (*Hint*: How is the number of leaves in the entire tree related to the number of leaves in the left and right subtrees of the root?)

    (b) Test the function *LeafCount*. Generate binary trees using the procedure *GenerateBST* in Exercise 5 of Section 9.3, display them using *DisplayPreOrder* (see Exercise 5 of this section), and then count the leaves using *LeafCount*.

12. **(a)** Write a nonrecursive procedure *NonRecInorder* to perform inorder traversal. (Use a stack of pointers to eliminate the recursion.)

    (b) Test the procedure *NonRecInorder*. Generate binary trees using the procedure *GenerateBST* in Exercise 5 of Section 9.3 and then traverse them using *NonRecInorder*.

13. **(a)** Write a procedure *LevelByLevel* to traverse a tree level by level; that is, first visit the root, then all nodes on level 1 (children of the root), then all nodes on level 2, and so on. Nodes on the same level should be visited in order from left to right. (*Hint*: Write a nonrecursive procedure, and use a queue of pointers.)

    (b) Test the procedure *LevelByLevel*. Generate binary trees using the procedure *GenerateBST* in Exercise 5 of Section 9.3 and then traverse them using *LevelByLevel*.

14. Trace the execution of the procedure *RecBSTDelete* for the tree in Exercise 2 as it deletes the following nodes. For each, start with the original tree and draw the subtree that is being processed on each recursive call to *RecBSTDelete*.

    (a) 24   **(b)** 58   **(c)** 37   **(d)** 15   **(e)** 5

15. Write a program to process a BST whose nodes contain characters. The user should be allowed to select from the following menu of options:

    I followed by a character: To insert a character
    S followed by a character: To search for a character
    TI: for inorder traversal
    TP: for preorder traversal
    TR: for postorder traversal
    QU: to quit

16. Write a *spell checker*, that is, a program that reads the words in a piece of text and looks up each of them in a *dictionary* to check its spelling. Use a BST to store this dictionary, reading the list of words from a file. While checking the spelling of words in a piece of text, the program should print a list of all words not found in the dictionary.

17. In Section 7.7 we designed a program for constructing a ***text concordance***, which is an alphabetical listing of all the distinct words in a piece of text. The basic storage structure for such a concordance was an array of pointers to ordered linked lists, one for words beginning with A, another for words beginning with B, and so on. Write a program that reads a piece of text, constructs a concordance that contains the distinct words that appear in the text and for each word, the line (or page) number of its first occurrence, and then allows the user to search for this concordance. Use an array of pointers to BSTs as a storage structure for the concordance.

18. Extend the program in Exercise 17, so that an ordered linked list of *all* occurrences of each word is stored. When the concordance is searched for a particular word, the program should display the line (or page) numbers of all occurrences of this word. The data structure used for the concordance is thus constructed from a good sample of those we have been studying: an *array* of *binary search trees*, each of whose nodes stores a *record*, one of whose fields is a *string* and another of whose fields is an *ordered linked list.*

19. (Project) For a certain company, the method by which the pay for each employee is computed depends on whether that employee is classified as an *Office* employee, a *Factory* employee, or a *SalesRep*. Suppose that a file of employee records is maintained in which each record is a variant record containing the following information for each employee:

Name (string).
Social security number (string).
Age (integer).
Number of dependents (integer).
Employee code (character O, F, S, representing *Office, Factory,* and *SalesRep*, respectively).
Hourly rate if employee is *Factory.*
Annual salary if employee is *Office.*
A base pay (real) and a commission percentage (real) if employee is *SalesRep.*

Write a menu-driven program that allows the user to select at least the following options:

GET: Get the records from the employee file and store them in a binary search tree, sorted so that the names are in alphabetical order.

INS: Insert the record for a new employee into the BST.

UPD: Update the record of an employee already in the tree.

RET: Retrieve and display the record for a specified employee (by name or by social security number).

LIS: List the records (or perhaps selected items in the records) in order. This option should allow the following suboptions:

ALL—to list for all employees
OFF—to list for only *Office* employees
FAC—to list for only *Factory*
SAL—to list for only *SalesRep*

SAV: Copy the records from the BST into a permanent file.
DEL: Delete the record of an employee from the BST.

9.5   Application of Binary Trees: Huffman Codes

In Section 9.2 we indicated how a binary tree can be used in various encoding and decoding problems. In particular we showed part of a binary tree for the Morse code, which represents each character by a sequence of dots and dashes. Unlike ASCII and EBCDIC coding schemes, in which the length of the code is the same for all characters, Morse code uses variable-length sequences. In this section we consider another coding scheme, Huffman codes, that uses variable-length codes.

The basic idea in these variable-length coding schemes is to use shorter codes for those characters that occur more frequently and longer codes for those used less frequently. For example, 'E' in Morse code is a single dot, whereas 'Z' is represented as $- - \cdot \cdot$. The objective is to minimize the expected length of the code for a character. This reduces the number of bits that must be sent when transmitting encoded messages. These variable-length coding schemes are also useful when compressing data because they reduce the number of bits that must be stored.

To state the problem more precisely, suppose that some character set $\{C_1, C_2, \ldots, C_n\}$ is given, and certain weights $w_1, w_2, \ldots, w_n$ are associated with these characters; w_i is the weight attached to character C_i and is a measure (e.g., probability or relative frequency) of how frequently this character occurs in messages to be encoded. If $l_1, l_2, \ldots, l_n$ are the lengths of the codes for characters $C_1, C_2, \ldots, C_n$, respectively, then the **expected length** of the code for any one of these characters is given by

$$\text{expected length} = w_1 l_1 + w_2 l_2 + \cdots + w_n l_n = \sum_{i=1}^{n} w_i l_i$$

As a simple example, consider the five characters A, B, C, D, and E, and suppose they occur with the following weights (probabilities):

character	A	B	C	D	E
weight	0.2	0.1	0.1	0.15	0.45

In Morse code with a dot replaced by 0 and a dash by 1, these characters are encoded as follows:

Character	Code
A	01
B	1000
C	1010
D	100
E	0

Thus the expected length of the code for each of these five letters in this scheme is

$$0.2 \times 2 + 0.1 \times 4 + 0.1 \times 4 + 0.15 \times 3 + 0.45 \times 1 = 2.1$$

Another useful property of some coding schemes is that they are **immediately decodable.** This means that no sequence of bits that represents a character is a prefix of a longer sequence for some other character. Consequently, when a sequence of bits is received that is the code for a character, it can be decoded as that character immediately, without waiting to see whether subsequent bits change it into a longer code for some other character. Note that the preceding Morse code scheme is not immediately decodable because, for example, the code for E (0) is a prefix of the code for A (01), and the code for D (100) is a prefix of the code for B (1000). (For decoding, Morse code uses a third "bit," a pause, to separate letters.) A coding scheme for which the code lengths are the same as in the preceding scheme and that is immediately decodable is as follows:

Character	Code
A	01
B	0000
C	0001
D	001
E	1

The following algorithm, given by D. A. Huffman in 1952, can be used to construct coding schemes that are immediately decodable and for which each character has a minimal expected code length:

HUFFMAN'S ALGORITHM

(* Accepts: A set of n characters $\{C_1, C_2, \ldots, C_n\}$ and a set of weights $\{w_1, w_2, \ldots, w_n\}$, where w_i is the weight of character C_i.

Function: Constructs a binary code for a given set of characters for which the expected length of the bit string for a given character is minimal.

Returns A collection of n bit strings representing codes for the characters. *)

1. Initialize a list of one-node binary trees containing the weights w_1, w_2, ..., w_n, one for each of the characters C_1, C_2, ..., C_n.
2. Do the following $n - 1$ times:
   a. Find two trees T' and T'' in this list with roots of minimal weights w' and w''.
   b. Replace these two trees with a binary tree whose root is $w' + w''$, and whose subtrees are T' and T'', and label the pointers to these subtrees 0 and 1, respectively:

3. The code for character C_i is the bit string labeling a path in the final binary tree from the root to the leaf for C_i.

As an illustration of Huffman's algorithm, consider again the characters A, B, C, D, and E with the weights given earlier. We begin by constructing a list of one-node binary trees, one for each character:

The first two trees to be selected are those corresponding to letters B and C, since they have the smallest weights, and these are combined to produce a tree having weight $0.1 + 0.1 = 0.2$ and having these two trees as subtrees:

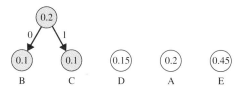

From this list of four binary trees, we again select two of minimal weights, the first and the second (or the second and the third), and replace them with another tree having weight $0.2 + 0.15 = 0.35$ and having these two trees as subtrees:

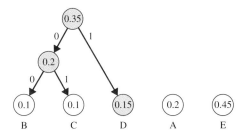

From this list of three binary trees, the first two have minimal weights and are combined to produce a binary tree having weight $0.35 + 0.2 = 0.55$ and having these trees as subtrees:

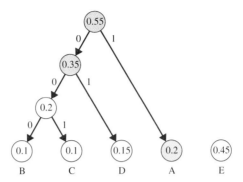

The resulting binary tree is then combined with the one-node tree representing E to produce the final Huffman tree:

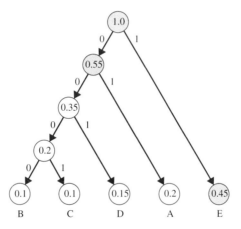

The Huffman codes obtained from this tree are as follows:

Character	Huffman Code
A	01
B	0000
C	0001
D	001
E	1

As we calculated earlier, the expected length of the code for each of these characters is 2.1.

A different assignment of codes to these characters for which the expected length is also 2.1 is possible because at the second stage we had two choices for trees of minimal weight:

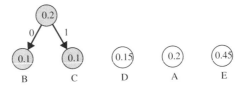

We selected the first and second trees from this list, but we could have used the second and third:

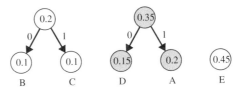

At the next stage, the resulting list of two binary trees would have been

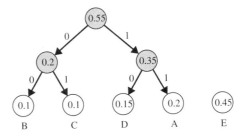

and the final Huffman tree would be

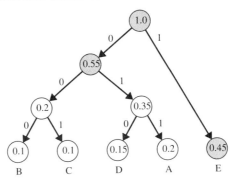

The assignment of codes corresponding to this tree is

Character	Huffman Code
A	011
B	000
C	001
D	010
E	1

The immediate decodability property of Huffman codes is clear. Each character is associated with a leaf node in the Huffman tree, and there is a unique path from the root of a tree to each leaf. Consequently, no sequence of bits comprising the code for some character can be a prefix of a longer sequence of bits for some other character.

Because of this property of immediate decodability, a decoding algorithm is easy:

HUFFMAN DECODING ALGORITHM

(∗ Accepts: A Huffmann tree and a bit string representing some
                       message that was encoded using the Huffman tree.
    Function: Decodes the message.
    Output: The decoded message. ∗)

1. Initialize pointer p to the root of the Huffman tree.
2. While the end of the message string has not been reached, do the following:
    a. Let x be the next bit in the string.
    b. If $x = 0$ then
          Set p equal to its left child pointer.
       Else
          Set p equal to its right child pointer.
    c. If p points to a leaf then
              i. Display the character associated with that leaf.
             ii. Reset p to the root of the Huffman tree.

As an illustration, suppose that the message string

0 1 0 1 0 1 1 0 1 0

is received and that this message was encoded using the second Huffman tree constructed earlier. The pointer follows the path labeled 010 from the root of this tree to the letter D and is then reset to the root:

$$\boxed{0 \quad 1 \quad 0} \quad 1 \quad 0 \quad 1 \quad 1 \quad 0 \quad 1 \quad 0$$
$$\quad\quad D$$

The next bit, 1, leads immediately to the letter E:

$$\boxed{0 \quad 1 \quad 0}\boxed{1} \quad 0 \quad 1 \quad 1 \quad 0 \quad 1 \quad 0$$
$$\quad\quad D \quad\; E$$

The pointer p next follows the path 011 to the letter A,

$$\boxed{0 \quad 1 \quad 0}\boxed{1}\boxed{0 \quad 1 \quad 1} \quad 0 \quad 1 \quad 0$$
$$\quad\quad D \quad\; E \quad\;\; A$$

and finally the path 010 to the letter D again:

$$\boxed{0 \quad 1 \quad 0}\boxed{1}\boxed{0 \quad 1 \quad 1}\boxed{0 \quad 1 \quad 0}$$
$$\quad\quad D \quad\; E \quad\;\; A \quad\quad D$$

The program in Figure 9.2 implements this decoding algorithm. The procedure *BuildDecodingTree* initializes a tree consisting of a single node and then reads letters and their codes from a code file and constructs the decoding tree. For each letter in the file, it calls procedure *AddToTree* to follow a path determined by the code of the character, creating nodes as necessary. When the end of the code string is reached, the character is inserted in the last (leaf) node created on this path. The procedure *Decode* is then called to read a message string of bits from *MessageFile* and to decode it using the decoding tree. Procedure *PrintTree* is included in this program simply to give an idea of what the tree looks like. It is basically nothing more than an *RNL* traversal of the tree. It prints the tree "on its side" without the directed arcs and 0/1 labels. We leave it to the reader to draw these in and then rotate the tree 90 degrees so it has its usual orientation.

```
PROGRAM HuffmanDecoding (input, output, CodeFile, MessageFile);

(************************************************************

   Input (file):    Text files CodeFile and MessageFile.
   Function:        Decodes a message in MessageFile using a Huffman
                    decoding tree.  Allowed characters and their
                    codes (assumed to have been assigned using
                    Huffman's algorithm) are read from CodeFile.
   Output (screen): A graphical representation of the Huffman tree
                    and the decoded message.

************************************************************)

CONST
#include 'STRING-CONST'   (* StringLimit *)

TYPE
#include 'STRING-TYPE'    (* String *)
   BitString = String;
   BinTreeElementType = char;
   BinTreePointer = ^BinTreeNode;
   BinTreeNode = RECORD
                   Data : BinTreeElementType;
                   LChild, RChild : BinTreePointer;
                 END;
   BinaryTreeType = BinTreePointer;

VAR
   CodeFile,               (* file containing characters and their codes *)
   MessageFile : text;     (* file containing message to be decoded *)
   Root : BinTreePointer;  (* pointer to root of decoding tree *)

#include 'STRING-OPS'     (* ReadString *)
```

Figure 9.2

Figure 9.2 (*cont.*)

```
PROCEDURE BuildDecodingTree (VAR Root : BinaryTreeType;
                            VAR CodeFile : text);

   (*******************************************************************

      Input (file):   Text file CodeFile.
      Function:       Reads characters and their codes (assumed to be
                      found using Huffman's algorithm) from CodeFile
                      and constructs the Huffman decoding tree.
      Output (param): A pointer to the Root of the Huffman tree.

   *******************************************************************)

   VAR
      Ch,                   (* character read from CodeFile *)
      Blank : char;         (* blank read (and ignored) in CodeFile *)
      Code : BitString;     (* Huffman code for Ch *)

   PROCEDURE AddToTree (Ch : char; Code : BitString; CodeLen : integer;
                        Root : BinaryTreeType);

      (*******************************************************************

         Input (param):  A character Ch, a bit string Code, an integer
                         CodeLen, and a pointer to the Root of a
                         Huffman decoding tree.
         Function:       Creates a node for character Ch whose Code is
                         a bit string of length CodeLen and adds it to
                         the Huffman decoding tree with root node
                         pointed to by Root.
         Output (param): Modified Huffman tree with specified Root.

      *******************************************************************)

      VAR
         i : integer;       (* index in Code *)
         TempPtr,           (* pointer to new node(s) *)
         p : BinTreePointer; (* pointer to nodes in path labeled by Code *)

   BEGIN (* AddToTree *)
      i := 1;
      p := Root;
      WHILE i <= CodeLen DO
         IF Code[i] = '0' THEN                (* descend left *)
            BEGIN
               IF p^.LChild = NIL THEN        (* create node along path *)
                  BEGIN
                     new (TempPtr);
                     TempPtr^.Data := '*';
                     TempPtr^.LChild := NIL;
                     TempPtr^.RChild := NIL;
                     p^.LChild := TempPtr
                  END (* IF *);
               i := i + 1;
               p := p^.LChild
            END (* IF 0 *)
```

Figure 9.2 (*cont.*)

```
            ELSE IF Code[i] = '1' THEN              (* descend right *)
                BEGIN
                    IF p^.RChild = NIL THEN         (* create node along path *)
                        BEGIN
                            new (TempPtr);
                            TempPtr^.Data := '*';
                            TempPtr^.LChild := NIL;
                            TempPtr^.RChild := NIL;
                            p^.RChild := TempPtr;
                        END (* IF *);
                    i := i + 1;
                    p := p^.RChild
                END (* ELSE IF 1 *);
        p^.Data := Ch
    END (* AddToTree *);

BEGIN (* BuildDecodingTree *)
    new (Root);
    Root^.Data := '*';
    Root^.LChild := NIL;
    Root^.RChild := NIL;
    reset (CodeFile);
    WHILE NOT eof(CodeFile) DO
        BEGIN
            read (CodeFile, Ch, Blank);
            ReadString (CodeFile, Code);
            AddToTree (Ch, Code, Length(Code), Root)
        END (* WHILE *)
END (* BuildDecodingTree *);

PROCEDURE PrintTree (Root : BinaryTreeType; Indent : integer);

(*****************************************************************

    Input (param):   A pointer to the Root of a binary tree and an
                     integer Indent.
    Function:        Uses recursion to display a binary tree.    The
                     tree is displayed "on its side" with each level
                     indented by a specified value Indent, but with
                     no arcs sketched in.
    Output (screen): Graphical representation of the binary tree.

*****************************************************************)

BEGIN (* PrintTree *)
    IF Root <> NIL THEN
        BEGIN
            PrintTree (Root^.RChild, Indent + 8);
            writeln (Root^.Data:Indent);
            PrintTree (Root^.LChild, Indent + 8)
        END (* IF *)
END (* PrintTree *);
```

Figure 9.2 (*cont.*)

```
PROCEDURE Decode (Root : BinaryTreeType; VAR MessageFile : text);

   (***********************************************************************

      Input (param):    A Pointer to Root of a Huffman decoding tree.
      Input (file):     The text file MessageFile.
      Function:         Reads a message (string of bits) from
                        MessageFile and decodes it using the Huffman
                        decoding tree.
      Output (screen):  Decoded message.

   ***********************************************************************)

   VAR
      Bit : char;              (* next message bit *)
      p : BinTreePointer;      (* pointer to trace path in decoding tree *)
   BEGIN (* Decode *)
      reset (MessageFile);
      WHILE NOT eof(MessageFile) DO
         BEGIN
            p := Root;
            WHILE (p^.LChild <> NIL) OR (p^.RChild <> NIL) DO
               BEGIN
                  read (MessageFile, Bit);
                  write (Bit);
                  IF Bit = '0' THEN
                     p := p^.LChild
                  ELSE IF Bit = '1' THEN
                     p := p^.RChild
                  ELSE
                     writeln ('Illegal bit:  ', Bit, ' -- ignored');
                  IF eoln(MessageFile) THEN
                     readln (MessageFile);
               END (* WHILE *);
            writeln ('--', p^.Data)
         END (* WHILE *)
   END (* Decode *);

BEGIN (* main program *)
   BuildDecodingTree (Root, CodeFile);
   PrintTree(Root, 8);
   writeln; writeln;
   Decode (Root, MessageFile);
END (* main program *).
```

Figure 9.2 (*cont.*)

Listing of CodeFile:

```
A 1101
B 001101
C 01100
D 0010
E 101
F 111100
G 001110
H 0100
I 1000
J 11111100
K 11111101
L 01111
M 01101
N 1100
O 1110
P 111101
Q 111111100
R 1001
S 0101
T 000
U 01110
V 001100
W 001111
X 111111101
Y 111110
Z 11111111
```

Listing of MessageFile:

```
000010010110011010010
01100111011010000101
11011001101011001100110110001100001110
```

Figure 9.2 (*cont.*)

Sample run:

```
                                                          Z
                                                  *
                                                      *
                                                          X
                                          *
                                                      *
                                                          Q
                                                  *
                                                      *
                                                          K
                                      *
                                      *
                                                          J
                              *
                          *
                                      Y
                      *
                              *
                                      P
              *
                                      F
          *
                  O
      *
              *
                  A
  *
          E
      *
              R
          *
              I
*
                  L
          *
                  U
      *
                  M
          *
                  C
      *
              S
          *
              H
  *
                          W
                  *
                          G
              *
                          B
          *
                          V
      *
                  D
  *
          T
```

Figure 9.2 (*cont.*)

```
000--T
0100--H
101--E
1001--R
101--E
0010--D
01100--C
1110--O
1101--A
000--T
0101--S
1101--A
1001--R
101--E
01100--C
1110--O
01101--M
1000--I
1100--N
001110--G
```

Exercises

1. Demonstrate that Morse code is not immediately decodable by showing that the bit string 100001100 can be decoded in more than one way.

2. Using the first Huffman code given in this section (A = 01, B = 0000, C = 0001, D = 001, E = 1), decode the following bit strings:

   (a) 000001001
   (b) 001101001
   (c) 000101001
   (d) 00001010011001

3. Construct the Huffman code for the Pascal reserved words and weights given in the following table:

Words	Weight
begin	.30
end	.30
for	.05
if	.20
while	.15

4. Repeat Exercise 3 for the following table of letters and weights:

Character	Weight
a	.20
b	.10
c	.08
d	.08
e	.40
f	.05
g	.05
h	.04

5. Using the Huffman code developed in Exercise 4, encode the following message: "feed a deaf aged hag."

6. Repeat Exercise 3 for the following table of Pascal reserved words and weights (frequencies):

Words	Weight
begin	22
case	2
do	20
downto	2
else	10
end	24
for	5
goto	1
if	20
repeat	4
then	20
to	3
until	4
while	15
with	2

7. Write a procedure that reads a table of letters and their weights and constructs a Huffman code for these letters.

8. Use the procedure of Exercise 7 in a program that encodes a message that the user enters.

9. (Project) Write a program to compress a text file using a Huffman code and to decompress a file generated using this code. The program should first read through the text file and determine the number of occurrences of each character in the file and the total number of characters in the file. The weight of each character will be the frequency count for that character. The program should then use these weights to construct the Huffman codes for the characters in the file. It should then read the file again and encode it using these Huffman codes and generate a file containing this encoded data. Compute the compression ratio, which is the number of bits in the compressed file divided by the total number of bits in the original file (eight times the number of characters in the file). The program should also provide the option of decompressing a file that was encoded using this Huffman code.

10

Sorting

In this chapter we consider the problem of sorting a list,

$$X_1, X_2, \ldots, X_n$$

that is, arranging the list elements so that they (or some key fields in them) are in ascending order,

$$X_1 \leq X_2 \leq \cdots \leq X_n$$

or in descending order

$$X_1 \geq X_2 \geq \cdots \geq X_n$$

We begin by considering some of the sorting schemes typically studied in introductory programming courses. Although these are for the most part fairly easy to understand and to implement in programs, they are not very efficient, especially for large data sets. Thus we also look at two of the more efficient sorting schemes, heapsort and quicksort.

10.1 Some O(n^2) Sorting Schemes

One classification of sorting schemes consists of three categories: *selection sorts, exchange sorts,* and *insertion sorts.* We begin our discussion of sorting algorithms by considering one simple sorting scheme from each of these categories.

Selection Sorts. The basic idea of a selection sort of a list is to make a number of passes through the list or a part of the list and, on each pass, to select one element to be correctly positioned. For example, on each pass through a sublist, the smallest element in this sublist might be found and then moved to its proper location.

As an illustration, suppose that the following list is to be sorted into ascending order:

67, 33, 21, 84, 49, 50, 75

We scan the list to locate the smallest element and find it in position 3:

67 , 33 , 21 , 84 , 49 , 50 , 75

We interchange this element with the first element and thus properly position the smallest element at the beginning of the list:

21 , 33 , 67 , 84 , 49 , 50 , 75

We now scan the sublist consisting of the elements from position 2 on to find the smallest element:

21 , 33 , 67 , 84 , 49 , 50 , 75

and exchange it with the second element (itself in this case) and thus properly position the next-to-smallest element in position 2:

21 , 33 , 67 , 84 , 49 , 50 , 75

We continue in this manner, locating the smallest element in the sublist of elements from position 3 on and interchanging it with the third element, then properly positioning the smallest element in the sublist of elements from position 4 on, and so on until we eventually do this for the sublist consisting of the last two elements:

21 , 33 , 49 , 84 , 67 , 50 , 75

21 , 33 , 49 , 50 , 67 , 84 , 75

21 , 33 , 49 , 50 , 67 , 84 , 75

21 , 33 , 49 , 50 , 67 , 75 , 84

Positioning the smallest element in this last sublist obviously also positions the last element correctly and thus completes the sort.

An algorithm for this simple selection sort was given in Section 6.4 for lists stored in arrays:

SIMPLE SELECTION SORT FOR ARRAY-BASED LISTS

(* Accepts: A list of n elements stored in an array $X[1]$, $X[2], \ldots , X[n]$.

Function: Sorts the list into ascending order using simple selection sort.

Returns: The sorted list. *)

For $i = 1$ to $n - 1$ do the following:

(* On the ith pass, first find the smallest element in the sublist $X[i], \ldots , X[n]$. *)

   a. Set *SmallPos* equal to i.
   b. Set *Smallest* equal to $X[SmallPos]$.
   c. For $j = i + 1$ to n do the following:
     If $X[j] <$ *Smallest* then (* smaller element found *)
       i. Set *SmallPos* equal to j.
       ii. Set *Smallest* equal to $X[SmallPos]$.

(* Now interchange this smallest element with the element at the beginning of this sublist.*)

   d. Set $X[SmallPos]$ equal to $X[i]$.
   e. Set $X[i]$ equal to *Smallest*.

A version that can be used for linked lists is just as easy. We need only replace the indices i and j with pointers that move through the list and sublists. Using the notation introduced in Section 7.2 for abstract linked lists, we can express this algorithm as

SIMPLE SELECTION SORT FOR LINKED LISTS

(* Accepts: A list of elements stored in a linked list.

Function: Sorts the list into ascending order using simple selection sort.

Returns: The sorted list. *)

1. Initialize pointer p to the first node.
2. While $p \neq$ nil do the following:

(* First find the smallest element in the sublist pointed to by p. *)

   a. Set pointer *SmallPtr* equal to p.
   b. Set *Smallest* equal to *Data(SmallPtr)*.
   c. Set pointer q equal to *Next(p)*.
   d. While $q \neq$ nil do the following:
     i. If *Data(q)* $<$ *Smallest* then   (* smaller element found *)
       Set *SmallPtr* equal to q and *Smallest* equal to *Data(q)*.
     ii. Set q equal to *Next(q)*.

(* Now interchange this smallest element with the element in the node at the beginning of this sublist. *)

e. Set *Data(SmallPtr)* equal to *Data(p)*.
f. Set *Data(p)* equal to *Smallest*.
g. Set *p* equal to *Next(p)*.

In Section 6.4 we derived a worst-case computing time of O(n^2) for this sorting method. This is, in fact, the computing time for all cases. On the first pass through the list, the first item is compared with each of the $n - 1$ elements that follow it; on the second pass, the second element is compared with the $n - 2$ elements following it; and so on. A total of

$$(n - 1) + (n - 2) + \cdots + 2 + 1 = \frac{n(n - 1)}{2}$$

comparisons is thus required for any list, and it follows that the computing time is O(n^2) in all cases.

Exchange Sorts. Unlike selection sorts, in which some element is selected and then moved to its correct position in the list, exchange sorts systematically interchange pairs of elements that are out of order until eventually no such pairs remain and the list is therefore sorted. One simple example of an exchange sort is **bubble sort.** Although this sorting scheme is very inefficient, it is quite simple and is therefore commonly taught in introductory programming courses.

To illustrate bubble sort, consider again the list

67 , 33 , 21 , 84 , 49 , 50 , 75

On the first pass, we compare the first two elements, 67 and 33, and interchange them because they are out of order:

67 , 33 , 21 , 84 , 49 , 50 , 75

33 , 67 , 21 , 84 , 49 , 50 , 75

Now we compare the second and third elements, 67 and 21, and interchange them:

33 , 67 , 21 , 84 , 49 , 50 , 75

33 , 21 , 67 , 84 , 49 , 50 , 75

Next we compare 67 and 84 but do not interchange them because they are already in the correct order:

33 , 21 , 67 , 84 , 49 , 50 , 75

33 , 21 , 67 , 84 , 49 , 50 , 75

Next, 84 and 49 are compared and interchanged:

33 , 21 , 67 , 84 , 49 , 50 , 75

33 , 21 , 67 , 49 , 84 , 50 , 75

Then 84 and 50 are compared and interchanged:

33 , 21 , 67 , 49 , 84 , 50 , 75

33 , 21 , 67 , 49 , 50 , 84 , 75

Finally 84 and 75 are compared and interchanged:

33 , 21 , 67 , 49 , 50 , 84 , 75

33 , 21 , 67 , 49 , 50 , 75 , 84

The first pass through the list is now complete.

We are guaranteed that on this pass, the largest element in the list will "sink" to the end of the list, since it will obviously be moved past all smaller elements. But notice also that some of the smaller items have "bubbled up" toward their proper positions nearer the front of the list.

We now scan the list again, but this time we leave out the last item because it is already in its proper position.

33 , 21 , 67 , 49 , 50 , 75 , 84

The comparisons and interchanges that take place on this pass are summarized in the following diagram:

33 , 21 , 67 , 49 , 50 , 75 , 84

21 , 33 , 67 , 49 , 50 , 75 , 84

21 , 33 , 67 , 49 , 50 , 75 , 84

21 , 33 , 49 , 67 , 50 , 75 , 84

21 , 33 , 49 , 50 , 67 , 75 , 84

21 , 33 , 49 , 50 , 67 , 75 , 84

On this pass, the last element involved in an interchange was in position 5, which means that this element and all those that follow it have been properly positioned and can thus be omitted on the next pass.

On the next pass, therefore, we consider only the sublist consisting of the elements in positions 1 through 4:

21, 33, 49, 50, 67, 75, 84

In scanning this sublist, we find that no interchanges are necessary, and so we conclude that the sorting is complete.

The details of this sorting scheme are given in the following algorithm:

BUBBLE SORT

(* Accepts: A list of elements $X_1, X_2, \ldots, X_n$.
Function: Bubble-sorts the list into ascending order.
Returns: The sorted list. *)

1. Initialize *NumPairs* to $n - 1$.
   (* *NumPairs* is the number of pairs to be compared on the current pass. *)

2. Repeat the following steps:
   a. Set *Last* equal to 1.
      (* *Last* marks the location of the last element involved in an interchange. *)
   b. For $i = 1$ to *NumPairs* do:
          If $X_i > X_{i+1}$ then:
            i. Interchange X_i and X_{i+1}.
            ii. Set *Last* equal to i.
   c. Set *NumPairs* equal to $Last - 1$.
   Until *NumPairs* = 0.

The worst case for bubble sort occurs when the list elements are in reverse order because in this case, only one item (the largest) is positioned correctly on each pass through the list. On the first pass through the list, $n - 1$ comparisons and interchanges are made, and only the largest element is correctly positioned. On the next pass, the sublist consisting of the first $n - 1$ elements is scanned; there are $n - 2$ comparisons and interchanges; and the next largest element sinks to position $n - 1$. This continues until the sublist consisting of the first two elements is scanned, and on this pass, there is one comparison and interchange. Thus, a total of $(n - 1) + (n - 2) + \cdots + 1 = n(n - 1) / 2$ comparisons and interchanges is required. The instructions that carry out these comparisons and interchanges are the instructions in the algorithm executed most often. It follows that the worst-case computing time for bubble sort is O(n^2). The average computing time is also O(n^2), but this is considerably more difficult to show.

Insertion Sorts. Insertion sorts are based on the same idea as the algorithms for inserting new elements into ordered linked lists described in Chapter 7: repeatedly insert a new element into a list of already sorted elements so that the resulting list is still sorted.

The method used is similar to that used by a card player when putting cards into order as they are dealt. To illustrate, suppose that the first card dealt is a 7. (We will ignore all other attributes, such as suit or color.) This card is trivially in its proper place in the hand:

When the second card is dealt, it is inserted into its proper place, either before or after the first card. For example, if the second card is a 2, it is placed to the left of the 7:

When the third card is dealt, it is inserted into its proper place among the first two cards so that the resulting three-card hand is properly ordered. For example, if it is a 4, the 7 is moved to make room for the 4, which must be inserted between the 2 and the 7:

This process continues. At each stage the newly dealt card is inserted into the proper place among the cards already in the hand so that the newly formed hand is ordered:

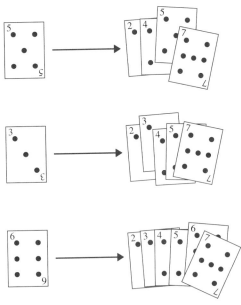

The following algorithm describes this procedure for lists stored in arrays. At the ith stage, X_i is inserted into its proper place among the already sorted

$X_1, X_2, \ldots, X_{i-1}$. We do this by comparing X_i with each of these elements, starting from the right end, and shifting them to the right as necessary. We use array position 0 to store a copy of X_i to prevent "falling off the left end" in these right-to-left scans.

LINEAR INSERTION SORT

(* Accepts: A list of n elements stored in an array $X[1], X[2], \ldots,$
                $X[n]$.

   Function: Sorts the list into ascending order using linear insertion sort.

   Returns: The sorted list.

   Note: Position 0 in the array is used to store the list element being inserted. *)

For $i = 2$ to n do the following:

    (* Insert $X[i]$ into its proper position among $X[1], \ldots, X[i - 1]$. *)
      a. Set *NextElement* equal to $X[i]$.
      b. Set $X[0]$ equal to *NextElement*.
      c. Set j equal to i.
      d. While *NextElement* $< X[j - 1]$ do the following:

          (* Shift element to right to open up spot. *)
          i. Set $X[j]$ equal to $X[j - 1]$.
          ii. Decrement j by 1.

    (* Now drop *NextElement* into the open spot. *)
      e. Set $X[j]$ equal to *NextElement*.

The following sequence of diagrams demonstrates this algorithm for the list 67, 33, 21, 84, 49, 50, 75. The sorted sublist produced at each stage is highlighted.

67,	33,	21,	84,	49,	50,	75	Initial sorted sublist of 1 element
33,	67,	21,	84,	49,	50,	75	Insert 33 to get 2-element sorted sublist
21,	33,	67,	84,	49,	50,	75	Insert 21 to get 3-element sorted sublist
21,	33,	67,	84,	49,	50,	75	Insert 84 to get 4-element sorted sublist
21,	33,	49,	67,	84,	50,	75	Insert 49 to get 5-element sorted sublist
21,	33,	49,	50,	67,	84,	75	Insert 50 to get 6-element sorted sublist
21,	33,	49,	50,	67,	75,	84	Insert 75 to get 7-element sorted sublist

The worst case for linear insertion sort is once again the case in which the list elements are in reverse order. Inserting $X[2]$ requires two comparisons (with $X[1]$ and then with $X[0]$), inserting $X[3]$ requires three, and so on. The total number of comparisons is thus

$$2 + 3 + \cdots + n = \frac{n(n + 1)}{2} - 1$$

so the computing time is again O(n^2). This is also the average-case computing time, since one would expect that on the average, the item being inserted must be compared with one half the items in the already sorted sublist.

Linear insertion sort can also be used with linked lists. For singly linked lists, however, the algorithm obviously is quite different from the preceding one because we have direct access to only the first element. Combining the basic techniques of *LinkedInsert* and *OrderedLinearSearch* from Chapter 7 to obtain an insertion sort algorithm for linked lists is not difficult and is left as an exercise.

Evaluation of These Sorting Schemes. All of the sorting algorithms that we have considered have the same computing time, O(n^2), in the worst and average cases, and so this measure of efficiency provides no basis for choosing one over the others. More careful analysis together with empirical studies, however, reveals that their performance is not the same in all situations.

The primary virtue of simple selection sort is its simplicity. It is too inefficient, however, for use as a general sorting scheme, especially for large lists. The source of this inefficiency is that it requires O(n) time to search for the next item to be selected and positioned. A better selection sort, known as *heapsort*, uses a more efficient search algorithm, which gives this sorting scheme a computing time of O($n \log_2 n$). Heapsort is described in detail in the next section. One weakness of both of these selection sorts, however, is that they perform no better for lists that are almost sorted than they do for totally random lists. Many applications involve lists that are already partially sorted, and for such applications, therefore, other sorting schemes may be more appropriate.

Bubble sort (as described here) does perform better for partially sorted lists because it is able to detect when a list is sorted and does not continue making unnecessary passes through the list. As a general sorting scheme, however, it is very inefficient because of the large number of interchanges that it requires. In fact, it is the least efficient of the sorting schemes we have considered and has virtually nothing to recommend its use. A two-way version described in the exercises performs only slightly better. The exchange sort known as *quicksort* described in Section 10.3 has average computing time O($n \log_2 n$) and is one of the most efficient general-purpose sorting schemes.

Linear insertion sort also is too inefficient to be used as a general-purpose sorting scheme. However, the low overhead that it requires makes it better than simple selection sort and bubble sort. In fact, empirical studies indicate that of all the sorting schemes we consider, it is the best choice for small lists (with a maximum of fifteen to twenty elements) and for lists that are already partially sorted. Two more efficient insertion sorts, *binary insertion sort* and *Shell sort*, are described in the exercises.

In summary, there is no such thing as one universally good sorting scheme. For small lists, linear insertion sort performs well. For lists in general, quicksort, Shell sort, or heapsort is the method of choice. The following table, taken from the video *Sorting Out Sorting*,[1] demonstrates this for randomly generated

[1] *Sorting Out Sorting* is a 30-minute video available from the Media Center of the University of Toronto that provides a fascinating visual comparison of the performance of nine sorting algorithms, three selection sorts, three exchange sorts, and three insertion sorts.

lists of size 500:

Sorting Algorithm	Type of Sort	Sorting Time (seconds)
Simple selection	Selection	69
Heapsort	Selection	18
Bubblesort	Exchange	165
Two-way bubble sort	Exchange	141
Quicksort	Exchange	6
Linear insertion	Insertion	66
Binary insertion	Insertion	37
Shell sort	Insertion	11

Exercises

1. For the following array X, show X after each of the first two passes of simple selection sort to arrange the elements in ascending order:

i	1	2	3	4	5	6
$X[i]$	30	50	70	10	40	60

2. (a) For the following array X, show X after each of the first two passes of bubble sort to arrange the elements in descending order:

i	1	2	3	4	5	6
$X[i]$	60	50	70	10	40	20

   (b) How many passes will bubble sort make all together?
   (c) In what situations will bubble sort make the most interchanges?

3. (a) Linear insertion sort has just correctly positioned $X[3]$ in the following array X:

i	1	2	3	4	5	6
$X[i]$	20	40	60	30	10	50

   Show X after each of $X[4]$ and $X[5]$ is correctly positioned.
   (b) In what situation will linear insertion sort make the fewest interchanges?

4. The basic operation in the simple selection sort algorithm is to scan a list $X_1, \ldots, X_n$ to locate the smallest element and to position it at the beginning of the list. A variation of this approach is to locate both the smallest and the largest elements while scanning the list and to position them at the beginning and the end of the list, respectively. On the next scan this process is repeated for the sublist $X_2, \ldots, X_{n-1}$, and so on.

(a) Using the array X in Exercise 1, show X after the first two passes of this double-ended simple selection sort.

(b) Write an algorithm to implement this double-ended simple selection sort, and determine its computing time.

5. The double-ended selection sort algorithm described in Exercise 4 can be improved by using a more efficient method for determining the smallest and largest elements in a (sub)list. One such algorithm is known as ***Min-Max Sort***[2]:

Consider a list $X_1, \ldots, X_n$, where n is even.

  1. For i ranging from 1 to n **div** 2, compare X_1 with X_{n+1-i} and interchange them if $X_i > X_{n+1-i}$. This establishes a "rainbow pattern" in which $X_1 \leq X_n$, $X_2 \leq X_{n-1}$, $X_3 \leq X_{n-2}$, and so on and guarantees that the smallest element of the list is in the first half of the list and that the largest element is in the second half.

  2. Repeat the following for the list $X_1, \ldots, X_n$, then for the sublist $X_2, \ldots, X_{n-1}$, and so on:

    a. Find the smallest element X_S in the first half and the largest element X_L in the second half, and swap them with the elements in the first and last positions of this (sub)list, respectively.

    b. Restore the rainbow pattern by comparing X_S with X_{n+1-S} and X_L with X_{n+1-L}, interchanging as necessary.

(a) For the following array X, show X after step 1 is executed, and then after each pass through the loop in step 2:

i	1	2	3	4	5	6	7	8	9	10
$X[i]$	30	80	90	20	60	70	10	100	50	40

(b) Write a program to implement this sorting algorithm.

6. Write a recursive procedure to implement simple selection sort.

7. Write a recursive procedure to implement bubble sort.

8. Write a bubble sort algorithm that is appropriate for a linked list.

9. A variation of bubble sort called ***two-way bubble sort*** alternates left-to-right scans with right-to-left scans of the unsorted sublists. On left-to-right scans, X_i is interchanged with X_{i+1} if $X_i > X_{i+1}$ so that larger elements are moved toward the right end of the sublist. On the right-to-left scans, X_{i+1} is interchanged with X_i if $X_{i+1} < X_i$ so that smaller elements are moved toward the left end of the sublist. Scans are repeated until no interchanges are made on one of these scans.

[2] Narayan Murthy, "Min-Max Sort: A Simple Method," *CSC '87 Proceedings* (Association of Computing Machinery, 1987).

   (a) For the array X in Exercise 5, show X at the end of each left-to-right pass and each right-to-left pass through the list.
   (b) Write an algorithm to implement this two-way bubble sort and determine its computing time.

10. Write an insertion sort algorithm for a linked list.

11. In **binary insertion sort**, a binary search is used instead of a linear search to locate the position in the sorted sublist $X[1]$, $X[2]$, . . . , $X[i - 1]$ where the next item $X[i]$ is to be inserted.

   (a) Write an algorithm for binary insertion sort.
   (b) For the following array X, show X after each of the elements $X[i]$, $i = 2, 3, . . . , 10$ is inserted into the sorted sublist $X[1]$, . . . , $X[i - 1]$ using binary insertion sort. Keep a count of how many times array elements are shifted to the right.

i	1	2	3	4	5	6	7	8	9	10
$X[i]$	100	90	60	70	40	20	50	30	80	10

   (c) Repeat **(b)** but use linear insertion sort.

12. Linear insertion sort performs best for small lists or partially sorted lists. **Shell sort** (named after Donald Shell) is an insertion sort that uses linear insertion sort to sort small sublists to produce larger partially ordered sublists. Specifically, one begins with a "gap" of a certain size g and then uses linear insertion to sort sublists of elements that are g apart, first $X[1], X[1 + g], X[1 + 2g], . . .$, then the sublist $X[2], X[2 + g], X[2 + 2g], . . .$, then $X[3], X[3 + g], X[3 + 2g]$, . . . , and so on. Next the size of the gap g is reduced, and the process is repeated. This continues until the gap g is 1, and the final linear insertion sort results in the sorted list.

   (a) For the array X in Exercise 11, show X after each of the sublists of elements that are g apart has been sorted using linear insertion sort. Use $g = 4$ and then reduce it to $g = 1$.
   (b) Write a program to sort a list of items using this Shell sort method, beginning with a gap g of the form $\dfrac{3^k - 1}{2}$ for some integer k and dividing it by 3 at each stage.

13. A binary search tree can also be used to sort a list. We simply insert the list elements into a BST, initially empty, and then use an inorder traversal to copy them back into the list. Write an algorithm for this **treesort** method of sorting, assuming that the list is stored in

   (a) an array.
   (b) a linked list.

14. Write a procedure to implement the treesort algorithm of Exercise 13. Use the procedure in a program that reads a collection of student numbers and names and then uses the treesort procedure to sort them so that the student numbers are in ascending order.

15. Each of the sorting schemes described in this section requires moving list elements from one position to another. If these list elements are records containing many fields, then the time required for such data transfers may be unacceptable. For such lists of large records, an alternative is to use an ***index table*** that stores the positions of the records and to move the entries in this index rather than the records themselves. For example, for an array $X[1], \ldots, X[5]$ of records, an array *Index* is initialized with $Index[1] = 1$, $Index[2] = 2, \ldots,$ $Index[5] = 5$. If it is necessary while sorting these records to interchange the first and third records as well as the second and fifth, we interchange the first and third elements and the second and fifth elements of the index table to obtain $Index[1] = 3$, $Index[2] = 5$, $Index[3] = 1$, $Index[4] = 4$, $Index[5] = 2$. At this stage, the records are arranged in the *logical* order $X[Index[1]], X[Index[2]], \ldots,$ $X[Index[5]]$, that is, $X[3], X[5], X[1], X[4], X[2]$. Write a program that reads the records in *UsersFile* (see Appendix E) and stores them in an array. Then sort the records so that the resources used to date are in descending order, using one of the sorting schemes in this section together with an index table.

16. If possible with your version of Pascal, write a program that compares the execution times of various $O(n^2)$ sorting algorithms described in this section for randomly generated lists of integers. (See Exercise 5 of Section 3.6 and footnote 2 in Section 5.2.)

10.2 Heaps and Heapsort

In the preceding section we looked at three sorting algorithms, simple selection sort, bubble sort, and linear insertion sort, all of which have worst-case and average-case computing time $O(n^2)$, where n is the size of the list being sorted. As we noted, there are other schemes with computing time $O(n \log_2 n)$ and thus in most cases are more efficient than these three. In fact, it can be shown that any sorting scheme based on comparisons and interchanges like those we are considering must have a worst-case computing time of at least $O(n \log_2 n)$. In this section we describe one of these, known as ***heapsort***, which, as we mentioned, is a selection sort. It was discovered by John Williams in 1964 and uses a new data structure called a *heap* to organize the list elements in such a way that the selection can be made efficiently.[3]

---

[3] J. W. J. Williams, "Algorithm 232: Heapsort," *Communication of the Association of Computing Machinery* 7 (1964): 347–348.

A ***heap*** is a binary tree with the following properties:

1. It is *complete*; that is, each level of the tree is completely filled, except possibly the bottom level, and in this level, the nodes are in the leftmost positions.
2. The data item stored in each node is greater than or equal to the data items stored in each of its children. (Of course, if the data items are records, then some key field in these records must satisfy this condition.)

For example, the first of the binary trees that follow is a heap; the second binary tree is not, because it is not complete; the third binary tree is complete, but it is not a heap because the second condition is not satisfied.

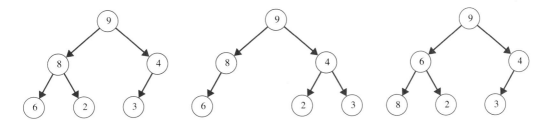

To implement a heap, we could use a linked structure like that for binary trees, but an array can be used more effectively. We simply number the nodes in the heap from top to bottom, numbering the nodes on each level from left to right

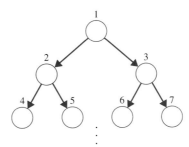

and store the data in the *i*th node in the *i*th location of the array. The completeness property of a heap guarantees that these data items will be stored in consecutive locations at the beginning of the array. Such an array *Heap* might be declared by

```
const
    HeapLimit = ... ;          (* limit on number of nodes in the heap *)

type
    HeapElementType = ... ;  (* a type of data items in the heap *)
    HeapType = array[1..HeapLimit] of HeapElementType;

var
    Heap : HeapType;
```

The items in the heap

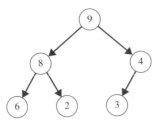

are then stored as follows: *Heap*[1] = 9, *Heap*[2] = 8, *Heap*[3] = 4, *Heap*[4] = 6, *Heap*[5] = 2, *Heap*[6] = 3.

Note that in such an array implementation, it is easy to find the children of a given node: The children of the *i*th node are at locations 2*∗i* and 2*∗i* + 1. Similarly, the parent of the *i*th node is easily seen to be in location *i* **div** 2.

An algorithm for converting a complete binary tree into a heap is basic to most other heap operations. The simplest instance of this problem is a tree that is almost a heap, in that both subtrees of the root are heaps but the tree itself is not, for example,

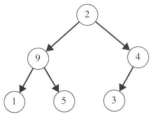

As this tree is complete and both subtrees are heaps, the only reason it is not a heap is that the root item is smaller than one (in fact, both) of its children. The first step, therefore, is to interchange this root with the larger of its two children, in this case, the left child:

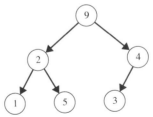

This guarantees that the new root will be greater than both of its children and that one of its subtrees, the right one in this case, will still be a heap. The other subtree may or may not be a heap. If it is, the entire tree is a heap, and we are finished. If it is not, as in this example, we simply repeat this "swapdown" procedure on this subtree. This process is repeated until at some stage, both subtrees of the node being examined are heaps; the process is repeated only a finite number of times because eventually we will reach the bottom of the tree.

For the general problem of converting a complete binary tree to a heap, we begin at the last node that is not a leaf, apply the swap-down procedure to convert the subtree rooted at this node to a heap, move to the preceding node, and swap down in that subtree, and so on, working our way up the tree until we reach the root of the given tree. The following sequence of diagrams illustrates this ''heapify'' process; the subtree being heapified at each stage is highlighted.

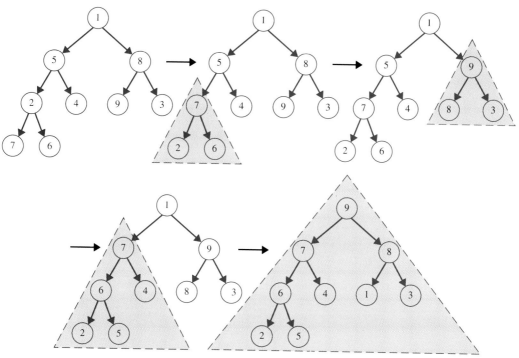

An algorithm to implement the swapdown process is as follows:

SWAPDOWN

(* Accepts: A complete binary tree stored in positions 1 through n of the array *Heap* with root at location r and with left and right subtrees that are heaps.
  Function: Converts the tree to a heap.
  Returns: A heap stored in array *Heap*. *)

1. Initialize a boolean variable *Done* to false and an index c (* child *) to $2 * r$.
2. While not *Done* and $c \leq n$ do the following:

     (* Find the largest child. *)
     a. If $c < n$ and $Heap[c] < Heap[c + 1]$ then
        Set c equal to $c + 1$.

     (* Interchange node and largest child if necessary, and move down to the next subtree. *)
     b. If $Heap[r] < Heap[c]$ then
          i. Swap $Heap[r]$ and $Heap[c]$.
          ii. Set r equal to c.
          iii. Set c equal to $2 * c$.
        Else
          Set *Done* to true.

An algorithm for converting any complete binary tree to a heap is then easy to write:

HEAPIFY

(* Accepts: A complete binary tree stored in positions 1 through *n* of array *Heap*.

   Function: Converts the tree to a heap.

   Returns: A heap stored in array *Heap*. *)

For $r = n$ **div** 2 down to 1 do: (* start at last nonleaf *)

   Apply *SwapDown* to the subtree rooted at location *r*.

To see how these algorithms can now be used to sort a list stored in an array, consider the following list:

$$35, \ 15, \ 77, \ 60, \ 22, \ 41$$

We think of the array storing these items as a complete binary tree:

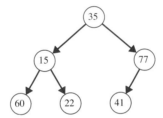

and we use the *Heapify* algorithm to convert it to a heap:

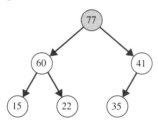

This puts the largest element in the list at the root of the tree, that is, at position 1 of the array. We now use the strategy of a selection sort and correctly position this largest element by placing it at the end of the list and turn our attention to sorting the sublist consisting of the first five elements. In terms of the tree, we are exchanging the root element and the rightmost leaf element and then "pruning" this leaf from the tree, as indicated by the dotted arrow in the following diagram:

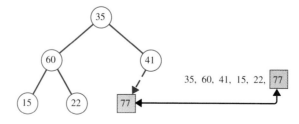

Quite obviously, the tree that results when we perform this root–leaf exchange, followed by pruning the leaf, usually is not a heap. In particular, the five-node tree that corresponds to the sublist 35, 60, 41, 15, 22 is not a heap. However, since we have changed only the root, the tree is almost a heap in the sense described earlier; namely, each of its subtrees is a heap. Thus we can use the *SwapDown* algorithm rather than the more time-consuming *Heapify* algorithm to convert this tree to a heap:

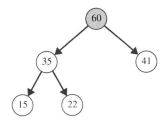

Now we use the same technique of exchanging the root with the rightmost leaf to correctly position the second largest element in the list, and then we prune this leaf from the tree to prepare for the next stage:

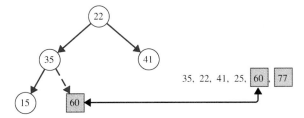

Now we use *SwapDown* to convert to a heap the tree corresponding to the sublist consisting of the first four elements:

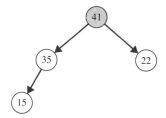

and do the root–leaf exchange and the leaf pruning to correctly position the third largest element in the list:

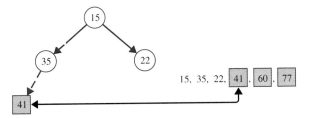

Next the three-node tree corresponding to the sublist 15, 35, 22 is converted to a heap using *SwapDown*

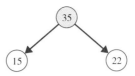

and the roof–leaf exchange and pruning operations are used to correctly position the next largest element in the list:

Finally, the two-node tree corresponding to the two-element sublist 22, 15 is converted to a heap:

and one last root–leaf swap and leaf pruning are performed to correctly position the element 22, which obviously also correctly positions the smallest element 15 at the beginning of the list:

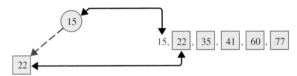

The following algorithm summarizes this simple but efficient sorting scheme, known as *heapsort:*

HEAPSORT

(∗ Accepts: A list of n elements stored in an array $X[1]$, $X[2]$, . . . , $X[n]$.
Function: Heapsorts the list so the elements are in ascending order.
Returns: The sorted list. ∗)

1. Consider X as a complete binary tree and use the *Heapify* algorithm to convert this tree to a heap.
2. For $i = n$ down to 2, do the following:
   a. Interchange $X[1]$ and $X[i]$, thus putting the largest element in the sublist $X[1]$, . . . , $X[i]$ at the end of the sublist.
   b. Apply the *SwapDown* algorithm to convert to a heap the binary tree corresponding to the sublist stored in positions 1 through $i - 1$ of X.

In the introduction to this section we claimed that the computing time of heapsort is $O(n \log_2 n)$. To see this, we must first analyze the *SwapDown* and *Heapify* algorithms.

In *SwapDown*, the number of items in the subtree considered at each stage is one half the number of items in the subtree at the preceding stage. Thus, by an analysis similar to that for binary search trees, the worst-case computing time for this algorithm is quite easily seen to be $O(\log_2 n)$. Since the *Heapify* algorithm executes *SwapDown* $n/2$ times, its worst-case computing time is $O(n \log_2 n)$. *Heapsort* executes *Heapify* one time and *SwapDown* $n - 1$ times; consequently, its worst-case computing time is $O(n \log_2 n)$.

The program in Figure 10.1 implements the *Heapsort* algorithm and the *Heapify* and *SwapDown* algorithms that it uses.

```
PROGRAM SortWithHeapsort (input, output);

(*********************************************************************

     Input (keyboard): A list of integers.
     Function:         Reads and counts a list of integers, sorts
                       them using the heapsort algorithm, and then
                       displays the sorted list.
     Output (screen):  The sorted list of integers.

*********************************************************************)

CONST
   EndDataFlag = -9999;
   HeapLimit = 100;

TYPE
   HeapElementType = integer;
   HeapType = ARRAY[1..HeapLimit] OF HeapElementType;

VAR
   Item : HeapType;       (* list of items to be sorted *)
   Temp : HeapElementType; (* temporary item read *)
   NumItems,              (* number of items *)
   i : integer;           (* index *)

PROCEDURE Swap (VAR A, B : HeapElementType);

   (*********************************************************************

       Input (param):  Items A and B.
       Function:       Interchanges A and B.
       Output (param): Modified A and B.

   *********************************************************************)

   VAR
      Temp : HeapElementType; (* temporary location used to swap A and B *)

   BEGIN (* Swap *)
      Temp := A;
      A := B;
      B := Temp
   END (* Swap *);
```

Figure 10.1

Figure 10.1 (cont.)

```
PROCEDURE Heapsort (VAR X : HeapType; n : integer);

   (*******************************************************************

      Input (param):   A list of n items stored in an array
                       X[1], X[2],..., X[n].
      Function:        Heapsorts the list so the items are in
                       ascending order.
      Output (param):  The sorted list.

   ******************************************************************)

VAR
   i : integer;             (* index *)

PROCEDURE SwapDown (VAR Heap : HeapType; r, n : integer);

   (*******************************************************************

      Input (param):   A complete binary tree stored in positions
                       r..n of array Heap with left and right
                       subtrees that are heaps.
      Function:        Converts the tree to a heap.
      Output (param):  A heap stored in Heap[r],..., Heap[n].

   ******************************************************************)

   VAR
      Child : integer;   (* largest child *)
      Done : boolean;    (* signals when swapping down is complete *)

   BEGIN (* SwapDown *)
      Done := false;
      Child := 2 * r;
      WHILE (NOT Done) AND (Child <= n) DO
         BEGIN
            (* Find the largest child *)

            IF Child < n THEN
               IF Heap[Child] < Heap[Child + 1] THEN
                  Child := Child + 1;

            (* Interchange node and largest child if necessary
               and move down to the next subtree. *)

            IF Heap[r] < Heap[Child] THEN
               BEGIN
                  Swap (Heap[r], Heap[Child]);
                  r := Child;
                  Child := 2 * Child
               END (* IF *)
            ELSE
               Done := true
         END (* WHILE *)
   END (* SwapDown *);
```

Figure 10.1 (cont.)

```
PROCEDURE Heapify (VAR Heap : HeapType; n : integer);

    (*******************************************************************

        Input (param):   A complete binary tree stored in positions
                         1..n of array Heap.
        Function:        Converts the tree to a heap.
        Output (param):  A heap stored in positions 1..n of array
                         Heap.

    ******************************************************************)

    VAR
        r : integer;        (* index *)

    BEGIN (* Heapify *)

        FOR r := n DIV 2 DOWNTO 1 DO
            SwapDown (Heap, r, n)
    END (* Heapify *);

    BEGIN (* Heapsort *)
        (* Convert tree represented by X[1], ..., X[n] into a heap *)

        Heapify (X, n);

        (* Repeatedly put largest item in root at end of list, prune
           it from the tree, and apply SwapDown to rest of tree *)

        FOR i := n DOWNTO 2 DO
            BEGIN
                Swap (X[1], X[i]);
                SwapDown (X, 1, i - 1)
            END (* FOR *)
    END (* Heapsort *);

BEGIN (* main program *)
    NumItems := 0;
    writeln ('Enter the list of items, ', EndDataFlag:1,
             ' to signal the end of the data.');
    writeln ('Maximum of ', HeapLimit:1, ' items allowed.');
    read (Temp);
    WHILE (Temp <> EndDataFlag) AND (NumItems < HeapLimit) DO
        BEGIN
            NumItems := NumItems + 1;
            Item[NumItems] := Temp;
            read (Temp)
        END (* WHILE *);
    readln;
    Heapsort (Item, NumItems);
    writeln ('Sorted list:');
    FOR i := 1 TO NumItems DO
        writeln (Item[i])
END (* main program *).
```

Figure 10.1 (cont.)

Sample run:

```
Enter the list of items, -9999 to signal the end
of the data.  Maximum of 100 items allowed.
23 56 98 102 44
-9999
Sorted list:
    23
    44
    56
    98
   102
```

In this section we emphasized the role of heaps in sorting. As a data structure, a heap is a viable alternative to binary search trees in organizing some collections of data. Unlike BSTs, heaps do not become lopsided as items are inserted or removed from the structure. Heaps can also be used to implement priority queues, which were described in Section 5.1 and in the exercises of 5.2. These applications of heaps are examined in more detail in the exercises.

Exercises

1. Convert each of the following binary trees to a heap using the *Heapify* algorithm if possible, or explain why it is not possible:

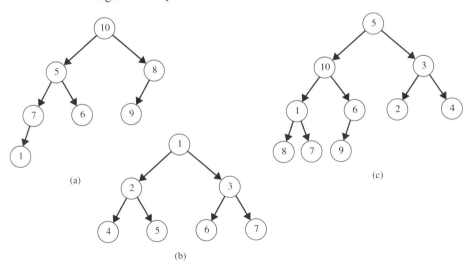

2. Using diagrams like those in this section, trace the action of heapsort on the following lists:

(a) 7, 1, 6, 5, 4, 2, 3   (b) 1, 7, 2, 6, 3, 5, 4
(c) 7, 6, 5, 4, 3, 2, 1   (d) 1, 2, 3, 4, 5, 6, 7

3. (a) Four calls to *SwapDown* must be made to heapify the following array *X*. Show *X* after each of the first two calls.

i	1	2	3	4	5	6	7	8	9
X[*i*]	20	15	31	10	67	50	3	49	26

(b) For the following array *X*, show the contents of *X* after each of the first two iterations of the loop:

for *i* := 8 **downto** 2 **do**
   begin
     Swap (*X*[1], *X*[*i*]);
     SwapDown (*X*, 1, *i* − 1)
   end (* **for** *);

i	1	2	3	4	5	6	7	8
X[*i*]	99	88	55	77	22	33	44	66

4. (a) Design an efficient algorithm for inserting an item into a heap having *n* elements to produce a heap with *n* + 1 elements. (*Hint*: Put the item in location *n* + 1 and then . . .)

(b) Design an efficient algorithm for deleting an item at location *Loc* from a heap having *n* nodes to produce a heap with *n* -- 1 nodes.

(c) Determine the computing times for the algorithms in parts (a) and (b).

5. Describe how a heap can be used to implement a priority queue.

6. Write a procedure to search a heap for a given item.

7. Write procedures implementing the insert and delete algorithms of Exercise 4. Use these procedures in a program that reads records containing an employee number and an hourly rate for several employees and that stores these in a heap, using the employee number as the key field. The program should then allow the user to insert or delete records and, finally, to use heapsort to sort the updated list so that the employee numbers are in ascending order and display this sorted list.

10.3 Quicksort

In Section 10.1 we noted that an exchange sort repeatedly interchanges elements in lists and sublists until no more interchanges are possible. In the case of bubble sort, consecutive items are compared and possibly interchanged on each pass through the list, which means that many interchanges may be needed to move an element to its correct position. In this section we consider the exchange sort developed by C. A. R. Hoare known as *quicksort,* which is more efficient than bubble sort because a typical exchange involves elements that are far apart so that fewer interchanges are required to correctly position an element.

The basic idea of quicksort is to choose some element called a *pivot* and then to perform a sequence of exchanges so that all elements that are less than this pivot are to its left and all elements that are greater than the pivot are to its right. This correctly positions the pivot and divides the (sub)list into two smaller sublists, each of which may then be sorted independently in the *same* way. This *divide-and-conquer* strategy leads naturally to a recursive sorting algorithm.

As an illustration, consider the following list of test scores:

75, 70, 65, 84, 98, 78, 100, 93, 55, 61, 81, 68

Suppose, for simplicity, that we select the first number 75 as the pivot. We must rearrange the list so that 70, 65, 55, 61, and 68 are to the left of 75 (but not necessarily in the order listed here) and the numbers 84, 98, 78, 100, 93, and 81 are to the right of 75.

The only thing we require of this rearrangement is that all the numbers in the sublist to the left of 75 be less than or equal to 75 and that those in the right sublist be greater than 75. We do not care how the elements in each of these sublists are themselves ordered. And it is precisely this flexibility that makes it possible to do this rearrangement very efficiently.

We carry out two searches, one from the right end of the list for elements less than or equal to the pivot 75 and the other from the left end for elements greater than 75. In our example, the first element located on the search from the right is 68, and that on the search from the left is 84:

75, 70, 65, 84, 98, 78, 100, 93, 55, 61, 81, 68

These elements are then interchanged:

75, 70, 65, 68, 98, 78, 100, 93, 55, 61, 81, 84

The searches are then resumed, from the right to locate another element less than or equal to 75 and from the left to find another element greater than 75:

75, 70, 65, 68, 98, 78, 100, 93, 55, 61, 81, 84

and these elements, 61 and 98, are interchanged:

75, 70, 65, 68, 61, 78, 100, 93, 55, 98, 81, 84

A continuation of the searches next locates 78 and 55:

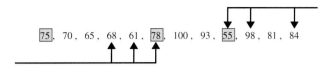

and interchanging them yields:

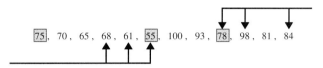

Now, when we resume our search from the right, we locate the element 55 that was found on the previous search from the left:

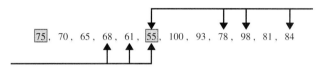

The "pointers" for the left and right searches have thus met, and this signals the end of the two searches. We now interchange 55 and the pivot 75:

55, 70, 65, 68, 61, 75, 100, 93, 78, 98, 81, 84

Note that all elements to the left of 75 are now less than 75 and that all those to its right are greater than 75, and thus the pivot 75 has been properly positioned.

The left sublist

55, 70, 65, 68, 61

and the right sublist

100, 93, 78, 98, 81, 84

can now be sorted *independently, using any sorting scheme desired.* Quicksort uses the same scheme we have just illustrated for the entire list; that is, these sublists must themselves be split by choosing and correctly positioning one pivot element (the first) in each of them. The following procedure *Split* can be used for this. It assumes that the list is stored in an array and uses the procedure *Swap* from the program of Figure 10.1 to interchange two list elements:

procedure *Split* (**var** *X* : *ListType*; *First, Last* : *integer*;
                 var *Pos* : *integer*);

(∗ Accepts: An array *X* and indices *First* and *Last*.
     Function: Rearranges *X*[*First*], . . . , *X*[*Last*] so that the *Pivot*
                 element is properly positioned.
     Returns: The rearranged list and the final position *Pos* of
                 Pivot. ∗)

```
var
    Left,                           (* index for searching from the left *)
    Right : integer;                (* index for searching from the right *)
    Pivot : ListElementType;        (* pivot element *)

begin (* Split *)
    Pivot := X[First];(* choose pivot and initialize indices for left and
                              right searches *)
    Left := First;
    Right := Last;
    while Left < Right do (* While searches haven't met *)
        begin
            (* Search from the right for element <= Pivot *)
            while X[Right] > Pivot do
                Right := Right - 1;

            (* Search from the left for element > Pivot *)
            while (Left < Right) and (X[Left] <= Pivot) do
                Left := Left + 1;

            (* Interchange elements if searches haven't met *)
            if Left < Right then
                Swap (X[Left], X[Right])
        end (* while *);

    (* End of searches; place pivot in correct position *)

    Pos := Right;
    X[First] := X[Pos];
    X[Pos] := Pivot
end (* Split *);
```

A recursive procedure to sort a list using quicksort is now easy to write:

```
procedure Quicksort (var X : ListType; First, Last : integer);

    (* Accepts:   An array X and indices First and Last.
       Function:  Quicksorts array elements X[First], . . . , X[Last] so they
                  are in ascending order.
       Returns:   The sorted list. *)

var
    Pos : integer;                  (* final position of pivot *)

begin (* Quicksort *)
    if First < Last then            (* list has more than one item *)
        begin
            Split (X, First, Last, Pos);        (* split into two sublists *)
            Quicksort (X, First, Pos - 1);  (* sort left sublist *)
            Quicksort (X, Pos + 1, Last)    (* sort right sublist *)
        end (* if *)
    (* else list has 0 or 1 element and requires no sorting *)
end (* Quicksort *);
```

This procedure is called with a statement of the form

Quicksort (*X*, 1, *n*)

where $X[1]$, $X[2]$, . . . , $X[n]$ is the list of elements to be sorted.

The following sequence of treelike diagrams traces the action of *Quicksort* as it sorts the list of integers:

$$8, \quad 2, \quad 13, \quad 5, \quad 14, \quad 3, \quad 7$$

In each tree, a circle indicates an element that has been correctly positioned at an earlier stage, a shaded circle indicating the current pivot. Rectangles represent sublists to be sorted, and a highlighted rectangle indicates the next sublist to be sorted.

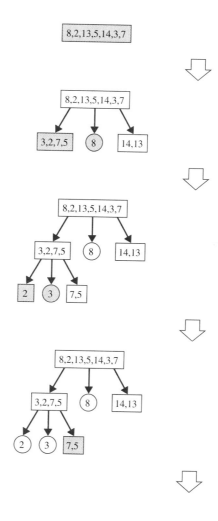

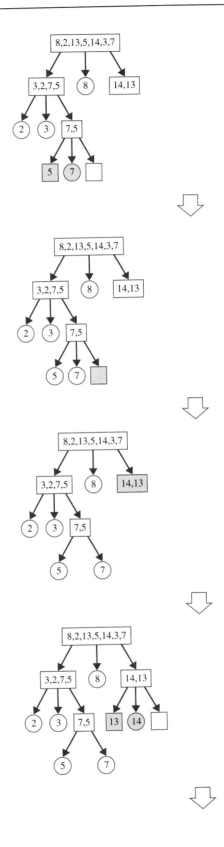

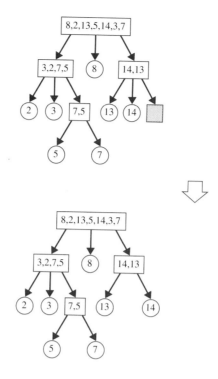

The worst case for quicksort occurs when the list is already ordered or the elements are in reverse order. The worst-case computing time is $O(n^2)$, and the average-case computing time is $O(n \log_2 n)$. Although a rigorous derivation of these computing times is rather difficult, we can see intuitively why they are correct by considering the treelike diagrams used to describe the action of *Quicksort*. At each level of the tree, the procedure *Split* is applied to several sublists, whose total size is, of course, at most n; hence, each of the statements in the while loop of *Split* is executed at most n times on each level. The computing time for quicksort is thus $O(n \cdot L)$, where L is the number of levels in the tree. In the worst case, one of the sublists produced by *Split* is always empty, so that the tree has n levels. It follows that the worst-case computing time is $O(n^2)$. If, however, the two sublists produce by *Split* are approximately the same size, the number of levels will be approximately $\log_2 n$, thus giving $O(n \log_2 n)$ as the computing time in the average case.

A number of changes can be made in quicksort to improve its performance. The first of these is to select the pivot at each stage more carefully in an attempt to produce more even splitting. One common method is the **median-of-three rule,** which selects the median of the first, middle, and last elements in each sublist as the pivot. In practice, it is often the case that the list to be sorted is already partially ordered, and then it is likely that the median-of-three rule will select a pivot closer to the middle of the sublist than will the "first-element" rule.

A second improvement is to switch to a faster sorting method when the sublist is small. We noted in Section 10.1, for example, that insertion sort is one of the best sorting schemes for small lists, say, of size up to fifteen or twenty. Thus we might modify quicksort so that insertion sort is used when *Last* − *First* is less than 20.

Quicksort is a recursive procedure, and as we have seen (see Section 6.5), a stack of activation records must be maintained by the system to manage recursion. The deeper the recursion is, the larger this stack will become. The depth of the recursion and the corresponding overhead involved can be reduced if we first sort the smaller sublist at each stage, rather than always selecting the left sublist. If quicksort is to be used extensively, it may even be worthwhile to remove recursion by writing it iteratively, as described in the exercises.

Exercises

1. For the following array *X*, show the contents of *X* after the procedure reference *Split* (*X*, 1, 10, *SplitPos*) is executed, and give the value of the array index *SplitPos*:

i	1	2	3	4	5	6	7	8	9	10
X[*i*]	45	20	50	30	80	10	60	70	40	90

2. Draw a sequence of trees like those in the text to illustrate the actions of *Split* and *Quicksort* while sorting the following lists:

   (a) E, A, F, D, C, B   **(b)** A, B, C, F, E, D
   (c) F, E, D, C, B, A   **(d)** A, B, C, D, E, F

3. One of the lists in Exercise 2 shows why the compound boolean condition is needed to control the search from the left in procedure *Split*. Which list is it? What would happen if we were to omit the boolean expression *Left* < *Right*?

4. The procedure *Quicksort* always sorts the left sublist before the right. The size of the stack used to implement the recursion required by *Quicksort* is reduced if the shorter of the two sublists is the first to be sorted. Modify *Quicksort* to do this.

5. As noted in the text, one way that quicksort can be improved is to use some other sorting algorithm to sort small sublists. For example, linear insertion sort is one of the fastest sorting schemes for lists having up to twenty elements. Modify *Quicksort* to use insertion sort if the sublist has fewer than *LBound* elements for some constant *LBound* and to use quicksort otherwise.

6. An alternative to the approach in Exercise 5 is simply to ignore all sublists with fewer than *LBound* elements, not splitting them further. When execution of the quicksort algorithm terminates, the file will not be sorted. It will be nearly sorted, however, in that it will contain small unordered groups of elements, but all of the elements in each such group will be smaller than those in the next group. One then

simply sorts the list using linear insertion sort. Modify *Quicksort* to incorporate this modification.

7. The procedure *Split* always selects the first element of the sublist to position. If the list is already sorted or nearly sorted, this is a poor choice for a pivot. As noted in the text, an alternative method for choosing the pivot and one that works better for partially sorted lists is the *median-of-three rule*, in which the median of the first, middle, and last elements in the list is selected. (The median of three numbers a, b, and c, arranged so that $a \leq b \leq c$ is the middle number b.) Modify *Split* to use this median-of-three rule.

8. As we saw in Section 6.5, recursion is usually implemented using a stack; parameters, local variables, and return addresses are pushed onto the stack when a recursive subprogram is called, and values are popped from the stack upon return from the subprogram. Generally, we can transform a recursive subprogram into a nonrecursive one by maintaining such a stack within the subprogram itself. Use this approach to design a nonrecursive version of procedure *Quicksort*; use a stack to store the first and last positions of the sublists that arise in quicksort.

9. The ***median*** of a set with an odd number of elements is the middle value if the data items are arranged in order. An efficient algorithm to find the median that does not require first ordering the entire set can be obtained by modifying the quicksort algorithm. We use procedure *Split* to position a pivot element. If this pivot is positioned at location $(n + 1)/2$, it is the median; otherwise, one of the two sublists produced by *Split* contains the median, and that sublist can be processed recursively. Write a procedure to find the median of a list using this method.

10. The technique described in Exercise 9 for finding the median of a set of data items can easily be modified to find the kth smallest element in the set. Write such a procedure.

11

Sorting and Searching Files

In the sorting and searching schemes considered up to now, we have assumed that the collection of items to be processed is stored in internal memory and can thus be accessed very quickly. The storage capacity of main memory may be too small, however, for large collections of student records, motor vehicle registrations, telephone listings, and so on. These kinds of collections must be stored in external memory such as magnetic tapes or disks, which have larger storage capacities but for which the access time is considerably greater. These collections of data items are called *files*, and the individual items are usually called *components* or *records*.

There are two basic types of files: *sequential* and *direct* (or *random*) *access.* In a sequential file the data items must be accessed in the order in which they are stored; that is, to access any particular component, we must start at the beginning of the file and pass through all the components that precede it. In contrast, each item in a direct access file can be accessed directly by specifying its location, usually by means of a component number. Direct access files can, however, be processed sequentially when necessary, by simply accessing the components in order by component number.

Standard Pascal supports only sequential files, but many other versions support both kinds. In this chapter we review the file capabilities provided in standard Pascal and consider several important file-processing problems, including sorting and updating. We also describe how direct access files are supported in other versions of Pascal.

11.1 Sequential Files in Standard Pascal

As a data structure, a *file* is a collection of related data items, usually stored in external memory, for which the basic operations are input and output; that is, information can be read from the file and/or written to the file. Usually the programmer is not concerned with the details of the actual device on which the data is stored because these details are handled by the operating system. Instead, the programmer deals with the *logical* structure of the file, that is, with the relationship among the items stored in the file and with the algorithms

504

needed to process them. As we noted in the introduction, files can be classified as sequential or direct access. In this section we describe how sequential files are implemented in standard Pascal.

The files used in Pascal programs up to this point have been ***text files.*** These are files whose components are characters and these characters are organized into lines. The predefined file type *text* is a standard type identifier used to declare text files. The standard system files *input* and *output* associated with the standard input and output devices are examples of text files. The predefined procedures *readln, writeln, eoln,* and *page* may be used only with text files.

Pascal also supports ***binary files,*** whose components may be of any type, simple or structured, except that they may not be of file type. The general form for a file declaration is

   file of *component-type*

where *component-type* specifies the type of the file components. For example, the declarations

    type
      IntegerFile = **file of** *integer;*
      BankRecord = **record**
                AcctNumber : *integer;*
                Balance : *real*
            end;
      FileOfBankRecords = **file of** *BankRecord;*

    var
      Memo : *text;*
      NumFile : *IntegerFile;*
      AcctFile : *FileOfBankRecords;*

declare that *Memo* is a text file, *NumFile* is a file whose components are integers, and *AcctFile* is a file whose components are records of type *Bank-Record.* The declarations

    type
      ShortString = **packed array**[1..12] **of** *char;*
      LongString = **packed array**[1..24] **of** *char;*
      DeptType = (*Factory, Office, Sales*);
      EmployeeRecord = **record**
                Number : *integer;*
                LastName,
                FirstName : *ShortString;*
                MidInitial : *char;*
                StreetAddress,
                CityState : *LongString;*
                PhoneNumber : *ShortString;*
                Gender : *char;*

> *Age*,
> *Dependents* : *integer*;
> *Dept* : *DeptType*;
> *Union* : *boolean*;
> *HourlyRate* : *real*
> **end;**
> *FileType* = **file of** *EmployeeRecord*;
>
> **var**
> *EmpFile* : *FileType*;

declare that *EmpFile* is a file whose components are of type *EmployeeRecord*.

Binary files such as *NumFile*, *AcctFile*, and *EmpFile* can usually be created only by a program, and access to the components of such files is possible only within a program. Attempting to list the file contents by using some system command or to access them by using a text editor usually results in "garbage" output or some error message. The characters that make up a text file are stored using some coding scheme such as ASCII or EBCDIC, as described in Section 2.2, and when a text file is listed, these codes are automatically converted to the corresponding characters by the terminal, printer, or other output device. On the other hand, the components of binary files are stored using the internal representation scheme for the particular computer being used, and this representation usually cannot be correctly displayed in character form by the output device.

To illustrate, consider the integer 27195. If the usual binary representation described in Section 2.2 is used, this integer would be stored internally in a 16-bit word as the bit string

0110101000111011

and this would also be its representation in a file of type integer such as *NumFile:*

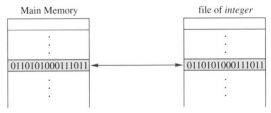

In a text file, however, it would be stored as a sequence of codes for the five characters '2', '7', '1', '9', '5':

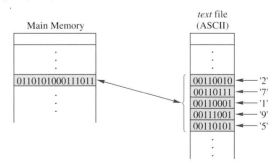

As these diagrams suggest, information can be transferred between main memory and a binary file more rapidly than between main memory and a text file, as it is already in a form that requires no decoding or encoding. Also, data items are usually stored more compactly in a binary file using their internal representation than in a text file using their external representation in one of the standard coding schemes.

Files may be either ***temporary*** or ***permanent.*** Temporary files are work files that exist only during execution of a program that creates and processes them, whereas permanent files also exist before and/or after program execution. In standard Pascal, the names of all file variables associated with permanent files must be listed in the file list of the program heading. Some other versions, such as Turbo Pascal, use no file list in the program heading, and some special predefined procedure such as *close* is used to make files permanent.

Two predefined procedures are provided for opening files so that their components can be accessed: *reset* and *rewrite*. The *reset* procedure is called with a reference of the form

   reset (*file-variable*);

although some versions allow or require a modified reference of the form

   reset (*file-variable*, *file-name*);

where *file-name* is the name of an actual data file in secondary memory that is to be associated with *file-variable*. For example, to open a file *EmpFile* for input, the statement

   reset (*EmpFile*);

is used in standard Pascal or perhaps

   reset (*EmpFile*, 'EMPFILE1.DAT');

in some other version if 'EMPFILE1.DAT' is the actual name of the file to be used as *EmpFile* in the program.

Each file to be used for output (except the standard file *output*) must be opened by referencing the procedure *rewrite*,

   rewrite (*file-variable*);

or using one of the variations provided in other versions, such as

   rewrite (*file-variable*, *file-name*);

The procedure *rewrite* creates an empty file into which components can be written; *any previous contents that the specified file may have had are erased!*

Information can be written into a file previously opened for output using the predefined procedure *write* in a reference of the form

   write (*file-variable*, *output-list*);

and for text files, but *only for text files*, the procedure *writeln* may also be used:

> *writeln (file-variable, output-list)*;

Each item in *output-list* must be compatible with the type of the components specified for the file variable, except in the case of text files, to which values of type *char*, *boolean*, *integer*, *real*, or string type may be written.

The program in Figure 11.1 illustrates how the procedure *write* is used in the creation of the binary file *AcctFile*. Here *AcctRec* is a record variable of type *BankRecord*, and the values of the fields are entered by the user during execution (and are thus read from the text file *input*). The statement

> *write (AcctFile, AcctRec)*;

writes these records to the file *AcctFile*.

```
PROGRAM CreateAcctFile1 (input, output, AcctFile);

(*********************************************************************

    Input (keyboard):  Values for the fields of a record of type
                       BankRecord.
    Function:          Creates the binary file AcctFile whose
                       components are records of type BankRecord.
                       The fields of a record AcctRec are entered by
                       the user during execution, and the procedure
                       write is used to write AcctRec to AcctFile.
    Output (file):     The binary file AcctFile.
    Output (screen):   A message signaling that file creation is
                       complete.

*********************************************************************)

TYPE
    BankRecord = RECORD
                     AcctNumber : integer;
                     Balance : real
                 END;
    FileOfBankRecords = FILE OF BankRecord;

VAR
    AcctRec : BankRecord;              (* record entered by user *)
    AcctFile : FileOfBankRecords;      (* binary file created *)
```

Figure 11.1

Figure 11.1 (cont.)

```
BEGIN
    rewrite (AcctFile);
    writeln ('Enter zero account number and balance to stop.');
    write ('Acct # and balance?  ');
    readln (AcctRec.AcctNumber, AcctRec.Balance);
    WHILE (AcctRec.AcctNumber > 0) DO
        BEGIN
            write (AcctFile, AcctRec);
            write ('Acct # and balance?  ');
            readln (AcctRec.AcctNumber, AcctRec.Balance)
        END (* WHILE *);
    writeln ('Creation of AcctFile completed')
END.
```

Sample run:

```
Enter zero account number and balance to stop.
Acct # and balance?  1141 2297.45
Acct # and balance?  1590  888.32
Acct # and balance?  1611  335.82
Acct # and balance?  1612   55.70
Acct # and balance?  1658 8923.48
Acct # and balance?  1701  620.46
Acct # and balance?  1722 1001.56
Acct # and balance?  1747 2937.52
Acct # and balance?  1751    5.02
Acct # and balance?  1788  192.86
Acct # and balance?  0 0
Creation of AcctFile completed
```

As we noted in Section 5.1, transfer of information between main memory and secondary memory is considerably slower than transfer from one location in main memory to another. Program execution degrades unacceptably if processing must be suspended each time a data item is to be transferred to or from secondary memory. For this reason, special segments of main memory known as *input/output buffers* are used as "holding" areas to facilitate file input/output.

To illustrate, consider the statement

write (AcctFile, AcctRec)

used in the program of Figure 11.1 to write the record *AcctRec* to *AcctFile*. This output to *AcctFile* actually takes place in two stages. The value of *AcctRec* is first copied into a special variable called a **file buffer variable** or **file window** that has the same type as the file components:

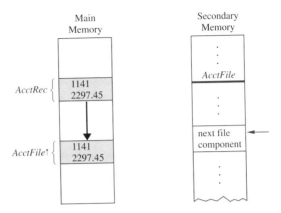

The second stage of output to *AcctFile* is to transfer this record from the file buffer variable into the file itself. While this is being done, processing of other statements in the program can continue.

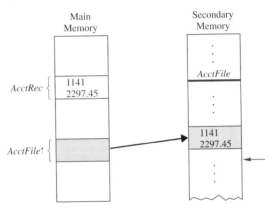

This buffer variable is created automatically by the declaration of the file variable, and is denoted by affixing an up arrow (↑) or a carat (∧) to the file variable:

   file-variable↑   or   *file-variable*∧

In our example, therefore, the variable

   AcctFile↑

is the buffer variable. It is of type *BankRecord* and may be used in the same manner as is any other record variable of this type.

   The assignment of a value to a file buffer variable carries out only the first stage of output to a file. It does not actually write this value into the associated file; rather, it merely copies the value into the memory location(s) assigned to this buffer variable. The second stage can then be performed using the predefined procedure *put*. This procedure is called with a statement of the form

    put (*file-variable*)

and transfers the value of the buffer variable *file-variable*↑ to the associated
file *file-variable*. This value is actually transferred rather than copied, and consequently, after this statement is executed, *file-variable*↑ is undefined.

In general, an output statement of the form

    write (*file-variable*, *item-1*, *item-2*, . . . , *item-n*)

is equivalent to the following *n* pairs of statements:

    file-variable↑ := *item-1*;
    put (*file-variable*);
    file-variable↑ := *item-2*;
    put (*file-variable*);

        .
        .
        .

    file-variable↑ := *item-n*;
    put (*file-variable*)

For example, the program in Figure 11.1 for creating the binary file *AcctFile*
can be written to make use of the file buffer variable and the procedure *put*,
as shown in Figure 11.2.

```
PROGRAM CreateAcctFile2 (input, output, AcctFile);

(*******************************************************************

   Input (keyboard): Values for the fields of a record of type
                     BankRecord.
   Function:         Creates the binary file AcctFile whose
                     components are records of type BankRecord.
                     The fields of the file buffer variable AcctFile^
                     are entered by the user during execution, and
                     the procedure put is used to transfer this
                     record to AcctFile.

   Output (file):    The binary file AcctFile.
   Output (screen):  A message signaling that file creation is
                     complete.

********************************************************************)
```

Figure 11.2

Figure 11.2 (cont.)

```
TYPE
   BankRecord = RECORD
                    AcctNumber : integer;
                    Balance : real
                END;
   FileOfBankRecords = FILE OF BankRecord;

VAR
   AcctFile : FileOfBankRecords;   (* binary file created *)

BEGIN
   rewrite (AcctFile);
   writeln ('Enter zero account number and balance to stop.');
   write ('Acct # and balance?  ');
   readln (AcctFile^.AcctNumber, AcctFile^.Balance);
   WHILE (AcctFile^.AcctNumber > 0) DO
      BEGIN
         put (AcctFile);
         write ('Acct # and balance?  ');
         readln (AcctFile^.AcctNumber, AcctFile^.Balance)
      END (* WHILE *);
   writeln ('Creation of AcctFile completed')
END.
```

For a text file, the buffer variable is of type *char*. When a value of some other allowed type—*integer*, *real*, *boolean*, string—is written to a text file, it is converted to the appropriate string of characters, and these characters are successively written to the file using the file buffer. In the case of the procedure *writeln*, this stream of characters is followed by an end-of-line character. Note that *writeln* cannot be used for binary files because they have no line structure.

A component of a file that has been opened for input with the procedure *reset* can be read using the procedure *read* in a reference of the form

> read (*file-variable, input-list*)

and for text files, and *only for text files* (because binary files have no line structure),

> readln (*text-file-variable, input-list*)

Here *input-list* is a list of variables whose types are compatible with the types of components in the specified file, with the usual exception for text files that allows reading values of type *char*, *boolean*, *integer*, and *real*.

As an example of file input, suppose that we wish to examine the contents of the nontext file *AcctFile* created by the program of Figure 11.1 or 11.2. Once this file has been opened for input with the procedure *reset*, the statement

> read (*AcctFile, AcctRec*);

can be used to read a component of *AcctFile* and assign it to the variable *AcctRec* of type *BankRecord*, and the values of the two fields of *AcctRec* can then be displayed:

writeln (*AcctRec.AcctNumber*:5, *AcctRec.Balance*:10:2)

In the program in Figure 11.3 these two statements are repeated until the end-of-file mark in *AcctFile* is encountered. This end-of-file mark is automatically placed at the end of each file created by a Pascal program.

```
PROGRAM ReadAcctFile1 (output, AcctFile);

(*******************************************************************

   Input (file):    The binary file AcctFile whose components are
                    records of type BankRecord.
   Function:        Reads and displays the contents of the binary
                    file AcctFile created by the program of Figure
                    11.1 or 11.2.
   Output (screen): The fields of the records in AcctFile.

 *******************************************************************)

TYPE
   BankRecord = RECORD
                   AcctNumber : integer;
                   Balance : real
                END;
   FileOfBankRecords = FILE OF BankRecord;

VAR
   AcctFile : FileOfBankRecords;   (* nontext file displayed *)
   AcctRec : BankRecord;           (* record in AcctFile *)

BEGIN
   reset (AcctFile);
   writeln ('Contents of AcctFile:');
   WHILE NOT eof(AcctFile) DO
      BEGIN
         read (AcctFile, AcctRec);
         writeln (AcctRec.AcctNumber:5, AcctRec.Balance:10:2)
      END (* WHILE *)
END.
```

Figure 11.3

Figure 11.3 (cont.)

Sample run:

```
Contents of AcctFile:
  1141    2297.45
  1590     888.32
  1611     335.82
  1612      55.70
  1658    8923.48
  1701     620.46
  1722    1001.56
  1747    2937.52
  1751       5.02
  1788     192.86
```

File input, like file output, is a two-stage process that uses the file buffer variable (file window). When a file such as *AcctFile* is opened for input,

    reset (*AcctFile*);

the first file component is copied into the file buffer variable *AcctFile↑*. Later, when the statement

    read (*AcctFile, AcctRec*);

is executed, the value of this buffer variable is copied to the record variable *AcctRec*:

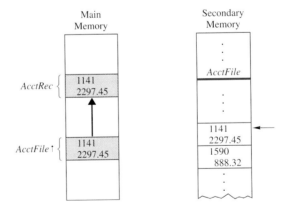

Then, while execution of the program continues, the next file component is copied from the file into the file buffer variable in preparation for the next time a value must be read:

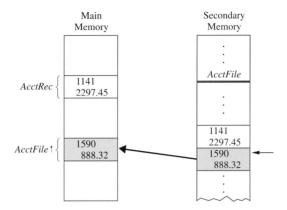

This buffer variable thus always contains a copy of the next component of the associated file, providing a "window" through which the *next* file component may be accessed. We can see what is coming without actually reading the next component.

The statement

read (AcctFile, AcctRec);

is equivalent to the pair of statements

AcctRec := *AcctFile↑*;
get (AcctFile);

where *get* is a predefined procedure that copies the next file component into the associated buffer variable. In general, *get* is called with a statement of the form

get (file-variable)

and an input statement of the form

read (file-variable, variable-1, variable-2, . . . , variable-n)

is equivalent to the *n* pairs of statements:

variable-1 := *file-variable↑*;
get (file-variable);
variable-2 := *file-variable↑*;
get (file-variable);

   .
   .
   .

variable-n := *file-variable↑*;
get (file-variable)

The program in Figure 11.4 is a modification of the program in Figure 11.3 for reading the nontext file *AcctFile*. The statement

> *writeln (AcctFile↑.AcctNumber:5, AcctFile↑.Balance:10:2);*

displays each file component directly rather than first transferring it to a record variable *AcctRec* and then displaying its value. The statement

> *get (AcctFile)*

then copies the next file component into the file buffer variable *AcctFile↑*.

```
PROGRAM ReadAcctFile2 (output, AcctFile);

(*****************************************************************

   Input (file):    The binary file AcctFile whose components are
                    records of type BankRecord.
   Function:        Reads and displays the contents of the binary
                    file AcctFile created by the program of Figure
                    11.1 or 11.2.  The procedure get is used to
                    retrieve these records.
   Output (screen): The fields of the records in AcctFile.

*****************************************************************)

TYPE
   BankRecord = RECORD
                   AcctNumber : integer;
                   Balance : real
                END;
   FileOfBankRecords = FILE OF BankRecord;

VAR
   AcctFile : FileOfBankRecords;   (* nontext file displayed *)

BEGIN
   reset (AcctFile);
   writeln ('Contents of AcctFile:');
   WHILE NOT eof(AcctFile) DO
      BEGIN
         writeln (AcctFile^.AcctNumber:5, AcctFile^.Balance:10:2);
         get (AcctFile)
      END (* WHILE *)
END.
```

Figure 11.4

When the procedure *read* (or *readln*) is used to read an integer or a real value from a text file, the characters are transferred one at a time to the file buffer variable, and the numeric equivalent of the string of characters representing the number in the file is formed. Leading blanks and leading end-of-line characters are ignored, and characters are transferred and converted until some character that cannot belong to a string representing an integer or a real number is encountered.

When an end-of-line character is encountered in a text file, the value of

> *eoln(file-variable)*

becomes true (it is false otherwise), and a blank is placed in the file window. This blank is read as the next component, unless it is bypassed by using a statement of the form

> *get (file-variable)*

A statement of the form

> *readln (file-variable)*

may also be used to bypass an end-of-line character because it is equivalent to

> **while not** *eoln(file-variable)* **do**
>   *get (file-variable)*;
> *get (file-variable)*

In either case, the file window *file-variable*↑ will contain the first character of the next line.

The procedures *get* and *read* (and *readln* for text files) copy the next file component into the file window unless the end of the file has been reached. In this case, the value of

> *eof(file-variable)*

becomes true (it is false otherwise), and the file buffer variable is undefined. Any subsequent calls to the procedures *get* and *read* result in an error, because such calls attempt to access information beyond the end of the file.

As an illustration, note the use of the *eof* function and file buffer variables in the following procedure, which copies the contents of one file into another:

procedure *CopyFile* (**var** *FromFile, ToFile* : *FileType*);

   (∗ Input: *FromFile.*
         Function: Copies the contents of *FromFile* into *ToFile.*
         Output: *ToFile.* ∗)

  begin (∗ *CopyFile* ∗)
    while not *eof*(*FromFile*) **do**
      begin
        ToFile↑ := *FromFile*↑;
        put (*ToFile*);
        get (*FromFile*)
      end (∗ **while** ∗)
  end (∗ *CopyFile* ∗);

This procedure copies one component at a time from *FromFile* to *ToFile*. This is necessary because the contents of a file can be accessed only one component at a time; it is not possible to copy one file into another file by using an assignment statement of the form *file-1* := *file-2*.

One consequence is that files used as parameters, as in the procedure *CopyFile*, must be variable parameters. Using value parameters is not allowed, because this would require copying an entire actual file into the corresponding formal file parameter. Corresponding actual file parameters and formal file parameters must have the same type, and as for the other predefined data structures in Pascal, this requirement means that they must be declared by the same or equivalent type identifiers (see footnote 2 in Section 2.4).

To illustrate, consider the problem of appending new information to an existing file. In Pascal we cannot simply open the file for output and then write the new information to the file, because the procedure *rewrite* erases any previous contents of a file. (Turbo Pascal provides the procedure *append* to open a file so that output can be appended to it.) Instead, the original file must be opened for input, some work file must be opened for output, and the contents of the original file must be copied into this work file. The new information can then be written at the end of this work file.

If it is not necessary to keep a permanent copy of the original file, the contents of this work file can be copied back to the original file when updating has been completed. In this case, the work file can be a temporary file. This is the approach taken in the program of Figure 11.5, which uses the temporary *WorkFile* to append new account records to the file *AcctFile* created earlier. The procedure *CopyFile* given in the preceding section is used to carry out the necessary file transfers. Note that although the temporary file *WorkFile* is not included in the file list of the program heading because it is not a permanent file, it is declared and opened in the usual manner.

```
PROGRAM AppendToAcctFile (input, output, AcctFile);

(****************************************************************

    Input (file):      The binary file AcctFile whose components are
                       records of type BankRecord.
    Input (keyboard): Values for the fields of a record of type
                       BankRecord.
    Function:          Reads account records entered by the user and
                       adds these records to the end of the previously
                       created AcctFile.  The contents of AcctFile are
                       first copied into the temporary file WorkFile,
                       the new records are appended to WorkFile, and
                       the contents of WorkFile are then copied back
                       to AcctFile.  The contents of AcctFile are then
                       verified by reading and displaying each record
                       in it.
    Output (screen):   A message signaling that file creation is
                       complete.
    Output (file):     The modified binary file AcctFile.

****************************************************************)


TYPE
   BankRecord = RECORD
                    AcctNumber : integer;
                    Balance : real
                END;
   FileOfBankRecords = FILE OF BankRecord;
   FileType = FileOfBankRecords;

VAR
   WorkFile,                       (* temporary file of account records *)
   AcctFile : FileOfBankRecords;   (* nontext file being appended to *)

PROCEDURE CopyFile (VAR FromFile, ToFile : FileType);

   (****************************************************************

      Input (file):  FromFile.
      Function:      Copies the contents of FromFile into ToFile.
      Output (file): ToFile.

   ****************************************************************)

   BEGIN (* CopyFile *)
      reset (FromFile);
      rewrite (ToFile);
      WHILE NOT eof(FromFile) DO
         BEGIN
            ToFile^ := FromFile^;
            put (ToFile);
            get (FromFile)
         END (* WHILE *)
   END (* CopyFile *);
```

Figure 11.5

Figure 11.5 (cont.)

```
BEGIN (* main program *)

   (* Copy contents of AcctFile to WorkFile *)

   CopyFile (AcctFile, WorkFile);

   (* Append new records to the end of WorkFile *)

   writeln ('Enter zero account number and balance to stop.');
   write ('Acct # and balance?  ');
   readln (WorkFile^.AcctNumber, WorkFile^.Balance);
   WHILE (WorkFile^.AcctNumber > 0) DO
      BEGIN
         put (WorkFile);
         write ('Acct # and balance?  ');
         readln (WorkFile^.AcctNumber, WorkFile^.Balance);
      END (* WHILE *);

   (* Now copy the contents of WorkFile to AcctFile *)

   CopyFile (WorkFile, AcctFile);

   (* Finally, verify the contents of AcctFile *)

   reset (AcctFile);
   writeln;
   writeln ('Contents of AcctFile:');
   WHILE NOT eof(AcctFile) DO
      BEGIN
         writeln (AcctFile^.AcctNumber:5, AcctFile^.Balance:10:2);
         get (AcctFile)
      END (* WHILE *)
END (* main program *).
```

Sample run:

```
Enter zero account number and balance to stop.
Acct # and balance?  1793 1505.67
Acct # and balance?  1801  622 63
Acct # and balance?  1888 3562.87
Acct # and balance?  1919  275.00
Acct # and balance?  1925  428.56
Acct # and balance?  0 0
```

Figure 11.5 (cont.)

```
Contents of AcctFile:
1141    2297.45
1590     888.32
1611     335.82
1612      55.70
1658    8923.48
1701     620.46
1722    1001.56
1747    2937.52
1751       5.02
1788     192.86
1793    1505.67
1801     622.63
1888       0.00
1793    1505.67
1801     622.00
1888    3562.87
1919     275.00
1925     428.56
```

11.2 Sequential Files in Turbo Pascal

There are a number of differences between the file-processing features of standard Pascal and those of Turbo Pascal. In this section we briefly describe how files are processed in Turbo Pascal.

Program Heading. Although not required in Turbo Pascal, it is good practice to include all file variables used in a program (including the standard text files *input* and *output*) in the file list of the program heading. Standard Pascal requires that all file variables associated with permanent files be included in this list, but Turbo Pascal makes no distinction between permanent and temporary files.

File Declarations. Both Turbo and standard Pascal support text files and binary files. Each file must be declared as a file variable in the declaration part of the program. The predefined type identifier *text* is used to specify the types of file variables associated with text files, and declarations for binary files have the form

file of *component-type*

Associating File Variables with Actual Files. In Turbo Pascal, before a file can be opened for input or output in a program, it must be associated with a disk file by calling the predefined procedure *assign* in a statement of the form

assign (*file-variable, file-name*);

This statement establishes a connection between the *file-variable* used to refer to the file within the program with the actual data file *file-name* stored on disk so that all subsequent input/output will be carried out using this disk file. For example,

> *assign (EmpFile, 'A:EMPFILE1.DAT');*

associates the file variable *EmpFile* with the file EMPFILE1.DAT stored on the disk in the A drive. If *file-name* is the empty string, the standard file *input* or *output* will be associated with *file-variable*.

Opening Files for Input. In both standard and Turbo Pascal, each file from which data values are to be read must first be opened for input by calling the predefined procedure *reset* with a statement of the form

> *reset (file-variable);*

Each such procedure call resets the data pointer to the beginning of the specified file. (The standard system file *input* need not be opened for input.)

Opening Files for Output. Each file to which data values are to be written must first be opened for output. In both Turbo and standard Pascal this can be done by calling the predefined procedure *rewrite* with a statement of the form

> *rewrite (file-variable);*

and in Turbo Pascal, the predefined procedure *append* may also be used. It is called with a statement of the form

> *append (file-variable);*

Each call to the procedure *rewrite* empties the specified file, so that any previous contents of the file are destroyed. A call to *append* positions the data pointer at the end of the file so that values will be appended to the file. (The standard system file *output* need not be opened for output.)

File Input. In both Turbo and standard Pascal, information can be read from a file using the procedure *read* in a statement of the form

> *read (file-variable, input-list);*

and the procedure *readln* may also be used for text files:

> *readln (file-variable, input-list);*

In either case, if *file-variable* is omitted, values are read from the standard system file *input*.

File Output. In both Turbo and standard Pascal, output can be directed to a file using the procedure *write* in a statement of the form

> *write (file-variable, output-list)*;

and the procedure *writeln* may also be used for text files:

> *writeln (file-variable, output-list)*;

In either case, if *file-variable* is omitted, values are written to the standard system file *output*.

File Buffer Variable (File Window), *get, put.* The file buffer variable (file window) *file-variable*↑ associated with a *file-variable* and the procedures *get* and *put* for managing its contents provided in standard Pascal are not supported in Turbo Pascal. Thus the procedure *write* must be used for all output to a binary file. To create a binary file like the file of bank records in the preceding section, therefore, the program in Figure 11.1 can be used, provided that calls to the procedures *assign* and *close* are added to the statement part:

```
begin
    assign (AcctFile, 'A:ACCTFIL1.DAT');
    rewrite (AcctFile);
    writeln ('Enter zero account number and balance to stop.');
    write ('Acct # and balance? ');
    readln (AcctRec.AcctNumber, AcctRec.Balance);
    while AcctRec.AcctNumber > 0 do
      begin
        write (AcctFile, AcctRec);
        write ('Acct # and balance? ');
        readln (AcctRec.AcctNumber, AcctRec.Balance)
      end (* while *);
    close (AcctFile)
end.
```

A program like that in Figure 11.2 cannot be used, however, since it uses the file buffer variable and the procedure *put* to create the file.

Also, the procedure *read* must be used in Turbo Pascal for all input from a binary file. Thus a program like that in Figure 11.3 can be used to read the contents of a binary file, provided that a call to the procedure *assign* is placed before the reference to the procedure *reset*:

```
assign (AcctFile, 'A:ACCTFIL1.DAT');
reset (AcctFile);
        .
        .
        .
```

but a program like that in Figure 11.4 that uses the file window and the procedure *get* cannot be used.

The *eof* Function.   The predefined function *eof* may be used in both Turbo and standard Pascal in a reference of the form

eof(file-variable)

to detect the end of an input file. It returns the value *true* if the data pointer is positioned at the end of the file and returns the value *false* otherwise.

The *eoln* Function.   The predefined function *eoln* may be used in both Turbo and standard Pascal in a reference of the form

eoln(file-variable)

to detect the end of a line in an input text file. It returns the value *true* if the data pointer is positioned at the end of a line and returns the value *false* otherwise. Unlike standard Pascal, however, the end-of-line mark in Turbo Pascal consists of two characters, a return character followed by a line-feed character, and these characters are not read and interpreted as blanks.

Closing Files.   In Turbo Pascal, after output to a file is completed, it should be closed by calling the predefined procedure *close* with a statement of the form

close (file-variable)

Failure to do so may result in the loss of data values because they might not be transferred from the output buffer to the file.

Copying Files.   In both Turbo and standard Pascal, the contents of one file cannot be copied to another by using an assignment statement of the form *file-variable-1 := file-variable-2*. Rather, the components must be copied one at a time. In Turbo Pascal, however, because file buffers and the procedures *get* and *put* are not provided, a procedure like *CopyFile* in the preceding section must be modified to use the procedures *read* and *write*:

```
procedure CopyFile (var FromFile, ToFile : FileType);

   (* Input:     FromFile.
      Function:  Copies the contents of FromFile into ToFile. The type
                 of the components in these files is ComponentType.
      Output:    ToFile. *)

   var
     Component : ComponentType;

   begin (* CopyFile *)
     while not eof(FromFile) do
       begin
         read (FromFile, Component);
         write (ToFile, Component)
       end (* while *)
   end (* CopyFile *);
```

Files as Parameters. In both Turbo and standard Pascal, formal parameters that represent files must be variable parameters.

11.3   File Updating

One important file-processing problem is file updating, that is, changing the contents of a file by inserting new records into the file, by deleting some records from the file, or by modifying existing records in the file. We have already considered several instances of this problem. For example, the program developed in Section 1.6 copied financial aid information from a text file into an array of records. The user could then modify any number of these records, and these records were written back into a file after the updating was completed. In other applications in which items of information in a file were processed, we copied these items into linked lists (see Section 7.7), a binary search tree (see Section 9.3), or a hash table (see Section 8.6). In all of these examples we assumed that the file was small enough that its contents could be copied and stored in their entirety in main memory. In this section we consider a file-updating problem in which no such assumption is made. In particular, we consider the problem of modifying the records in a master file using the information in a transaction file, where both files are to be processed sequentially. For example, the master file may be an inventory file that is to be updated with a transactions file containing the day's sales and returns; or the master file may be a file of student records that is to be updated with a transaction file containing student grades for a given semester.

Here we consider the particular problem of updating the account records in a master file *AcctFile* using the information in the transaction file *TransFile*, which records the deposits in and withdrawals from customer accounts for a given day. An entry is made in this transactions file each time a deposit or withdrawal is made, and consequently, there may be several entries in this file for a given account. On the other hand, there will undoubtedly be some accounts for which no transactions are recorded.

This type of updating of sequential files can be done most easily and efficiently if both files have been previously sorted (using some sorting scheme like that in the next section) so that the values in some common key field appear in ascending (or descending) order. An algorithm for performing such file updating is as follows:

> **ALGORITHM FOR UPDATING A MASTER FILE**
> **USING A TRANSACTIONS FILE**
>
> (∗ Input: Two files, *MasterFile* and *TransFile*. It is assumed that the
>   records in these fields are ordered so that values in some
>   common key field are in ascending order and that all
>   values in *TransFile* are valid.
>   Function: Updates records in *MasterFile* with information from
>   *TransFile* to produce *NewMasterFile*.
>   Output: The file *NewMasterFile*. ∗)

1. Read the first record from *MasterFile* and assign it to *MasterRec*.
2. Read the first record from *TransFile* and assign it to *TransRec*.
3. Initialize a boolean variable *EndOfUpdate* to false.
4. While not *EndOfUpdate* do the following updating:
   Compare the key fields of *MasterRec* and *TransRec*. If they match, do the following:
   a. Update *MasterRec* using the information in *TransRec*.
   b. If the end of *TransFile* has been reached, set *EndOfUpdate* to true; otherwise read the next value for *TransRec* from *TransFile*.
   If the key fields do not match, do the following:
   a. Write *MasterRec* to *NewMasterFile*.
   b. Read a new value for *MasterRec* from *MasterFile*.
5. Because the last updated master record has not been written, write *MasterRec* to *NewMasterFile*.
6. Copy any remaining records in *MasterFile* into *NewMasterFile*.

The program in Figure 11.6 uses this algorithm to update the contents of *AcctFile* with the entries in *TransFile* and produces *NewAcctFile*. Also shown are the contents of two small files used in a sample run and the updated file produced. (The listings of these nontext files were obtained using programs like those in Figures 11.3 and 11.4.)

```
PROGRAM AcctFileUpdate (AcctFile, TransFile, NewAcctFile);

(*******************************************************************

   Input (file):  Binary files AcctFile and TransFile whose
                  components are records of type BankRecord.  Both
                  files are sorted so that the account numbers are
                  in ascending order.
   Function:      Updates the entries in the master file AcctFile
                  with the entries in the transactions file
                  TransFile.  The records in AcctFile contain the
                  account number and current balance for customers;
                  those in Transfile contain the account number and
                  amount of deposit (+) or withdrawal (-) recorded
                  during some transaction.  The updated records are
                  written to the output file NewAcctFile.
   Output (file): The file NewAcctFile.

********************************************************************)
```

Figure 11.6

Figure 11.6 (cont.)

```
TYPE
   BankRecord = RECORD
                     AcctNumber : integer;
                     Balance : real
                 END;
   Transaction = RECORD
                     TransNumber : integer;
                     Amount : real
                 END;
   MasterFile = FILE OF BankRecord;
   TransactionFile = FILE OF Transaction;

VAR
   AcctRec : BankRecord;          (* record from AcctFile *)
   TransRec : Transaction;        (* record from TransFile *)
   AcctFile,                      (* account file being updated *)
   NewAcctFile : MasterFile;      (* updated account file *)
   TransFile : TransactionFile;   (* file of transactions *)
   EndOfTransFile : boolean;      (* signals end of TransFile *)

BEGIN
   reset (AcctFile);
   reset (TransFile);
   rewrite (NewAcctFile);

   (* Read first record from each file *)

   read (AcctFile, AcctRec);
   read (TransFile, TransRec);

   (* Update records of AcctFile with records of TransFile *)

   EndOfTransFile := false;
   WHILE NOT EndOfTransFile DO
      BEGIN
         WITH AcctRec, TransRec DO
            IF AcctNumber = TransNumber THEN      (* id-numbers match *)
               BEGIN
                  Balance := Balance + Amount;
                  IF eof(TransFile) THEN
                     EndOfTransFile := true
                  ELSE
                     read (TransFile, TransRec)
               END (* IF *)
            ELSE                                  (* no match *)
               BEGIN
                  write (NewAcctFile, AcctRec);
                  read (AcctFile, AcctRec)
               END (* ELSE *)
      END (* WHILE *);

   (* Write AcctRec to NewAcctFile; then copy any
      remaining records from AcctFile *)

   write (NewAcctFile, AcctRec);
   WHILE NOT eof(AcctFile) DO
      BEGIN
         read (AcctFile, AcctRec);
         write (NewAcctFile, AcctRec)
      END (* WHILE *)
END.
```

Figure 11.6 (cont.)

Contents of AcctFile:

```
1141    2297.45
1590     888.32
1611     335.82
1612      55.70
1658    8923.48
1701     620.46
1722    1001.56
1747    2937.52
1751       5.02
1788     192.86
```

Contents of TransFile:

```
1590     111.89
1590     -50.00
1590     -23.39
1658   -1111.11
1701    -200.00
1701    -100.00
1701    -200.00
1701     -50.00
1701     -50.00
1747      12.48
1747      50.00
```

Contents of NewAcctFile:

```
1141    2297.45
1590     926.82
1611     335.82
1612      55.70
1658    7812.37
1701      20.46
1722    1001.56
1747    3000.00
1751       5.02
1788     192.86
```

Exercises

1. Each of the following standard Pascal programs is intended to read a text file *InFile* in which each line contains an integer and to find the sum of all the integers in the file. Explain why each fails to do so.

(a) *reset (InFile)*;
    Sum := 0;
    while not *eof(InFile)* **do**
      begin
        read (InFile, Number);
        Sum := *Sum* + *Number*
      end (* **while** *);

(b) *reset (InFile)*;
    Sum := 0;
    readln (InFile, Number);
    while not *eof(InFile)* **do**
      begin
        Sum := *Sum* + *Number*;
        readln (InFile, Number)
      end (* **while** *);

(c) *reset (InFile)*;
    Sum := 0;
    repeat
      get (InFile);
      Sum := *Sum* + *InFile*↑
    until *eof(InFile)*;

2. Each of the following standard Pascal program segments is intended to display all nonblank characters in the text file *InFile*, with no error resulting. For each, describe a text file for which it fails.

(a) *reset (InFile)*;
    read (InFile, Ch);
    repeat
      if *InFile*↑ = ' ' **then**
        get (InFile)
      else
        begin
          writeln (InFile↑);
          get (InFile)
        end (* **else** *)
    until *eof(InFile)*;

(b) *reset (InFile)*;
    read (InFile, Ch);
    while not *eof(InFile)* **do**
      begin
        while *Ch* = ' ' **do**
          read (InFile, Ch);
        writeln (Ch);
        read (InFile, Ch)
      end (* **while** *);

(c) *reset (InFile)*;
    read (InFile, Ch);
    while not *eof(InFile)* **do**
      begin
        if *Ch* <> ' ' **then**
          writeln (Ch);
        read (InFile, Ch)
      end (* **while** *);

In each of the following exercises, the files *InventoryFile*, *InventoryUpdate*, *UsersFile*, *StudentFile*, and *StudentUpdate* are to be processed as files of records (*not* as text files). See Appendix E for descriptions of the records in these files.

3. Write a program to search *InventoryFile* to find an item with a specified stock number. If a match is found, display the item name and the number currently in stock; otherwise, display a message indicating that it was not found.

4. At the end of each month, a report is produced that shows the status of the account of each user in *UsersFile*. Write a program to read the current date and produce a report of the following form:

```
               USER ACCOUNTS--09/30/91
                                  RESOURCE          RESOURCES
    USER NAME          USER-ID      LIMIT             USED
    - - - - - - - - - - - - - - - - - - - - - - - - - - - - - -
    Joseph Miltgen     100101       $750             $381
    Isaac Small        100102       $650             $599***
         .                .           .                .
         .                .           .                .
         .                .           .                .
```

where the three asterisks (***) indicate that the user has already used 90 percent or more of the resources available to him or her.

5. Write a program to update *InventoryFile* with *InventoryUpdate* to produce a new inventory file. Each record in *InventoryFile* for which there is no record in *InventoryUpdate* with a matching item number should remain unchanged. Each record with one or more corresponding records in *InventoryUpdate* should be updated with the entries in the update file. For transaction code R, the number of items returned should be added to the number in stock. For transaction code S, the number of items sold should be subtracted from the number currently in stock; if more items are sold than are in stock, display a message showing the order number, stock number, item name, and how many should be back ordered (that is, the difference between the number ordered and the number in stock), and set the number currently in stock to zero.

6. (Project) Write a program to read the files *StudentFile* and *StudentUpdate* and produce an updated grade report. This grade report should show

   (a) The current date.
   (b) The student's name and student number.
   (c) A list of the names, grades, and credits for each of the current courses under the headings COURSE, GRADE, and CREDITS.
   (d) Current GPA (multiply credits by numeric grade—A = 4.0, A− = 3.7, B+ = 3.3, B = 3.0, . . . , D− = 0.7, F = 0.0—for each course to find the number of honor points earned for that course; sum these to find the total number of new honor points, and then divide the total number of new honor points by the total number of new credits to give the current GPA, rounded to two decimal places).

(e) Total number of credits taken (old credits from *StudentFile* plus total number of new credits).

(f) New cumulative GPA (first calculate old honor points = old credits times old cumulative GPA and then new cumulative GPA = sum of old honor points and new honor points divided by updated total credits.)

7. (Project) Write a ***text editor*** that performs editing operations on the lines of a text file. Include commands of the following forms in the menu of options:

F *n*	Find and display the *n*th line of the file.
P *n*	Print *n* consecutive lines, beginning with the current line.
M *n*	Move ahead *n* lines from the current line.
T	Move to the top line of the file.
C/*string1*/*string2*/	Change the current line by replacing *string1* with *string2*.
L *string*	Search the file starting from the current line to find a line containing *string*.
D *n*	Delete *n* consecutive lines, beginning with the current line.
I *line*	Insert the given *line* after the current line.

8. (Project) Write a program to implement a computer dating service. It should accept a person's name, sex, and interests (sports, music preference, religion, and the like) and then search a file containing records having these items of information to find the person(s) of the opposite sex who has the most interests in common with the given individual.

9. (Project) Write a menu-driven program that uses *StudentFile* and *StudentUpdate* and allows (some of) the following options. Write a separate procedure for each option so that options and the corresponding procedures can be easily added or removed.

1. Locate a student's permanent record when given his or her student number and print it in a nice format.
2. Same as option 1, but locate the record when given his or her name.
3. Print a list of all student names and numbers in a given class (1, 2, 3, 4, 5).
4. Same as option 3, but for a given major.
5. Same as option 3, but for a given range of cumulative GPAs.
6. Find the average cumulative GPAs for all

   (a) females   (b) males   (c) students with a specified major
   (d) all students. (These are suboptions of menu option 6.)

7. Produce updated grade reports having the following format:

```
                    GRADE REPORT--SEMESTER 1
                           12/23/91

                       DISPATCH UNIVERSITY
           10103 James L. Johnson
                                    GRADE              CREDITS
           -----------------------------------------------------
           ENGL 176                   C                    4
           EDUC 268                   B                    4
           EDUC 330                   B+                   3
           PE 281                     C                    3
           ENGR 317                   D                    4
           Cumulative Credits:        33
           Current GPA:               2.22
           Cumulative GPA             2.64
```

(See Exercise 6 for descriptions of these last items.)

8. Same as option 7, but instead of producing grade reports, produce a new permanent file containing the updated total number of credits and new cumulative GPAs.
9. Produce an updated file when a student (a) drops or (b) adds a new course.
10. Produce an updated file when a student (a) transfers to or (b) withdraws from the university.

11.4 Mergesort

Sorting schemes can be classified as **internal** or **external**, according to whether the collection of data items to be sorted is stored in main memory or in secondary memory. The sorting schemes described in the preceding chapter were internal sorts. In this section we describe two versions of a popular external sorting scheme known as **mergesort.**

As the name suggests, the basic operation in mergesort is **file merging**, that is, combining two files that have previously been sorted so that the resulting file is also sorted. As a simple illustration, suppose that *File1* contains eight integers in increasing order:

File1: 15 20 25 35 45 60 65 70

and *File2* contains five integers in increasing order:

File2: 10 30 40 50 55

In practice, of course, files contain many more items, and each item is usually a record containing several different types of information, and as we have commented before, sorting is then based on some key field within these records.

To merge files *File1* and *File2* to produce sorted *File3*, we read one element from each file, say, X from *File1* and Y from *File2*:

File1: | 15 | 20 25 35 45 60 65 70
↑
X

File2: | 10 | 30 40 50 55
↑
Y

We compare these items and write the smaller, in this case Y, to *File3*:

File3: 10

and then read another value for Y from *File2*:

File1: | 15 | 20 25 35 45 60 65 70
↑
X

File2: 10 | 30 | 40 50 55
↑
Y

Now X is smaller than Y, so it is written to *File3*, and a new value for X is read from *File1*:

File1: 15 | 20 | 25 35 45 60 65 70
↑
X

File2: 10 | 30 | 40 50 55
↑
Y

File3: 10 15

Again, X is less than Y, so it is written to *File3*, and a new value for X is read from *File1*:

File1: 15 20 | 25 | 35 45 60 65 70
↑
X

File2: 10 | 30 | 40 50 55
↑
Y

File3: 10 15 20

Continuing in this manner, we eventually read the value 60 for X and the last value of *File2*, 55, for Y:

File1: 15 20 25 35 45 | 60 | 65 70
↑
X

File2: 10 30 40 50 | 55 |
↑
Y

File3: 10 15 20 25 30 35 40 45 50

Because $Y < X$, we write Y to *File3*:

File3:   10 15 20 25 30 35 40 45 50 55

Because the end of *File2* has been reached, we simply copy the remaining items in *File1* to *File3* to complete the merging:

File3:   10 15 20 25 30 35 40 45 50 55 60 65 70

The general algorithm for merging two sorted files is

MERGE

(∗ Input: Sorted files *File1* and *File2*.
Function: Merges sorted files *File1* and *File2*, giving *File3*.
Output: *File3*. ∗)

1. Open *File1* and *File2* for input, *File3* for output.
2. Read the first element X from *File1* and the first element Y from *File2*.
3. Repeat the following until the end of either *File1* or *File2* is reached:
   If $X < Y$, then
      (i) Write X to *File3*.
      (ii) Read a new X value from *File1*.
   Otherwise:
      (i) Write Y to *File3*.
      (ii) Read a new Y value from *File2*.
4. If the end of *File1* was encountered, copy any remaining elements from *File2* into *File3*. If the end of *File2* was encountered, copy the rest of *File1* into *File3*.

To see how the merge operation can be used in sorting a file, consider the following file F containing sixteen integers:

F: 75 55 15 20 85 30 35 10 60 40 50 25 45 80 70 65

We begin by copying the elements of F alternatively into two other files $F1$ and $F2$:

F1:   75 15 85 35 60 50 45 70

F2:   55 20 30 10 40 25 80 65

We now merge the first one-element subfile of $F1$ with the first one-element subfile of $F2$ to give a sorted two-element subfile of F:

F1:   \[75\] 15 85 35 60 50 45 70

F2:   \[55\] 20 30 10 40 25 80 65

F: \[55 75\]

Next the second one-element subfile of $F1$ is merged with the second one-element subfile of $F2$ and is written to F:

```
F1:   75  15  85  35  60  50  45  70
F2:   55  20  30  10  40  25  80  65
F:    55  75  15  20
```

This merging of corresponding one-element subfiles continues until the end of either or both of the files *F1* and *F2* is reached. If either file still contains a subfile, it is simply copied into *F*:

```
F:  55 75 | 15 20 | 30 85 | 10 35 | 40 60 | 25 50 | 45 80 | 65 70
```

As the highlighted blocks indicate, the file *F* now consists of a sequence of two-element subfiles. We again split it into files *F1* and *F2*, copying these two-element subfiles alternately to *F1* and *F2*:

```
F1:  55 75 | 30 85 | 40 60 | 45 80
```

```
F2:  15 20 | 10 35 | 25 50 | 65 70
```

Now we merge corresponding subfiles in *F1* and *F2* to produce four-element sorted subfiles in *F*:

```
F:  15 20 55 75 | 10 30 35 85 | 25 40 50 60 | 45 65 70 80
```

Now, using four-element subfiles, we again split *F* by copying subfiles alternately to *F1* and *F2*:

```
F1:  15 20 55 75 | 25 40 50 60
```

```
F2:  10 30 35 85 | 45 65 70 80
```

and then merge corresponding four-element subfiles to produce eight-element sorted subfiles in *F*:

```
F:  10 15 20 30 35 55 75 85 | 25 40 45 50 60 65 70 80
```

The next splitting into files *F1* and *F2* produces

```
F1:  10 15 20 30 35 55 75 85
```

```
F2:  25 40 45 50 60 65 70 80
```

and merging corresponding eight-element subfiles in *F1* and *F2* produces one sorted sixteen-element sorted subfile in *F*, so that *F* has now been sorted:

```
F:  10 15 20 25 30 35 40 45 50 55 60 65 70 75 80 85
```

In this example, the size of *F* is a power of 2, so that all the subfiles produced by the split and merge operations have the same size, and this size is also a power of 2. In general, this will be true for all of the subfiles except possibly for the last one, which may have fewer elements. Although this means that some care must be exercised in checking for the ends of files and subfiles in this version of mergesort, known as ***binary mergesort***, it does not present any serious difficulties in designing the required split and merge algorithms.

A more serious criticism of binary mergesort is that it restricts itself to subfiles of sizes 1, 2, 4, 8, . . . , 2^k, where $2^k \geq$ size of F and must therefore always go through a series of k split–merge phases. If sorted subfiles of other sizes are allowed, the number of phases can be reduced in those situations where the file contains longer "runs" of elements that are already in order. A version of mergesort that takes advantage of these "natural" sorted subfiles (in contrast to the "artificial" sizes and subfiles created by binary mergesort) is called ***natural mergesort***, naturally.

As an illustration of natural mergesort, consider again the file F used to demonstrate binary mergesort:

$$F: \quad 75 \quad 55 \quad 15 \quad 20 \quad 85 \quad 30 \quad 35 \quad 10 \quad 60 \quad 40 \quad 50 \quad 25 \quad 45 \quad 80 \quad 70 \quad 65$$

Notice that several segments of F consist of elements that are already in order

$$F: \quad \boxed{75} \; \boxed{55} \; \boxed{15 \quad 20 \quad 85} \; \boxed{30 \quad 35} \; \boxed{10 \quad 60} \; \boxed{40 \quad 50} \; \boxed{25 \quad 45 \quad 80} \; \boxed{70} \; \boxed{65}$$

and that these sorted subfiles subdivide F in a natural way.

We begin as before by copying subfiles of F alternately to two other files, $F1$ and $F2$, but using these natural subfiles rather than requiring that at each stage, their sizes be a power of 2:

$$F1: \quad \boxed{75} \; \boxed{15 \quad 20 \quad 85} \; \boxed{10 \quad 60} \; \boxed{25 \quad 45 \quad 80} \; \boxed{65}$$

$$F2: \quad \boxed{55} \; \boxed{30 \quad 35} \; \boxed{40 \quad 50} \; \boxed{70}$$

We now identify the natural sorted subfiles in each of $F1$ and $F2$:

$$F1: \quad \boxed{75} \; \boxed{15 \quad 20 \quad 85} \; \boxed{10 \quad 60} \; \boxed{25 \quad 45 \quad 80} \; \boxed{65}$$

$$F2: \quad \boxed{55} \; \boxed{30 \quad 35 \quad 40 \quad 50 \quad 70}$$

Notice that although the subfiles of $F1$ are the same as those copied from F, the last three subfiles written to $F2$ have combined to form a larger subfile.

Now, proceeding as in binary mergesort, we merge the first subfile of $F1$ with the first one in $F2$ to produce a sorted subfile in F:

$$F: \quad \boxed{55 \quad 75}$$

and then merge the second subfiles:

$$F: \quad \boxed{55 \quad 75} \; \boxed{15 \quad 20 \quad 30 \quad 35 \quad 40 \quad 50 \quad 70 \quad 85}$$

Since we have now reached the end of $F2$, we simply copy the remaining subfiles of $F1$ back to F:

$$F: \quad \boxed{55 \quad 75} \; \boxed{15 \quad 20 \quad 30 \quad 35 \quad 40 \quad 50 \quad 70 \quad 85} \; \boxed{10 \quad 60} \; \boxed{25 \quad 45 \quad 80} \; \boxed{65}$$

Now we again split F, alternately copying sorted subfiles to $F1$ and $F2$:

$F1$: | 55 75 | 10 60 | 65 |

$F2$: | 15 20 30 35 40 50 70 85 | 25 45 80 |

This time we see that two subfiles of $F1$ combine to form a larger subfile:

$F1$: | 55 75 | 10 60 65 |

$F2$: | 15 20 30 35 40 50 70 85 | 25 45 80 |

As before, we merge corresponding subfiles of $F1$ and $F2$, writing the results back to F:

F: | 15 20 30 35 40 50 55 70 75 85 | 10 25 45 60 65 80 |

In the next phase, splitting F produces files $F1$ and $F2$, each of which contains only one sorted subfile, and thus they are themselves completely sorted files:

$F1$: | 15 20 30 35 40 50 55 70 75 85 |

$F2$: | 10 25 45 60 65 80 |

Consequently, when we perform the merge operation in this phase, F will be a sorted file:

F: | 10 15 20 25 30 35 40 45 50 55 60 65 70 75 80 85 |

Notice that one fewer split–merge phase was required here than in binary mergesort.

The splitting operation in natural mergesort is carried out by the following algorithm:

SPLIT ALGORITHM FOR NATURAL MERGESORT

(* Input: File F.
    Function: Splits file F into files $F1$ and $F2$ by copying natural sorted
              subfiles of F alternately to $F1$ and $F2$.
    Output: Files $F1$ and $F2$. *)

1. Open the file F for input and the files $F1$ and $F2$ for output.
2. While the end of F has not been reached, do the following:
    a. Copy a sorted subfile of F into $F1$ as follows: Repeatedly read
       an element of F and write it into $F1$ until the next element in F
       is smaller than this copied item or the end of F is reached.
    b. If the end of F has not been reached, copy the next sorted
       subfile of F into $F2$ in a similar manner.

And the following algorithm implements the merge operation illustrated in the example:

MERGE ALGORITHM FOR NATURAL MERGESORT

(* Input: Files *F1* and *F2*.

    Function: Merges corresponding sorted subfiles in *F1* and *F2* back into file *F. NumSubFiles* is the number of sorted subfiles produced in *F*.

    Output: File *F*. *)

1. Open files *F1* and *F2* for input, *F* for output.
2. Initialize *NumSubFiles* to 0.
3. While neither the end of *F1* nor the end of *F2* has been reached, do the following:
    a. While no end of a subfile in *F1* or in *F2* has been reached, do the following:
       If the next element in *F1* is less than the next element in *F2*, then copy the next element from *F1* into *F* ; otherwise, copy the next element from *F2* into *F*.
    b. If the end of a subfile in *F1* has been reached, then copy the rest of the corresponding subfile in *F2* to *F*; otherwise, copy the rest of the corresponding subfile in *F1* to *F*.
    c. Increment *NumSubFiles* by 1.
4. Copy any subfiles remaining in *F1* or *F2* to *F*, incrementing *NumSubFiles* by 1 for each.

An algorithm for natural mergesort consists of simply calling these two algorithms repeatedly until the file is sorted:

NATURAL MERGESORT

(* Input: File *F*.

    Function: Sorts a file *F* using two auxiliary files *F1* and *F2*.

    Output: Sorted file *F*. *)

Repeat the following steps:

1. Call the *Split* algorithm to split *F* into files *F1* and *F2*.
2. Call the *Merge* algorithm to merge corresponding subfiles in *F1* and *F2* back into *F*.

Until *NumSubFiles* = 1

Mergesort can also be used as an internal sorting method for lists. The split and merge algorithms can easily be modified to use arrays or linked lists in place of the files *F, F1*, and *F2*.

The worst case for natural mergesort occurs when the items are in reverse order. In this case, natural mergesort functions in exactly the same way as binary mergesort does, using subfiles of sizes 1, 2, 4, 8, and so on. It follows that to sort a file or list of *n* items, $\log_2 n$ split and merge operations are required and each of the n items must be examined in each of them. Hence, in the worst case, and as can be shown for the average case also, the computing time of natural mergesort is $O(n \log_2 n)$.

The standard Pascal program in Figure 11.7 uses natural mergesort to sort the employee file *EmpFile* described in Section 11.1 using the key field *Number* so that the employee records are arranged in such a way that the employee numbers are in ascending order. In this program, procedure *Mergesort* has the structure indicated in the following diagram:

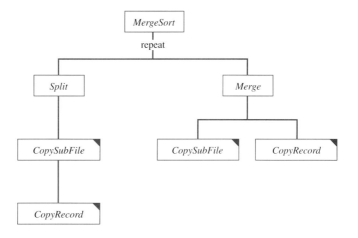

Procedures *Split* and *Merge* implement the split and merge algorithms. Both use the procedures *CopyRecord* and *CopySubFile* to copy one item or a sorted subfile, respectively, from one file to another. Also included in Figure 11.7 is a listing of employee numbers in their original order and a listing in the order produced by the program. These listings were obtained by adding procedures similar to the programs in Figures 11.3 and 11.4 for reading and displaying information in binary files.

```
PROGRAM SortWithMergesort (output, EmpFile);

(************************************************************************

   Input (file):    The binary file EmpFile whose components are
                    records of type EmployeeRecord.
   Function:        Sorts EmpFile using the natural mergesort
                    algorithm to produce NewEmpFile.
   Output (file):   The sorted file EmpFile.
   Output (screen): Message indicating that sorting is complete.

************************************************************************)
```

Figure 11.7

Figure 11.7 (cont.)

```
TYPE
   ShortString = PACKED ARRAY[1..12] OF char;
   LongString = PACKED ARRAY[1..24] OF char;
   DeptType = (Factory, Office, Sales);
   EmployeeRecord =  RECORD
                        Number : integer;
                        LastName,
                        FirstName : ShortString;
                        MidInitial : char;
                        StreetAddress,
                        CityState : LongString;
                        PhoneNumber : ShortString;
                        Sex : char;
                        Age,
                        Dependents : integer;
                        Dept : DeptType;
                        Union : boolean;
                        HourlyRate : real
                     END;
   FileType = FILE OF EmployeeRecord;

VAR
   EmpFile : FileType;           (* external file to be sorted *)

PROCEDURE Mergesort (VAR F : FileType);

   (*********************************************************************

      Input (file):  F.
      Function:      Mergesorts file F.
      Output (file): Sorted file F.

   *********************************************************************)

   VAR
      F1, F2 : FileType;       (* auxiliary files used in mergesort *)
      NumSubfiles : integer;   (* number of subfiles in F *)

   PROCEDURE CopyRecord (VAR FromFile, ToFile : FileType;
                         VAR EndSubfile : boolean);

      (*****************************************************************

         Input (file):  FromFile.
         Function:      Copies one record from FromFile to ToFile
                        and checks if the field Number in the next
                        record in FromFile is smaller than that in
                        the record just copied.
         Output (file): ToFile.
         Output (param): Boolean value EndSubFile, which is true if
                        the end of a subfile in FromFile has been
                        reached and is false otherwise.

      *****************************************************************)
```

Figure 11.7 (cont.)

```
    BEGIN (* CopyRecord *)
        IF NOT eof(FromFile) THEN
            BEGIN
                read (FromFile, ToFile^);
                IF eof(FromFile) THEN
                    EndSubFile := true
                ELSE
                    EndSubFile := (FromFile^.Number < ToFile^.Number);
                put (ToFile)
            END (* IF *)
        ELSE
            EndSubFile := true
    END (* CopyRecord *);

PROCEDURE CopySubFile (VAR FromFile, ToFile : FileType;
                       VAR EndSubFile : boolean);

    (******************************************************************

        Input (file):  FromFile.
        Function:      Copies a sorted subfile from FromFile to
                       ToFile.
        Output (file): ToFile.

    ******************************************************************)

    BEGIN (* CopySubFile *)
        EndSubfile := false;
        WHILE NOT EndSubfile DO
            CopyRecord (FromFile, ToFile, EndSubfile)
    END (* CopySubFile *);

PROCEDURE SplitFile (VAR F, F1, F2 : FileType);

    (******************************************************************

        Input (file):  F.
        Function:      Splits file F into files F1 and F2 by
                       copying natural sorted subfiles of F
                       alternately to F1 and F2.
        Output (file): F1 and F2.

    ******************************************************************)

    VAR
        FileNum : 1..2;        (* # of file being written to *)
        EndSubfile : boolean;  (* indicates end of subfile *)
```

Figure 11.7 (cont.)

```
BEGIN (* SplitFile *)

   (* Open the files *)

   reset (F);
   rewrite (F1);
   rewrite (F2);

   (* Split the file *)

   FileNum := 1;
   WHILE NOT eof(F) DO
      BEGIN
         CASE FileNum OF
               1 : CopySubFile (F, F1, EndSubfile);
               2 : CopySubFile (F, F2, EndSubfile)
         END (* CASE *);

         (* Switch to other file *)

         FileNum := 3 - FileNum
      END (* WHILE *)
END (* SplitFile *);

PROCEDURE Merge (VAR F, F1, F2 : FileType; VAR NumSubfiles : integer);

   (*****************************************************************

      Input (file):  F1 and F2.
      Function:      Merges corresponding sorted subfiles in F1
                     and F2 back into file F.  NumSubFiles is the
                     number of sorted subfiles produced in F.
      Output (file): F.

   *****************************************************************)

VAR
   EndSubfile1,               (* indicates end of subfile in F1 *)
   EndSubfile2 : boolean;     (*      "        "    "    "    " F2 *)

BEGIN (* Merge *)

   (* Open the files *)

   reset (F1);
   reset (F2);
   rewrite (F);

   (* Now merge subfiles of F1 & F2 into F *)

   NumSubfiles := 0;
   WHILE NOT (eof(F1) OR eof(F2)) DO
      BEGIN
         EndSubfile1 := false;
         EndSubfile2 := false;
```

Figure 11.7 (cont.)

```
                  (* merge two subfiles *)

                  REPEAT
                     IF F1^.Number < F2^.Number THEN
                        CopyRecord (F1, F, EndSubfile1)
                     ELSE
                        CopyRecord (F2, F, EndSubfile2)
                  UNTIL EndSubfile1 OR EndSubfile2;

                  (* copy rest of other subfile *)

                  IF EndSubfile1 THEN
                     CopySubFile (F2, F, EndSubfile2)
                  ELSE
                     CopySubFile (F1, F, EndSubfile1);
                  NumSubfiles := NumSubfiles + 1
               END (* WHILE *);

            (* Now copy any remaining subfiles in F1 or F2 to F *)

            WHILE NOT eof(F1) DO
               BEGIN
                  CopySubFile (F1, F, EndSubfile1);
                  NumSubfiles := NumSubfiles + 1
               END (* WHILE *);
            WHILE NOT eof(F2) DO
               BEGIN
                  CopySubFile (F2, F, EndSubfile2);
                  NumSubfiles := NumSubfiles + 1
               END (* WHILE *);
         END (* Merge *);

   BEGIN (* Mergesort *)
      NumSubfiles := 0;
      REPEAT
         SplitFile (F, F1, F2);
         Merge (F, F1, F2, NumSubfiles)
      UNTIL NumSubfiles = 1
   END (* Mergesort *);

BEGIN (* main program *)
   Mergesort(EmpFile);
   writeln ('Sorting completed')
END (* main program *).
```

Employee numbers in original file:

```
2101
3592
1868
1045
2990
```

Figure 11.7 (cont.)

Employee numbers in sorted file:

```
1045
1868
2101
2990
3592
```

The preceding program uses the look-ahead property provided by the file window to examine the next record in a file without actually reading it. In versions of Pascal such as Turbo Pascal that do not provide the file window, the program must be modified to simulate this look-ahead feature.

Exercises

1. Using diagrams like those in the text, show the various splitting–merging stages of binary mergesort for the following lists of numbers:

   (a) 13, 57, 39, 85, 70, 22, 64, 48
   (b) 13, 57, 39, 85, 99, 70, 22, 48, 64
   (c) 13, 22, 57, 99, 39, 64, 57, 48, 70
   (d) 13, 22, 39, 48, 57, 64, 70, 85
   (e) 85, 70, 65, 57, 48, 39, 22, 13

2. Repeat Exercise 1 but use natural mergesort.

3. Write a program that uses natural mergesort, appropriately modified, to sort a list stored in an array.

4. Proceed as in Exercise 3, but for a linked list. For the merge operation, merge the two linked lists by simply changing links rather than actually copying the list elements into a third list.

5. Suppose that we sort a list of records in which some of the values in the key field may be the same. A sorting scheme is said to be *stable* if it does not change the order of such records. For example, consider a list of records containing a person's name and age that is to be sorted so that the ages are in ascending order. Suppose that

comes before

| Smith | 39 |

in the original list (with possibly several records between them). For a stable sorting scheme, Doe's record still comes before Smith's after the list is sorted. Determine whether each of the following is a stable sorting method:

(a) Simple selection sort
(b) Bubble sort
(c) Linear insertion sort
(d) Heapsort
(e) Quicksort
(f) Binary mergesort
(g) Natural mergesort

6. One variation of the mergesort method is to modify the splitting operation as follows: Copy some fixed number of elements into main memory, sort them using an internal sorting method such as quicksort, and write this sorted list to *F1*; then read the same number of elements from *F* into main memory, sort them internally, and write this sorted list to *F2*; and so on, alternating between *F1* and *F2*. Write procedures for this modified mergesort scheme, using quicksort to sort internally the sublists containing *Size* elements for some constant *Size*.

7. Write a procedure to carry out a ***three-way merge***, that is, a procedure that merges three sorted files to form another sorted file.

8. Use the procedure in Exercise 7 to merge three files of records containing names and phone numbers, sorted so that the names are in alphabetical order. For duplicate entries in the files, put only one entry in the final file.

9. Use the procedure in Exercise 7 in a program that performs a ***ternary mergesort***, which differs from binary mergesort in that three files rather than two are used to split a given file.

10. Modify the program in Figure 11.7 to use binary mergesort instead of natural mergesort.

11. (Project) Write a program to read titles of books or magazine articles and prepare a KWIC (Key Word In Context) index. Each word in a title, except for such simple words as AND, OF, THE, and A, is considered to be a keyword. The program should read the titles and construct a file containing the keywords together with the corresponding title, sort the file using the mergesort method, and then display the KWIC index. For example, the titles

    FUNDAMENTALS OF PROGRAMMING
    PROGRAMMING FUNDAMENTALS FOR DATA STRUCTURES

should produce the following KWIC index:

DATA STRUCTURES // PROGRAMMING FUNDAMENTALS FOR
FUNDAMENTALS FOR DATA STRUCTURES // PROGRAMMING
OF PROGRAMMING
PROGRAMMING FUNDAMENTALS FOR DATA STRUCTURES
// FUNDAMENTALS OF
STRUCTURES // PROGRAMMING FUNDAMENTALS FOR DATA

12. If possible with your version of Pascal, write a program to compare the computing times of binary mergesort and natural mergesort for files of randomly generated integers. (See Exercise 5 of Section 3.6 regarding how to measure execution time, and footnote 2 in Section 5.2 concerning random number generation.)

13. *Polyphase sort* is another external sorting scheme of the mergesort variety. A simple version of it begins by merging one-element subfiles in two files, *F1* and *F2*, forming sorted subfiles of size 2 in a third file, *F3*. However, only enough subfiles are merged to empty one of *F1* and *F2*—say, *F1*. The remaining one-element subfiles in *F2* are then merged with the two-element subfiles in *F3* to produce subfiles of length 3 and are written to *F1* until *F2* becomes empty. The remaining two-element subfiles of *F3* are then merged with three-element subfiles of *F2* to form subfiles of length 5 in *F1* until *F3* becomes empty. This process continues until the sorting is complete.

Note that the sequence of subfile lengths in polyphase sort is 1, 1, 2, 3, 5, 8, 13, 21, 34, . . . , the sequence of *Fibonacci numbers* (see Section 6.1). The final subfile length (which is also the size of the original file *F3* to be sorted) must therefore be some Fibonacci number f_n. It also follows that the sizes of the initial files *F1* and *F2* must be the two Fibonacci numbers f_{n-1} and f_{n-2}, which precede f_n. Rewrite the program in Figure 11.7 to sort *EmpFile* using polyphase sort, adding "dummy" subfiles to either *F*1 or *F*2 if necessary to make their sizes two consecutive Fibonacci numbers and removing them when sorting is completed.

11.5 Direct Access Files

Direct access or *random access files* are files in which each component can be accessed directly by specifying its location in the file, thus making it possible to read or write components anywhere in the file. A direct access file can be thought of, therefore, as a very large array that is stored in secondary memory instead of in main memory (so access to its components is slower than for arrays). In this section we describe some of the techniques used in processing direct access files. As we have noted, standard Pascal does not support direct access files, but many other versions do. In the examples of this section we use the direct access file features provided in Turbo Pascal.

A direct access file cannot be a text file, but any other type of file is allowed. Before its components can be accessed, the file variable used to refer to the file in the program must be associated with the name of a disk file that contains the actual data to be processed, using the procedure *assign* in the usual way. The file must then be opened for input/output by using either of the procedures *reset* or *rewrite*, as described earlier. Also, the procedure *close* should be used to close the file after input/output is completed.

Once a direct access file has been opened, any particular component can be accessed by using the predefined procedure *seek*. It is called with a statement of the form

    seek (file-variable, component-number)

where *component-number* is an integer expression specifying the number of the component to be located in the file; the numbering of the components begins with 0. Seeking a component whose number is one more than the number of the last component is permitted, and this positions the data pointer at the end of the file so that a new component can be added there. Using a component number that is larger than this or that is negative is an error.

The predefined Turbo Pascal functions *FilePos* and *FileSize* are useful in positioning the data pointer in a direct access file. A reference to *FilePos* has the form

    FilePos(file-variable)

and returns a value of type *longint* that is the number of the component at which the data pointer is currently positioned. *FileSize* is referenced with an expression of the form

    FileSize(file-variable)

Its value is of type *longint* and is the number of components in the file, 0 if the file is empty. A reference to *seek* of the form

    seek (FileSize(file-variable))

thus positions the data pointer at the end of the file.

Once a component has been located with *seek*, the procedure *read* can be used to read this component. For example, to read the record of the employee that is the *RecNum*th component in *EmpFile*, we can use the statements

    seek (EmpFile, RecNum);
    read (EmpFile, EmpRec);

The procedure *write* can be used to replace the component at which the data pointer is currently positioned. For example, to modify some of the fields such as the pay rate in the employee record that is the *RecNum*th component of *EmpFile*, we can use

```
seek (EmpFile, RecNum);
read (EmpFile, EmpRec);
with EmpRec do
  begin
    writeln ('Employee # ', Number);
    write ('Enter new hourly pay rate: ');
    readln (HourlyRate)
  end (* with *);
seek (EmpFile, RecNum);
write (EmpFile, EmpRec);
```

Note that it is necessary to call *seek* to reposition the data pointer at the *RecNum*th component, since the *read* procedure advances it to the next component.

Of course, to access a particular component in a direct access file, it is necessary to know its component number. For example, suppose we wish to locate the record for an employee whose number *NumDesired* has been entered by the user during program execution. If the file were constructed so that the *n*th record in the file corresponded to the employee whose number is *n*, then the task would be trivial. However, this is not likely because, for example, if social security numbers were used for employee numbers, the record for employee 567–34–9999 would be stored in the 567,349,999th record in the file, but most of the file components numbered 0 through 567,349,998 would probably not be used.

Of course we could just adapt linear search to files:

```
Pos := 0;
Found := False;
while not Found and (Pos < NumRecords) do
  begin
    seek (EmpFile, Pos);
    read (EmpFile, EmpRec);
    if EmpRec.Number = NumDesired then
      Found := true
    else
      Pos := Pos + 1
  end (* while *);
```

But this searches the file sequentially and does not take advantage of the fact that we have direct access to each component.

An alternative strategy might be to use a hash function *h* so that *h*(*NumDesired*) is the number of the file component where this employee's record should be found and, if it is not, to search for it using a search strategy consistent with the way the hash table was created.

If the file has been sorted so the employee numbers are in ascending order, for example, by using mergesort, then binary search could be used, since we have direct access to each file component:

```
First := 0;
Last := NumRecords ;
Found := False;
while not Found and (First <= Last ) do
   begin
      Pos := (First + Last) div 2;
      seek (EmpFile, Pos);
      read (EmpFile, EmpRec);
      if NumDesired < EmpRec.Number then
         Last := Pos − 1
      else if NumDesired > EmpRec.Number then
         First := Pos + 1
      else
         Found := true
end (* while *);
```

One difficulty with most of these search techniques is the large number of file components that must be transferred from secondary memory to main memory, where they can be examined by the search procedure. Such transfers may be prohibitively time-consuming, especially if the records are large.

An alternative is to use an **index** to establish a correspondence between key values and component numbers. This index is a list of key values stored in main memory—in an array, for example—arranged in the same order as they appear in the file. Thus the location of a given key value in this list is the same as the number of the corresponding record in the file. We search this index for some particular key value using some internal search method such as binary search, and its position in this index is the number of the desired record in the file:

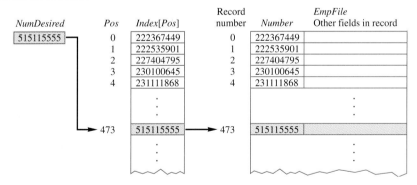

This record can then be fetched using only one transfer from secondary memory to main memory.

The file update program in Figure 11.8 illustrates the use of an index to locate an employee record in a direct access file *EmpFile*. This index is stored in the array *Index*, which is constructed by reading the employee numbers from the file *EmpNumberFile*. This program assumes that the files *EmpFile* and *EmpNumberFile* are sorted with employee numbers in ascending order, so that binary search can be used to locate an employee number entered by the user in this index. Once the record for that employee is retrieved from *EmpFile*, the user can then modify it. For simplicity, this program allows a change only in the hourly rate, but it can easily be modified to allow changes in the other fields of the employee records.

```
PROGRAM EmployeeFileUpdate (input, output, EmpFile, EmpNumFile);

(*******************************************************************

    Input (file):       The binary file EmpFile whose components are
                        records of type EmployeeRecord and the text
                        file EmpNumFile containing employee numbers.
    Input (keyboard):   File name and new hourly rates for employeees.
    Function:           Update a direct access file EmpFile.  An
                        employee number is entered by the user; the
                        number of the record in EmpFile for this
                        employee is looked up in Index; the record is
                        retrieved and displayed; modifications are
                        made; and the updated record is then
                        rewritten to the file.
    Output (file):      Updated file EmpFile.
    Output (screen):    Contents of employee records and various
                        messages.

    Note:               This is a Turbo Pascal program.

********************************************************************)

CONST
    MaxRecNum = 100;

TYPE
    DeptType = (Factory, Office, Sales);
    EmployeeRecord =  RECORD
                        Number : integer;
                        LastName,
                        FirstName : string;
                        MidInitial : char;
                        StreetAddress,
                        CityState,
                        PhoneNumber : string;
                        Gender : char;
                        Age,
                        Dependents : integer;
                        Dept : DeptType;
                        Union : boolean;
                        HourlyRate : real
                      END;
    FileType = FILE OF EmployeeRecord;
    IndexArray = ARRAY[0..MaxRecNum] of integer;
```

Figure 11.8

Figure 11.8 (cont.)

```
VAR
   EmpFile : FileType;          (* direct access employee file *)
   EmpNumFile : text;           (* file of employee numbers *)
   EmpRec : EmployeeRecord;     (* an employee record *)
   RecNum,                      (* number of a record in EmpFile *)
   LastRecNum,                  (* number of last record in EmpFile *)
   EmpNum : integer;            (* employee number *)
   Index : IndexArray;          (* index for EmpFile *)
   Found : boolean;             (* signals if entry found in Index *)

PROCEDURE ConstructIndex (VAR EmpNumFile : text; VAR Index : IndexArray;
                          VAR Last : integer);

   (*****************************************************************

      Input (file):     The binary file EmpFile whose components are
                        records of type EmployeeRecord.
      Input(keyboard):  Name of file.
      Function:         Constructs an Index of employee numbers by
                        reading them in order from EmpNumberFile.
      Output (param):   The array Index and the number Last of the last
                        record in EmpFile.

   *****************************************************************)

   VAR
      FileName : string;   (* actual name of employee number file *)

   BEGIN (* ConstructIndex *)
      write ('Name of file of employee numbers?  ');
      readln (FileName);
      assign (EmpNumFile, FileName);
      reset (EmpNumFile);
      Last := -1;
      WHILE NOT eof(EmpNumFile) DO
         BEGIN
            Last := Last + 1;
            readln (EmpNumFile, Index[Last]);
         END (* WHILE *)
   END (* ConstructIndex *);
```

Figure 11.8 (cont.)

```
PROCEDURE Search (VAR Index : IndexArray; Last, EmpNumber : integer;
                  VAR Found : boolean; VAR Location : integer);

    (****************************************************************

        Input (param):   A zero-based array Index, the position Last of
                         the last element in the array, and an employee
                         number EmpNum.
        Function:        Uses a binary search to look EmpNum up in Index
                         which has first entry in location 0 and last
                         entry in location Last.
        Output (param):  Found is true and Location is the position of
                         EmpNum in Index if the search is successful;
                         otherwise Found is false.

    ****************************************************************)

    VAR
        First,              (* first item in sublist being searched *)
        Middle : integer;   (* middle item in sublist *)

    BEGIN (* Search *)
        First := 0;
        Found := false;
        WHILE (First <= Last) AND (NOT Found) DO
            BEGIN
                Middle := (First + Last) DIV 2;
                IF EmpNum < Index[Middle] THEN
                    Last := Middle - 1   (* EmpNum in first half of sublist *)
                ELSE IF EmpNum > Index[Middle] THEN
                    First := Middle + 1  (* EmpNum in last half of sublist *)
                ELSE
                    BEGIN                        (* EmpNum found *)
                        Found := true;
                        Location := Middle
                    END (* IF *)
            END (* WHILE *)
    END (* Search *);

PROCEDURE Update (VAR EmpFile: FileType; Index : IndexArray);

    (****************************************************************

        Input (file):     The file EmpFile of employee records.
        Input (param):    The array Index.
        Input (keyboard): File name and new hourly rates for employees.
        Function:         Updates hourly rates for employees in EmpFile.
                          User enters an employee number that is looked
                          up in Index.  Its location in Index is then
                          used as the number of the employee's record in
                          the direct access file EmpFile.
        Output (file):    Updated file EmpFile.
        Output (screen):  Employee records and messages to the user.

    ****************************************************************)

    VAR
        FileName : string;          (* actual name of employee file *)
```

Figure 11.8 (cont.)

```
     BEGIN (* Update *)
        (* open EmpFile *)
        write ('Name of file to be updated?  ');
        readln (FileName);
        assign (EmpFile, FileName);
        reset (EmpFile);
        (* update the file *)
        writeln ('Enter negative employee number to stop.');
        writeln;
        write ('Employee #?  ');
        readln (EmpNum);
        WHILE EmpNum > 0 DO
           BEGIN
              Search (Index, LastRecNum, EmpNum, Found, RecNum);
              IF NOT Found THEN
                 writeln ('No such employee number')
              ELSE
                 BEGIN
                    seek (EmpFile, RecNum);
                    read(EmpFile, EmpRec);
                    WITH EmpRec DO
                       BEGIN
                          writeln (Number, ' ', FirstName, ' ', MidInitial,
                                      '. ', LastName);
                          writeln ('Hourly rate:  $', HourlyRate:4:2);
                          write ('New hourly rate?  $');
                          readln (HourlyRate);
                       END (* WITH *);
                    seek (EmpFile, RecNum);
                    write (EmpFile, EmpRec)
                 END (* ELSE *);
              writeln;
              write ('Employee #?  ');
              readln (EmpNum)
           END (* WHILE *);
        writeln;
        writeln ('File updating completed');
        close(EmpFile)
     END (* Update *);

BEGIN (* main program *)
   ConstructIndex (EmpNumFile, Index, LastRecNum);
   Update (EmpFile, Index)
END (* main program *).
```

Sample run:

```
Name of file of employee numbers?  EMPNUMS.DAT
Name of file to be updated?  DAEMPFILE.DAT
Enter negative employee number to stop.

Employee #?  1868
1868 Mary A. Smith
Hourly rate:  $9.76
New hourly rate?  $9.95
```

Figure 11.8 (cont.)

```
Employee #?  1868
1868 Mary A. Smith
Hourly rate:  $9.95
New hourly rate?  $9.95

Employee #?  3591
No such employee number

Employee #?  3592
3592 Alfred E. Newman
Hourly rate:  $4.00
New hourly rate?  $4.10

Employee #?  -1

File updating completed
```

In file update programs like that in Figure 11.8, it may well be the case that the number of records is so large that even the index is too large to store in main memory and/or that searching it is not practical. One common alternative, known as *indexed sequential search*, uses a smaller index by having each entry refer to a block of consecutive file components rather than to an individual component. More precisely, the *i*th entry in the index is the largest key value in the *i*th block of components, where we assume the file has been

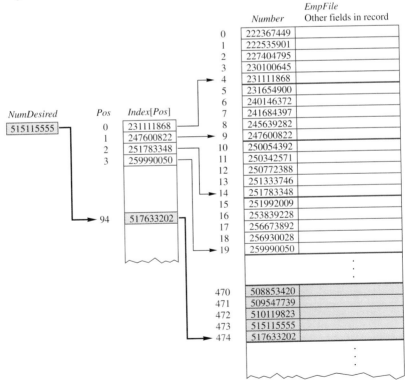

Figure 11.9

previously sorted so that the key values are in ascending order. To locate the record containing a particular key value, we search the index for the first entry that is greater than or equal to the desired key. Its position in the index determines the block in the file where the desired record should be found, and we can search this block sequentially to locate it or to determine that it is not in the file. This is illustrated in Figure 11.9 for *EmpFile*, where a block size of 5 is used.

The file may be so large that even this index is too large. For the index to be sufficiently small, it may be necessary to use a large block size to keep the number of index entries manageable. But now, large parts of the file will have to be searched sequentially, and so we are back again to the problem of slow transfer of information from secondary memory to main memory. However, what has been done once can be done again! We simply construct a secondary index that acts as an index to the primary index for the file. This is illustrated in Figure 11.10, where blocks of size 5 are used for the file and blocks of size 3 in the primary index.

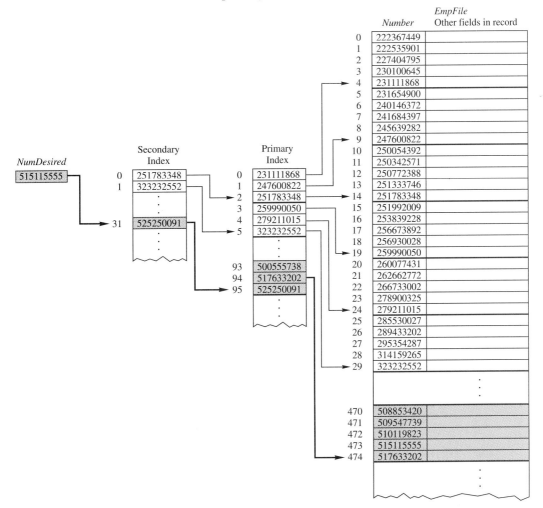

Figure 11.10

Exercises

1. Write procedures *ReadDirect* and *WriteDirect* that simulate direct access file input/output using only sequential access. *ReadDirect* should accept a file variable and a record number *n* and should return the *n*th record in the file or signal a read error if there is no such record. *WriteDirect* should accept a file variable, a record number *n*, and a record and should modify the file by replacing the *n*th record in the file with this record.

2. Information about computer terminals in a computer network is maintained in a direct access file. The terminals are numbered 1 through 100, and information about the *n*th terminal is stored in the *n*th record of the file. This information consists of a terminal type (string), the building in which it is located (string), its transmission rate (integer), an access code (character), and the date of last service (month, day, year). Write a program to read a terminal number, retrieve and display the information about that terminal, and modify the date of last service for that terminal.

3. Write a program similar to that in Figure 11.8 for processing *InventoryFile*, considered as a direct access file of records described in Appendix E. The program should first construct an index that contains item numbers as key values. (For this, you might first write a "pre-processor" program that reads through *InventoryFile*, regarded as a sequential file, and constructs a file containing the item numbers. Note that the records in *InventoryFile* are arranged so that the item numbers are in ascending order.) The program should then allow the user to enter item numbers, and it should retrieve the information in the file for that item. This search should be carried out using a binary search of the index.

4. Write a program like that in Exercise 3 for retrieving information from *InventoryFile*, but use a hash table for the index. For the rather small sample *InventoryFile* in Appendix E, you might use a hash table of size 11 and hashing function *h(item-number)* = (last three digits of *item-number*) **mod** 11.

5. Write a program like that in Exercise 3 for retrieving information from *InventoryFile*, but use an indexed sequential search like that described in this section.

6. Write a program like that in Exercise 3 for retrieving information from *InventoryFile*, but use two indices, a primary index and a secondary index, as described in this section.

7. (Project) In each of the examples and exercises considered thus far, it has been assumed that the file has been sorted so that the key values in the records are in ascending order. This makes it possible to use the position of a key value in the index as the number of the corresponding

record in the file. If new records are added to the file or removed from the file, however, both the file and the index must be sorted with each insertion or deletion if this approach is to be used. An alternative approach, requiring that only the index be kept sorted, is to include with each key value in the index the number of the corresponding record. A new record can then be inserted at any "free" location in the file. The key value of this record, together with this location, is then inserted into the index. The free locations in the file can be managed as a linked stack. (The nodes of this linked stack might be records in the file and the record numbers used to link them together.) When a record is deleted from the file, it is pushed onto the free stack, and its entry is removed from the index.

Use this indexing scheme in a menu-driven program that will manage a database of records in *InventoryFile*. The program should support at least the following operations:

(0) Display the menu.
(1) Insert a new record into the (possibly empty) database.
(2) Search the database for an item with a given number, and retrieve information about that item.
(3) Search the database for an item with a given number, and change the information (not the item number) in the record for that item.
(4) Search the database to delete the record for an item with a given number.
(5) Print a list of records for all items for which the number in stock has fallen below the minimum inventory level.
(6) Update all records in *InventoryFile* with the information in the file *InventoryUpdate*.
(7) Quit.

8. (Project) Proceed as in Exercise 7, but use a binary search tree for the index and support only the following options:

(0) Display the menu.
(1) Insert a new record into the (possibly empty) database.
(2) Search the database for an item with a given number, and retrieve information about that item.
(3) Search the database for an item with a given number, and change the information (not the item number) in the record for that item.
(4) Quit.

9. (Project) Extend the program in Exercise 8 to allow the additional options:

(4) Search the data base to delete the record for an item with a given number.
(5) Print a list of records for all items for which the number in stock has fallen below the minimum inventory level.
(6) Update all records in *InventoryFile* with the information in the file *InventoryUpdate*.
(7) Quit.

12 Trees

In Chapter 9 we introduced trees and showed how a special kind of binary tree, a binary search tree (BST), can be used to carry out a binary search in a linked structure. We also considered several operations on binary trees, including traversal, insertion, and deletion, and how trees can be used to construct an efficient code known as a Huffman code. In Chapter 10 we described the heap data structure, another special kind of binary tree, and used it to transform an inefficient selection sort algorithm into one of the more efficient internal sorting schemes. In this chapter, we begin by examining more advanced operations on binary trees, namely, balancing and threading. General trees, in which each node may have any number of children, are a natural extension of binary trees and are also discussed in this chapter.

12.1 Tree Balancing: AVL Trees

As we observed in Chapter 9, the order in which items are inserted into a binary search tree determines the shape of the tree and how efficiently this tree can be searched. For example, the BST that results when the abbreviations of states NY, IL, GA, RI, MA, PA, DE, IN, VT, TX, OH, and WY are inserted into an empty tree in this order is

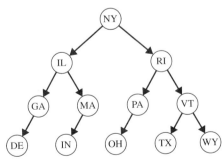

For such nicely balanced trees, the search time is $O(\log_2 n)$, where n is the number of nodes in the tree. If the abbreviations are inserted in the order DE,

558

GA, IL, IN, MA, MI, NY, OH, PA, RI, TX, VT, WY, however, the BST degenerates into a linked list for which the search time is O(*n*):

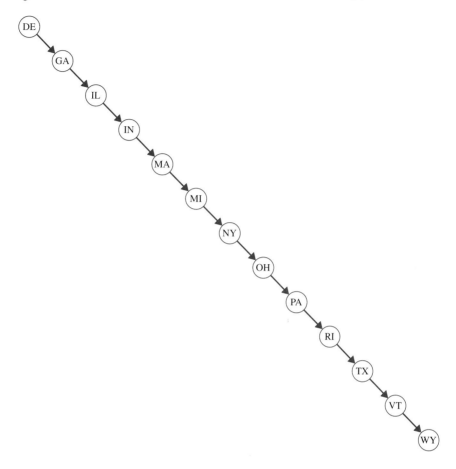

In this section we describe a technique developed in the 1960s by the two Russian mathematicians, Georgii Maksimovich Adel'son-Vel'skii and Evgenii Mikhailovich Landis, for keeping a binary search tree balanced as items are inserted into it. The trees that result are usually called *AVL trees*, in their honor.

In a binary tree, the ***balance factor*** of a node *x* is defined as the height of the left subtree of *x* minus the height of *x*'s right subtree. Recall that the height of a tree is the number of levels in it. A binary search tree is said to be an *AVL* or ***height-balanced tree*** if the balance factor of each node is 0, 1, or −1. For example, the following are AVL trees, and the balance factor of each node is shown in the node:

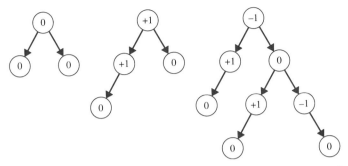

The following are not AVL trees, and the nodes whose balance factors are different from 0, 1, or −1 are highlighted:

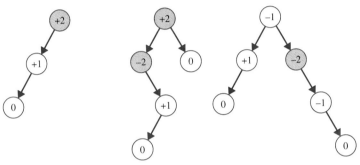

To illustrate the technique for constructing an AVL tree, we consider again the example of a BST containing state abbreviations. Suppose that we begin with an empty tree into which the first abbreviation inserted is RI, giving the following balanced tree:

In this one node tree, both the state abbreviation and the balance factor are shown in the node. If the next abbreviation inserted is PA, the result is still a balanced tree:

If DE is inserted next, an unbalanced tree results:

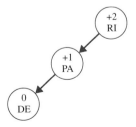

A *right rotation* of the subtree rooted at the node RI yields the balanced tree:

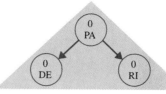

Inserting GA next does not unbalance the tree:

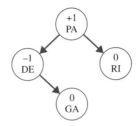

But an unbalanced tree results if OH is inserted next:

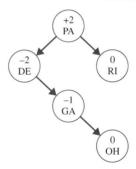

Performing a *left rotation* of the nodes in the subtree rooted at DE rebalances the tree:

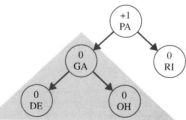

Inserting MA next produces another unbalanced tree:

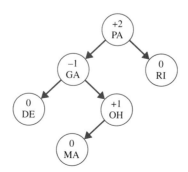

Rebalancing this tree requires a double *left–right rotation*. We first perform a left rotation of the nodes in the left subtree of PA,

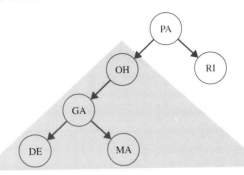

and follow this with a right rotation of the tree rooted at PA:

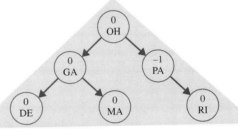

Inserting IL and then MI does not unbalance the tree,

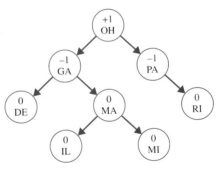

but inserting IN does:

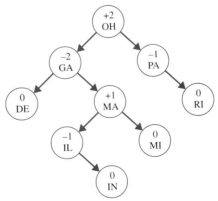

In this case, a double *right–left rotation* rebalances the tree. We first perform a right rotation of the nodes in the right subtree of GA,

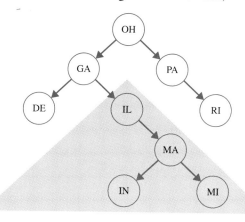

and then follow this with a left rotation of the subtree rooted at GA:

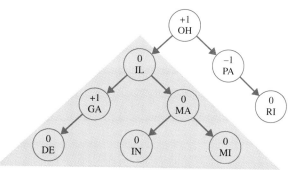

Inserting NY produces an unbalanced tree,

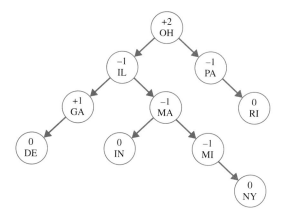

which requires a double left–right rotation for rebalancing, first, a left rotation of the nodes in the left subtree of OH,

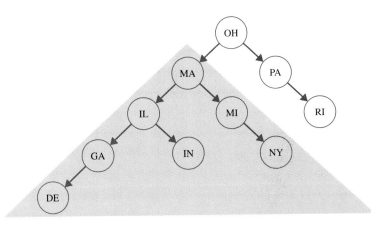

followed by a right rotation of the nodes in the subtree rooted at OH:

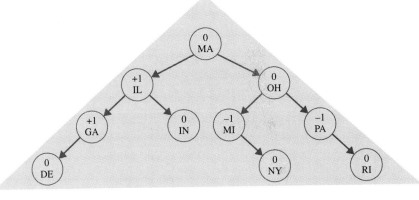

Inserting VT next causes an imbalance,

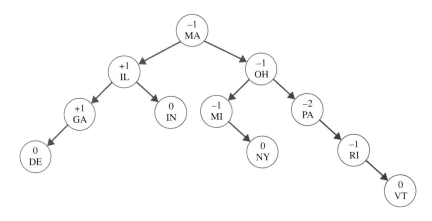

but this tree is easily rebalanced by a simple left rotation of the subtree rooted at PA:

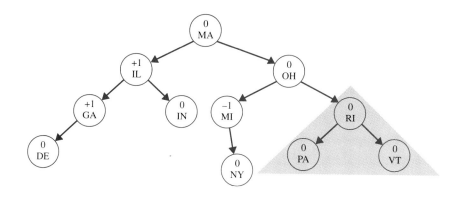

Insertion of the last two abbreviations TX and WY does not unbalance the tree, and the final AVL tree obtained is

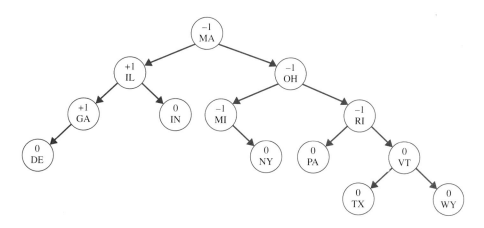

As this example demonstrates, when a new item is inserted into a balanced binary tree, the resulting tree may be unbalanced. It also demonstrates that the tree can be rebalanced by transforming the subtree rooted at the node that is the nearest ancestor of the new node having balance factor ± 2. This transformation can be carried out using one of the following four types of rotations:

1. *Simple right rotation*: This rotation is used when the new item is in the left subtree of the left child B of the nearest ancestor A with balance factor $+2$.
2. *Simple left rotation*: This rotation is used when the new item is in the right subtree of the right child B of the nearest ancestor A with balance factor -2.
3. *Left–right rotation*: This rotation is used when the new item is in the right subtree of the left child B of the nearest ancestor A with balance factor $+2$.
4. *Right–left rotation*: This rotation is used when the new item is in the left subtree of the right child B of the nearest ancestor A with balance factor -2.

Each of these rotations can be carried out by simply resetting some of the links. For example, consider a simple right rotation, which is used when the item is inserted in the left subtree of the left child B of the nearest ancestor A with balance factor $+2$. A simple right rotation can be accomplished by simply resetting three links:

1. Reset the link from the parent of A to B.
2. Set the left link of A equal to the right link of B.
3. Set the right link of B to point A.

The following sequence of diagrams illustrates:

Balanced Subtree Before Insertion

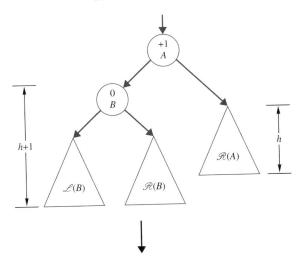

Unbalanced Subtree After Insertion

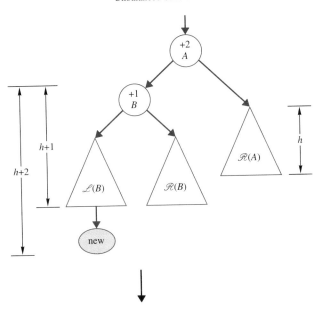

Rebalanced Subtree After Simple Right Rotation

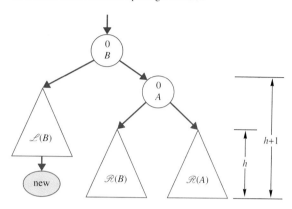

The corresponding simple left rotation can also be carried out by resetting three links and is left as an exercise.

The double rotations can be carried out with at most five link changes. For example, consider a left–right rotation, which is used when the item is inserted in the right subtree of the left child B of the nearest ancestor A with balance factor $+2$. The left rotation can be accomplished by resetting three links:

1. Set the left link of A to point to the root C of the right subtree of B.
2. Set the right link of B equal to the left link of C.
3. Set the left link of C to point to B.

and the right rotation by resetting three links:

4. Reset the link from the parent of A to point to C.
5. Set the left link of A equal to the right link of C.
6. Set the right link of C to point to A.

Note that the link change in step 5 cancels that in step 1, so that in fact only five links must be reset.

The following diagrams show this left–right rotation in the three possible cases: (1) B has no right child before the new node is inserted, and the new node becomes the right child C of B; (2) B has a right child C, and the new node is inserted in the left subtree of C; and (3) B has right child C, and the new node is inserted in the right subtree of C.

Case 1: Balanced Subtree Unbalanced Subtree
Before Insertion After Insertion

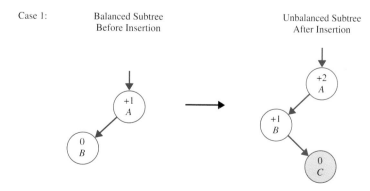

Balanced Subtree After Left-Right Rotation

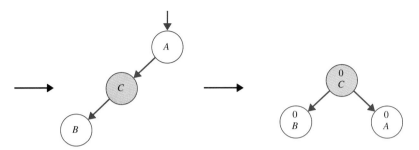

Case 2:   Balanced Subtree Before Insertion

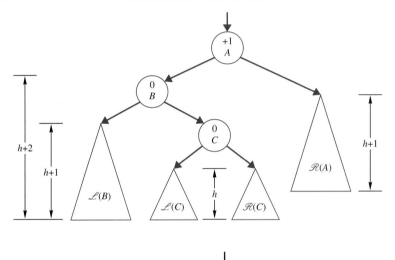

Unbalanced Subtree After Insertion

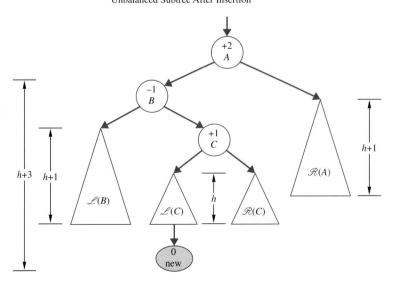

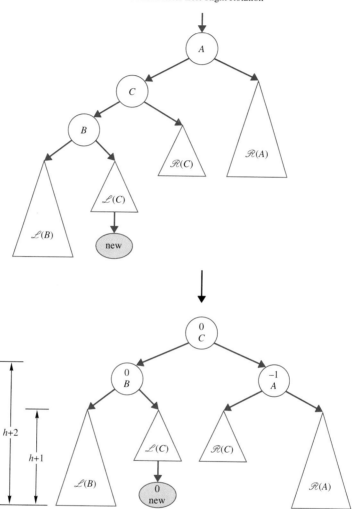

Balanced Subtree After Left-Right Rotation

Case 3:   Balanced Subtree Before Insertion

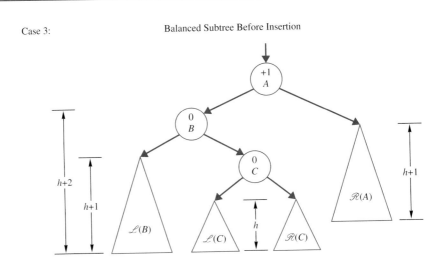

Unbalanced Subtree After Insertion

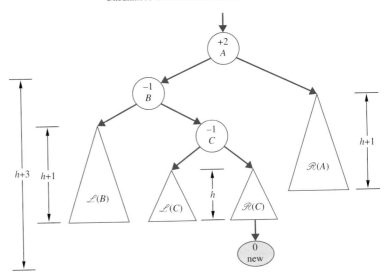

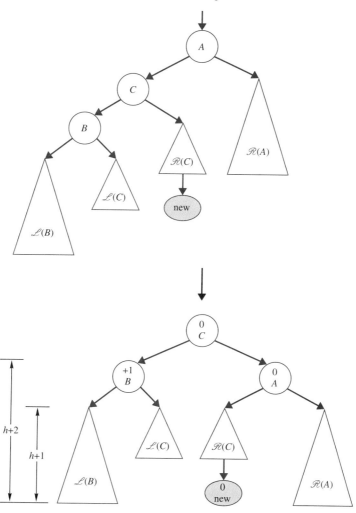

Balanced Subtree After Left-Right Rotation

The corresponding right–left rotations can also be accomplished with at most five link changes and are left as exercises.

Empirical studies have indicated that on the average, rebalancing is required for approximately 45 percent of the insertions. Roughly one half require double rotations.

Using an AVL tree to store data items rather than allowing the binary tree to grow haphazardly when new items are inserted guarantees that the search time will be $O(\log_2 n)$. There is obviously some overhead involved in rebalancing, but if the number of search operations is sufficiently greater than the number of insertions, the faster searches will compensate for the slower insertions.

Exercises

1. For each of the following, trace the construction of the AVL tree that results from inserting the Pascal reserved words in the given order. Show the tree and balance factors for each node before and after each rebalancing.

   (a) **label, const, type, array, procedure, begin, end**
   (b) **array, of, record, set, with, case, end**
   (c) **div, mod, not, and, or, in, nil**
   (d) **or, not, mod, in, div, and**
   (e) **begin, end, if, then, else, case, while, do, repeat, until, for, to, downto, with**

2. Proceed as in Exercise 1, but for the following collections of numbers:

   (a) 22, 44, 88, 66, 55, 11, 99, 77, 33
   (b) 11, 22, 33, 44, 55, 66, 77, 88, 99
   (c) 99, 88, 77, 66, 55, 44, 33, 22, 11
   (d) 55, 33, 77, 22, 11, 44, 88, 66, 99
   (e) 50, 45, 75, 65, 70, 35, 25, 15, 60, 20, 40, 30, 55, 10, 80

3. Draw diagrams for a simple left rotation similar to those in the text for the simple right rotation. Also describe what links must be reset to accomplish this rotation.

4. Draw diagrams for a right–left rotation similar to those in the text for the left-right rotation. Also describe what links must be reset to accomplish this rotation.

12.2 Threaded Binary Search Trees

In the preceding section we described a scheme for keeping a binary search tree balanced as it is being constructed. The objective in tree balancing is to produce a BST that can be searched efficiently. Another important tree operation is traversal, and in Section 9.4 we described recursive procedures for performing inorder, preorder, and postorder traversals. In this section we show how special links called *threads* make simple and efficient nonrecursive traversal algorithms possible.

If a binary tree has n nodes, then the total number of links in the tree is $2n$. Since each node except the root has exactly one incoming arc, it follows that only $n - 1$ of these links point to nodes; the remaining $n + 1$ links are nil. Thus more than one half of the links in the tree are not used to point to other nodes. A **threaded binary search tree** is obtained when these unused links are used to point to certain other nodes in the tree in such a way that traversals or other tree operations can be performed more efficiently.

To illustrate, suppose that we wish to thread a BST like the following in such a way that a simple and efficient iterative algorithm for inorder traversal can be developed:

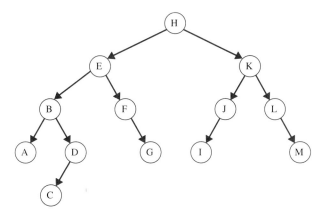

The first node visited in an inorder traversal is the leftmost leaf, that is, the node containing A. Since A has no right child, the next node visited in this traversal is its parent, the node containing B. We can use the right pointer of node A as a thread to its parent to make this backtracking in the tree easy. This thread is shown as the dotted line from A to B in the following diagram:

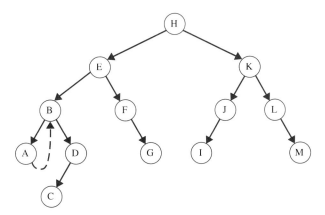

The next node visited is C, and since its right pointer is nil, it also can be used as a thread to its parent D:

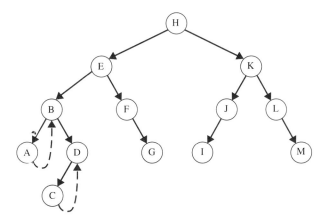

Since the right pointer in node D is again nil, it can be used as a thread to its successor, which in this case is the node containing E:

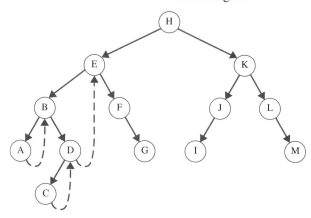

The next nodes visited are E, F, and G, and since G has a nil right pointer, we replace it with a thread to its successor, the node containing H:

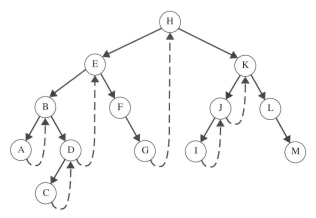

We next visit node H and then node I. Since the right pointer of I is nil, we replace it with a thread to its parent J, and since its right link is nil, we replace this link with a thread to its parent K. Since no other nodes except the last one visited (M) have nil right pointers, we obtain the final ***right-threaded BST***:

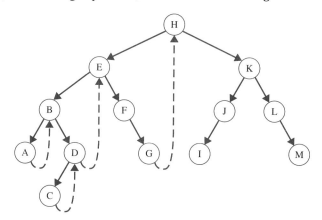

The following algorithm summarizes this process of right-threading a binary search tree:

ALGORITHM TO RIGHT-THREAD A BST

(* Accepts: A binary search tree.
     Function: Right-threads the binary search tree. Each thread links a
               node to its inorder successor.
     Returns: A right-threaded BST. *)

Perform an inorder traversal of the BST. Whenever a node x with a nil right pointer is encountered, replace this right link with a thread to the inorder successor of x. The inorder successor of such a node x is its parent if x is a left child of its parent; otherwise, it is the nearest ancestor of x that contains x in its left subtree.

An iterative algorithm for traversing a right-threaded binary search tree is now straightforward:

ALGORITHM FOR INORDER TRAVERSAL
OF A RIGHT-THREADED BST

(* Accepts: A right-threaded BST in which each thread connects
                       a node and its inorder successor.
     Function: Carries out an inorder traversal of the BST.
     Returns/Output: Depends on the kind of processing done when a
                       node is visited.

     Note: $LLink(p)$ and $RLink(p)$ denote the left and right
                  links in the node pointed to by p. *)

1. Initialize a pointer p to the root of the tree.
2. While p is not nil do the following:
   a. While $LLink(p)$ is not nil,
      Replace p by $LLink(p)$.
   b. Visit the node pointed to by p.
   c. While $RLink(p)$ is a thread do the following:
      i. Replace p by $RLink(p)$.
      ii. Visit the node pointed to by p.
   d. Replace p by $RLink(p)$.

Note that this algorithm requires being able to distinguish between right links that are threads and those that are actual pointers to right children. This suggests adding a boolean field *RightThread* in the record declarations like those in Section 9.2 for nodes of a BST. While the tree is being threaded, *RightThread* will be set to true if the right link of a node is a thread and will be set to false otherwise. Declarations like the following are thus appropriate for threaded binary search trees:

type
    ThrBSTElementType = ... ; (* type of data items in the nodes *)
    ThreadedTreePointer = ↑*ThreadedTreeNode*;
    ThreadedTreeNode = **record**
                        Data : *ThrBSTElementType*;
                        LLink, *RLink* : *ThreadedTreePointer*;
                        RightThread : *boolean*
                end;
    ThreadedBST = *ThreadedTreePointer*;

Procedures to implement the algorithms given in this section for threading a BST and traversing a threaded BST are quite straightforward and are left as exercises.

Exercises

1. Show the threaded BST that results from right-threading the following binary search trees:

   (a) The BST in Exercise 2 of Section 9.4.
   (b) The first BST containing state abbreviations in Section 12.1.
   (c) The final AVL tree containing state abbreviations in Section 12.1.
   (d) The BST obtained by inserting the following Pascal reserved words in the order given: **file, real, boolean, array, set, record, integer, char**.
   (e) The BST obtained by inserting the following Pascal reserved words in the order given: **array, boolean, char, file, integer, real, record, set**.
   (f) The BST obtained by inserting the following Pascal reserved words in the order given: **set, record, real, integer, file, char, boolean, array**.
   (g) The BST obtained by inserting the following Pascal reserved words in the order given: **end, begin, if, then, case, else, while, do, repeat, until, with, for, downto, to**.

2. Write a procedure to implement the inorder traversal algorithm for a right-threaded BST given in the text.

3. Write a procedure to implement the right-threading algorithm for a BST given in the text.

4. (a) Give an algorithm similar to that in the text for threading a binary tree, but to facilitate preorder traversal.
   (b) For each of the binary trees in Exercise 1, show the binary tree threaded as described in part (**a**).

5. Give an algorithm for carrying out a preorder traversal of a binary tree threaded as described in part (**a**).

6. Consider a binary tree that is threaded to facilitate inorder traversal. Give an algorithm for finding the preorder successor of a given node in such an inorder-threaded binary tree. Do *not* rethread the tree to facilitate preorder traversal as described in Exercise 4.

7. Proceeding as in Exercise 6, give an algorithm for carrying out a preorder traversal of an inorder-threaded binary tree.

8. The right-threading algorithm given in the text right-threads an existing BST. It is also possible to construct a right-threaded BST by inserting an item into a right-threaded BST (beginning with an empty BST) in such a way that the resulting BST is right-threaded.

   (a) Give such an insertion algorithm.
   (b) Trace the algorithm with the Pascal reserved words given in Exercise 1(**d**), showing the right-threaded BST after each word is inserted.
   (c) Repeat part (**b**) for the words in Exercise 1(**g**).

9. Give an algorithm to delete a node from a right-threaded BST so that the resulting BST is also right-threaded.

10. A *fully-threaded* BST replaces not only nil right links with threads to inorder successors, as described in the text, but also nil left links with threads to inorder predecessors. Show the fully-threaded BST for each of the BSTs in Exercise 1.

11. (a) Give an algorithm to fully thread a BST, as described in Exercise 10.
    (b) Write an algorithm to insert a node into a fully-threaded BST so that the resulting BST is also fully threaded.
    (c) Write an algorithm to find the parent of a given node in a fully-threaded BST.

12. Write a program that uses the techniques of Section 12.1 to construct a BST, threads it using the procedure of Exercise 3, and then traverses it using the procedure of Exercise 2.

13. Proceed as in Exercise 12, but implement the insertion algorithm of Exercise 8 and use this to construct the threaded BST.

12.3   Tries, B-Trees, and Other Trees

Until now we have confined our attention to binary trees, those in which each node has at most two children. In many applications, however, allowing more than two children is necessary or at least desirable. For example, in a *genealogical tree* such as the following, it is not the case that each person has a maximum of two children:

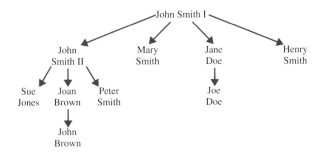

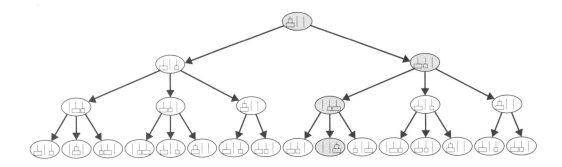

Game trees that are used to analyze games and puzzles do not have the binary property. The following tree showing the various configurations possible in the Tower of Hanoi problem with two disks (see Section 6.2) is a simple illustration of such a game tree:

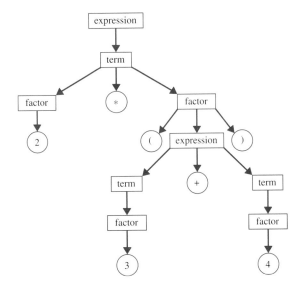

Parse trees constructed during the compilation of a program are used to check the program's syntax. For example, in Section 6.2 we considered the parse tree for the expression $2 * (3 + 4)$, and the following tree could be the parse tree constructed by a Pascal compiler for the statement

if $x < 0$ **then**
    Flag := 1

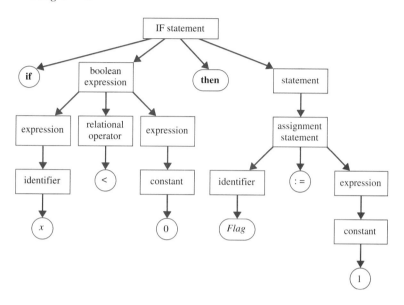

The searching technique used for binary search trees has also been extended to general trees. One method of organizing a general search tree is called a ***trie*** (derived from the word *retrieval* but pronounced "try"). In the search of a BST for a particular item, the search path descends to the left subtree of a particular node if the item is less than the data value in that node; otherwise, it descends to the right subtree. These are the only two options. A trie is a general tree, however, so that at a given node, there may be several different directions that a search path may follow, and in general, this results in shorter search paths because there are fewer levels in the tree.

To illustrate, suppose we wish to store a collection of words to be used as a dictionary in a spell-checker program. As this program checks a document, it must examine each word and search the dictionary for a match, signaling a possible spelling error if no match is found. Because this dictionary must be consulted many times, efficient searching is critical, and thus it is natural to organize the dictionary as a trie.

Each node of the trie stores one letter. The first-level nodes store all the first letters of the words in the dictionary; those on the second level store all the second letters of the words in the dictionary; and so on. As a simple illustration, consider a dictionary containing the following words: APE, CAT, COD, COW, DEER, DOE, DOG, DOVE, HORSE, and ZEBRA. This list of words can be stored in the following trie:

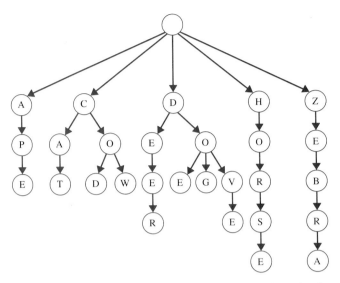

Note that the search time for each word is proportional to the length of that word, and since short words occur more frequently than do long words, this should result in good overall performance for the spell-checker program. One difficulty with this trie is that some words are prefixes of other words. For example, suppose that CATTLE is to be added to this dictionary. If we simply add three nodes with the letters T, L, and E, respectively, to the path of nodes for CAT, then there is no way to check the spelling of the word CAT. One solution is to add a dummy character such as $ to the end of each word so that no word is a prefix of any other word. Thus the trie, with CATTLE added, would be

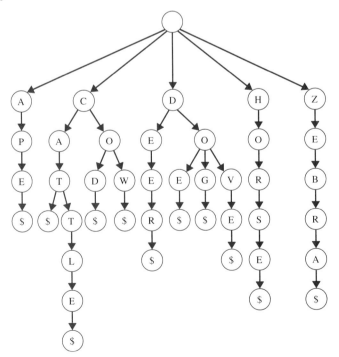

BSTs and tries are data structures used in ***internal searching schemes***, that is, those in which the data set being searched is small enough that all of it can be stored in main memory. A B-tree is one data structure that is useful in ***external searching***, where the data is stored in secondary memory. A ***B-tree of order m*** is a general tree satisfying the properties:

1. All the leaves are on the same level.
2. The root has at least two children and at most *m* children; all other internal (nonleaf) nodes have at least *m/2* children and at most *m* children.
3. The number of data items stored in each internal node is one less than the number of children, and these values partition the data items that are stored in the children.

To illustrate, the following is a B-tree of order 5 that stores integers:

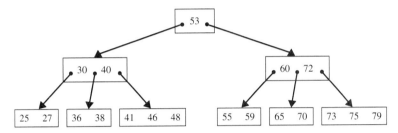

To search this tree for the value 36, we begin at the root and compare 36 with the data items stored in the root. In this B-tree, the single item 53 is stored in the root, and 36 is less than 53, so we next search the left subtree:

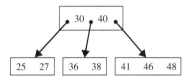

Comparing 36 with the data items 30 and 40 stored in the root of this subtree, we find that 36 is between these values, indicating that 36 is in the middle subtree:

$$\boxed{36 \quad 38}$$

Examining the data items in the root of this subtree, we locate the value 36.

The basic step in constructing a B-tree of order *m* is to begin with a single node and to insert values into this node until it becomes full, that is, until it contains *m* − 1 items. When the next item is inserted, the node is split into two nodes, one storing the items less than the median and the other storing those greater than the median. The median itself is stored in a parent having these two nodes as children.

As an illustration, the preceding B-tree of order 5 can be constructed as follows: Suppose the first integers inserted are 25, 40, 41, and 27. These are arranged in ascending order and are stored in the root node of a one-node tree:

$$\boxed{25 \quad 27 \quad 40 \quad 41}$$

Suppose the next item to be inserted is 55. Because the root node is full, it must be split into two nodes, one containing 25 and 27, which are less than the median 40, and the other containing values greater than the median, 41 and 55:

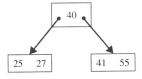

Next 36, 46, and 60 can be inserted into the leaves:

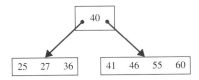

If 53 is inserted, the rightmost leaf must be split:

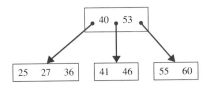

Now 38, 73, 48, and 72 are inserted into leaves; no splitting is necessary:

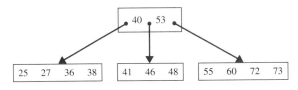

The insertion of 79 forces a splitting of the rightmost leaf:

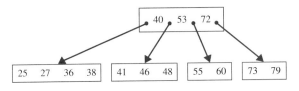

Now 59, 65, and 75 can be inserted into the leaves with no splitting, but the insertion of 30 causes the leftmost leaf to split:

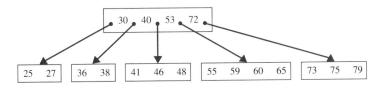

Finally, 70 is inserted into the fourth leaf, causing a split. When the median 60 is inserted into the parent node, which is the root, it also must be split, and the resulting B-tree is

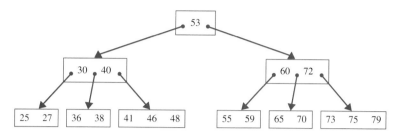

As noted earlier, B-trees are useful for organizing data sets stored in secondary memory, such as files and databases stored on a magnetic disk. In such applications, nodes in the B-tree typically store one file block, the maximum amount of information that can be retrieved in one access. This maximizes the number of data items stored in each node and the number of children. This, in turn, minimizes the depth of the B-tree and hence the length of a search path. Because one disk access is required at each level along the search path, the number of data transfers from the disk is also minimized.

In practice, when the data items are large records, modified B-trees in which only the leaves store complete records are used; internal nodes store certain key values in these records because only the key values are used in searching. Also, the leaves may be linked together to reduce still further the number of disk accesses required.

Because general trees arise in a variety of applications, we must consider what structures might be used to implement them. One implementation is a natural extension of the implementation for binary trees using a multiply linked structure. A node in such a structure representing a general tree has several link fields rather than just two,

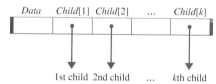

where k is the maximum number of children that a node may have. Its declaration thus has the form

```
const
    MaxChildren = ... ;     (* maximum number of children per node *)

type
    TreeElementType = ... ;     (* type of data items in nodes *)
    TreePointer = ↑TreeNode;
    TreeNode = record
                    Data : TreeElementType;
                    Child : array[1..MaxChildren] of TreePointer
                end;
    TreeType = TreePointer;
```

The problem with this linked representation is that each node must have one link field for each possible child, even though most of the nodes will not use all of these links. In fact, the amount of "wasted" space may be quite large. To demonstrate this, suppose that a tree has n nodes with a maximum of 5 children per node. The linked representation will thus require n nodes, each having 5 link fields, for a total of $5n$ links. In such a tree, however, there are only $n - 1$ directed arcs, and thus only $n - 1$ of these link fields are used to connect the nodes. This means that $5n - (n - 1) = 4n + 1$ of the link fields are nil; thus the fraction of unused link fields is

$$\frac{4n + 1}{5n}$$

which is approximately equal to 4/5; that is, approximately 80 percent of the link fields are nil.

It is possible, however, to represent any tree using nodes that have only two link fields, that is, by a binary tree. We use one of these fields to link siblings together (that is, all the children of a given node) in the order in which they appear in the tree, from left to right. The other link in each node points to the first node in this linked list of its children. For example, the tree

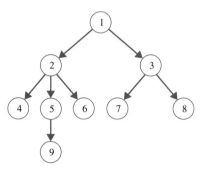

can be represented by the binary tree

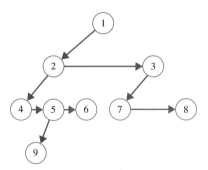

or, if it is drawn in the more customary manner,

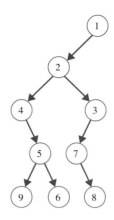

In this binary tree, node x is a left child of node y if x is the leftmost child of y in the given tree, and x is the right child of y if x and y are siblings in the original tree.

When a binary tree is used in this manner to represent a general tree, the right pointer in the root always is nil because the root never has a right child. (Why?) This allows us to use a binary tree to represent not merely a single tree but an entire *forest*, which is a collection of trees. We simply set the right pointer to the root of the binary tree for the next tree in the forest. For example, the following forest

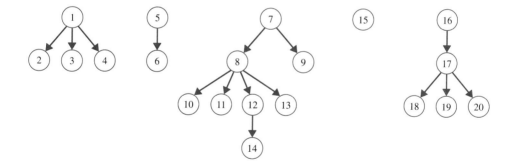

can be represented by the single binary tree:

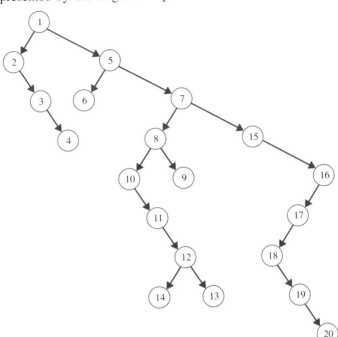

One especially attractive feature of this representation of general trees is that we have studied binary trees in some detail and have developed algorithms for processing them. These algorithms can thus be used to process general trees, as described in the exercises; in particular, the traversal algorithms can be used to traverse general trees and forests.

A third representation of general trees is based on the fact that trees are special cases of a more general structure known as a ***directed graph***. Directed graphs are considered in the next chapter, and any of the implementations described there can also be used for trees.

Exercises

1. Draw a trie to store the following set of words: A, AM, AN, AND, BAT, BE, BEEN, BET, BEFORE, BEHIND, BIT, BITE, BUT, BYTE, CAT, COT, CUT.

2. Draw a trie to store the following set of integers: 1, 12, 123, 1234, 12345, 27, 35, 41, 423, 424, 4244, 479.

3. Draw the B-tree of order 3 that results when the following letters are inserted in the order given: C, O, R, N, F, L, A, K, E, S.

4. Construct the B-tree of order 5 that results when the following integers are inserted in the order given: 261, 381, 385, 295, 134, 400, 95, 150, 477, 291, 414, 240, 456, 80, 25, 474, 493, 467, 349, 180, 370, 257.

5. Represent each of the following general trees or forests by binary trees:

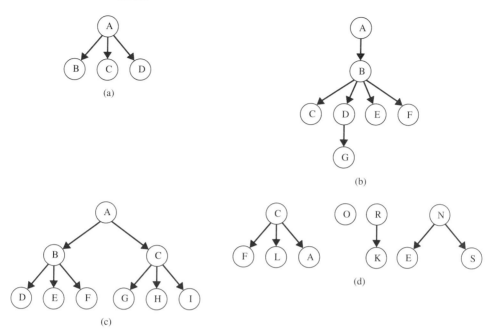

(a)

(b)

(c)

(d)

6. Write a procedure to print in ascending order the data items stored in a trie.

7. Write a program that reads words and constructs a tree to store these words. The program should then allow the user to enter a word and should search the trie for this word.

8. Incorporate the procedure of Exercise 6 into the program of Exercise 7.

9. Write a spell-checker program like that in Exercise 16 of Section 9.4, but use a trie to store the dictionary rather than a BST.

10. Write appropriate declarations for a B-tree.

11. Write a procedure to search a B-tree for a given item.

12. Write a procedure to print in ascending order (of keys) the items stored in a B-tree.

13. Write a program that reads words and constructs a B-tree to store these words. The program should then allow the user to enter a word and should search the B-tree for this word.

14. Incorporate the procedure of Exercise 12 into the program of Exercise 13.

13
Graphs and Digraphs

As we noted in Chapter 9 and in the preceding chapter, a tree is a special case of a more general structure known as a *directed graph*, or simply *digraph*. Directed graphs differ from trees in that they need not have a root node and there may be several (or no) paths from one vertex to another. They are useful therefore in modeling communication networks and other networks in which signals, electrical pulses, and the like flow from one node to another along various paths. In other networks there may be no direction associated with the links, and these can be modeled using *undirected graphs*, or simply *graphs*. In this chapter we consider how both directed and undirected graphs can be represented as well as algorithms for some of the basic graph operations such as searching and traversal.

13.1 Directed Graphs

A *directed graph*, or *digraph*, like a tree, consists of a finite set of elements called *vertices*, or *nodes*, together with a finite set of directed arcs that connect pairs of vertices. For example, a directed graph having five vertices numbered 1, 2, 3, 4, 5, and eight directed arcs joining vertices 1 to 2, 1 to 4, 1 to 5, 2 to 3, 2 to 4, 3 to itself, 4 to 2, and 4 to 3 might be pictured as

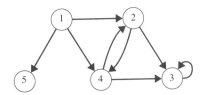

Trees are special kinds of directed graphs and are characterized by the fact that one of their nodes, the root, has no incoming arcs and every other node can be reached from the root by a unique path, that is, by following one and only one sequence of consecutive arcs. The preceding digraph does have a "rootlike" node with no incoming arcs, namely, vertex 1, but there are many different paths from vertex 1 to vertex 3, for example:

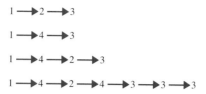

Applications of directed graphs are many and varied. Digraphs are used to analyze electrical circuits, develop project schedules, find shortest routes, analyze social relationships, and construct models for the analysis and solution of many other problems. For example, the following directed graph illustrates how digraphs might be used to plan the activities that must be carried out and the order in which they must be done for a (simplified) construction project:

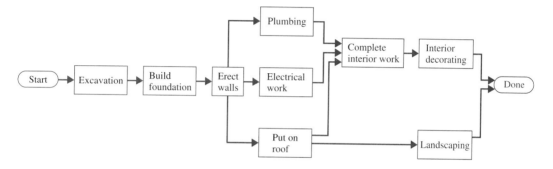

Similarly, flowcharts used to represent algorithms are directed graphs.

There are several common ways of implementing a directed graph using data structures already known to us. One of these is the *adjacency matrix* of the digraph. To construct it, we first number the vertices of the digraph 1, 2, ..., n; the adjacency matrix is then the $n \times n$ matrix Adj, in which the entry in row i and column j is 1 (or true) if vertex j is *adjacent* to vertex i (that is, if there is a directed arc from vertex i to vertex j), and is 0 (or false) otherwise. For example, the adjacency matrix for the digraph

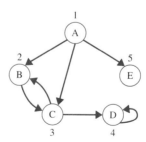

with nodes numbered as shown is

$$Adj = \begin{bmatrix} 0 & 1 & 1 & 0 & 1 \\ 0 & 0 & 1 & 0 & 0 \\ 0 & 1 & 0 & 1 & 0 \\ 0 & 0 & 0 & 1 & 0 \\ 0 & 0 & 0 & 0 & 0 \end{bmatrix}$$

For a **weighted digraph** in which some "cost" or "weight" is associated with each arc (for example, in a digraph modeling a communication network), the cost of the arc from vertex i to vertex j is used instead of 1 in the adjacency matrix.

This matrix representation of a directed graph is straightforward and is useful in a variety of graph problems. For example, with this representation, it is easy to determine the **in-degree** and the **out-degree** of any vertex, that is, the number of edges coming into or emanating from that vertex, respectively. The sum of the entries in row i of the adjacency matrix is obviously the out-degree of the ith vertex, and the sum of the entries in the ith column is its in-degree.

The matrix representation of a digraph is also useful in path-counting problems. For example, suppose we wish to count the number of paths of length 2 from vertex i to vertex j in a digraph G. Such a path will exist if and only if there is some vertex k such that there is an arc from vertex i to vertex k and an arc from vertex k to vertex j.

This means that both the i, k entry and the k, j entry of the adjacency matrix of G must be 1. Since the i, j entry of Adj^2 is the sum of the products of the entries in the ith row with those in the jth column, each such vertex k contributes 1 to the sum. Thus, the i, j entry of Adj^2 will be the number of paths of length 2 from vertex i to vertex j. In general, the i, j entry of the kth power of Adj, Adj^k, indicates the number of paths of length k from vertex i to vertex j. For example, for the preceding digraph,

$$Adj^3 = \begin{bmatrix} 0 & 1 & 1 & 2 & 0 \\ 0 & 0 & 1 & 1 & 0 \\ 0 & 1 & 0 & 2 & 0 \\ 0 & 0 & 0 & 1 & 0 \\ 0 & 0 & 0 & 0 & 0 \end{bmatrix}$$

The entry in position 1, 4 is 2, indicating that there are 2 paths of length 3 from vertex 1 (A) to vertex 4 (D): A $\rightarrow$ B $\rightarrow$ C $\rightarrow$ D and A $\rightarrow$ C $\rightarrow$ D $\rightarrow$ D.

There are, however, some deficiencies in this representation. One is that it does not store the data items in the vertices of the digraph, the letters A, B, C, D, and E in our example. But this difficulty is easily remedied; we need only create an auxiliary array $Data$ and store the data item for the ith vertex in $Data[i]$. For our example, therefore, the two arrays

$$Adj = \begin{bmatrix} 0 & 1 & 1 & 0 & 1 \\ 0 & 0 & 1 & 0 & 0 \\ 0 & 1 & 0 & 1 & 0 \\ 0 & 0 & 0 & 1 & 0 \\ 0 & 0 & 0 & 0 & 0 \end{bmatrix} \qquad Data = \begin{bmatrix} A \\ B \\ C \\ D \\ E \end{bmatrix}$$

completely characterize the digraph.

Another deficiency of the adjacency matrix representation is that this matrix is often **sparse**, that is, it has many zero entries, and thus considerable space is "wasted" in storing these zero values. We can alleviate this problem by adapting one of the representations of sparse matrices described in Section 8.8. For example, modifying the representation of a sparse matrix as an array of pointers to linked row-lists gives rise to the **adjacency list representation** for digraphs. The directed graph is represented by an array of pointers $V[1]$, $V[2], \ldots , V[n]$, one for each vertex in the digraph. Each array element $V[i]$ points to a head node that stores the data item for that vertex and also contains a pointer to a linked list of **vertex nodes**, one for each vertex adjacent to node i. Each vertex node has two fields: an integer field, which stores the number of that vertex, and a link field, which points to the next vertex node in this adjacency list.

The adjacency list representation of the digraph

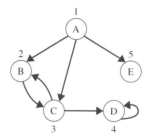

can thus be pictured as follows:

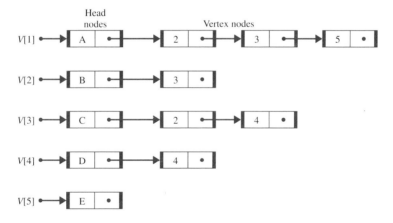

Note that the numbers in these vertex nodes are the numbers of the columns in the adjacency matrix in which 1's appear. These nodes thus play the same role as the nodes in the row lists of the sparse matrix representation considered in Chapter 8.

This adjacency list representation of a digraph can be implemented in Pascal with declarations of the form

const
    MaxVertices = . . . ;   (∗ maximum number of vertices in digraph ∗)

type
  DigraphElementType = ... ;   (* type of data items in vertices *)
  VertexNumber = 1..*MaxVertices*;
  AdjPointer = ↑*VertexNode*;
  VertexNode = **record**
                        Vertex : *VertexNumber*;
                        Next : *AdjPointer*
                  end;
  HeadNode = **record**
                        Data : *DigraphElementType*;
                        Next : *AdjPointer*
                  end;
  HeadPointer = ↑*HeadNode*;
  ArrayOfPointers = **array**[*VertexNumber*] **of** *HeadPointer*;

var
  V : *ArrayOfPointers*;

If we prefer a single declaration for the nodes, we can use a variant record such as

  Node = **record**
                  Next : *AdjPointer*;
                  case *Tag* : *boolean* **of**
                      true : (*Vertex* : *VertexNumber*);   (* vertex node *)
                      false : (*Data* : *DigraphElementType*)   (* head node *)
            end;

To construct these adjacency lists for a digraph, we might proceed as follows:

ALGORITHM TO CONSTRUCT ADJACENCY LISTS

For *i* ranging from 1 to the number of vertices do:

1. Obtain a head node pointed to by *V*[*i*] and initialize its *Next* field to nil.
2. Read the data item to be stored in this vertex into the data field *V*[*i*]↑.*Data* of this head node.
3. For each vertex adjacent to vertex *i* do:
   a. Read the number of that vertex.
   b. Insert this number into a linked list of vertex nodes pointed to by *V*[*i*]↑.*Next* using one of the insertion algorithms in Chapter 7.

In the next section we use this adjacency list representation in a program to find the shortest path joining two specified nodes in a directed graph. The procedure *MakeDigraph* in the program in Figure 13.1 implements the preceding algorithm for constructing such a representation.

13.2 Searching and Traversing Digraphs

One of the basic operations we considered for trees was traversal, visiting each node exactly once, and we described three standard orders for binary trees: inorder, preorder, and postorder. Traversal of a tree is always possible if we begin at the root, because every other node is *reachable* from this root via a sequence of consecutive arcs. In a general directed graph, however, there may not be a vertex from which every other vertex can be reached, and thus it may not be possible to traverse the entire digraph, regardless of the start vertex. Consequently, we must first look at the problem of determining which nodes in a digraph are reachable from a given node. Two standard methods of searching for such vertices are *depth-first search* and *breadth-first search.* We illustrate these methods first for trees, as these terms are more descriptive in this special case.

To illustrate depth-first search, consider the following tree:

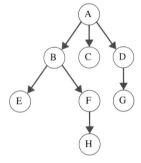

If we begin at the root, we first visit it and then select one of its children, say B, and then visit it. Before visiting the other children of A, however, we visit the descendants of B in a depth-first manner. Thus we select one of its children, say E, and visit it:

A, B, E

Again, before visiting the other child of B, we must visit the descendants of E. Because there are none, we backtrack to B and visit its other child F and then visit the descendants of F:

A, B, E, F, H

Because all of B's descendants have now been visited, we can now backtrack to A and begin visiting the rest of its descendants. We might select C and its descendants (of which there are none):

A, B, E, F, H, C

and finally, visit D and its descendants:

A, B, E, F, H, C, D, G

A breadth-first search of this tree, beginning at the root, first visits the root and each of its children, say, from left to right:

A, B, C, D

The children of these first-level nodes are then visited:

A, B, C, D, E, F, G

and finally, the children of the second-level nodes E, F, and G are visited:

A, B, C, D, E, F, G, H

A depth-first search of a general directed graph from a given start vertex is similar to that for trees. We visit the start vertex and then follow directed arcs as "deeply" as possible to visit the vertices reachable from it that have not already been visited, backtracking when necessary. For example, a depth-first search of the digraph

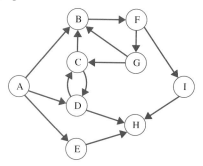

beginning at vertex A might first visit vertices A, B, F, I, and H. We then backtrack to F and from there visit G, from which we can reach vertices C and D (as well as B, F, I, and H, but they have already been visited). Finally, we backtrack to A, from which we can reach the last unvisited vertex E, thus visiting the vertices in the order

A, B, F, I, H, G, C, D, E

A depth-first search starting at B can visit the vertices

B, F, I, H, G, C, D

but we cannot reach vertices A and E.

This description suggests a recursive algorithm for depth-first search because at each stage, after visiting a vertex, we select some unvisited vertex adjacent to it (if there are any) and use it as the start vertex for a depth-first search. Such an algorithm is

DEPTH-FIRST SEARCH ALGORITHM

(* Accepts: A digraph and a vertex v.

Function: Performs a depth-first search of the digraph to visit all vertices reachable from the given start vertex v.

Returns/output: Depends on the type of processing done when a vertex is visited. *)

1. Visit the start vertex v.
2. For each vertex w adjacent to v do the following:
   If w has not been visited, apply the depth-first search algorithm with w as the start vertex.

Assuming the declarations for the adjacency list representation of a digraph given earlier, we can implement this algorithm with the following procedure:

```
procedure DepthFirstSearch (V : ArrayOfPointers;
                            var Unvisited : SetOfVertices;
                            Start : VertexNumber);
```

(* Accepts: An array V of pointers to the adjacency lists of a digraph, a set *Unvisited*, which contains the numbers of all vertices not yet visited, and a vertex number *Start*.

Function: Performs a depth-first search of the digraph, beginning at vertex *Start*.

Returns: The updated set *Unvisited*.

Output: Depends on the type of processing done when a vertex is visited. *)

```
var
   CurrPtr : AdjPointer;        (* pointer to node in adjacency list *)
   NewStart : VertexNumber;     (* start vertex for next depth-first search *)

begin (* DepthFirstSearch *)
   (* Insert statements here to process V[Start]↑.Data *)
   Unvisited := Unvisited − [Start];

   (* Traverse its adjacency list, performing depth-first searches from
      each unvisited node in it *)
   CurrPtr := V[Start]↑.Next;
   while CurrPtr <> nil do
      begin
         NewStart := CurrPtr↑.Vertex;
         if NewStart in Unvisited then
            DepthFirstSearch (V, Unvisited, NewStart);
         CurrPtr := CurrPtr↑.Next
      end (* while *)
end (* DepthFirstSearch *);
```

Here *Unvisited* is a set of type *SetOfVertices* = **set of** *VertexNumber*, which would be initialized before procedure *DepthFirstSearch* is called by the statement

> *Unvisited* := [1..*NumVertices*];

where *NumVertices* is the number of vertices in the digraph.

In a breadth-first search of the preceding directed graph

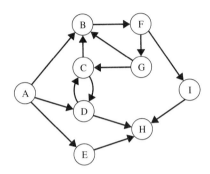

beginning at A, we visit A and then all those vertices adjacent to A:

A, B, D, E

We then visit all vertices adjacent to B, D, and E:

A, B, D, E, F, C, H

Continuing, we visit nodes adjacent to F, C, and H. G and I are adjacent to F, so we visit them:

A, B, D, E, F, C, H, G, I

A, B, and D are adjacent to C, but these vertices have already been visited, and no vertices are adjacent to H. Since all of the vertices have been visited, the search terminates.

A breadth-first search beginning at B might first visit B and F, then G and I, followed by H and C, and finally D:

B, F, G, I, H, C, D

Since A and E are not reachable from B, the search terminates.

In a depth-first search, we follow a path from the start vertex until we reach a vertex all of whose adjacent vertices have already been visited. We then backtrack to the last previously visited vertex along this path so that vertices adjacent to it can be visited. Storing the nodes along this path in a stack makes this backtracking possible. In the recursive procedure *Depth-FirstSearch*, this stack is automatically maintained, as described in Section 6.5.

In a breadth-first search, however, we visit the vertices level by level, and while visiting each vertex on some level, we must store it so we can return to it after completing this level, so that the vertices adjacent to it may be visited. Because the first vertex visited on this level should be the first one to which we return, a queue is an appropriate data structure to use to store the vertices. The following algorithm for breadth-first search uses a queue in this manner:

BREADTH-FIRST SEARCH ALGORITHM

(∗ Accepts: A digraph and a vertex v.
   Function: Performs a breadth-first search of the digraph to visit all vertices reachable from the given start vertex.
Returns/output: Depends on the type of processing done when a vertex is visited. ∗)

1. Visit the start vertex.
2. Initialize a queue to contain only the start vertex.
3. While the queue is not empty do the following:
     a. Remove a vertex v from the queue.
     b. For all vertices w adjacent to v do the following:
        If w has not been visited then:
          i. Visit w.
          ii. Add w to the queue.

The following table traces the execution of this algorithm for the preceding digraph:

Step(s)	v	Visit	Queue
1, 2	—	A	A
3a	A		—
3b	A	B, D, E	B D E
3a	B		D E
3b	B	F	D E F
3a	D		E F
3b	D	C, H	E F C H
3a	E		F C H
3b	E		F C H
3a	F		C H
3b	F	G, I	C H G I
3a	C		H G I
3b	C		H G I
3a	H		G I
3b	H		G I
3a	G		I
3b	G		I
3a	I		—
3b	I		—

Search algorithms like those for depth-first searches are basic to many other algorithms for processing directed graphs. For example, to traverse a digraph, we can repeatedly apply one of these searches, selecting new start vertices when necessary, until all of the vertices have been visited. Thus one possible traversal algorithm is

DIGRAPH TRAVERSAL ALGORITHM

(* Accepts: A digraph.
Function: Traverses the digraph, visiting each vertex exactly once. A depth-first search is the basis of the traversal.
Returns/output: Depends on the type of processing done when a vertex is visited. *)

1. Initialize a set *Unvisited* to contain the numbers of all the vertices in the digraph.
2. While *Unvisited* is not empty, do the following:
   a. Select a start vertex from this set *Unvisited.*
   b. Use the depth-first search algorithm to visit all vertices reachable from this start vertex.

Another class of problems for which we can design algorithms using one of the search algorithms consists of ***routing problems***. For example, consider a directed graph that models an airline network in which the vertices represent cities and the directed arcs represent flights connecting these cities. We may be interested in determining the most direct route between two cities, that is, the route with the fewest intermediate stops. In terms of a digraph modeling such a network, we must determine the length of a shortest path, one composed of a minimum number of arcs, from a start vertex to a destination vertex. An algorithm for determining such a shortest path is an easy modification of the breadth-first search algorithm:

SHORTEST PATH ALGORITHM

(* Accepts: A digraph and a *Start* vertex and a *Destination* vertex.
Function: Finds a shortest path from vertex *Start* to vertex *Destination* in the digraph.
Output: The vertices on a shortest path from *Start* to *Destination* or a message indicating that *Destination* is not reachable from *Start.* *)

1. Visit *Start* and label it with 0.
2. Initialize *Distance* to 0.
3. Initialize a queue to contain only *Start.*
4. While *Destination* has not been visited and the queue is not empty, do the following:
   a. Remove a vertex v from the queue.
   b. If the label of v is greater than *Distance*, increment *Distance* by 1.
   c. For each vertex w adjacent to v:
      If w has not been visited, then
         i. Visit w and label it with *Distance* + 1.
         ii. Add w to the queue.

5. Increment *Distance* by 1.
6. If *Destination* has not been visited then
    Display 'Destination not reachable from start vertex'.
    Else find the vertices $P[0], \ldots, P[Distance]$ on the shortest path as
    follows:
    a. Initialize $P[Distance]$ to *Destination*.
    b. For each value of k ranging from $Distance - 1$ down to 0:
        Find a vertex $P[k]$ with $P[k + 1]$ adjacent to it and with la-
        bel k.

The following table traces the execution of the first part of this algorithm as it
finds the shortest path from vertex A to vertex H in the preceding digraph:

Step(s)	v	Distance	Queue	Labels for A B C D E F G H I
1, 2, 3		0	A	0
4	A	0	B D E	0 1 1 1
4	B	1	D E F	0 1 1 1 2
4	D	1	E F C H	0 1 2 1 1 2 2
4	E	1	F C H	0 1 2 1 1 2 2

Step 6 then determines a sequence of vertices on a path from A to H, for example, $P[2] = $ 'H', $P[1] = $ 'D', $P[0] = $ 'A'.

The program in Figure 13.1 uses this algorithm to solve the airline network
problem just described. The procedure *MakeDigraph* constructs the adjacency
list representation of the network using the algorithm given earlier, reading the
necessary information from *NetworkFile*. Each city is identified by both number
and name, and the *i*th line of the file contains the name of the *i*th city followed
by the numbers of all vertices adjacent to the *i*th vertex. The user then enters
the name of a start city and the name of a destination, and the procedure
FindPath is called to find the shortest path from the start vertex to the destination vertex if there is one. It assumes the existence of a package for processing queues as described in Section 5.2. The compiler directive #include
'QUEUE-CONST' inserts the necessary constant definitions into the CONST
section of the procedure *FindPath*; #include 'QUEUE-TYPE' inserts the necessary type definitions into its TYPE section, including the type *QueueType*;
#include 'QUEUE-VAR' inserts the declaration of the boolean variable
QueueError into its variable section; and the directive #include 'QUEUE-OPS'
inserts the basic-processing procedures *CreateQ*, *AddQ*, and *RemoveQ* and the
function *EmptyQ* into its subprogram section.

```
PROGRAM ShortestPath (input, output, NetworkFile);

(*********************************************************************

    Input (file):      A text file NetworkFile containing network
                       information.
    Input (keyboard):  Several Start and Destination vertices and a
                       user Response that controls repetition.
    Function:          Finds the most direct route in an airline
                       network from a given start city to a given
                       destination city.  An adjacency list
                       implementation is used for the network, and the
                       information needed to construct it is read from
                       NetworkFile.
    Output (screen):   Names of Cities along the shortest path.

    Note:              Certain constant, type, function and procedure
                       declarations from the string ADT package must
                       be inserted into the declaration part.  The
                       compiler directive #include inserts these items
                       from the three files STRING-CONST, STRING-TYPE,
                       and STRING-OPS.


*********************************************************************)


CONST
    MaxVertices = 25;       (* maximum number of vertices in digraph *)
#include 'STRING-CONST'  (* StringLimit *)

TYPE
#include 'STRING-TYPE'    (* String *)
    DigraphElementType = String;
    VertexNumber = 0..MaxVertices;
    AdjPointer = ^VertexNode;
    VertexNode = RECORD
                     Vertex : VertexNumber;
                     Next : AdjPointer
                 END;
    HeadNode = RECORD
                   Data : DigraphElementType;
                   Next : AdjPointer
               END;
    HeadPointer = ^HeadNode;
    ArrayOfPointers = ARRAY[VertexNumber] OF HeadPointer;
    Path = ARRAY[VertexNumber] OF VertexNumber;

VAR
    V : ArrayOfPointers;      (* array of pointers to adjacency lists *)
    NetworkFile : text;       (* file containing network information *)
    NumVertices,              (* number of vertices in digraph *)
    k,                        (* index *)
    Start,                    (* number of start city *)
    Destination,              (* number of destination city *)
    Distance : VertexNumber;  (* length of shortest path P *)
    P : Path;                 (* shortest path from Start to Destination *)
    Response : char;          (* user response *)

#include 'STRING-OPS'        (* ReadString *)
```

Figure 13.1

Figure 13.1 (cont.)

```
PROCEDURE MakeDigraph (VAR NetworkFile : text; VAR V : ArrayOfPointers;
                       VAR NumVertices : VertexNumber);

    (**********************************************************************

        Input (file):    A text file NetworkFile containing network
                         information.
        Function:        Constructs an adjacency list representation of a
                         network stored in NetworkFile.  The ith line of
                         the file contains the data item to be stored in
                         the head node followed by a list of the numbers
                         of all vertices adjacent to vertex #i.
        Output (param):  The array V of pointers to adjacency lists and
                         NumVertices, the number of vertices.

    **********************************************************************)

    VAR
        HeadPtr : HeadPointer; (* pointer to head node *)
        VertPtr : AdjPointer;  (* pointer to vertex node *)


BEGIN (* MakeDigraph *)
    reset (NetworkFile);
    NumVertices := 0;
    WHILE NOT eof(NetworkFile) DO
        BEGIN
            new (HeadPtr);
            ReadString (NetworkFile, HeadPtr^.Data);
            HeadPtr^.Next := NIL;
            WHILE NOT eoln(NetworkFile) DO
                BEGIN
                    new(VertPtr);
                    read (NetworkFile, VertPtr^.Vertex);
                    VertPtr^.Next := HeadPtr^.Next;
                    HeadPtr^.Next := VertPtr
                END (* WHILE *);
            readln (NetworkFile);
            IF NumVertices < MaxVertices THEN
                BEGIN
                    NumVertices := NumVertices + 1;
                    V[NumVertices] := HeadPtr
                END (* IF *)
            ELSE
                writeln ('Too many vertices')
        END (* WHILE *)
END (* MakeDigraph *);
```

Figure 13.1 (cont.)

```
PROCEDURE FindPath (V : ArrayOfPointers;
                    NumVertices, Start, Destination : integer;
                    VAR P : Path; VAR Distance : VertexNumber);

   (*****************************************************************

      Input (param):    An array V of pointers to adjacency lists for
                        some digraph, the number NumVertices of vertices,
                        and vertex numbers Start and Destination.
      Function:         Finds a shortest path in the digraph from vertex
                        Start to Destionation.
      Output (param): An array P of vertices along this shortest path.
      Note:             Certain constant, type, variable, function and
                        procedure declarations from the queue ADT
                        package must be inserted into the declaration
                        part.  The compiler directive #include inserts
                        these items from the four files QUEUE-CONST,
                        QUEUE-TYPE, QUEUE-VAR, and QUEUE-OPS.



      *****************************************************************)


   CONST
#include 'QUEUE-CONST'          (* QueueLimit, MaxIndex *)

   TYPE
      QueueElementType = VertexNumber;
#include 'QUEUE-TYPE'           (* QueueArray and QueueType *)

   VAR
#include 'QUEUE-VAR'            (* QueueError *)
      Vert,                     (* one of the vertices *)
      k : VertexNumber;         (* index *)
      DistLabel : ARRAY[VertexNumber] OF integer;
                                (* distance labels for vertices *)
      PredLabel : Path;         (* predecessor labels for vertices *)
      Queue : QueueType;        (* queue of vertices *)
      ptr : AdjPointer;         (* pointer to run through adjacency list *)

#include 'QUEUE-OPS'            (* CreateQ, EmptyQ, AddQ, RemoveQ *)

   BEGIN (* FindPath *)
      (* Initialize all vertices as unvisited (DistLabel = -1) *)
      FOR k := 1 TO NumVertices DO
         DistLabel[k] := -1;

      (* Perform breadth first search from Start to find Destination,
         labeling vertices with distances from Start as we go *)
```

Figure 13.1 (cont.)

```
        DistLabel[Start] := 0;
        Distance := 0;
        CreateQ (Queue);
        AddQ (Queue, Start);
        WHILE (DistLabel[Destination] < 0) AND NOT EmptyQ(Queue) DO
            BEGIN
                RemoveQ (Queue, Vert);
                IF DistLabel[Vert] > Distance THEN
                    Distance := Distance + 1;
                ptr := V[Vert]^.Next;
                WHILE ptr <> NIL DO
                    BEGIN
                        IF DistLabel[ptr^.Vertex] < 0 THEN
                            BEGIN
                                DistLabel[ptr^.Vertex] := Distance + 1;
                                PredLabel[ptr^.Vertex] := Vert;
                                AddQ(Queue, ptr^.Vertex)
                            END (* IF *);
                        ptr := ptr^.Next
                    END (* WHILE *)
            END (* WHILE *);
        Distance := Distance + 1;

        (* Now reconstruct the shortest path if there is one *)

        IF DistLabel[Destination] < 0 THEN
            writeln ('Destination not reachable from start vertex')
        ELSE
            BEGIN
                P[Distance] := Destination;
                FOR k := Distance - 1 DOWNTO 0 DO
                    P[k] := PredLabel[P[k + 1]]
            END (* ELSE *)
    END (* FindPath *);

BEGIN (* main program *)
    MakeDigraph(NetworkFile, V, NumVertices);
    REPEAT
        write ('Number of start city?   ');
        readln (Start);
        write ('Number of destination?  ');
        readln (Destination);
        FindPath (V, NumVertices, Start, Destination, P, Distance);
        writeln ('Shortest path is:');
        FOR k := 0 TO Distance - 1 DO
            BEGIN
                writeln(P[k]:3, ' ', V[P[k]]^.Data);
                writeln ('        |');
                writeln ('        v');
            END (* FOR *);
        writeln(Destination:3, ' ', V[Destination]^.Data);
        writeln;
        write ('More (Y or N)?  ');
        readln (Response)
    UNTIL NOT (Response IN ['y', 'Y'])
END (* main program *).
```

Figure 13.1 (cont.)

Listing of NetworkFile:

```
LOS ANGELES
3 4 6
SAN FRANCISCO
1 3 4
DENVER
1 2 3
CHICAGO
3 8
BOSTON
4 6
NEW YORK
4 7 8
MIAMI
8 3 5
NEW ORLEANS
1 7
```

Sample run:

```
Number of start city?   5
Number of destination?  1
Shortest path is:
  5 BOSTON
     |
     v
  6 NEW YORK
     |
     v
  8 NEW ORLEANS
     |
     v
  1 LOS ANGELES

More (Y or N)?  N
```

A classic routing problem that is of both practical and theoretical interest is the *traveling salesman problem*. In this problem, a weighted digraph with vertices representing cities and the cost of an arc representing the distance between the cities must be traversed using a path of minimal total cost. The practical importance of this problem should be obvious. It is also an important problem in theoretical computer science because the only known algorithms for solving it have worst-case computing time $O(2^n)$, and as we noted in Section 6.4, such exponential computing times are practical for only very small values of n (the number of cities). In fact, the traveling salesman problem belongs to the large class of problems known as *NP-complete problems*, for which no algorithms with worst-case polynomial computing times have been found. These problems are equivalent problems in that if a polynomial time algorithm could be found for *any one* of the problems in this class, then the existence of polynomial time algorithms for *all* of the other problems would be guaranteed!

Exercises

1. For each of the following, find the adjacency matrix *Adj* and the data matrix *Data* for the given digraph:

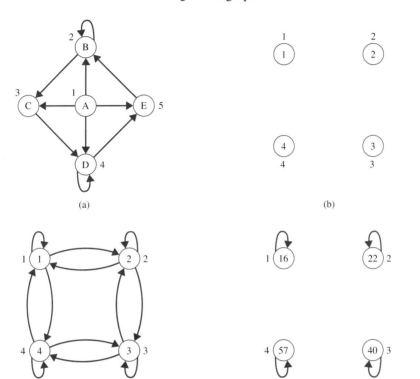

(a)

(b)

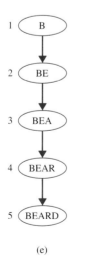

(c)

(d)

(e)

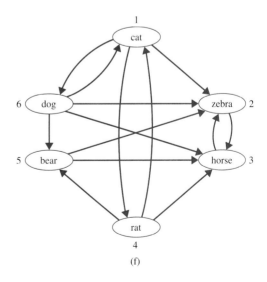

(f)

2. A simple alternative to the adjacency list representation for a directed graph is to use a linked list of head nodes containing data items and pointers to the adjacency lists rather than an array of pointers to these head nodes. Write an algorithm to construct this *linked adjacency list representation.*

3. For each of the following, find the directed graph represented by the given adjacency matrix *Adj* and the data matrix *Data*:

(a) $Adj = \begin{bmatrix} 0 & 1 & 0 & 1 & 0 \\ 1 & 1 & 1 & 0 & 0 \\ 0 & 0 & 0 & 0 & 1 \\ 0 & 1 & 0 & 0 & 1 \\ 0 & 0 & 0 & 0 & 0 \end{bmatrix}$, $Data = \begin{bmatrix} A \\ B \\ C \\ D \\ E \end{bmatrix}$

(b) $Adj = \begin{bmatrix} 0 & 1 & 1 & 1 \\ 0 & 0 & 1 & 1 \\ 0 & 0 & 0 & 1 \\ 0 & 0 & 0 & 0 \end{bmatrix}$, $Data = \begin{bmatrix} CAT \\ RAT \\ BAT \\ DOG \end{bmatrix}$

(c) $Adj = \begin{bmatrix} 1 & 1 & 1 \\ 1 & 1 & 1 \\ 1 & 1 & 1 \end{bmatrix}$, $Data = \begin{bmatrix} 111 \\ 222 \\ 333 \end{bmatrix}$

(d) $Adj = \begin{bmatrix} 1 & 0 & 1 & 0 & 0 & 0 & 1 \\ 0 & 0 & 1 & 1 & 1 & 0 & 0 \\ 0 & 0 & 1 & 1 & 0 & 0 & 1 \\ 1 & 1 & 1 & 1 & 1 & 1 & 1 \\ 0 & 0 & 0 & 0 & 0 & 0 & 0 \\ 0 & 0 & 1 & 1 & 0 & 0 & 1 \\ 1 & 0 & 0 & 0 & 0 & 1 & 0 \end{bmatrix}$, $Data = \begin{bmatrix} Alpha \\ Beta \\ Gamma \\ Delta \\ Mu \\ Pi \\ Rho \end{bmatrix}$

4. For each of the directed graphs in Exercise 1, give its adjacency list representation.

5. For each of the directed graphs in Exercise 3, give its adjacency list representation.

6. For each of the directed graphs in Exercise 1, give its linked adjacency list representation (see Exercise 2).

7. For each of the following adjacency lists, draw the directed graph represented:

(a)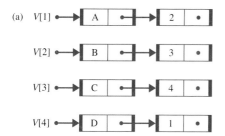

(b)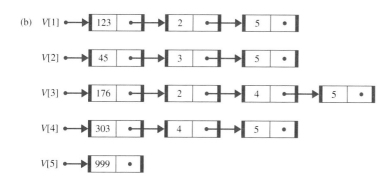

(c)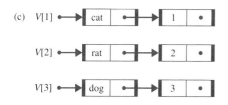

(d)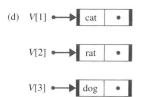

(e)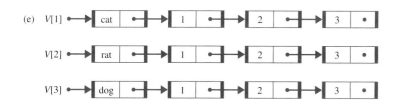

(f)

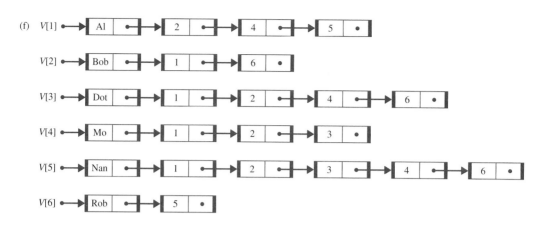

8. For each of the following algorithms, construct a trace table, using the digraph in Exercise 1(a). Each time it is necessary to select a node to visit and there is more than one possibility, select the node labeled with the smallest number.

   (a) Depth-first traversal starting at vertex 1.
   (b) Depth-first traversal starting at vertex 2.
   (c) Breadth-first traversal starting at vertex 1.
   (d) Breadth-first traversal starting at vertex 2.
   (e) Shortest path from vertex 2 to vertex 5.

9. For each of the following algorithms, construct a trace table, using the digraph in Exercise 1(f). Each time it is necessary to select a node to visit and there is more than one possibility, select the node labeled with the smallest number.

   (a) Depth-first traversal starting at vertex 1.
   (b) Depth-first traversal starting at vertex 2.
   (c) Breadth-first traversal starting at vertex 1.
   (d) Breadth-first traversal starting at vertex 2.
   (e) Shortest path from vertex 4 to vertex 6.

10. For the following graph, construct a trace table for each of the following algorithms. Each time it is necessary to select a node to visit and there is more than one possibility, select the node containing the letter that comes earliest in the alphabet.

    (a) Depth-first traversal starting at vertex A.
    (b) Depth-first traversal starting at vertex F.
    (c) Breadth-first traversal starting at vertex A.
    (d) Breadth-first traversal starting at vertex F.
    (e) Shortest path from vertex A to vertex E.
    (f) Shortest path from vertex A to vertex H.
    (g) Shortest path from vertex G to vertex C.
    (h) Shortest path from vertex J to vertex I.
    (i) Shortest path from vertex J to vertex A.

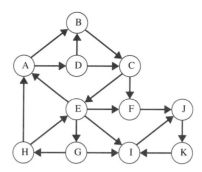

11. Write a program that traverses a directed graph using both a depth-first search and a breadth-first search, where the directed graph is represented by its adjacency matrix.

12. Proceed as in Exercise 11, but use the adjacency list representation for the directed graph.

13. Rewrite the program *ShortestPath* in Figure 13.1, but use the adjacency matrix representation for the digraph.

14. If A is an $n \times n$ adjacency matrix for a directed graph G, then the entry in the ith row and jth column of A^k is equal to the number of paths of length k from the ith vertex to the jth vertex in this digraph. The *reachability matrix* R of G is the $n \times n$ matrix defined by

$$R = I + A + A^2 + \cdots + A^{n-1}$$

where I is the $n \times n$ identity matrix having ones on the diagonal and zeros off. In G, there is a path from vertex i to vertex j if and only if the entry in row i and column j of R is nonzero. Write a program to find the reachability matrix for a directed graph.

15. An alternative to the method of Exercise 14 for determining reachability is to use "boolean multiplication and addition," that is, **and** and **or** operations, in carrying out the matrix computations ($0 = false$, $1 = true$). Rewrite the program in Exercise 14 to find this form of the reachability matrix.

16. *Warshall's algorithm* provides a more efficient method for calculating the boolean form of the reachability matrix described in Exercise 15:

    1. Initialize R to A and k to 1.
    2. While $k \leq n$ and R is not all ones do the following:
        a. For i ranging from 1 to n with $i \neq k$:
            If the entry in the ith row and kth column of R is 1, then replace row i with (row i) **or** (row k).
        b. Increment k by 1.

Use Warshall's algorithm to find the reachability matrix for the following digraph:

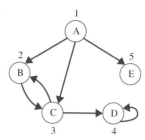

17. Write a program to find the reachability matrix of a digraph using Warshall's algorithm.

13.3 Graphs

A *graph*, sometimes called an *undirected graph*, consists of a finite set of elements called *vertices*, or *nodes*, together with a finite set of *edges*, which connect pairs of distinct vertices. Thus, a graph differs from a digraph in that no direction is associated with the edges, and since the vertices connected by an edge must be distinct, no loops joining a vertex to itself are allowed. For example, the following diagram shows a graph having five vertices with edges joining vertices 1 and 2, 1 and 4, 1 and 5, 2 and 4, 3 and 4, and 4 and 5:

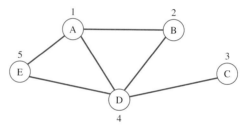

Such graphs are useful in modeling electrical circuits, structures of chemical compounds, communication systems, and many other networks in which no direction is associated with the links.

Like digraphs, graphs may be represented by either adjacency matrices or adjacency lists. For example, the adjacency matrix for the preceding graph is

$$Adj = \begin{bmatrix} 0 & 1 & 0 & 1 & 1 \\ 1 & 0 & 0 & 1 & 0 \\ 0 & 0 & 0 & 1 & 0 \\ 1 & 1 & 1 & 0 & 1 \\ 1 & 0 & 0 & 1 & 0 \end{bmatrix}$$

where a 1 in row i and column j indicates the existence of an edge joining the ith and jth vertices. Because these edges are undirected, there also is a 1 in row j and column i; thus the adjacency matrix for an undirected graph is always *symmetric*. This means that the entries on one side of the diagonal (from the upper left corner to the lower right corner) are redundant. Also, since undirected graphs have no loops, all entries on the diagonal of the adjacency matrix are 0. Consequently, the adjacency matrix is not a very efficient representation of an undirected graph.

The adjacency list representation for the preceding graph is

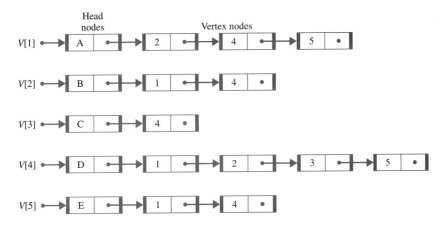

Like the adjacency matrix, this representation is also not very efficient because redundant information is stored. If an edge joins vertices i and j, then a vertex node containing vertex i appears in the adjacency list for vertex j, and a vertex node containing vertex j appears in the adjacency list for vertex i.

A more efficient representation of a graph uses *edge lists*. Each *edge node* in one of these lists represents one edge in the graph and has the form

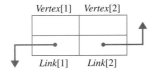

where *Vertex*[1] and *Vertex*[2] are vertices connected by an edge, *Link*[1] points to another edge node having *Vertex*[1] as one endpoint, and *Link*[2] points to another edge node having *Vertex*[2] as an endpoint. An array V of pointers to head nodes storing the data items in the vertices is also used; the head node pointed to by $V[i]$ also contains a link field that points to an edge node having the ith vertex as one of its endpoints. The edge list representation for the preceding graph,

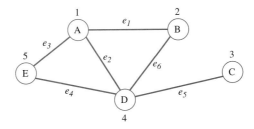

where we have labeled the edges e_1, e_2, . . . , e_6 as indicated, might thus be pictured as follows:

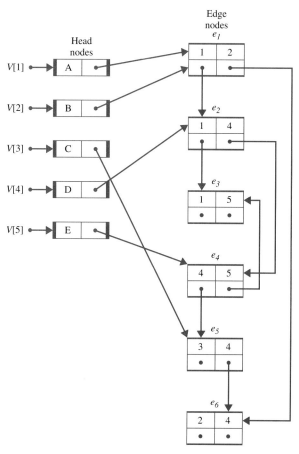

Depth-first search, breadth-first search, traversal, and other algorithms for processing graphs are similar to those for digraphs. For example, the program in Figure 13.2 uses a depth-first search to determine whether a graph is **connected**, that is, whether there is a path from each vertex to every other vertex. Procedure *BuildGraph* constructs the edge-list representation of the graph, and procedure *DepthFirstSearch* marks those vertices that are reachable from vertex 1. Other algorithms for processing graphs are left as exercises.

```
PROGRAM Connectedness (input, output);

(*********************************************************************

    Input (keyboard):   Number of vertices and number of edges in some
                        graph, labels for the vertices, and endpoints
                        of the edges.
    Function:           Determines whether a graph is connected.  The
                        edge-list implementation is used for the graph.
    Output (screen):    Message indicating whether the graph is
                        connected and if not, some vertex and a list of
                        vertices that cannot be reached from it.

*********************************************************************)

CONST
    MaxVertices = 25;                   (* maximum number of vertices in graph *)

TYPE
    VertexNumber = 1..MaxVertices;
    EdgePointer = ^EdgeNode;
    EdgeNode = RECORD
                    Vertex : ARRAY[1..2] OF VertexNumber;
                    Link : ARRAY[1..2] OF EdgePointer;
               END;
    DigraphElementType = char;
    HeadNode = RECORD
                    Data : DigraphElementType;
                    Next : EdgePointer
               END;
    HeadPointer = ^HeadNode;
    ArrayOfPointer = ARRAY[VertexNumber] OF HeadPointer;
    VertexSet = SET OF VertexNumber;

VAR
    i,                              (* index *)
    NumVertices : VertexNumber;     (* number of vertices *)
    NumEdges : integer;             (* number of edges *)
    V : ArrayOfPointer;             (* pointers to edge lists *)
    Unvisited : VertexSet;          (* set of unvisited vertices *)
```

Figure 13.2

Figure 13.2 (cont.)

```
PROCEDURE BuildGraph (VAR V : ArrayOfPointer;
                      VAR NumVertices : VertexNumber
                      VAR NumEdges : integer);

(*******************************************************************

    Input (keyboard): Number of values and number of edges in some
                      graph, labels for the vertices and endpoints
                      of the edges.
    Function:         Constructs the edge-list representation of the
                      graph.
    Output (param):   An array V of pointers to edge lists, the
                      number NumVertices of vertices, and the number
                      NumEdges of edges.
    Output (screen):  Message indicating too many vertices and
                      various user prompts.

********************************************************************)

    VAR
        i, j,                       (* indices *)
        EndPt : VertexNumber;       (* endpoint of an edge *)
        EdgePtr : EdgePointer;      (* pointer to edge node *)

    BEGIN (* BuildGraph *)

        write ('Enter number of vertices:  ');
        readln (NumVertices);
        IF NumVertices > MaxVertices THEN
            writeln ('Too many vertices')
        ELSE
            BEGIN
                (* create head nodes *)
                writeln ('Enter labels of vertices, 1 per line:');
                FOR i := 1 TO NumVertices DO
                    BEGIN
                        new (V[i]);
                        V[i]^.Next := NIL;
                        write ('Vertex ', i:1, ':  ');
                        readln (V[i]^.Data);
                        V[i]^.Next := NIL
                    END (* FOR *);

                (* create edge lists *)
                write ('Enter number of edges:      ');
                readln (NumEdges);
                FOR i := 1 TO NumEdges DO
                    BEGIN
                        new (EdgePtr);
                        write ('Endpoints of edge ', i:1, ':  ');
                        FOR j := 1 TO 2 DO
                            BEGIN
                                read (EndPt);
                                (* insert new edge node at beginning
                                   of edge list for EndPt *)
                                EdgePtr^.Vertex[j] := EndPt;
                                EdgePtr^.Link[j] := V[EndPt]^.Next;
                                V[EndPt]^.Next := EdgePtr
                            END (* FOR *);
                        readln;
                    END (* FOR *)
            END (* ELSE *)
    END (* BuildGraph *);
```

Figure 13.2 (cont.)

```
PROCEDURE DepthFirstSearch (V : ArrayOfPointer; Start : VertexNumber;
                            VAR Unvisited : VertexSet);

(*********************************************************************

   Input (param):   An array V of pointers to edge lists for some
                    graph, a vertex number Start, and the set
                    Unvisited of (all) vertices.
   Function:        Depth-first searches a graph represented by edge
                    lists and visits all vertices in Unvisited that
                    are reachable from vertex Start.
   Output (param):  The set Unvisited of all vertices not reachable
                    from vertex Start.

*********************************************************************)

VAR
    Ptr : EdgePointer;          (* pointer to run through edge list *)
    StartEnd,                   (* one endpoint of an edge *)
    OtherEnd,                   (* other endpoint of edge *)
    NewStart : VertexNumber;    (* new starting vertex for DepthFirstSearch *)

    BEGIN (*  DepthFirstSearch *)
       Unvisited := Unvisited - [Start];
       Ptr := V[Start]^.Next;
       WHILE (Unvisited <> [ ]) AND (Ptr <> NIL) DO
          BEGIN
             StartEnd := 1;
             OtherEnd := 2;
             IF Ptr^.Vertex[1] <> Start THEN
                BEGIN
                   StartEnd := 2;
                   OtherEnd := 1
                END (* IF *);
             NewStart := Ptr^.Vertex[OtherEnd];
             IF NewStart IN Unvisited THEN
                 DepthFirstSearch (V, NewStart, Unvisited);
             Ptr := Ptr^.Link[StartEnd]
          END (* WHILE *)
    END (* DepthFirstSearch *);

BEGIN (* main program *)
   BuildGraph (V, NumVertices, NumEdges);
   Unvisited := [1..NumVertices];
   DepthFirstSearch (V, 1, Unvisited);
   write ('Graph is');
   IF Unvisited = [ ] THEN
      writeln (' connected')
   ELSE
      BEGIN
         writeln (' not connected;  vertices not reachable from');
         write (V[1]^.Data, ' are:  ');
         FOR i := 1 TO NumVertices DO
            IF i IN Unvisited THEN
                write (V[i]^.Data, '  ');
         writeln
      END (* ELSE *)
END (* main *).
```

Figure 13.2 (cont.)

Sample runs:

```
Enter number of vertices:  5
Enter labels of vertices, 1 per line:
Vertex 1:  A
Vertex 2:  B
Vertex 3:  C
Vertex 4:  D
Vertex 5:  E
Enter number of edges:     6
Endpoints of edge 1:   1 2
Endpoints of edge 2:   1 4
Endpoints of edge 3:   1 5
Endpoints of edge 4:   2 4
Endpoints of edge 5:   3 4
Endpoints of edge 6:   4 5
Graph is connected


Enter number of vertices:  5
Enter labels of vertices, 1 per line:
Vertex 1:  A
Vertex 2:  B
Vertex 3:  C
Vertex 4:  D
Vertex 5:  E
Enter number of edges:     2
Endpoints of edge 1:   1 4
Endpoints of edge 2:   5 4
Graph is not connected;  vertices not reachable from
A are:  B  C
```

Exercises

1. For each of the following graphs, give its

    (i) adjacency matrix representation.
    (ii) adjacency list representation.
    (iii) edge-list representation.

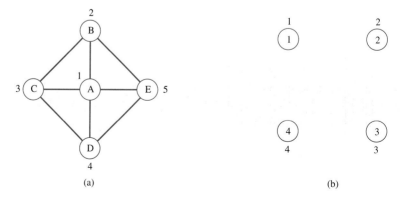

(a)　　　　　　　　　　　　　　(b)

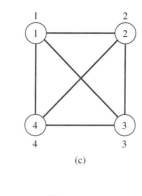

(c)

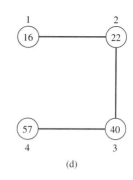

(d)

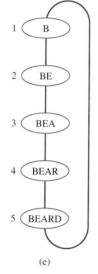

(e)

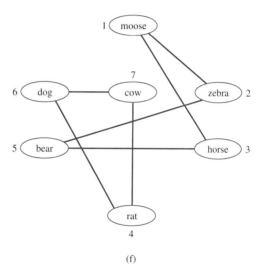

(f)

2. The linked adjacency list representation for directed graphs described in Exercise 2 of Section 13.2 can also be used for undirected graphs. Write an algorithm to construct such a linked adjacency list representation.

3. Give the linked adjacency list representation for each of the graphs in Exercise 1 (see Exercise 2).

4. For each of the following adjacency matrices, draw the graph represented:

(a) $Adj = \begin{bmatrix} 0 & 1 & 0 & 1 & 0 \\ 1 & 0 & 1 & 0 & 0 \\ 0 & 1 & 0 & 0 & 1 \\ 1 & 0 & 0 & 0 & 1 \\ 0 & 0 & 1 & 1 & 0 \end{bmatrix}$

(b) $Adj = \begin{bmatrix} 0 & 1 & 1 & 1 \\ 1 & 0 & 1 & 1 \\ 1 & 1 & 0 & 1 \\ 1 & 1 & 1 & 0 \end{bmatrix}$

(c) $Adj = \begin{bmatrix} 0 & 0 & 0 \\ 0 & 0 & 0 \\ 0 & 0 & 0 \end{bmatrix}$

$$\textbf{(d)} \ Adj = \begin{bmatrix} 0 & 0 & 1 & 0 & 0 & 0 & 1 \\ 0 & 0 & 1 & 1 & 1 & 0 & 0 \\ 1 & 1 & 0 & 1 & 0 & 0 & 1 \\ 0 & 1 & 1 & 0 & 1 & 1 & 1 \\ 0 & 1 & 0 & 1 & 0 & 0 & 0 \\ 0 & 0 & 0 & 1 & 0 & 0 & 1 \\ 1 & 0 & 1 & 1 & 0 & 1 & 0 \end{bmatrix}$$

5. For each of the following adjacency lists, draw the graph represented:

(a)

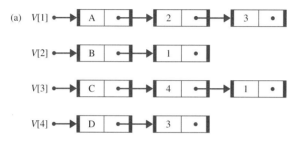

(b)

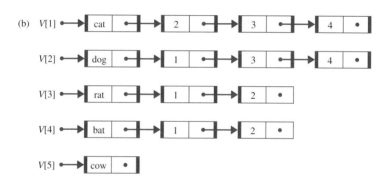

(c)

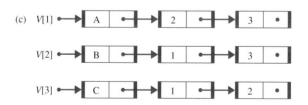

(d) $V[1] \longrightarrow \boxed{A \ | \ \bullet}$

$V[2] \longrightarrow \boxed{B \ | \ \bullet}$

$V[3] \longrightarrow \boxed{C \ | \ \bullet}$

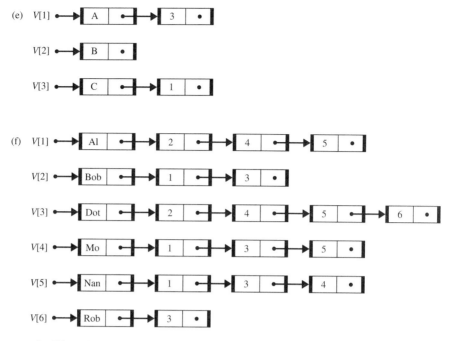

6. Give the edge-list representation for each of the graphs whose adjacency lists are given in Exercise 5.

7. Rewrite the program *Connectedness* in Figure 13.2 using the adjacency matrix representation for the graph.

8. Proceed as in Exercise 7, but use the adjacency list representation.

9. Proceed as in Exercise 7, but use the linked adjacency list representation described in Exercise 2.

10. Consider the following operations to be performed on a graph:

    (a) Insert a new vertex, given a specification of all vertices adjacent to it.
    (b) Search a graph for a vertex that stores a given data item, and retrieve information about that item and/or update the information.
    (c) Delete a vertex containing a given data item and all edges incident to it.
    (d) Find all vertices adjacent to a given vertex.

    Using one of the representations for graphs described in this section, including that in Exercise 2, or devising one of your own, give algorithms that implement these operations.

11. Write a program that reads and stores the names of persons and the names of job positions in the vertices of a graph. Two vertices will

be connected if one of them represents a person and the other a job position for which that person is qualified. The program should allow the user to specify one of the following options:

(1) Insert (a) a new applicant or (b) a new job position into the graph.
(2) Delete (a) an applicant or (b) a job position from the graph.
(3) List all persons qualified for a specified job position.
(4) List all job positions for which a specified person is qualified.

Use the algorithms developed in Exercise 10 to implement these operations.

12. Write a program to determine whether a graph contains a *cycle*, that is, a path connecting some vertex to itself. Use an adjacency matrix to represent the graph.

13. Modify the program in Exercise 12 so that an adjacency list representation is used for the graph.

14. Modify the program in Exercise 12 so that an edge-list representation is used for the graph.

15. Modify the program in Exercise 12 so that a linked adjacency list representation is used for the graph (see Exercise 2).

16. A *spanning tree* T for a graph G is a subgraph of G containing all the vertices of G but containing no cycles. (A *subgraph* of a graph G has a vertex set and an edge set that are subsets of the vertex set and the edge set of G, respectively.) The following algorithm can be used to find a spanning tree T for a graph G:

   1. Initialize the vertex set V_T of T equal to the vertex set V_G of G and the edge set E_T of T to the empty set.
   2. While there is an edge e in the edge set E_G of G such that $E_T \cup \{e\}$ forms no cycle in T, add e to E_T.

Write a program to find a spanning tree for a graph.

17. *Kruskal's algorithm* finds the spanning tree of minimal cost in a weighted graph. It is a simple modification of the algorithm in Exercise 16: In step 2, add the edge e of minimal cost that does not create a cycle. Write a program that implements Kruskal's algorithm.

14

Object-Oriented Programming

Object-oriented programming (OOP) is a relatively new method for designing and implementing software systems. Its goals are to improve programmer productivity by making it easier to reuse and extend software and to manage its complexity, thereby reducing the cost of developing and maintaining software.

For several years, Smalltalk was the only true object-oriented programming language, and the term *object-oriented programming* was first used to describe its programming environment. More recently, the object-oriented languages C++, based on the C language, Actor, and Turbo Pascal 5.5 and 6.0 have appeared, making object-oriented programming methods more generally available. The popularity of this new programming paradigm should continue to increase and it may become the *modus operandi* in programming and system development. In this chapter we describe the object-oriented approach in general and then show how it is implemented in Turbo Pascal 5.5 and 6.0.

14.1 Introduction to Object-Oriented Programming

The Pascal language was designed to facilitate the development of structured programs. As we know, such structured programs are easier to develop and maintain than unstructured ones are, and as a result, structured programming techniques are widely used. As the complexity of software systems increased, it became necessary to divide them into simpler modules that could be developed, compiled, and tested separately before they were integrated to form larger systems. This led to the introduction of new structures into programming languages such as modules in Modula-2, units in Turbo Pascal, and packages in Ada. As the number and complexity of software systems has continued to increase, it has become clear that development cost can be reduced if portions of existing software can be extended and reused in developing new software systems. This notion of software *extensibility* and *reusability* together with the techniques of structured and modular programming are fundamental concepts in object-oriented programming.

Languages such as Smalltalk, C++, Actor, and Turbo Pascal 5.5 and 6.0 have three important properties that characterize them as true object-oriented programming languages: *encapsulation, inheritance,* and *polymorphism* with the related concept of *late* or *dynamic binding.* In this section we describe and illustrate each of these fundamental characteristics.

A central theme of this text is the study of abstract data types. Recall that an ADT consists of a collection of related data items together with basic operations used to process these items. Since both the data and the operations are integral parts of a single entity, a programming language that supports ADTs should make it possible to encapsulate these in a single structure. We have seen that **encapsulation** is not one of the strengths of standard Pascal; one part of our ADT packages had to be inserted into the constant section of a program, other parts into the type and variable sections, and procedures and functions for the basic operations into the subprogram section. We have also said that units in Turbo Pascal, modules in Modula-2, and packages in Ada make it possible to encapsulate ADTs.

These programming languages also provide better support for the other important aspect of encapsulation, namely, the separation of the definition of an ADT from its implementation. A unit in Turbo Pascal consists of an interface part in which the ADT is defined and an implementation part that contains the functions and procedures for its basic operations. Similarly, a module in Modula-2 consists of a definition part and an implementation part, and a package in Ada consists of a specification part and a body (implementation part). In each case the interface or definition part contains **public** information that is accessible outside the structure, and the implementation part contains **private** information that is accessible only within the structure. This separation of a data type's definition from its implementation makes it possible to hide the private implementation details so that a user of the ADT is forced to process the data items using only the basic operations defined for that type. Another benefit of this separation is that the implementation of an ADT may be changed without having to change the programs, subprograms, modules, or units that use the ADT.

In object-oriented programming languages, encapsulation is provided by *classes*, which have the encapsulation property together with the public–private separation that it entails. A variable that is declared to be of a specific class is called an *object*, and the operations that are defined on it are called *methods*, which play the same role as procedures and functions in non-object-oriented languages. The process of calling one of these methods to modify the data stored in the object is referred to as *sending a message* to the object. For example, if a stack is implemented as a class and S is an object of this class, then to retrieve the top element of S, we send a message to S instructing it to pop its top element. Similarly, to add a new element to this stack, we send a message to S telling it to push an element onto itself. Note the shift from a procedure/function-oriented approach to a data-oriented one: Instead of passing the stack S to a procedure or function that performs some operation on S, we send a message to the object (data) S asking it to perform an operation on itself. Object-oriented programming thus focuses on the data to be processed rather than on the subprograms that do the processing.

Classes also provide the second important property of object-oriented programming, ***inheritance***. A class can be defined to be a ***subclass*** of another class, and this subclass then inherits the characteristics of the parent class. For example, suppose that some application requires the use of stacks having some limited size. We could, of course, define a completely new abstract data type for such restricted stacks, but its definition would duplicate much of the definition of an ordinary stack. The object-oriented approach is to define a new class of restricted stacks as a subclass *RestrictedStack* of the class *Stack* of standard stacks and *reuse* some of the characteristics inherited from the ancestor class. For example, the storage structure used to store the stack elements and the methods for checking if a stack is empty and for popping an element from a stack are the same for restricted stacks as for standard stacks and can thus be reused. The create and push operations, however, are different for the two kinds of stacks, and so it is necessary to define new create and push methods for restricted stacks that will *override* the create and push methods inherited from the class of standard stacks. Because restricted stacks have a limited size, we must add a new size field to the storage structure, and because they may become full, we must also add a new method that checks for a stack-full condition.

Polymorphism (from the Greek, meaning "many forms") and the related concept of ***late*** or ***dynamic binding*** is the third important property of object-oriented programming. A ***polymorphic method*** is one that has the same name for various classes, but has different implementations in these classes. For example, suppose that in addition to the subclass *RestrictedStack*, another class *PriorityQueue* is needed in which the elements are ordered, with the largest one at the top of the stack. All three classes, *Stack*, *RestrictedStack*, and *PriorityQueue*, will have a method named *Push*, but it obviously must be implemented differently for each of them. We could of course use different names for this method, but it is standard practice to use *Push*. Dynamic or late binding occurs when some polymorphic method is defined for various classes, but the actual code for that method is not determined (bound to that method) until execution time. This is in contrast with ***early*** or ***static binding*** in which a method's code is bound to that method at compile time.

In summary, object-oriented programming focuses on how abstract data types are encapsulated using classes and how these classes can be organized in hierarchies so that their common properties can be reused by subclasses by means of inheritance and shared by means of polymorphism, especially using late binding. In this section we examined the class *Stack* and the subclasses *RestrictedStack* and *PriorityQueue*. Some applications, however, require additional levels of abstraction. For example, we may wish to consider a rather general class called *LinkedStructure* and at least two subclasses, *LinkedList* and *BST* (binary search tree). The class *LinkedList* may in turn have several subclasses, such as *CircularLinkedList*, *SymmetricallyLinkedList*, *Queue*, and *Stack* with its two subclasses, *RestrictedStack* and *PriorityQueue*. The following diagram displays this hierarchy of classes:

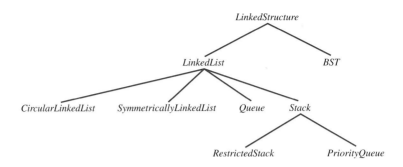

14.2   Object-Oriented Programming in Turbo Pascal 5.5 and 6.0

Classes are implemented in Turbo Pascal 5.5 and 6.0 using **_object types_**. Definitions of object types have a format similar to that of records:

> **object**
>   *field-list*
>   *method-list*
> **end**:

or for a subclass of some *ancestor-class*,

> **object** (*ancestor-class*)
>   *field-list*
>   *method-list*
> **end**;

Here, *field-list* has the same form as for records:

> *list-of-field-identifiers-1 : type-1*;
> *list-of-field-identifiers-2 : type-2*;
>   .
>   .
>   .

These fields store the data items of the class. The *method-list* is a list of the procedure and function headings of subprograms that will implement the basic methods of the class.

To illustrate, consider the class *Stack* of the previous section. An object type definition that we will use to implement this class is

> *Stack* = **object**
>   *Store : StackStorage*;   (∗ stores stack elements ∗)
>   *Error : boolean*;   (∗ set to true if a method fails ∗)
>   **procedure** *Create*;
>   (∗ Initialize the stack as an empty stack. ∗)

> **function** *Empty* : *boolean*;
>> (∗ Checks if the stack is empty. ∗)
>
> **procedure** *Push* (*Item* : *ElementType*);
>> (∗ Pushes *Item* onto the stack. ∗)
>
> **procedure** *Pop* (**var** *Item* : *ElementType*);
>> (∗ Pops *Item* from the stack. ∗)
>
> **end**;

Here, *StackStorage* and *ElementType* are type identifiers (perhaps other object types) that have been previously defined. The field list in this object type definition consists of the two fields *Store*, which is the storage structure used to store the stack's elements, and *Error*, which is used to signal if some method fails. *Create*, *Empty*, *Push*, and *Pop* are the methods that will perform the basic stack operations.

Such object type definitions are usually placed in a type section in the interface part of a unit, and the complete procedures and functions to implement the methods are placed in the implementation part of this unit. In the heading of these subprograms, the method name is qualified by the object type name. Thus, for example, the complete definition of procedure *Create* might be

> **procedure** *Stack.Create*;
>
>> **begin** (∗ *Create* ∗)
>>> *Store* := **nil**;
>>> *Error* := *false*
>> **end** (∗ *Create* ∗);

Complete definitions of the other methods *Empty*, *Push*, and *Pop* are also straightforward and are given in the unit *StackClass* shown in Figure 14.1.

To complete the definition of the class *Stack*, the type identifiers *ElementType* and *StackStorage* must be defined and made accessible to *StackClass*. A definition of *ElementType* could be placed within *StackClass* itself; however, this would require modifying this unit each time the type of stack elements is changed. This may not be possible because the user may not have access to the source code for *StackClass*. Even if the source code is available, it is generally not good practice to modify software that has already been developed and tested. For these reasons, *StackClass* has been designed so that the user defines *ElementType* in a separate unit *ElementInfo*, and *Stack-Class* imports *ElementType* from this unit.

The type identifier *StackStorage* could be defined within the unit *StackClass*. However, since the interface part of a unit ordinarily contains only information needed by the user to use a class correctly and not implementation details like those for a storage structure, we have opted to hide the definition of *StackStorage* in a separate unit *StackStorageStructure*. Figure 14.1 contains a listing of this unit together with the unit *ElementInfo*.

```
UNIT StackClass;

(*******************************************************************

    Imports:  The type ElementType of stack elements from the unit
              ElementInfo, and the storage structure StackStorage used to
              store the stack from the unit StackStorageStructure.
    Function: Defines the class Stack.
    Exports:  The object type Stack whose methods are Create (to
              initialize the stack as an empty stack),  Empty (to check
              if the stack is empty), Push (to push an element onto the
              stack), and Pop (to pop an element from the stack.)

    *******************************************************************)

    INTERFACE

    USES ElementInfo,               (* import ElementType *)
         StackStorageStructure;     (* import StackStorage *)

    TYPE
       Stack = OBJECT
                  Store : StackStorage; (* stores stack elements *)
                  Error : boolean;       (* set to true if a method fails *)
                  PROCEDURE Create;
                     (* Initialize the stack as an empty stack. *)
                  FUNCTION Empty : boolean;
                     (* Checks if the stack is empty. *)
                  PROCEDURE Push (Item : ElementType);
                     (* Push Item onto the stack. *)
                  PROCEDURE Pop (VAR Item : ElementType);
                     (* Pop Item from the stack. *)
               END;

    IMPLEMENTATION

    PROCEDURE Stack.Create;

       BEGIN (* Create *)
          Store := NIL;
          Error := false
       END (* Create *);

    FUNCTION Stack.Empty;

       BEGIN (* Empty *)
          Empty := (Store = NIL);
          Error := false
       END (* Empty *);

    PROCEDURE Stack.Push (Item : ElementType);

       VAR
          TempPtr : StackPointer;
```

Figure 14.1

Figure 14.1 (cont.)

```
      BEGIN (* Push *)
         new (TempPtr);
         TempPtr^.Data := Item;
         TempPtr^.Next := Store;
         Store := TempPtr;
         Error := false
      END (* Push *);

   PROCEDURE Stack.Pop (VAR Item : ElementType);

      VAR
         TempPtr : StackPointer;

      BEGIN (* Pop *)
         IF Stack.Empty THEN
            BEGIN
               writeln ('*** Attempt to pop from an empty stack ***');
               Error := true
            END
         ELSE
            BEGIN
               Error := false;
               Item := Store^.Data;
               TempPtr := Store;
               Store := Store^.Next;
               dispose (TempPtr)
            END (* ELSE *)
      END (* Pop *);

   END (* StackClass*).

(*################################################################*)
(*################################################################*)

UNIT StackStorageStructure;

(********************************************************************

   Imports:   The type ElementType of stack elements from the unit
              ElementInfo.
   Function:  Sets up the storage structure for a stack as a linked
              stack.
   Exports:   Type StackStorage (and types StackNode and
              StackPointer).

********************************************************************)

INTERFACE

USES ElementInfo;
```

Figure 14.1 (cont.)

```
TYPE
   StackPointer = ^StackNode;
   StackNode = RECORD
                     Data : ElementType;
                     Next : StackPointer
                 END;
   StackStorage = StackPointer;

IMPLEMENTATION

END (*StackStorageStructure *).

(*#################################################################*)
(*#################################################################*)

UNIT ElementInfo;

(*****************************************************************

   Function: Defines the type ElementType of stack elements.
   Exports:  Type ElementType.

   ************************************************************)


INTERFACE

TYPE
   ElementType = ... ;   (* type of stack elements -- set by user *)

IMPLEMENTATION

END (* ElementInfo *).
```

The object type *Stack* can then be imported into a program by using a **uses** clause in the usual manner and then using *Stack* to specify the type of variables, for example,

>   **var**
>   *S* : *Stack*;

Since the type of the variable *S* is a class, *S* is an *object*. The fields of an object are accessed in the same manner as the fields of a record are, that is, by attaching the object's name as a prefix to the field identifier; for example,

>   **if** *S.Error* **then**
>   *writeln* ('Stack error—cannot proceed');

The **with** statement may also be used for objects; thus,

>   **with** *S* **do**
>   **if** *Error* **then**
>   *writeln* ('Stack error—cannot proceed');

is equivalent to the preceding **if** statement.

Messages are sent to an object by using references to the object's methods of the form

>   *object.method*

For example, *S* is initialized by sending it the message

>   *S.Create*;

and the message

>   *S.Pop* (*Item*)

instructs *S* to pop an item from its stack.

The program in Figure 14.2 illustrates the declaration and use of objects. It is a modification of the base-conversion program in Figure 4.2. It imports *ElementType* from the unit *ElementInfo* in which the user has defined *ElementType* to be *integer* or 0..1, for example. It also imports the object type *Stack* from the unit *StackClass* and defines *StackOfRemainders* to be an object of this type. *StackOfRemainders* is initialized by sending it the message

>   *StackOfRemainders.Create*;

As each remainder is generated, it is added to this stack by sending the message

>   *StackOfRemainders.Push* (*Remainder*);

to *StackOfRemainders* to push this remainder onto its stack. After all of the remainders have been calculated and stored in the stack, the message

>   *StackOfRemainders.Pop* (*Remainder*)

is sent repeatedly to the object *StackOfRemainders* to pop an element from its stack, which is then displayed, until the message

>   *StackOfRemainders.Empty*

returns a value of true, signaling that the stack is empty.

```
PROGRAM BaseTenToBaseTwo (input, output);

(*******************************************************************

    Input (keyboard): A positive integer in base-ten notation and a user
                      response.
    Function:         Converts the base-ten representation of a positive
                      integer to base two and then displays this
                      base-two representation.  It uses an object
                      StackOfRemainders of type Stack to store and
                      process these remainders.
    Output (screen):  Base-two representation of the input integer.
    Imports:          The (user-defined) type ElementType of stack
                      elements from the unit ElementInfo and the object
                      type Stack from the unit StackClass.


*******************************************************************)


USES ElementInfo, StackClass;

VAR
    Number : LongInt;            (* the number to be converted *)
    Remainder : ElementType;     (* remainder when Number is divided by 2 *)
    StackOfRemainders : Stack;   (* stack of remainders *)
    Response : char;             (* user response *)

BEGIN
    REPEAT
        write ('Enter positive integer to convert:  ');
        readln (Number);
        StackOfRemainders.Create;
        WHILE Number <> 0 DO
            BEGIN
                Remainder := Number MOD 2;
                StackOfRemainders.Push (Remainder);
                Number := Number DIV 2
            END (* WHILE *);
        write ('Base two representation:  ');
        WHILE NOT StackOfRemainders.Empty DO
            BEGIN
                StackOfRemainders.Pop (Remainder);
                write (Remainder:1)
            END (* WHILE *);
        writeln; writeln;
        write ('More (Y or N)?  ');
        readln (Response)
    UNTIL NOT (Response IN ['Y', 'y'])
    END.
```

Figure 14.2

Figure 14.2 (cont.)

Sample Run:

```
Enter positive integer to convert:   31
Base two representation:   11111

More (Y or N)?   Y
Enter positive integer to convert:   12345
Base two representation:   11000000111001

More (Y or N)?   N
```

This example illustrates how classes can be implemented using units and object types and more generally how they can be used to encapsulate abstract data types. The second important characteristic of object-oriented programming, *inheritance*, is also supported in Turbo Pascal 5.5 and 6.0 by using the second form of object type definition to implement subclasses:

> **object** (*ancestor-class*)
>   *field-list*
>   *method-list*
> **end**;

When an object is declared to have this type, it inherits all the fields and methods of the ancestor class.

To demonstrate inheritance, consider the class of restricted stacks described in the preceding section. Recall that a restricted stack is like an ordinary stack except that there is a limit on the number of elements that a restricted stack can hold. If we define the class *RestrictedStack* as a subclass of the class *Stack*, it inherits the fields *Store* and *Error* together with the methods *Create*, *Empty*, *Push*, and *Pop*. The fields *Store* and *Error* and the methods *Empty* and *Pop* will be reused because they are the same for both kinds of stacks. However, the method *Push* is different for restricted stacks, since it adds an element to a restricted stack only if there is room, and it sets *Error* to true otherwise. The method *Create* is also different, since it must initialize the size of the restricted stack to zero. This means that the new methods *Create* and *Push* must be defined to override the corresponding inherited methods. An appropriate object type definition for this subclass is therefore

> *RestrictedStack* = **object** (*Stack*)
>   **procedure** *Create*;
>   (∗ Initialize the restricted stack as an empty
>   stack. ∗)
>   **procedure** *Push* (*Element* : *ElementType*);
>   (∗ Pushes *Element* onto the restricted stack,
>   provided there is room for it. ∗)
>   **end**;

If an object is declared to have this type,

> **var**
>   *R* : *RestrictedStack*;

messages to *R* like

> *R.Empty*;

and

> *R.Pop* (*Item*);

invoke the methods *Empty* and *Push* defined in the ancestor class *Stack*. The messages

> *R.Create*

and

> *R.Push* (*Item*);

invoke the methods *Create* and *Push* for the object type *RestrictedStack* and not the corresponding methods in *Stack*.

A complete unit to implement the class RestrictedStacks is given in Figure 14.3. Also shown is a listing of the unit *StackInfo* in which the user sets the limit *StackLimit* on the size of restricted stacks.

```
UNIT RestrictedStackClass;

(************************************************************************

    Imports:  The constant StackLimit from StackInfo, type ElementType
              from ElementInfo, and the object type Stack from
              StackClass.
    Function: Defines the class RestrictedStack as a subclass of the
              class Stack from the unit StackClass.  It reuses the
              fields Store and Error and the methods Empty and Pop; the
              methods Create and Push are overridden.
    Exports:  The object type RestrictedStack.

 *********************************************************************** )

    INTERFACE

    USES StackInfo,        (* import StackLimit *)
         ElementInfo,      (* import ElementType *)
         StackClass;       (* import ancestor class Stack *)
```

Figure 14.3

Figure 14.3 (cont.)

```
    TYPE
        RestrictedStack = OBJECT (Stack)
                            PROCEDURE Create;
                              (* Initialize the restricted stack
                                 as an empty stack. *)
                            PROCEDURE Push (Item : ElementType);
                              (* Push Item onto the stack,
                                 provided there is room. *)
                          END;

    IMPLEMENTATION

    VAR
       Size : integer;     (* current size of stack *)

    PROCEDURE RestrictedStack.Create;

       BEGIN (* Create *)
          Store := NIL;
          Size := 0;
          Error := false
       END (* Create *);

    PROCEDURE RestrictedStack.Push (Item : ElementType);

       BEGIN (* Push *)
          IF Size = StackLimit THEN
             BEGIN
                writeln ('*** Stack limit of ', StackLimit:1,
                         ' exceeded ***');
                Error := true
             END (* IF *)
          ELSE
             BEGIN
                Inc(Size);
                Stack.Push (Item)
             END (* ELSE *)
       END (* Push *);

    END (* RestrictedStackClass *).

(*##############################################################*)
(*##############################################################*)

UNIT StackInfo;

INTERFACE

CONST
    StackLimit = ...; (* limit on size of restricted stack -- set by user *)

IMPLEMENTATION

END (* StackInfo *).
```

Note that in implementing *Push* for restricted stacks, we have used only the public information for the class *Stack* and not any of the private implementation details. There are several reasons for this. The first and most important is that a basic principle of object-oriented programming is to reuse software that has already been developed and tested. A second reason is that implementation details are hidden and are thus not ordinarily available (because source code for them is not available). Finally, using only public information from the ancestor class ensures that if the implementation of the ancestor class is changed, no changes are needed in the implementation of the subclass.

Even if a method from an ancestor class is being overridden in a subclass, it still is accessible in this subclass, but in this case it is necessary to qualify the method's name with the class name. Thus, in defining *Push* for *RestrictedStack*, the method *Push* from the class *Stack* is invoked by using the qualified identifier

Stack.Push

This is necessary because when resolving method calls, the compiler first searches within the subclass for a method having the specified name. If there is such a method, it is used; otherwise, the search continues up through the ancestor classes. Thus, for a restricted stack, an unqualified reference to the method *Push* produces a recursive call to the method *Push* within this subclass rather than to the method *Push* in the ancestor class *Stack*.

To illustrate the use of this subclass *RestrictedStack*, suppose that in the base-conversion program of Figure 14.2, integers are being converted to binary but there is a limit on the number of bits allowed in the binary representation. This means that if the size of the stack used to store the digits of the base-two representation exceeds this limit, an overflow occurs. The program in Figure 14.4 checks this condition. It uses a restricted stack to store the binary digits rather than a standard stack like the program in Figure 14.2.

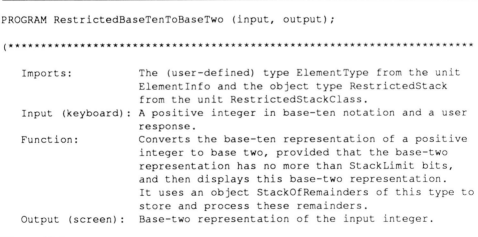

```
PROGRAM RestrictedBaseTenToBaseTwo (input, output);

(***********************************************************************

    Imports:          The (user-defined) type ElementType from the unit
                      ElementInfo and the object type RestrictedStack
                      from the unit RestrictedStackClass.
    Input (keyboard): A positive integer in base-ten notation and a user
                      response.
    Function:         Converts the base-ten representation of a positive
                      integer to base two, provided that the base-two
                      representation has no more than StackLimit bits,
                      and then displays this base-two representation.
                      It uses an object StackOfRemainders of this type to
                      store and process these remainders.
    Output (screen):  Base-two representation of the input integer.
```

Figure 14.4

Figure 14.4 (cont.)

```
    Note:                  The class RestrictedStack is a subclass of the
                           class Stack defined in the unit StackClass.


  ********************************************************************)

USES ElementInfo, RestrictedStackClass;

VAR
    Number : LongInt;           (* the number to be converted *)
    Remainder : ElementType;    (* remainder when Number is divided by 2 *)
    StackOfRemainders : RestrictedStack;
                                (* stack of remainders *)
    Response : char;            (* user response *)

BEGIN
    REPEAT
       write ('Enter positive integer to convert:  ');
       readln (Number);
       StackOfRemainders.Create;
       WHILE Number <> 0 DO
          BEGIN
             Remainder := Number MOD 2;
             StackOfRemainders.Push (Remainder);
             Number := Number DIV 2
          END (* WHILE *);
       IF StackOfRemainders.Error THEN
          writeln ('*** WARNING:  Some bits were lost in the following');
       write ('Base two representation:  ');
       WHILE NOT StackOfRemainders.Empty DO
          BEGIN
             StackOfRemainders.Pop (Remainder);
             write (Remainder:1)
          END (* WHILE *);
       writeln; writeln;
       write ('More (Y or N)?  ');
       readln (Response)
    UNTIL NOT (Response IN ['Y', 'y'])
END.
```

Sample run:

```
Enter positive integer to convert:  12345
Base two representation:  11000000111001

More (Y or N)?  N
Enter positive integer to convert:  12345
Base two representation:  11000000111001

More (Y or N)?  Y
Enter positive integer to convert:  123456
Base two representation:  11110001001000000

More (Y or N)?  Y
Enter positive integer to convert:  1234567
*** Stack limit of 20 exceeded ***
*** WARNING:  Some bits were lost in the following
Base two representation:  00101101011010000111

More (Y or N)?  N
```

As another illustration of inheritance, we consider priority queues, as described in Section 5.1. Recall that these are lists in which the elements are arranged in such a way that those with the highest priority are removed before those of lower priority. We assume that these elements are records, one of whose fields *Priority* stores an integer representing the priority of that element. If we modify the push operation for stacks so that an element is inserted below all those with higher priority, then it, together with the usual create, empty, and pop operations, can be used to process these elements. It makes sense, therefore, to make *PriorityQueue* a subclass of the class *Stack*, reuse the methods *Create*, *Empty*, and *Pop*, and override the method *Push*. An appropriate definition for this subclass is thus

$$PriorityQueue = \textbf{object} \ (Stack)$$
$$Push \ (Item : ElementType)$$
$$(* \ \text{Add } Item \text{ to the stack so that it is below}$$
$$\text{all elements of higher priority. } *)$$
$$\textbf{end};$$

The unit *PriorityQueueClass* in Figure 14.5 contains this type definition together with the complete procedure *Push*.

```
UNIT PriorityQueueClass;

(*********************************************************************

    Imports:   The type ElementType from the unit ElementInfo and the
               object type Stack from the unit StackClass.
    Function:  Defines the class PriorityQueue as a subclass of the
               class Stack from the unit StackClass.  It inherits the
               fields Store and Error and the methods Create, Empty, and
               Pop; the method Push is overridden.
    Exports:   The object type PriorityQueue.

*********************************************************************)

INTERFACE

USES ElementInfo,      (* import ElementType *)
     StackClass;       (* import ancestor class Stack *)

TYPE
   PriorityQueue = OBJECT (Stack)
                   PROCEDURE Push (Item : ElementType);
                      (* Add Item to the stack so that it is below
                          all elements of equal or higher priority. *)
                   END;

IMPLEMENTATION
```

Figure 14.5

Figure 14.5 (cont.)

```
PROCEDURE PriorityQueue.Push (Item : ElementType);

    VAR
        TempStack : Stack;
                    (* temporary stack to store higher priority elements *)
        TopElement : ElementType;
                    (* top stack element *)
        HigherPriority : boolean;
                    (* checks priority condition *)

    BEGIN (* Push *)
        (* Remove elements until one of lower priority is found or
            stack is empty; store these elements in the temporary
            stack TempStack. *)
        TempStack.Create;
        HigherPriority := true;
        WHILE NOT Empty AND HigherPriority  DO
            BEGIN
                Pop (TopElement);
                HigherPriority := TopElement.Priority >= Item.Priority;
                IF HigherPriority THEN
                    TempStack.Push (TopElement)
                ELSE
                    Stack.Push (TopElement);
            END (* WHILE *);

        (* Add the new element to the stack, and then put all
            those from TempStack on top of it. *)

        Stack.Push (Item);
        WHILE NOT TempStack.Empty DO
            BEGIN
                TempStack.Pop (TopElement);
                Stack.Push (TopElement)
            END (* WHILE *)
    END (* Push *);

END (* PriorityQueueClass *).
```

The third characteristic of object-oriented programming is *polymorphism*, which is the property of a method's having the same name but different implementations in various classes. For example, there is a method named *Push* for each of the three classes *Stack*, *RestrictedStack*, and *PriorityQueue*, but its implementations in these classes are different; thus, *Push* is a polymorphic method. Similarly, *Create* is polymorphic, because its implementation is different for the class *Stack* than it is for *RestrictedStack*.

In these examples, the different versions of the polymorphic method *Push* were obtained by overriding the definition of *Push* from the class *Stack* in the subclasses *RestrictedStack* and *PriorityQueue* so that *Push* has different implementations for each of these classes. Since three different procedures are given in these implementations, the compiler can generate a separate piece of code for each of these three versions of *Push*. This is therefore an example of *early* or *static binding*; the compiler binds the code for one version to the method

Push in the class *Stack*, the code for another version to the method *Push* in the subclass *RestrictedStack*, and yet a different piece of code to the method *Push* in the subclass *PriorityQueue*.

There is a problem with early binding, however. To illustrate, suppose we wish to add a new method *RepeatedPush* to each of the classes *Stack*, *RestrictedStack*, and *PriorityQueue*, which can be used to push more than one copy of an element onto the structures in these classes. The code for this method is the same for each class:

procedure *RepeatedPush* (*Item* : *ElementType*; *Num* : *integer*);

    var
      i : *integer*;   (* index *)

    begin (* *RepeatedPush* *)
      for *i* := 1 **to** *Num* **do**
        Push (*Item*)
    end (* *RepeatedPush* *);

It seems reasonable, therefore, simply to add this method to the class *Stack* from which it can be inherited and used by the subclasses *RestrictedStack* and *PriorityQueue*, but this does not work. To see why, consider an object of each of these classes:

    var
      S : *Stack*;
      R : *RestrictedStack*;
      PQ : *PriorityQueue*;
      Element : *ElementType*;
      N : *integer*;

Sending the message *RepeatedPush* to *S*,

    S.RepeatedPush (*Item*, *N*);

pushes *N* copies of *Item* onto *S*, as expected. However, similar messages to the restricted stack *R* or to the priority queue *PQ*,

    R.RepeatedPush (*Item*, *N*);
    PQ.RepeatedPush (*Item*, *N*);

do not produce the expected results.

To demonstrate this, suppose that in the base-conversion problem we have been considering, all of the binary representations must have the same number of bits; for example, sixteen bits are commonly used to store integers, and thirty-two bits are used for long integers. The program in Figure 14.4 can easily be modified to obtain such representations. We need only count the bits as they are generated and then use the new method *RepeatedPush* to push the required number of leading zeros onto the stack of remainders, by sending the message

    StackOfRemainders.RepeatedPush (0, *NumBits* − *Count*)

where *Count* is the number of bits generated and stored in the restricted stack and *NumBits* is the total number of bits in the binary representation. The program in Figure 14.6 uses this approach to obtain such representations.

```
PROGRAM RestrictedBaseTenToBaseTwo (input, output);

(*************************************************************************

   Imports:          The (user-defined) type ElementType from the unit
                     ElementInfo and the object type RestrictedStack
                     from the unit RestrictedStackClass.
   Input (keyboard): A positive integer in base-ten notation, the number
                     NumBits of bits in the binary representation, and a
                     user response.
   Function:         Converts the base-ten representation of a positive
                     integer to a base-two representation having NumBits
                     bits and then displays this base-two representation.
                     It uses an object StackOfRemainders of type
                     RestrictedStack to store and process the remainders.
   Output (screen):  Base-two representation of the input integer.

   Note:             The class RestrictedStack is a subclass of the
                     class Stack defined in the unit StackClass.

 *************************************************************************)

USES ElementInfo, RestrictedStackClass;

VAR
   Number : LongInt;            (* the number to be converted *)
   NumBits : integer;           (* number of bits in binary representation *)
   Remainder : ElementType;     (* remainder when Number is divided by 2 *)
   StackOfRemainders : RestrictedStack;
                                (* stack of remainders *)
   Count : integer;             (* count of remainders *)
   Response : char;             (* user response *)

BEGIN
   write ('How many bits do you want in the binary representations? ');
   readln (NumBits);
   REPEAT
      write ('Enter positive integer to convert:  ');
      readln (Number);

      (* First convert Number to base two *)
      StackOfRemainders.Create;
      Count := 0;
      WHILE Number <> 0 DO
         BEGIN
            Remainder := Number MOD 2;
            StackOfRemainders.Push (Remainder);
            IF NOT StackOfRemainders.Error THEN
               Inc (Count);
            Number := Number DIV 2
         END (* WHILE *);
```

Figure 14.6

Figure 14.6 (cont.)

```
        (* Add leading 0's to obtain a representation
           having exactly NumBits bits *)
        StackOfRemainders.RepeatedPush (0, NumBits - Count);
        IF StackOfRemainders.Error THEN
            writeln ('*** WARNING:  Some bits were lost in the following');
        write ('Base two representation:  ');
        WHILE NOT StackOfRemainders.Empty DO
            BEGIN
                StackOfRemainders.Pop (Remainder);
                write (Remainder:1)
            END (* WHILE *);
        writeln; writeln;
        write ('More (Y or N)?  ');
        readln (Response)
   UNTIL NOT (Response IN ['Y', 'y'])
END.
```

Sample run:

```
How many bits do you want in the binary representations? 16
Enter positive integer to convert:  63
Base two representation:  0000000000111111

More (Y or N)?  Y
Enter positive integer to convert:  1
Base two representation:  0000000000000001

More (Y or N)?  N
```

Based on this sample run we may be tempted to conclude that the program and units are correct. However, this is not the case, as the following sample run shows:

Sample run:

```
How many bits do you want in the binary representations? 32
Enter positive integer to convert:  63
Base two representation: 00000000000000000000000000111111

More (Y or N)? Y
Enter positive integer to convert:  1
Base two representation:  00000000000000000000000000000001

More (Y or N)?  Y
Enter positive integer to convert:  1234567
*** Stack limit of 20 exceeded ***
Base two representation:  00000000000000101101011010000111

More (Y or N)?  N
```

The third conversion shows that the stack limit was set at 20 in the unit *StackInfo*, which means that no more than twenty elements can ever be pushed onto the restricted stack *StackOfRemainders*. The output clearly indicates, however, that in each case thirty-two bits were somehow pushed onto the stack, even though the size of the stack was exceeded. This happened because the definition of *RepeatedPush* in the class *Stack* uses the method *Push* from this class and consequently, the code generated by the compiler and bound to *RepeatedPush* contains the code for the method *Push* in the class *Stack*. Any reference to *RepeatedPush* in the subclass *RestrictedStack* must use this same code, which means that the wrong version of *Push* is being used, so that the stack limit is ignored when pushing elements onto the stack. This is also the case for the subclass *PriorityQueue*. Any reference to *RepeatedPush* in an object of this subclass uses *Push* from the ancestor class *Stack* rather than the *Push* from *PriorityQueue*, with the result that copies of an element are added at the top, regardless of the element's priority.

There are two possible solutions to this problem. One is to override the method *RepeatedPush* in the subclasses *RestrictedStack* and *PriorityQueue*. This requires, however, using the same procedure (except for the name) in the implementation of *RepeatedPush* in all three of these classes. But this solution violates the spirit of object-oriented programming because it repeats rather than reuses methods that have been previously defined.

A better solution is to give one definition of the method *RepeatedPush* but to have code for the appropriate version of *Push* inserted when *RepeatedPush* is called, so that for the message

    S.RepeatedPush (*Item, N*);

the code for *Push* from the class *Stack* is used in *RepeatedPush*, but for the message

    R.RepeatedPush (*Item, N*);

the code for *Push* from the subclass *RestrictedStack* is used, and for the message

    PQ.RepeatedPush (*Item, N*);

the code for *Push* from the subclass *PriorityQueue* is inserted into *RestrictedPush*. This means, however, that code cannot be bound to *RepeatedPush* at compile time but must be generated for it during execution when the type of the object can be determined. This late or dynamic binding is accomplished in object-oriented languages by using virtual methods. A ***virtual method*** is one whose code is bound to the method's name during execution rather than at compile time.

In Turbo Pascal 5.5 and 6.0, a method is made virtual by appending the reserved word **virtual** to its heading in the definition of the object type. For example, to make *Push* a virtual method in the class *Stack* so that the method *RepeatedPush* will function correctly in this class and in its subclasses, we must modify the earlier definition of the object type *Stack*:

```
Stack  =  object
              Store : StackStorage;         (* stores stack elements *)
              Error : boolean;              (* sets to true if a method fails *)
              constructor Create;
                   (* Initialize the stack as an empty stack. *)
              function Empty : boolean;
                   (* Checks if the stack is empty. *)
              procedure Push (Item : ElementType); virtual;
                   (* Pushes Item onto the stack. *)
              procedure Pop (var Item : ElementType);
                   (* Pops Item from the stack. *)
              procedure RepeatedPush (Item : ElementType;
                                      Num : integer);
                   (* Push Num copies of Item onto the stack. *)
          end;
```

Note that we have also replaced the reserved word **procedure** with the reserved word **constructor** in the declaration of method *Create*. This is necessary because late binding requires that certain tables of information be constructed when the object is created. If we replace the definition of the object type *Stack* in the unit of Figure 14.2 and replace **procedure** with **constructor** in the heading of *Create* in the unit's implementation part, the resulting unit can be used in the same way as before. Figure 14.7 shows the resulting unit.

```
UNIT StackClass;

(*********************************************************************

   Imports:   The type ElementType of stack elements from the unit
              ElementInfo, and the storage structure StorageType used to
              store the stack from the unit StackStorageStructure.
   Function:  Defines the class Stack.
   Exports:   The object type Stack whose methods are Create (to
              initialize the stack as an empty stack),  Empty (to check
              if the stack is empty), Push (to push an element onto the
              stack), Pop (to pop an element from the stack), and
              RepeatedPush (to push several copies of an element onto
              the stack).

*********************************************************************)
```

Figure 14.7

Figure 14.7 (cont.)

```
INTERFACE

USES ElementInfo,             (* import ElementType *)
     StackStorageStructure;   (* import StorageType *)

TYPE
   Stack = OBJECT
               Store : StackStorage; (* stores stack elements *)
               Error : boolean;       (* set to true if a method fails *)
               CONSTRUCTOR Create;
                  (* Initialize the stack as an empty stack. *)
               FUNCTION Empty : boolean;
                  (* Checks if the stack is empty. *)
               PROCEDURE Push (Item : ElementType); VIRTUAL;
                  (* Push Item onto the stack. *)
               PROCEDURE Pop (VAR Item : ElementType);
                  (* Pop Item from the stack. *)
               PROCEDURE RepeatedPush (Item : ElementType;
                                       Num : integer);
                  (* Push Num copies of Item onto the stack. *)
           END;

IMPLEMENTATION

CONSTRUCTOR Stack.Create;

   BEGIN (* Create *)
      Store := NIL;
      Error := false
   END (* Create *);

FUNCTION Stack.Empty;

   BEGIN (* Empty *)
      Empty := (Store = NIL);
      Error := false
   END (* Empty *);

PROCEDURE Stack.Push (Item : ElementType);

   VAR
      TempPtr : StackPointer;

   BEGIN (* Push *)
      new (TempPtr);
      TempPtr^.Data := Item;
      TempPtr^.Next := Store;
      Store := TempPtr;
      Error := false
   END (* Push *);
```

Figure 14.7 (cont.)

```
PROCEDURE Stack.Pop (VAR Item : ElementType);

    VAR
        TempPtr : StackPointer;

    BEGIN (* Pop *)
        IF Stack.Empty THEN
            BEGIN
                writeln ('*** Attempt to pop from an empty stack ***');
                Error := true
            END
        ELSE
            BEGIN
                Error := false;
                Item := Store^.Data;
                TempPtr := Store;
                Store := Store^.Next;
                dispose (TempPtr)
            END (* ELSE *)
    END (* Pop *);

PROCEDURE Stack.RepeatedPush (Item : ElementType; Num : integer);

    VAR
        i : integer;

    BEGIN (* RepeatedPush *)
        FOR i := 1 TO Num DO
            Push (Item)
    END (* RepeatedPush *);

END (* StackClass*).
```

Similar changes must be made in the definitions of the subclasses *RestrictedStack* and *PriorityQueue*. In particular, the method *Push* must be made virtual in each case, and the reserved word **procedure** in the definitions of the method *Create* must be replaced with the reserved word **constructor**. Figures 14.8 show the resulting unit for the class of restricted stacks.

```
UNIT RestrictedStackClass;

(*********************************************************************

   Imports:   The constant StackLimit from StackInfo, type ElementType
              from ElementInfo, and the object type Stack from
              StackClass.
   Function:  Defines the class RestrictedStack as a subclass of the
              class Stack from unit StackClass.  It inherits the fields
              Store and Error, the methods Create, Empty, and Pop, and
              the virtual method RepeatedPush.  The method Push is
              overridden; Size is a field to store the current size of
              the stack; and Full is a method to check for a stack-full
              condition.
   Exports:   The object type Restricted Stack.

*********************************************************************)

   INTERFACE

   USES StackInfo,        (* import StackLimit *)
        ElementInfo,      (* import ElementType *)
        StackClass;       (* import ancestor class Stack *)

   TYPE
       RestrictedStack = OBJECT (Stack)
                           Size : integer;
                           FUNCTION Full : boolean;
                               (* Checks if the stack is full *)
                           CONSTRUCTOR Create;
                               (* Initialize the restricted stack
                                  as an empty stack *)
                           PROCEDURE Push (Item : ElementType); VIRTUAL;
                               (* Push Item onto the stack,
                                  provided there is room *)
                         END;

   IMPLEMENTATION

   FUNCTION RestrictedStack.Full : boolean;

      BEGIN (* Full *)
         Full := (Size = StackLimit);
         Error := false
      END (* Full *);

   CONSTRUCTOR RestrictedStack.Create;

      BEGIN (* Create *)
         Store := NIL;
         Size := 0;
         Error := false
      END (* Create *);
```

Figure 14.8

Figure 14.8 (cont.)

```
PROCEDURE RestrictedStack.Push (Item : ElementType);

   BEGIN (* Push *)
      IF Full THEN
         BEGIN
            writeln ('*** Stack limit of ', StackLimit:1,
                     ' exceeded ***');
            Error := true
         END (* IF *)
      ELSE
         BEGIN
            Inc(Size);
            Stack.Push (Item)
         END (* ELSE *)
   END (* Push *);

END (* RestrictedStackClass *).
```

After these changes are made, a sample run of the program in Figure 14.6 produces the following output:

Sample run:

```
How many bits do you want in the binary representations? 32
Enter positive integer to convert:   31
*** Stack limit of 20 exceeded ***
*** Stack limit of 20 exceeded ***
*** Stack limit of 20 exceeded ***
*** Stack limit of 20 exceeded ***
*** Stack limit of 20 exceeded ***
*** Stack limit of 20 exceeded ***
*** Stack limit of 20 exceeded ***
*** Stack limit of 20 exceeded ***
*** Stack limit of 20 exceeded ***
*** Stack limit of 20 exceeded ***
*** Stack limit of 20 exceeded ***
*** Stack limit of 20 exceeded ***
*** WARNING: Some bits were lost in the following
Base two representation: 00000000000000011111

More (Y or N)? N
```

This output shows that *RepeatedPush* for objects of type *RestrictedStack* now does use the method *Push* for this class. When *RepeatedPush* attempted to push twelve leading zeros onto the restricted stack *StackOfRemainders*, the method *Push* for restricted stacks was referenced twelve times, and each reference produced a message that the stack limit was exceeded. The twenty bits in the final base-two representation rather than the thirty-two bits obtained before also demonstrate that the correct method *Push* has been used.

References to the method *RepeatedPush* in a program that uses objects of type *Stack* use the method *Push* for the class *Stack*. Thus, if we change the **uses** clause in the program of Figure 14.6 to

    uses *ElementType, StackClass*;

and the declaration of the variable *StackOfRemainders* to

    StackOfRemainders : Stack

execution of the program produces

```
How many bits do you want in the binary representations? 32
Enter positive integer to convert:   31
Base two representation:   00000000000000000000000000011111

More (Y or N)? N
```

Similarly, if *Push* were made virtual in the unit *PriorityQueueClass*, then references to *RepeatedPush* in a program that used objects of type *PriorityQueue* would use the method *Push* for the class *PriorityQueue*.

In this section we have illustrated the basic elements of object-oriented programming as implemented in Turbo Pascal. It must be emphasized, however, that this has been only an introduction to the whole area of OOP and that there is much more that could be said. Nevertheless, the notions of encapsulation, inheritance, and polymorphism introduced in this chapter are fundamental concepts underlying all of object-oriented programming, and this programming paradigm can be used effectively only if these basic ideas are thoroughly understood.

Exercises

1. Name and define the fundamental concepts of object-oriented programming.

2. Another basic operation that is useful for stacks is one that retrieves the top stack element without removing it from the stack. Write a unit to implement a subclass *ExtendedStack* of the class *Stack* that adds a new method *GetTopElement* to those inherited from *Stack*. The new method should be implemented using only the public methods from *Stack*. Also write a program to test the unit.

3. Proceed as in Exercise 2 but add a method *Dump* to empty a stack and display its contents.

4. Proceed as in Exercise 3, but add a method *Print* that displays the contents of a stack without emptying it.

5. Write a unit that implements the class *LookAheadStack* as a subclass of the class *Stack*. A look-ahead stack differs from a standard stack only in the push method. An element, which is a record, is added to the stack by the push method only if the value in its priority field is greater than the value in the priority field of the top stack element. Also write a program to test the unit.

6. Write a unit that implements the class *Scroll* as a subclass of the class *Stack*. (See Section 5.1 for the definition of a scroll.) Also write a program to test the unit.

7. Modify the units *StackStorageStructure* and *StackClass* to use the array-based implementation of stacks described in Section 4.2.

8. If *StackStorageStructure* and *StackClass* are modified as described in Exercise 7, what changes must be made in the unit

  (a) *RestrictedStackClass*?
  (b) *PriorityQueueClass*?

9. Imitating the object type *Stack* considered in this chapter, write a unit to implement the class *Queue*, which implements the ADT queue. Use a linked list to store the queue elements, as described in Section 8.1. Also write a program to test the unit.

10. Proceed as in Exercise 9 but use the array-based implementation of queues described in Section 5.2.

11. Rewrite the drill-and-practice program considered in Section 5.1 using the class *Queue* developed in Exercise 9 or 10.

12. Write a unit that implements the class *Deque* as a subclass of the class *Stack* or the class *Queue* of Exercise 11. Also write a program to test the unit. (See Section 5.1 for the definition of a deque.)

13. Write a unit that implements the class *LinkedList*, as described in Section 7.6. Also write a program to test the unit.

14. Write a unit that implements the class *ComplexNumber*, as described in Exercise 6 of Section 2.5. Also write a program to test the unit.

15. Write a unit that implements the class *RationalNumber*, as described in Exercise 7 of Section 2.5. Also write a program to test the unit.

A

ASCII and EBCDIC

ASCII and EBCDIC codes of printable characters

Decimal	Binary	Octal	Hexadecimal	ASCII	EBCDIC
32	00100000	040	20	SP (Space)	
33	00100001	041	21	!	
34	00100010	042	22	''	
35	00100011	043	23	#	
36	00100100	044	24	$	
37	00100101	045	25	%	
38	00100110	046	26	&	
39	00100111	047	27	' (Single quote)	
40	00101000	050	28	(	
41	00101001	051	29	)	
42	00101010	052	2A	*	
43	00101011	053	2B	+	
44	00101100	054	2C	, (Comma)	
45	00101101	055	2D	- (Hyphen)	
46	00101110	056	2E	. (Period)	
47	00101111	057	2F	/	
48	00110000	060	30	0	
49	00110001	061	31	1	
50	00110010	062	32	2	
51	00110011	063	33	3	
52	00110100	064	34	4	
53	00110101	065	35	5	
54	00110110	066	36	6	
55	00110111	067	37	7	
56	00111000	070	38	8	
57	00111001	071	39	9	
58	00111010	072	3A	:	
59	00111011	073	3B	;	
60	00111100	074	3C	<	
61	00111101	075	3D	=	
62	00111110	076	3E	>	
63	00111111	077	3F	?	
64	01000000	100	40	@	SP (Space)
65	01000001	101	41	A	
66	01000010	102	42	B	

Decimal	Binary	Octal	Hexadecimal	ASCII	EBCDIC
67	01000011	103	43	C	
68	01000100	104	44	D	
69	01000101	105	45	E	
70	01000110	106	46	F	
71	01000111	107	47	G	
72	01001000	110	48	H	
73	01001001	111	49	I	
74	01001010	112	4A	J	¢
75	01001011	113	4B	K	. (Period)
76	01001100	114	4C	L	<
77	01001101	115	4D	M	(
78	01001110	116	4E	N	+
79	01001111	117	4F	O	|
80	01010000	120	50	P	&
81	01010001	121	51	Q	
82	01010010	122	52	R	
83	01010011	123	53	S	
84	01010100	124	54	T	
85	01010101	125	55	U	
86	01010110	126	56	V	
87	01010111	127	57	W	
88	01011000	130	58	X	
89	01011001	131	59	Y	
90	01011010	132	5A	Z	!
91	01011011	133	5B	[	$
92	01011100	134	5C	\	*
93	01011101	135	5D	]	)
94	01011110	136	5E	∧	;
95	01011111	137	5F	_ (Underscore)	¬ (Negation)
96	01100000	140	60	`	- (Hyphen)
97	01100001	141	61	a	/
98	01100010	142	62	b	
99	01100011	143	63	c	
100	01100100	144	64	d	
101	01100101	145	65	e	
102	01100110	146	66	f	
103	01100111	147	67	g	
104	01101000	150	68	h	
105	01101001	151	69	i	
106	01101010	152	6A	j	∧
107	01101011	153	6B	k	, (Comma)
108	01101100	154	6C	l	%
109	01101101	155	6D	m	_ (Underscore)
110	01101110	156	6E	n	>
111	01101111	157	6F	o	?
112	01110000	160	70	p	
113	01110001	161	71	q	
114	01110010	162	72	r	
115	01110011	163	73	s	
116	01110100	164	74	t	
117	01110101	165	75	u	
118	01110110	166	76	v	
119	01110111	167	77	w	
120	01111000	170	78	x	
121	01111001	171	79	y	
122	01111010	172	7A	z	:

Decimal	Binary	Octal	Hexadecimal	ASCII	EBCDIC
123	01111011	173	7B	{	#
124	01111100	174	7C	|	@
125	01111101	175	7D	}	' (Single quote)
126	01111110	176	7E	~	=
127	01111111	177	7F		,,
128	10000000	200	80		
129	10000001	201	81		a
130	10000010	202	82		b
131	10000011	203	83		c
132	10000100	204	84		d
133	10000101	205	85		e
134	10000110	206	86		f
135	10000111	207	87		g
136	10001000	210	88		h
137	10001001	211	89		i
.	.	.	.		.
.	.	.	.		.
145	10010001	221	91		j
146	10010010	222	92		k
147	10010011	223	93		l
148	10010100	224	94		m
149	10010101	225	95		n
150	10010110	226	96		o
151	10010111	227	97		p
152	10011000	230	98		q
153	10011001	231	99		r
.	.	.	.		.
.	.	.	.		.
162	10100010	242	A2		s
163	10100011	243	A3		t
164	10100100	244	A4		u
165	10100101	245	A5		v
166	10100110	246	A6		w
167	10100111	247	A7		x
168	10101000	250	A8		y
169	10101001	251	A9		z
.	.	.	.		.
.	.	.	.		.
192	11000000	300	C0		}
193	11000001	301	C1		A
194	11000010	302	C2		B
195	11000011	303	C3		C
196	11000100	304	C4		D
197	11000101	305	C5		E
198	11000110	306	C6		F
199	11000111	307	C7		G
200	11001000	310	C8		H
201	11001001	311	C9		I
.	.	.	.		.
.	.	.	.		.
208	11010000	320	D0		}
209	11010001	321	D1		J

Decimal	Binary	Octal	Hexadecimal	ASCII	EBCDIC
210	11010010	322	D2		K
211	11010011	323	D3		L
212	11010100	324	D4		M
213	11010101	325	D5		N
214	11010110	326	D6		O
215	11010111	327	D7		P
216	11011000	330	D8		Q
217	11011001	331	D9		R
.	.	.	.		.
.		.	.		.
.	.	.	.		.
224	11100000	340	E0		\
225	11100001	341	E1		
226	11100010	342	E2		S
227	11100011	343	E3		T
228	11100100	344	E4		U
229	11100101	345	E5		V
230	11100110	346	E6		W
231	11100111	347	E7		X
232	11101000	350	E8		Y
233	11101001	351	E9		Z
.	.	.	.		.
.		.	.		.
.	.	.	.		.
240	11110000	360	F0		0
241	11110001	361	F1		1
242	11110010	362	F2		2
243	11110011	363	F3		3
244	11110100	364	F4		4
245	11110101	365	F5		5
246	11110110	366	F6		6
247	11110111	367	F7		7
248	11111000	370	F8		8
249	11111001	371	F9		9
.	.	.	.		.
.	.	.	.		.
.		.	.		.
255	11111111	377	FF		

ASCII codes of control characters

Decimal	Binary	Octal	Hexadecimal	Character
0	00000000	000	00	NUL (Null)
1	00000001	001	01	SOH (Start of heading)
2	00000010	002	02	STX (End of heading and start of text)
3	00000011	003	03	ETX (End of text)
4	00000100	004	04	EOT (End of transmission)
5	00000101	005	05	ENQ (Enquiry—to request identification)
6	00000110	006	06	ACK (Acknowledge)
7	00000111	007	07	BEL (Ring bell)
8	00001000	010	08	BS (Backspace)
9	00001001	011	09	HT (Horizontal tab)
10	00001010	012	0A	LF (Line feed)
11	00001011	013	0B	VT (Vertical tab)
12	00001100	014	0C	FF (Form feed)
13	00001101	015	0D	CR (Carriage return)
14	00001110	016	0E	SO (Shift out—begin non-ASCII bit string)
15	00001111	017	0F	SI (Shift in—end non-ASCII bit string)
16	00010000	020	10	DLE (Data link escape—controls data transmission)
17	00010001	021	11	DC1 (Device control 1)
18	00010010	022	12	DC2 (Device control 2)
19	00010011	023	13	DC3 (Device control 3)
20	00010100	024	14	DC4 (Device control 4)
21	00010101	025	15	NAK (Negative acknowledge)
22	00010110	026	16	SYN (Synchronous idle)
23	00010111	027	17	ETB (End of transmission block)
24	00011000	030	18	CAN (Cancel—ignore previous transmission)
25	00011001	031	19	EM (End of medium)
26	00011010	032	1A	SUB (Substitute a character for another)
27	00011011	033	1B	ESC (Escape)
28	00011100	034	1C	FS (File separator)
29	00011101	035	1D	GS (Group separator)
30	00011110	036	1E	RS (Record separator)
31	00011111	037	1F	US (Unit separator)

EBCDIC codes of control characters

Decimal	Binary	Octal	Hexadecimal	Character
0	00000000	000	00	NUL (Null)
1	00000001	001	01	SOH (Start of heading)
2	00000010	002	02	STX (End of heading and start of text)
3	00000011	003	03	ETX (End of text)
4	00000100	004	04	PF (Punch off)
5	00000101	005	05	HT (Horizontal tab)
6	00000110	006	06	LC (Lower case)
7	00000111	007	07	DEL (Delete)
10	00001010	012	0A	SMM (Repeat)
11	00001011	013	0B	VT (Vertical tab)
12	00001100	014	0C	FF (Form feed)
13	00001101	015	0D	CR (Carriage return)
14	00001110	016	0E	SO (Shift out—begin non-ASCII bit string)
15	00001111	017	0F	SI (Shift in—end non-ASCII bit string)
16	00010000	020	10	DLE (Data link escape—controls data transmission)
17	00010001	021	11	DC1 (Device control 1)
18	00010010	022	12	DC2 (Device control 2)
19	00010011	023	13	DC3 (Device control 3)
20	00010100	024	14	RES (Restore)
21	00010101	025	15	NL (Newline)
22	00010110	026	16	BS (Backspace)
23	00010111	027	17	IL (Idle)
24	00011000	030	18	CAN (Cancel—ignore previous transmission)
25	00011001	031	19	EM (End of medium)
26	00011010	032	1A	CC (Unit backspace)
28	00011100	034	1C	IFS (Interchange file separator)
29	00011101	035	1D	IGS (Interchange group separator)
30	00011110	036	1E	IRS (Interchange record separator)
31	00011111	037	1F	IUS (Interchange unit separator)
32	00100000	040	20	DS (Digit select)
33	00100001	041	21	SOS (Start of significance)
34	00100010	042	22	FS (File separator)
36	00100100	044	24	BYP (Bypass)
37	00100101	045	25	LF (Line feed)
38	00100110	046	26	ETB (End of transmission block)
39	00100111	047	27	ESC (Escept)
42	00101010	052	2A	SM (Start message)
45	00101101	055	2D	ENQ (Enquiry—to request identification)
46	00101110	056	2E	ACK (Acknowledge)
47	00101111	057	2F	BEL (Ring bell)
50	00110010	062	32	SYN (Synchronous idle)
52	00110100	064	34	PN (Punch on)
53	00110101	065	35	RS (Record separator)
54	00110110	066	36	UC (Upper case)
55	00110111	067	37	EOT (End of transmission)
60	00111100	074	3C	DC4 (Device control 4)
61	00111101	075	3D	NAK (Negative acknowledge)
63	00111111	077	3F	SUB (Substitute a character for another)

B Pascal Reserved Words, Standard Identifiers, and Operators

Reserved Words

and	end	mod	repeat
array	file	nil	set
begin	for	not	then
case	forward	of	to
const	function	or	type
div	goto	packed	until
do	if	procedure	var
downto	in	program	while
else	label	record	with

Standard Identifiers

Predefined Constants

false   *true*   *maxint*

Predefined Types

boolean   *char*   *integer*   *real*   *text*

Predefined Files

input   *output*

Predefined Functions

abs	*exp*	*sin*
arctan	*ln*	*sqr*
chr	*odd*	*sqrt*
cos	*ord*	*succ*
eof	*pred*	*trunc*
eoln	*round*	

Predefined Procedures

dispose	*put*	*unpack*
get	*read*	*write*
new	*readln*	*writeln*
pack	*reset*	
page	*rewrite*	

Operators

Unary Arithmetic Operators

Operator	Operation	Type of Operand	Type of Result
+	unary plus	integer real	integer real
−	unary minus	integer real	integer real

Binary Arithmetic Operators

Operator	Operation	Type of Operands	Type of Result
+	addition	integer or real	integer if both operands are integer, otherwise real
−	subtraction	integer or real	integer if both operands are integer, otherwise real
*	multiplication	integer or real	integer if both operands are integer, otherwise real
/	division	integer or real	real
div	integer division	integer	integer
mod	modulo	integer	integer

Relational Operators

Operator	Operation	Type of Operands	Type of Result
=	equality	simple, string, set, or pointer	boolean
<>	inequality	simple, string, set, or pointer	boolean
<	less than	simple or string	boolean
>	greater than	simple or string	boolean
<=	less than or equal to, or subset	simple, string, or set	boolean
>=	greater than or equal to, or superset	simple, string, or set	boolean
in	set membership	first operand: ordinal type second operand: set type	boolean

Boolean Operators

Operator	Operation	Type of Operands	Type of Result
and	conjunction	boolean	boolean
not	negation	boolean	boolean
or	disjunction	boolean	boolean

Set Operators

Operator	Operation	Type of Operands	Type of Result
+	set union	set type	same as operands
−	set difference	set type	same as operands
*	set intersection	set type	same as operands

Assignment Operators

Operator	Operation	Type of Operands
:=	assignment	any type except file types

C

Syntax Diagrams

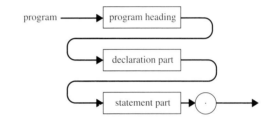

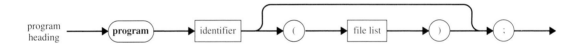

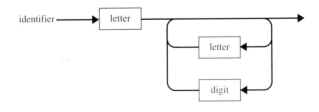

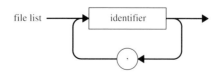

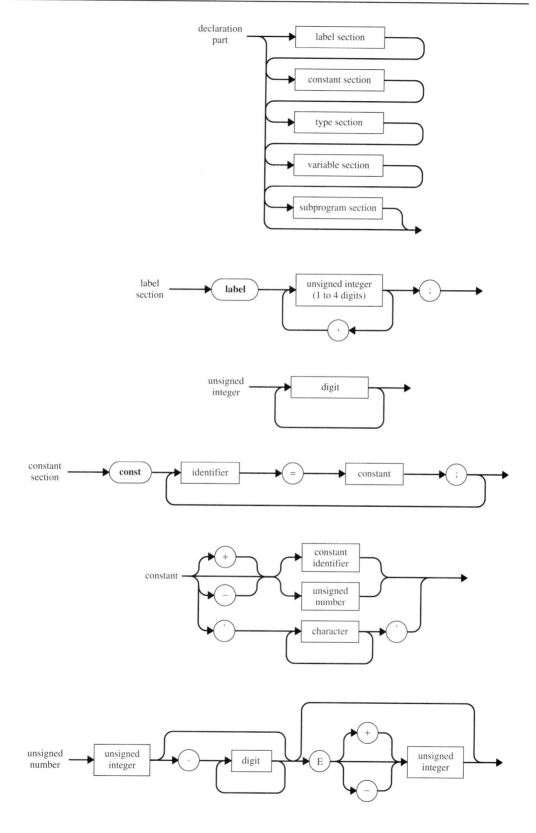

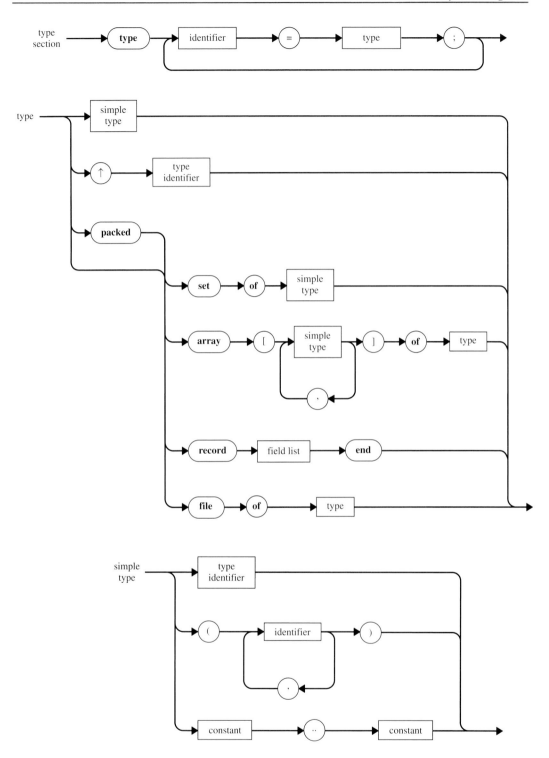

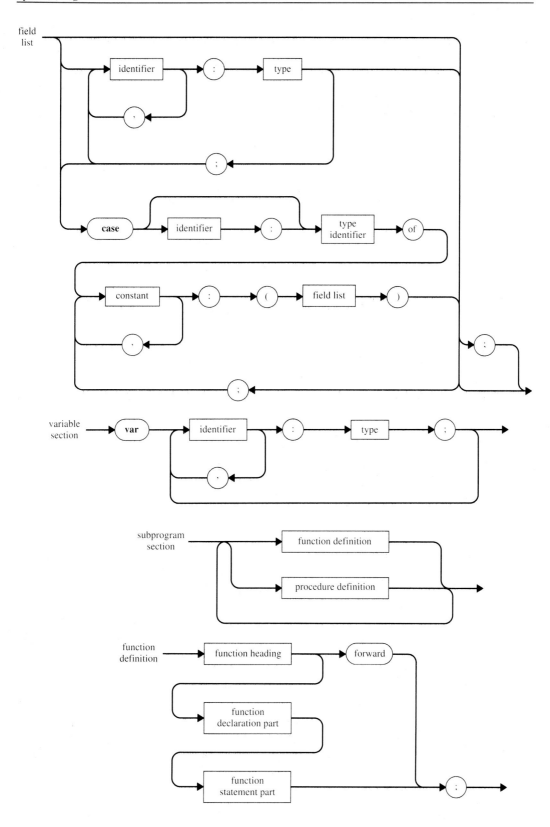

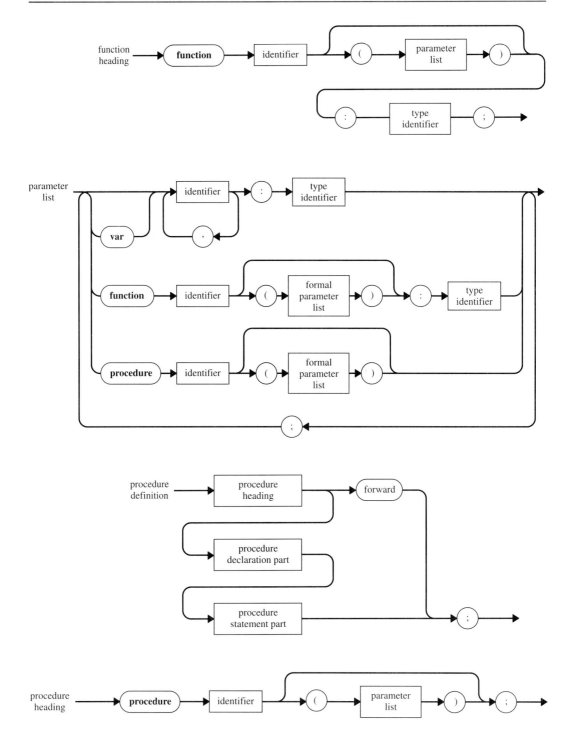

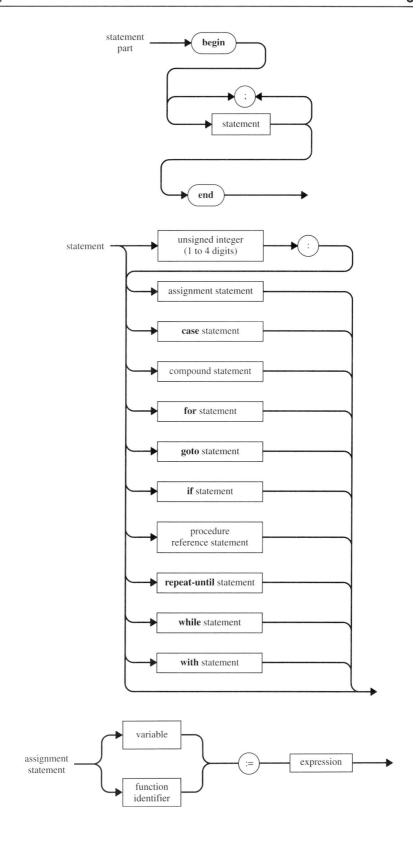

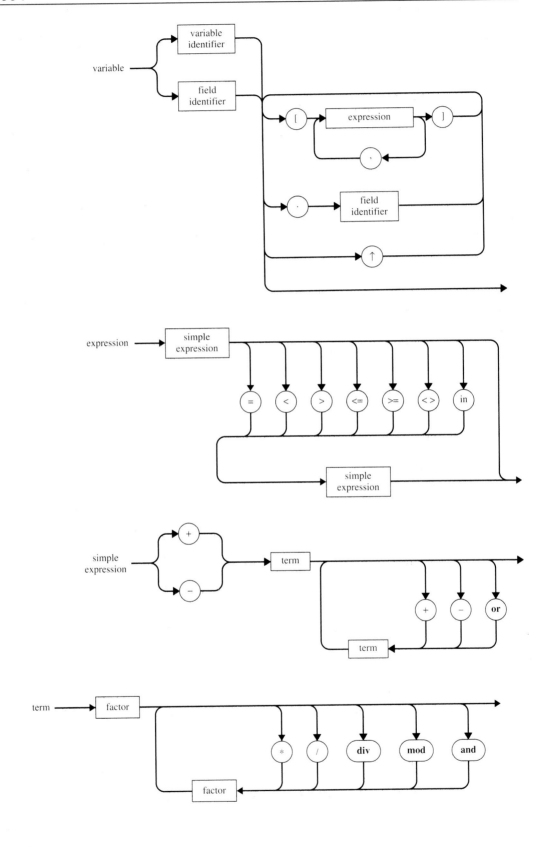

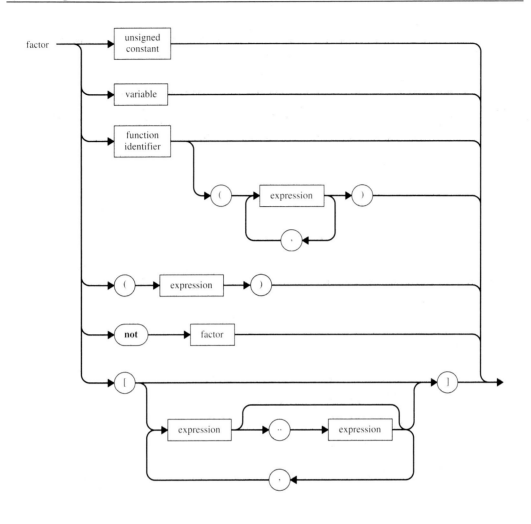

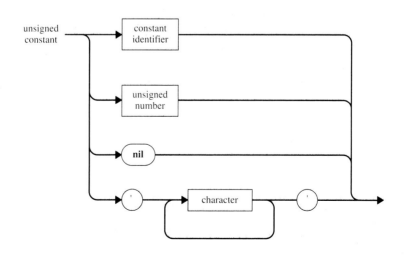

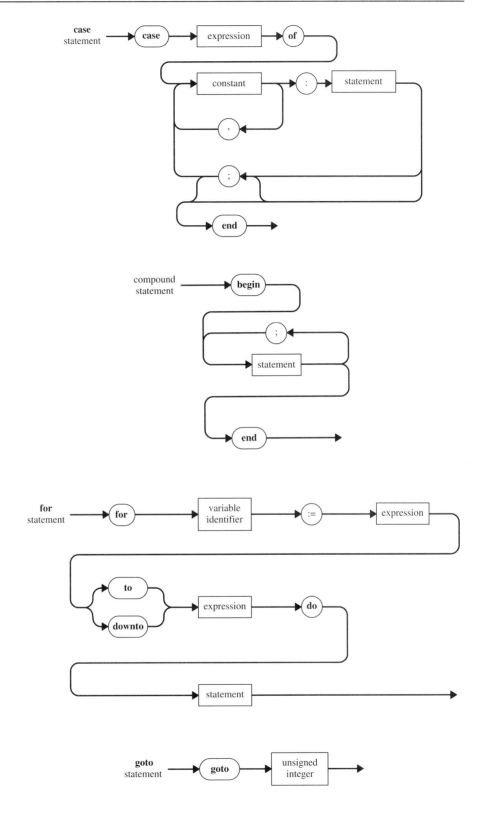

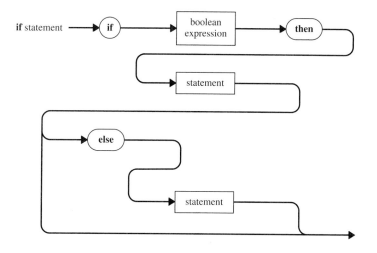

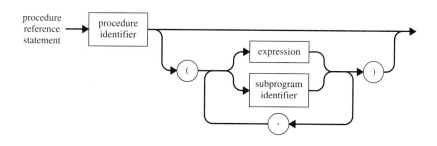

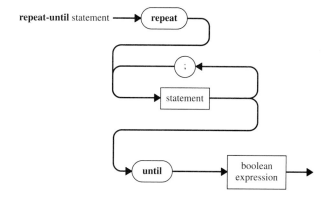

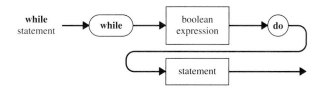

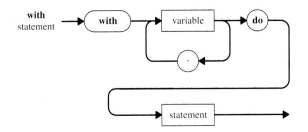

D

Pascal Predefined Functions and Procedures

Predefined Functions

Function	Description	Type of Argument	Type of Value
$abs(x)$	absolute value of x	integer or real	same as argument
$arctan(x)$	inverse tangent of x (value in radians)	integer or real	real
$chr(x)$	character whose ordinal number is x	integer	character
$cos(x)$	cosine of x (in radians)	integer or real	real
$eof(f)$	end-of-file function	file	boolean
$eoln(f)$	end-of-line function	text	boolean
$exp(x)$	exponential function e^x	integer or real	real
$ln(x)$	natural logarithm of x	integer or real	real
$odd(x)$	true if x is odd, false otherwise	integer	boolean
$ord(x)$	ordinal number of x	ordinal	integer
$pred(x)$	predecessor of x	ordinal	ordinal
$round(x)$	x rounded to nearest integer	real	integer
$sin(x)$	sine of x (in radians)	integer or real	real
$sqr(x)$	x^2	integer or real	same as argument
$sqrt(x)$	square root of x	integer or real	real
$succ(x)$	successor of x	ordinal	ordinal
$trunc(x)$	x truncated to its integer part	real	integer

Predefined Procedures

Procedure	Description
dispose (P) *dispose (P, tag-value-list)*	Releases the memory location pointed to by pointer variable *P*, leaving *P* undefined. The second form may be used for variant records.
get (F)	Advances the data pointer in file *F* to the next component and assigns this component to the file buffer variable *F↑*.
new (P) *new (P, tag-value-list)*	Acquires a memory location and assigns its address to pointer variable *P*. The second form may be used for variant records.
pack (U, First, P)	Copies the elements of the unpacked array *U*, beginning at position *First*, to the packed array *P*.
page (F)	Causes a system-dependent effect on the text file *F* so that subsequent text written to *F* will be on a new page if *F* is printed on a suitable output device.
put (F)	Transfers the contents of the buffer variable *F↑* to the file *F*.
read (F, input-list)	Reads values from the file *F* and assigns these to the variables in the input list. If *F* is not specified, the standard file *input* is assumed.
readln (F, input-list)	Reads values from the text file *F*, assigns these to the variables in the input list, and then advances the data pointer in *F* past the next end-of-line mark. If *F* is not specified, the standard file *input* is assumed.
reset (F)	Opens the file *F* for input, positions the data pointer in *F* at the first file component, and assigns this component to the file buffer variable *F↑*.
rewrite (F)	Creates the empty file *F* and opens it for output. Any previous contents of *F* are destroyed.
unpack (P, U, First)	Copies the elements of the packed array *P*, beginning at position *First*, to the unpacked array *U*.
write (F, output-list)	Writes the values of the items in the output list to file *F*. If *F* is not specified, the standard file *output* is assumed.
writeln (F, output-list)	Writes the value of the items in the output list to text file *F* followed by an end-of-line mark. If *F* is not specified, the standard file *output* is assumed.

E

Sample Data Files

Several exercises in the text use the files *InventoryFile*, *InventoryUpdate*, *LeastSquaresFile*, *StudentFile*, *StudentUpdate*, and *UsersFile*. This appendix describes the contents of these files and gives a sample listing for each.

InventoryFile
Item number: an integer
Number currently in stock: an integer in the range 0 through 999
Unit price: a real value
Minimum inventory level: an integer in the range 0 through 999
Item name: a 25-character string

File is sorted so that item numbers are in increasing order.

Sample *InventoryFile*

```
1011  20   54.95   15  TELEPHOTO POCKET CAMERA
1012  12   24.95   15  MINI POCKET CAMERA
1021  20   49.95   10  POL. ONE-STEP CAMERA
1022  13  189.95   12  SONAR 1-STEP CAMERA
1023  15   74.95    5  PRONTO CAMERA
1031   9  279.99   10  8MM ZOOM MOVIE CAMERA
1032  15  310.55   10  SOUND/ZOOM 8MM CAMERA
1041  10  389.00   12  35MM SLR XG-7 MINO. CAM.
1042  11  349.95   12  35MM SLR AE-1 PENT. CAM.
1043  20  319.90   12  35MM SLR ME CAN. CAM.
1044  13  119.95   12  35MM HI-MATIC CAMERA
1045  20   89.99   12  35MM COMPACT CAMERA
1511   7  129.95    5  ZOOM MOVIE PROJECTOR
1512   9  239.99    5  ZOOM-SOUND PROJECTOR
1521  10  219.99    5  AUTO CAROUSEL PROJECTOR
1522   4  114.95    5  CAR. SLIDE PROJECTOR
2011   4   14.95    5  POCKET STROBE
2012  12   48.55   10  STROBE SX-10
2013  10   28.99   15  ELEC.FLASH SX-10
3011  13   32.99   15  TELE CONVERTER
```

```
3012 14  97.99  15 28MM WIDE-ANGLE LENS
3013 13  87.95  15 135MM TELEPHOTO LENS
3014  8 267.95   5 35-105 MM ZOOM LENS
3015  7 257.95   5 80-200 MM ZOOM LENS
3111  4  67.50   5 HEAVY-DUTY TRIPOD
3112 10  19.95   5 LIGHTWEIGHT TRIPOD
3511 10 159.99   5 35MM ENLARGER KIT
4011  4  35.98   5 40X40 DELUXE SCREEN
4012 10  44.98   5 50X50 DELUXE SCREEN
5011 17   4.29  25 120-SLIDE TRAY
5012 33   2.95  25 100-SLIDE TRAY
5021 12   6.25  15 SLIDE VIEWER
5031 12  55.95  10 MOVIE EDITOR
6011 10  59.95   5 CONDENSER MICROPHONE
6111 80   0.89 100 AA ALKALINE BATTERY
7011 19  19.79  20 GADGET BAG
8011 45   1.49  50 135-24 COLOR FILM
8021 60   0.99  50 110-12 COLOR FILM
8022 42   1.45  50 110-24 COLOR FILM
8023 37   0.59  25 110-12 B/W FILM
8024 43   0.95  25 110-24 B/W FILM
8031 44   0.89  50 126-12 COLOR FILM
8032 27   0.59  25 126-12 B/W FILM
8041 39   6.89  50 8MM FILM CASSETTE
8042 25  11.89  20 16MM FILM CASSETTE
9111 10 959.99  12 COMBINATION CAMERA KIT
```

InventoryUpdate
Order number: three letters followed by four digits
Item number: an integer (same as those in *InventoryFile*)
Transaction code: a character (S = sold, R = returned)
Number of items sold or returned: an integer in the range 0 through 999

File is sorted so that item numbers are in increasing order. (Some items in *InventoryFile* may not have update records; others may have more than one.)

Sample *InventoryUpdate*

CCI7543	1012S	2		BTP5396	3013S	1
LTB3429	1012S	7		GFL4913	3013S	8
DJS6762	1021S	9		EHQ7510	3013S	7
NQT1850	1022S	1		QQL6472	3013S	5
WYP6425	1023S	4		SVC6511	3014S	4
YOK2210	1023R	2		XJQ9391	3014S	4
QGM3144	1023S	1		ONO5251	3111S	3
NPQ8685	1031S	5		CXC7780	3111S	1
MAP8102	1031S	13		VGT8169	3112S	8
JRJ6335	1031S	1		IMK5861	3511S	2
UWR9386	1032S	3		QHR1944	3511S	1
TJY1913	1032S	11		ZPK6211	4011S	2
YHA9464	1041S	5		VDZ2970	4012S	6

SYT7493	1041S	3		BOJ9069	5011S	6
FHJ1657	1042S	7		MNL7029	5011S	9
OJQ1221	1043S	8		MRG8703	5021S	10
UOX7714	1043S	2		DEM9289	5021S	1
ERZ2147	1043S	7		BXL1651	5031S	2
MYW2540	1044S	1		VAF8733	6111S	65
UKS3587	1045S	2		UYI0368	7011S	2
AAN3759	1045S	2		VIZ6879	8011S	16
WZT4171	1045S	12		GXX9093	8011S	19
TYR9475	1511S	1		HHO5605	8021S	41
FRQ4184	1511S	1		BOL2324	8021S	49
TAV3604	1512S	2		PAG9289	8023S	15
DCW9363	1522S	1		MDF5557	8023S	17
EXN3964	1522R	1		IQK3388	8024S	12
OIN5524	1522S	1		OTB1341	8024S	28
EOJ8218	1522S	1		SVF5674	8031S	24
YFK0683	2011S	2		ZDP9484	8031S	15
PPX4743	2012S	4		OSY8177	8032S	15
DBR1709	2013S	4		GJQ0185	8032S	8
JOM5408	2013S	3		VHW0189	8041S	20
PKN0671	2013S	1		WEU9225	8041S	6
LBD8391	3011S	9		YJO3755	8041S	8
DNL6326	3012S	9				

LeastSquaresFile
This is a text file in which each line contains a pair of real numbers representing
the *x* coordinate and the *y* coordinate of a point.

Sample *LeastSquaresFile*

2.18	1.06		5.63	8.58
7.46	12.04		8.94	15.27
5.75	8.68		7.34	11.48
3.62	4.18		6.55	9.92
3.59	3.87		4.89	7.07
7.5	12.32		9.59	15.82
7.49	11.74		1.81	0.45
7.62	12.07		0.99	-0.71
7.39	12.17		4.82	6.91
1.88	0.58		9.68	16.24
6.31	10.09		1.21	-0.22
2.53	2.04		4.54	5.64
5.44	8.25		1.48	0.3
1.21	-0.76		6.58	9.8
9.07	15.5		3.05	3.56
3.95	5.0		6.19	9.62
9.63	17.01		6.47	9.83
9.75	16.91		8.13	10.75
9.99	16.67		7.31	11.73
3.61	4.69		0.33	-1.93
9.06	15.0		5.12	7.41
5.03	6.62		5.23	7.73
4.45	6.12		7.14	11.02

4.54	5.89	1.27	-0.21
0.92	-1.02	2.51	1.59
0.82	-1.5	5.26	7.86
2.62	2.1	4.74	6.19
5.66	8.53	2.1	2.12
8.05	13.05	5.27	7.73
8.99	14.85	2.85	2.63
5.12	7.03	1.99	1.09
3.85	4.43	8.91	15.03
6.08	9.21	2.19	1.21
1.42	0	1.6	-0.05
2.58	2.38	8.93	15.12
5.99	9.42	3.19	3.56
0.63	-1.63	3.37	3.64
9.98	17.25		

StudentFile
Student number: an integer
Student's last name: a 15-character string
Student's first name: a 10-character string
Student's middle name: a character
Hometown: a 25-character string
Phone number: a 7-character string
Sex: a character (M or F)
Class level: a 1-digit integer (1, 2, 3, 4, or 5 for special)
Major: a 4-character string
Total credits earned to date: an integer
Cumulative GPA: a real value

File is arranged so that student numbers are in increasing order.

Sample *StudentFile*

```
10103JOHNSON        JAMES     L
WAUPUN, WISCONSIN        7345229M1ENGR 15 3.15
10104ANDREWS        PETER     J
GRAND RAPIDS, MICHIGAN   9493301M2CPSC 42 2.78
10110PETERS         ANDREW    J
LYNDEN, WASHINGTON       3239550M5ART  63 2.05
10113VANDENVANDER   VANNESSA  V
FREMONT, MICHIGAN        5509237F4HIST110 3.74
10126ARISTOTLE      ALICE     A
CHINO, CALIFORNIA        3330861F3PHIL 78 3.10
10144LUCKY          LUCY      L
GRANDVILLE, MICHIGAN     7745424F5HIST 66 2.29
10179EULER          LENNIE    L
THREE RIVERS, MICHIGAN   6290017M1MATH 15 3.83
10191NAKAMURA       TOKY      O
CHICAGO, ILLINOIS        4249665F1SOCI 12 1.95
10226FREUD          FRED      E
```

```
LYNDEN, WASHINGTON        8340115M1PSYC 15 1.85
10272SPEARSHAKE      WILLIAM    W
GRAND RAPIDS, MICHIGAN   2410744M5ENGL102 2.95
10274TCHAIKOVSKY     WOLFGANG   A
BYRON CENTER, MICHIGAN   8845115M3MUSC 79 2.75
10284ORANGE          DUTCH      V
GRAAFSCHAAP, MICHIGAN    3141660M2ENGR 42 2.98
10297CAESAR          JULIE      S
DENVER, COLORADO         4470338F4HIST117 3.25
10298PSYCHO          PRUNELLA   E
DE MOTTE, INDIANA        5384609F4PSYC120 2.99
10301BULL            SITTING    U
GALLUP, NEW MEXICO       6632997M1EDUC 14 1.95
10302CUSTER          GENERAL    G
BADLANDS, SOUTH DAKOTA   5552992M3HIST 40 1.95
10303FAHRENHEIT      FELICIA    O
SHEBOYGAN, WISCONSIN     5154997F2CHEM 40 3.85
10304DEUTSCH         SPRECHEN   Z
SPARTA, MICHIGAN         8861201F5GERM 14 3.05
10307MENDELSSOHN     MOZART     W
PEORIA, ILLINOIS         2410744M3MUSC 76 2.87
10310AUGUSTA         ADA        B
LAKEWOOD, CALIFORNIA     7172339F2CPSC 46 3.83
10319GAUSS           CARL       F
YORKTOWN, PENNSYLVANIA   3385494M2MATH 41 4.00
10323KRONECKER       LEO        P
TRAVERSE CITY, MICHIGAN  6763991M3MATH 77 2.75
10330ISSACSON        JACOB      A
SILVER SPRINGS, MD       4847932M5RELI 25 2.99
10331ISSACSON        ESAU       B
SILVER SPRINGS, MD       4847932M5RELI 25 2.98
10339DEWEY           JOHANNA    A
SALT LAKE CITY, UTAH     6841129F2EDUC 41 3.83
10348VIRUS           VERA       W
SAGINAW, MICHIGAN        6634401F4CPSC115 3.25
10355ZYLSTRA         ZELDA      A
DOWNS, KANSAS            7514008F1ENGL 16 1.95
10377PORGY           BESS       N
COLUMBUS, OHIO           4841771F2MUSC 44 2.78
10389NEWMANN         ALFRED     E
CHEYENNE, WYOMING        7712399M4EDUC115 0.99
10395MEDES           ARCHIE     L
WHITINSVILLE, MA         9294401M3ENGR 80 3.10
10406MACDONALD       RONALD     B
SEATTLE, WASHINGTON      5582911M1CPSC 15 2.99
10415AARDVARK        ANTHONY    A
GRANDVILLE, MICHIGAN     5325912M2ENGR 43 2.79
10422GESTALT         GLORIA     G
WHEATON, ILLINOIS        6631212F2PSYC 42 2.48
10431GOTODIJKSTRA    EDGAR      G
CAWKER CITY, KANSAS      6349971M1CPSC 15 4.00
10448REMBRANDT       ROBERTA    E
SIOUX CENTER, IOWA       2408113F1ART  77 2.20
10458SHOEMAKER       IMELDA     M
HONOLULU, HAWAII         9193001F1POLS 15 3.15
10467MARX            KARL       Z
HAWTHORNE, NEW JERSEY    5513915M3ECON 78 2.75
10470SCROOGE         EBENEZER   T
```

```
TROY, MICHIGAN            8134001M4SOCI118 3.25
10482NIGHTINGALE    FLORENCE  K
ROCHESTER, NEW YORK       7175118F1NURS 15 3.15
10490GAZELLE        GWENDOLYN D
CHINO, CALIFORNIA        3132446F2P E  43 2.78
10501PASTEUR        LOUISE    A
WINDOW ROCK, ARIZONA     4245170F1BIOL 16 3.10
10519ELBA           ABLE      M
BOZEMAN, MONTANA         8183226M3SPEE 77 3.40
10511LEWIS          CLARK     N
NEW ERA, MICHIGAN        6461125M4GEOG114 3.37
10515MOUSE          MICHAEL   E
BOISE, IDAHO             5132771M5EDUC 87 1.99
10523PAVLOV         TIFFANY   T
FARMINGTON, MICHIGAN     9421753F1BIOL 13 1.77
10530CHICITA        JUANITA   A
OKLAHOMA CITY, OK        3714377F5ENGL 95 2.66
10538BUSCH          ARCH      E
ST LOUIS, MISSOURI       8354112M3ENGR 74 2.75
10547FAULT          PAIGE     D
PETOSKEY, MICHIGAN       4543116F5CPSC 55 2.95
10553SANTAMARIA     NINA      P
PLYMOUTH, MASSACHUSETTS 2351881F1HIST 15 1.77
10560SHYSTER        SAMUEL    D
EVERGLADES, FLORIDA      4421885M1SOCI 13 1.95
10582YEWLISS        CAL       C
RUDYARD, MICHIGAN        3451220M3MATH 76 2.99
10590ATANASOFF      ENIAC     C
SPRINGFIELD, ILLINOIS    6142449F1CPSC 14 1.88
10597ROCKNE         ROCKY     K
PORTLAND, OREGON         4631744M4P E 116 1.98
10610ROOSEVELT      ROSE      Y
SPRING LAKE, MICHIGAN    9491221F5E SC135 2.95
10623XERXES         ART       I
CINCINATTI, OHIO         3701228M4GREE119 3.25
10629LEIBNIZ        GOTTFRIED W
BOULDER, COLORADO        5140228M1MATH 13 1.95
10633VESPUCCI       VERA      D
RIPON, CALIFORNIA        4341883F5GEOG 89 2.29
10648PRINCIPAL      PAMELA    P
ALBANY, NEW YORK         7145513F1EDUC 14 1.75
10652CICERO         MARSHA    M
RAPID CITY, SD           3335910F3LATI 77 2.87
10657WEERD          DEWEY     L
DETROIT, MICHIGAN        4841962M4PHIL115 2.99
10663HOCHSCHULE     HORTENSE  C
LINCOLN, NEBRASKA        7120111F5EDUC100 2.70
10668EINSTEIN       ALFRED    M
NEWARK, NEW JERSEY       3710225M2ENGR 41 2.78
10675FIBONACCI      LEONARD   O
NASHVILLE, TENNESSEE     4921107M4MATH115 3.25
10682ANGELO         MIKE      L
AUSTIN, TEXAS            5132201M4ART 117 3.74
10688PASCAL         BLAZE     R
BROOKLYN, NEW YORK       7412993M1CPSC 15 1.98
```

StudentUpdate
Student number: an integer (same as those used in *StudentFile*)
For each of five courses:
    Course name: a seven-character string (e.g., CPSC131)
    Letter grade: a two-character string (e.g., A −, B +, C♭)
    Course credit: an integer

File is sorted so that student numbers are in increasing order. There is one update record for each student in *StudentFile*.

Sample *StudentUpdate*

```
10103ENGL176C 4EDUC268B 4EDUC330B+3P E 281C 3ENGR317D 4
10104CPSC271D+4E SC208D-3PHIL340B+2CPSC146D+4ENGL432D+4
10110ART 520D 3E SC259F 1ENGL151D+4MUSC257B 4PSYC486C 4
10113HIST498F 3P E 317C+4MUSC139B-3PHIL165D 3GEOG222C 3
10126PHIL367C-4EDUC420C-3EDUC473C 3EDUC224D-3GERM257F 4
10144HIST559C+3MATH357D 3CPSC323C-2P E 246D-4MUSC379D+4
10179MATH169C-4CHEM163C+4MUSC436A-3MATH366D-2BIOL213A-4
10191SOCI177F 4POLS106A 4EDUC495A-3ENGR418B+2ENGR355A 4
10226PSYC116B 3GERM323B-4ART 350A 4HIST269B+4EDUC214C+3
10272ENGL558A-4EDUC169D+3PSYC483B+4ENGR335B+2BIOL228B 4
10274MUSC351B 4PSYC209C-4ENGR400F 1E SC392A 4SOCI394B-3
10284ENGR292D 4PSYC172C 4EDUC140B 4MATH274F 4MUSC101D+4
10297HIST464F 1HIST205F 1ENGR444F 1MATH269F 1EDUC163F 1
10298PSYC452B 3MATH170C+4EDUC344C-2GREE138C-2SPEE303A-3
10301EDUC197A 4P E 372B 3ENGR218D 4MATH309C 4E SC405C-4
10302CHEM283F 1P E 440A 2MATH399A-3HIST455C-4MATH387C-3
10303HIST111D-3ART151 C+3ENGL100C-3PSYC151D+3PE104  A-1
10304GERM526C-2CHEM243C 4POLS331B-4EDUC398A 3ENGR479D+4
10307MUSC323B+3MATH485C 4HIST232B+4EDUC180A 3ENGL130B+4
10310CPSC264B 2POLS227D+3ENGR467D-3MATH494D-4ART 420C+4
10319MATH276B 2E SC434A 3HIST197B-4GERM489B-2ART 137C-3
10323MATH377D-4EDUC210D 4MATH385D-4ENGR433C 2HIST338A-4
10330HIST546C+3E SC440B+3GREE472C+3BIOL186B 4GEOG434C+2
10331HIST546C 3E SC440B+3GREE472C 3BIOL186B+4GEOG434C+2
10339EDUC283B 3CPSC150B 3ENGR120D 4CPSC122F 4ART 216B 4
10348CPSC411C-3HIST480C+4PSYC459B 4BIOL299B+4ECON276B+3
10355ENGL130C-3CPSC282C+4CPSC181A-4CPSC146C-4SOCI113F 1
10377SOCI213D+3PSYC158D 4MUSC188C 3PSYC281D-4ENGR339B+4
10389EDUC414D+4PSYC115C-2PSYC152D-4ART 366D-3ENGR366F 4
10395ENGR396B 4HIST102F 3ENGL111A 4PSYC210D-2GREE128A 4
10406CPSC160C+4CPSC233C 1LATI494C+3ENGL115C-3MATH181A 3
10415ENGR287C 4EDUC166B-4EDUC106A-3P E 190F 3MATH171B-3
10422PSYC275A-4MATH497A 4EDUC340F 1GERM403C-4MATH245D+4
10431CPSC187D-4CPSC426F 4ENGR476B-4BIOL148B+3CPSC220F 3
10448ART 171D+3CPSC239C-3SOCI499B-4HIST113D+3PSYC116C 4
10458POLS171F 1CPSC187C+4CHEM150B 2PHIL438D-4PHIL254D 4
10467ECON335D-3E SC471B+4MATH457C+3MATH207C 2BIOL429D 4
10470MUSC415C+3POLS177C 3CPSC480A 4PSYC437B 3SOCI276D 4
10482ENGL158D-4EDUC475B 3HIST172B-2P E 316F 4ENGR294A-3
10490P E 239F 4ENGL348F 3LATI246F 4CPSC350F 4MATH114F 1
10501BIOL125F 4CPSC412F 3E SC279F 4ENGR153F 2ART 293F 1
10519SPEE386B+4HIST479C 4PSYC249B-2GREE204B-4P E 421A 1
```

```
10511E SC416B 3MATH316D-4MATH287C 2MATH499A-4E SC288D 3
10515EDUC563D+3PHIL373D-3ART 318B 4HIST451F 1ART 476C+3
10523BIOL183D-2HIST296D+4HIST380B+4ENGR216C 4MATH412B-2
10530ENGL559F 1EDUC457D+4CPSC306A 3ENGR171B+1CPSC380A 4
10538ENGR328A-4ENGR336C 3EDUC418D+3PHIL437B+4CPSC475D 4
10547CPSC537A-4ART 386D 4HIST292D-4ENGR467A-4P E 464B+4
10553HIST170A-4SOCI496D-3PHIL136B+4CPSC371D-4CPSC160A-1
10560SOCI153D+3MATH438D+4CPSC378C 4BIOL266F 3EDUC278D+3
10582MATH388A-3P E 311B 3ECON143D 4MATH304C+3P E 428C+4
10590CPSC134B-3E SC114B+3CPSC492C 4ENGL121C 4ENGR403A-4
10597P E 423A-3BIOL189D+3PHIL122D-4ENGL194C-4SOCI113D+3
10610E SC594C-3PHIL344F 4CPSC189B+2ENGR411D-3MATH241A 4
10623GREE412B-4ENGL415D-3ENGL234D-4MATH275F 1SOCI124B+3
10629MATH137D 2MATH481F 3E SC445F 1MATH339D 4ART 219B+4
10633GEOG573B 4ENGL149C+4EDUC113B+4ENGR458C-2HIST446D+4
10648EDUC132D+4MUSC103D-4ENGL263C 4ENGL134B+4E SC392A 3
10652LATI363F 3BIOL425F 1CPSC267C 4EDUC127C+3MATH338B 4
10657PHIL429F 1ART 412D-4MUSC473B-4SOCI447C-4MATH237D+2
10663EDUC580B-4ENGR351B+4SOCI283D 4ART 340C 4PSYC133D+3
10668ENGR274B+4SOCI438C 1P E 327C 4BIOL158A 4EDUC457A-4
10675MATH457A 4ENGR114C 4CPSC218C 3E SC433C-3PSYC243C+1
10682ART 483D+3GERM432C 3ENGL103B+4MUSC169C-3SOCI381C-2
10688CPSC182F 1HIST371C+4PSYC408F 1MUSC214B+4MATH151C 3
```

UsersFile
Identification number: an integer
User's name: A 30-character string in the form Last Name, First Name
Password: a 5-character string
Resource limit (in dollars): an integer of up to four digits
Resources used to date: a real value

File is arranged so that identification numbers are in increasing order.

Sample *UsersFile*:

```
10101MILTGEN, JOSEPH             MOE
 750 380.81
10102SMALL, ISAAC               LARGE
 650 598.84
10103SNYDER, SAMUEL             R2-D2
 250 193.74
10104EDMUNDSEN, EDMUND          ABCDE
 250 177.93
10105BRAUNSCHNEIDER, CHRISTOPHER BROWN
 850 191.91
10106PIZZULA, NORMA             PIZZA
 350 223.95
10107VANDERVAN, HENRY           VAN
 750 168.59
10108FREELOADER, FREDDIE        RED
 450  76.61
10109ALEXANDER, ALVIN           GREAT
 650 405.04
```

```
10110MOUSE, MICHAEL              EARS
  50   42.57
10111LUKASEWICZ, ZZZYK          RPN
 350   73.50
10112CHRISTMAS, MARY            NOEL
 850   33.28
10113SINKEY, CJ                 TRAIN
 750  327.53
10114NIJHOFF, LARAN            KKID
 550  382.03
10115LIESTMA, STAN              SAAB
 650   38.36
10116ZWIER, APOLLOS             PJ
 350  249.48
10117JAEGER, TIM                BIKE
 250  246.73
10118VANZWALBERG, JORGE         EGYPT
 850  466.95
10119JESTER, COURTNEY           JOKER
 450  281.16
10120MCDONALD, RONALD           FRIES
 250   35.00
10121NEDERLANDER, BENAUT        DUTCH
 550   28.82
10122HAYBAILER, HOMER           FARM
 850   37.32
10123SPEAR, WILLIAM             SHAKE
 450  337.01
10124ROMEO, JULIET              XOXOX
 150  100.19
10125GREEK, JIMMY               WAGER
 250    0.03
10126VIRUS, VERA                WORM
 750   67.35
10127BEECH, ROCKY               BOAT
 950  256.18
10128ENGEL, ANGEL               WINGS
 150   16.39
10129ABNER, LIL                 DAISY
 950   89.57
10130TRACY, DICK                CRIME
 550  392.00
10131MCGEE, FIBBER              MOLLY
 750  332.12
10132BELL ,ALEXANDER            PHONE
 850  337.43
20101COBB, TYRUS                TIGER
  50   32.81
20102GEORGE, RUTH               BABE
 350  269.93
20103DESCARTES, RONALD          HORSE
 250  109.34
20104EUCLID, IAN                GREEK
 350   63.63
20105DANIELS, EZEKIEL           LIONS
 350  128.69
20106TARZAN, JANE               APES
 150  100.31
```

```
20107HABBAKUK, JONAH          WHALE
 950 183.93
20108COLUMBUS, CHRIS          PINTA
 850 202.24
20109BYRD, RICHARD            NORTH
 550 168.49
20110BUNYAN, PAUL             BABE
 550 333.47
20111CHAUCER, JEFF            POEM
 950  37.02
20112STOTLE, ARI              LOGIC
 750 337.74
20113HARRISON, BEN            PRES
 550 262.97
20114JAMES, JESSE             GUNS
 250  58.81
20115SCOTT, FRANCINE          FLAG
 350 168.11
20116PHILLIPS, PHYLLIS        GAS66
 650 322.22
20117DOLL, BARBARA            KEN
 350  26.34
20118FINN, HUCK               TOM
 350  22.86
20119SAWYER, TOM              HUCK
 950 460.30
20120NEWMANN, ALFRED          MAD
 450 116.00
20121SIMPLE, SIMON            SAYS
 550 486.05
20122SCHMIDT, MESSER          PLANE
 250  35.31
20124LUTHER, CALVIN           REF
 777 666.66
20125YALE, HARVARD            IVY
 150 127.70
```

F

Miscellany

In the main part of this text we mentioned some special features of Pascal that were not described in detail. For completeness they are briefly described in this appendix.

Functions and Procedures as Parameters

Subprograms considered in the main part of the text have involved two kinds of formal parameters: value parameters and variable parameters. In addition to these kinds of parameters, Pascal also allows functions and procedures as parameters.

As an illustration of the use of ***function parameters***, consider a function *Integral* that approximates the area of the region under the graph of a function $f(x)$ for $a \leq x \leq b$, by subdividing this region into n rectangles and summing the areas of these rectangles (see Figure F.1). This subprogram *ApproxArea* must have the formal parameters a, b, and n, which are ordinary value parameters, and a function parameter f. When *ApproxArea* is referenced, actual parameters of real type are associated with the formal parameters a and b; an actual parameter of integer type is associated with the formal parameter n; and an actual function is associated with the formal parameter f.

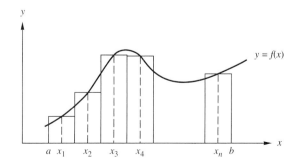

Figure F.1

Function parameters are designated as such by a function heading (without the closing semicolon) within the formal parameter list. Thus an appropriate heading for *ApproxArea* is

function *ApproxArea*(**function** $f(x : real)$: *real*;
$a, b : real$; $n : integer)$: *real*;

Here **function** $f(x : real)$: *real* specifies that f is a function parameter denoting a function whose formal parameter and value are of real type. The corresponding actual function parameter must be a function having a real formal parameter and a real value. For example, if *Poly* is a real-valued function with a real parameter,

Area := *ApproxArea*(*Poly*, 0, 1.5, 20)

is a valid function reference. Note that only the name of the actual function parameter is given; it is not accompanied by its own actual parameters.

Figure F.2 shows a program that uses the function *ApproxArea* to calculate the area under the graph of the function *Poly* defined by $Poly(x) = x^2 + 3x + 2$ for $0 \le x \le 4$.

```
PROGRAM AreaUnderCurve (input, output);

(*******************************************************************

    Input (keyboard): Endpoints of an interval and number of
                      subintervals.
    Function:         Uses the function ApproxArea to calculate the
                      area under the graph of the function Poly.
    Output (screen):  Approximate area.

*******************************************************************)

VAR
    Left, Right : real;          (* endpoints of an interval *)
    NumSubintervals : integer;   (* number of subintervals *)

FUNCTION Poly(x : real) : real;

    (***************************************************************

        Input (param):  Real argument x.
        Function:       Defines the function for which area is being
                        calculated.
        Output (Poly):  The value Poly(x).

    ***************************************************************)

    BEGIN (* Poly *)
        Poly := sqr(x) + 3 * x + 2;
    END (* Poly *);
```

Figure F.2

```
FUNCTION ApproxArea (FUNCTION f(x : real): real;
                     a, b : real; n : integer) : real;

   (*********************************************************************

        Input (param):        A real-valued function f of a real
                              variable, real numbers a and b, and
                              integer n.
        Function:             Approximates area under the graph of the
                              function f over the interval [a, b] using
                              n subintervals.  The function is evaluated
                              at the midpoints of the subintervals.
        Output (ApproxArea): Returns the approximate value of the
                              area.

   *********************************************************************)

   VAR
      x,            (* midpoint of a subinterval *)
      Deltax,       (* size of subintervals *)
      Sum : real;   (* sum of areas of rectangles *)

   BEGIN (* ApproxArea *)
      Deltax := (b - a) / n;
      Sum := 0;
      x := a + Deltax / 2;
      WHILE x <= b DO
         BEGIN
            Sum := Sum + f(x);
            x := x + Deltax
         END (* WHILE *);
      ApproxArea := Sum * Deltax
   END (* ApproxArea *);

BEGIN (* main program *)
   writeln ('Endpoints and # subintervals:');
   readln (Left, Right, NumSubintervals);
   writeln ('Approximate area = ',
            ApproxArea(Poly, Left, Right, NumSubintervals):8:6)
END (* main program *).
```

Sample runs:

```
Endpoints and # subintervals:
0 4 4
Approximate area = 53.000000


Endpoints and # subintervals:
0 4 8
Approximate area = 53.250000


Endpoints and # subintervals:
0 4 500
Approximate area = 53.333312
```

Procedures may also be used as parameters in subprograms. In this case, a formal parameter is designated as a ***procedure parameter*** by including a procedure heading (without the closing semicolon) in the formal parameter list.

If *F* is a formal function or procedure parameter and *A* is the corresponding actual parameter, then the following rules apply:

1. *A* must be defined within the program; it may not be a predefined function or procedure.
2. If *F* denotes a function whose value is of type *T*, then *A* must also denote a function whose value is of type *T*.
3. If

$$Flist\text{-}1 : type\text{-}1;\ Flist\text{-}2 : type\text{-}2;\ \ldots\ ;\ Flist\text{-}n : type\text{-}n$$

is the formal parameter list of *F*, then the formal parameter list of *A* must have the form

$$Alist\text{-}1 : type\text{-}1;\ Alist\text{-}2 : type\text{-}2;\ \ldots\ ;\ Alist\text{-}n : type\text{-}n$$

where each *Flist-i* and *Alist-i* contain the same number of parameters, and all of these parameters are value parameters, all are variable parameters, all are function parameters, or all are procedure parameters. (In the case of function or procedure parameters, they must also satisfy these same rules.)

To illustrate Rule 2, consider the following procedure heading:

procedure *Demo* (**procedure** *F*(*x, y* : *integer*; **var** *V* : *real*));

The heading of the procedure defining the actual procedure *A* corresponding to *F* could be

procedure *A* (*Num1, Num2* : *integer*; **var** *Alpha* : *real*);

but it could not be any of the following:

procedure *A* (*Num1, Num2* : *integer*; **var** *Num3* : *integer*);
procedure *A* (*Num1* : *integer*; **var** *Alpha* : *real*);
procedure *A* (*Num1, Num2* : *integer*; *Alpha* : *real*);
procedure *A* (*Num1* : *integer*; *Num2* : *integer*; **var** *Alpha* : *real*);

Statement Labels and the *goto* Statement

Pascal provides two statements for implementing repetition structures: the **while** statement for constructing pretest loops in which the termination test is at the top of the loop, and the **repeat-until** statement for constructing posttest loops in which the termination test is made at the bottom of the loop. More general repetition structures can also be implemented in Pascal. In these structures there may be several termination tests and they may be placed anywhere within the body of the loop, or there may be no termination test at all, in which case the loop is an ***infinite loop***.

A ***repeat-forever*** loop is an example of an infinite loop. It can be constructed in Pascal as a while loop,

> **while** *true* **do**
>> body of the loop

or as a repeat loop:

> **repeat**
>> body of the loop
>
> **until** *false*

When these statements are executed, the body of the loop is executed repeatedly. Since the termination test is never false in the first case and is never true in the second, these loops will never terminate. Such infinite loops may be useful in some special applications. For example, control programs in an operating system are meant to run forever. Similarly, a program might use a nonterminating loop to continually collect data from a device monitoring some process such as the operation of a nuclear reactor.

Most programs, however, are not intended to execute forever; consequently, most loops must contain some mechanism for terminating repetition. To illustrate, consider a program for which the input data may contain errors and where provision must be made to detect these errors. When an error is found, control might be passed to some other part of the program for error handling and/or execution of the program terminated. These abnormal situations can be handled easily by using statement labels and the **goto** statement. For example, if all the data values processed by a program are no greater than 100, the following while loop might be used:

> **while** *true* **do**
>> **begin**
>>> *read* (*Data*);
>>> **if** *Data* > 100 **then goto** 50;
>>> (∗ else process *Data* ∗)
>>>
>>> .
>>> .
>>> .
>>
>> **end** (∗ **while** ∗)
>
> 50: *writeln* ('∗∗∗ Bad data value ∗∗∗', *Data*);
>
>> .
>> .
>> .

In this example, 50 is a ***statement label.*** Such labels must be declared in the label section in the declaration part of the program. This section has the form

>   **label**
>   *label-1, label-2, . . . , label-n;*

and it must be the first section in the declaration part. Each *label-i* must be a positive integer of up to four digits and can be used to label only one statement. Control can then be transferred to that statement by using a **goto** statement of the form

>   **goto** *label-i*

In the preceding example, if a data value greater than 100 is read, control is transferred to the statement with label 50. A label section such as the following must therefore be used to define this statement label:

>   **label** 50;

The statement label 50 followed by a colon (:) can then be attached as a prefix to any statement in the program unit in which this label section appears. In our example, it is attached to an output statement that displays an error message.

A statement of the form

>   **if** *boolean-expression* **then goto** *statement-label*

can be placed anywhere within a loop to cause an exit from it. For example,

>   **while** *true* **do**
>   **begin**
>   *statement-sequence-1*;
>   **if** *boolean-expression* **then goto** ##;
>   *statment-sequence-2*
>   **end** (∗ **while** ∗);
>   ##: *next-statement*

If *statement-sequence-1* is omitted, this loop is a pretest loop; if *statement-sequence-2* is omitted, it is a posttest loop; if both *statement-sequence-1* and *statement-sequence-2* are present, it is a ***test-in-the-middle loop***. The loop might also contain multiple exits

>   **while** *true* **do**
>   **begin**
>   *statement-sequence-1*;
>   **if** *boolean-expression-1* **then goto** ##;
>   *statement-sequence-2;*
>   **if** *boolean-expression-2* **then goto** ##;
>   .
>   .
>   .

> *statement-sequence k*;
> **if** *boolean-expression-k* **then goto** ##;
> *statement-sequence-k + 1*
> **end** (* **while** *);
> ##: *next-statement*

In most applications, however, while and repeat-until loops are preferred because the logical flow in such single-exit loops is easier to follow than it is in loops that allow multiple exits. Moreover, loops having the termination test at the top or at the bottom of the loop are easier to read and understand than are those that allow exits in the middle.

The familiar scope rules for identifiers in Pascal programs also apply to statement labels. Thus the ***fundamental scope principle for labels*** is

> The scope of a statement label is the program unit in which it is declared.

More specifically, the three basic ***scope rules for labels*** are

1. A statement label declared in a program unit is not accessible outside that unit.
2. A global statement label is accessible in any subprogram in which that label is not declared locally.
3. Statement labels declared in a subprogram can be accessed by any subprogram defined within it, provided that the label is not declared locally in the internal subprogram.

The Procedure *page*

The procedure *page* is designed to insert page breaks into the output produced by a program. This procedure is called with a statement of the form

> *page* (*file-name*)

or

> *page*

In the second form, the standard file *output* is assumed. The effect of a call to procedure *page* is system dependent, and one must determine the details by consulting the system reference manuals. The Pascal standard states only that

> *Page* (*f*) shall cause an implementation-defined effect on the textfile *f*, such that subsequent output to *f* will be on a new page if the textfile is printed on a suitable device and shall perform an implicit *writeln*.

Alternative Forms of Procedures *new* and *dispose*

Alternative forms of reference to the procedures *new* and *dispose* may be used for variant records. The procedure *new* may be called with a statement of the form

> *new (pointer, tag-value-1, tag-value-2, . . . , tag-value-n)*

Here *tag-value-1, tag-value-2, . . . , tag-value-n* represent values of tag fields in increasingly nested variant parts of the record; that is, this procedure reference may be used to allocate a memory location for a record having the structure

>   **record**
>   *fixed-part-1*;
>   **case** *tag-field-1* : *tag-type-1* **of**
>   .
>   .
>   .
>   *tag-value-1* : (*fixed-part-2*;
>   **case** *tag-field-2* : *tag-type-2* **of**
>   .
>   .
>   .
>   *tag-value-2* : (*fixed-part-3*;
>   **case** *tag-field-3* : *tag-type-3* **of**
>   .
>   .
>   .
>   *tag-value-3* : (. . .
>   .
>   .
>
>   **end**;

When a memory location is allocated for a variant record with a procedure call of the form

> *new (pointer)*

it is sufficiently large to store the largest variant in that record. If it is known that a record with a particular variant is being processed, the alternative form of the procedure call may be used. This allows the system to allocate a location whose size is appropriate to that variant. To illustrate, consider the following declarations:

>   **type**
>   *NameString* = **packed array**[1..20] **of** *char*;
>   *EmployeeRecord* = **record**

Name : *NameString*;
Age, Dependents : *integer*;
case *EmpCode* : *char* **of**

'F' : (∗ Factory employee ∗)
(*DeptCode* : *char*;
HourlyRate : *real*);
'O' : (∗ Office employee ∗)
(*Salary* : *real*);
'S' : (∗ Salesperson ∗)
(*MileageAllowance* : *integer*;
BasePay, CommissionRate : *real*)
end;

If it is known that a location is needed to store the record of an office employee (*EmpCode* is O) and that *P* is to point to this location, the procedure reference

new (*P*, 'O')

may be used.

When a memory location is allocated in this manner, however, it may then be used only for a record with this particular structure, that is, to store a record for an office employee. Also, to dispose of this memory location, an alternative form of reference to the procedure *dispose* is required. For this example, it would be

dispose (*P*, 'O')

The form for *dispose* that corresponds to the general form of the procedure reference for *new* is

dispose (*pointer, tag-value-1, tag-value-2, . . . , tag-value-n*)

The alternative forms of procedure references to *new* and *dispose* allow the system (but do not require it) to allocate memory more efficiently for variant records. When each of the variant parts is about the same size, however, there is no real advantage in using these alternative forms.

The Procedures *pack* and *unpack*

The procedures *pack* and *unpack* transfer elements between unpacked arrays and packed arrays. The procedure *pack* is called with a statement of the form

pack (*unpackedarray, first, packedarray*)

where *unpackedarray* is the unpacked array and *first* is the position of the first element of *unpackedarray* to be transferred to the packed array *packed array*. For example, to read a string into a packed array, one could declare an unpacked array *Buffer*,

> *Buffer* : **array**[1..*StringLimit*] **of** *char*;

read characters into *Buffer*,

> **for** *i* := 1 **to** *StringLimit* **do**
>   **if not** *eoln* **then**
>   *read* (*Buffer*[*i*])
>   **else**
>   *Buffer*[*i*] := ' ';
> *readln*;

and then transfer these to the string variable *Str* of type **packed array** [1 .. *StringLimit*] **of** *char*:

> *pack* (*Buffer*, 1, *Str*);

The procedure *unpack* transfers the elements from a packed array to an unpacked array. This procedure is called with a statement of the form

> *unpack* (*packedarray, unpackedarray, first*)

where *packedarray* is the packed array whose elements are to be transferred to the unpacked array *unpackedarray; first* denotes the position in *unpacked-array* where the first element of *packedarray* is to be placed.

For both of the procedures *pack* and *unpack*, the component type of the two arrays must be the same, but the indices may be of different ordinal types. The number of array elements transferred is the number of elements in the packed array. Consequently, the segment of the unpacked array to which or from which values are being transferred must be at least as large as the number of elements in the packed array.

Arrays of any type may be packed. In particular, packing may be useful in processing boolean arrays, since the boolean constants *false* and *true* are normally represented internally as 0 and 1, each of which may be stored in a single bit. A 32-bit memory word can, therefore, store 32 boolean constants. The declaration

> **type**
>   *Barray* = **packed array**[1..100] **of** *boolean*;

therefore, allows memory to be allocated more efficiently than

> **type**
>   *Barray* = **array**[1..100] **of** *boolean*;

G

Turbo Pascal

There are several popular versions of Pascal that vary somewhat from the ANSI/IEEE standard version of Pascal assumed in this text. In this appendix we summarize the major variations and extensions in Turbo Pascal, a popular version of Pascal for microcomputers that was developed and marketed by Borland International.

Basic Pascal

- *Additional data types.* In addition to type *integer*, the integer types *byte*, *shortint*, *word*, and *longint* are provided. Their ranges of values are given in the following table:

Type	Range
byte	0 through 255
shortint	-128 through 127
integer	-32768 through 32767
word	0 through 65535
longint	-2147483648 through 2147483647

For processing reals, the types *real, single, double,* and *extended* are provided, as is *comp* for processing integers stored in a real format. (The special compiler directive {$N} for numeric processing must be turned on when using types *single, double, extended,* and *comp*. This is all that is required if your machine has an 8087 chip. If it does not, a special emulation directive {$E} can be turned on to provide 8087 emulation in software.) For these types the ranges and number of significant digits are given in the following table:

Type	Range	Significant Digits
real	2.9E−39 through 1.7E + 38	11−12
single	1.5E−45 through 3.4E + 38	7−8
double	5.0E−324 through 1.7E + 308	15−16
extended	3.4E−4932 through 1.1E + 4932	19−20
comp	$1 - 2E + 63$ through $2E + 63 - 1$	19−20

Turbo Pascal also provides the type **string** for processing strings of characters. Strings are limited to 255 characters.

- *Alternative representations of numbers.* Integers may be expressed in hexadecimal notation obtained by placing a dollar sign ($) in front of its hexadecimal representation.

- *Predefined constants. Maxint* has the value 32767, and *MaxLongInt* has the value 2147483647.

- *Reserved words.* The following are additional reserved words in Turbo Pascal: **absolute, external, implementation, inline, interface, interrupt, shl, shr, string, unit, uses,** and **xor.**

- *Identifiers.* An identifier consists of a letter followed by any number of additional letters, digits, or underscores (__); only the first 63 characters are used.

- *Arithmetic operators.* The value of i **mod** j is the remainder that results when i is divided by j. Also, i **div** j is defined for all nonzero integers i and j. The shift operators **shl** and **shr** shift the bits in the binary representation of an integer a specified number of positions to the left or right, respectively. For example, 4 **shl** 6 = 256 and 256 **shr** 6 = 4. **Shl** and **shr** have the same priorities as the multiplication and division operators. The boolean operators **not, and, or,** and **xor** may also be used to perform bitwise boolean operations on integer values (see the Turbo Pascal notes for boolean operators).

- *Arithmetic functions. Frac, int,* and *pi* are predefined arithmetic functions; $frac(x)$ returns the fractional part of the real or integer parameter x; $int(x)$ returns the integer part; and *pi* returns the value of π.

- *Program heading.* In Turbo Pascal, the program heading is optional.

- **Uses** *clause.* A Turbo Pascal program may contain a **uses** clause of the form

> **uses** *unit-name*

which precedes the declaration part of the program. This clause makes available all of the constants, types, variables, procedures, and functions that are defined in the specified unit (see the Turbo Pascal notes for units).

- *Declaration part.* The sections of the declaration part may appear any number of times and in any order.

- *Typed constants.* Turbo Pascal allows typed constants. These are not true constants but are, in fact, variables whose initial values are specified in a modified form of the usual constant declaration. For example,

```
const
   Sum : integer = 0;
   Radius : real = 2.5;
   Code : char = 'A';
```

declares the integer variable *Sum* and initializes it to 0; the real variable *Radius* and initializes it to 2.5; and the character variable *Code* and initializes it to 'A'.

- *Increment and decrement operations.* Turbo Pascal provides two special procedures that can be used to increment or decrement integer variables. These procedures have the forms

  Inc (variable, step)
  Dec (variable, step)

  where *variable* is an integer variable whose value is to be incremented by *step*, and *step* is an integer-valued expression. For example, the assignment statement

  Sum := Sum + Counter

  can also be written

  Inc (Sum, Counter)

  If the step size is omitted in these statements, it is taken to be 1. For example,

  Dec (Counter)

  is an alternative to the assignment statement

  Counter := Counter − 1

Control Structures

- *Boolean operators.* In addition to **not, and,** and **or,** the exclusive-or operator **xor** is provided; *P* **xor** *Q* is true if exactly one of *P* or *Q* is true and is false otherwise. Also, these four boolean operators may be applied bitwise to integer values (0 = false, 1 = true). For example,

  $$14 \textbf{ and } 23 = 0000000000001110_2 \textbf{ and } 0000000000010111_2$$
  $$= 0000000000000110_2 = 6$$

  Similarly, 14 **or** $23 = 31$ and 14 **xor** $23 = 25$.
- **case** *statement.* Ranges of values may be specified in the form

  first-value..last-value

  in label lists of a **case** statement. Also, a **case** statement may have an **else** clause; for example,

  ```
  case Class of
       1 : writeln ('Freshman');
       2..4 : writeln ('Upperclassman')
      else
           writeln ('Special')
  end (* case *)
  ```

If the value of the selector is not in any of the label lists, the statement in the **else** clause will be executed; if no **else** clause is present, execution will "fall through" the **case** statement and continue with the next statement. This example also illustrates that subrange notation may be used in label lists to indicate a range of consecutive values.

● **for** *statement.* When execution of a **for** statement is completed, the control variable retains its last value.

Procedures, Functions, and Units

● *Additional functions and procedures.* In addition to the standard predefined Pascal procedures and functions, the string functions *concat, copy, length,* and *pos,* and the string procedures *delete* and *insert* described in Section 3.3, Turbo Pascal provides a number of others. These include the function *Random* and the procedure *Randomize* for generating random numbers:

● *Random, Random(Num).* This function generates random numbers. The first form returns a random real number in the interval [0, 1), and the second returns a random integer value in the interval [0, *Num*).

● *Randomize.* This procedure initializes the random number generator with a random value.

The string functions *concat, copy, length,* and *pos* and the string procedures *delete* and *insert* described in Section 3.3 are also provided. In addition there are a number of special graphics subprograms.

● *Function and procedure parameters.* The declarations of function and procedure parameters differ from those in standard Pascal. For example, consider the function *ApproxArea* in Figure F.2 of Appendix F, which approximates the area of the region under the graph of $f(x)$ for $a \leq x \leq b$ using n subintervals, where f, a, b, and n are parameters. In standard Pascal, the heading of such a function might be

> **function** *ApproxArea* (**function** $f(x : real) : real$;
> $a, b : real$; $n : integer$) $: real$;

Here **function** $f(x : real) : real$ specifies that f is a function parameter denoting a function whose formal parameter and value are of real type. The corresponding actual function parameter must be a real-valued function having a real formal parameter. In Turbo Pascal, the function *ApproxArea* would be written

> **function** *ApproxArea* ($f : RealFunction$;
> $a, b : real$; $n : integer$) $: real$;

The type identifier *RealFunction* must be defined in a type section in the declaration part of the program. In this example, the type section might have the form

> **type**
> *RealFunction* = **function**($x : real$) $: real$;

The type identifier *RealFunction* can then be used to specify that the value of a formal parameter (or variable or other identifier) is a function having one parameter of type *real* and whose value is of type *real*. (Whenever a function or procedure is used as a parameter, the compiler directive {$F+ } must be included in the program, or alternatively, the Force Far Calls option in the Compiler submenu of the main menu Options must be turned on.)

● *Units.* A unit has three parts: a heading that names the unit, an interface part that describes the processing done by this unit, and an implementation part that specifies how this processing is carried out.

> unit heading
> interface part
> implementation part

The **unit heading** consists of the reserved word **unit** followed by the name of the unit:

> **unit** *name*;

The **interface part** begins with the reserved word **interface**, which is followed by an optional uses clause and a modified form of the declaration part of a program:

> **interface**
> **uses** clause (optional)
> declaration part (modified)

The **uses** clause has the same form as in a program and specifies other units that contain special items to be used in this unit; these items are also available to any programs or other units that use this unit. In the declaration part, constant, variable, and type (and label) sections have the usual forms, but the subprogram sections contain only headings of the procedures and functions defined in this unit.

The **implementation part** of a unit consists of the reserved word **implementation** followed by an optional **uses** clause, a declaration part, and an initialization part:

> **implementation**
> **uses** clause (optional)
> declaration part
> initialization part

The **uses** clause has the usual form and specifies other units that contain special items to be used in this unit. However, unlike the case in which the **uses** clause appears in the interface part, these items are not available to programs or other units that use this unit. The various sections of the declaration part have the usual forms. One of the subprogram sections must contain the complete procedure and function definitions for those procedures and functions whose headings were given in the interface part. The headings in these definitions must, of course, be the same as those in the interface part. The *initialization part* may be trivial, consisting simply of the reserved word **end,** or it may have the same form as the statement part of a program. In the second case, the statements in this statement part are executed before those in any program or other unit in which this unit is used. In either case, a period follows the initialization part to mark the end of the unit.

Once a unit has been compiled, a program (or another unit) can use items from it simply by specifying the unit's name in a **uses** clause. Thus, if a **uses** clause of the form

> **uses** *name*;

is inserted after the program heading in a program, the constants, types, variables, functions and procedures defined in the specified unit can be used within that program.

Input/Output

- *Opening a file.* Before a permanent file can be opened with the procedures *reset, rewrite* or *append*, a name must be assigned to it with the procedure *assign*. This procedure is called with a statement of the form

> *assign (file-variable, file-name)*

where *file-name* is the actual name of the data file stored in secondary memory to be associated with *file-variable*.
- *Closing a file.* When input from or output to a file is completed, the file should be closed by calling the procedure *close* with a statement of the form

> *close (file-variable)*

Failure to do this may result in loss of data in the file, inability to access it, or some other misfortune.

Ordinal Data Types

- *Type conversion.* Any ordinal type identifier *OrdType* may be used as a function to convert a value of any other ordinal type to the value of type *OrdType* having the same ordinal number. For example, for the declarations

> **type**
>   *DaysOfWeek = (Sunday, Monday, Tuesday, Wednesday,*
>   *Thursday, Friday, Saturday);*
>   *FaceCard = (Jack, Queen, King);*
>   *CardRange = 1..13;*

$integer(Queen) = CardRange(Queen) = 1, DaysOfWeek(2) = Tues-$
day, and $FaceCard(Sunday) = Jack$.

- *Range checking.* The range-checking compiler option must be enabled (or equivalently, the compiler directive {$R + } included in the program) for range checking to be performed.
- *Inc and Dec.* The procedures *Inc* and *Dec* may be used with any ordinal types.

Arrays

In Turbo Pascal, there are only a few variations from and extensions to the array-processing features of standard Pascal:

- *Range checking.* The range-checking compiler option must be enabled (or equivalently, the compiler directive {$R + } included in the program) for range checking to be performed.
- *Array constants.* An array variable may be initialized as a typed constant by using a declaration of the form

> **const**
>   *array-name* : *array-type* = (*list-of-array-elements*);

For example, the declarations

> **type**
>   *DigitType* = 0..9;
>   *NumeralType* = '0'..'9';
>   *NumeralArray* = **array**[*DigitType*] **of** *NumeralType*;
>
> **const**
>   *Numeral* : *NumeralArray* = ('0', '1', '2', '3', '4',
>   '5', '6', '7', '8', '9');

initialize the array *Numeral* with $Numeral[0] = '0'$, $Numeral[1] = '1'$, ..., $Numeral[9] = '9'$. An alternative form of constant section could also have been used:

> **const**
>   *Numeral* : *NumeralArray* = '0123456789';

Similar declarations can be used to initialize multidimensional arrays. In this case, nested parentheses enclose the array elements in each dimension, with the innermost constants corresponding to the rightmost dimensions. For example, to initialize a two-dimensional array *A* so that

$$A = \begin{bmatrix} 1 & 2 & 3 \\ 2 & 4 & 6 \\ 3 & 6 & 9 \end{bmatrix}$$

we could use

> **const**
>   *RowLimit* = 3;
>   *ColumnLimit* = 3;
>
> **type**
>   *Matrix* = **array**[1..*RowLimit*, 1..*ColumnLimit*] **of** *integer*;
>
> **const**
>   *Mat* : *Matrix* = ((1, 2, 3), (2, 4, 6), (3, 6, 9));

- *Packed Arrays.* Although the reserved word **packed** is allowed, it has no effect, since arrays are packed automatically whenever possible. Consequently, the procedures *pack* and *unpack* are not provided in Turbo Pascal.

  As noted in the text, many versions of Pascal include a predefined string type and a number of predefined string functions and procedures. In particular, this is true of Turbo Pascal, which also has the following variations and extensions.

- *String type.* String declarations using the predefined type *string* have the form *string*[*n*], where *n* is an integer constant in the range 1 through 255 indicating the maximum length of strings of this type. This maximum length must always be specified; no default value is provided. Strings are implemented as character arrays having index type 0..*n*. The individual characters are stored in positions 1 through *n*, and position 0 scores *chr*(*length*), where *length* is the current length of the string. Thus, if *Str* is a string variable, *length*(*Str*) is equivalent to *ord*(*Str*[0]).

- *Strings and characters.* Characters and strings of length 1 are compatible, and character arrays may be viewed as strings of constant length. When a character array appears in a string expression, it is converted to a string with length equal to the (fixed) size of the array. As in standard Pascal, a string constant may be assigned to a character array, provided that they have the same length, but string variables and computed values of string expressions may not be.

- *String functions.* In addition to the string functions *concat*, *copy*, *length*, and *pos* and the string procedures *delete* and *insert* described in Section 3.3, Turbo Pascal provides the following:

- + *operator.* Concatenation may also be accomplished by use of the + operator. For example, 'John' + 'Henry' + 'Doe' yields the string 'John Henry Doe'.

- **val** *procedure.* The procedure call *val*(*numeral, number, error*) converts the value of the string expression *numeral* representing an integer or real numeral to the corresponding numeric value *number*. For example, *val*('123', *Number, Error*) assigns the integer value 123 to *Number*. *Error* is an integer variable for which a value of 0 is returned if there is no conversion error; if an error occurs, *number* is undefined, and the value of *error* is the position of the first erroneous character in *numeral*.

- *str procedure*. The procedure call *str(number, numeral)* converts the integer or real value *number* to the string of characters representing the corresponding *numeral*. For example, *str(123, Numeral)* assigns the string '123' to string variable *Numeral*.

Records

- *Record constants*. A record variable may be initialized as a typed constant by using a declaration of the form

    const
        record-name : *record-type* = (*list-of-field-constants*);

    where each field constant has the form *field-name* : *field-value*. For example, the declarations

    type
      Point = **record**
            X, Y : *real*
          end;
    const
      Origin : *Point* = (*X* : 0, *Y* : 0);

    initializes the record variable *Origin*, with both *Origin.X* and *Origin.Y* equal to 0.

Sets

- *Restrictions on sets*. The maximum number of elements in a set is 256. The ordinal values of the base type may be in the range 0..255.
- *Set constants*. A set variable may be initialized as a typed constant by means of a declaration of the form

    const
      set-name : *set-type* = *set-constant*;

    for example,

    type
      LetterSet = **set of** 'a'..'z';

    const
      Vowels : *LetterSet* = ['a', 'e', 'i', 'o', 'u'];

Files

- *Opening/closing files*. As described in Section 11.2, in Turbo Pascal a file must be assigned a name with the procedure *assign* before it is opened with *reset* or *rewrite*, and a file should be closed with the procedure *close* when input from or output to it has been completed.

- **get and put.** The standard predefined procedures *get* and *put* are not provided. Instead, all file input and output uses *read* and *write*. Consequently, file buffer variables are not used in Turbo Pascal.

- *Direct access files.* Direct access files are opened in the usual manner using the *assign, reset,* and *rewrite* procedures. The procedure *seek* is used to position the file pointer, as described in Section 11.5.

- *Additional procedures and functions.* There are a number of other predefined procedures for processing files, including

  - **erase.** *erase* (*file-variable*) erases the specified file. The file should be closed before it is erased.

  - **flush.** *flush* (*file-variable*) empties the buffer associated with the specified file.

  - **rename.** *rename* (*file-variable, str*) renames the specified file with the string *str.*

Two additional predefined functions, *filepos* and *filesize*, are also provided:

- *filepos*(*file-variable*) is the current position of the file pointer in the specified file.

- *filesize*(*file-variable*) is the number of components in the specified file. Since components are numbered beginning with zero, the value of this function is one more than the number of the last component in the file.

Pointers

Pointer variables can be processed as in standard Pascal except that the alternative forms of reference to procedures *new* and *dispose* for variant records, as described in Appendix F, are not allowed.

Miscellany

- *Procedure **page**.* This procedure is not provided in Turbo Pascal.

- *Procedures **new** and **dispose**.* The alternative forms of reference to procedures *new* and *dispose* for variant records, as described in Appendix F, are not allowed.

Answers to Selected Exercises

Section 1.6 (p. 41)

13. $Row := 0$;
    $Found := false$;
    while not $Found$ **and** $(Row < n)$ **do**
      begin
        $Row := Row + 1$;
        $Col := 0$;
        while not $Found$ **and** $(Col < n)$ **do**
          begin
            $Col := Col + 1$;
            if $Mat[Row, Col] = Item$ **then**
              $Found := true$
          end (* **while** *)
      end (* **while** *);
    if $Found$ **then**
      writeln ('Item found')
    else
      writeln ('Item not found');

16. **(1)** More than one statement per line.
    (2) Global variables rather than parameters are used to pass information to and from the procedure.
    (3) Nondescriptive variable names.
    (4) Not structured.
    (5) Poor use of spacing and no indentation.
    (6) Useless comments.

Section 2.2 (p. 55)

1. **(a)** 16448   **(d)** -16385

2. **(a)** 16448   **(d)** -16383

3. (a) -16320 **(d)** 16385

4. (a) $0.501953125 * 2^{-16} \cong -0.000007659$
   (d) $-0.5 * 2^{-15} \cong -0.000015259$

5. (a) (i) true   **(ii)** TT   **(iii)** FTFFFFFFFTFFFFFF
   (d) (i) true   **(ii)** TT   **(iii)** TTFFFFFFFFFFFFFFT

6. (a) (i) @@   **(ii)** (blank blank)

7. (a) 209   **(d)** 4095

8. (a) 69   **(d)** 4095

9. (a) 11010001   **(d)** 111111111111

10. (a) 1000101   **(d)** 111111111111

11. (a) 52   **(d)** 777777

12. (a) 2A   **(d)** 3FFFF

13. (a) (i) 1100011   **(ii)** 143   **(iii)** 63

14. (a) (i) 0.1   **(ii)** 0.4   **(iii)** 0.8

15. (a) (i) $0.\overline{1001}$ **(ii)** $0.\overline{4631}$ **(iii)** $0.\overline{9}$

16. (a) (i) 0000000001100011   **(d) (i)** 1111111100000001

17. (a) (i) 0101000000010000   **(d) (i)** 0100000000001011

     (ii) same   **(ii)** same

18. (a)   B   E
      0100001001000101
   (d)   M   r   blank   D   o   e
      0100110101110010 0010111000100000 0100010001101111 0110010

Section 2.3 (p. 72)

1. (a) (i) 20   **(v)** 4
   (b) (i) $A[4]$ is stored in words   **(ii)** $A[5]$ is stored in byte 1 of
          $b+6$ and $b+7$.   word $b+2$.

2. (a) (i) $A[i]$ is stored in word $b + 2(i - 1)$.

3. (a) $M[0,9]$ is stored in words   **(e)** $M['F',1]$ is stored in words
       116 and 117.   150 and 151.

4. (a) $M[0,9]$ is stored in words 164 and 165.

(e) $M['F',1]$ is stored in words 110 and 111.

6. $M[i, j] = \text{Base}(M) + [(i - l_1) + (j - l_2)m]n$,
where $m = u_1 - l_1 + 1$.

10. $M[i, j] = b + ((i - 1)i / 2) + (j - 1)$

12. $M[i, j] = \text{base}(M) + 2i + j - 3$

Section 2.5 (p. 92)

1. (a) *CivTimeRec* = **record**
                        Hours : 1..12;
                        Minutes,
                        Seconds : 0..59;
                        AMPM : (*AM*, *PM*)
                    end;

(d) *AngleRec* = **record**
                        Degrees : 0..359;
                        Minutes,
                        Seconds : 0..59
                    end;

(g) *String* = **packed array**[1..15] **of** *char*;
        StyleType = (*TwoDoor*, *FourDoor*, *StationWagon*, *OtherStyle*);
        ColorType = (*red*, *black*, *blue*, *yellow*, *brown*, *OtherColor*);
        AutomobileRec = **record**
                        Make : *String*;
                        Model : *String*;
                        Style : *StyleType*;
                        Color : *ColorType*
                    end;

2. (b) *NameString* = **packed array** [1..20] **of** *char*;
        NumberString = **packed array**[1..11] **of** *char*;
        Color = (*blue*, *brown*, *green*, *other*);
        MaritalStatus = (*Married*, *Single*);
        Date = **record**
                        Month : 1..12;
                        Day : 1..31;
                        Year : 1900..2000
                    end;
        PersonalInfo = **record**
                        Name : *NameString*;
                        Birthday : *Date*;
                        Age : *integer*;
                        Sex : *char*;
                        SocSecNumber : *NumberString*;
                        Height, *Weight* : *integer*;
                        EyeColor : *Color*;

           case *MarStat* : *MaritalStatus* **of**
             Married : (*NumChildren* : *integer*);
             Single : ( )
        end;

(d) *DateRecord* = **record**
           Day : 1..31;
           Month : 1..12;
           Year : 1900..2000
        end;
     String = **packed array**[1..20] **of** *char*;
     Conditions = (*Clear, PartlyCoudy, Cloudy, Stormy*);
     StormType = (*Snow, Rain, Hail*);
     CloudType = (*Cumulus, Stratus, Nimbus, Cirrus*);
     WeatherRecord = **record**
           Date : *DateRecord*;
           City, State, Country : *String*;
           case *WeatherCondition* : *Conditions* **of**
             Clear : ( );
             Cloudy : (*CloudLevel* : *real*;
               Clouds : *CloudType*);
        PartlyCloudy : (*PercentClouds* : *real*);
         Stormy : (**case** *Storm* : *StormType* **of**
             Snow : (*Depth* : *real*);
             Rain : (*Amount* : *real*);
             Hail : (*Size* : *real*))
     end;

Section 2.6 (p. 99)

1. (a)

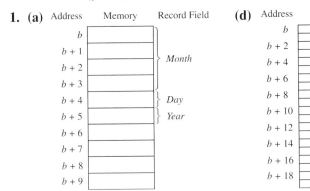

2. (a) const
     N = 99;

Section 2.8 (p. 118)

1. (a) [1..7, 9, 11]   **(d)** [2, 4, 6, 11, 12]
    (g) [5, 7, 8]   **(j)** [1..9, 11, 12]
   (m) [8]   **(p)** [1, 3, 5, 7]

type
 SetOfNumbers = **set of** 1..*N*;

var
 Even, Odd : *SetOfNumbers*;
 Number : *Integer*;

Even := [ ];
for *Number* := 1 to *N* **div** 2 **do**
 Even := *Even* + [2 * *Number*];
Odd := [1..*N*] − *Even*;

(d) const
 N = 999;

type
 Numbers = 1..*N*;
 NumberSet = **set of** *Numbers*;

var
 LargeEvenPrimes : *NumberSet*;

LargeEvenPrimes := [ ];

(g) type
 Months = (*January, February, March, April, May, June, July,*
       August, September, October, November,
       December);
 SetOfMonths = **set of** *Months*;

var
 JMonths : *SetOfMonths*;

JMonths := [*January, June, July*];

(j) type
 DaysOfWeek = (*Sunday, Monday, Tuesday, Wednesday,*
         Thursday, Friday, Saturday);
 SetOfDays = **set of** *DaysOfWeek*;

var
 WeekDays : *SetOfDays*;

WeekDays := [*Monday..Friday*];

Section 2.9 (p. 122)

1. (a) 01010101010101010101
  (d) 01110101010101010101
  (g) 00000000000000000000

2. procedure *Union* (**var** *A, B, Result* : *SetArray*; *First, Last* : *integer*);

    var
      x : *integer*;

    begin (∗ *Union* ∗)
      for *x* := *First* **to** *Last* **do**
        Result[*x*] := *A*[*x*] **or** *B*[*x*]
    end (∗ *Union* ∗);

3. One method of representation is to let S[0] correspond to 0.0, S[1] to 0.1, ... , S[10] to 1.0, ... , S[100] to 10.0. Then set S[30], S[31], ... , S[40] to true, all others to false.

Section 3.2 (p. 142)

1. (a) function *Length* (*Str* : *String*) : *integer*;

    var
      i : *integer*;

    begin (∗ *Length* ∗)
      i := *StringLimit*;
      while *Str*[*i*] <> *EndOfStringMark* **do**
        i := *i* + 1;
      Length := *i*
    end (∗ *Length* ∗);

7. (a) procedure *DisplayString* (*S* : *String*);

    var
      i : *integer*;

    begin (∗ *DisplayString* ∗)
      for *i* := *S.Start* **to** *S.Start* + *S.Length* − 1 **do**
        write (*Storage*[*i*]);
      writeln
    end (∗ *DisplayString* ∗);

Section 3.5 (p. 161)

3. (a) 0554 1486 2112

5. 0295

Section 3.6 (p. 172)

1. (a) 0 1 1 0 2 0 2 0 1 1 0   **(f)** 0 1 0 1 3 0 2

2. (a)

Instruction	*PrefixFound*	*k*	*j*	*Next* Value Computed
Initially	false	0	1	$Next[1] = 0$
2a	false	0	1	
2b	false	0	1	
2c	false	1	2	
2d	false	1	2	$Next[2] = 1$
2a	false	1	2	
2b	false	0	2	
2c	false	1	3	
2d	false	1	3	$Next[3] = 1$
2a	false	1	3	
2b	false	0	3	
2c	false	1	4	
2d	false	1	4	$Next[4] = 0$
2a	false	1	4	
2b	true	1	4	
2c	true	2	5	
2d	true	2	5	$Next[5] = 2$
2a	false	2	5	
2b	false	0	5	
2c	false	1	6	
2d	false	1	6	$Next[6] = 0$
2a	false	1	6	
2b	true	1	6	
2c	true	2	7	
2d	true	2	7	$Next[7] = 2$
2a	false	2	7	
2b	false	0	7	
2c	false	1	8	
2d	false	1	8	$Next[8] = 0$
2a	false	1	8	
2b	true	1	8	
2c	true	2	9	
2d	true	2	9	$Next[9] = 1$
2a	false	2	9	
2b	true	2	9	
2c	true	3	10	
2d	true	3	10	$Next[10] = 1$
2a	false	3	10	
2b	true	3	10	
2c	true	4	11	
2d	true	4	11	$Next[11] = 0$

Section 4.3 (p. 195)

1. (a) $S.Top = 2$
$S.Element[5] = ?$ (? = undefined)
$S.Element[4] = ?$
$S.Element[3] = 37$
$S.Element[2] = 59$
$S.Element[1] = 10$

3. (a) **procedure** *GetTopElement* (*Stack* : *StackType*;
                                    TopElement : *StackElementType*);

> **begin** (* *GetTopElement* *);
>   *StackError* := *EmptyStack*(*Stack*);
>   **if not** *StackError* **then**
>   **begin**
>   *Pop* (*Stack*, *TopElement*);
>   *Push* (*Stack*, *TopElement*);
>   **end** (* **if** *)
>   **else**
>   *writeln*('Empty stack')
> **end** (* *GetTopElement* *);

(b) **procedure** *GetTopElement* (*Stack* : *StackType*;
                              TopElement : *StackElementType*);

> **begin** (* *GetTopElement* *);
>   *StackError* := *Stack.Top* = 0;
>   **if not** *StackError* **then**
>   *TopElement* := *Stack.Element*[*Stack.Top*]
>   **else**
>   *writeln*('Empty stack')
> **end** (* *GetTopElement* *);

8. 123, 132, 213, 231, and 321 are possible; 312 is not.

Section 4.4 (p. 209)

1. (a) $-7.\overline{3}$ **(d)** 12.0   **(g)** 12.0   **(j)** 8.0

2. (a) Before "/" is read: Before "*" is read:

| 8 |
| 32 |

| 5 |
| 4 |

Value of RPN expression is 20

3. (a) $A B * C + D -$ **(d)** $A B C D + / +$
(g) $A B - C - D - E -$

4. (a) Before "C" is read: Before "–' is read:

Stack is | / | Stack is | / |
         |_+_| |_+_|

Accumulated output is $A\ B$ Accumulated output is $A\ B\ C$

Before "D" is read:
Stack is | – |
         |___|

Accumulated output is $A\ B\ C\ /\ +$

Final RPN expression is $A\ B\ C\ /\ +\ D\ -$

5. (a) $(A\ -\ (B\ +\ C))\ *\ D$ **(d)** $((A\ +\ B)\ -\ C)\ /\ (D\ *\ E)$
   (g) $A\ /\ ((B\ /\ C)\ /\ D)$

6. (a) (i) -15 **(iv)** 15
   (b) (i) $A\ B\ C\ \sim\ +\ *$ **(iii)** $A\ \sim\ B\ \sim\ *$

7. (a) $A\ B$ **and** C **or**   **(e)** $A\ B\ =\ C\ D\ =$ **or**

8. (a) $-\ +\ *\ A\ B\ C\ D$ **(d)** $+\ A\ /\ B\ +\ C\ D$
   (g) $-\ -\ -\ -\ A\ B\ C\ D\ E$

9. (a) -24.5 **(d)** -2.0
   (g) 55.0

10. (a) $(A\ +\ B)\ *\ (C\ -\ D)$ **(d)** $A\ -\ (B\ -\ C)\ -\ D$
   (g) $(A\ *\ B\ +\ C)\ /\ (D\ -\ E)$

Section 5.2 (p. 225)

1. $Q.Front\ =\ 1,\ Q.Rear\ =\ 4$
   $Q.Element[0]\ =\ 'A',\ Q.Element[1]\ =\ 'B',\ Q.Element[2]\ =\ 'C',$
   $Q.Element[3]\ =\ 'A',$
   $Q.Element[4]$ is undefined.

3. (b) function $QSize(Q\ :\ QueueType)\ :\ integer;$

```
    var
      Count : integer;

    begin (* QSize *)
      Count := 0;
      while not EmptyQueue(Q) do
        begin
          Count := Count + 1;
          RemoveQ(Q)
        end (* while *);
      QSize := Count
    end (* QSize *);
```

(d) **function** *QSize*(*Q* : *QueueType*) : *integer*;
      var
        Count : *integer*;

      begin (∗ *QSize* ∗)
        Count := *Q.Rear* − *Q.Front*;
        if *Count* < 0 **then**
          Count := *Count* + *QueueLimit*;
        QSize := *Count*
      end (∗ *QSize* ∗);

9. **(a)** 123, 132, 213, 231, and 312 are possible; 321 is not.

12. **procedure** *AddQ* (**var** *Queue*: *QueueType*;
                    Item : *QueueElementType*);

    begin (∗ *AddQ* ∗)
      with *Queue* **do**
        if *Count* <> *QueueLimit* **then**
          begin
            QueueError := *false*;
            Element[*Rear*] := *Item*;
            Rear := (*Rear* + 1) **mod** *QueueLimit*;
            Count := *Count* + 1
          end (∗ **if** ∗)
        else
          begin
            writeln ('∗∗∗ Attempt to insert in a full queue ∗∗∗');
            QueueError := *true*
          end (∗ **else** ∗)
    end (∗ *AddQ* ∗);

    procedure *RemoveQ* (**var** *Queue* : *QueueType*;
                      var *Item* : *QueueElementType*);

    begin (∗ *RemoveQ* ∗)
      if not *EmptyQ*(*Queue*) **then**
        with *Queue* **do**
          begin
            QueueError := *false*;
            Item := *Element*[*Front*];
            Front := (*Front* + 1) **mod** *QueueLimit*;
            Count := *Count* − 1
          end (∗ **with** ∗)
      else
        begin
          writeln ('∗∗∗ Attempt to insert in a full queue ∗∗∗');
          QueueError := *true*
        end (∗ **else** ∗)
  end (∗ *AddQ* ∗);

Section 6.1 (p. 256)

1. (a) (i) (blank line)
             ABC
   (b) (i) (blank line)
             HGFEDC
   (c) (i) CBA
   (d) (i) CBA
             ABC

3. (a) *Hint*: Q ('m', 2) produces as output
             (blank line)
             L
             M
             N
   (c) *Hint*: Q ('m', 2) produces as output
             ML
             (blank line)
             N
             (blank line)

4. (b) $n * x$

5. (b) function $F(x : real; n : Cardinal) : real$;

        begin (* F *)
          $F := n * x$
        end (* F *);

7. (b) function $SumArray(A : ArrayType; n : integer) : integer$;

        begin (* $SumArray$ *)
          if $n < 1$ **then**
            $SumArray := 0$
          else
            $SumArray := SumArray(A, n - 1) + A[n]$
        end (* $SumArray$ *);

3. (a) $A * B$

(d) $(A * B) * C$

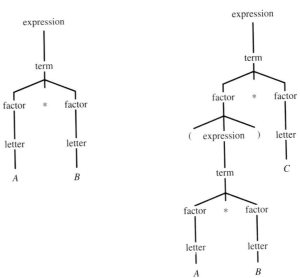

4. (a)

Active Procedure	Position	Symbol	Valid	Action
Main Program	0			Call *CheckForExpression.*
CheckForExpression	0			Call *CheckForTerm.*
CheckForTerm	0			Call *CheckForFactor.*
CheckForFactor	0			Call *GetChar* to get next symbol.
	1	A		*GetChar* increments *Position* and returns.
	1	A	true	*Valid* set to true; return to *CheckForTerm.*
CheckForTerm	1	A	true	Call *GetChar* to get next symbol.
	2	$*$		*GetChar* increments *Position* and returns.
	2	$*$	true	Call *CheckForFactor.*
CheckForFactor	2	$*$	true	Call *GetChar* to get next symbol.
	3	B		*GetChar* increments *Position* and returns.
	3	B	true	*Valid* set to true; return to *CheckForExpression.*
CheckForExpression	3	B	true	Call *GetChar* to get next symbol.
	4	$\$$		*GetChar* increments *Position* and returns.
	3	$\$$	true	"Unget" a character.
Main program	3			

Section 6.3 (p. 279)

4. function *Factorial*(*n* : *integer*) : *integer*;

    begin (∗ *Factorial* ∗)
      if *n* = 0 **then**
        Factorial := 1
      else
        Factorial := *n* ∗ *Factorial*(*n* − 1)
    end (∗ *Factorial* ∗);

Proof of correctness:
    I: The input consists of a nonnegative integer *n*.
    O: The function terminates, and when it does, the value of the function is *n*!.
    Anchor step: If *n* = 0, then *Factorial* := 1 is executed, and 0! = *n*! = 1, so O is satisfied.
    Induction step: Now assume that for some nonnegative integer *k*, the function terminates for *n* = *k* and returns the correct value *k*!. If *n* = *k* + 1, then the statement *Factorial* := *n* ∗ *Factorial* (*n* − 1) is executed. So *Factorial* := (*k* + 1) ∗ *Factorial*(*k*). By the induction hypothesis, *Factorial*(*k*) terminates and equals *k*!. So *Factorial*(*k* + 1) = (*k* + 1) ∗ *Factorial*(*k*) = (*k* + 1) ∗ *k*! = (*k* + 1)!, so O is true for *n* = *k* + 1.

Section 6.4 (p. 292)

1. (a) O(n^3)

4. (a) O(n)   **(d)** O(n^2)

Section 7.1 (p. 302)

2. (a) procedure *FindMean* (*List* : *ListType*; *NoValue* : *ListElementType*;
                                         var *Mean* : *real*);

    var
      Sum : *real*;
      Num : *integer*;

    begin (∗ *FindMean* ∗)
      Sum := 0;
      Num := 0;
      with *List* **do**
        for *i* := 1 **to** *ListLimit* **do**
          if *Element*[*i*] <> *NoValue* **then**
          begin
            Num := *Num* + 1;
            Sum := *Sum* + *Element*[*i*]
          end (∗ **if** ∗);
      if *Num* <> 0 **then**
        Mean := *Sum* / *Num*

```
        else
            Mean := 0
    end (* FindMean *);
```

3. (a) const
      MaxDegree = ...; (* maximum degree of polynomials)
    type
      CoefType = ...; (* type of coefficients *)
      PolyRec = **record**
                  Degree : *integer*;
                  Coef : **array**[0..*MaxDegree*] **of** *CoefType*;
           end;
  (b) **procedure** *ReadInfo* (**var** *Poly* : *PolyRec*);

      var
        i : *integer*;

      begin (* *ReadInfo* *)
        with *Poly* **do**
          begin
            write ('Enter degree of this polynomial: ');
            readln (*Degree*);
            writeln ('Enter the coefficients in ascending order: ');
            for *i* := 0 **to** *Degree* **do**
              begin
                write ('Enter coefficient of $x\wedge$, *i*:1, ':');
                readln (*Coeff*[*i*])
              end (* **for** *)
          end (* **with** *)
      end (* *ReadInfo* *);

Section 7.2 (p. 309)

1. Algorithm to count the nodes in a linked list:

  1. Set *Count* = 0 and *Ptr* = *List*.
  2. While *Ptr* <> nil, do the following:
    a. Increment *Count*.
    b. Set *Ptr* = *Next*(*Ptr*).

5. The complexity of the algorithm in Exercise 1 is $O(n)$, where n is the length of the list.

Section 7.3 (p. 319)

2.

Array Index	Data	Next
1	J	4
FreePtr → 2	Z	7
3	C	6
4	P	0
List → 5	B	3
6	F	1
7	K	8
8	Q	9
9	?	10
10	?	0

6. (a) **function** *Length*(*List* : *LinkedList*) : *integer*;

> **var**
>   *Count* : *integer*;
>   *Ptr* : *ListPointer*;
>
> **begin** (∗ *Length* ∗)
>   *Count* := 0;
>   *Ptr* := *List*;
>   **while** *Ptr* <> *NilValue* **do**
>   **begin**
>   *Ptr* := *Node*[*Ptr*].*Next*;
>   *Count* := *Count* + 1
>   **end** (∗ **while** ∗);
>   *Length* := *Count*
> **end** (∗ *Length* ∗);

(b) **function** *Length*(*List* : *LinkedList*) : *integer*;

> **begin** (∗ *Length* ∗)
>   **if** *List* = 0 **then**
>   *Length* := *NilValue*
>   **else**
>   *Length* := 1 + *Length*(*Node*[*List*].*Next*)
> **end** (∗ *Length* ∗);

Section 7.5 (p. 329)

1. (a) Values of pointer variables cannot be displayed.
   (c) *P1* and *Q1* are not bound to the same type.

2. (a) 123
       456
   (d) error—*P3↑* is not a record with a field *Data*.

3. (a)

   (d) Error occurs—*P4↑.Next↑.Data* is undefined because *P4↑.Next* is nil.

4. (a) **function** *Length*(*List* : *LinkedList*) : *integer*;

> **var**
>   *Count* : *integer*;
>   *Ptr* : *ListPointer*;
>
> **begin** (∗ *Length* ∗)
>   *Count* := 0;
>   *Ptr* := *List*;

```
      begin (* Length *)
        Count := 0;
        Ptr := List;
        while Ptr <> nil do
          begin
            Ptr := Ptr↑.Next;
            Count := Count + 1
          end (* while *);
        Length := Count
      end (* Length *);
```

(b) **function** *Length(List : LinkedList) : integer;*

```
      begin (*Length *)
        if List = nil then
          Length := 0
        else
          Length := 1 + Length(List↑.Next)
      end (* Length *);
```

Section 8.2 (p. 364)

3. procedure *CreateQ* (**var** *Queue : QueueType*);

```
      begin (* CreateQ *)
        Queue.Front := nil;
        Queue.Rear := nil;
        QueueError := false
      end (* CreateQ *);
    function EmptyQ(Queue : QueueType);

      begin (* EmptyQ *)
        EmptyQ := Queue.Front = nil;
        QueueError := false
      end (* EmptyQ *);
```

10. procedure *CreateCList* (**var** *CList : CircLinkedListType*);

```
      var
        TempPtr := CListPointer;

      begin (* Create *)
        new (CList);
        CList↑.Next := CList;
        CListError := false
      end (* Create *);
```

procedure *CLInsert* (*CList : CircLinkedListType;*
                           PredPtr : CListPointer;
                           Item : CListElementType);

```
      var
        TempPtr: CListPointer;
```

```
        begin (* CLInsert *)
          new (TempPtr);
          TempPtr↑.Data := Item;
          TempPtr↑.Next := PredPtr.Next;
          PredPtr↑.Next := TempPtr;
          CListError := false
        end (* CLInsert*);
```

12. **procedure** *AddQ* (**var** *CQueue* : *QueueType*;
                            Item : *QueueElementType*);

```
        var
          TempPtr : QueuePointer;

        begin (* AddQ *)
          new (TempPtr);
          TempPtr↑.Data := Item;
          if EmptyQ(CQueue) then
              TempPtr↑.Next := TempPtr
          else
            begin
              TempPtr↑.Next := CQueue↑.Next;
              CQueue↑.Next := TempPtr
            end (* else *);
          CQueue := TempPtr;
          QueueError := false
        end (* AddQ *);
```

Section 8.3 (p. 373)

1. O(*mn*)

5. **function** *CardinalNumber*(*A* : *SetType*) : *integer*;

```
        var
          i := integer;
          PtrA : SetPointer;

        begin (* CardinalNumber *)
          PtrA := A↑.Next;
          i := 0;
          while PtrA <> nil do
            begin
              i := i + 1;
              PtrA := PtrA↑.Next
            end (* while *);
          CardinalNumber := i
        end (* CardinalNumber *);
```

Section 8.4 (p. 382)

4. **(a)** **function** *Length*(*S* : *StringType*) : *integer*;

> **begin** (∗ *Length* ∗)
>   *Length* := *S.Length*
> **end** (∗ *Length* ∗);

Section 8.6 (p. 395)

1.

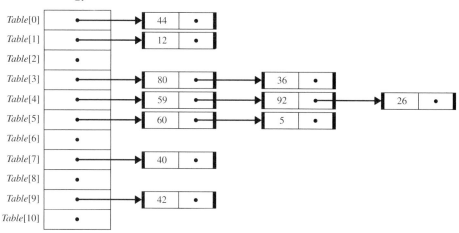

Section 8.7 (p. 406)

1. **(a)** I   **(e)** *P1*

2. **(b)** *P1↑.BLink↑.Data* := 'M';
          P1↑.FLink↑.Data := 'S';

3. **(b)** *P2↑.BLink↑.BLink↑.BLink↑.Data* := 'M';
          P2↑.BLink↑.Data := 'S';

4. **(a)** B   **(e)** *P1*

5. **(b)** *new* (*TempPtr*);
          TempPtr↑.Data:= 'L';
          TempPtr↑.BLink := *P1*;
          TempPtr↑.FLink := *P1↑.FLink*;
          P1↑.FLink := *TempPtr*;
          TempPtr↑.FLink↑.BLink := *TempPtr*;
          P1↑.FLink↑.FLink↑.Data := 'A';

6. **(b)** *new* (*TempPtr*);
          TempPtr↑.Data:= 'L';
          TempPtr↑.BLink := *P2↑.BLink ↑.BLink*;

$TempPtr\uparrow.FLink := P2\uparrow.BLink;$
$TempPtr\uparrow.BLink\ \uparrow.FLink := TempPtr;$
$TempPtr\uparrow.FLink\uparrow.BLink := TempPtr;$
$P2\uparrow.BLink\uparrow.Data := \text{'A'};$

Section 8.8 (p. 415)

2. (a)

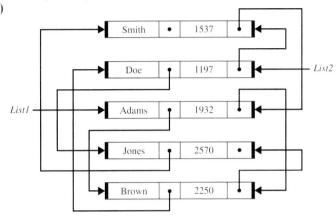

(b)

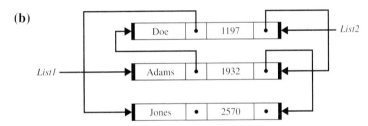

9. (a) **type**

  $MatElementType = integer;$
  $MatNodePointer = \uparrow MatNodeType;$
  $MatNodeType = $ **record**

    $Col : integer;$
    $Data : MatElementType;$
    $Next : MatNodePointer$

  end;
  $RowArray = $ **array**$[1..MaxRows]$ **of** $MatNodePointer;$

  var

  $A : RowArray;$

16. (a)

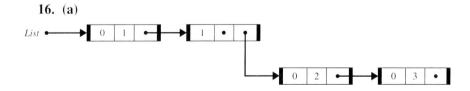

17. (a) $7 + (3x + 5x^3)y - 17y^2$

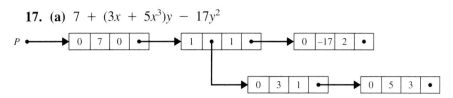

Section 9.1 (p. 423)

1. (a) 5, 7

2. procedure *LinearSearch* (**var** *X* : *ListType*; *n* : *integer*;
  Item : *ListElementType*;
  var *Found* : *boolean*;
  var *Loc* : *integer*);

  begin (∗ *LinearSearch* ∗)
   Loc := 1;
   X[*n* + 1] := *Item*;
   while *Item* <> *X*[*Loc*] **do**
    Loc := *Loc* + 1;
   Found := (*Loc* <= *n*)
  end (∗ *LinearSearch* ∗);

Section 9.3 (p. 437)

2. (a)   **(b)**

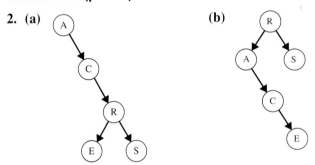

3. (a)

i	1	2	3	4	5	6	7	8	9	10	11	12	13	14	15
T[*i*]	A		C				R							E	S

(b)

i	1	2	3	4	5	6	7	8	9	10	11	12	13	14	15
T[*i*]	R	A	S		C					E					

Section 9.4 (p. 453)

1. (a) (i)

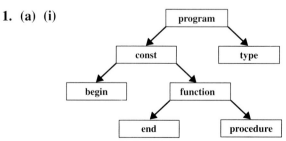

(b) (i) Inorder: **begin, const, end, function, procedure, program, type**

Preorder: **program, const, begin, function, end, procedure, type**

Postorder: **begin, end, procedure, function, const, type, program**

2. (a)

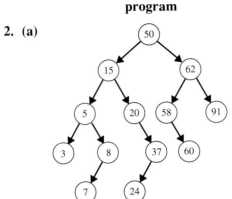

3. (a) 3, 5, 8, 15, 20, 24, 37, 50, 58, 60, 62, 91

6. (a) Preorder: − − A B C
Postorder: A B − C −

8. (i)

1	program
2	const
3	type
4	begin
5	function
6	
7	
8	
9	
10	end
11	procedure
12	

9. (i)

1	−
2	−
3	C
4	A
5	B

Section 9.5 (p. 470)

2. (a) BAD   **(c)** CAD

3. *Note:* Other answers than the one given here are possible.

begin	10
end	11
for	000
if	01
while	001

Section 10.1 (p. 481)

1. After first pass:

i	1	2	3	4	5	6
$X[i]$	10	50	70	30	40	60

2. (a) After first pass:

i	1	2	3	4	5	6
$X[i]$	50	60	10	40	20	70

3. (a) After $X[4]$ is positioned:

i	1	2	3	4	5	6
$X[i]$	20	30	40	60	10	50

4. (a) After first pass:

i	1	2	3	4	5	6
$X[i]$	10	50	60	30	40	70

5. After first pass through the loop:

i	1	2	3	4	5	6	7	8	9	10
$X[i]$	10	50	40	20	60	70	30	90	80	100

9. (a) At end of first left-to-right pass:

i	1	2	3	4	5	6	7	8	9	10
$X[i]$	30	80	20	60	70	10	90	50	40	100

At end of first right-to-left pass:

i	1	2	3	4	5	6	7	8	9	10
$X[i]$	10	30	80	20	60	70	40	90	50	100

Section 10.2 (p. 494)

2. (d)

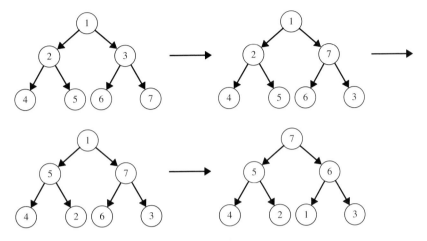

3. (a) After first call:

i	1	2	3	4	5	6	7	8	9
$X[i]$	20	15	31	49	67	50	3	10	26

(b) After first pass through the loop:

i	1	2	3	4	5	6	7	8
$X[i]$	88	77	55	66	22	33	44	99

Section 10.3 (p. 502)

2. (b)

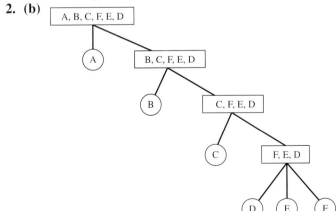

5. procedure *QuickSort* (**var** *X* : *ListType*; *First, Last* : *integer*);

   var
     Pos : *integer*;

   begin (**QuickSort **)
     Split (*X, First, Last, Pos*);
     if *Pos* − *First* < *LBound* **then**
       InsertionSort (*X, First, Pos* − 1)
     else
       QuickSort (*X, First, Pos* − 1);
     if *Last* − *Pos* < *LBound* **then**
       InsertionSort (*X, Pos* + 1, *Last*)
     else
       QuickSort (*X, Pos* + 1, *Last*)
   end (* *QuickSort* *);

Section 11.3 (p. 529)

1. (a) Attempts to read beyond the end of the file when the data pointer is positioned at the last end-of-line mark.

2. (a) Fails for all text files whose first character is not a blank.

Section 11.4 (p. 544)

1. (a)

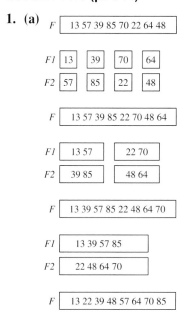

2. (a)

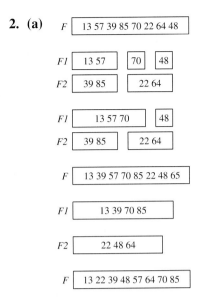

F 13 57 39 85 70 22 64 48

F1 13 57 | 70 | 48
F2 39 85 | 22 64

F1 13 57 70 | 48
F2 39 85 | 22 64

F 13 39 57 70 85 22 48 65

F1 13 39 70 85

F2 22 48 64

F 13 22 39 48 57 64 70 85

5. (a) Not stable.
   (d) Not stable.

Section 11.5 (p. 556)

1. procedure *ReadDirect* (**var** *F* : *FileType*; *n* : *integer*;
                          var *RecordN* : *RecordType*;
                          var *ReadError* : *boolean*);

    var
      i : *integer*;

    begin (∗ *ReadDirect* ∗)
      reset (*F*);
      i := −1;
      while (*i* < *n*) **and not** *eof*(*F*) **do**
        begin
          i := *i* + 1;
          read (*F*, *RecordN*)
        end (∗ **while** ∗);
      ReadError := *i* < *n*
    end (∗ *ReadDirect* ∗);

Section 12.1 (p. 572)

1. (c)

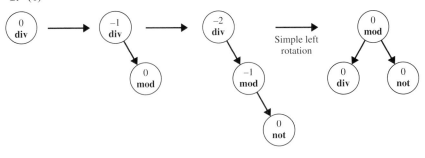

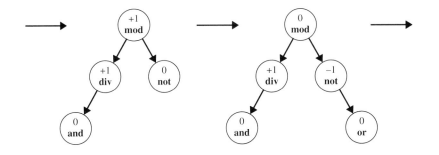

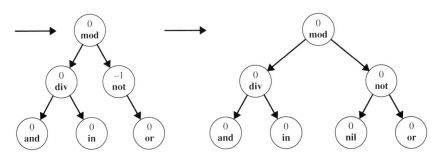

2. (a) The final AVL tree is

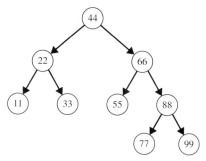

Section 12.2 (p. 576)

1. (b)

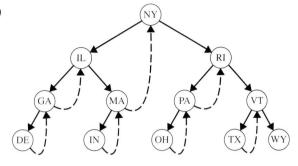

4. (b) For Exercise 1(b):

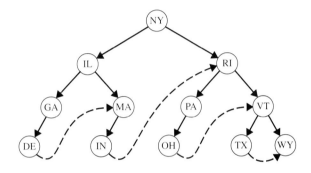

10. (b)

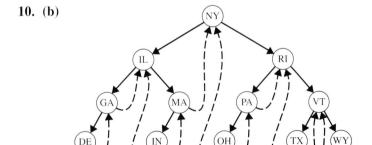

Section 12.3 (p. 586)

2.

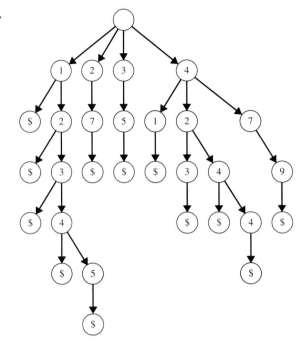

5. (a)

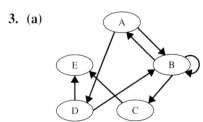

Section 13.2 (p. 605)

1. (a) $Adj = \begin{bmatrix} 0 & 1 & 1 & 1 & 1 \\ 0 & 1 & 1 & 0 & 0 \\ 0 & 0 & 0 & 1 & 0 \\ 0 & 0 & 0 & 1 & 1 \\ 0 & 1 & 0 & 0 & 0 \end{bmatrix}$ $Data = \begin{bmatrix} A \\ B \\ C \\ D \\ E \end{bmatrix}$

3. (a)

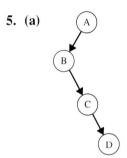

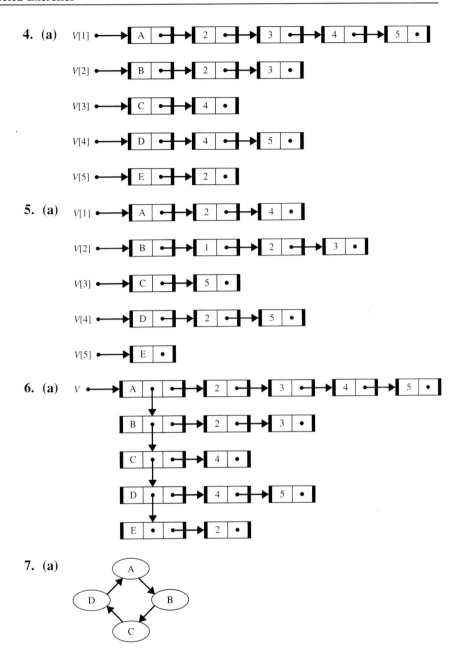

4. (a)

$V[1] \longrightarrow$ A | • | → | 2 | • | → | 3 | • | → | 4 | • | → | 5 | •

$V[2] \longrightarrow$ B | • | → | 2 | • | → | 3 | •

$V[3] \longrightarrow$ C | • | → | 4 | •

$V[4] \longrightarrow$ D | • | → | 4 | • | → | 5 | •

$V[5] \longrightarrow$ E | • | → | 2 | •

5. (a)

$V[1] \longrightarrow$ A | • | → | 2 | • | → | 4 | •

$V[2] \longrightarrow$ B | • | → | 1 | • | → | 2 | • | → | 3 | •

$V[3] \longrightarrow$ C | • | → | 5 | •

$V[4] \longrightarrow$ D | • | → | 2 | • | → | 5 | •

$V[5] \longrightarrow$ E | •

6. (a)

$V \longrightarrow$ A | • | • | → | 2 | • | → | 3 | • | → | 4 | • | → | 5 | •

B | • | • | → | 2 | • | → | 3 | •

C | • | • | → | 4 | •

D | • | • | → | 4 | • | → | 5 | •

E | • | • | → | 2 | •

7. (a)

Section 13.3 (p. 616)

1. (a) (i) $Adj = \begin{bmatrix} 0 & 1 & 1 & 1 & 1 \\ 1 & 0 & 1 & 0 & 1 \\ 1 & 1 & 0 & 1 & 0 \\ 1 & 0 & 1 & 0 & 1 \\ 1 & 1 & 0 & 1 & 0 \end{bmatrix}$ $Data = \begin{bmatrix} A \\ B \\ C \\ D \\ E \end{bmatrix}$

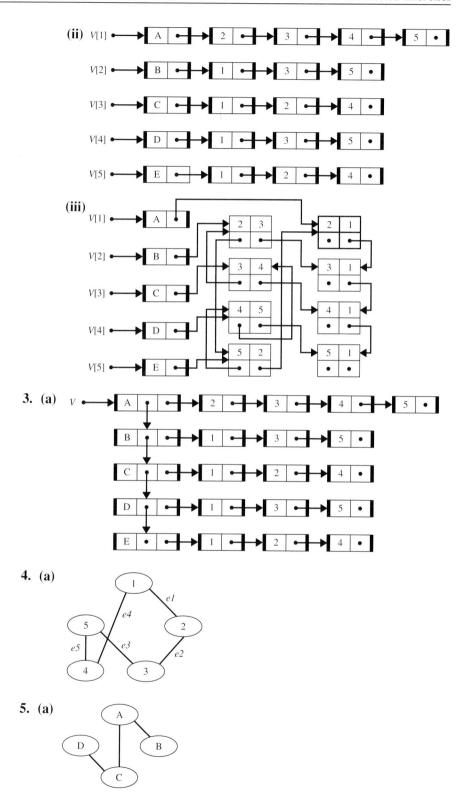

6. (a)

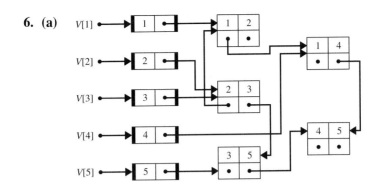

INDEX

Pascal Reference Chart

Statements	Example
Assignment	*Count* := 0; *Wages* := *RoundCents*(*Hours* * *Rate*); *DeptCode* := 'A'; *OverTime* := (*Hours* > 40); *ProductName* := 'Ford-Carburetor'; *Letters* := ['A'..'F', 'P', 'S']; *EmpRec* := *InFile*↑; *EmpRec.Number* := 12345; *TempPtr* := **nil**; *FirstPtr*↑.*Data* := *ProductName*;

Sequential
  Compound
	begin
	  Wages := *RoundCents*(*Hours* * *Rate*);
	  OverTime := *false*
	end;

Selection
  if
	if *Hours* <= 40 **then**
	  Wages := *RoundCents*(*Hours* * *Rate*)
	else
	  begin
	    OverTime := *true*;
	    Wages := *RoundCents*(*HoursLimit* * *Rate* +
	      OTMult * *Rate* * (*Hours* − *HoursLimit*))
	  end (* **else** *);

case	**case** *DeptCode* **of**
	  'o', 'O' : *Dept* := *Office*;
	  'f', 'F' : *Dept* := *Factory*;
	  's', 'S' : *Dept* := *Sales*
	end (* **case** *);